WORLD POPULATION CONTROL

Symposia of the
Columbia Human Rights Law Review
available as hardcover books

Legal Rights of Children:
Status, Progress and Proposals

Surveillance, Dataveillance and Personal Freedoms:
Use and Abuse of Information Technology

World Population Control:
Rights and Restrictions

WORLD POPULATION CONTROL

RIGHTS AND RESTRICTIONS

Edited by the staff of
Columbia Human Rights
Law Review

Family Service Association of America
New York

Pages 11-205 and 515-575 were originally published as
pages 273-534 of the COLUMBIA HUMAN RIGHTS LAW REVIEW,
Volume 6, Number 2, copyright © 1975 by *Columbia
Human Rights Law Review,* which is published in association
with the Columbia University Institute of Human Rights.
Reprinted with permission.

Pages 209-512 were originally published as pages 1-268
of the COLUMBIA HUMAN RIGHTS LAW REVIEW, Volume 7,
Number 1, copyright © 1975 by the United Nations Fund
for Population Activities. Reprinted with permission.

This first hardcover edition published by
Family Service Association of America
44 East 23rd Street, New York, N.Y. 10010

International Standard Book Number: 0-87304-143-7
Library of Congress Catalog Card Number: 75-27963

Printed in the United States of America

CONTENTS

PART I

POLICY ISSUES IN THE U.S.A.

Introduction

By
Sanda M. Kayden* and Ilene P. Karpf*

As the scholars and authors who have contributed to this issue of the *Columbia Human Rights Law Review* point out, the formulation of population policies ranks as one of the most critical issues of contemporary society. As world interest in this area grows, the need for legal involvement becomes more obvious. But to date legal participation has posed more questions than it has offered solutions.

Two competing interests must be reconciled in the development of a workable population program, and both are treated in this symposium. On one hand, there is the concern of the international community and the individual state in the formulation and implementation of a population plan. On the other, there is the responsibility to respect the individual's freedom and to guarantee each individual's rights of choice in matters of reproduction.

Many experts, taking a societal perspective, call for a comprehensive population strategy. As Paul Erlich pointed out in his doomsday prediction, if the current rate of population growth were to continue, within several thousand years, "everything in the universe would be converted into people and the diameter of the ball of people would be expanding with the speed of light!"[1] The need for a global approach to population planning is beginning to be recognized. However, nations do tend to formulate their own goals and to act independently. The realization of world cooperation in population planning will be no small achievement. Certainly the problems facing developing countries are linked to those confronting the developed countries. For example, the developed nations' demand for natural resources diverts them from use in less industrialized nations. Only recently has the United States begun to recognize its role in the problem and to experience for itself some of the effects of world overpopulation. Some of these include the "shortages"—of

---

* Staff Members, Columbia Human Rights Law Review.
1. P. ERLICH & A. ERLICH, POPULATION, RESOURCES, ENVIRONMENT: ISSUES IN HUMAN ECOLOGY 41-42 (1970).

food, adequate housing, natural resources, and energy. Air, water, and noise pollution are other ill effects of an expanding population. One means of dealing with these problems might be by better planning within each field. However, many experts are urging an approach that would also encourage a decline in the birth rate. A decrease in the number of potential consumers would lessen the pressure to expand, to cut down in quality, and to waste resources.

Where do various countries in the world stand today in their treatment of population issues? In the United States there is no national body of law to deal with the subject comprehensively. Generally regulation is left to the fifty states subject to the requirements of the Constitution. Several recent United States Supreme Court decisions[2] have addressed the constitutional issues involved in population planning. Much remains to be done, however, to give these decisions practical effect and to create a comprehensive plan of population growth in the United States. Several smaller scale programs have been instituted by the federal government. In 1968, the President's Committee on Population and Family Planning was created. Former President Nixon's Message on Population in 1968 gave total support to the Agency for International Development's (A.I.D.) programs on population control. A.I.D.'s activities included research grants for development of birth control devices, although most of its activities centered on international issues. In 1970, the Commission on Population Growth and the American Future was created, and that same year Congress passed the Family Planning Services and Population Resources Act. This was the first major bill to provide for federal monetary support for family planning and population research.[3]

The United States has also taken an active role in international population control through A.I.D. which funds population and family planning programs throughout the world. In 1971, over 95 million dollars were spent by A.I.D. in maintaining a field staff and supplying financial assistance to other countries seeking to develop population control systems. There is little doubt that A.I.D. is the largest single supporter of population and family planning programs in the world.

The United States has not acted alone in its activities to encourage population control on an international level. An active role has been taken by the United Nations, as well as by private organizations such as the International Planned Parenthood Federation. On December 10, 1966, twelve countries signed the Declaration on Population by World Leaders which accepted family planning as a basic human right. Eighteen more nations

2. These cases include Doe v. Bolton, 410 U.S. 179 (1973) and Roe v. Wade, 410 U.S. 113 (1973), both of which dealt with the right to an abortion; and Eisenstadt v. Baird, 405 U.S. 438 (1972) and Griswold v. Connecticut, 381 U.S. 479 (1965), both of which treated the right of access to contraceptives.

3. A detailed explanation of federal legislation in this area can be found in P. PIETROW, WORLD POPULATION CRISIS: UNITED STATES RESPONSES (1973).

agreed to the Declaration the following year. Formal United Nations recognition of the basic right of family planning was first announced in the Declaration adopted during the United Nations Conference on Human Rights in Teheran in May, 1968.

A year later, the General Assembly adopted the U.N. Declaration on Social Progress and Development. This document was the first United Nations resolution to call for direct action on the part of national governments. The Document states that each country should provide its families not only with the knowledge of but also with the means for family planning as well.[4]

Several branches of The United Nations in particular have participated in the area of population planning. The United Nations Educational, Scientific and Cultural Organization (UNESCO) maintains advisory services on regional and national projects as well as conducting teacher training programs. The World Health Organization (WHO) operates research and training programs in the field of population control, and UNICEF is authorized to include contraceptives in supplies sent to countries participating in its child care programs.[5]

Though the nations of the world are beginning to realize that population planning is of concern to them all, developing an international strategy for action is fraught with numerous problems. Each country has its own laws concerning birth control, abortion and sterilization. The local culture and religious beliefs of each nation must be considered before planning a comprehensive population program.

Aside from the efforts of A.I.D. and the United Nations, most countries are plotting their own destinies in this area. The modern trend has been toward a liberalization of laws dealing with birth control and abortion, allowing individuals more freedom of the choice in their private lives. In December, 1974, the National Assembly approved a bill which made France the first Catholic country in the world to permit abortions during the first trimester of pregnancy. East Germany passed an abortion law in 1972 which gives the total decision-making power to the woman during the first twelve weeks of conception. However, in a few countries which have had liberalized laws for many years, the birth rate has fallen so dramatically that the process has been reversed and the laws have been made more stringent. In Rumania, Czechoslovakia and Hungary, to stimulate population growth, abortion laws have been changed and incentives are being offered to induce couples to produce more children.

The need for a higher birth rate is in sharp contrast to conditions existing in India, in parts of Africa and in many Asian countries where the

---

4. U.N. Declaration on Social Progress and Development art. 22b.
5. A complete survey of the United Nations activities in the field of population planning can be found in D. PARTON, POPULATION IN THE UNITED NATIONS SYSTEM (1973).

governments are attempting through legislation, education and incentives to reduce the birth rate dramatically.

India intends to integrate family planning services with other health care facilities on a village by village level. More than 130,000 field workers will be involved in the population control effort.[6] Previously, India had concentrated its efforts on using incentives during a voluntary sterilization program.

A population program developed by A.I.D., the national government and private agencies in the Philippines is also being overhauled. Though more than 2,000 local clinics were established to educate people and to distribute birth control devices, the response has been minimal. In this predominantly Roman Catholic country, the government's official position is opposed to abortion as a method of birth control.[7]

Legal involvement in world population problems is in its initial stages of development. Whether a uniform system of population planning will be formulated or whether the fragmented approach will be furthered is impossible to determine. However, in some areas, such as family planning, the trend is toward uniformity. After family planning was declared to be a fundamental human right by the United Nations,[8] "a legal duty on the part of each government to see that laws and policies which conflict with the implementation of such rights be amended or abolished and that new laws and policies be adopted to conform with and further these rights"[9] was created. Certainly the challenge has been put to the international community to coordinate a population program. What will come of this challenge remains to be seen.

In addition to the issue of a global approach to population planning there remains the problem of how to develop methods for planning population growth without impinging on the individual's rights of choice. Indeed, the United Nations Conference on Human Rights in Teheran has categorized family planning as a basic human right.[10] The Proclamation stated that "parents have a basic human right to determine freely the number and the spacing of their children."[11] Another Resolution added that "a right to adequate education and information in this respect" exists for all "couples."[12]

The magnitude of the conflict between man and mankind is emphasized by considering some of the areas of behavior affected by legal action to control population. Current questions on abortion include the timing of the abortion (raising questions about the status of the fetus—is it an individual with legal

---

6. N.Y. Times, Nov. 24, 1974, § 1, at 8.

7. N.Y. Times, Dec. 15, 1974, § 1, at 11.

8. U.N. Conference on Human Rights, Teheran. U.N. Doc. A/Conf. 32/41. Resolution XVIII on Human Rights Aspects of Family is reprinted in 63 AM. J. INT'L L. 678-79, 674-77 (1969).

9. Lee, *Law and Family Planning*, 2 STUDIES IN FAMILY PLANNING 81 (1971).

10. Lee, *Law, Human Rights and Population: A Strategy for Action*, 12 VA. J. INT'L L. 309 (1972).

11. Teheran, Proclamation on Human Rights, *supra* note 8.

12. *Id.*

rights or do the mother's rights supercede those of the fetus); the father's legal position of power to prevent or force an abortion to occur; the state's power to regulate abortion procedures; the constitutionality of such state laws that do attempt to regulate abortion; the rights of the married versus the unmarried woman; the rights of a minor to an abortion; the position of powerful religious groups in controlling abortion laws; and the importance of the role played by physicians and hospitals in interpreting the mandates of existing laws. A recent issue in the United States has arisen concerning the responsibilities of a physician to maintain the life of an aborted fetus where the mother requested the abortion.

The right to adequate means of preventing conception, that is, to contraceptive devices and sterilization, has also received the attention of the world community. Access to contraceptive devices poses some of the same questions as does the question of the availability of abortion. For example, should there be restrictions which distinguish between married and unmarried persons, or minors and adults? Who should be the judge of quality and safety of presently marketed contraception devices? Is a once-a-month pill for women technically a method of preventing contraception or is it really another form of abortion? How can we guarantee inexpensive and adequate distribution of and education about these devices to those who need them? Here, the law must keep pace with technical advances in the medical profession as they occur.

Although the use of contraceptives is essentially a matter for individual choice, sterilization is a technique for birth control that has focused on the use of force. Can a government legally impose sterilization on its citizens to prevent population growth? Can or should it use sterilization to decrease the number of citizens who carry an undesirable genetic trait? If sterilization is permissible, when should a person be sterilized—at a certain age, or after a specific number of children have been born to a family? Should sterilization be performed on men or women or on both sexes? How can sterilization be prevented from being used to control certain races, religious groups, minority groups, and the poor? Another question concerns the freedom to choose to be sterilized. To what degree should the government regulate in this area? May a physician or hospital refuse to sterilize those who request the operation?

Population planning is not limited to the period of pre-natal controls. As a result of relatively recent advances in medicine and science, human beings are living longer than ever before. The future may bring even greater extensions of the average life span and more questions about the meaning of "life" and when it should be terminated. Already the law is being asked to define the point at which a person is legally dead. Should the law remove any prohibitions on suicide? How should the law deal with euthanasia and who should have the ultimate decision as to when a person may be permitted to die?

Beyond birth and death concerns is the obvious legal interference with "life" as it exists already. Marital laws can affect the birth rate by lowering or raising the permissible age for marriage. Zoning is a useful method for exercising social and governmental control over population. Unfortunately, it can be employed for negative goals as well as for positive ones. Countries all have their own laws for immigration and emigration. Certain groups of citizens can be forced to leave a country, while others be "discouraged" from departing. Enticement may be offered in the form of taxation benefits in order to attract new citizens to enter a country. Human experimentation is yet another means of "life control." The permitting of a disease to go untreated for the sake of medical knowledge, in an uninformed and unconsented-to situation such as the well-publicized Tuskeegee syphilis experiments, raise crucial issues about the individual's control over his or her own body. At this time the questions are only beginning to be formulated. Unfortunately the answers do not come as readily.

Naturally, as concern over the issue of population grows, more demands will be placed on the laws of individual nations and of the world community in general to provide solutions to the questions at hand. How these issues will be resolved may well prove to be a crucial factor in determining the future of man's role on this planet.

Abortion, Conscience and the Constitution: An Examination of Federal Institutional Conscience Clauses

By
Harriet F. Pilpel* and Dorothy E. Patton**

As the United States Supreme Court made clear in Doe v. Bolton, *it is not only complete proscription of abortion which is unconstitutional, but governmental erection of barriers which 'unduly restrict' the rights of the woman.*[1]

In January, 1973 the United States Supreme Court ruled for the first time on the constitutionality of state criminal abortion statutes. In *Roe v. Wade*[2] the Court held that statutes which prohibited all abortions except those done to save the life of the woman unconstitutionally violated the woman's right of privacy.[3] In the companion case, *Doe v. Bolton,*[4] the Court

---

* Mrs. Pilpel is a senior member of a New York City law firm. She is also a vice-chairman of the American Civil Liberties Union and General Counsel to the Planned Parenthood Federation of America, Incorporated.

** Associate Editor, Columbia Human Rights Law Review.

1. Doe v. Hale Hospital, 500 F. 2d 144, 146 (1st Cir. 1974) *cert. denied* 43 U.S.L.W. 3413 (U.S. Jan. 27, 1975), *citing* Doe v. Bolton, 410 U.S. 179, 198 (1973).

2. 410 U.S. 113 (1973) [hereinafter cited as *Roe*].

3. At the time of the Court's decision, two general types of abortion law were in effect in the different states. Prohibitory statutes prohibited all abortions except those done to save the life of the woman. Statutes of this type had been enacted in nearly all jurisdictions starting in the early 1800's. However, some of these prohibitory laws had been replaced before the *Roe* and *Doe* decisions by so-called American Law Institute type statutes which followed Model Penal Code Sec. 230.2 (Proposed Official Draft, 1962). These laws permitted abortions not only to save the life of the woman but also where 1) continuance of the pregnancy would impair the physical or mental health of the mother or 2) there was a likelihood the child would be born with a physical or mental defect, or 3) the pregnancy resulted from rape, incest or other felonious intercourse.

In *Roe* the Court invalidated a prohibitory statute and said:
[The Texas abortion statute] sweeps too broadly. The statute makes no distinction between abortions performed early in pregnancy and those performed later, and it limits to a single reason, "saving" the mother's life, the legal justification for the procedure. The statute, therefore, cannot survive the constitutional attack made upon it here. 410 U.S. at 164.

4. 410 U.S. 179 (1973) [hereinafter cited as *Doe*].

invalidated a number of abortion-restricting statutory regulations.[5] Congress reacted swiftly. Eight days after *Roe* and *Doe* were handed down, an abortion-prohibiting constitutional amendment was introduced in the House of Representatives; subsequently, Congress considered other amendments to the Constitution and to federal laws. Although the 93rd Congress adjourned without acting on any of the proposed Constitutional amendments, it did enact several abortion-limiting laws. Some of these laws took the form of "entity conscience clauses." Such clauses in effect state that where abortion or sterilization are against the "conscience" of a hospital or other entity, that entity may refuse to perform these medical procedures. For many women and families such laws may constitute a barrier which limits the constitutional right which the Supreme Court recognized in *Roe* to decide whether or not to terminate a pregnancy.[6] This article discusses the recently enacted entity conscience clauses and examines them in terms of constitutional rights.

I.   The Constitutional Right of Privacy and Human Reproduction

The Supreme Court has ruled that the Constitution reserves to the individual rights of reproductive choice. Emphasizing that legislation relating to human procreation "involves one of the basic civil rights of man,"[7] the Supreme Court has applied the fourteenth amendment and the privacy doctrine[8] to invalidate state legislation which limited individual rights of choice in matters of human reproduction. In an early decision, *Skinner v. Oklahoma*,[9] the Court held that, as to the defendant, a statute which authorized court-ordered sterilization of some habitual criminals violated the equal protection guarantee.[10] In other more recent decisions the Court has

5. In *Doe* the Court examined regulations in an ALI abortion law which, unlike the prohibitory statute at issue in *Roe*, permitted abortions but promulgated regulations which in a variety of ways limited access to the abortion procedure. The Supreme Court invalidated regulations which required that abortions be conducted in accredited hospitals, that a hospital abortion committee approve all abortions, and that two other physicians confirm the performing physician's judgment concerning the need for the abortion. The Court also invalidated a regulation prohibiting abortions in Georgia for non-residents.

6. In *Roe v. Wade* the Court said:
> This right of privacy . . . founded in the Fourteenth Amendment's concept of personal liberty and restrictions on state actions, as we feel it is . . . is broad enough to encompass a woman's decision whether or not to terminate her pregnancy [citations omitted]. 410 U.S. at 153.

7. Skinner v. Oklahoma, 316 U.S. 535, 541 (1942) [hereinafter cited as *Skinner*].

8. The meaning of the constitutionally based right to privacy was first specifically invoked in Griswold v. Connecticut, 381 U.S. 479 (1965), wherein the Court invalidated a Connecticut anti-contraceptive statute. Justice Douglas traced the origin and development of the privacy doctrine through constitutional text and court decisions. The Court ruled that the Constitution protects certain private areas of activity against state interference. *See* note 19 *infra*.

9. 316 U.S. 535 (1942).

10. *But see* Buck v. Bell, 274 U.S. 200 (1927), wherein the U.S. Supreme Court upheld court-ordered sterilization of a feeble-minded woman.

invalidated, primarily on due process grounds, legislation which sought to prevent individuals from limiting their own procreative capacity: in *Griswold v. Connecticut*[11] and *Eisenstadt v. Baird*,[12] the Court held unconstitutional statutory provisions which limited the access of individuals to contraceptive information and materials, and in *Roe v. Wade*[13] and *Doe v. Bolton*,[14] the Court voided statutory provisions which prohibited abortion except to save the life of the woman as well as provisions which imposed conditions severely limiting access to the abortion procedure.[15]

Although the separate decisions treated different forms of birth limiting methods—sterilization in *Skinner*, contraception in *Griswold* and *Eisenstadt*, abortion in *Roe* and *Doe*—these decisions as a group affirm the "fundamental" character of the right of individuals to choose whether they will or will not bear children. In *Eisenstadt v. Baird*,[16] Mr. Justice Brennan, speaking for the Court, succinctly framed this principle when he said:

> If the right of privacy means anything, it is the right of the *individual*, married or single, to be free from unwarranted governmental intrusion in matters so fundamentally affecting a person as the decision whether to bear or beget a child.[17]

The Court's affirmation of individual rights in this area necessarily reduces governmental authority to intermeddle. Emphasizing that cases such as *Roe* and *Skinner* are concerned with *who*, the individual or the state, makes decision regarding individual procreation, one commentator has observed that "the Court's plain concern in cases like *Roe* and *Griswold v. Connecticut* [has been] . . . with freedom from governmental control."[18] Thus, Supreme Court rulings on state legislation which impinged on freedom of reproductive choice have affirmed that choices regarding child-bearing are reserved by the Constitution to the individual (in the case of abortion with her doctor) and, conversely, that government's power in this regard is very limited.

Although the early decisions, particularly *Griswold*, stirred interest and debate mainly among constitutional scholars,[19] *Roe v. Wade*[20] and *Doe v. Bolton*,[21] the Court's most recent decisions on these issues, have had a

11. 381 U.S. 479 (1965) [hereinafter cited as *Griswold*].
12. 405 U.S. 438 (1972) [hereinafter cited as *Eisenstadt*].
13. 410 U.S. 113 (1973).
14. 410 U.S. 179 (1973).
15. *See* notes 3 and 5 *supra*.
16. 405 U.S. 438 (1972).
17. *Id.* at 453.
18. Tribe, *Forward: Toward a Model of Roles in the Due Process of Life and Law*, 87 HARV. L. REV. 1, 42 (1973).
19. *See, e.g.*, *Symposium on the Griswold Case and the Right of Privacy*, 64 MICH. L. REV. 197-288 (1966).
20. 410 U.S. 113 (1973).
21. 410 U.S. 179 (1973).

profound impact on local and national politics and on judicial and legislative decisions concerning abortion and other forms of birth limitation.[22] On the one hand, state legislatures have responded to *Roe* and *Doe* by repealing criminal abortion statutes and enacting new legislation purportedly conforming to the rules and guidelines[23] set out in *Roe* and *Doe*.[24] Further, state and federal courts have applied the principles developed in *Roe* and *Doe* to invalidate state statutes and hospital regulations which precluded abortions or which were unconstitutionally impermissive with regard to them.[25]

On the other hand, the Supreme Court abortion decisions have also prompted proposals for legislation and constitutional amendments which would forbid or restrict abortions and abortion-related activities, and thereby nullify the Court's decisions. For example, some state legislatures reduced the liberalizing effect of the abortion statutes enacted in response to *Roe* by including in those laws restrictive provisions such as husband or parental consent requirements, reporting requirements, waiting periods and "conscience clauses."[26] More significantly, although *Roe* and *Doe* involved state,

---

22. *See* sections II and III *infra.*

23. *See* note 81 *infra.*

24. The essential features of these new laws are catalogued in the FAMILY PLANNING/ POPULATION REPORTER, Vol. 2, No. 6 (1973), Vol. 3, No. 1 (1974), and Vol. 3, No. 2 (1974).

25. *See* section III *infra.*

26. For example, post-*Roe* Utah legislation requires the consent of parents for an abortion to be performed on a minor and the consent of the husband in a number of situations:

. . .Inasmuch as various persons have an interest in and through an unborn child, before an abortion may be performed written consent to the performance of such abortion must be given by the following individuals:

(1) In all cases such consent must be given by the woman upon whom the abortion is to be performed.

(2) If the woman upon whom the abortion is to be performed is married at the time of the performance of the abortion, such consent must be given by her husband.

(3) If the woman upon whom the abortion is to be performed was married at the time of conception but was divorced between conception and the time that the abortion is to be performed such consent must be given by her husband at the time of conception.

(4) If the pregnant woman is unmarried and under eighteen years of age, such consent must be given by the parents or guardian of such pregnant woman.

(5) In all cases, consent must be given by the father of the fetus. Where the father is unknown or cannot be located, the pregnant woman must file with the court at the time of the hearing specified in the next section an affidavit under oath so stating, and showing to the court that she has taken all reasonale efforts to identify him or locate him.

(6) In all other cases not covered by subsections (2), (3), (4), and (5) above, application must be made to the district court for consent to the performance of such abortion.

UTAH CODE ANN. § 76-7-304 (Supp. 1973). This statute was invalidated in Doe v. Rampton, 366 F. Supp. 189 (D. Utah 1973), *vacated and remanded for reconsideration in light of Roe v. Wade,* 410 U.S. 950 (1973). *See* text accompanying notes 128-32 *infra.* Indiana has a similar parental consent requirement. BURNS IND. REV. STAT. ANN. § 10-108 (Supp. 1974). In Nevada, the physician performing the abortion must provide written justification for his conclusion that the pregnancy would endanger the life of the mother or would seriously impair her physical or

rather than federal laws, the Congressional reaction to these decisions was swift and far-reaching. In the wake of *Roe* and *Doe*, the 93rd Congress had pending before it numerous abortion-limiting amendments to the federal Constitution and to federal legislation. Most of the proposed constitutional amendments would operate by applying the due process and equal protection clauses to unborn offspring;[27] other proposed amendments would return the abortion question to the states. The statutory proposals would operate by prohibiting the use of federal funds for abortions and abortion-related purposes.[28] Although the 93rd Congress rejected some of the abortion-limiting proposals, and allowed others to lapse with its adjournment,[29] it did enact a few abortion and sterilization limiting laws. In some cases—for example, the National Research Service Award Act of 1974[30]—the anti-abortion provisions are part of legislation that is concerned with the funding of health and medical programs to which abortion provisions are naturally related. In other instances—for example, the Legal Services Corporation Act of 1974[31]—anti-abortion provisions have been added to legislation not directly related to health and medicine.

---

emotional health. NEV. REV. STAT. ch. 442, § 442.250 (1973). Vermont requires that all abortions be reported by physicians, hospitals or funeral directors. VERMONT REV. STAT. ANN. tit. 18, §§ 5521, 5522 (Supp. 1974). *See also* Doe v. Israel 358 F. Supp. 1193 (D.R.I. 1973) and Ward v. Poelker, 495 F.2d 1349 (8th Cir. 1974).

27. For example, Senator Buckley of New York proposed an amendment which would permit abortions only if necessary to save the life of the mother.

> SECTION 1: With respect to the right to life the word 'person', as used in this Article and in the Fifth and Fourteenth Articles of Amendment to the Constitution of the United States, applies to all human beings, including their unborn offspring at every stage of their biological development, irrespective of age, health, function or condition of dependency. SEC. 2. This article shall not apply in an emergency when a reasonable medical certainty exists that continuation of the pregnancy will cause the death of the mother . . . .

S.J. Res. 119, 93rd Cong., 1st Sess. (1973). 119 Cong. Rec. 9976 (daily ed. May 31, 1973).

Representative Hogan of Maryland proposed an amendment which prohibited all abortions.

> SECTION 1: Neither the United States nor any State shall deprive any human being, from the moment of conception, of life without due process of law; nor deny to any human being, from the moment of conception, within its jurisdiction, the equal protection of the laws . . . .

H.R.J. Res. 261, 93rd Cong., 1st Sess. (1973). 119 Cong. Rec. 571 (daily ed. Jan. 30, 1973).

Each of these amendments depends on a conclusion that the Constitution protects life from the moment of conception. *See* Doe v. Israel, 358 F. Supp. 1193 (D.R.I. 1973), invalidating a post-*Roe* Rhode Island statute based on the legislature's "factual" determination that life begins at conception. *See also* Roe v. Wade wherein the U.S. Supreme Court rejected a similar argument: "[We] do not agree that, by adopting one theory of life, [the state] may override the rights of the pregnant woman that are at stake." 410 U.S. at 162. Consideration of the proposed constitutional amendments is beyond the intended scope of this article.

28. *See* section II *infra.*

29. *See* text accompanying notes 53-62 *infra.*

30. Pub. L. 93-348, §§ 213, 214 (July 12, 1974). *See* text accompanying notes 49-50 *infra.*

31. Pub. L. 93-355 § 1007 (b) (8), (July 25, 1974). *See* text accompanying note 51 *infra.*

A significant characteristic of this legislation is provisions which allow individuals or entities receiving federal funds to refuse to participate in the performance of abortions or sterilizations if such participation is against the religion or "conscience" of the individual or entity. Such provisions are termed individual and entity "conscience clauses" because they permit individuals and entities to so refuse for religious and moral reasons—that is, according to the dictates of conscience. Conscience clauses or comparable abortion-limiting provisions were enacted as parts of the Church Amendment to the Health Services Extension Act of 1973,[32] the National Research Service Award Act of 1974,[33] the Legal Services Corporation Act of 1974,[34] and the Foreign Aid Assistance Act of 1973.[35] In addition, the House and the Senate separately approved other anti-abortion amendments which failed to survive subsequent congressional action.[36]

Such statutory provisions are fast becoming an integral part of legislation which funds the federal health programs through which individuals may seek abortions and sterilizations. It has been argued that the effect of these federal institutional conscience clauses is to enable some federally funded institutions to limit the constitutional right of the individual to choose whether or not to bear children. The purpose of this article is to consider whether entity conscience clauses are constitutional in the light of relevant legal and constitutional principles.

It should be clearly understood at the outset that the validity of conscience clauses insofar as they apply to individuals is not in question here. An individual has a fundamental right not to engage in any activity—abortion, sterilization or any other activity—which would be against his or her conscience.[37] It does not follow, however, that all "entities" necessarily have similar rights of conscience: if they are public, that is government entities or if their connection with government is such as to render their action "state action",[38] they may not infringe constitutionally protected rights. This article focuses only on those conscience clauses which purport to exempt govern-

---

32. 42 U.S.C. § 300a-7 (1974). *See* text accompanying notes 43-48 *infra*.
33. Pub. L. 93-348, §§ 213, 214 (July 12, 1974). *See* text accompanying notes 49-50 *infra*.
34. Pub. L. 93-355, § 1007 (b) (8) (July 25, 1974). *See* text accompanying note 51 *infra*.
35. Pub. L. 93-189, § 2 (Dec. 17, 1973). *See* text accompanying note 52 *infra*.
36. *See* text accompanying notes 53-62 *infra*.
37. Referring to entity and individual conscience clauses, a New York Civil Liberties Union attorney noted the following distinctions:
> A totally different issue, and one which is not in dispute here, is the right of individuals to refuse to perform or participate in such procedures. No civil libertarian could conceivably support a court order directing a physician to perform an abortion or sterilization which is religiously or morally impermissible to that individual.

Gutman, *Can Hospitals Constitutionally Refuse to Permit Abortions and Sterilizations?*, 2 FAMILY PLANNING/POPULATION REPORTER 146 (1973).
38. *See* section III *infra*.

ment entities or entities connected with government from requirements of the Constitution.

Courts reviewing entity conscience clause legislation will almost certainly look to two lines of cases to determine the validity of these statutory provisions. One line of cases arose from civil rights litigation involving the general question of hospital policies which limit constitutionally protected rights. These cases, like the challenges to abortion and sterilization laws, were brought in the federal courts under the federal civil rights statute, 42 U.S.C. Section 1983.[39] The second source to which courts will refer is the developing case law, based on the aforementioned civil rights cases, arising out of recent litigation involving abortion and sterilization-limiting regulations and statutes.[40] Consideration of the newly enacted institutional conscience clauses in light of civil rights and procreation case law discloses the constitutional infirmity inherent in the recently enacted conscience clauses insofar as they apply to government or government-connected entities.

II.   ABORTION AND STERILIZATION PROHIBITIONS AND CONSCIENCE CLAUSES IN FEDERAL LEGISLATION

The first congressional prohibition against the use of particular federal funds for abortions appeared in legislation enacted three years before the *Roe* decision. The Family Planning Services and Population Research Act of 1970[41] authorizes funding for family planning programs and for research on reproductive biology and contraceptive technology through federal funding of training grants and contracts with public and private institutions. This law, however, contains an outright ban on the use of these funds in "programs where abortion is a method of family planning."[42] Although not a conscience clause, this provision suggested possible congressional opposition to abortion even before *Roe* was decided.

As we have pointed out above, subsequent to the January, 1973 Supreme Court abortion decisions, anti-abortion and anti-sterilization limitations have been added to several federal laws and bills. The first post-*Roe* legislation of this type, the Church Amendment,[43] was in part a response to a 1972

---

39. Hereinafter cited as section 1983. *See* note 51 *infra.*
40. *See* section III *infra.*
41. 42 U.S.C. §§ 300-300a-6 (1974).
42. 42 U.S.C. § 300a-6 (1974): "None of the funds appropriated under this title shall be used in programs where abortion is a method of family planning."
43. Health Programs Extension Act of 1973, § 401 (b) (c), 42 U.S.C. § 300a-7 (1974): (a) The receipt of any grant, contract, loan, or loan guarantee under the Public Health Service Act, the Community Mental Health Centers Act, or the Developmental Disabilities Services and Facilities Construction Act by any individual or

federal court decision which had enjoined a denominational hospital's attempt
to prohibit the use of its facilities for the performance of sterilization
surgery.[44] The court had entered the injunction after finding that "the fact
that the defendant [St. Vincent's Hospital] is the beneficiary of the receipt of
Hill-Burton Act [hospital construction] funds is alone sufficient to support an
assumption of jurisdiction" under section 1983,[45] the basic civil rights action
statute. The Church Amendment precluded federal jurisdiction in such cases
by prohibiting "any court from finding state action on the part of a hospital
which receives Hill-Burton [or other named federal][46] funds and using that
finding as a basis for requiring the hospital to make its facilities available for
the performance of sterilization procedures or abortions."[47] This limitation on
section 1983 relief enabled hospitals to refuse for reasons of conscience to
admit abortion and sterilization patients.

In addition to these provisions which purport to allow hospitals and
other entities to exercise their "conscience," section 401(c)[48] of the Church
Amendment prohibits hospitals from discharging staff members because of
their beliefs concerning abortion and sterilization. In this way, the legislation
protects individual physicians and other health personnel from retaliatory
action and insures that they may act in accord with their religious convictions
in this regard.

Congress expanded the scope of the Church Amendment in 1974.
Section 214 of the National Research Service Award Act of 1974[49] added an

---

entity does not authorize any court or any public official or other public authority to
require—
 (1) such individual to perform or assist in the performance of any sterilization procedure or abortion if his performance or assistance in the performance of
such procedure or abortion would be contrary to his religious beliefs or moral
convictions; or
 (2) such entity to—
 (A) make its facilities available for the performance of any sterilization
procedure or abortion if the performance of such procedure or abortion in such
facilities is prohibited by the entity on the basis of religious beliefs or moral
convictions, or
 (B) provide any personnel for the performance or assistance in the performance of any sterilization procedure or abortion if the performance or assistance in
the performance of such procedure or abortion by such personnel would be
contrary to the religious beliefs or moral convictions of such personnel.
 44. Taylor v. St. Vincent's Hospital, Civ. No. 1090 (D. Mont. 1972), rev'd 369 F. Supp.
948 (D. Mont. 1973). Cited in H.R. Rep. No. 227, 93rd Cong., 1st Sess. (1973).
 45. 1973 U.S. CODE CONGRESSIONAL AND ADMINISTRATIVE NEWS 1473, 1477, citing the
Hill-Burton Act 42 U.S.C. §§ 291-291z (1974).
 46. See note 43 supra.
 47. Watkins v. Mercy Medical Center, 364 F. Supp. 799, 801 (D. Idaho 1973).
 48. Health Programs Extension Act of 1973, § 401 (c), 42 U.S.C. § 300a-7 (1974).
 49. National Research Service Award Act of 1974, Pub. L. 93-348, § 214 (d) (July 12,
1974):
 (d) No individual shall be required to perform or assist in the performance of
any part of a health service program or research activity funded in whole or in part
under a program administered by the Secretary of Health, Education, and Welfare

individual conscience clause which allows hospital personnel to refuse to participate in *any* health service program—not only those funded through the programs named in the Church Amendment and not only abortion and sterilization—supported through biomedical or behavioral research grants and contracts administered by the Secretary of Health, Education, and Welfare. In this way, Congress broadened the conscience clause provisions of the Church Amendment to cover medical services and research other than abortion and sterilization and extended the right of individuals to refuse to participate in abortion and sterilizations to personnel in a broader range of HEW supported programs than those named in the 1973 amendment.[50]

Other recent federal legislation utilizes the conscience clause principle but less comprehensively, and with less specificity than the Church Amendment. The Legal Services Corporation Act of 1974,[51] for example, limits abortion-related litigation in federally-funded poverty law programs by prohibiting the use of the program's funds in litigation intended to compel the performance of abortions against institutional and individual consciences. Also Congress has restricted the use of U.S. funds for abortion in foreign aid programs. The Foreign Aid Assistance Act of 1973[52] authorizes expenditures for family planning in foreign countries but prohibits the use of the AID funds there appropriated to "pay for the performance of abortions as a method of family planning or to motivate or coerce any person to practice abortion."

Significantly, however, Congress refused to approve other abortion restricting proposals, including some which both houses actively considered and which either the House or the Senate separately approved. For example, the Senate rejected, and the Conference Committee deleted from the final bill, the House-approved Froehlich Amendment[53] to the Headstart, Economic Opportunity, and Community Partnership Act of 1974,[54] an act to extend Office of Economic Opportunity programs through fiscal 1977. The

---

if his performance or assistance in the performance of such part of such program or activity would be contrary to his religious beliefs or moral convictions.

50. In addition to the individual conscience clause, the Act includes provisions concerning medical ethics in federally funded programs. One provision relates to the protection of human research subjects and precludes HEW support for research on living fetuses before or after an induced abortion unless the research is intended to assure the survival of the fetus. National Research Service Award Act of 1974, Pub. L. 93-348, § 213 (July 12, 1974).

51. Pub. L. 93-355, § 1007 (b) (8), (July 25, 1974):

  (b) No funds made available by the Corporation under this title, either by grant or contract may be used

  (8) to provide legal assistance with respect to any proceeding or litigation which seeks to procure a non-therapeutic abortion or to compel any individual or institution to perform an abortion, or assist in the performance of an abortion, or provide the facilities for the performance of an abortion, contrary to the religious beliefs or moral convictions of such individual or institution.

52. Pub. L. 93-189, § 2 (Dec. 17, 1973).

53. H.R. 14449, 93rd Cong., 2d Sess. *See* 120 Cong. Rec. 4471 (daily ed. May 29, 1974).

54. Headstart, Economic Opportunity and Community Partnership Act of 1974, Pub. L. 93-644 (Jan. 4, 1975), 1974 U.S. CODE CONGRESSIONAL AND ADMINISTRATIVE NEWS 7329 (1975).

Froehlich Amendment would have prohibited financial assistance for abortions or sterilizations under the family planning provisions in that act. The House-Senate conferees also refused to include in the 1975 Labor-HEW appropriations bill[55] the Senate-approved Bartlett Amendment.[56] The Bartlett Amendment was intended to prohibit the use of medicaid funds to pay for abortions unless the abortion was necessary to save the life of the mother. There were also unsuccessful attempts to broaden the Church Amendment through an entity conscience clause[57] applicable to all institutions supported by HEW grants and contracts.[58] However, despite the failure of this legislation to win final approval in the 93rd Congress, it illustrates the potential breadth of institutional conscience clauses and the attendant practical and constitutional limitations of such legislation. For example, Senate bill S. 3713,[59] a proposed amendment to the Health Professions Educational Assistance Act of 1974[60] included the following institutional conscience clause:

> No entity shall be required to make its facilities available for the performance of any health service program or research activity funded in whole or in part by the Department of Health, Education and Welfare if such performance is prohibited by the entity on the basis of religious belief or moral convictions.[61]

Legislation of this type would allow all HEW funded hospitals, clinics and other facilities where abortions and sterilizations might be performed to refuse to admit patients seeking these medical services. The full significance of this broad language was elaborated in the Minority Report of the Senate Committee on Labor and Public Welfare which had considered the bill:

> This sweeping provision exempts any institution or corporation from participating in any health service program or research

55. Pub. L. 93-517 (Dec. 7, 1974), 1974 U.S. CODE OF CONGRESSIONAL AND ADMINISTRATIVE NEWS 6587 (1974).
56. H.R. 15580, 93rd Cong., 2d Sess. *See* 120 Cong. Rec. 16,839 (daily ed. Sept. 17, 1974).
57. *See* notes 49-50 *supra*, for a discussion of 1974 amendments adding an individual "conscience clause" to the Church Amendment.
58. S. 3713, 93rd Cong., 2d Sess. § 1 (d) (2) (1974) was proposed as an amendment to the Health Professions Education Assistance Act of 1974, S. 3585, 93rd Cong., 2d Sess. (1974). Originally, the Senate had approved an entity conscience clause in the National Health Services Award Act of 1974, but the House-Senate conferees rejected that provision and reported out the individual conscience clause only. A comparable conscience clause was then added to the proposed Health Professions Educational Assistance Act and was approved by the House-Senate conferees. However, because the conferees could not agree on other features of the legislation Congress did not complete action on the bill before adjournment. 1974 Cong. Quart. 3434.
59. S. 3713, 93rd Cong., 2d Sess. § 1 (d) (2), (1974). *See* 120 Cong. Rec. 11640 (daily ed. June 27, 1974).
60. S. 3585, 93rd Cong., 2d Sess. (1974). *See* note 48 *supra*.
61. S. 3713, 93rd Cong., 2d Sess., § 3 (1) (d) (2) (1974).

activity which the entity chooses to reject on moral or religious grounds. This blanket exemption applies to agencies and institutions which are wholly owned and operated by Federal, State, and county or municipal governments as well as to entities which are privately owned and controlled. It applies to entities which are fully, mostly or partially funded by public funds. It does not differentiate between secular and sectarian institutions. It makes no exceptions for life or death emergencies or for the situations in which the entity is the only geographically available source of medical care. It fails to mention what criteria or sets of criteria are to be used in assessing what would constitute the moral or religious beliefs [of] an entity or corporation.[62]

In sum, entity conscience clauses such as those enacted in the Church Amendment and the Legal Services Corporation Act and those proposed in S. 3713 seek to immunize from legal attack federally funded hospitals which refuse to admit patients seeking abortions and sterilizations. Their effect is to restrict "the right of the *individual* . . . to be free from unwarranted governmental intrusion"[63] in matters of reproductive choice. Congress enacted these laws despite the principle that a constitutional amendment rather than a mere act of Congress is required to abrogate any part of the Constitution. Insofar as these conscience clauses permit public facilities or private facilities whose activities legally constitute "state action" to be free of constitutional restrictions, they are clearly ineffective and unconstitutional.

III. THE PRESENT LAW AS TO STATE STATUTES AND REGULATIONS RELATING TO THE AVAILABILITY OF ABORTIONS AND STERILIZATIONS

In many recent cases abortion-seeking plaintiffs and their physicians have used Section 1983[64] to challenge abortion and sterilization-limiting regulations and statutes. To maintain an action under this section, the plaintiff must establish that he has been deprived of a civil right and that this deprivation was caused by persons "acting under color of" state law. To meet

---

62. SENATE COMM. ON LABOR AND PUBLIC WELFARE, S. Rep. No. 1133, 93rd Cong., 2d Sess. § 8 (1974), Minority views of Messrs. Javits, Stafford, and Hathaway.
63. 405 U.S. at 453. See note 12 *supra*.
64. 42 U.S.C. § 1983 (1974):
Every person who, under color of any statute, ordinance, regulation, custom, or usuage, of any State or Territory subjects, or causes to be subjected, any citizen of the United States or other persons within the jurisdiction thereof to the deprivation of any rights, privileges or immunities secured by the Constitution and laws, shall be liable to the person injured in an action of law, suit in equity, or other proper proceedings for redress.

the first of these requirements, plaintiffs have alleged violations of the equal protection or due process guarantees of the fourteenth amendment. To meet the second requirement when public hospitals were defendants, plaintiffs have asserted that there was state action because such hospitals were government controlled and financed. When private hospitals were defendants, the state action claim was based on allegations that the state was involved in the activities and conduct of the private institution through government subsidies, exemptions and/or regulations.

The application of the law of state action in abortion and sterilization cases has resulted in three lines of decisions. First, some federal courts have held that public officials and institutions, including public hospitals, may not promulgate administrative regulations which limit access to abortions or sterilizations, either through regulations of medicaid payments or through selective admissions policies.[65] Second, some courts have ruled that private hospitals, may if they wish, prohibit hospital admissions and procedures for purposes of abortion and sterilization.[66] Finally, a third group of decisions maintains this distinction between public and private hospitals in the context of conscience clauses contained in state abortion statutes.[67] An examination of these three groups of decisions will reveal some of the factors and principles against which the validity and applicability of congressional abortion and sterilization-limiting legislation may be measured.

A. *Public Hospitals*

Since none of the federal entity conscience clauses limit their intended scope to particular categories of hospitals, each clause presumably applies to all hospitals, including public hospitals. The result is that entity conscience clauses authorize public institutions to forbid the exercise of constitutionally protected rights. Such legislative authorization is contrary to nearly seventy years of case law prohibiting public officials and instrumentalities from infringing constitutionally protected rights.[68] Chief Justice Warren, speaking

---

65. *See* text accompanying notes 75-95 *infra.*
66. *See* text accompanying notes 110-114 *infra.*
67. *See* text accompanying notes 123-135 *infra.*
68. In Ex parte Young, 209 U.S. 123 (1908), the Supreme Court broadened the applicability of section 1983 by applying the state action principle to order a state attorney general not to enforce a state law, thereby making state officials responsible for the consequences of their "individual conduct" performed pursuant to state law. Since then, section 1983 has been successfully invoked to protect individual rights against public officials such as police officers (Monroe v. Pape, 365 U.S. 167 (1961)), public school officials (Harkless v. Sweeney Independent School Dist., 427 F.2d 319 (5th Cir. 1970)), and public hospital administrators (Hodgson v. Anderson, 378 F. Supp. 1008 (D. Minn. 1974)). Recently in Bruno v. City of Kenosha, 412 U.S. 507 (1973), the Supreme Court held that section 1983 does not authorize equitable actions against a city. This decision does not appear to preclude equitable actions against public officials, however. *See* United Farmworkers v. City of Del Ray Beach, 493 F.2d 799 (5th Cir. 1974) and Cason v. City of Jacksonville, 497 F.2d 949 (5th Cir. 1974).

for a unanimous Court, restated this principle in *Cooper v. Aaron*,[69] wherein the Supreme Court ordered the Little Rock School Board to proceed with desegregation plans. The Court said:

> [T]he prohibitions of the Fourteenth Amendment extend to all actions of the state denying equal protection of the laws, whatever the agency of the State taking the action . . . or whatever the guise in which it is taken.[70]

This well-accepted interpretation of the fourteenth amendment allows civil rights actions against public instrumentalities such as school boards, universities, and hospitals.[71] The cases involving hospitals are particularly pertinent because they involve public hospital limitations on constitutionally protected rights.

In keeping with the historical origin and purpose of civil rights legislation in the last century, and as a result of civil rights activism in this century, the leading cases on this question of denial of constitutional rights by public institutions have involved racial discrimination. In *Foster v. Mobile County Hospital Board*,[72] and *Meredith v. Allen County War Memorial Hosp. Comm'n.*,[73] black physicians brought civil rights actions against public hospitals which had denied them staff privileges. In these cases, the courts held that public hospital conduct—here racially discriminatory staffing policies—violate the fourteenth amendment.

More recently in cases where race has not been a factor, courts have relied on these race discrimination precedents to invalidate abortion and sterilization-limiting policies promulgated by statute, ordinance or hospital regulation. One group of cases involves statutory or administrative regulations limiting medicaid payments for abortions and sterilizations; the second group involves government or public hospital policies which allow hospitals to refuse to admit patients for abortions and sterilizations. A brief examination of these cases follows.

Prior to the Supreme Court abortion decisions, New York enacted a law permitting abortions during the first two trimesters[74] and, as a result, the early challenges to restrictive regulations involved New York hospitals. In *Klein v. Nassau County Medical Center*,[75] an indigent woman sought an injunction against enforcement of a state adminstrative directive which allowed medicaid payments for "medically indicated" abortions, but did not

---

69. 358 U.S. 1 (1958).

70. *Id.* at 17.

71. *See* text accompanying notes 72-95 *infra*.

72. 398 F.2d 227 (5th Cir. 1968).

73. 397 F.2d 33 (5th Cir. 1968).

74. N.Y. PENAL LAW § 125.05 (McKinney Supp. 1972).

75. 347 F. Supp. 496 (E.D.N.Y. 1972), *vacated and remanded for reconsideration in light of Roe v. Wade*, 412 U.S. 925 (1973).

allow payment for "elective" abortions. Ruling that the regulation violated the equal protection guarantee of the fourteenth amendment, the court said:

> [Indigent women alone were] subjected to State coercion to bear children which they do not wish to bear, and no other women similarly situated are so coerced. Other women . . . have complete freedom to make the choice . . . uninhibited by any State action.[76]

The Supreme Court vacated the *Klein* judgment, and remanded the case for reconsideration in the light of *Roe v. Wade*. In similar cases arising after *Roe* and *Doe*, several courts have utilized an equal protection rationale to invalidate medicaid limiting regulations. Like *Klein*, *Doe v. Wolgemuth*[77] and *Doe v. Rose*,[78] involved challenges to state medicaid regulations which forbade medicaid reimbursement for elective abortions. In both cases the courts ruled that such state regulations violated the equal protection guarantee of the federal Constitution because they precluded medical assistance for otherwise eligible poor persons *solely when they sought an abortion*. For example, the court in *Rose* observed that under the Utah regulations in issue "an indigent pregnant woman [was] entitled to *medical* services and care for her *pregnancy* . . . ." but not for an elective abortion.[79] Thus, the equal protection rationale adopted in these cases does not depend on wealth-based discrimination: rather the courts reject a classification which distinguishes between women electing abortion and those electing to carry their pregnancies to term. In dictum, these courts have also alluded to the due process principles developed in *Roe*. For example, in *Doe v. Wolgemuth*[80] the court drew on the distinction between pregnancy trimesters elaborated in *Roe*,[81] and ruled that the Pennsylvania regulations were overly broad because they regulated the elective abortion decision during all three trimesters in violation of the

---

76. 347 F. Supp. at 500.
77. 376 F. Supp. 173 (W.D.Pa. 1974).
78. 499 F.2d 1112 (10th Cir. 1974).
79. *Id.* at 1113 (emphasis added).
80. 376 F. Supp. 173 (W.D.Pa. 1974).
81. In Roe v. Wade, 410 U.S. 113, 164 (1973), the Supreme Court set out guidelines in which it suggested the permissible level of governmental regulation of decisions concerning abortion varied according to the different stages of pregnancy:
   (a) For the stage prior to approximately the end of the first trimester the abortion decision and its effectuation must be left to the medical judgement of the pregnant woman's attending physician.
   (b) For the stage subsequent to approximately the end of the first trimester, the State, in promoting its interest in the health of the mother, may, if it chooses, regulate the abortion procedure in ways that are reasonably related to maternal health.
   (c) For the stage subsequent to viability the State, in promoting its interest in the potentiality of human life, may, if it chooses, regulate, and even proscribe, abortion except where it is necessary, in appropriate medical judgement, for the preservation of the life or health of the mother.

standard set out in *Roe v. Wade*. Federal courts have invalidated restrictive medical regulations of this type in Utah,[82] South Dakota,[83] Ohio,[84] and Connecticut.[85]

A second group of cases involves challenges to public hospitals which refuse to admit abortion and sterilization patients. In another pre-*Roe* New York decision, *McCabe v. Nassau County Medical Center*,[86] the court had invalidated regulations which based the availability of sterilization procedures on a woman's age and present number of children, thereby preventing the plaintiff in that case from obtaining low-cost sterilization surgery at the Center. Such regulations, the court concluded, constituted state action and were unconstitutional on equal protection grounds as well as on the ground of deprivation of the right of marital privacy.

The leading decision on this question after *Roe* is *Hathaway v. Worchester Memorial Hospital*.[87] There, the court held that a public hospital's policy prohibiting sterilizations violated the equal protection guarantee since the hospital permitted other, similar procedures:

[I]t is clear under *Roe* and *Doe* that a complete ban on a surgical procedure relating to the fundamental interest in the pregnancy decision is far too broad when other comparable surgical procedures are performed.

. . .

[O]nce the state has undertaken to provide general short-term hospital care, as here, it may not constitutionally draw the line at medically indistinguishable surgical procedures that impinge on fundamental rights.[88]

The First Circuit reaffirmed this principle and expanded it to invalidate an abortion-prohibiting regulation in *Doe v. Hale Hospital*.[89] In *Ward v. Poelker*,[90] the court invalidated a St. Louis ordinance which imposed stringent regulations on abortion clinics, requiring, among other things, an abortion permit listing the names and medical experience of all physicians and nurses performing the abortion. Here the court concluded that the regulation was overbroad with respect to the *Roe* trimester schedule and noted that the

82. Doe v. Rampton, 366 F. Supp. 189 (D. Utah), *vacated and remanded for reconsideration in light of Roe v. Wade*, 410 U.S. 950 (1973).
83. Doe v. Westby, 383 F. Supp. 1143 (D.S.D. 1974).
84. Roe v. Ferguson,— F. Supp. — (S.D. Ohio 1974).
85. Roe v. Norton, 380 F. Supp. 726 (D. Conn. 1974).
86. 453 F.2d 698 (2d Cir. 1971).
87. 475 F.2d 701 (1st Cir. 1973).
88. *Id.* at 706.
89. 500 F.2d 144 (1st Cir. 1974), *cert. denied* 43 U.S.L.W. 3413 (U.S. Jan. 27, 1975).
90. 495 F.2d 1349 (8th Cir. 1974).

city did not impose this requirement on any other medical or surgical procedure. Similar abortion-limiting regulations promulgated by public hospitals have also been invalidated by courts in the Seventh and Eighth Circuits.[91]

In *Orr v. Koefoot*[92] the standards developed in the foregoing cases were extended to apply to a state university hospital which was not a general public hospital and which defended its restrictive abortion policy (15 allowed per week) as necessary to meet the requirements of its "conservative medical teaching program." Acknowledging that as a teaching institution the defendant might legitimately regulate admission policies to promote research and educational objectives, the court nevertheless found that state action was present, and held that the restrictive abortion policy was invalid. Noting that numerical limits applied only to abortions and not to any other hospital procedures, the court found that the limitation on abortions benefited "neither the State nor the goals of the University, while on the other hand, it intrudes on basic 'fundamental' rights."[93]

The above cases disclose the judicial response to some of the methods which public agencies have adopted to prevent women from obtaining abortion and sterilization services. In each case the court has held that the agency's conduct was state action for purposes of Section 1983. Further, the courts have refused to allow regulations which provided public benefits for pregnancies and therapeutic abortions, but not for elective abortions. These decisions have also utilized the fundamental rights rationale developed in *Roe*. Some of the guiding factors were summarized in *Nyberg v. City of Virginia*.[94] After pointing out that the Supreme Court abortion decisions involved *criminal* abortion statutes rather than non-criminal hospital regulations, the court said:

> [T]hose decisions cannot be read so narrowly. As the several noncriminal cases cited by the court in *Roe v. Wade* point out, the issue is the existence of certain fundamental rights. If any of the defined fundamental rights is found to be present the state must then show 'compelling state interest' if it wishes to limit or regulate. . . .

---

91. Hodgson v. Anderson, 378 F. Supp. 1008 (D. Minn. 1974); Doe v. Mundy, 378 F. Supp. 731 (E.D.Wisc. 1974); Nyberg v. City of Virginia, 495 F.2d 1342 (8th Cir. 1974), *appeal dismissed* 419 U.S. 891, 42 L. Ed. 2d 136 (1974). *See also* Poe v. Charlotte Memorial Hospital, 374 F. Supp. 1302 (W.D.N.C. 1974), wherein the court ruled that a physician was entitled to a hearing before a public hospital could discontinue his staff privileges because of abortion-related activities; *also* Doe v. General Hospital of the District of Columbia, U.S.D.C. D.C. Civ. No. 573-70, wherein the court enjoined Washington's only public hospital from refusing to grant first trimester abortions to eligible women.

92. 377 F. Supp. 673 (D. Neb. 1974).

93. *Id.* at 683.

94. 495 F.2d 1342 (8th Cir. 1974), *appeal dismissed* 419 U.S. 891, 42 L. Ed. 2d 136 (1974).

The trial court here, as did the First Circuit in *Hathaway*, felt required to hold that an outright ban on nontherapeutic abortions (Hathaway dealt with a municipal hospital's ban on sterilization operations) was unconstitutional under the teachings of *Roe* and *Doe*. We agree.[95]

Thus, courts in the First, Second, Third, Sixth, Seventh, Eighth, and Tenth circuits have ruled that public hospitals and public officials may not promulgate regulations, informal policies, or resolutions which discriminate against some users of the facility by prohibiting the performance of elective abortions or sterilizations, and that state medicaid laws and regulations may not discriminate against women seeking elective sterilizations and abortions. Such restrictive regulations, of course, are not being enacted by Congress when it enacts institutional conscience clauses. But these are the kinds of regulations which a public hospital might claim it has the right to promulgate under conscience clause legislation applicable to abortion and sterilization. If conscience clause legislation can constitutionally be so utilized, public hospitals could adopt regulations of a type which many federal courts have held to be in violation of the due process and equal protection guarantees of the Constitution and the teachings of *Roe* and *Doe*. Clearly if conscience clauses were thus invoked, they too would run afoul of constitutional guarantees.

B. *Private Hospitals*

The fourteenth amendment and the Civil Rights Act (Section 1983) apply only to government action and do not reach purely private conduct. However, when private conduct and governmental activity become intertwined, courts will examine the private conduct to determine if the state is involved to such an extent that the private conduct has become ."clothed in" or "impressed with" state action. In cases involving private hospitals, federal jurisdiction under the civil rights act is generally based on the theory that the state's involvement with the hospital makes the state and the hospital "joint venturers" in some activity. This principle was elaborated in *Burton v. Wilmington Parking Authority*[96] where the Supreme Court said:

> It is clear. . .that 'Individual invasion of individual rights is not the subject-matter of the amendment,' [citing the Civil Rights Cases] and that private conduct abridging individual rights does no violence to the Equal Protection Clause *unless to some significant extent the State in any of its manifestations* has been found to have become involved in it . . . . Only by sifting facts and

---

95. *Id.* at 1345-46.
96. 365 U.S. 715 (1961). The Court held that the fourteenth amendment prohibited racial discrimination by the operator of a private restaurant leased in a state owned and operated building.

weighing circumstances can the non-obvious involvement of the State in private conduct be attributed its true significance.[97]

The case by case approach suggested in the Court's stress on "shifting facts and weighing circumstances" led first to court decisions which, like those involving public hospitals, applied the fourteenth amendment to prohibit racially discriminatory staffing policies in private hospitals. For example, in *Simkins v. Moses H. Cone Memorial Hospital*,[98] a black physician challenged the defendants' discriminatory staffing policies. The Fourth Circuit reversed a district court decision finding no state action and held, instead, that the defendant hospitals, though private, were instrumentalities of the government and therefore were subject to the strictures of the fifth and fourteenth amendments. The court based its conclusion on government involvement and participation in the hospitals' activities through "massive use of public funds [Hill-Burton hospital construction funds, 42 U.S.C. § 291-291z (1974)] and extensive state-federal sharing in the common plan. . . ."[99]

Courts have also found state action because of government involvement with private hospitals other than through direct financing such as Hill-Burton grants. The leading decision on this point is *Eaton v. Grubbs*,[100] a case like *Simkins* in which a black physician challenged discriminatory hospital staffing policies. Relying on *Burton v. Wilmington Parking Authority*[101] and *Simkins v. Moses H. Cone Memorial Hospital*,[102] the court found state action in the form of tax exemptions, use of eminent domain to secure additional land for the hospital, capital construction subsidies, and a lease provision and trust agreement requiring the hospital to operate for the benefit of the city and county. Acknowledging that the separate elements might not individually constitute state action, the court found, nevertheless, that the total record created involvement sufficient for a finding of state action under section 1983.

Simkins and *Eaton* are both Fourth Circuit decisions involving racially discriminatory hospital staffing policies. The principles developed in these cases have been broadened in other circuits and applied in cases where racial discrimination was not a factor. For example, in *Sams v. Ohio Valley General Hospital Ass'n*,[103] the court held that a hospital receiving federal funds unconstitutionally discriminates against patients from neighboring geographic regions when it denies staff privileges to physicians from different, but neighboring regions. Further, in *Citta v. Delaware Valley Hospital*,[104] a staff

---

97. *Id.* at 722 (emphasis added).
98. 323 F.2d 959 (4th Cir. 1963), *cert. denied* 376 U.S. 938 (1964) [hereinafter cited as *Simkins*].
99. *Id.* at 967.
100. 329 F.2d 710 (4th Cir. 1964).
101. 365 U.S. 715 (1961). *See* note 96 *supra.*
102. 323 F.2d 959 (4th Cir. 1963), *cert. denied* 376 U.S. 938 (1964).
103. 413 F.2d 826 (4th Cir. 1969).
104. 313 F. Supp 301 (E.D.Pa. 1970).

privileges case where racial discrimination was not an issue, the court held that the physician's allegation that he had been denied a proper hearing constituted a claim for relief under section 1983. Basing jurisdiction on the hospital's receipt of Hill-Burton hospital construction funds, the court said:

> We proceed from the well-established principle that the receipt of Hill-Burton funds carries with it the obligation to observe Federal Constitutional mandates. Disregard of these mandates constitutes state action, for the Act trusts the State to maintain a fair and just governance of [those] hospitals accepting the aid of legislation. . . .[105]

Further, this principle was restated and applied to a claimed violation of first amendment rights. In *Holmes v. Silver Cross Hospital of Joliet, Ill.*[106] an administrator claimed that the hospital and its physicians had violated section 1983 by compelling a blood transfusion for the decedent against his religious convictions. In rejecting a defense that the defendants had not acted under color of state law, the court said:

> Where state and private goals, functions and activities have become so intertwined as to become indistinguishable . . . actions for the deprivation of civil rights have been upheld since the alternative would allow states to circumvent the policies of section 1983 by funneling funds and actions through private instrumentalities.[107]

Thus, where private hospitals have been defendants in civil rights actions, mainly staff privileges cases, some federal courts have held that the receipt of federal and local funds and the fact of government regulations and benefits may make the action of a private hospital "state action" for purposes of section 1983 jurisdiction.[108] Courts have applied this rule broadly, employing it not only in race discrimination cases but also in non-racial discrimination cases involving claimed violations of due process, equal protection, and first amendment rights. Where, however, private hospitals have been defendants in abortion and sterilization cases, the tendency of the courts has been to dismiss the actions brought on the ground that state action was not involved.

---

105. *Id.* at 307.
106. 340 F. Supp. 125 (N.D.Ill. 1972).
107. *Id.* at 132.
108. *See also* Sosa v. Board of Managers of Valverde Memorial Hospital, 437 F.2d 173 (5th Cir. 1971); Meyer v. Massachusetts Eye and Ear Infirmary, 330 F. Supp 1328 (D. Mass. 1971); O'Neill v. Grayson County War Memorial Hospital, 427 F.2d 1140 (6th Cir. 1973); Christhilf v. Annapolis Emergency Hospital Assn., Inc., 476 F.2d 174 (4th Cir. 1974); Schlein v. The Milford Hospital, 383 F. Supp. 1263 (D. Conn. 1974). *But see* cases cited in text accompanying notes 111-121 *infra*.

The decisions in these cases also rest on precedents developed in cases involving racial discrimination. The leading United States Supreme Court decision is *Moose Lodge No. 107 v. Irvis*,[109] a case in which the Court limited the applicability of the state "involvement" theory as a basis for finding state action for purposes of federal jurisdiction in civil rights cases. In *Moose Lodge*, the Court held that racial discrimination toward a guest by a private club was not actionable under section 1983 since the claimed involvement, in this case issuance of a liquor license, was not sufficient to make that state a joint participant. The Court said:

> [Our holdings] indicate that where the impetus for the discrimination is private, the State must have 'significantly involved itself with invidious discriminations' . . . in order for the discriminatory action to fall within the ambit of the constitutional prohibition.[110]

The requirement for a nexus between the state's involvement and the allegedly unconstitutional private conduct has also controlled the disposition of some cases involving public regulation and financing of private educational institutions and private hospitals. The private college cases have involved the due process claims of suspended students. For example, in *Powe v. Miles*[111] the court ruled that Alfred University's action in suspending student protesters did not amount to state action for purposes of section 1983, even though there was state involvement through contracts, regulations, and financing. Because the state's involvement was not related to the deprivation of the students' rights, the students were not entitled to relief.[112]

Similarly, challenges to publicly funded private hospitals which denied staff privileges have also on occasions failed because the action challenged was

---

109. 407 U.S. 163 (1972).
110. *Id.* at 173.
111. 407 F.2d 73 (2d Cir. 1968).
112. The court said:
The contention that New York's regulation of educational standards in private schools, colleges, and universities . . . makes their acts in curtailing protest and disciplining students the acts of the state is equally unimpressive. It overlooks the essential point—that the state must be involved not simply with some activity of the institution alleged to have inflicted injury upon a plaintiff, but with the activity that caused the injury.

. . .

We perceive no basis for holding that the grant of scholarships and . . . financing . . . imposes on the State a duty to see that Alfred's overall policies with respect to demonstrations and discipline conform to First and Fourteenth Amendment standards so that state inaction might constitute an object of attack. 407 F.2d at 81.
See Grafton v. Brooklyn Law School, 478 F.2d 1137 (2d Cir. 1973); Blackburn v. Fisk, 443 F.2d 121 (6th Cir. 1971). *Cf.* Goss v. Lopez, 43 U.S.L.W. 4181 (U.S. Jan. 22, 1975) wherein the Supreme Court ruled that the due process clause of the fourteenth amendment requires that high school officials provide notice and an opportunity to be heard to students faced with the possibility of suspension for misconduct.

found not to amount to state action. In these cases, as in the school cases, the courts have emphasized that the state's involvement must be directly related to the alleged constitutional violation. For example, in *Mulvihill v. Butterfield Memorial Hospital*,[113] a physician staff privileges case, the court said:

> The state must be involved not simply with some activity of the institution alleged to have inflicted the injury . . . . but with the activity that caused the injury. 'Putting the point another way, the state action, not the private action, must be the subject of the complaint.'[114]

These cases seem to reject the precedents followed by those courts which hold that state action may be based on the cumulative effects of various forms of state involvement such as financing, regulation, and tax exemption. They conclude, instead, that partial public financing is not enough: for action to be found to be state action in violation of the Constitution the activities of the state must be directly related to or involved with the activities which give rise to the alleged violation.

Recently, several federal courts have followed this line of cases and have allowed private hospitals receiving public funds to enforce abortion and sterilization-prohibiting regulations. In *Taylor v. St. Vincent's Hospital*,[115] *Doe v. Bellin Memorial Hospital*[116] and *Greco v. Orange Memorial Hospital Corp.*,[117] the courts upheld private hospital policies forbidding the performance of sterilizations and abortions in the hospitals' facilities. And in *Watkins v. Mercy Medical Center*[118] and *Barrett v. United Hospital*[119] the courts upheld the right of private hospitals to refuse to reappoint physicians whose views or conduct with respect to the abortion issue did not conform to the anti-abortion policies of these hospitals. The courts deciding these cases have emphasized the requirement for a nexus between the government aspects and the precise policy complained of to warrant holding a private entity subject to constitutional guarantees applicable only to state action. For example, in ruling that a private hospital's abortion prohibiting policy did not amount to state action, a federal district court said:

> There is no claim that the state has sought to influence hospital

---

113. 329 F. Supp. 1020 (S.D.N.Y. 1971).

114. *Id.* at 1023, *citing* Powe v. Miles, 407 F.2d 73, 81 (2d Cir. 1968). *See also* Jackson v. Norton-Children's Hospitals, Inc., 487 F.2d 502 (6th Cir. 1973), *cert. denied* 416 U.S. 1000 (1974); *also* Ward v. St. Anthony's Hospital, 476 F.2d 471 (10th Cir. 1973). *But see* cases cited in text accompanying notes 98-108 *supra*.

115. Civ. No. 1090 (1972), *rev'd* 369 F. Supp. 948 (D. Mont. 1973).

116. 479 F.2d 756 (7th Cir. 1973).

117. 374 F. Supp. 227 (E.D.Tex. 1974).

118. 364 F. Supp. 799 (D.Idaho 1973).

119. 376 F. Supp. 791 (S.D.N.Y. 1974).

policy respecting abortions, either by direct regulation or by discriminatory application of its powers or its benefits. Insofar as actions of the State of Wisconsin or its agents is disclosed in the record, the State has exercised no influence whatsoever on the decision of the defendants which plaintiffs challenge in this litigation.[120]

In *Chrisman v. Sisters of St. Joseph of Peace*,[121] an action brought by a woman seeking sterilization at a denominational hospital, the court followed the same line of reasoning and held that it lacked jurisdiction under section 1983 because the state was not involved with the challenged hospital regulation. Significantly, the court also rejected the plaintiff's claim that the Church Amendment was constitutionally invalid as a violation of the Establishment Clause of the first amendment to the United States Constitution. The court concluded that the Church Amendment was itself neutral and that it protected "the freedom of religion of those with religious or moral scruples against sterilizations and abortions."[122] Since in the opinion of the court there was no valid first amendment claim, the court found the Church Amendment to be a valid limitation on the power of the federal courts to grant equitable relief in abortion and sterilization cases.

In contrast to the public hospital abortion decisions, the holdings in each of these private hospital cases affirm the conscience clause principle. That is, in each case hospitals were allowed to enforce abortion and sterilization restricting regulations, and the fact of federal funding and other forms of state involvement did not materially influence the courts' decisions. It is notable that in three of these cases, the courts referred to the Church Amendment to support the finding of no state action. In one of them, the court upheld the Church Amendment against a first amendment claim.

C. Court Decisions on Entity Conscience Clauses in State Legislation

It has been argued that in *Doe v. Bolton*,[123] there is dictum recognizing the validity of entity conscience clauses.[124] Unlike the restrictive Texas statute at issue in *Roe v. Wade*, the Georgia statute at issue in *Doe* was a more liberal law which permitted abortions for several reasons to protect the woman's health, not just her life. For this reason, the challenge to the law was based not on its main provisions but rather on numerous regulatory provi-

120. 479 F.2d 756, 761 (7th Cir. 1973).
121. 506 F.2d 308 (9th Cir. 1974).
122. *Id.* at 312.
123. 410 U.S. 179 (1973).
124. *See, e.g.*, Doe v. Bellin Memorial Hospital, 479 F.2d 756, 760 (7th Cir. 1973) and Chrisman v. Sisters of St. Joseph, 506 F.2d 308 (9th Cir. 1974).

sions, many of which the district court and the Supreme Court ultimately found to be unduly restrictive. However, neither court voided the institutional conscience clause in section 26-1201 (e).[125] Rather, the Supreme Court apparently relied on this clause to support invalidation of an abortion committee requirement in the statute. After objecting to the committee requirement, the Court said:

> And the hospital itself is otherwise fully protected. Under Section 26-1202 (e) the hospital is free not to admit a patient for an abortion. It is even free not to have an abortion committee . . . . These provisions obviously are in the statute in order to afford appropriate protection to the individual and to the *denominational* hospital. Section 26-1202(e) affords adequate protection to the hospital. . . .[126]

Some courts and commentators have interpreted this passage as a validation of the institutional conscience clause principle.[127] It would seem, however, that such an assumption is unwarranted for two reasons. First, the plaintiffs in *Doe* did not challenge the conscience clause regulation (it was challenged only in amicus briefs), and second, the Supreme Court's dictum on this point names *denominational* hospitals only, even though the statutory language does not itself specify any particular type of hospital. Thus, although there may be dictum in *Doe* to the effect that such clauses are not invalid as applied to denominational hospitals, the Supreme Court has not ruled squarely on the question nor has it said anything at all on the question of the validity of such a clause as applied to a non-denominational hospital.

Although there are no definitive decisions on the validity of institutional conscience clauses in federal legislation, some of the factors affecting the constitutionality of similar provisions in state legislation are elaborated in two recent federal court decisions. Both cases involved challenges to state abortion laws enacted after the United States Supreme Court abortion decisions, and both suggest that conscience clauses cannot Constitutionally be utilized by *all* hospitals to refuse abortions or voluntary sterilization. In *Doe v. Rampton*,[128] a three-judge court invalidated a 1973 Utah statute which contained a detailed all-inclusive series of conscience clauses which read:

> 76-7-306. Physician, hospital employee or hospital not required to participate in abortion.
> (1) [Individual conscience clause].
> (2) Nothing in this part shall require a hospital to admit any

125. GA. LAWS § 26-1201(e) (1968).
126. 410 U.S. at 197-8 (emphasis added).
127. *See* note 105 *supra*.
128. 366 F. Supp. 189 (D.Utah 1973).

patient under the provisions hereof for the purpose of having an abortion.

(3) [Same language, but specifying private hospital].

(4) [Same language, but specifying denominational hospital].[129]

The first of the three opinions in *Doe v. Rampton* held that section 76-7-306 was totally invalid because it was broad enough to make abortions impossible to obtain in any trimester. The judge said:

> [S]urely the state may not, as Utah attempts to do in Section 76-7-302, provide that every woman who desires an abortion in Utah must seek the services of a physician licensed and regulated by the state and that the majority of women who desire an abortion in Utah must seek the facilities of a state licensed and regulated hospital and then provide, as in this section, that all such physicians and hospitals may deny their services and facilities to every such woman in every circumstance.[130]

Another judge on the panel concluded that the individual and denominational hospital conscience clauses in subsections (1) and (4), respectively, were valid, but absent more facts, he withheld judgment on the "hospital" (undefined) and private hospital conscience clauses in subsections (2) and (3).[131] The third judge stated that the statute was invalid but his reasons related to legislative motive and tactics, rather than to substantive legal principles.[132]

Hodgson v. Anderson,[133] was an action challenging the constitutionality of the 1973 Minnesota abortion law. That law included an institutional conscience clause which provided that no person, hospital or institution will be:

> coerced, held liable, or discriminated against in any manner because of a refusal to perform, accommodate or assist or subject to abortion for any reason.[134]

The court invalidated several other restrictive provisions of the statute it regarded as overly restrictive and partially invalidated the entity conscience clause by ruling that the clause was invalid insofar as it applied to public hospitals. The court said:

---

129. *Id.* at 196, *citing* U.C.A. § 76-7-306 (1953).
130. 366 F. Supp. at 193.
131. *Id.* at 204.
132. *Id.* at 178-9.
133. 378 F. Supp. 1008 (D. Minn. 1974).
134. *Id.* at 1014, *citing* MINN. STAT. § 145.414 (1974).

The provisions of Section 145.414 are overbroad and invalid as applied to public hospitals whose facilities are sought for first and second stage abortions and constitute state interference of the kind prohibited by the Supreme Court in *Roe v. Wade.* With respect to Section 145.414, we conclude the law as determined by the Eighth Circuit in *Nyberg [v. City of Virginia* 495 F.2d 1347] to be dispositive.

'[T]he hospital facilities must be made available for abortion services, as they are for other medical procedures, to those physicians and their patients who have a right to and request such facilities.'[135]

Thus, the *Hodgson* court specifically invalidated a statutory conscience clause as it applied to public institutions. Many other challenges to the applicability of conscience clauses to public hospitals and to private hospitals with attributes sufficient to make their action "state action" are presently in process and others are planned.

IV. Conclusion

The expenditure of public funds on the national and local levels as an instrument for accomplishing social, political, and economic policy objectives has increased substantially since the end of the Second World War. However, statutes which purport to allow the receipt or use of government "largesse" as a basis for the recipients of such funds to restrict constitutionally protected rights of others raise serious constitutional questions. This, of course, is the specific intent of the institutional conscience clauses and the related abortion-restricting provisions: they purport to permit public *and* private hospitals to refuse to perform abortions (and sterilizations) in direct defiance of the United States Supreme Court rulings prohibiting all but very limited governmental regulation of the abortion procedure in the first and second trimesters of pregnancy.

A number of federal courts have invalidated anti-abortion and anti-sterilization regulations and policies such as those which the federal institutional conscience clauses would permit if they are read literally. The courts have found that restrictive abortion and sterilization regulations promulgated by public hospitals are constitutionally invalid because they infringe rights of privacy, and/or because they are overbroad in relation to the trimester schedule set out in *Roe v. Wade*, and/or because they unreasonably discriminate against one class of patients—that is, those seeking abortions and

---

135. 378 F. Supp. at 1018, *citing* Nyberg v. City of Virginia, 495 F.2d 1342 (8th Cir. 1974), *appeal dismissed* 419 U.S. 891, 42 L. Ed. 2d 136 (1974).

sterilizations—in violation of the equal protection guarantee of the federal Constitution. Whatever the rationale, each of the courts appears to have recognized that prohibitive and highly restrictive regulation of voluntary sterilizations and abortions by public hospitals are acting inconsistently with the Supreme Court's abortion decisions. As the court said in *Nyberg v. City of Virginia:*

> It would be a non sequitur to say that the abortion decision and its effectuation is an election to be made by the physician and his patient without interference by the state and then allow the state through its public hospitals to effectively bar the physician from using state facilities to perform the operation.[136]

The law, insofar as it applies to private hospitals, is less clear. Many courts have held that public funding, regulation, and other forms of involvement are not sufficient without more to warrant the action of a private hospital being regarded as "state action", and have refused to assume jurisdiction in order to redress grievances flowing from even absolute anti-sterilization and anti-abortion edicts. Other courts, however, have vindicated constitutional claims against private hospitals in cases "[W]here state and private goals, functions and activities have become so intertwined as to become indistinguishable."[137] The precedents which find state action on the part of publicly funded private hospitals which act inconsistently with the federal Constitution make clear that any other conclusion would "allow states to circumvent the policies of section 1983 by funneling funds and actions through private instrumentalities."[138]

In any event, it appears now to be established that prohibitive and overly restrictive abortion and sterilization policies on the part of a public hospital violate the provisions of the fourteenth amendment. Similarly, if a hospital, although in some respects private (e.g., a voluntary nonprofit association), is characterized by the indicia which courts have held render the hospital's activities "state action", the hospital's refusal to admit abortion and sterilization patients, like a refusal to admit or treat blacks, would be unconstitutional whether or not such refusal reflected the "religious belief" or "moral conviction" of the hospital. Where there is a detailed and substantial showing of public funding, public regulation and public function, many courts tend to find that private entities are engaged in "state action" which renders them subject to constitutional guarantees.

What then is the purpose and effect of the entity conscience clauses?

---

136. 495 F.2d 1342, 1346 (8th Cir. 1974), *appeal dismissed* 419 U.S. 891, 42 L. Ed. 2d 136 (1974).
137. Holmes v. Silver Cross Hospital of Joliet, Ill., 340 F. Supp. 125, 132 (N.D.Ill. 1972).
138. *Id.*

They are superfluous with respect to private entities whose action would not be considered "state action" anyway. In the absence of a sufficient number of public indicators of state action, such entities may follow their "religious belief" and "moral conviction" as they see fit free of constitutional constraint—and they do not need the entity conscience clauses to do so. But if, on the other hand, public entities or private entities whose action would otherwise be considered state action are involved, an institutional conscience clause cannot transform their action into non-state action. In other words, no conscience clause can put a state action hospital, public or private, beyond the reach of the constitutional guarantee of freedom of choice as to child bearing.

The conclusion is plain: the receipt of federal funds cannot be made the basis for insulating any entity receiving them from otherwise applicable constitutional guarantees. If this were not so, "entities" like schools and hospitals which receive HEW funds could on that ground alone refuse to serve or treat, for example, any black person or any persons of any other minority group by asserting that to do so would, because of that person's race, creed, color, national origin or sex, offend its "religious belief" or "moral convictions." Since the institutional conscience laws are superfluous in relation to purely private hospitals and unconstitutional with reference to public and "state action" private hospitals, they serve no useful purpose and they create and encourage confusion and litigation. It is hoped that responsible legislators and administrators will avoid such clauses in the future.

Pregnancy and Abortion in Adolescence: A Comparative Legal Survey and Proposals for Reform*

By
Luke T. Lee** and John M. Paxman***

OUTLINE

* This article is a revised version of a background paper prepared for the World Health Organization Symposium on Pregnancy and Abortion in Adolescence, held in Geneva, 24-28 June 1974.

** J.D., Ph.D., Director, Law and Population Programme, Fletcher School of Law and Diplomacy.

*** J.D., Research Associate in International Law, Fletcher School of Law and Diplomacy.

I. INTRODUCTION

(1) 18-year old single girl; lives with brother. On admission claimed to be nulliparous and to be menstruating. Admitted with TETANUS. On examination by gynecologist sixth day of hospital stay, her breasts were active, os uteri patulous, uterus not bulky. Died eighth day; autopsy confirmed abortion.

(4) 15-year old single girl lived with father. Procurement with oral drugs from chemists and relations. No tetanus. On admission Anaemic + +; T. 99.6 to 102.2°F. High vaginal swab; pus cells+ +, occasional Gram + cocci. Culture (anaerobic and aerobic) sterile. Died within 24 hours. Autopsy confirmation.

(12) 16-year old housewife lived with father. Admitted with Tetanus due to attempt to procure abortion at 26 weeks; had injections from a nurse 4 days before, and died within 24 hours of admission. Autopsy; male foetus, crown-rump length 21.4 cm.

These are three case summaries of eighteen deaths attributed to procured abortion among 161 patients aged 12-20 admitted the Lagos University Teaching Hospital in the 1963-67 period.[1] The high mortality rate of 11.2% in one of the best staffed and equipped hospitals in Nigeria bespeaks the serious health hazard posed by teen-age pregnancy and abortion in that West African country.

From another continent, with another perspective, we find a recent study showing that 55% of nonvirgin adolescents interviewed in the United States confessed that neither they nor their partners used any birth control method, nor did they do anything else to reduce the risk of pregnancy at the time of first sexual intercourse. Of this same group of girls, 19% indicated as a regular birth control method: "I just trusted to luck that I wouldn't become pregnant;" Eight percent stated: "I didn't think about whether or not I might become pregnant." The resultant pregnancy rates of 11% for nonvirgin girls aged 13-15 and 28% for those aged 16-19 should have come as no surprise.[2] Every year, more than 200,000 girls aged 17 and under—one in ten—give

1. *See* Akingba and Gbajimo, *Procured Abortion: Counting the Cost*, 7 JOURNAL OF THE NIGERIA MEDICAL ASSOCIATION, No. 3, at 17, 26 (1970).
2. Sorensen and Hendin, *Adolescent Sexuality in Contemporary America: A Survey of Teenage Attitudes and Practices*, Boston Globe, Feb. 18, 1973 (Magazine), at 6-10. *Adapted from* THE SORENSEN REPORT: ADOLESCENT SEXUALITY IN CONTEMPORARY AMERICA (1973).

birth, and the divorce rate among teenagers is three times the national average.[3]

The modern version of "Madame Butterfly" as teen-age "temporary wives" of servicemen stationed overseas presents another dimension of the adolescent pregnancy problem. Often abandoned to overcrowded orphanages, the offspring grow up physically conspicuous and emotionally disturbed amidst the taunts of their schoolmates, whether in Europe or in Asia. According to a recent study made in West Germany, a country which until recently had a restrictive abortion law,[4] 65% of some 8,000 children of half-black parentage are growing up psychologically retarded, shy and inhibited.[5] In racially monolithic Japan, only a handful of half-black children have broken through the high walls of prejudice, winding up mainly in the entertainment field.[6] Similar stigmas attach to children whose fathers are Caucasian. Even under the Confucian concept of tightly knit families, South Korea's "half-castes" are considered "outcastes," and their presence reminds many Koreans of the shame of widespread prostitution.[7]

Dissimilar though the above situations may seem, as far as adolescents are concerned, they share a common theme: a lack of concern for basic human rights. Specifically, the following rights as set out in United Nations documents were ignored:

(a) the right to adequate education and information on family planning;[8]

(b) the right of access to the means of practicing family planning;[9] and,

(c) the right of children, whether born in or out of wedlock, to equal status under the law and to adequate support from natural parents.[10]

It should be noted that human rights, by definition, "attach to all human beings equally, whatever their nationality,"[11] and, as such, impose not only a

---

3. N.Y. Times, May 5, 1974, § 4, at 5, col. 2. *See also,* Cohn and Lieberman, *Family Planning and Health: Congruent Objectives of Malthus and Spock,* 64 AM. J. PUB. HEALTH 225-229 (1974).

4. According to reports, the lower house of the West German Parliament recently approved a bill which would legalize abortion during the first three months of pregnancy thus superseding the former century-old statute. Washington Post, Apr. 27, 1974, at A24, col. 1. However, the application of the new law was suspended at the request of the Lord of Baden-Wiirtenburg by the Constitutional Court at Karlsruh on June 21, 1974. The application of Baden-Wiirtenburg is based on Article 2 of the Constitution which provides that: "Every person has the right to life and to physical integrity."

5. *The Abandoned,* NEWSWEEK MAGAZINE, Feb. 13, 1967, at 50.

6. *Id.* The estimates of the number of mixed bloods fathered during the post-war American occupation of Japan range from the low Japanese official figure 4,000 to 50,000.

7. *Confucius' Outcasts: South Korea,* TIME MAGAZINE, Dec. 10, 1965, at 43.

8. Proclamation of Teheran, Final Act of the International Conference on Human Rights, para. 16, and Resolution XVIII (1968) on the Human Rights Aspects of Family Planning, adopted by the Conference on Human Rights at Teheran on 12 May 1968.

9. U.N. Declaration on Social Progress and Development, Art. 22(b), G.A. Res. 2542, 24 U.N. GAOR, Supp. 18, at 45, U.N. Doc. A/7388 (1969).

10. Declaration of the Rights of the Child, Principle 1, G.A. Res. 1386, 14 U.N. GAOR, Supp. 16, at 19, U.N. Doc. A/4354 (1959).

11. Waldock, *Human Rights in Contemporary International Law and the Significance of the European Convention,* 11 INT'L AND COMP. L.Q. 3 (Supp. 1965).

moral, but also a legal responsibility upon states "to see to it that laws and policies contradictory to this right should be amended or abolished, and new ones adopted in conformity with and in promotion of this right."[12] Cast in such a light several important questions arise:

> What are the consequences of the denial of such rights, especially to adolescents to whom society necessarily owes a greater duty of protection than it does to adults?
>
> How does law affect the rights of adolescents in matters which concern pregnancy and abortion?
>
> What role should law assume in protecting the rights of minors?
>
> What paramount interests are we seeking to protect?
>
> Lastly, what corrective reform measures should be undertaken?

It should be noted at the outset that no universal legal model exists for dealing with adolescent pregnancy and abortion. The law of each jurisdiction is a function of national and cultural preferences and varies accordingly. There is, however, a common thread which runs through the laws of the various jurisdictions—human rights, especially the rights of the child—whose potential for contributing to the solution of the problem of adolescent pregnancy and abortion deserves to be explored.

The purpose of this paper is thus to define the various legal issues which are relevant to the problem of adolescent pregnancy and abortion, particularly from the viewpoint of human rights.

II. The Legal Status of Adolescents

A. *Definition of "Adolescents"*

There is no consensus with respect to the definition of "minors" or "adolescents." Legal minimum ages vary not only according to sex, but also according to purposes, such as marriage, civil majority, criminal responsibility, voting right, military service, alcoholic beverages, etc.[13] For each of the purposes, the ages differ from country to country and, in a federal structure, such as that of the United States, from state to state.

For the purposes of this paper, therefore, the terms "minor," "adolescent," and "teenager" are used interchangeably to denote a person who, by the laws of her country, is below the age at which she is judged competent in reaching independent decisions on specified matters otherwise allowed to adults.

---

12. Letter by Vicente Abad Santos, Secretary of Justice of the Philippines, to Dean Irene Cortes of the University of the Philippines, College of Law, March 16, 1972.

13. *See* App. I for a compilation, covering 48 countries, of the ages at which various rights attach.

B. *Status in Civil Matters*

Historically, the legal status of minors in *civil* matters has been quite different from that of adults. The law universally bestows a protective civil status upon minors which insulates them from the flightiness of their decisions and from outside coercion on the theory that they "lack the capacity to act because their physical, mental and moral development is incomplete."[14] The rationale which underlies this essentially paternalistic view was reiterated in a court decision rendered in the United States a little more than a decade ago:

> At common law infants (under 21) do not possess the power to exercise the same legal rights as adults. The disabilities are really privileges, which the law gives them, and which they may exercise for their own benefit, the object of the law being to secure infants from damaging themselves or their property by their own improvident acts or prevent them from being imposed on others.[15]

This special legal status cuts two ways. On one hand, it sponsors an attitude which gives minors special protections that are not available to adults. For example, a minor may void at his option most contracts he has entered into. It was in the area of child employment that some of the first "protective" laws regarding minors were passed in the United States. After repeated attempts to quell the practice of employing youths in hazardous industries, the passage of the Fair Labor Standards Act of 1938[15a] triggered a wealth of state legislation aimed at prohibiting the employment of youths under 18 in hazardous industries and limiting the hours that youths under 16 could work.[16] The simultaneous enactment of compulsory education laws acted as a means of protecting minors by ensuring that a child would not be sent to work before a certain age.

On the other hand, many of the benefits available to adults through the exercise of choice are not available to minors without parental consent. This is particularly true in the area of medical treatment where the paternalistic concern for the welfare of the minor and the standards governing the tort liability of medical personnel come together to generally bar medical treatment absent parental consent, except in emergency cases. To a certain extent, then, minors are held hostage to the will of their parents or guardians.

It is in fact the law relating to medical treatment of minors that most directly affects the problems of adolescent pregnancy and abortion. Until recently, the near-universal rule has been that minors must have the consent of their parents before they receive medical treatment. In the absence

---

14. J. PORRAS GARCÍA, PROTECCIÓN DE MENORES EN MATERIA CIVIL 23 (Mexico, 1964).
15. Dixon v. United States, 197 F. Supp. 803 (W.D.S.C., 1961).
15a. P.L. 87-30, 75 Stat. 65.
16. U.S. DEP'T OF LABOR, 3 THE CHILD 17-18 (1938).

thereof, the actions of the medical practitioner in treating a minor may constitute an assault and battery.

This rule is increasingly being made subject to exceptions. First, the "emancipated minor rule" now recognizes that a minor who is emancipated from parental control—married minors or those who live separately from their parents, earn their own living, and make their own decisions on important matters—can consent to medical treatment. Second, a mature minor rule has also been established which permits minors of sufficiently advanced maturity and knowledge to do the same.[17] Third, in the face of problems related to venereal disease, drug abuse and teenage pregnancy, a few countries have legislated into existence general "health services to minors acts" which permit underaged persons to seek and consent to medical help without parental consent.[18] Though these inroads have been slight to date, there is a trend in the direction of granting more decision-making power to minors where medical treatment is involved.

There is also a body of law which is slowly growing out of situations where the minor is in need of medical intervention and the parents refuse to permit such treatment.[19] The necessity of performing blood transfusions, amputations, and other types of corrective surgery have given rise to a series of cases in which courts have exercised their *parens patriae* power and have stepped in to determine that the best interest of the child dictates that the treatment be authorized. This type of judicial intervention is often narrowly circumscribed, but courts will use their authority to authorize treatment if the facts support the need.

C. *Status Under Criminal Law*

Despite the fact that minors had traditionally been treated differently in civil matters, it was only at the beginning of the twentieth century that recognition was given to the concept that as far as the criminal law was concerned minors also differed from adults. On the basis of their mental, physical and emotional differences, it was argued that the interests of all would best be served if minors were given specialized treatment for violations of the criminal law. Prior to the twentieth century, courts with criminal jurisdiction had dealt with juvenile and adult offenders under the same set of rules and punishment. There is one English case, for example, which shows that as late as 1852, two children, one age two, the other age six, were haled

---

17. The "mature minor" rule has yet to gain universal acceptance.
18. Miss. Code Ann. §§ 7129-81 *et. seq.* (Supp. 1966).
19. An example of the former reluctance of courts to intervene is shown by the decision In re Hudson, 13 Wash. 2d 673, 126 P.2d 765 (Sup. Ct. 1942) (parental refusal to permit amputation of a club arm). But in In re Rotkowitz, a New York Court declared a child, who needed surgery to correct a deformed leg but whose parents split on consent, neglected and ordered the operation performed. 175 Misc. 948, 25 N.Y.S. 2d 624 (Dom. Rel. Ct. 1941).

into court for "laying snares" to trap game. They were fined and told that if
they failed to pay they would be imprisoned for 30 days.[20] Other examples of
rigorous treatment can be found. In 1828, 13-year-old boy was hanged for
murder in New Jersey.[21] During the mid-nineteenth century, signs of the
shift in theory were made apparent by legislation in several countries which
began to afford specialized treatment for the criminal acts of minors. This
change came into widespread acceptance in the early 1900's, when juvenile
courts or other institutions, such as the child welfare boards which specialized
in treating minors, were first established.[22] It was then that the theory and
practice of treating minors became one of protection and rehabilitation rather
than punishment through imprisonment, the basis being that a minor differs
in intellectual and emotional maturity from an adult. As a result, the notion
persists that minors should not be stigmatized for what would otherwise be
criminal acts.

  While attempts to provide successful rehabilitative treatment to minors
have produced uneven results, the distinctive treatment between adults and
minors is now virtually universal. Under the recently revised Penal Code of
the German Democratic Republic, youths aged 14 to 18 are given sentences
with special care taken to shape their development in a "positive direction"
and help them gain a sense of "social responsibility" to the end that they
become "useful" citizens.[23] The so-called special legal status of a minor under
criminal law was evidenced also by an observation made in an opinion of the
Supreme Court of Ghana regarding the sentencing of a 15-year-old girl who
had been convicted of procuring an abortion. The Court said that "by reason
of the age of the girl," the trial court was precluded from imposing the prison
sentence required under the statute.[24] It is of interest to note, however, that
the girl was tried in a criminal court under the Offences Against the Person
Act, which makes no distinctions for age or legal status.[25]

  While it can be seen that the law, both civil and criminal, affords to
minors a "privileged" status by acknowledging their right to proper care,
education, employment protection, and special guidance and rehabilitation for
illegal acts, the reality is sometimes quite different. Under the guise of
protective legal status, minors have been denied many of the most fundamental of rights. For example, in the United States, juveniles were long denied

  20. 2 THE CHILD AND THE STATE 328 (G. Abbot ed. 1947).
  21. Hofmann and Pilpel, *The Legal Rights of Minors,* 20 PEDIATRIC CLINICS OF NORTH
AMERICA 991 (1973).
  22. O. NYQUIST, JUVENILE JUSTICE 138-142 (1960).
  23. Penal Code of the German Democratic Republic, Jan. 12, 1968, Art. 65.
  24. Boateng v. The State, 1964 Ghana Law Reports 602, 604 (1964).
  25. The public debate which surrounded the trial of Marie Clair Chevalier in Bobigny,
France, is suggestive of this dilemma. The 16-year old girl was tried along with her mother for
having arranged for an abortion after refusing to bear the child. Marie Clair was acquitted by the
judge but the mother was convicted and given a suspended fine as punishment, despite the strict
French law. *See* Boston Globe, Nov. 24, 1972, at 52, col. 1.

the constitutional rights of persons accused of crimes, such as the right to counsel. As seen above, under the law requiring parental consent to medical treatment, adolescents are often thwarted in their attempts to seek help. Lastly, while in many countries the social welfare benefits are available to minors and adults alike, in other countries the rights of minors are unclear. In sum, the trenchant observation made by Justice Fortas of the United States Supreme Court may have correctly characterized the legal limbo in which minors are found. He wrote:

> [T]here may be grounds for concern that the child [juvenile] receives the worst of both worlds: that he gets neither the protections accorded to adults nor the solicitous care and regenerative treatment postulated for children.[26]

It would seem fitting that attempts be made to review and clarify the legal status of minors vis-à-vis the subject matter of pregnancy and abortion.

III. Laws Affecting Pregnancy and Abortions in Adolescence

A. *Sex Education and Information*

Reference was made at the beginning of this paper to the high mortality rate connected with abortion during adolescence at the Lagos University Teaching Hospital. It is significant to note that one of the two remedies proposed for preventing unwanted pregnancies lay in the dissemination of sex information to parents and teachers, as well as young poeple.[27] Similar recommendations have appeared elsewhere. The so-called Lane Report, published in the United Kingdom in 1974, emphasized in broad terms the role that sex education should play in the prevention of unwanted pregnancies and thus the tendency to seek out abortions:

> A public educated to a more mature and responsible attitude toward sexual behaviour and to contraception will be the most sure guarantee that recourse is made less often to therapeutic abortion of unwanted pregnancies.[28]

It would seem fair to assert that most of the educational systems in the world permit some form of instruction in the curriculum concerning human reproduction. Many countries have laws or regulations similar to those in

---

26. Kent v. United States, 383 U.S. 541, 546 (1966).
27. Akingba and Gbajimo, *supra* note 1 at 28.
28. Report of the Committee on the Working of the Abortion Act, Cmnd. No. 5579, p. 185 (1974).

effect in Costa Rica, which establish a policy that the curriculum should include sex education not only on the physiological and biological aspects, but also on the psychological, ethical and religious perspectives.[29] What is less certain is whether such instruction includes specific mention of contraception. In some instances, discussion of contraception within the structure of the school curriculum may be barred by other legislation which relates specifically to the dissemination of all types of information on that subject. The prime example of this type of legislation is the French Law of July 31, 1920. While no longer the law in France, many francophone African countries have retained the law even upon attaining independence by enacting "reception" statutes which took over in whole or in part in the former French law.[30] In Chad, Section 3 of the French Law of July 31, 1920, was lifted, almost *in toto*, and made part of Article 98 of the Chad Law No. 28 of December 29, 1965.[31] Drawing its inspiration from the early French statute, Article 98, paragraph 2 of the Chad law makes the dissemination of "contraceptive or anti-natalist propaganda" through speeches in public places, or by placing in "public channels" books, written material, drawings, pictures or posters a criminal offense punishable by imprisonment of from one to six months and a fine of from 24,000 to 1,200,000 francs.

Dissemination of birth control information was banned in Italy under Section 553 of the Penal Code until 1971, when the Italian Constitutional Court declared the law unconstitutional in the *de Marchi* case. The Court decision stated in part:

> . . . the problem of family planning has, at the present period of history, become so important socially and concerns such a broad scope of interests, that in the light of the public awareness and of the gradual widening of health education it can no longer be considered an offense to public morals to discuss various aspects of the problem publicly, to disseminate information concerning it, or to promote contraceptive practices.[32]

In a small but growing number of countries sex education is being made compulsory. Such is the case in Sweden where information on contraception is provided in school to pupils between the ages of 14 and 16.[33] The recent

---

29. Exec. Decree No. 26 (March 18, 1970). Courses on sex education and hygiene are to be given during the first three years of secondary school. CÓDIGO SANITARIO, Art. 219.

30. Here we cite as examples the laws of Cameroon, Chad, Congo-Brazzaville, Central African Republic, Guinea, Niger and Upper Volta.

31. JOURNAL OFFICIEL DE LA RÉPUBLIQUE DE TCHAD, Jan. 1, 1966, at 13.

32. Corte Constituzionale, Sentenza No. 49, at 5 (March 16, 1971).

33. B. LINNER, SEX AND SOCIETY IN SWEDEN, App. D, at 142-145 (1967). A recent Danish law has also made sex education compulsory but it has been reported that the law is being challenged before the European Commission on Human Rights. SEICUS Report, No. 5, at 6 (1973).

interest in decreasing the high number of abortions in Hungary has led the Government there to require that sex education, including instruction on contraception, be included in the school curriculum as of September 1974.[34] The new Philippine Constitution places the responsibility for population control squarely on the shoulders of the Government.[35] The Population Act of 1971[36] has made contraception a national policy, and schools have been ordered to cooperate in disseminating birth control information,[37] despite the lack of a special law on sex education. Thus, contraception information is given at the secondary school level. In furtherance of the national policy, the Philippine municipality of Tiwi, Albay has enacted an ordinance which requires that before a marriage license is issued to a couple they must present a certificate from the municipal health officer to the effect that they have completed a family planning orientation course.[38]

Many countries have no laws, regulations or decisions which address the issue of sex education and contraception. This is so irrespective of whether a country has a pro-natalist or anti-natalist population policy, though admittedly more interest tends to be shown in contraception where anti-natalist policies exist. In their absence Governments have had to grope for ways to fill the void. Though Kenya has adopted a general policy as part of its Development Plan of 1970-74 aimed at reducing its rate of population growth, the Government has yet to take formal action as to sex education in the schools. What sex education there has been to date is provided by the Family Planning Association. The practice has been for the Association to approach secondary schools and colleges with offers to give lectures on family planning. In this manner some sex education is being given to adolescents.[39]

It is apparent from a survey of the literature that sex education is at once a sensitive and controversial subject. The nature of public opinion has often inhibited the implementation of an organized program of sex education in many countries, not the least among them the United States and the United Kingdom. The surge of public sensitivity to sex education is more often than not affected by cultural and religious factors. In Pakistan, where under Article 2 of the Constitution, Islam is declared the state religion, nothing which is offensive to Islamic religious principles can be taught in the schools. In the absence of an agreement on the part of Islamic scholars as to the compatibility

34. Decision No. 1040/1973/X.18 of the Council of Ministers, *Magyar Közlöny*, Oct. 18, 1973, No. 71, Sec. 11/A, para. 1; Sec. III, paras. 1-6.
35. Art. XV, § 10.
36. Republic Act. No. 6365, *as revised by* Pres. Decrees No. 69 and 79 (1972).
37. General Order 18 of December 1972.
38. Resolution No. 37, Ordinance No. 5 (March 13, 1973).
39. This information was provided by Professor U. U. Uche of the Faculty of Law, University of Nairobi, for an on-going study entitled THE WORLD'S LAWS ON SEX EDUCATION, which has been undertaken by Edmund H. Kellogg, Jan Stepan and David Kline at the request at SEICUS.

of sex education for minors with Islam, any attempt to teach contraception would of necessity have to be undertaken with caution.[40]

Though as noted above, French law has typically reflected the attitude that information regarding contraception not be disseminated,[41] recent recognition of the need for a freer flow of this type of information, particularly to teenagers, has provided the impetus for a change in French policy and law. The proposal for a Higher Council on Sex Education, Birth Control and Family Planning made in Law No. 73-639 of July 11, 1973, was implemented by a decree issued on January 5, 1974. Among other things the Council is charged with ensuring that the youth receives suitable sex education. But rather than make sex education mandatory, France has taken a middle course. Under the scheme, sex education, including instruction on contraception and ethical matters, will be provided outside of a compulsory school time in special groups which will meet with parental consent.[42]

The critical reader will note that the foregoing discussion presupposes the existence of two conditions, neither of which necessarily exists in all countries: (1) that education is available to all adolescents, and (2) that the majority of adolescents remain in school until a time when sex education, especially pertaining to contraception, is given—normally during the secondary years as the students enter adolescence. Nonfulfillment of these conditions is evident in information from Mexico. While primary education is obligatory in Mexico, it is estimated that from 13 to 18% of the youths there do not attend school at all,[43] and of those who go to school, only 44% finish the primary grades. This type of statistic serves to emphasize the uneven opportunity afforded to adolescents to obtain information regarding human sexuality in general and contraception specifically.

The laws and policies governing education affect adolescents in two other important ways. First, until very recently, it was the policy in the United States to force pregnant teenagers to give up their schooling, at least until the baby was born. As noted recently, "[p]regnancy is a major reason for dropping out of school. Most school systems do not permit pregnant students to continue attending regular classes."[44] In many cases the rationale which is cited to support enforcement of the rule is based on the idea that it is not proper for teenagers to see a pregnant peer. There is reason to believe that little consideration is given as to what policy would really best serve the interests of the student. Similar rules are in effect in many other countries and have an obvious impact on a young girl's decision regarding what to do

---

40. Country tabulation for Pakistan in study mentioned in note 39 *supra*.

41. *See* text accompanying notes 29-31 *supra*.

42. MINISTERE DE L'EDUCATION NATIONALE, INFORMATION SEXUELLE A L'ECOLE 5 (1974) (brochure prepared for parents).

43. G. CORNEJO, A. KELLER, S. LERNER, L. AZUARA, LEY Y POBLACION EN MEXICO 84 (1974).

44. Foltz, *Pregnancy and Special Education*, 62 AM. J. PUB. HEALTH 1612 (1972).

about pregnancy. For example, there is a decision of the Supreme Court of Ghana in which a young school girl was prosecuted for seeking an abortion. The recitation of the facts in the case revealed that she sought the abortion because of her desire to "finish her school."[45] In a later study made in Ghana of females who procured abortions because of unwanted pregnancies it was found that only 13% knew about contraception.[46]

The current and widespread practice of expelling pupils who become pregnant runs counter to the concept of helping adolescents. Aside from the fact that these rules provide a high inducement for seeking an abortion, it contradicts a concern for human rights.[47] Therefore, such practices should be reviewed.

Second, by providing increased educational opportunities, the status of women is enhanced in the long run and tends to lead to widening job opportunities for them and increasing their role outside the home. This in turn would have the effect of delaying marriage and reducing the number of children in view of the inverse relationship between educational level and fertility.[48] The importance of laws in this field is summed up in the Pakistan Second Five Year Plan:

> Educated women can comprehend the possibilities of family planning more readily; gainfully employed women tend to marry later and to have fewer children. . . . The motivation for fewer children and more abundant life is more important than more dissemination of knowledge of the means of contraception.[49]

In sum, it is important that legislation, regulations and policies governing education and dissemination of contraceptive information be re-examined

45. Boateng v. The State, 1964 Ghana Law Reports 602, 609 (1964). In Nigeria the desire to complete school training which necessarily gives rise to the fear of dismissal from school or from business was found to be the principal motivating rationale for inducing abortion. In a study made of 71 cases of induced abortion, 68% cited fear of dismissal as the reason why they sought abortions. Akingba and Gbajimo, *supra* note 1. As a cultural insight it is interesting to note that in many African countries what is generally called the "bride price" is directly proportional to the amount of education that a woman has received. J. B. AKINGBA, THE PROBLEM OF UNWANTED PREGNANCIES IN NIGERIA TODAY 102-103 (1971).

46. D. A. Ampofo, *The Dynamics of Induced Abortion and the Social Implication for Ghana*, 9 GHANA MEDICAL JOURNAL 295 (1970).

47. The IPPF Conference on the Medical and Social Aspects of Abortion in Africa (1973) made similar observations. For a brief report of the Conference *see* ABORTION RESEARCH NOTES, Supp. No. 8 (Feb. 1974).

48. It has been estimated that in Pakistan if no woman married below the age of 18 the fertility rate would be reduced by 15% due to the fact that at present more than half of the women have three or more children before reaching 20. F. Rahman and Lee, *Pakistan*, in POPULATION AND LAW (L. T. Lee and A. Larson, eds. 1971), (hereinafter Lee/Larson). *See also* E. DRIVER, DIFFERENTIAL FERTILITY IN INDIA (1963); D. KLINE AND W. McCANN, LAW EDUCATION AND POPULATION 12-16 (Paper presented at the UNESCO Workshop on the Teaching of Population Dynamics in Law Schools, Paris, Feb. 18-22, 1974).

49. GOVERNMENT OF PAKISTAN, SECOND FIVE-YEAR PLAN (1960-1965) at 334-35 (1960).

in light of the resolution unanimously adopted at the UN Conference on Human Rights in Tehran: namely, that couples have the right to be sufficiently instructed and informed on family planning.[50]

B.   *Contraception*

That access to contraceptives by adolescents as well as the probability of contraceptive failures is directly relevant to pregnancy and abortion is self-evident. However, the laws governing all aspects of contraception, *e.g.*, importation, distribution, sale, advertisement, and prescription or insertion of contraceptives, are in a state of utter dissarray.[51] For example, advertisement of contraceptives is prohibited in Eire,[52] but vasectomy is legal in Dublin; while in Stockholm, contraceptives are aggressively advertised, but vasectomy is allowed only on narrow grounds.[53]

In India, the pill is not available in the government program, although abortion and sterilization are legal; however, in Malaysia the reverse is true. In Japan, abortion is widely used but the pill is illegal for contraceptive purposes and IUD's severely restricted in their use.[54]

Also, sale of contraceptives is prohibited in Spain, as it is in Eire[55] or was in France (except in the case of condoms) prior to the law of 1967.[56]

---

50. We are not insensitive to arguments which would narrowly interpret "couples" and "family planning" so as to exclude adolescents, or at least unmarried ones. We see such views as unnecessarily restrictive and have chosen to adopt a more liberal interpretation.

51. To emphasize the contradictions which exist in the law in this and related areas, we point to the laws of the State of New York. There a person can buy contraceptives at age 16, but one cannot consent to intercourse until age 17. Moreover, one cannot get married without parental consent until age 18. One is almost forced to ask quizzically what minors do with the contraceptives during the year they wait to become 17. N.Y. Educ. Law, § 6811(8) (McKinney Supp. 1971); N.Y. Penal Law, § 130.05(3) (9) (McKinney 1967); N.Y. Dom. Rel. Law, § 15 (McKinney Cum. Supp. 1971).

52. *See* Criminal Law Amendment Act, 1935, § 17, Censorship of Publications Act of 1929, §§ 16, 17 (1) and Censorship of Publications Act of 1946, §§ 7(b) and 9(b). The Irish Supreme Court decided on December 19, 1973 in the *McGee* case that the ban on imports of contraceptives for private use was unconstitutional. *See* The Times (London), Dec. 20, 1973, p. 4, col. 1.

53. Swedish Association for Sex Education, *Sweden* in Lee/Larson, *supra* note 49, at 181-187.

54. M. Potts, Health Related Legislation and Family Planning 1 (Background paper prepared for UNESCO Workshop on Teaching of Population Dynamics in Law Schools, Paris, February 1974). According to information received from Dr. Minoru Muramatsu of the Institute of Public Health in Tokyo by the Transnational Research Institute, the IUD was approved by the Japanese Government "as a valid contraceptive" in August 1974.

55. Spain: Penal Code, § 416, para. 3 bans sale of all "objects which are able to avoid pregnancy." Eire: Criminal Law Amendment Act, 1935 makes it a criminal offense "to sell, or expose, offer, advertise or keep for sale . . . any contraceptive." The law in Eire is evaded by giving the contraceptives away free of charge. Two family planning groups were recently acquitted of charges of violating this law because they mailed information and contraceptives to two young girls. The court found that these mailings did not violate the law because they did not constitute a sale as specified under the law.

56. Law 67-1176, § 3, para. 5; § 7/11(1a).

Sweden[57] and China,[58] by contrast, actually require pharmacists to maintain stocks of contraceptives. Until July 1970, Massachusetts laws had prohibited the sale of "any drug, medicine, instrument or article whatever for the prevention of conception"—except in the case of married persons to whom registered physicians could prescribe, and registered pharmacists could provide, such drugs or articles for contraception.[59] In fact, until 1965, the State of Connecticut had even prohibited the *use* of contraceptives.[60]

The laws of many countries not only restrict the insertion of IUD's or prescription of oral pills to medical doctors,[61] but, in addition, prohibit the latter from providing such services to minors without parental consent.[62] Under the provisions of the 1967 French law, unmarried minors must have the consent of one of their parents before they can acquire contraceptives.[63]

Though some countries are updating their laws concerning contraceptives, many laws are still vestiges of "legal imperialism" reflective of bygone pronatalist policies of erstwhile colonial powers.[64] These laws continue to hold sway in many developing countries long after they attain independence, despite the fact that even some of the former colonial powers have already changed their own laws because of their incompatibility with human rights and the realities which spring from human behavior.

The picture painted is at best bleak and confusing. While events are moving rapidly toward granting wider access to contraceptives, most adolescents who are sexually active are forced to go without the protections afforded to adults.[65] This ought not to be the case. Reason dictated that steps be taken

---

57. *Sweden*, in Lee/Larson, *supra* note 48, at 181-84.

58. Lee, *Law and Family Planning*, 2 STUDIES IN FAMILY PLANNING, No. 4, at 83 (1971).

59. Eisenstadt v. Baird, 405 U.S. 438 (1972).

60. Griswold v. Connecticut, 381 U.S. 475 (1965).

61. Stepan and Kellogg, *The World's Laws on Contraceptives*, 22 AM. J. COMP. L. 615 (1974).

62. *Id.* at 642.

63. The French Assembly recently passed by an overwhelming margin a law which authorizes general distribution of contraceptives. The requirement of parental and medical consent has been abolished under the act because the lack of birth control among young girls had caused a great number of social tragedies and illegal abortions. N.Y. Times, June 29, 1974, p. 3, col. 1. Final approval of the bill was given in late November, with the cost of making contraceptives widely available to be absorbed by the Social Security system. N.Y. Times, Nov. 28, 1974, p. 2, col. 4.

64. Laws in francophone Africa exemplify this tendency. *See generally* WOLF, ANTI-CONTRACEPTION LAWS IN SUB-SAHARAN FRANCOPHONE AFRICA: SOURCES AND RAMIFICATIONS (Laws and Population Monograph No. 15, 1973).

65. Practices in one urban area of the United States highlight the absurdity and the lack of sensitivity to the problems under discussion here. As late as 1970, the health service agencies in the District of Columbia refused to give birth control information to girls under 18—even with parental consent—unless they had already had a baby, an abortion or a miscarriage. D. Bazelon, *Beyond Control of the Juvenile Court*, 21 JUVENILE COURT JUDGES 42 (1972). Similar "stunning indications" to the effect that as many as 56% of the teenagers surveyed in New York were seeking pregnancy tests or abortions have provided the impetus for the creation of a multi-million

to protect those active teenagers from the greater dangers—physical as well as psychological—associated with pregnancy and abortion. Special attention should be given to the establishment of programs which offer counseling and assistance to teenagers regarding contraception.

C. *Minimum Age of Marriage*

For the purpose of marriage—another subject relevant to pregnancy and abortion—the minimum ages usually make a distinction between minor boys and minor girls. For example, the most universally used ages are 18 and 16 for boys and girls, respectively. Such minimum ages of marriage are in force in Algeria, Australia, Bangladesh, Brazil, Egypt, Ivory Coast, Jamaica, Japan, South Korea, the Netherlands, Norway, and the U.S.S.R. But the ages are set as low as 14 and 12 in Chile, Spain, Venezuela, and parts of Canada, and as high as 21 and 18 in Niger and parts of the United States.[66]

However, what the law may stipulate as the minimum age of marriage is no guarantee as to reality. The effectiveness of the law depends upon a number of forces—social custom, religion, status of women, economic condition, educational and employment opportunities, as well as enforcement machinery. The last refers to the existence not only of a group of dedicated and efficient judicial and administrative cadres, but also supportive legislation without which the minimum marriage age law would prove illusory. For example, how could the minimum age be ascertained in the absence of a compulsory registration of births? What motivation is there to comply with the minimum marriage age requirement without an effective compulsory education and minimum age for child labor? What kind of self-enforcement incentive exists in the citizenry, such as its sense of patriotism and concern for the common good?

Depending upon the make-up of these forces, the average age of marriage may fall below or exceed the minimum marriage age. Thus, despite the 1929 Child Marriage Restraint Act, as amended in 1949, and the 1955 Hindu Marriage Act, both of which set the minimum age at 18 for boys and 15 for girls, the Indian statutes were not generally enforced because of the lack of marriage and birth registration, as well as mild punishment or penalty for violation.[67] Notwithstanding the passage of the Muslim Family Laws Ordinance in 1961, raising the minimum marriage age for girls to 16, the estimated marriage age, according to a report in 1968, was only 13.5 in

dollar program to provide birth-control information and devices to teenagers there. N.Y. Times, July 23, 1974, p. 33, col. 1. The American College of Obstetricians and Gynecologists in recommending that legal barriers to contraceptives for minors be removed has taken the position that pregnancy should not be the price that a minor must pay for contraception. (Adopted May 1971.)

66. For a more complete listing of the minimum marriage ages throughout the world, *see* Patrikios, *Why?*, UNESCO COURIER, October 1973, pp. 24, 26-27.

67. Singh, *India*, in Lee/Larson, *supra* note 48, at 115.

Dacca[68] and 14.9 in East Pakistan (now Bangladesh) as a whole.[69] And the practice of child marriage continues, though now to a lesser extent than before.[70]

In the case of China, however, intensification of campaigns stressing the virtues of late marriages—men should not marry before reaching 28 and women not before 25—has apparently brought the actual marriage age considerably above the official minimum ages of 20 and 18, respectively, as stipulated in the 1950 marriage law.[71]

Whether reform of the laws governing minimum age of marriage alone will lessen the problems related to teenage pregnancy and abortions is subject to considerable doubt. Several countries are presently advocating revising the minimum age upward. But it would seem that if these reforms are not preceded or accompanied by other changes, such as widespread informational campaigns and the provision of better educational and occupational alternatives for teenagers, they are doomed to failure. In societies where social customs in favor of early marriage are deeply ingrained, it will take more than a mere change in legislation to alter community attitudes. In any event, societies which cannot count on the tool of mass mobilization of resources in this area will also have trouble inculcating new attitudes among the people.

D. *Family Allowances*

Among the factors influencing the decision of a minor to seek abortion or permit the pregnancy to run its course is the availability of family or child allowances. By 1967, 64 countries had instituted programs providing ·such allowances.[72]

Following the depression of the 1930's, many governments assumed a greater responsibility for the economic and social well-being of their people, and the introduction of family allowance programs became widespread in the post-war period. The United States and Japan are now the only two industrialized nations without a general family allowance program.

Eligibility for a family allowance is determined in most cases by age and order of birth. Thus, some countries only start payments for the second or third child born, and a few countries have imposed an upper limit on the number of children within any one family for whom the allowances will be granted. Some countries vary the amount of the allowance as the number or

68. Reported in the Morning News Dacca of December 9, 1968.

69. Rahman and Lee, *Pakistan* in Lee/Larson, *supra* note 48, at 141.

70. *See generally*, B. N. Sampath, *Child Marriage: Revision of Marriageable Age and its Effective Implementation*, 3 LAWASIA 387 (1972).

71. HUANG YU-CHAN, CHUNG-KUNG CHIH-YU YUNG-TUNG (Birth Control in Communist China) 130 (1967).

72. MEASURES, POLICIES AND PROGRAMMES AFFECTING FERTILITY, WITH PARTICULAR REFERENCE TO NATIONAL FAMILY PLANNING PROGRAMMES, U.N. Doc. No. ST/SOA/Series A/51 at 17-26 (1972), (hereinafter U.N. MEASURES).

age of children increases or grant supplementary allowances while the children are attending school. In some countries the system of family allowances is related to employment, by means of a payroll tax, which may have a depressing effect on wages or an inflationary effect on prices. If marriage grants may be analogized to family allowances, we may also mention here outright grants on the occasion of marriage, as in the case of Portugal, or interest-free loans that are increased if the bride gives up her employment or are partially cancelled with the birth of each child, as in the case of Spain. Because of the great variety of possible systems it is statistically difficult to make useful comparisons of allowances paid and their impact on the decision of a pregnant minor to give birth to a child.

A comparative study of birth rates in Sweden and Norway after the last war suggested that the evidence concerning Sweden did not "exclude the possibility that family allowances have had some [positive] effect upon fertility in young marriages." Such effect was not present in Norway, where payments begin only with the second child and are not part of a comprehensive family program as they are in Sweden.[73]

It may be safely stated, however, that the impact of family allowances on minors' decisions to bear children would depend on the size of the payments per child. Where the size of payment exceeds or approximates the actual cost of bringing forth, rearing, and educating a child, it may act as a stimulant to fertility, as is reputed to be the case in post-war France, especially in increasing the frequency of births of second and third parity. On the other hand, if the payment is only nominal, the causal relationship between family allowances and fertility may be tenuous at best, as seems to be the case in most of the developing countries.

Since France has consciously resorted to family allowances as a means of stimulating its fertility rate, it is useful to study its system and development.[74] The French system had its roots in the late 19th century when employers took the initiative of giving maternal assistance to families. In 1932 legislation came into being which made it mandatory for employers to pay contributions to an "employer's compensation bank" to support the payment of bonuses to employees. The décret-loi of July 29, 1939, succeeded in altering the concept of family allowances from that of bonuses and made them available to everyone except independent workers. The Law of August 27, 1946, brought the control of the allowance fund under the central government as part of the social security system, and the allowances were based on number of children, ages, working status, etc. The payments take the form of straight family

73. Gille, *Scandinavian Family Allowances: Demographic Aspects*, 1 EUGENICS QUARTERLY 188-89 (1954); U.N. MEASURES, *supra* note 72, at 36.

74. The information in the text is drawn from Jacques Doublet and Hubert de Villedary, LAW AND POPULATION GROWTH IN FRANCE 34-35 (Law and Population Monograph Series No. 12, 1973).

allowances, which lessen economic pressures of children in the homes, and "sole support" allowances, which are designed to keep the mother at home. Included in the overall allowance program are payments for maternity and prenatal care. The maternity allowance is made for the purpose of encouraging fertility and thus specifically preventing abortion. The prenatal allowances are made prior to the birth of the child. The Law of January 3, 1972, increased the "sole support" allowance to enable the mother to remain at home if she chooses. That law also established a new allowance for child care expenses.

Under the Civil Service Statute in Costa Rica, employees of the government whose monthly income does not exceed ₡300 (colones) are entitled to an allowance of ₡15 for each child.[75] Because the family allowance scheme in the Soviet Union has remained unchanged since 1947, despite rising wages, benefits paid to unmarried mothers upon the birth of the first child and to married mothers beginning with the fourth child, are thought to be of little significance.[76] On the other hand, Romania and Bulgaria have in the past few years sharply increased the benefits available for the first few children in an attempt to increase the birth rate in those countries.[77] By Decree No. 61 of the Council of Ministers of 28 December 1967 the lump sum payments in Bulgaria were revised as follows: $10 for the first child; $100 for the second; and $250 for the third. In addition, monthly child allowances are paid to all eligible families as follows: $2.50 for the first child; $7.50 for second; and $17.30 for third. Mothers of "illegitimate" children receive $5 per month for the first child, with payments for subsequent children equal to those of other families. These payments continue until the child reaches 16 years of age. In Romania, each family receives a salary supplement of 130 lei per month (about $7.15) for each child under 15.

A recent comparative study seems to suggest that the impact of family allowances on the birth rate in Bulgaria was not overwhelming. Part of the difficulty in trying to assess the impact arises from the fact that changes in the abortion law coincided with increases in family allowances. However, there appears to be some correlation between higher monetary incentives and increases in fertility in the urban areas. But in rural Bulgaria the birth rates have fallen steadily since 1969. The cause of the rise in fertility in Romania is equally difficult to determine. Though the crude birth rate in 1972 was 18.8—more than four points above the 1966 rate when abortion laws were made more restrictive and family allowances increased—it is unlikely that the

---

75. Universidad de Costa Rica, Projecto *Drecho y Poblacion* in EL DERECHO Y LA POBLACION EN COSTA RICA 14-15 (1973).
76. B. Q. Madison, SOCIAL WELFARE IN THE SOVIET UNION 208-09 (1968).
77. H. P. David, FAMILY PLANNING AND ABORTION IN THE SOCIALIST COUNTRIES OF CENTRAL AND EASTERN EUROPE 65, 132 (1970).

monetary incentives have played a significant role in the slight long-term increase.[78]

In the United Kingdom,[79] upon satisfaction of the National Insurance contribution conditions by the mother or father, a lump sum payment of £25 is paid for each child that lives for at least 12 hours after birth. As the payment is linked to birth of the child, it covers all children. Where contribution requirements are not satisfied, the assistance may still be given but may vary depending upon the circumstances of the family or unwed mother. Family allowances are available on a weekly basis but only for the second and subsequent children.

The family allowance schemes are to a certain extent a luxury participated in by the developed countries. Of the 35 countries surveyed in the mid-1960's, 17 spent more than 1% of their national income on family allowance payments. Of the 17, only Chile could be classified as a developing country.[80] In Chad, Dahomey and Gabon, the influence of the French family allowance system and pronatalist policies can be seen but the scope of the family allowance protection is very limited. For example, in Dahomey only 5% of the children eligible for payments are protected by the system.[81] Thus, in many of the countries the monetary incentives for carrying a child full term are minimal and would appear to have little impact.

A recent comparison of family allowance programs done by Jacques Doublet for the International Labour Organisation illustrates how a family allowance scheme's impact on fertility is subject to the vagaries of the situation in each country. According to Doublet, a comparison between the birth rate of Ghana, a country which has an active family planning program but no family allowance system, and the Ivory Coast, where a family allowance program has been in effect for years, leads to a rather unexpected result: the Ivory Coast has a birth rate and natural growth rate slightly lower than that of Ghana.[82]

Both maternity benefits and income tax exemptions for dependent children may be considered as forms of family allowances, hence factors in minors' decisions regarding pregnancy and abortion. Such manipulations of maternity benefits as changing the amount of birth grants, delivery or hospital

---

78. For a detailed discussion of the effect of monetary incentives on the birth rates in these countries *see* R. J. MCINTYRE, PRONATALIST PROGRAMS IN EASTERN EUROPE 12-16 (paper presented at the annual meeting of the Population Association of America, New York, Apr. 20, 1974).

79. D. M. KLOSS and B. L. RAISBECK, LAW AND POPULATION GROWTH IN THE UNITED KINGDOM, 39 (Law and Population Monograph Series No. 11, 1973).

80. U.N. MEASURES, *supra* note 72, at 21, Table 1.

81. *Id.* at 23, Table 3.

82. A summary of the study may be found in a short article by Max Wilde, *Family Allowances and Fertility* in 1 PEOPLE, No. 3, at 24-25 (1974).

costs,[83] provisions of pre- and post-natal care, and length of maternity leave with pay, may have some influence on minors' decisions in bearing children.

The maternity leave policy under the civil service scheme in Nigeria in theory grants three months' leave with pay to pregnant employees. But the policy is evidently applied unevenly. According to Akingba, the methods of granting payment vary without reason. Some employees get the leave with full pay; others at only half. Those women employed by quasi-governmental institutions (corporations, universities) forfeit their annual leave for the period they are out on maternity leave. Some government agencies demand proof of a marriage certificate before leave will be granted. The application of the policy seems to be subject to the vagaries of individual preference. Those who are employed in Nigeria's private sector are far worse off. Many of the employers are reluctant to grant leave with pay. Some have strongly stated policies against pregnancy among employees, at least until they have worked for a year. There is at least one case reported where the mother had to be treated for a severe case of tetanus which resulted from an abortion she acquired in order to keep her employment.[84]

A recent amendment to the Philippine Woman and Child Labor Law requires that maternity leave be granted to "any pregnant woman employee" who has worked for an employer for at least six months out of the past twelve. The leave, with full pay, takes effect two weeks before delivery and continues until four weeks after. The amendment also empowered the Secretary of Labor to formulate a regulation requiring employers to establish nurseries at the place of work for the benefit of the working women.[85]

As for income tax exemptions, many countries provide some system of easing the financial burden of persons who must make additional expenditures resulting from having more children. Tax exemptions are, however, a less perceptible addition to the family wealth than family allowances. For example, exemption per child up to four children under the Income Tax Act, 1973 in Kenya is 180 shillings. As the shilling is worth only 14 cents (U.S dollars), that would put the annual exemption at $25. Uche has attempted to assess the impact of such tax breaks on fertility. His study, based on interviews with 350 selected adults in 1973-74, showed the following relationships between tax relief and fertility behavior.[86]

---

83. Since 1969 Singapore has been assessing an *accouchement* fee at Government Maternity Hospitals on women with the delivery of the third child. SINGAPORE FAMILY PLANNING AND POPULATION BOARD, FOURTH ANNUAL REPORT, 1969 3.

84. A short discussion of the policies in effect in Nigeria can be found in J. B. AKINGBA, THE PROBLEM OF UNWANTED PREGNANCIES IN NIGERIA TODAY 107-14 (1971).

85. Presidential Decree No. 148, March 26, 1973. The essence of this decree became part of the Labor Code, Art. 131 by a decree issued May 1, 1974.

86. U. U. UCHE, LAW AND POPULATION GROWTH IN KENYA 28, Table 7 (Law and Population Monograph Series No. 22, 1974). The monograph is derived from a larger two-volume study, THE LAW RELATING TO THE GROWTH AND CONTROL OF POPULATION IN KENYA,

Questions	Yes %	No %	No Opin- ion %	Refused Comment %	Other %
Do you consider the relief provisions in deciding your family size	25.4	61.7	5.1	7.1	.6
Would you consider having more children if the level of relief was higher than it is	32.3	41.7	10.3	14.6	1.1
Would you limit your family size if the Act had no relief provisions	20.3	52.9	8.0	16.6	2.3

While the levels of the exemptions are so low as to be somewhat neutral in their present effect, the responses of the survey seem to suggest that an increase in the tax exemption for children would have a positive effect on the decision to increase family size.

In assessing the effect of family allowances, maternity benefits and income tax exemptions upon minors' decisions to have or not to have children, it is important to note that: (1) family allowances are effectively available only in the developed countries and only if they constitute substantial and meaningful sums; (2) maternity benefits are most commonly available to persons in civil service, and at present most minors do not have access to those types of jobs; and (3) tax exemptions cannot be taken advantage of in most developing countries since minimum taxable income is already far above the average *per capita* income.

E.   *Out-of-Wedlock Births*

If the opportunity to marry is not available to the pregnant adolescent, and abortion is not a viable option, she will invariably carry the child to term and give birth to a so-called "illegitimate" child. In the United States such births represent a large portion of the total births to teenagers. Of the 600,000 children born to women under 20 years of age in 1968, 160,000 were born out-of-wedlock—a figure which represents nearly 50% of the total number of "illegitimate" births.[87] As adolescents have become more sexually active, the number of illegitimate births for that age group has risen. According to Zelnick and Kantner, during 1965-68 the illegitimacy rate among girls 15-19 rose by 18%.[88]

---

prepared by Uche under a grant from the Interdisciplinary Communications Program of the Smithsonian Institution.

87. U.S. BUREAU OF THE CENSUS, STATISTICAL ABSTRACT OF THE UNITED STATES 50, Table 58 (1970).

88. D. Hardin, *Recent Trends in Illegitimacy—Implications for Practice,* 49 CHILD WELFARE 375 (1970).

Under English common law, the child of an unwed mother was the child of no one and had no rights of inheritance.[89] This view has been maintained by many states in the United States, although the laws vary from state to state. Though a few of the states have adopted laws which give the "illegitimate" child rights (support, inheritance, etc.) similar to those of "legitimate" children, in many others the former is the subject of discrimination insofar as legal protection is concerned.

Since the adoption of the Declaration of the Rights of the Child in 1959,[90] which calls for the elimination of discrimination against children born out-of-wedlock, there has been a gradual movement toward a complete equality of children born in and out of wedlock. In the United States, for example, the 1965 amendments to the Social Security Act contained provisions for children born out-of-wedlock to receive social security benefits.[91] Many of the services provided under the Act are given federal funding only if they are available without regard to status, age or parenthood. And the Aid to Families with Dependent Children (AFDC) program distributes cash to unwed mothers and their dependent children.[92] Recently, the Commission on Population Growth and the American Future included among its recommendations the revision of state laws and practices so as to insure that "all children, regardless of the circumstances of their birth, be accorded fair and equal status socially, morally and legally." The inequality in treatment has at least in part been caused by the unfounded belief that by penalizing the out-of-wedlock births, such births would decrease, illicit sex would be discouraged, and the traditional family institution would be strengthened. However, such causal relationships have not been borne out by fact, even in countries which have removed discrimination against out-of-wedlock births.[93]

For example, the law in Norway was altered in 1915 so as to afford to the "illegitimate" children rights nearly equal to those of the "legitimate."[94] The law included a provision whereby every child would have the benefit of establishing paternity. Neither the giving of equal rights to "illegitimate" children nor the subsequent extension of medical, social and financial benefits to unwed mothers after 1915 have brought about the doom of the family institution or increased "illegitimacy."

89. 10 AM. JUR. 2D Bastards § 62 (1963).

90. See note 10 supra. The fundamental law in West Germany with regard to illegitimacy predated the thrust of the U.N. declaration by stating that: Illegitimate children shall be provided by legislation with the same opportunities for their physical and spiritual development and their position in society as are enjoyed by legitimate children. Basic Law of the Federal Republic of Germany of 23 May 1949, BGBl, Part 1, at 1, Art. 6, para. 5 (1949).

91. Social Security Act, 42 U.S.C. §§ 416(H)(3) (1965).

92. Cutright, AFDC, Family Allowances and Illegitimacy, 2 FAMILY PLANNING PERSPECTIVES, No. 4, at 4 (1970).

93. See generally, V. SAARIO, STUDY OF DISCRIMINATION AGAINST PERSONS BORN OUT OF WEDLOCK (1967).

94. For a lengthy discussion of the Norwegian experience, see H. D. KRAUSE, ILLEGITIMACY: LAW AND SOCIAL POLICY (1971).

This comports with what Phillips Cutright has observed: a lack of correlation between the rates of "illegitimacy" and the percentage of GNP devoted to social security costs (health insurance, family allowances, pensions, unemployment benefits, etc.). Among the countries studied, West Germany and Czechoslovakia—with the highest percentage of GNP devoted to social security expenditures—had only the average rates of "illegitimacy." Of Spain, Japan, Portugal and the United States—countries which expended the lowest percentage of GNP on social security costs—the first two had only average "illegitimacy" rates, the latter two above average.[95]

With respect to the treatment given under the law to children born in and out of wedlock, the Costa Rican Constitution[96] requires the parents to give the latter equal treatment. Moreover, the Constitution confers upon everyone the right to know who their parents are and prohibits any differentiation based on filiation. Thus, the legal distinction and discrimination present in other countries between children born in and out of wedlock has been eliminated. A regulation of the Ministry of Labor and Social Welfare recently assigned the duty of ensuring equal treatment under the law to the Department of Family Social Services.

While the legal machinery and theory are present in Costa Rica to protect the rights of the "illegitimate" child, the reality of the situation is another matter. Paternity petitions are seldom granted and there are apparently enormous problems in enforcing the legal provisions. In 1970, for example, 6,500 "illegitimate" births were registered but only 27 paternity investigations were initiated. Even more revealing is the fact that during the period of 1949-1967, the Court of Cassation granted only 60 paternity petitions. Professor Elizabeth Odio concludes therefore that the constitutionally protected right is illusory and of little practical meaning.[97]

Prior to January 3, 1972, French law made a distinction between the rights of "legitimate" and "illegitimate" children. The pre-1972 situation dated back to the Civil Code of 1804, but had slowly been evolving to its present position of equality of treatment. The Law of November 16, 1912, made it easier to establish paternity and thus to receive maintenance. And while children who were born of adulterous or incestuous relationships could not have access to the courts to establish paternity, they were entitled to receive maintenance under the Law of July 15, 1955. The 1972 law drastically changed the "illegitimacy" law by stressing equality of treatment for all children. Under that law the new Article 334 of the Civil Code now states:

---

95. Cutright, *Illegitimacy: Myths, Causes, Cures,* 3 FAMILY PLANNING PERSPECTIVES, No. 1, at 29 (1971).

96. Arts. 53-54. For further discussion, *see* EL DERECHO Y LA POBLACION EN COSTA RICA, *supra* note 75, at 37-38.

97. E. Odio, *Law and Population in Costa Rica,* in POPULATION AND THE ROLE OF LAW IN THE AMERICAS 39 (Law and Population Monograph Series No. 18, 1974).

The illegitimate child has in general the same rights and the same duties as the legitimate child.

Even if the paternal filiation is not established under Article 342, the new child has a cause of action to demand support "from the man who had relations with his mother during the legal period of conception."[98]

"Illegitimacy" has assumed serious proportions in the United Kingdom[99] where the percentage of out-of-wedlock births has nearly doubled in the past twenty years. According to the First Report of the Select Committee on Science and Technology (1971), fully 8.3% of all births were "illegitimate." This despite the relaxation of laws governing abortion and contraception. The financial problems of a mother of an "illegitimate" child have been reduced somewhat by the aid given by voluntary agencies and the state. The unwed mother is now able to receive the same benefits as other mothers. A goodly number of unwed mothers in the United Kingdom place their babies "in care." Over 3,000 "illegitimate" children born in 1967 were placed under the jurisdiction of the state for care and keeping. This indicates either a desire of the mother not to be burdened by the child or an inadequacy of the system of aid given to unwed mothers. It is most likely occasioned by a combination of the two factors.

F. *Adoption*

The decision of minors to resort to abortion or to carry the pregnancy to term may hinge upon the availability of adoption and the ease of the adoption procedures under the law. That adoption may serve as a possible alternative to abortion was underscored in a recent study by the Council of Europe, citing the fact that in France only 4,500 adoption applications can be met out of 30,000 each year.[100]

A recently enacted state abortion statute in the United States has taken a unique approach to this situation. The law, while setting forth that no abortion may be performed without the woman's "voluntary and informed written consent," establishes that the standard for "informed" is that she be given, among other information, the names and addresses of two adoption agencies.[101] This is apparently done in an attempt to educate the woman as to the alternatives to abortion.

On the whole, adoption is governed entirely by statutes, with the best

---

98. For a fuller discussion of these laws *see* Doublet and Villedary, *supra* note 74, at 37-42.

99. Kloss and Reisbeck, *supra* note 79.

100. *See* COUNCIL OF EUROPE, POPULATION AND VOCATIONAL TRAINING DIVISION, WORKING PARTY OF DEMOGRAPHIC EXPERTS—FERTILITY, LEGISLATION DIRECTLY OR INDIRECTLY AFFECTING FERTILITY IN EUROPE. (Report on the Conclusions and Recommendations of the meeting held in Strasbourg, 5-7 December 1973), Doc. GT/DEM/Fecondite (74) 1, at 15.

101. Bill No. H30, signed into law in Utah on Feb. 14, 1974. For a brief discussion of the new Utah law *see* 3 FAMILY PLANNING/POPULATION REPORTER, No. 3, at 56 (1974).

interests of the child controlling, but lacking in uniformity. Usually, the consent of the natural parent or parents, as well as adopting parents, is required.

To facilitate adoption across national boundaries, the United Nations is in the throes of deciding whether to convene a "United Nations Conference for an International Convention on Adoption Law."[102] As a prelude, the Social Development Division is presently preparing a study titled, "Comparative Analysis of Adoption Laws" which will survey the existing legislation or the lack thereof, and the differences in the existing laws now in force throughout the world.

G.   *Abortion*

1. Introduction

The clear trend toward younger and childless women selecting abortion as a method of dealing with pregnancy, especially in Eastern Europe, was noted by Mehlan as early as 1965.[103] With few exceptions, the more recent data support this observation as to the world-wide increase in younger women seeking abortion.

According to Dr. Egon Szabady, Deputy President of the Central Statistical Office and Chairman of the Demographic Committee of the Hungarian Academy of Sciences, the 1956 regulations sparked what he termed an "abortion epidemic,"[104] which has brought about the tightening of the law governing abortion procedures there in 1973. In 1970 of the 192,300 abortions performed, 195 were done on elementary school girls (14 and under) and 18,000 were performed on high school girls (15-19). During that same year a study showed that 7,063 young women between the ages of 15-19 filed applications with the abortion committee in Budapest. That figure represents 3.5% of female population of high school age. By 1972 the percentage of abortions performed on women under 20 years of age had jumped to 14.4%.[105] The experience in the United States has been similar. Statistics kept by a physician who performed abortions over a 30-year period indicate that between 1955-1964 the percentage of young women between the ages of 15 and 19 on whom he performed abortions rose from 9% of the total to 19%.[106]

---

102. General Assembly Resolution 3028 (XXVII).

103. K. H. Mehlan, *Reducing the Abortion Rate and Increasing Fertility by Social Policy in the German Democratic Republic*, 2 PROCEEDINGS OF THE WORLD POPULATION CONFERENCE, Belgrade, 1965, 226, § 11 (1967).

104. Nepszava (Newspaper), Dec. 31, 1973.

105. C. Tietze and D. Dawson, *Induced Abortion: A Factbook*, 14 REPORTS ON POPULATION/FAMILY PLANNING 18, Table 4 (1973).

106. R. Spenser, *The Performance of Non-Hospital Abortions*, 1 ABORTION IN A CHANGING WORLD 222 (R. Hall ed. 1970) (hereinafter Hall).

Even before abortion in the State of New York was made free of its legal restraints, fully 25% of the legal abortions in 1970-71, at 60 teaching hospitals and 6 free clinics were performed on women who were less than 20.[107] During 1967-69 of the abortions in California under the therapeutic abortion law, 4,515 were performed on girls 19 and under—a figure which represented fully 30% of all such abortions.[108]

The rise in the number of abortions granted to young and unmarried women in Sweden is one of the major elements in the rise of the total number of abortions. Since 1956 the total number of abortions performed on women of the 15-19 age group has quadrupled, and after 1964 the shift has been toward abortions for young women. In 1960 only 10.7% of the abortions legally performed in Sweden were on women 19 or less. By 1972 the percentage had increased to 23.5%. A study of abortions in Ankara, Turkey, in 1967 revealed that of the 1,385 women admitted for post-abortion treatment, 16.8% were less than 20.[109]

Of the criminal abortions (246) treated in Siriraj Hospital (Thailand) in 1971, 17.8% of the patients were under 20, and two-thirds of those were single.[110]

Though Tietze and Dawson have noted the rise in teenage abortions, they also observe that there is a correlation between that rise and the increase of teenagers in the population. But even when the data are computed on an age-specific basis, those abortions obtained by women under 20 showed the greatest increase.[111]

But not all countries have experienced this marked increase in teenage abortion, at least those which were legally performed and for which there are statistics available. In Japan, where abortion is readily available, abortions performed on teenagers dropped from 17,022 in 1950 to 12,217 in 1964, and teenage abortion dropped from 2.1% of the total number in 1968 to 1.9% in 1972. The fact is most likely traceable to the increase in use of contraceptives among teenagers. But while the number of teenage abortions was declining, the number of abortions per 1,000 live births for that age group was increasing from 302 in 1950 to 745 a decade later. This shows an increasing tendency for the young woman to use abortion as a back-up method during that period of time. This trend has since stabilized itself.[112]

107. C. Tietze and S. Lewit, *Early Medical Complications of Legal Abortion: Highlights of the Joint Program for the Study of Abortion* in ABORTION AND THE LAW (J. Butler ed. 1972).

108. C. Tietze and D. Dawson, *supra* note 105, at 18.

109. I. Nazer, *Abortion in the Near East*, in Hall, *supra* note 106, at 271-72, particularly Table 3. Nazer was citing a study made by Erenus titled PROVOKED ABORTION (1967).

110. S. Koesawang, *Investigation of Illegal Abortion Cases Admitted to Siriraj Hospital (Bangkok)* in STERILIZATION AND ABORTION PROCEDURES 43 (Proceedings of the First Meeting of the IGCC Expert Group Working Committee on Sterilization and Abortion, Pancing, Malaysia, Jan. 3-5, 1973).

111. Tietze and Dawson, *supra* note 105, at 19-20, Table 5.

112. D. CALLAHAN, ABORTION: LAW, CHOICE AND MORALITY 286, Table 21 (1970).

In some societies the problem of teenage abortion is relatively insignificant. In Taiwan only 1.3% of the induced abortions occurred among young women under 19.[113] Just 2.7% of the abortions done in Singapore in 1972 were on women 19 or less.[114]

In a 1965 study by Fournier of 596 women admitted for abortion treatment at social security and public welfare hospitals in Mexico, 280 were treated for provoked (induced) abortion. But only 10 out of the entire study sample were teenagers.[115] The annual percentage of abortions in the USSR among teenagers runs below 2%.[116]

The statistical data available on the subject of marital status of teenagers who seek abortions indicates the extent to which unmarried teenagers opt to have abortions. While there are some variances between countries, there is a tendency for married teenagers not to select the abortion alternative as a method of handling pregnancy.

	Percentage of total abortions for ages 19 or less[117]	Percentage of ages 19 or less single at time of abortion[118]
Czechoslovakia, 1971	8.5	81.2
Denmark, 1969	16.6	96.4
England and Wales, 1971	22.1	97.1
Hungary, 1971	9.0	74.3
United States, 1970/71	29.4	93.3

2. Legal Provisions Governing Recourse to Abortion

Even the most cursory examination of the abortion laws presently in force throughout the world will reveal the tremendous differences that exist. In Belgium, Ireland, the Philippines, some countries of Latin America and in many countries which were formerly under British rule, abortion is a criminal offense for which there are no exceptions. Many countries—Algeria, Malaysia, and Paraguay, among these—permit abortion only when it is necessary to save the life of the pregnant woman. Others, such as Cameroon, Thailand, and El Salvador, permit abortion where there is evidence that the pregnancy is the result of rape, incest, or other illicit intercourse. A growing number of countries, particularly in Scandinavia and Eastern Europe, permit abortion

---

113. L. P. Chow, *Abortion in Taiwan*, in 1 Hall, *supra* note 106, at 254, Table 2.

114. Tietze and Dawson, *supra* note 105, at 18.

115. M. M. Fournier, *El Aborto Criminal Como Problema Social: Su Prevencion*, 1 Planeacion Familiar 4-5 (1967).

116. *Induced Abortion as a Public Health Problem in Europe*, 27 WHO Chronicle, 525-30 (1973).

117. Tietze and Dawson, *supra* note 105, at 18-19, Table 4.

118. *Id.* at 28, Table 11. For a succinct review of some of the statistical aspects of abortion among teenagers, *see* J. van der Tak, Abortion, Fertility and Changing Legislation: An International Review 97-101 (1974).

for a wide variety of socio-medical reasons. A handful of countries have authorized abortion where a young woman is below a certain age. Still fewer have made abortion available virtually on demand. These various grounds for abortion will be discussed separately: abortion on request, medical-eugenic indications, socio-economic indications and humanitarian indications.

(a) *Abortion on Request*

The terms "abortion on request" or "abortion on demand" are actually misnomers for there are invariably certain conditions, formalities or procedures to be observed or fees to be paid. It is generally taken to mean the elimination of the need to specify any ground for abortion within a specified period of gestation.[119]

The restrictive abortion law in the Soviet Union was amended and relaxed on September 2, 1954, when a decree of the Presidium of the Supreme Soviet abolished criminal penalties for women who consented to the interruption of pregnancy. Under a further decree of November 23, 1955, abortions were permitted if done by qualified personnel in medical facilities. The commentary accompanying the decree notes "in order to give women the possibility of deciding by themselves the question of motherhood" the Presidium of the Supreme Soviet "has decided to repeal the previous law on abortions." The abortion on request nature of the Soviet decree was limited somewhat when a Ministry of Health Instruction on December 28, 1955, provided a list of "contraindications," under which no abortion may be performed, including:

(i)   acute or chronic gonorrhea;

(ii) acute or chronic inflammatory conditions of the sexual organs;

(iii) purulent foci, irrespective of localization;

(iv) acute infectious diseases; and

(v)   a previous abortion within the preceding six months.

In the Soviet Union, legal abortions for whatever reason are now free for employed women and cost 5 rubles for non-employed women (U.S. $6.67).[120] Special permissions are required if pregnancies are more than 12 weeks old. Abortions are now subject to penalties only when performed in unauthorized institutions, in unsanitary conditions, or by unauthorized persons.

The People's Republic of China now not only permits abortion on request, but also provides abortion as a free public service, thus implementing in full the 1969 United Nations Declaration on Social Progress and

---

119. WHO, ABORTION LAWS: A SURVEY OF CURRENT WORLD LEGISLATION 10 (1971).

120. According to up-dated version of Henry David's FAMILY PLANNING AND ABORTION IN THE SOCIALIST COUNTRIES OF CENTRAL AND EASTERN EUROPE (now in press).

Development calling on U.N. members to provide the people with not only the knowledge, but also the "means necessary to enable them to exercise their right to determine freely and responsibly the number and spacing of their children."[121]

While the texts of Chinese laws or regulations on abortion are not available, the major official central government statements were made in 1954 when abortion was first permitted under restrictive conditions and in 1957 when many of these restrictions were lifted.

According to reports received at that time restrictions pertaining to age, number of children and administrative procedures on applications for abortion were to be removed.[122] Later instructions have included the following:

> [Abortion] may be performed when contraceptive measures have failed or *when the woman is pregnant without taking these measures but is unfit to give birth (for various reasons, such as too frequent intervals between births, multiple pregnancies, economic conditions and relationships of work).* Generally it should not be carried out if the pregnancy exceeds two months.[123]

A recent report by Faundes and Luukkainen confirmed that induced abortion is performed free on request in the People's Republic of China. They described the procedure as follows:

> As soon as a woman realizes that she is missing a period, she attends the clinic. . . . If a positive diagnosis is made on the first visit and the patient declares that she does not want to have the baby, she is immediately taken to the appropriate ward where she waits for her turn to have an abortion. . . .[124]

Due to the landmark decision in *Roe v. Wade,*[124a] which involved the issue of the constitutionality of a Texas statute forbidding abortion except to save the woman's life, the abortion laws in the United States were altered to permit abortion on request during the first trimester. The decision was based on the essential fact that the decision to have an abortion during the first three months of pregnancy "lies with the woman and her doctor."

In Denmark, a law which authorizes free abortion until the twelfth week of gestation was adopted in 1973. The decision whether to have an abortion is left entirely up to the woman. One of the important new features of the

---

121. G. A. Res. 2542, 24 U.N. GAOR, Suppl. 18, at 45, U.N. Doc. A/7388 (1969).

122. *Special Report from Peking,* Wen-hui Pao, Shanghai, Apr. 12, 1957.

123. *Planning Childbirth and Promoting Late Marriage,* 5 MEDICAL AND HEALTH DATA, (1970) (emphasis added).

124. A. Faundes and T. Luukkainen, *Health and Family Planning Services in the Chinese People's Republic,* 3 STUDIES IN FAMILY PLANNING, No. 7, at 173 (Supp. 1972).

124a. 410 U.S. 113 (1973).

Danish law is the provision which permits women who are less than 18 years of age to consent to the abortion.[125] This makes an inroad into the customary practice of having the parents consent before medical treatment can be given to minors.

The Tunisian Government recently liberalized its abortion law to allow the artifical interruption of pregnancy if "performed during the first three months in a hospital, a health center, in an authorized clinic by a duly authorized practitioner."[126] The German Democratic Republic and Austria also have legislation which leaves decision about abortion during the first three months of pregnancy entirely up to the woman.[127]

(b) Medical-Eugenic Indications

A survey of the laws governing abortion practice indicates a vast difference in both the explicitness and the types of medical indications which are considered to support the performance of an abortion. The Czech ordinance, for example, sets forth in great detail the list of pathological conditions which can be considered to create a hazard to the life of the woman if pregnancy is permitted to continue.[128] In Sri Lanka (Ceylon) an exception from criminal liability is made where the miscarriage was brought about "in good faith for the purpose of saving the life of the woman."[129]

Until 1972, the Indian Criminal Law permitted abortion on the same extremely narrow ground of saving the life of the mother. But the Medical Termination of Pregnancy Bill of 1971 has nullified the provisions of the Penal Code as they pertained to doctors, thus making it possible for a registered

125. Law on Abortion, June 13, 1973, No. 350, *Lovtidende A*, 1973-NR. XXXII, p. 993. A similar law has just been passed in Sweden to become effective Jan. 1, 1975. Law of July 9, 1974 [1974] SFS 596. Under the law until the twelfth week a woman may request an abortion and the decision is solely hers to make. Medical personnel are prevented from influencing her decision, except on narrowly defined medical grounds. (§ 1) A doctor's refusal to perform an abortion during this time without notifying the State Directorate of Health and Welfare of the reasons is punishable by up to six months imprisonment (§ 9). Between the 13th to the 18th week, permission of the medical authorities will have to be obtained (§ 3). LIBRARY OF CONGRESS, EUROPEAN LAW DIVISION, REPORT: ABORTION LEGISLATION IN DENMARK AND SWEDEN 13-16 (1974).

126. Decret-loi No. 73-2, Sept. 26, 1973. As Tunisia was the first country under French influence to liberalize its law, it will be interesting to see what impact the recent French National Assembly's approval of a liberal abortion law will have on these former French colonies. The law, which will most probably go into effect in early 1975, in essence will allow any permanent resident who is "distressed" by a pregnancy to have an abortion during the first ten weeks. N.Y. Times, Nov. 28, 1974, p. 1, col. 4.

127. German Democratic Republic: *Gestzblatt der Deutscher Demokratischen Republik*, Part I, 15 March 1972, No. 5, pp. 89-90. Austria: Kalis and David, *Abortion Legislation: A Summary International Classification, 1974*, in ABORTION RESEARCH: INTERNATIONAL EXPERIENCE 16 (David ed. 1974).

128. Appendix to Instruction of Ministry of Health No. 72/1962 Sb. NV. A copy of the list may be found in Lee/Larson, *supra* note 48, at 254-61.

129. Penal Code, § 303.

medical practitioner to perform an abortion if, in good faith, he comes to the conclusion that:

(i) the continuance of the pregnancy would involve a risk to the life of the pregnant woman or of grave injury to her physical or mental health; or

(ii) there is a substantial risk that if the child were born, it would suffer from such physical or mental abnormalities as to be seriously handicapped.[130]

Under the Turkish Regulations of 12 June 1967, among the indications authorizing therapeutic abortions is the consideration of whether there is a substantial risk of fetal deformity or danger to succeeding generations. Specifically, an abortion may be performed if: (1) the means used to treat a disease during pregnancy—use of cortisone—is likely to prejudice the development of the fetus; (2) if X-ray or radioisotope treatment is liable to affect the embryo or fetus; (3) if either the father or the mother have hereditary mental diseases; (4) if parents have already had children with mental retardation due to chromosomal defect; (5) if, during the first three months of pregnancy the mother had rubella, viral hepatitis, toxoplasmos, varicella or other serious viral infections.[131]

Many countries which were once under British rule have statutes patterned after Section 58 of the Offences Against the Persons Act, 1861, which allowed no specific exceptions for therapeutic abortion. The Jamaican law makes it a crime to give a pregnant woman "any poison or other noxious thing" or use "any means whatsoever" to procure a miscarriage.[132] That statute and others of its type presently in force in Guyana, Barbados, and Trinidad and Tobago do not provide any specific exceptions for such medical intervention as therapeutic abortion. The no-exception aspects of these statutes have been affected somewhat by the decision in *Rex v. Bourne*,[133] the first reported case in which the early abortion statute was judicially interpreted. The decision forms the foundation upon which rests the generally accepted legality of therapeutic abortion in the United Kingdom, and hence in former British colonies. The case arose as a test case in 1938, when a prominent gynecologist performed an abortion on a 14-year-old girl who had been raped by several soldiers and had consequently become pregnant. The operation was performed openly, with the consent of the girl's parents and with notice to the prosecuting authorities. Bourne felt at the time that if the pregnancy were allowed to continue, it would severely endanger the mental

130. Medical Termination of Pregnancy Bill, § 32(b) (1971).
131. Decision No. 6/8305 of 12 June 1967 of Council of Ministers, Annex I. *See also* WHO, *supra* note 113, at 43.
132. Offences Against the Person Act, Arts. 65-66 (1861), *as amended* (1969).
133. [1938] 3 All E.R. 615; [1939] 1 K.B. 687.

health of the girl. While taking notice of the absence of any statutory exemptions in favor of abortion, Judge Macnaghten ruled that such an exemption was implied by the word "unlawfully" in the statute in that one who was qualified could "lawfully" act to induce a miscarriage. In his remarks to the jury, Macnaghten stated that where the doctor is of the opinion that "the probable consequences of the pregnancy will make the woman a physical or mental wreck,"[134] the jury could find a good faith defense. Bourne was acquitted and consequently the legal justification for therapeutic abortion was established in the United Kingdom.

The law in some countries allows an abortion to be performed if it is necessary to preserve the health of the woman. For example, Section 86 of the Penal Code of Argentina was amended in 1967 permitting a licensed physician to induce an abortion if the woman consents and if there is a serious danger to the life or health of the woman and no other measures will avert the danger.[135] Similarly, as a practical matter, in Iran a pregnancy may be terminated if three physicians certify that its continuance will endanger the woman's health.[136]

(c) *Socio-Economic Indications*

An increasing number of countries are including provisions within the laws governing abortion which permit the persons who have authority to grant abortions the power to weigh the impact of socio-economic factors in reaching their decision. The recent decision of the Hungarian Council of Ministers, Resolution No. 1040/1973/X.18, instituted as a ground for abortion the fact that the "woman is not living in a married state or has been living alone for at least six months." The authorities may also approve an application for abortion if the request was generated for "weighty social considerations." Such provisions give the people who screen abortion applications a great deal of latitude.[137]

According to the Decree of 26 April 1969, abortion in Yugoslavia may be approved in cases where "it can be reasonably expected that the pregnant woman will find herself placed, as a result of the birth of the child, in difficult personal, family or material conditions,"[138] which cannot by other means be avoided. Under the Danish law, as recently adopted, after the twelfth week of

134. *Id.* at 619. A similar doctrine of necessity was read into the early German Penal Code. The case there involved the prosecution of a doctor who performed an abortion on a woman who threatened to commit suicide if she did not get an abortion. Decision of the Reichsgericht in Criminal Matters (I. Strafsenat) of March 11, 1927, g. Dr. St., 61 RGst. 242 (1928).
135. Law No. 17567 of Dec. 6, 1967.
136. Penal Code §§ 181-83 (1962 ed.).
137. Magyar Közlöny, Oct. 18, 1973, 774-78, paras. 2(1)(b) and 2(2)(d).
138. Section 4. *See* 20 INTERNATIONAL DIGEST OF HEALTH LEGISLATION 573 (1969) (hereinafter IDHL).

pregnancy an abortion may be authorized in cases where because of age (16 or less) or immaturity, the woman is for the time being incapable of caring properly for her child.[139]

Also classified as socio-economic indications are grounds of a combined economic and health nature, with the former clearly predominant. The law in Japan is a case in point. Article 14(1) of the Eugenic Protection Law of 1948, as amended, authorizes a designated physician to perform an abortion "at his discretion" if a mother's "health may be affected seriously by the continuation of pregnancy or by delivery, from the physical or economic viewpoint." Although "economic" reasons alone would not, according to the letter of the law, constitute a sufficient ground for abortion, the difficulty or impossibility of proving conclusively their serious adverse effect upon health has resulted in such a liberal interpretation of the law that, in practice, even wealthy *and* healthy women may obtain abortions. Most of the operations for induced abortions have indeed been performed on this ground.[140]

The United Kingdom Abortion Act of 1967 permits two registered medical practitioners to determine whether

> the continuance of the pregnancy would involve risk to the life of the pregnant woman, or of injury to the physical or mental health of the woman or any existing children of her family, greater than if the pregnancy were terminated; . . .[141]

In addition to the fact that the health test is to be applied, the Act allows consideration of the pregnant woman's "actual or reasonably foreseeable environment." While this does not create a "social" ground for termination, since it requires the presence of health considerations—present or foreseeable—factors of a social or economic nature, including the woman's marital status and existing family size, may be taken into account in reaching the decision.

The Indian Medical Termination of Pregnancy Bill has a similar provision permitting social and economic factors to play a part in the decision. In addition, there is another interesting feature of the Indian legislation. Although the new Indian abortion law, which was passed in August 1971, and went into effect in April 1972, does not stipulate contraceptive failure explicitly as a ground for abortion, Explanation II to Article 3(2), which authorizes abortion if continued pregnancy would involve a risk of grave injury to the mental health of the woman, provides:

> Where any pregnancy occurs as a result of failure of any device or

---

139. *See* note 120 *supra*, Chap. I, para. 3.

140. M. Muramatsu, Some Facts About Family Planning in Japan 9 (1955).

141. Laws of Great Britain, Eliz. 2, c. 87, § 1, para. 1(a) (1967); 19 IDHL, *supra* note 138, at 887 (1968).

method used by any married woman or her husband for the purpose of limiting the number of children, the anguish caused by such unwanted pregnancy may be presumed to constitute a grave injury to the mental health of the pregnant woman.

Although on its face the legislative explanation applies only to married women, it is of significance to adolescents in India because child marriage is still prevalent.

(d) *Humanitarian Indications*

A number of countries permit abortion to be performed for what are deemed to be humanitarian reasons. Article 1 of the Swedish statute (prior to the 1974 reform), which represents the prototype of this category, has been described as authorizing abortion in cases where

. . . a woman has become pregnant as the result of rape, other criminal coercion or incestuous sexual intercourse . . .[142]

Similar provisions exist in the laws governing interruption of pregnancy in at least 25 countries.

Under the Penal Code of Cameroon, in cases where the pregnancy has resulted from rape, an abortion performed by a medical practitioner does not violate the abortion law if the facts of the case have been verified by the public prosecutor's office.[143] As Professor Louis B. Schwartz has observed:

The rape justification . . . conforms to widely held moral views. It seems to many people intolerable that a woman who has been the victim of . . . assault should be compelled to bear the child of her ravisher.[144]

Where a woman is below a certain statutory age, she is not legally capable, in view of her immaturity, of giving valid consent to intercourse. This gives rise to the concept of "statutory rape." Because of the potential usefulness of this legal fiction in dealing with teenage pregnancy, it is desirable to explore the implications of this approach. Section 203.2(3) of the American Law Institute's Model Penal Code proposed that a pregnancy could

---

142. NATIONAL BOARD OF HEALTH, SWEDISH LAWS ON STERILIZATION, ABORTION AND CASTRATION (Summary) (1963), Law No. 172 of March 20, 1964, *amending* Law No. 318 of June 17, 1938, 17 IDHL, *supra* note 138, at 117 (1966).
143. Penal Code, Art. 339; 20 IDHL, *supra* note 138, at 397-98. A recent IPPF Conference on Abortion in Africa suggested that "[c]onception due to contraceptive failure, rape, or *conception in a minor—which is by implication the result of rape*—might also be considered as reasons for abortion." ABORTION RESEARCH NOTES, Supp. No. 8 (Feb. 1974).
144. L.B. SCHWARTZ, THE TERRIBLE CHOICE: THE ABORTION DILEMMA 55 (1968).

be terminated where the pregnancy resulted from rape or other "felonious intercourse." The explanatory note to that section included the following:

> An illicit intercourse with a girl below the age of 16 shall be deemed felonious for purposes of this subsection.

The legal presumption which accompanies this statement of policy is that the young girl lacks the capacity to fully comprehend the nature and long-range implications of sexual intercourse. This presumption has been challenged in some quarters by the argument that an under-age girl who is sexually active is likely to be both aware of the danger of pregnancy and familiar with the various methods of preventing that result.[145] But that notion, in turn, is contradicted by current research findings which show, among other things, that the type of knowledge which teenagers have concerning contraception and fertility is grossly inaccurate, and that there are considerable legal and practical barriers relating to their access to contraceptives.[146]

It is important to remember that the criminal law sanctions for statutory rape have traditionally centered on vindicating society's apparent outrage at the violation of the minor's body. Cast in such a light the law has concerned itself only with the punishment of the violation. It has traditionally overlooked the fact that the act of statutory rape carries with it the possibility of later pregnancy. Therefore, an important dichotomy arises—one which should be ameliorated. Despite the overriding concern of the law in treating, rehabilitating minors and thus in minimizing the negative effects which are endemic to adolescent experience, in a majority of cases the girl who becomes pregnant does not get the protection from the law which should normally be forthcoming if the law's rationale for protecting minors were evenly applied. What normally happens is that the law treats the minor girl as "promiscuous" or "incorrigible" rather than treating her as a victim of her own immaturity and thus granting to her the type of protection that she really needs. The end product of this dichotomy is that the pregnant teenager, though she cannot legally consent to intercourse, must carry her baby to term and then be legally responsible for its care.[147]

The rationale which supports the desirability of using the statutory rape theory as a basis for treatment of pregnant minors is premised on the same

---

145. Note, *Forcible and Statutory Rape*, 62 YALE L.J. 55, 78 (1952). It has been observed by an English judge that: "There are many girls under sixteen who know full well what it is all about and can properly consent." R. v. Howard, [1965] 3 All E.R. 684, 685 (C.C.A.). If this is so, and practically we must assume the fact, might there not be reason for believing that they can also consent to an abortion?

146. M. BAIZERMAN, C. SHEEHAN, D. ELLISON, *et. al.*, PREGNANT ADOLESCENTS: A REVIEW OF LITERATURE WITH ABSTRACTS, 1960-1970 (1971).

147. Shopper, *Psychiatric and Legal Aspects of Statutory Rape, Pregnancy and Abortion*, 1 JOURNAL OF PSYCHIATRY AND LAW 275-95 (1973).

type of common-sense view which supports the rape justification for abortion among adult women as stated above. While there are differences between the rape of an adult woman and the statutory rape of a minor, they are only of degree.

There are at present a number of countries which have incorporated into their abortion laws provisions aimed at dealing with the problem of statutory rape. The Greek law on abortions approves them if there is evidence of either rape or the seduction of a girl under 16.[148] The Swedish[149] and Finnish[150] laws authorize abortion if the woman is under the ages of 15 and 16, respectively. In Thailand the statutory rape age is 13,[151] and in such a case abortion is not a crime as long as it is performed by a "medical practitioner." Wider use of the statutory rape ground for abortion could provide a useful method for dealing with the adolescent pregnancy problem that is at once on sound legal footing and humane. It would be particularly useful in countries where the rape justification is one of but a few exceptions to the otherwise general prohibition against abortion.[152]

Lastly, the laws of Jordan and Lebanon provide a rather unique humanitarian basis for abortion, though it may not be a basis for totally avoiding the criminal sanction. The abortion statutes in these countries extend the doctrine of mitigating circumstances to abortions which are undertaken to protect the woman's reputation or to protect her family's honor.[153]

(e) *Consent*

The majority of the world's abortion laws are silent on the issue of the age at which a person can consent to have such an operation. For example, the Swiss law makes the consent of the pregnant woman an essential requirement of the abortion law, but does not stipulate the age for consent other than stating that if the woman is incapable of making judgment, the consent can be

---

148. Penal Code, Art. 304 (Law No. 1492, 1950).

149. *See* note 142 *supra* (1963).

150. Act on Induced Abortion, No. 239, Mar. 24, 1970, § 1. For an English translation of the law *see* 21 IDHL, *supra* note 138, at 699-705 (1970).

151. Penal Code, § 305.

152. Presently available statistics reveal that in the past the rape criterion has not been relied on often as a ground to justify abortion. A 1965 national survey in Japan showed that only 0.3% of the induced abortions were performed because pregnancy resulted from rape. JAPAN'S EXPERIENCE IN FAMILY PLANNING—PAST AND PRESENT 71, 78 (M. Muramatsu ed. 1967). In Sweden during 1967 less than 1% of the abortions were based on the rape justification. Callahan, *supra*, note 112, at 195, Table 8. The lowness of the percentages may reflect the fact that the abortion procedures are so liberal in those two countries that the rape criterion is not used. But they also reflect the fact that pregnancy resulting from rape has a low incidence of occurrence. Such would not necessarily be the case where a minor becomes pregnant. Technically she has under law been raped, albeit "statutorily."

153. Jordan: Penal Code, Art. 318 (Law No. 85 of 1951); Lebanon: Penal Code, Art. 545 (Legislative Decree No. NL/340, Mar. 31, 1943).

given by her legal representative.[154] By an amendment in 1952, the Japanese law merely requires the consent of the woman or her spouse for an abortion to be performed.[155] Where laws do not specifically require consent, however, there is often a legal presumption that consent is required before an abortion can be performed. In most instances the rules governing consent for an abortion are found in legal principles from sources other than the abortion statutes. Only a few statutes specify the persons competent to give consent and, for the purposes of abortion among adolescents, the age under which parental or guardians' consent is required. The Bulgarian statute stipulates that if the young woman on whom an abortion is to be performed is less than 18 years of age the consent of the parents must be obtained.[156] The restrictive Moroccan law requires the consent of the spouse or, in his absence, a written notice from the chief medical officer of the prefecture or province certifying that treatment is necessary to safeguard the mother's health.[157] From its language, it is not clear whether this statute is contemplating the possibility of adolescent pregnancy and abortion. Under the governing regulations, therapeutic abortion for minors in Turkey cannot be performed unless the parents' consent has been given.[158] But if the delay in obtaining the consent will place the woman's health in jeopardy, the requirement can be dispensed with. The recently enacted statute in India indicates that:

(a) No pregnancy of a woman, who has not attained the age of eighteen years, or who, having attained the age of eighteen years, is a lunatic, shall be terminated except with the consent in writing of her guardian.

(b) Save as otherwise provided in clause (a), no pregnancy shall be terminated except with the consent of the pregnant woman.[159]

The recently felt need of teenagers to obtain medical services, especially in terms of contraception and abortion in England and the United States has triggered several changes in the laws concerning treatment of minors and their ability to consent to the same. Under traditional legal theory minors are incapable of rendering an informed consent, and the common law permitted minors to receive medical treatment in the absence of parental consent in but few circumstances: in emergencies, and where the parent refused to consent to a medical treatment which was sorely needed to maintain the minor's

154. Penal Code, Art. 120.

155. Law No. 156 of July 13, 1948, *with amendments to* Apr. 21, 1966, 16 IDHL, *supra* note 138, at 69 (1965).

156. Council of Ministers Decree No. 61 of Dec. 28, 1967 and Ministry of Public Health and Social Welfare, Instruction No. 188 of Feb. 16, 1968, *as amended*, May 4, 1972.

157. Crown Decree No. 181-66 of July 1, 1967, *amending* Arts. 453 and 455 of the Penal Code. 19 IDHL, *supra* note 138, at 217 (1967).

158. *See* note 131 *supra*.

159. *See* note 130 *supra*, § 3 (4).

health.[160] This view has been sustained on the notion that minors as a class lack the knowledge, maturity and judgment necessary to satisfy the standards set for rendering consent. However, during this century courts began to fashion what has come to be known as the "mature minor" rule, as a response to the apparent arbitrariness of the earlier common law.[161] This rule permits a minor near majority who has the mentality sufficient to understand the nature and import of the medical treatment he is about to undergo to give valid consent. The common law rules have been changed somewhat by recent legislation. While the age of majority in England is 18, through Section 8 of the Family Law Reform Act 1969, the "consent of a minor who has attained the age of sixteen years to any surgical . . . treatment . . . shall be as effective as it would be if he were of full age." Where a minor has consented to a treatment, the law states it is unnecessary to obtain the parent's consent before going forward with the procedure consented to.

Other inroads have been made into the traditional doctrine. Though therapeutic abortion legislation was passed in 1967 in California, it took four years to settle the question concerning whether the pregnant minor could consent to the operation. After much litigation the California Supreme Court, in *Ballard v. Anderson*, finally held that the statute authorized an unmarried minor who was "of sufficient maturity to give an informed consent" to give effective legal consent to a therapeutic abortion.[162] The opinion in *Ballard* did emphasize nevertheless that the burden of convincing medical authorities that the consent is "informed" fell on the minor. If the teenager fails to convince medical personnel that she has the required "understanding and maturity," they may refuse to perform the therapeutic abortion.

A portion of the California statute governing medical treatment of minors presently reads:

> [A]n unmarried pregnant minor may give consent to the furnishing of hospital, medical, or surgical care related to her pregnancy, and such consent shall not be subjected to disaffirmance because of minority.[163]

Despite the broad language used in the statute in granting to minors the right to consent, a recent opinion from the Attorney General reiterated the fact that the consent must be "informed."[164] This is in accord with the legal principles which govern the subject of consent.

160. For short but excellent discussions of the common law backgrounds as well as recent statutory developments *see* Wadlington, *Minors and Health Care: The Age of Consent*, 11 OSGOODE HALL L.J. 115 (1973); Skegg, *Consent to Medical Procedures on Minors*, 30 MODERN L. REV. 370 (1973); Hoffman and Pilpel, *supra* note 21, at 989.

161. Wadlington, *supra* note 160, at 117-20.

162. Ballard v. Anderson, 4 Cal. 3d 873, 484 P.2d 1345, 95 Cal. Rptr. 1 (1971).

163. CAL. CIV. CODE § 34.6.

164. A brief synopsis of the opinion may be found in 3 FAMILY PLANNING/POPULATION REPORTER, No. 3, at 52 (1974).

In June of 1972 the State of New York put into effect a law which made it possible for certain young patients to consent to medical treatment. The statute sets the age for consenting at 18, unless the patient is married or a parent and dispenses with parental consent requirement if the attempts to secure the consent of the parents would increase the risk of the youth's life or health.[165] While the law does not specifically mention abortion, the New York City hospital rules allow not only females, 17 years of age and older, to consent to the operation, but also those teenagers who are "emancipated," that is, those who are self-supporting or living away from home and make most of their own decisions.[166]

In *Roe v. Wade*,[167] the United States Supreme Court did not deal with the question of the capacity of minors to consent to abortion, although many of the medical treatment statutes in the United States specifically exclude abortion as one type of treatment to which minors can consent.[168] Nevertheless, the trend is toward the adoption of statutes allowing certain minors to consent to medical treatment under all conditions. As of 1972, thirteen states had passed the "comprehensive" type of statute. Under the liberal Alabama statute, for example, consent may be given to any legally authorized "medical" treatment by any person who is "fourteen or older . . . or is pregnant."[169]

On the other hand, at least eighteen states have statutes which require parental consent for abortion in all or some cases involving minors. Recently, however, a three-judge federal panel declared that the parental consent requirement of the Florida abortion statute[170] was unconstitutional. While the panel took note of the fact that parental interests may be of a compelling nature, they also observed that the Florida statute gave parents the authority to withhold consent for abortions for no reason at all or for reasons that could be unrelated to the paramount interests of the pregnant teenager.[171]

The decision of the court was based on the principle enunciated in *Roe v. Wade* that the state has no authority to interfere with a woman's right of privacy during the first trimester of pregnancy. In its opinion, the court emphatically stated that

165. N.Y. PUB. HEALTH L. § 2504 (1) (Cum. Supp. 1972-73). *See also* Pilpel, *Minor's Rights to Medical Care*, 36 ALBANY L. REV., 462, 469 (1972).
166. Hoffman and Pilpel, *supra* note 21, at 990.
167. 410 U.S. 113, 165 n.67 (1973).
168. *See, e.g.,* language of the new Indiana statute Bill No. S334 *as cited in* 2 FAMILY PLANNING/POPULATION REPORTER, No. 6, at 150 (1973).
169. ALA. CODE ANN., tit. 22, § 104 (15-17) (Cum. Supp. 1972).
170. 15A FLA. STAT. ANN. § 458.22(3)(b) (Cum. Supp. 1973).
171. The flip side of this formulation—the case where the parents attempt to force the minor to have an abortion—has also been litigated. After considering all of the traditional bases for parental control, a Maryland court held that the pregnant teenager had the right to bear her child full term even though such a course of action was contrary to the will of her parents. In re Smith, 16 Md. App. 209, 295 A.2d 238 (1972). In a similar vein, it has been held that the teenager's mother cannot offer her daughter's baby for adoption. The power to consent to adoption rests with the adolescent mother. Matter of Presler, 171 Misc. 559 (N.Y. Sup. Ct. 1939).

. . . pregnant women under 18 years of age cannot under law be distinguished from ones over 18 years of age in reference to "fundamental," "personal," constitutional rights.[172]

3. Illegal Abortions

In many countries the pregnant teenager who elects to have an abortion is faced, due to the restrictive nature of the laws, with seeking an illegal abortion. Of an abortion performed on a 17-year-old Chilean woman, the following autobiographical account records the problems and dangers which confront the teenager in seeking out an abortionist and having it done in inferior conditions:

> She dissolved some pills in lukewarm water in a lavatory, and then poured the water through the *sonda* into my womb. My impression is that this is supposed to dissolve the foetus inside the mother's womb. I always have had my abortions between one and two months of pregnancy. Never after that. . . . [Later] a friend came to my house and said, "You're shivering with cold." I said, "Throw a blanket over me because I'm dying of cold." Then my friend said, "Look, Cristina, I'm going to take you to the hospital because otherwise you're going to die here." I told her, "Let me stay here because by now I've had enough of this business, so many kids and so many problems that I don't know what to do." . . . My womb was so infected that the doctors couldn't touch me. One doctor wanted to treat me and the other didn't. One said to the other, "If you send her back home she'll die on the way." So they operated on me, scraping my womb clean, almost without anesthesia as a kind of punishment. They scraped and scraped as if they were cleaning the inside of a watermelon. Then they asked me who did this to me and I could tell them nothing. One must not talk in these situations, and I really wasn't lying because I didn't know where this woman lived nor did I ever see her again. This woman had no license, but I was desperate to find someone. . . .[173]

Despite the difficulty of measuring precisely the rates and risks of illegal abortion, the following estimates nevertheless reflect the magnitude of the

---

172. Coe v. Gerstein, Civ. No. 51-1250 (S.D. Fla., filed August 14, 1973). For a more elaborate discussion of the constitutional issues and rationales supporting the ability of minors to consent to abortion, *see* Pilpel and Zuckerman, *Abortion and the Rights of Minors*, 23 CASE W. RES. L. REV. 779, 792-806 (1973) and Note, *Implications of the Abortion Decisions: Post Roe and Doe Litigation and Legislation*, 74 COLUM. L. REV. 237, 242-47 (1974).

173. Gall, *Birth, Abortion and the Progress of Chile*, 19 FIELDSTAFF REPORTS, No. 2, at 7-8 (1972).

problem posed by illegal abortion. In Egypt, for example, it has been estimated that 40% of hospital admissions for deliveries and pregnancy complications were actually for abortions and their complications.[174] Recent records of two university hospitals suggest the existence of one abortion for every two births, notwithstanding the restrictive nature of the Egyptian Penal Code on abortion.[175] Reports from Turkey indicate that, during the late 1950's and early 1960's, there were 500,000 abortions and 10,000 deaths each year from abortion operations, few of which took place in hospitals because of their illegality.[176]

In Italy, the annual number of interrupted pregnancies during the 1960's reportedly fluctuated around 150,000, a large number of which were illegal abortions.[177] Two other estimates have put the annual number of illegal abortions at a maximum of 500,000[178] and between 800,000 and 3,000,000,[179] respectively. High numbers of maternal deaths occur every year as a result of malpractices that run the gamut from the use of herbs to primitive, unsophisticated instruments.[180] In Chile, 8% of all hospital admissions have been for patients with post-abortal complications; these patients have occupied one-fourth of all maternity beds in Maternal Health Service hospitals.[181] The death rate in the late 1960's was estimated at 150-200 per 100,000 abortions, with most of the abortions being illegal.[182] Indeed, it is estimated that 50% of pregnancies in Latin America are currently terminated by illegal abortions—resulting in the death of four times as many women as in countries where abortions are legal.[183]

Of the numbers cited above, a statistically significant percentage must be assumed to be abortions performed on teenagers. In some countries, the percentage may run as high as 25%.[184]

Even in countries which have liberal abortion laws the problem of illegal

174. INTERNATIONAL PLANNED PARENTHOOD FEDERATION, INDUCED ABORTIONS 27 (1972) (hereinafter cited as IPPF).

175. El-Kammash and El-Kammash, in Lee/Larson, *supra* note 48, at 369.

176. *See* Dr. Nusret H. Fisek's statement, in 2 Hall, *supra* note 106, at 47.

177. G. FERRARI, REPORT ON ITALY 17 (Draft Working Paper for the International Union for the Scientific Study of Population's Committee on Legislation Directly or Indirectly Influencing Fertility in Europe; hereinafter cited as IUSSP Working Paper) (mimeo. 1972).

178. *Id.* at 19.

179. N.Y. Times, Jan. 16, 1973, at 30, col. 4. A recent study based on interviews with 558 31-year-old married women in low-income neighborhoods in Rome showed an incidence of 2 abortions for every 2 to 3 surviving children. *Id.*

180. Boston Globe, Jan. 20, 1973, at 2, col. 1.

181. H. Romero, *Chile*, in FAMILY PLANNING AND POPULATION PROGRAMS, A REVIEW OF WORLD DEVELOPMENTS 235-245 (1966); R. Roemer, *Abortion Law: The Approaches of Different Nations*, 57 AM. J. PUB. HEALTH 1906 (1967).

182. IPPF, *supra* note 174, at 27.

183. *See* Dr. Edwin M. Gold's statement in 2 Hall, *supra* note 106, at 45.

184. Before the decisions in Roe v. Wade and Doe v. Bolton, it was estimated that the number of illegal abortions each year was between 200,000 and 1,200,000. Recent statistics have indicated that abortions performed on teenagers represent between 20 and 25 percent of the total number of abortions performed illegally in the United States.

abortions has not been totally alleviated. While the liberalization of abortion laws has brought about a noticeable decline in the rates of illegal abortions, the practice continues.[185] Some of this can be attributed to the cumbersome, institutionalized manner through which legal abortions are screened and approved. This is particularly true of the Swedish system. Some women will simply seek an illegal abortion rather than go through the obstacle course established by the abortion regulations. Glanville Williams has written:

> . . . We are told that in Sweden the special hospital boards which hear applications for abortion allow only 40 percent of the applications. In addition to the 60 percent who are turned down, there is an unknown number of women who do not apply for legal abortions, either because they realize that their case does not fall within the rules, or because they cannot tolerate the formality and even humiliation of applying to a hospital board in a matter they regard as being uniquely their own affair. These are the women who go to illegal abortionists.[186]

On the other hand, those women who are denied legal abortions may be compelled to go forward and give birth to an "unwanted child." In such cases the mother is faced with having to deal with what has recently been classified as a "compulsory pregnancy." A compulsory pregnancy is said to occur whenever a woman is compelled by external circumstances to carry to full term a pregnancy which is unequivocally unwanted.[187] The effects of such forced circumstances have equally negative long-range implications for both the mother and the child.

A number of reports have demonstrated the consequences of denied abortions upon the women, the children, and the society at large.[188] In a Swedish study 120 children born after refusal by the authorities to grant permission for abortion were compared to paired controls of the same sex born either in the same hospital or district to mothers who had not applied for abortion. After a close observation for 21 years, the former group of children were found to have higher incidences of psychiatric disorder, delinquency, criminal behavior, and alcoholism. They were more often recipients of public welfare assistance, were more unfit for military service, and received less schooling than those in the control group. The study concluded that the very fact that a woman applied for legal abortion indicates that the prospective

185. L. T. Lee, *International Status of Abortion Legalization*, in THE ABORTION EXPERIENCE 340-41 (H. Osofsky and J. Osofsky eds., 1973).

186. *The Legalization of Medical Abortion*, 56 THE EUGENICS REV. 24 (1964).

187. *See generally*, M. B. Beck, *The Destiny of the Unwanted Child: The Issue of Compulsory Pregnancy* in ABORTION AND THE UNWANTED CHILD (C. Reiterman ed. 1971).

188. *See generally*, G. Hardin, *Abortion and Human Dignity* in CASE FOR LEGALIZED ABORTION NOW 12-13 (A. Guttmacher ed. 1967).

child, if carried to term, will have a greater likelihood of social and mental problems than his peers.[189]

From a psychiatric standpoint, we are told that single women in general, and students in particular, do better if they are allowed to have the abortion which they request. This was one of the conclusions made by a group of doctors, psychiatrists and sociologists in the United Kingdom. The study undertaken there revealed the somewhat surprising result that single girls still tended to perceive the use of contraceptives as being more immoral than the risking of an unwanted pregnancy and the possible consequences of abortion.[190]

From the criminal law point of view it seems undesirable to prosecute the woman who is forced due to personal circumstances to seek out a clandestine abortion. Experience has shown that the abortion laws have been ineffective in curtailing the rate at which women seek abortions. Attempts to enforce the laws have been exercises in futility. While this alone is not sufficient reason to vacate present abortion laws, to subject a woman to criminal punishment for being compelled to participate in such acts is Draconian and counter-productive. This is particularly true in countries which have very strict abortion laws, yet do not permit ready access to contraceptives. There is, no doubt, reason for placing criminal sanctions on those who perform the abortions—based on the rationale that unregulated abortions increase maternal deaths due to the wretched conditions under which they are customarily performed—but much could be accomplished if the aura of criminality were removed from the head of the woman. There is presently a discernible shift in that direction. In France, long famous for its restrictive abortion statute, President Giscard d'Estaing recently instructed prosecuting authorities not to prosecute women who have "had themselves aborted in a way contrary to the 1920 law."[191]

---

189. Forssman and Thuwe, *One Hundred and Twenty Children Born After Application for Therapeutic Abortion Refused: Their Mental Health, Social Adjustment and Educational Level Up to the Age of 21*, 42 ACTA PSYCHIATRICA SCANDINAVIA 71-88 (1966). The Swedish study has been criticized for a number of reasons, not the least of which was the fact that 20 percent of the experimental group were born out of wedlock. The preliminary results of a ten-year Czechoslovakian study have recently been released. That study attempted to avoid the pitfalls of the Forssman/Thuwe study, particularly by having less than 5 percent of the experimental group born out of wedlock. Some two hundred children born to women who had been denied abortions twice during 1961-1963 were compared to an equal number of controls with regard to physical and psychological development. The data suggest that children unwanted at conception tend to have a higher incidence of sickness, somewhat lower grades in school and "worse integration in their peer group" than others. Z. Dytrych, Z. Matejcek, H. P. David and H. L. Friedman, *Children Born to Women Denied Abortions: Initial Findings of a Matched Control Study in Prague, Czechoslovakia*, (paper presented at the annual meeting of the Population Association of America, New York, April 18, 1974). For a synopsis of the paper *see* 3 FAMILY PLANNING DIGEST, No. 6, at 10 (1974).

190. *See generally*, EXPERIENCE WITH ABORTIONS: A CASE STUDY OF NORTHEAST SCOTLAND (Horobin ed. 1913); Shopper, *supra* note 141.

191. Boston Globe, July 26, 1974, at 31, col. 5. This was also the recommendation of the

H. *Menstrual Regulation*

The recent development of the menstrual regulation techniques will undoubtedly have an impact on the subject of adolescent pregnancy. These techniques which may be used as a post-conceptive means of regulating fertility carry with them the promise of simplifying both the legal and medical barriers to abortion. Basically, there are two means for inducing menstruation now available: (1) use of prostaglandins—a substance which is naturally present at menstruation and childbirth; (2) the use of a flexible polyethylene cannula aspirator. Aside from the simplicity and safety of the method, the value of this procedure is that it can be used to ensure a non-pregnant state prior to the medical determination that a woman is pregnant. Many proponents of the menstrual regulation procedure are urging that it be used during the two weeks immediately following a missed period. Thus, a teenager who suspects that she is pregnant can ask to have the procedure performed and afterward be guaranteed that she is not, because any embryo which may have begun formation will have been eliminated.

The use of the technique raises several legal issues. While there is little doubt that the technique can be utilized presently in countries with liberal and moderate abortion laws, it remains to be seen whether the technique is a violation of the abortion laws which are restrictive. There is some evidence that it will not be illegal in countries where statutes require evidence of a pre-existing pregnancy before a violation of the law takes place.[192] Laws such as those now on the books in many countries of Latin America, in Egypt, Taiwan and Libya, among others, exact this requirement. Legislation which follows the French and earlier English models centers on the intent for which the technique is used. This fact will make it somewhat more difficult to use the method, free of threat of criminal prosecution, if it can be shown that the intent was to eliminate the "product of conception"[193] rather than to restore the menstrual cycle.

There is a probability that the menstrual regulators will become regarded as contraceptives rather than abortifacients, as has happened with the IUD and "morning after" pill. If this be so, then the procedure can be helpful in eliminating many of the stigmas which accompany abortion. Because most teenagers throughout the world do not have access to the traditional contraceptives, the menstrual regulation technique can be used to eliminate pregnancy among those young women who have conceived but have no desire to carry the pregnancy full term.

Symposium on Law and Population which was convened in Tunis, June 17-21, 1974. *See* Recommendations of the Symposium on Law and Population, at 21. As soon as the new French law goes into effect, the significance of this particular statement will be lessened.

192. L. T. Lee and J. M. Paxman, THE LEGAL ASPECTS OF MENSTRUAL REGULATION 21-25 (Law and Population Monograph Series No. 19, 1974).

193. *Id.* at 11-21.

IV.   CONCLUSIONS

The legal problems concerning adolescent pregnancy and abortion having been discussed in the foregoing space, a few general comments and recommendations for legal reform may be noted.

In the first place, we should place adolescent pregnancy and abortion in quantitative perspective: over 70% of females between the ages of 15 and 20 were already married in Chad, India, Mali, Nepal, Niger, Bangladesh, Pakistan and Tanzania. On the average, about 40% of women 15-19 years old were married in the countries in Africa, 30% in Asia, 15% in the Americas and Oceania, 9% in the Soviet Union and 7% in Europe. Only in a number of European countries and in French Guiana, Guadeloupe, Hong Kong, Japan, South Korea, Macau, Martinique and the Ryukyu Islands were fewer than 5% of women married between the ages of 15 and 20.[194] In general, the pattern in Western industrialized societies has been one of delayed marriage (mid-20's) and a high proportion of singles (10-20%), whereas in the developing countries, early (mid to late teens) and universal (all but 1 or 2%) marriage for girls has been the rule.[195]

The consequences of such early marriages are many, not the least of which are higher fertility rates and age gaps between males and females on entering marriage (8-10 years) than in the case of late marriage.[196] These will tend to accentuate the girls' already subordinate position in society—making the equality of the sexes more difficult.

In his background paper presented at the Second Asian Population Conference entitled "Law, Human Rights and Population: A Strategy for Action,"[197] one of the authors of the present study proposed the inclusion of the following fourteen human rights already embodied in the various United Nations instruments in a "Charter on Human Rights and Population:"

1. The right to adequate education and information on family planning.[198]
2. The right of access to the means of practicing family planning.[199]
3. The right to the equality of men and women.[200]

---

194. UN ECOSOC, STUDY ON THE INTERRELATIONSHIP OF THE STATUS OF WOMEN AND FAMILY PLANNING 71 (Report of the Special Rapporteur, Addendum, Doc. E/CN.6/575/Add. 1, Dec. 13, 1973).
195. *Id.* at 70.
196. *Id.* at 71.
197. UN Doc. POP/APC.2/BP/32; 12 VA. J. INT'L. L. 309 (1972).
198. Teheran Proclamation on Human Rights Resolution XVIII (1968).
199. U.N. Declaration on Social Progress and Development, Art. 22.
200. Universal Declaration of Human Rights, Art. 2; International Covenant on Civil and Political Rights, Art. 3; International Covenant on Economic, Social and Cultural Rights, Art. 3; and Declaration on the Elimination of Discrimination Against Women, Arts. 1, 4, 6, 9 and 10.

4. The right of children, whether born in or out of wedlock, to equal status under the law and to adequate support from natural parents.[201]
5. The right to work.[202]
6. The right to an adequate social security system, including health and old-age insurance.[203]
7. The right to freedom from hunger.[204]
8. The right to an adequate standard of living.[205]
9. The right to environmental protection.[206]
10. The right to liberty of movement.[207]
11. The right to privacy.[208]
12. The right of conscience.[209]
13. The right to separation of Church from State, law from dogma.[210]
14. The right to social, economic and legal reforms to conform with the above rights.[211]

Although much research remains to be done in terms of their legal implications, coordination and priority, the fourteen rights may nevertheless provide the basic considerations to which any attempt at legal reform in the area of adolescent, as well as adult, pregnancy and abortion should be directed.

As examples for the first five points, any review of laws affecting adolescent pregnancy and abortion should take into consideration the following:

(1) Are adolescents being adequately educated and informed on family planning in the present school system? (laws on education, obscenity, postal communication, etc.)

(2) Do they have access to the means (both services and contraceptives) of practicing family planning? (laws on public health, pharmacy, social security, etc.)

(3) Do female adolescents have the same legal status as that of males,

---

201. Declaration of the Rights of the Child, Principles 1, 4, 6, 9 and 10.
202. International Covenant on Economic, Social, and Cultural Rights, Art. 6.
203. *Id.* Art. 9.
204. *Id.* Art. 11(2).
205. *Id.* Art. 11(1).
206. *Id.* Art. 12(2)(b); Declaration of the U.N. Conference on the Human Environment, Principles 1, 8, 13, 15 and 16.
207. International Covenant on Civil and Political Rights, Art. 12.
208. *Id.* Art. 17.
209. *Id.* Art. 18(1).
210. *Id.* Arts. 18 and 26.
211. This right flows logically from the fact that human rights are *ipso facto* legal rights, entailing legal obligations on the part of governments to undertake the necessary reforms to conform with such rights.

particularly in the fields of education, job opportunity, remuneration and marriage and divorce? (laws on education, labor, family relations, etc.)

(4) Can adolescent parents in fact support adequately their children whether born in or out of wedlock? Are their children's rights adequately safeguarded where such support is not forthcoming? If not, what preventive measures or remedies? (laws on family or child allowances, adoption, bastardy, child-care centers, etc.)

(5) Are adolescent parents adequately prepared and trained to work? Would they have been better off to complete their schooling instead of being forced into the job market in order to support a family? What are the consequences to the society in terms of additional unskilled labor, unemployment or disguised unemployment? (laws on labor, vocational training, unemployment benefits, etc.)

The basis for providing adolescents with special and particularized treatment in the realm of pregnancy and abortion have already been enunciated, legally as well as medically. The law ostensibly seeks to ascertain the course of action that best serves the interests of the minor. Medicine has flatly asserted that the controlling premise is that "the youth's health is paramount to any other consideration."[212] Neither discipline has been entirely consistent in the application of their own self-imposed standards as in many cases they have worsened the dilemma which confronts pregnant adolescents, rather than aided in the resolution.

It can be seen from the foregoing discussion that our exploration into the legal aspects of adolescent pregnancy and abortion leads us through a complicated maze of oft-conflicting legislation and government policies. All too frequently the laws have remained oblivious to the actual needs of adolescents and their basic human rights. This is regrettable since any attempt at implementing the human rights standard must *a fortiori* take into account the special status of adolescents, the safeguarding of whose rights deserves particular vigilance.

This rather broad review of the legal implications of adolescent pregnancy and abortion has led us to the conclusion that there is a need to undertake a systematic compilation and review of the existing laws which affect the issue. Moreover, further research should be undertaken into the definition and implications of unwanted pregnancy among minors.

---

212. American Medical Association, *News*, Apr. 17, 1967.

APPENDIX

Age Ladder of Rights and Obligations

| | Marriage | | Civil | Criminal | |
	Boys	Girls	Majority	Responsibility	Vote
Algeria	18	16	21	18	19
Argentina	18	18	21	21	21
Australia	18	16	21	18	18
Bangladesh	18	16	21	18	18
Belgium	18	15	21	18	21
Brazil	18	16	21	21	18
Cameroon	18	15	21	18	21
Canada	14/16	12/16	18/19	16/18	18/19
Chile	14	12	21	18	18
Colombia	No Age Limit		boys 21		
			girls 18	18	21
Costa Rica	15	15	21	21	18
Czechoslovakia	18	18	18	18	18
Denmark	20	18	20	15	20
Egypt	18	16	21	21	21
Ethiopia	18	15	18	18	21
Finland	18	17	20	18	20
France	18	15	21	18	21
German Dem. Rep.	16	16	18	18	18
Germany Fed. Rep.	21	16	21	21	18
Ghana	18	13	21	21	21
Iran	15	15	18	18	18
Italy	16	14	21	18	21
Ivory Coast	18	16	21	18	21
Jamaica	18	16	21	16	18
Japan	18	16	20	20	20
Korea (Rep. of)	18	16	20	14	20
Laos	18	15	18	16	18
Madagascar	17	14	21	21	18
Mauritius	18	15	21	21	21
Mexico	16	14	18	18	18
Niger	21	18	21	18	21
Nigeria	14/18	14/18	21	17	21
Netherlands	18	16	21	18	18
New Zealand	16	16	20	17	20
Norway	18	16	20	16	20
Romania	18	18	18	18	18
Senegal	20	16	21	18	21
Singapore	18	18	21	16	21
Spain	14	12	21	16	21
Switzerland	20	18	20	20	20
Tanzania	18	15	18	18	18
Turkey	17	15	18	18	20

APPENDIX *(Continued)*

Age Ladder of Rights and Obligations

	Marriage		Civil	Criminal	
	Boys	Girls	Majority	Responsibility	Vote
United Kingdom	16	16	18	17	18
U.S.A.	14/21	12/18	18/21	18/17/16	18
U.S.S.R.	18	16/18	18	18	18
Venezuela	14	12	21	21	18
Yugoslavia	18	18	18	18	18
Zaire	18	18	21	21	18

Source: Patrikios, *Marriage Age 16, Civil Majority 18, Voting Age 21—Why? UNESCO Courier*, October 1973, pp. 26-27.

Legal Rights of Minors to Sex-Related Medical Care

By
Eve W. Paul*

Recent American social history has been dominated by the struggle of blacks and women to achieve equal status. There are many indications that the next great wave of social change will focus upon the legal rights of minors.

Minors[1] have traditionally been subject to many legal disabilities, perhaps the most dramatic of which is the denial to minors of effective control over their own bodies. The common law treated children in many respects as the property of their parents. In the area of medical care, in the absence of exceptional circumstances,[2] parental consent was required before a minor could obtain needed medical treatment.

A growing awareness of the medical problems related to sexual activity among minors[3] has spurred rapid changes in the law brought about by activity in both legislatures and courts. Moreover, the courts have made great strides in recognizing the constitutional rights of minors. This article will discuss

---

* B.A. Cornell, 1950, J.D. Columbia, 1952, is active in the field of population planning, and the author of many articles on the subject. She is currently associated with the New York firm of Greenbaum, Wolff & Ernst.

1. At common law, the minimum age of majority was 21. 42 AM. JUR. 2d, *Infants* § 1 (1969). This has been lowered by statute from 21 to 18 in forty states. Paul, Pilpel, and Wechsler, *Pregnancy, Teenagers and the Law*, 6 FAMILY PLANNING PERSPECTIVES No. 3, at 142 (1974).

2. There are generally four exceptions, three of which (emancipation, emergency, and the so-called "mature minor" exception) will be dealt with later in this article. The courts recently have been developing a fourth exception to the common law doctrine; that of the abused or neglected minor. In most cases where this exception has been applied, there existed an emergency situation with the minor in immediate need of care and a refusal by the parent to provide it. The courts thus ordered care to be provided against the parents' wishes. People ex rel Wallace v. Labrenz, 411 Ill. 618, 104 N.E.2d 769, *cert. denied* 344 U.S. 824 (1952). In most of the cases, the courts have required vaccination of children to effectuate a health regulation which was an integral part of a state mandatory schooling law. Cude v. State of Arkansas, 237 Ark. 927, 377 S.W.2d 816 (1964); Mannis v. State of Arkansas, 240 Ark. 42, 398 S.W.2d 206 (1966), *cert. denied* 384 U.S. 972. *See also* State v. Perricone, 37 N.J. 463, 181 A.2d 751, *cert. denied* 371 U.S. 890 (1962); In re Vasko, 238 App. Div. 128, 263 N.Y. Supp. 552 (2d Dep't 933); In re Rotkowitz, 175 Misc. 948, 25 N.Y.S. 2d 624 (Children's Ct. 1941); In re Sampson, 64 Misc. 2d. 658, 317 N.Y.S. 2d 641 (Fam. Ct. 1970), *aff'd* 37 App. Div. 2d 668, 323 N.Y.S.2d 253 (3d Dep't 1971) *aff'd*, 29 N.Y.2d 900, 328 N.Y.S.2d 686 (1972); In re Clark, 21 Ohio Op. 2d 86, 185 N.E. 2d 128 (Ohio Com. Pl. 1962). *See* text accompanying notes 41-54 *infra*.

3. M. Zelnik and J.F. Kantor, *The Probability of Premarital Intercourse*, 1 SOCIAL SCIENCE RESEARCH 3 (1972).

93

recent developments in the law relating to minors' access to sex-related medical care and the underlying constitutional issues.

I. THE PROBLEM

In a period of declining birthrates, out-of-wedlock births in the United States for women under 20 have continued to increase, numbering an estimated 150,000 in 1972.[4] Illegitimacy rates among teenagers have increased most sharply, and births to teenagers are becoming an even larger proportion of all births.[5]

Important reasons for this trend are the rising incidence of premarital intercourse at earlier ages[6] and the fact that only a very small percentage of sexually active teenagers are using the most effective methods of contraception.[7]

Yet the consequences of an unwanted pregnancy can be disastrous for a teenage girl and her child. If the pregnancy is carried to term, the mother faces greatly increased medical risks.[8] The death rate for teenage mothers and their babies is 30 percent higher than that for mothers age 20 to 24 and their babies.[9] The child also has a greater chance of being physically abused or neglected if it survives.[10]

---

4. RESEARCH DEPARTMENT, PLANNED PARENTHOOD FEDERATION OF AMERICA, INC., UNWANTED PREGNANCY AMONG SINGLE TEENAGERS 3.

5. National Center for Health Statistics, DHEW (NCHS), *Interval Between First Marriage and Legitimate First Birth, United States, 1964-66*, 18 MONTHLY VITAL STATISTICS REPORT, No. 12 (Supp. 1970); NCHS, *Summary Report, Final Natality Statistics, 1969*, 22 MONTHLY VITAL STATISTICS REPORT, No. 7 (Supp. 1973); and P. Cutright, *Illegitimacy in the United States, 1920-1968*, in WESTOFF AND PARKE, JR. (eds.), 1 COMMISSION ON POPULATION GROWTH AND THE AMERICAN FUTURE RESEARCH REPORTS 365 (1972).

6. Zelnik and Kantor, *supra* note 3, at 335.

7. Kantor and Zelnik, *Contraception and Pregnancy Experience of Young Unmarried Women in the United States*, 5 FAMILY PLANNING PERSPECTIVES 21 (1973).

8. *See* Day, *Factors Influencing Offspring*, 113 AM. J. DISEASES OF CHILDREN 179 (1967); Daniels, *Medical, Legal and Social Indications of Contraceptives for Teenagers*, 5 CHILD WELFARE 150 (1971); Wallace, *Teeanage Pregnancy*, AM. J. OBST. & GYNEC. (Aug. 15, 1965); Grant, *Biologic Outcomes of Adolescent Pregnancy: An Administrative Perspective*, in JOHNS HOPKINS UNIV. SCHOOL OF HYGIENE AND PUBLIC HEALTH, PERSPECTIVES IN MATERNAL AND CHILD HEALTH (1970). *See also:* BUTLER AND BONHAM, PERINATAL MORTALITY (1963); Heady and Morris, 66 J. OBS. & GYNEC. BRIT. EMP. 577 (1959); Yerushalmy, Bierman, Illsley, *The Social Correlates of Childbirth*, paper for Perinatal Research Committee, Association for the Aid of Crippled Children (1964); U.S. DEPT. OF HEALTH, EDUCATION AND WELFARE, INTERNATIONAL COMPARISON OF PERINATAL AND INFANT MORTALITY: THE UNITED STATES AND SIX WESTERN EUROPEAN COUNTRIES, Series 3, No. 6 (1967); Kessler, *Maternal and Infant Mortality*, PROCEEDINGS OF THE INTERNATIONAL PLANNED PARENTHOOD FEDERATION, Santiago, Chile (1967); Yerushalmy, Palmer, and Kramer, 55 PUBLIC HEALTH REPORTS 1195 (1940); Jaffe and Polgar, *Epidemiological Indications for Fertility Control*, JOURNAL OF THE CHRISTIAN MEDICAL ASSOCIATION OF INDIA 12 (1967); Pakter, Rosner, Jacobziner, and Greenstein, 51 AM. J. PUB. HEALTH 846 (1961).

9. Stryker, *Higher Mortality in Teen Pregnancies*, 4 GETTING IT TOGETHER . . ., No. 2 (Jan. 1974); Tietze, *Mortality with Contraception and Induced Abortion*, STUDIES IN FAMILY PLANNING 6 (Sept. 1969).

10. Gil, VIOLENCE AGAINST CHILDREN 109 (1970), (9.29 percent of abusing mothers in

The social consequences may be equally shattering. Precipitate marriage, school dropout, marital instability, poverty and dependency, all attend an unwanted pregnancy.[11]

Access to contraceptive advice and liberalized procedures for obtaining a legal abortion would be most effective in combatting these problems. But a minor seeking contraceptive advice or a legal abortion may discover that confidential medical services are not available to him or her, or that doctors and hospitals are reluctant to help at all, in the absence of parental consent.[12]

While some states have recognized that minors may need some protection because of their uncertain status, the statutes which have been promulgated for the purpose of "protecting" the minor are often arbitrary in their operation and effect.

In New York, for example, licensed pharmacies may sell contraceptives to minors 16 years of age or older;[13] under the penal statutes, the minimum age at which a female minor may give valid consent to sexual intercourse is 17.[14] Finally, men and women must be 18 to marry without parental consent.[15] This raises the interesting question of what a girl is supposed to do with the contraceptives she can purchase at age 16, until age 17 when she can consent to sexual intercourse, or age 18 when she can get married.[16]

II.   THE LEGAL DISABILITIES OF MINORS

Minors have long been subject to a variety of disabilities under the law. At common law, minors were said to lack the full capacity to contract,[17] to consent to medical treatment,[18] to marry,[19] to hold public office,[20] to acquire

---

1967 were younger than 20 years of age); U.S. BUREAU OF THE CENSUS, CURRENT POPULATION REPORTS, *Previous and Prospective Fertility: 1967* 29, Series P-20, No. 211 (only 2.4% of mothers 14-44 were younger than 20).

11. Pregnancy is the largest cause of school dropouts among teenagers in lower socioeconomic classes, according to one expert. *Hearings on S. 2108 and S. 2319 before a Subcomm. of the Sen. Comm. on Labor and Public Welfare,* 91st Cong., 1st & 2nd Sess. 69 (1970). *See also* CALLAHAN, ABORTION, LAW, CHOICE & MORALITY 67-71 (1970), and note 4 *supra.*

12. Potential liability may also hinder professional or semi-professional "counselors", *see* Note, *Counseling the Counselors: Legal Implications of Counseling Minors Without Parental Consent,* 31 MD. L. REV. 332 (1971).

13. N.Y. EDUC. LAW § 6811 (McKinney 1947).

14. N.Y. PENAL LAW § 130.05 (McKinney 1965).

15. N.Y. DOMESTIC RELATIONS LAW § 7 (McKinney 1964).

16. Pilpel and Wechsler, *Birth Control, Teenagers and the Law,* 3 FAMILY PLANNING PERSPECTIVES 37 (July 1971).

17. Young v. Sterling Leather Works, 91 N.J.L. 289, 102 A. 395 (1917).

18. Bonner v. Moran, 126 F.2d 121 (D.C. Cir. 1941).

19. State v. Ward, 204 S.C. 210, 28 S.E.2d 785 (1944); State v. Sellers, 140 S.C. 66, 134 S.E.873 (1926); Mangrum v. Mangrum, 310 Ky. 226, 220 S.W.2d 406 (1949).

20. In re Golding, 57 N.H. 146, 24 Am. R. 66 (1876); Harkreader v. State, 35 Tex. Cr. 243, 33 S.W. 117 (1895).

domicile,[21] to act as executor or administrator,[22] to make wills,[23] to act as agent or trustee[24] or to appoint agents or attorneys.[25]

Minors have received further differential treatment under statutes protecting their health and morals,[26] prescribing working conditions,[27] and denying them the right to consent to sexual intercourse.[28]

These disabilities are sometimes said to be personal privileges conferred on minors by the law. As such they constitute limitations on the legal capacity of infants, not to defeat their rights, but to shield and protect them from their own improvidence, or from the acts of others.[29]

In cases concerning medical treatment for sex-related problems these disabilities have, however, often worked to the minor's detriment, especially because the situation has been complicated by the minor's embarrassment and disinclination to disclose the problem to a parent.[30]

The informed consent of a patient, if competent, has always been a prerequisite to surgery.[31] If the patient was considered incompetent,[32] then the consent of someone else who would be legally authorized to consent under the circumstances was needed.[33]

At common law, the age of legal majority, and thus competence to consent, was fixed at 21.[34] The law assumed that a minor was not wise or mature enough to determine what his or her medical needs were. Thus, consent was left in the hands of the minor's older, and presumably wiser parent or guardian.[35] Accordingly, a physician rendering medical care without parental consent was in danger of a possible civil suit by the parent for assault and battery,[36] even if the contact was for the benefit of the minor.[37] The

---

21. In re Webb's Adoption, 65 Ariz. 176, 177 P.2d 222 (1947); In re Robben, 188 Kan. 217, 362 P.2d 29 (1961).

22. In re Tippet's Will, 13 N.Y.S.2d 971 (1939); In re Golenbiewski's Estate, 146 Ohio St. 551, 67 N.E.2d 328 (1946).

23. In re Martin's Estate, 1 Or. App. 260, 457 P.2d 662 (1969).

24. Schmidgall v. Engelke, 81 Ill. App. 2d 103, 224 N.E.2d 590 (1967).

25. Schroeder v. State, 252 So. 2d 270 (1971); People v. Bergerson, 271 N.Y.S.2d 236, 218 N.E.2d 288 (1966).

26. Ludwig v. Kirby, 13 N.J. Super. 116, 80 A.2d 239 (1951); Gabin v. Skyline Cabana Club, 54 N.J. 550, 258 A.2d 6 (1969).

27. N.Y. PENAL LAW § 130.05 (McKinney 1965).

28. Re Davidson, 223 Minn. 268, 272, 26 N.W.2d 223, 225 (1942).

29. Bonner v. Moran, 126 F.2d 121 (D.C. Cir. 1941).

30. Pratt v. Davis, 224 Ill. 300, 79 N.W. 562 (1906).

31. Ballard v. Anderson, 4 Cal.3d 873, 484 P.2d 1345 (1971); 23 HASTINGS L. REV. 1495, 1502 (1972).

32. BLACK'S LAW DICTIONARY 906 (4th ed. 1968): "Lack of ability, legal qualification, or fitness to discharge the required duty."

33. Bonner v. Moran, 126 F.2d 121 (D.C. Cir. 1941).

34. See James, The Age of Majority, 4 AM. J. LEG. HIST. 22 (1960).

35. "Infancy, along with incompetency, habitual drunkenness, and the like, are legal disabilities." Weber v. State, 267 App. Div. 325, 45 N.Y.S.2d 834, 836 (1944).

36. 70 C.J.S., Physicians & Surgeons § 48, at 968 (1951); SHARTEL & PLANT, THE LAW OF MEDICAL PRACTICE 25-26 (1959); Zoski v. Gaines, 271 Mich. 1, 260 N.W. 99 (1935); Rogers v.

physician was also in danger of a malpractice suit arising from a claim of performing an unauthorized operation.[38]

Physicians were thus often reluctant to provide medical care to minors without prior parental consent, and because of the necessity of parental notification, minors were often reluctant to seek medical care, especially if the medical problem was sex-related.[39]

However, the rule requiring parental consent has always been subject to a variety of exceptions.[40] Courts throughout the country have held that, when confronted with an "emergency which endangers the life or health of a minor," a physician need not wait to obtain parental consent before commencing treatment.[41] Exactly what the courts meant by an "emergency which endangers the life or health of a minor", has been subject to varying interpretations, however,[42] and the burden of proof is usually on the physician to prove the existing emergency.[43]

Another exception to the rule requiring parental consent which has been recognized by the courts is that of the "emancipated minor."[44] Since emancipation is viewed as an extinguishment of parental rights and duties, most

Sells, 178 Okla. 103, 61 P.2d 1018 (1936); Moss v. Rishworth, 222 S.W. 225 (Tex. Comm'n of App. 1920).

37. Zoski v. Gaines, 271 Mich. 1, 260 N.W. 99 (1935); Rogers v. Sells, 178 Okla. 103, 61 P.2d 1018 (1936).

38. "While an unauthorized operation is, in contemplation of law, an assault and battery, it also amounts to malpractice, even though negligence is not charged." Physicians' and Dentists' Business Bureau v. Dray, 8 Wash.2d 38, 111 P.2d 568, 569 (1941); and *see* Maercklein v. Smith 129 Col. 72, 266 P.2d 1095, 1098 (1954), (concerning an adult plaintiff who had given consent for a circumcision and received an unauthorized vasectomy instead); *See also* Brown v. Wood, 202 So.2d 125 (Fla. D. Ct. App. 1967).

39. The minor faced with parental refusal has two remedies: litigation against his parents, or seeking an order by the appropriate state agency acting *in loco parentis. See* In re Seiforth, 309 N.Y. 80, 127 N.E.2d 820 (1955). Either approach may be costly and time consuming. For a discussion of the problems involved, *see,* Note, *Judicial Power to Order Medical Treatment for Minors Over Objections of Their Guardians,* 14 SYR. L. REV. 84 (1962). At least 16 states have statutes allowing a doctor to breach the confidence of a minor patient without the patient's consent. *See* HEALTH SERVICES AND MENTAL HEALTH ADMINISTRATION, U.S. DEP'T OF HEALTH, EDUCATION & WELFARE, FAMILY PLANNING, CONTRACEPTION AND STERILIZATION: AN ANALYSIS OF LAWS AND POLICIES IN THE UNITED STATES (AS OF SEPTEMBER 1971), prepared by the Center for Family Planning Program Development, the Technical Assistance Division of Planned Parenthood-World Population, DHEW Publication No. (HSA) 74-16001, 77 (1974).

40. *See* note 1 *supra.*

41. Jackovach v. Yocom, 212 Iowa 914, 237 N.W. 444 (1931); Wells v. McGehee, 39 So.2d 196 (La. 1949); Luka v. Lowrie, 171 Mich. 122, 136 N.W. 1106 (1912); Sullivan v. Montgomery 155 Misc. 448, 279 N.Y.S. 575 (Sup. Ct. 1935); Browning v. Hoffman, 90 W. Va. 568, 111 S.E. 492 (1922).

42. *Compare* Jackovach v. Yocom, 212 Iowa 914, 237 N.W. 444 (1931) (emergency amputation of minor's arm required to preserve life); *with* Sullivan v. Montgomery, 155 Misc. 448, 279 N.Y.S. 575 (Sup. Ct. 1935) (setting a minor's dislocated ankle).

43. *See, e.g.,* Rogers v. Sells, 178 Okla. 103, 61 P.2d 1018 (1936); Moss v. Rishworth, 222 S.W. 225 (Tex. Comm'n of App. 1920). *Cf.* United States v. Vuitch, 402 U.S. 62 (1971).

44. Smith v. Seibly, 72 Wash. 2d 16, 431 P.2d 719 (1967); Bach v. Long Island Jewish Hospital, 49 Misc. 2d 297, 267 N.Y.S. 2d 289 (Sup. Ct. 1966).

courts would probably hold, even in the absence of a statute or judicial precedent, that a completely emancipated minor can consent to his or her own medical treatment.

An "emancipated minor" is usually defined as a minor who lives apart from his or her parents and is self-supporting.[45] Recent cases have held that a minor who contributes part of his or her own support may be emancipated even though still living at home.[46] Various events such as marriage[47] and military service[48] can effect the emancipation of a minor. However, a minor may be emancipated for some purposes but not for others.[49] Thus, a New York court recently held that while a minor was emancipated for the purpose of consenting to medical services, she was not emancipated for the purpose of altering her property rights.[50] And several states which recognize the emancipation exception to parental consent may still require such consent under specific abortion statutes.[51]

The most recent exception formulated by the courts has been that for the "mature minor," one who is sufficiently intelligent and mature to understand the nature and consequences of the medical treatment being sought.[52] A physician treating a "mature minor" will not be held liable, even though parental consent has not been obtained, provided that the treatment is for the minor's benefit.[53] The "mature minor" doctrine is a logical extension of the general rule requiring that physicians obtain "informed consent" from all patients before undertaking treatment. A "mature minor" can be defined as one who is capable of giving informed consent; this may depend in each case on the nature and seriousness of the medical treatment involved. Thus, in a recent Washington case, the exception was used to allow an eighteen year old minor to consent to a vasectomy because he was intelligent and mature

---

45. *See, e.g.*, Delaware L. & W. R. Co. v. Petrowsky, 250 F. 554, 559 (2d Cir. 1918), and Wallace v. Cox, 136 Tenn. 69, 188 S.W. 611 (1916).

46. *See, e.g.*, Cidis v. White, 71 Misc. 2d 481, 336 N.Y.S.2d 362 (Dist. Ct. 1972); Martinez v. Southern Pacific Co., 288 P.2d 868 (Cal. 1955); Wood v. Wood, 135 Conn. 280, 63 A.2d 586 (1948).

47. Crook v. Crook, 80 Ariz. 275, 296 P.2d 951 (1956); Estate of Hardaway, 26 Ill. App. 2d 493, 168 N.E.2d 796 (1960).

48. Niesen v. Niesen, 38 Wis. 2d 599, 157 N.W.2d 660 (1968).

49. Gillikin v. Burbage, 263 N.C. 317, 139 S.E.2d 753 (1965).

50. Bach v. Long Island Jewish Hospital, 49 Misc. 2d 297, 267 N.Y.S. 2d 289 (Sup. Ct. 1966). *And see* text accompanying notes 78-92 *infra*.

51. Such statutes may be unconstitutional under Roe v. Wade, 410 U.S. 113 (1973) and Doe v. Bolton, 410 U.S. 179 (1973). *See* Foe v. Vanderhoof, Civ. Act. No. 74-F-418 (D. Colo., Feb. 5, 1975). *See also* text accompanying notes 144-60 *infra*.

52. *See* Wadlington, *Minors and Health Care, The Age of Consent*, 11 OSGOODE HALL L.J. 115, 117-120 (1973).

53. Younts v. St. Francis Hospital, 205 Kan. 292, 469 P.2d 330 (1970); Bakker v. Welsh, 144 Mich. 632, 108 N.W. 94 (1906); Bishop v. Shurly, 237 Mich. 76, 211 N.W. 75 (1926); Gulf & Ship Island R.R. v. Sullivan, 155 Miss. 1, 119 So. 501 (1928); Lacey v. Laird, 166 Ohio St. 12, 139 N.E.2d 25 (1956); *see also* Bonner v. Moran, 126 F.2d 121 (D.C. Cir. 1941), and Smith v. Seibly, 72 Wash. 2d 16, 431 P.2d 719 (1967).

enough to understand and appreciate the consequences of the operation.[54] And in 1973, Judge Weinfeld of the Federal District Court for the Southern District of New York suggested a similar test in an abortion case. The surviving father of a pregnant minor sued a physician and clinic for performing an abortion on the girl without parental consent. Judge Weinfeld denied summary judgment for the plaintiff, declaring that whether the minor "was competent to exercise this right [to terminate her pregnancy] on her own behalf without her parents' consent presents an issue of fact."[55]

Courts have elected, in the few suits that have been brought, to rely on the above exceptions. The author knows of no case holding a physician liable for damages for supplying any medical service to a minor without parental consent where the minor was older than fifteen and the treatment was for the minor's benefit and performed with the minor's consent. Nevertheless, doctors, hospitals, and health agencies have been reluctant to treat minors without parental consent, fearing exposure to suits for technical assault or malpractice.[56]

III. REMEDIAL LEGISLATION

In recent years society has recognized the increased maturity of today's teenagers by adopting a variety of statutes broadening the rights of minors.

Following the adoption of the twenty-sixth amendment to the Constitution, enabling eighteen-year-olds to vote, almost all the states reduced the age of majority to eighteen.[57]

Furthermore, several states have enacted statutes specifically reducing the age at which a minor can consent to medical care. Thus, in Alabama, fourteen-year-olds can consent to medical care.[58] In Oregon[59] and (subject to certain conditions) California[60] and Colorado,[61] the age of consent for medical care has been reduced to fifteen. In South Carolina,[62] minors may consent to medical care at age sixteen, and in Connecticut,[63] Georgia,[64] Illinois,[65]

54. Smith v. Seibly, 72 Wash. 2d 16, 431 P.2d 719 (1967).
55. Modugno v. Monsey Medical Center, Civ. Act. No. 73-C-230 (S.D.N.Y. 1973).
56. See notes 35 and 37 supra.
57. The following jurisdictions retain a 21 year age of majority: Alabama (for females), Colorado, Mississippi, Missouri, Pennsylvania, South Carolina, and the District of Columbia.
58. Act No. 2281 (1971).
59. OREGON LAWS Ch. 381 (1971).
60. The minor must live separate and apart from his parents and manage his own financial affairs, regardless of his income. CAL. CIV. CODE § 34.6 (West Supp. 1971).
61. COLO. REV. STAT. ANN. § 41-2-13 (1971).
62. S. CAR. HEALTH CODE, Ch. 2, Art. 1.1, § 32-565 (1974).
63. Pub. Act 304 (effective Oct. 1, 1971).
64. GA. CODE ANN. § 88-2904 (1971).
65. ILL. ANN. STAT. Ch. 91, § 18.1 (Smith-Hurd 1972 Cum. Supp.).

Maryland,[66] New Jersey,[67] New York,[68] North Carolina,[69] Pennsylvania,[70] and Virginia,[71] the age of consent to medical care has been specifically reduced to eighteen.

The common law exceptions to the parental consent doctrine have been recognized by many states in statutory form. Eleven states have enacted comprehensive statutes enabling minors to consent to medical care.[72] Twelve states have codified the common law "emergency" exception only.[73] The "emancipation" exception is at least partially in effect in almost half the states, with twenty-one states having statutes emancipating married and/or pregnant minors for the purpose of consenting for their own medical care.[74] The "mature minor" exception has also been recognized by statute in a number of states.[75]

Many states have enacted legislation enabling minors to consent to medical care in certain specified situations, usually defined as the detection, prevention and treatment of venereal disease, pregnancy and drug abuse. Today, every state but Wisconsin has a law giving minors the right to consent

66. MD. ANN. CODE, art. 43, § 135 (1971).

67. 1972 LAWS, Ch. 81.

68. PUB. HEALTH LAW § 2504 (McKinney 1971).

69. N. CAR. GEN. STAT. § 90-21.5 (1971).

70. PA. STAT., tit. 35, § 10101 (1969).

71. House Bill 378 (1970).

72. Alabama, Act No. 2281 (1971); California, CAL. CIV. CODE §§ 25.6, 25.7, 34.5, 34.6, 34.7 (West Supp. 1971); Colorado, COLO. REV. STAT. ANN. § 41-2-13 (1971); Georgia, GA. CODE ANN. Ch. 88-29 (1971); Illinois, ILL. ANN. STAT. Ch. 91, §§ 18.1-18.7 (Smith-Hurd 1966 and Supp. 1972); Kentucky, KY. REV. STAT. § 214.185 (1972); Maryland, MD. ANN. CODE art. 43, § 135 (1971); Minnesota, LAWS Ch. 544 (1971); Mississippi, MISS. CODE ANN. § 7129-81 et seq. (Cum. Supp. 1971); North Carolina, N. CAR. GEN. STAT. §§ 90-21.1-90-21.5 (1971); Pennsylvania, PA. STAT. tit. 35, §§ 10101-10105 (1969).

73. Alabama, Act No. 2281 (1971); Georgia, GA. CODE ANN. § 88-2905 (1971); Illinois, ILL. ANN. STAT. Ch. 91, § 18.3 (Smith-Hurd Cum. Supp. 1972); Kentucky, KY. REV. STAT. § 214.185 (1972); Maryland, MD. ANN. CODE art. 43, § 135(a)(4) (1971); Massachusetts, MASS. ANN. LAWS Ch. 112, § 12E (Cum. Supp. 1971); Minnesota, LAWS Ch. 544, § 144.344 (1971); Mississippi, MISS. CODE ANN. § 7129-83 (Cum. Supp. 1971); New York, N.Y. PUB. HEALTH LAW § 2504 (McKinney Supp. 1972); North Carolina, N. CAR. GEN. STAT. § 90-21.1 (Cum. Supp. 1971); Rhode Island, R.I. GEN. LAWS ANN. § 23-51-1 (Supp. 1971) (any person sixteen or over or married).

74. Alabama, Act No. 2281 (1971); Arizona, ARIZ. REV. STAT. ANN. § 44-132 (1967); California, CAL. CIV. CODE §§ 25.6, 25.7, 34.6 (West Supp. 1971); Colorado, COL. REV. STAT. ANN. § 41-2-13 (1971); Deleware, DEL. CODE ANN. tit. 13, § 717 (Supp. 1970); Georgia, GA. CODE ANN. Ch. 88-29 (1971); Illinois, ILL. ANN. STAT. Ch. 91, § 18.1 (Smith-Hurd Cum. Supp. 1972); Indiana, IND. ANN. STAT. § 35-4409 (1969); Kentucky, KY. REV. STAT. § 214.185 (1972); Maryland, MD. ANN. CODE art. 43, § 135 (1971); Minnesota, LAWS Ch. 544, §§ 144.341, 144.342 (1971); Mississippi, MISS. CODE ANN. § 7129-81 (Cum. Supp. 1971); Missouri, MO. REV. STAT. § 431.065 (Cum. Supp. 1970); Montana, MONT. REV. CODES ANN. 69-6101 (1970); Nevada, NEV. REV. STAT. § 129.030 (1969); New Jersey, N.J. STAT. ANN. § 9:17A-1 (Supp. 1971); New Mexico, STAT. ANN. § 12-12-1 (1967); New York, N.Y. PUB. HEALTH LAW § 2504 (McKinney Supp. 1972); North Carolina, N.C. GEN. STAT. § 90-21.5(a) (1971); Pennsylvania, PA. STAT. tit. 35, § 10101 (Cum. Supp. 1971); South Carolina, S. CAR. CODE § 11-157 (Cum. Supp. 1970).

75. Paul, Pilpel and Wechsler, supra note 1, at 144.

for diagnosis and treatment of venereal disease,[76] and even Wisconsin teen-agers can give such consent once they have reached the age of majority, eighteen.

A recent national survey[77] found a "strong trend" in recent years for states to pass legislation "giving minors access to effective birth control services on their own consent and initiative." This trend is supported by almost three out of four Americans, according to a June, 1972 Gallup poll.[78] The liberalizing trend has been marked by the enactment of statutes in thirteen states[79] and the District of Columbia[80] specifically permitting broad categories[81] of minors to consent to contraceptive services. Twelve other states have statutes authorizing publicly sponsored family planning programs which may permit services to at least some minors without parental consent.[82]

In addition to state legislation, federal law since 1972 has required that family planning services be offered and provided to sexually active minors under the program of aid to needy families with children.[83] It is apparent from the legislative history that Congress intended to remove any practical impediment to the availability of such services which would be caused by the imposition of parental consent requirements.[84] Several states have incorporated this policy into their own legislation.[85]

At least one study has concluded that the increased availability of contraceptive information would help prevent teenage pregnancy:

There are no patterns of sexual promiscuity or cultural values supporting pregnancy outside of marriage.[86]

Rather, the study placed the blame on "limited knowledge of and access to

76. *Id.* at 142. Thirty-one states adopted such statutes between 1968 and 1971.

77. FAMILY PLANNING, *supra* note 39.

78. 1 FAMILY PLANNING/POPULATION REPORTER 11 (1973).

79. Paul, Pilpel and Wechsler, *supra* note 1, at 145.

80. Dist. of Col. Reg. No. 71-27 (1971).

81. Paul, Pilpel and Wechsler, *supra* note 1, at 145.

82. *Id.* The states are Alaska, Arkansas, Iowa, Kansas, Louisiana, Michigan, New Mexico, New York, Ohio, Oklahoma.

83. 42 U.S.C. § 602(a)(15(A)) (1974); Family Planning Services, 45 C.F.R. § 220.21 (1974).

84. The Senate Finance Committee Report on the Social Security Amendments of 1972 asserts that family planning services must be provided on a confidential basis, thus obviating any need for parental notification and consent. S. REP. NO. 1230, 92nd Cong., 2d Sess. 297 (1972).

85. *See, e.g.,* N.Y. SOCIAL SERVICES LAW § 350.1(e) (McKinney Supp. 1974), which provides that the State Department of Social Services must offer "to eligible persons of childbearing age, *including children who can be considered sexually active,*" such family planning services and supplies as those eligible persons may desire (emphasis added). *See also* CAL. WELFARE AND INSTITUTIONS CODE § 10053.5 (1972). A lawsuit has been brought in California challenging that provision under the Equal Protection clause of the Fourteenth Amendment on the grounds that it allows poor minors access to services which are denied to wealthy minors. *Cf.* Wolff v. State Bd. of Registration for the Healing Arts, 380 F. Supp. 1137 (E.D. Mo. 1974).

86. Furstenberg, Gardis and Mankowitz, *Birth Control: Knowledge and Attitudes Among Unmarried Pregnant Adolescents: A Preliminary Report,* 31 J. MARRIAGE & FAMILY 42 (1969).

contraception."[87] The United States Commission on Population Growth and the American Future has also recommended that

> birth control be made available to teenagers in appropriate facilities sensitive to their needs and concerns.[88]

State legislatures have looked with less favor upon abortions for minors. In forty-eight states and the District of Columbia, women may consent for an abortion upon reaching age eighteen. However, only sixteen states and the District of Columbia[89] have explicitly recognized the right of any younger minors to consent to an abortion. Furthermore, some states specifically prohibit abortion for minors in the absence of parental consent,[90] though many of these statutes have been or may be declared unconstitutional.[91] Twenty-one states have statutes enabling minors to consent to pregnancy-related medical treatment,[92] and this has been held to include the right to have an abortion,[93] and the right to refuse an abortion.[94] But eight of these statutes have provisions specifically excluding abortion.[95]

IV. CONSTITUTIONAL ISSUES

Recent developments point the way toward a constitutionally protected right of minors to access to sex-related medical care.

A. Minors as "Persons" under the Fourteenth Amendment

The Supreme Court in recent years has extended constitutional procedural safeguards and substantive rights to minors. The Court first applied due process criminal requirements to juvenile proceedings in 1967. In re Gault[96] dealt with a fifteen-year-old youth who had been committed to the

---

87. Id.

88. REPORT OF THE COMMISSION ON POPULATION GROWTH AND THE AMERICAN FUTURE 189 (Signet ed. 1972).

89. Paul, Pilpel and Wechsler, supra note 1, at 145.

90. Id.

91. See text accompanying notes 153-160 infra.

92. See note 73 supra.

93. Ballard v. Anderson, 95 Cal. Rptr. 1, 484 P.2d 1345 (1971).

94. In re Smith, 16 Md. App. 209, 295 A.2d 238 (1972).

95. Paul, Pilpel and Wechsler, supra note 1, at 146.

96. 387 U.S. 1 (1967). The ruling had been foreshadowed one year earlier, in Kent v. United States, 383 U.S. 541 (1966), where the Court reversed the conviction of a 16-year-old who had been tried before the United States District Court for the District of Columbia after the District of Columbia Juvenile Court had waived jurisdiction over him. The Supreme Court held that the order waiving jurisdiction was invalid because the Juvenile Court had not provided the juvenile with a hearing, with access to his social records and probation reports, or with a statement of the reasons for its decision.

Arizona State Industrial School "for the period of his minority," that is, until age twenty-one. The Court held that where a court's determination may result in a loss of personal liberty, certain due process requirements must be met. The Court declared that "neither the Fourteenth Amendment nor the Bill of Rights is for adults alone."[97] But the Court limited the rights it granted to notice of the charges, the right to counsel, confrontation and cross-examination of witnesses, and the privilege against self-incrimination.[98]

In subsequent cases, the Court has expanded the list of covered rights, holding that charges must be proved beyond a reasonable doubt where a juvenile is charged with an act which would be a crime if committed by an adult.[99] However, it has also since ruled that "trial by jury in the juvenile court's adjudicative stage is not a constitutional requirement,"[100] though such a procedure would be necessary for an adult charged with a similar offense.

Two years after *Gault*, the Court used the fourteenth amendment to prevent a restriction of free expression by minors. In *Tinker v. Des Moines School District*,[101] the Court upheld the right of public school students to wear black armbands in school as a protest against the Vietnam war, ruling that the armbands were protected expression which could not be forbidden in the absence of evidence that they would "substantially interfere with the work of the school or impinge upon the rights of other students."[102] Justice Fortas, writing for the majority, stated:

> Students in school as well as out of school are "persons" under our Constitution. They are possessed of fundamental rights which the State must respect, just as they themselves must respect their obligation to the State.[103]

Just what those rights are, however, will be determined on a case-to-case basis.

A recent Supreme Court decision established one such right by holding that high school students facing temporary suspension from a public school are entitled to notice and hearing either before or promptly following the suspension. In a five-to-four decision, the Court held that the students' right to attend public school classes is a liberty and property interest that qualifies for protection under the due process clause of the fourteenth amendment.[104]

Although the Supreme Court may be said to be steadily expanding the rights of minors against state encroachment, a somewhat different issue is

97. In re Gault, 387 U.S. at 13.
98. *Id.* at 16.
99. In re Winship, 397 U.S. 358 (1970).
100. McKeiver v. Pennsylvania, 403 U.S. 528, 545 (1971).
101. 393 U.S. 503 (1969).
102. *Id.* at 509.
103. *Id.* at 511.
104. Goss *v.* Lopez, 43 U.S.L.W. 4181 (Jan. 21, 1975).

presented by the rights of a minor vis-a-vis his or her parents or legal guardian. It has long been recognized that parents have the right to direct the upbringing and education of children under their control. Thus, the state may not require all children to attend public schools.[105] In *Wisconsin v. Yoder*,[106] the Supreme Court held that members of the Amish faith could not be compelled to send their children to any school beyond the eighth grade.

The parents in *Yoder* contended that their children's attendance at high school was contrary to the Amish religion and way of life. Dissenting, Justice Douglas took the position that the views of the children involved should be heard before deciding the case. He wrote:

> Where the child is mature enough to express potentially conflicting desires, it would be an invasion of the child's rights to permit such an imposition without canvassing his views.[107]

In support of his position in *Yoder*, Justice Douglas cited the Supreme Court's decision in *Prince v. Massachusetts*[108] affirming the conviction under a state's child labor laws of a woman who permitted her nine-year-old niece to distribute religious tracts in the streets. Writing for the majority in *Prince*, Justice Rutledge had pointed out that rights of parenthood are not beyond limitation, citing previous cases upholding the state's right to protect the child from ill health by requiring compulsory vaccination[109] and requiring a parent to obtain needed medical care for his child.[110]

The *Prince* case has also been cited for the proposition that "the power of the state to control the conduct of children reaches beyond the scope of its authority over adults."[111] That language was quoted by Justice Brennan writing for the majority in *Ginsberg v. New York*[112] where the Court upheld a conviction under a New York statute[113] for selling to a sixteen-year-old boy "girlie" magazines which were not obscene for adults.

Justice Brennan specified two interests which justified the limitations set by the statute on the availability of pornographic material to minors under seventeen: the interest of parents in discharging their responsibility for their children's well-being, and the independent interest of the state in the well-being of its youth.[114]

The Supreme Court recently agreed to decide another case involving

---

105. Pierce *v*. Society of Sisters, 268 U.S. 510 (1925).
106. 406 U.S. 205 (1972).
107. 406 U.S. at 242 (Douglas, J. dissenting).
108. 321 U.S. 158 (1944).
109. Jacobsen *v*. Massachusetts, 197 U.S. 11 (1905).
110. People *v*. Pierson, 196 N.Y. 201 (1903).
111. 321 U.S. at 170.
112. 390 U.S. 629 (1968).
113. N.Y. Penal Law § 484-h (McKinney 1964).
114. 390 U.S. at 639-640.

the issue of whether a different standard of obscenity can be applied to publications written and read by minors than would control adult literary efforts.[115] At issue in that case is a student newspaper called Corn Cob Curtain circulated at an Indianapolis high school, which was banned by school authorities as "obscene, filthy, indecent and defamatory." School system rules required the superintendent's approval before any student publication could be distributed.

School authorities maintained that the newspaper, if circulated, would produce "significant disruption of the normal educational process," but the federal district court granted the students an injunction against interference with their paper, saying it represented an unconstitutional prior restraint on freedom of the press.

Whatever the outcome of that case may be, the author's view is that the obscenity cases, where the interests of the state and the parents may be said to coincide, have limited impact on cases involving health care for minors where the minors' need for sex-related health services and the state's interest in filling that need may well conflict with parental views of morality. We proceed therefore to a discussion of the constitutional bases and state interests which have been asserted in support of or opposition to abortion and contraception.

B. *The Right of Privacy*

The right of all citizens to access to contraception and abortion has been among the most important issues raised in the development of a constitutional right to privacy. The existence of such a right, although recognized in the past,[116] was substantially broadened by the United States Supreme Court in 1965 in *Griswold v. Connecticut.*[117] While there is no explicit mention of privacy in the Constitution, the roots of such a right have been found in the first amendment,[118] the fourth and fifth amendments,[119] the ninth amendment,[120] and the first section of the fourteenth amendment.[121]

---

115. 43 U.S.L.W. (1974).

116. Union Pacific R. Co. *v.* Botsford, 141 U.S. 250, 251 (1891); Mapp v. Ohio, 367 U.S. 643, 656 (1961). Perhaps the most celebrated expression of this argument was made by Justice Brandeis in his dissenting opinion in Olmstead v. United States, 277 U.S. 438 (1928) (in which the Court held that the obtaining of evidence by means of a secret wiretap and the use of such evidence at trial did not violate the fourth amendment), where he described "the right to be let alone" as "the right most valued by civilized men." 277 U.S. at 478.

117. 381 U.S. 479 (1965).

118. Stanley v. Georgia, 394 U.S. 557 (1969) (regarding the right to possess obscene matter in one's own house) *and* NAACP v. Alabama, 357 U.S. 449 (1958) (denying the state's right to examine the civil rights organization's membership list).

119. Mapp v. Ohio, 367 U.S. 643 (1961).

120. Griswold v. Connecticut, 381 U.S. 479, 487 (1965) (Goldberg, J. concurring).

121. Pierce v. Society of Sisters, 268 U.S. 510 (1925) and Meyer v. Nebraska, 262 U.S. 390 (1923).

In *Griswold,* the Court invalidated a state statute which made the use of contraceptives a criminal offense. The Court held that the statute violated a constitutional right of privacy which the Court found in the penumbras of the Bill of Rights guarantees. However, because the emphasis in the decision was on the right of privacy within the marriage relationship[122] and because the statute restricted only the use and not the distribution of contraceptives, the full extent of the right remained unclear.

The confusion on this subject was evident in *Eisenstadt v. Baird,*[123] in which the Court held that a Massachusetts statute which distinguished between married and unmarried people for purposes of determining when the distribution of contraceptives was permissible violated the equal protection clause of the fourteenth amendment. Justice Brennan thus answered one of the questions which had remained after *Griswold,* but indicated that he still had doubts about the scope of that case, when he said in his opinion for the Court: "whatever the rights of the individual to access to contraceptives may be, the rights must be the same for the unmarried and the married alike."[124]

The following year, the Court handed down its decisions in the abortion cases, *Roe v. Wade*[125] and *Doe v. Bolton.*[126] In *Roe,* the Court considered the constitutionality of the Texas abortion statute[127] and came to the conclusions "that the right of personal privacy includes the abortion decision, but that this right is not unqualified and must be considered against important state interests in regulation."[128] The Court struck down the statute, which prohibited abortion except where necessary to save the life of the mother.

Three state interests were asserted and dealt with by the Court.[129] First was the state's interest in discouraging illicit sex. Since the state did not stress this argument, the Court disposed of it quickly. However, the argument may prove stronger when asserted with regard to minors.[130] The second interest was to protect the life of the mother. As the Court concluded that early abortion is safer than childbirth,[131] the Court held that no valid state interest could arise until the second trimester, when a limited rule-making authority could be granted to state legislatures.[132] The final state interest, protecting

---

122. Appellants had been convicted under an accessory statute for giving advice about contraceptives to married persons.

123. 405 U.S. 438 (1972).

124. *Id.* at 453.

125. 410 U.S. 113 (1973).

126. 410 U.S. 179 (1973).

127. TEXAS CIVIL STAT. ANN. art. 4512-1 *et seq.* (Vernon 1973).

128. 410 U.S. at 154.

129. 410 U.S. at 129, 148-56, 162-64.

130. *But compare* Eisenstadt v. Baird, 405 U.S. 438 (1972). *And see* text accompanying notes 161-163 *infra.*

131. 410 U.S. at 148-50, 163. The Court relied upon numerous studies cited in note 44 at page 149 of the majority opinion.

132. 410 U.S. at 162-66.

potential life, was held to arise only upon the fetus reaching viability.[133] However, the Court expressly reserved decision on the constitutionality of provisions which required consent for an abortion from the husband of a married minor, or the parents of an unmarried minor.[134]

In *Doe*, the Court considered the validity of a more modern Georgia statute[135] patterned on the American Law Institute's Model Penal Code.[136] The Supreme Court struck down the Georgia law, which permitted abortions only when a continuation of the pregnancy would endanger the health of the pregnant woman, when the fetus was likely to be born defective, or when the pregnancy resulted from rape. Georgia's law also required the written concurrence of two Georgia doctors in addition to the attending physician and advance approval by an abortion committee at an accredited hospital.[137] The Court based its conclusion largely on the fact that similar procedures were not required for other types of surgery.[138] Having decided in *Roe* that no interest in fetal life arises until the fetus is viable outside of the womb, the Court held that there was no valid justification for this different treatment. The procedures were also found to bear no reasonable relationship to the protection of the mother.[139] Here, again, there appears to be no reason to distinguish minors from adults, but the Court was not asked to address the issue.

C. *Privacy for Minors*

The Supreme Court has not yet addressed the issue of privacy with specific reference to the sex-related medical care of minors. However, several lower courts have suggested the favorable direction that is likely to be taken in the future.

Recently, a federal district court granted an injunction requested by a junior high school student against the school's implementation of a drug

133. *Id.* at 163-65.
134. *Id.* at 165, n.67.
135. GA. CODE ANN. §§ 26-1201-1203 (1970).
136. AMERICAN LAW INSTITUTE, MODEL PENAL CODE § 207.10 (1969). The ALI statute was adopted by approximately one-fourth of the states.
137. GA. CODE ANN. § 23-1201(b) (1970).
138. Doe v. Bolton, 411 U.S. 179, 193-200 (1973).
139. *Id.* at 195-200. The relative importance of state interests may be illustrated by comparing the Justices' votes in *Baird* with those in *Roe* and *Doe*. Justice White, who wrote a separate concurring opinion in *Baird*, dissented in the abortion cases. The apparent inconsistency can be explained since his opinion in *Baird* was based solely on the fact that the contraceptive involved there was vaginal foam, which had never been shown to be hazardous to health. The abortion statutes, however, fell squarely within the area which he felt the state should be free to regulate. Thus the emphasis in Justice White's opinions is on the right of the state to regulate as long as it has a valid reason for doing so rather than on the right of the individual to privacy.

Chief Justice Burger, on the other hand, dissented in *Baird*, rejecting Justice White's distinction between vaginal foam and other kinds of contraceptives and arguing for a broad state power to regulate where health is concerned. He reiterated that view in *Roe* and *Doe*, but voted with the majority on the ground that even a broad state regulatory power did not justify the limitations on privacy imposed by the specific statutes involved.

prevention program.[140] The program was designed to aid the school in identifying potential drug abusers by means of a questionnaire inquiring about family relationships and rearing. The injunction was issued on the ground that the program would violate the student's right of privacy. The court wrote: "The fact that the students are juveniles does not in any way invalidate their right to assert their Constitutional right to privacy."[141] It is worth noting that the student's mother supported him in this case, so there was no issue of parental consent involved. The case is important, however, because a minor's right to privacy (as opposed to the due process rights involved in *Gault* and the first amendment rights in *Tinker*) was recognized explicitly for the first time.

The Supreme Court has held that the right of privacy is a "fundamental right" which may not be restricted in the absence of a "compelling state interest."[142] Accordingly, the issue in each case must be whether a compelling state interest exists warranting invasion of the minor's privacy. As recently stated by a New York court, "the state must show a compelling state interest to justify treating juveniles differently from adults."[143]

The state interests generally cited in support of parental consent requirements are the protection of a minor from his or her own improvidence and the preservation of parental control. Neither consideration seems "compelling" where a sexually active teenager seeks contraception or abortion and is sufficiently intelligent to understand the nature and consequences of such health care. Such a minor is in practical effect "emancipated" from parental control as far as sexual behavior is concerned. Moreover, in view of the dangers—medical, psychological and social—of teenage pregnancy, it cannot be said to be in the best interests of a minor to force her into unwanted pregnancy—or, in the case of a boy, unwanted fatherhood.

Recognizing these facts, many courts have recently invalidated parental consent requirements for minors' abortions. In *In re P.J.*,[144] the Family Division of the District of Columbia Superior Court held that the common law requirement of parental consent was unconstitutionally applied to a seventeen-year-old girl whose mother was opposed to abortion on religious grounds. The court found that the girl's "degree of maturity and knowledge was such that she fully understood the nature of the proceedings, the nature of the operation, how the operation is performed, and the effect of such an operation," and concluded that, in those circumstances, to deny her an abortion "would be depriving her of a right guaranteed by the Constitution

140. Merriken v. Cressman, 364 F. Supp. 913 (E.D. Pa. 1973).
141. *Id.* at 918.
142. Roe v. Wade, 410 U.S. 113 (1973); Griswold v. Connecticut, 381 U.S. 479 (1965). *See also* Kramer v. Union Free School Dist., 395 U.S. 621, 627 (1969); Shapiro v. Thompson, 394 U.S. 618, 634 (1969); Sherbert v. Verner, 374 U.S. 398, 406 (1963).
143. People v. Schupf, N.Y. Law Journal, Dec. 5, 1974, p. 17 col. 5 (Sup. Ct. 1974).
144. 12 Crim. L. Rep. 2549 (D.C. Super. Ct., Feb. 6, 1973).

and Bill of Rights."[145] Both *Gault* and *Roe* were cited in support of this conclusion.[146]

In *Coe v. Gerstein*,[147] a federal district court struck down a statutory parental consent requirement[148] on the ground that it constituted an improper delegation of state power. The statute authorized parents to withhold consent without giving a reason for doing so, which meant that in some cases consent might be withheld out of concern for maternal health in the first trimester or for the fetus before the stage of viability. Under *Roe,* the state could not validly invoke those reasons in order to interfere with the abortion decision and, the court reasoned, the state may not delegate to parents the authority to do so. The court declared, "a pregnant woman under 18 years of age cannot, under the law, be distinguished from one over 18 years of age in reference to 'fundamental,' 'personal,' constitutional rights."[149]

Coe v. Gerstein reaches a good result, but the decision might equally well have been based on the ground that the state has no compelling interest that would justify a parental consent requirement. Moreover, the decision leaves open the possibility that a parental consent requirement could be constitutional in a more narrowly drafted statute. Given the court's reasoning, it seems that it would have to uphold a statute which authorized parents to withhold consent to their minor daughters' abortions as long as they gave a reason for withholding consent, and as long as the reason they gave was neither concern for maternal health in the first trimester nor protection of the fetus before it became viable.[150]

A parental consent requirement was invalidated as part of a sweeping attack on Utah's abortion law in *Doe v. Rampton*.[151] The court placed special emphasis on the legislature's apparent attempt to violate the mandate of *Roe*

---

145. *Compare* Wisconsin v. Yoder, 406 U.S. 205 (1973) (Douglas, J. dissenting in part).

146. As an alternate ground for its decision, the court found that the young woman would "suffer great and immediate harm to her physical and mental health if the pregnancy continued."

147. 376 F. Supp. 695 (S.D. Fla. 1973). An expedited appeal to the U.S. Supreme Court was rejected on procedural grounds, 417 U.S. 279 (1974), but an appeal to the Circuit Court of Appeals is pending at this writing.

148. The statute, FLA. STAT. ANN. § 458.22(3) (1972), required parental consent for unmarried women under 18 years of age, and spousal consent for all married woman except those whose husbands were voluntarily living apart from them. The court also struck down the spousal consent requirement on the same reasoning.

149. 376 F. Supp. at 698.

150. Religious grounds were advanced, and defeated, as such a reason in *In re P.J.* Parental religious beliefs provide grounds for denying educational rights to minors, and may affect other rights as well. Wisconsin v. Yoder, 406 U.S. 205 (1972). In *Yoder,* the Court relied on the arguments of the Amish parents that a high school education was against *their* religious beliefs, and did not consider the religious views of the affected children. The record only contained evidence with respect to the views of one of the three children whose parents brought the suit. It was for that reason that Justice Douglas dissented in part. *See* text accompanying notes 106-107 *supra.*

151. 366 F. Supp. 189 (D. Utah), *vacated,* 410 U.S. 950 (1973).

and *Doe*.[152] But the court did not address itself directly to the issue of abortions for minors.

A three-judge federal court in Kentucky has followed the *Coe v. Gerstein* and *Doe v. Rampton* decisions and invalidated provisions of a recently-enacted Kentucky abortion statute which required parental consent for all abortions performed on minors after the first trimester of pregnancy.[153] The court pointed out that since the state could not independently interfere to protect the fetus prior to viability, it could not do so indirectly by interfering on behalf of husbands or parents.[154]

The Supreme Court of Washington has also used these cases to declare unconstitutional under the due process and equal protection clauses that state's parental consent requirement for the abortion of minors.[155] The court wrote:

> Prima facie, the constitutional rights of minors, including the right of privacy, are coextensive with those of adults. Where minors' rights have been held subject to curtailment by the state in excess of that permissible in the case of adults it has been because some peculiar state interest existed in the regulation and protection of children, not because the rights themselves are of some inferior kind.[156]

The court proceeded to deal with the interests asserted by the state: protecting the health of the minor, protecting the potential life of the fetus, the assurance of an "adequately reflective and informed decision on the part of the minor woman, and the 'support of the family unit and parental authority.' "[157] The first two interests were adequately dealt with in *Roe* and *Doe*, the court said, noting that the danger of childbearing to the minor's health was even greater than that to a pregnant adult. The last interest was held not to be absolute, and, therefore, had to yield to the fundamental rights of the minor. With respect to the state's interest in assuring an informed decision by the patient, the court stated that the statute did not require an intelligent decision but instead allowed the parents an absolute veto, "not only where their judgment is better informed and considered than that of their daughter, but also where it is colored by personal religious belief, whim, or even hostility to her best interests."[158]

---

152. *Id.* at 198.
153. Wolfe v. Schroering, Civ. Act. No. C-74-186-L(8) (W.D. Ky., Nov. 20, 1974).
154. *Id.*, slip opinion at 9.
155. Washington v. Koome, Wash. Sup. Ct. No. 42645 (Jan. 7, 1975). The decision overturned the criminal conviction of a physician who had performed an abortion, despite parental opposition, on an unmarried sixteen-year-old.
156. *Id.*, slip opinion at 4.
157. *Id.* at 7.
158. *Id.* at 9. The court based its equal protection argument on two grounds. First, it held

Most recently, Judge Finesilver of the Federal District Court for Colorado has held unconstitutional a Colorado statute requiring parental consent for abortions performed on unmarried women under eighteen.[159] Several similar suits are currently pending in other jurisdictions.[160]

Contrary to the general trend of the cases is the 2-1 decision of a three-judge federal court in the Eastern District of Missouri in *Planned Parenthood v. Danforth.*[161] Upholding a 1974 Missouri abortion statute against attack on constitutional grounds, the court upheld among other provisions of the law a requirement of the consent of a parent or one in loco parentis for abortions performed on single women under 18. The majority ruled that "the state's interest in safeguarding the authority of the family relationship [is] a compelling basis for allowing regulation of a minor's freedom to consent to an abortion." Dissenting in part, Circuit Judge Webster said:

> I do not suppose it could be seriously argued that a minor could be made to submit to an abortion at the insistence of her parents [citing *In re Smith, supra*]. I cannot see why she would not be entitled to the same right of self-determination now explicitly accorded to adult women, provided she is sufficiently mature to understand the procedure and to make an intelligent assessment of her circumstances with the advice of her physician.

Another decision which fails to recognize minors' rights—this one in the area of contraception—is *Doe v. Planned Parenthood Association,*[162] where the Utah Supreme Court ruled that the Planned Parenthood Association of Utah could not be compelled to provide contraceptive services to females under 14 years of age and males under 16 years without parental consent. Overturning the trial court's ruling that the requirement of parental consent for such services was a violation of the right of privacy, the supreme court said that

---

that there was no basis for distinguishing as the statute did between married and unmarried minors of the same age. Second, it adopted the principle that abortion should be treated procedurally the same as other surgery.

159. Foe v. Vanderhoof, Civ. Act. No. 74-F-418 (D. Colo. Feb. 5, 1975).

160. *See, e.g.,* Baird v. Quinn, C.A. No. 74-4992-F (D. Mass., temporary restraining order issued Oct. 31, 1974); Noe v. Packel, C.A. No. 74-954 (W.D. Pa., temporary restraining order issued Oct. 9, 1974); Planned Parenthood et. al. v. Fitzpatrick, Civ. No. 74-2440 (E.D. Pa., preliminary injunction issued Oct. 10, 1974); Roe v. Rampton, Civ. No. 74-344 (C.D. Utah, complaint filed Nov., 1974). See Lady Jane v. Norton, Civ. No. 74-347 (D. Conn., temporary restraining order issued Oct. 29, 1974); Noe v. True, No. 74-1577 (6th Cir. opinion reversing dismissal issued Dec. 5, 1974); Doe v. Weinberger, No. C-74-2481 (N.D. Cal., complaint filed Nov. 26, 1974).

161. No. 74-416C(A) (E.D. Mo., 1974). On Feb. 18, 1975, the Supreme Court issued an injunction staying enforcement of the entire Missouri statute pending appeal of the decision. 43 U.S.L.W. 3451.

162. 29 Utah 2d 356, 510 P.2d 75 (1973).

the giving of information or contraceptive paraphernalia to a minor
child so as to avoid pregnancy from unlawful sexual relations would
certainly tend to make a child of immature judgment more likely
to commit the crime of fornication and to become infected with
venereal disease, to say nothing of the morals of the situation.[163]

The court rejected plaintiff's equal protection argument:

To give information and contraceptives to married people so as to
control the size of their families is one thing. To deny it to single
minor children is not a denial of the equal protection of the law, as
they are not in the same class with married people.[164]

It is not clear whether the court considered the critical word to be "single" or
"minor." If "single," then the holding seems irreconcilable with *Eisenstadt v.
Baird.*[165] If the critical word is "minor" however, the holding could be
defended under the reasoning of *Prince v. Massachusetts*[166] and *Ginsberg v.
New York*[167] that the state has greater power to control the actions of minors
than it has over adults.

However, as Judge Pierce recognized in *Population Services International v. Wilson,*[168] *Prince* and *Ginsberg* differ in important respects from the
situation where a minor seeks access to contraceptives. In the *Population
Services* case, plaintiffs sought injunctive relief against the enforcement of
§ 6811(8) of the New York Education Law[169] which, *inter alia*, made the sale
or distribution of contraceptives to minors under the age of sixteen (by anyone
except a physician) a misdemeanor.[170] In holding that plaintiffs had raised
sufficient constitutional questions to require submitting the case to a three-
judge district court, Judge Pierce wrote:

cogent arguments are advanced here that the prohibited articles
might serve as a positive good for the minors affected, in that
access to them might diminish the incidence of venereal disease
and unwanted pregnancy for persons in the affected age group.[171]

In the earlier cases, there was no such "positive" benefit for the minor.

---

163. *Id.* at 76.
164. *Id.* at 76.
165. 405 U.S. 438 (1972).
166. 321 U.S. 158 (1944).
167. 390 U.S. 629 (1968).
168. Civil No. 74-1572 (Oct. 23, 1974).
169. N.Y. EDUC. LAW, § 6811(8) (McKinney 1971).
170. Plaintiffs also challenged the prohibitions on the sale or distribution of contraceptives
by anyone other than a licensed pharmacist and on the advertisement or display of contraceptives.
171. Slip opinion at 14.

In *Prince,* as pointed out above,[172] the interest of the state in prohibiting child labor coincided with the health interest of the child and was found to outweigh the guardian's and child's protected right of religious expression. *Ginsberg* involved obscenity, which is not clearly protected by the first amendment. The right to privacy, as developed by the Supreme Court in *Griswold, Eisenstadt, Roe v. Wade,* and *Doe v. Bolton* appears to demand equal application to minors and virtually every case confronting the issue to date has so held.

V.   CONCLUSION

Although the rights of young people to access to sex-related medical services on their own consent have been greatly expanded by courts and legislatures in recent years, many young persons still encounter great difficulty in obtaining medical contraceptive services and even greater difficulty in terminating an unwanted pregnancy without parental consent. The right of minors to access to contraceptive services without parental consent has recently been endorsed by the American Bar Association[173] and by numerous physicians' groups,[174] and indeed has been established by statute in a number of states and mandated by federal law with respect to indigent sexually active youngsters.

Emerging constitutional doctrines of privacy and the rights of minors provide a solid basis for the development of a constitutional right of minors to access to sex-related health services, including contraception and abortion, without parental consent. Whatever interest the state or the parents have in protecting the minor from his or her own immaturity is adequately protected by the requirement that only minors who are sufficiently intelligent and mature to give informed consent be allowed to consent for any medical care, whether or not related to sex.

---

172. *See* text accompanying note 109 *supra.*

173. At its August, 1973, annual meeting, the American Bar Association called for the development of "affirmative legislation which will permit minors to receive contraceptive information and services."

174. The physician's right, free of legal barriers, to exercise his medical judgment in the provision of contraceptive care for the best interests of his minor patients has been endorsed by the American Medical Association, the American College of Obstetricians and Gynecologists, the American Academy of Pediatrics, the American Academy of Family Physicians and the Association of Planned Parenthood Physicians, the American College Health Association and the American Public Health Association.

Nor Piety Nor Wit: The Supreme Court on Abortion

By
Joseph W. Dellapenna*

Dead babies can take care of themselves
Alice Cooper

On January 22, 1973, the Supreme Court decided *Roe v. Wade*[1] and *Doe v. Bolton*.[2] Under these cases states are virtually precluded from placing any restrictions on abortions during the first trimester of pregnancy. States can regulate abortions performed during the second trimester, but only to protect the health of the mother. Only during the final trimester (after viability of the foetus) can states step in to protect the life of the unborn child—except where the life or health of the mother is endangered.

As even those who applaud the decisions admit,[3] the opinions sustaining these conclusions are confusing, mystifying and unpersuasive.[4] These cases capped one of the most rapid transformations of legal-moral judgments in history. Yet the controversy is not over. Rather it has gained intensity[5]—in part because of the exceptionally poor opinions purporting to justify the

---

* Associate Professor of Law, University of Cincinnati College of Law, LL.M in Public International and Comparative Law, George Washington University (1969); J.D., Detroit College of Law (1968); B.B.A., University of Michigan (1965).

1. 410 U.S. 113 (1973).
2. 410 U.S. 179 (1973).
3. *E.g.,* Ely, *The Wages of Crying Wolf: A Comment on Roe v. Wade,* 82 YALE L. J. 920 (1973); Tribe, *Forward: Toward a Model of Roles in the Due Process of Life and Law,* 87 HARV. L. REV. 1, 2-5 (1973) [hereinafter cited as Tribe]. Heyman & Barzelay, *The Forest and the Trees: Roe v. Wade and its Critics,* 53 B. U. L. REV. 765 (1973) are perhaps the only commentators to enthusiastically embrace the Court's apparent reasoning. They comment: "The language of the Court's opinon in *Roe* too often obscures the full strength of the four-step argument that underlies its decision." *Id.* at 765.
4. *See especially* Epstein, *Substantive Due Process By Any Other Name: The Abortion Cases,* 1973 SUP. CT. REV. 159; Viviera, *Roe and Wade: Substantive Due Process and the Right of Abortion,* 25 HAST. L. REV. 867 (1974).
5. *Cf.* Byrn, *The Abortion Amendments: Policy in the Light of Precedent,* 18 ST. L. U. L. J. 380, 380-82 (1974). For examples of recognition of this increased intensity felt by those favoring the outcome of *Wade* and *Bolton,* see Blair, *Abortion: Can We Lose Our Right to Choose?,* Ms. 92 (Oct. 1973); Sanders, *Enemies of Abortion,* HARPER'S 26 (Mar. 1974); Schardt, *New Threats: Saving Abortion,* CIVIL LIBERTIES 1 (Sept. 1973).

outcome commanded by the majority. Of course, persuasive analyses would not convince vociferous critics firmly committed to the losing side.[6] But there is a large group who stand on the middle ground of the controversy. Presently they find only confusion where they expect authoritative guidance. Searching analyses could swing this group decisively to one side of the controversy. Searching analyses might also revise the conclusions of the Court.

This paper will first summarize the Court's approach to the abortion cases. Then it shall examine the most thoughtful defense of the outcome of the cases: that of Lawrence Tribe.[7] Rather than simply recounting the analyses already advanced by critics and supporters of the Court's position, this paper shall examine the abortion issue from the larger perspective of the relationship of law and morality. This question is central to a proper resolution of the abortion controversy, but has been overlooked or ignored by most commentators and by the Court itself. The paper will then attempt to apply these principles to the abortion problem to suggest a reasonable outcome. Finally the paper will explore alternatives for implementing the solution proposed in the face of *Wade* and *Bolton*.

I.   WHAT THE COURT DID

In 1970 an unmarried Dallas bar waitress ("Jane Roe")[8] became pregnant. She was refused an abortion because she could not show that her life was endangered by continuation of the pregnancy as required by Texas Law.[9] Roe brought suit seeking a declaratory judgment that the Texas criminal abortion statute was unconstitutional. At about the same time an Atlanta housewife ("Mary Doe") with three living children became pregnant. Two of her children were in foster homes and the other had been placed for adoption because of the Does' poverty. Doe was denied an abortion under the Georgia statute,[10] which required a showing of a threat to maternal health from continuation of the pregnancy, that the pregnancy resulted from rape, or that there was great likelihood that the foetus would be born with "a grave, permanent, and irremediable mental or physical defect." The law also required approval by two consulting physicians and a hospital abortion commit-

6. *E.g.*, Byrn, *An American Tragedy: The Supreme Court on Abortion*, 41 FORDHAM L. REV. 807 (1973); Byrn, *supra* note 5; Loewy, *Abortive Reasons and Obscene Standards: A Comment on the Abortion and Obscenity Cases*, 52 N. CAR. L. REV. 223 (1973); Rice, *The Dred Scott Case of the Twentieth Century*, 10 HOUS. L. REV. 1054 (1973); Rice, *Overruling Roe v. Wade: An Analysis of the Proposed Constitutional Amendments*, 15 B.C. IND. AND COM. L. REV. 307 (1974).

7. Tribe, *supra* note 3.

8. The personal backgrounds of "Jane Roe" and "Mary Doe" are briefly summarized in TIME 50 (Feb. 5, 1973).

9. TEX. PENAL CODE arts. 1191-1194, 1196 (1948).

10. GA. CODE ANN. §§ 26-1201, to -1203 (1970 rev.).

tee. Mary Doe sought a declaratory judgment that the Georgia statute was unconstitutional in its entirety, and an injunction forbidding its enforcement. Both suits were joined by other individuals representing the medical or the social welfare professions, and were brought as class actions. Both plaintiffs won partial victories below.[11] On appeal, the Supreme Court eventually invalidated virtually all existing restrictions on abortions.[12]

While the litigation was proceeding, both babies were born and given up for adoption. The Texas barmaid and the Georgia housewife had to content themselves with having been the occasion for moving the United States from the most restrictive nations with regard to abortion to perhaps the most permissive.[13]

In *Roe v. Wade*, the Court faced several difficult issues. After hurdling several procedural barriers,[14] the majority proceeded to review the history of attitudes towards abortion from the ancient Near East down to today.[15] While the tone of the historical inquiry was that abortion has been generally accepted, except in aberrational periods like the late nineteenth century, in fact, the survey shows abortion to have been controversial throughout history—except for the last century or so, when it was generally condemned. The Court never made clear how this material was relevant to its disposition of the case. It simply presented the material and then dropped it.

The Court next turned to what the majority conceived as the principle issue in the case. This was the problem of balancing the personal, marital, familial and sexual privacy of the mother against the state interests.[16] The first

---

11. Roe v. Wade, 314 F. Supp. 1217 (N.D. Tex. 1970); Doe v. Bolton, 319 F. Supp. 1048 (N.D. Ga. 1970).

12. Roe v. Wade, 410 U.S. 113 (1973); Doe v. Bolton, 410 U.S. 179 (1973).

13. L. LADER, ABORTION (1966) and L. LADER, ABORTION II (1973) [hereinafter cited as LADER I and LADER II respectively], chronicles the extent of the transition and the many other fronts through which it was achieved.

14. The Court found standing and justiciability without mootness for Roe herself despite the prior birth of her child. The Court also avoided the abstention doctrine. The other parties were dismissed. 410 U.S. at 123-129. *See* Epstein, *supra* note 4, at 160-167 for a criticism of the cases on these grounds.

15. 410 U.S. at 130-147. *Cf.* Byrn, *supra* note 6, at 814-839; Quay, *Justifiable Abortion—Medical and Legal Foundations*, 49 GEO. L. J. 173 (1960), 395 (1961). The Court's analysis of this history is sometimes rather startling. Thus the Court concluded that the Hippocratic Oath (with its strong injunction against abortions) was "a Pythagorean manifesto and not the expression of an absolute standard of medical conduct," 410 U.S. at 132, *citing* L. EDELSTEIN, THE HIPPOCRATIC OATH (1943). The Court does not explain the subsequent acceptance of the Oath by the medical profession. Similarly the common law view of abortion is dismissed with dark hints that Coke's famous dictum that this was "a great misprision and no murder" was a conspiracy to foist his own peculiar views onto an unsuspecting nation, 410 U.S. at 134-136. How Coke could do this if his views really were different than those of the English legal profession is not made clear. *See also* Means, *The Phoenix of Abortional Freedom: Is a Penumbral or Ninth-Amendment Right About to rise from the Nineteenth-Century Legislative Ashes of a Fourteenth Century Liberty?*, 17 N.Y. L. FORUM 335 (1971) (the court relied very heavily on this article for its reconstruction of history). Viviera, *supra* note 4, at 872-874, raises doubts as to the relevance of these materials.

16. 410 U.S. at 129, 148-156, 162-164.

interest was discouraging illicit sex. Texas did not advance the argument, and the Court disposed of it quickly and easily.[17] The second interest was preservation of the mother's health. As the Court concluded that early abortion is safer than childbearing,[18] this policy was also disposed of easily. Believing the risk to maternal health to become substantial in the second trimester, the Court allocated a limited rulemaking competence to state legislatures at that time.[19] The third state interest was protecting prenatal life. This posed the critical question.[20] The Court noted doubts whether this was the original purpose of the statutes,[21] but passed over them without comment.[22] The majority disclaimed the ability to resolve the critical issue of what the state was seeking to protect—a human life or the mere potential for life[23]—but did not explain how it could assess the state's interest in protecting fetal life without answering that question. They contented themselves with treating the state's interest as one of protecting the potential for life[24]— which appears suspiciously like the resolution the Court denied having made.

Against these interests the Court weighed the mother's interest in controlling her life and her body.[25] This is part of the right of privacy which all agree exists in our Constitution despite the considerable confusion as to where it is found there.[26] The right is not absolute, but is subject to

17. In view of Eisenstadt v. Baird, 405 U.S. 438 (1972), it is doubtful if this interest would have received more extended treatment even if it had been argued by Texas.

18. 410 U.S. at 148-150, 163. *See also* Means, *The Law of New York Concerning Abortion and the Status of the Foetus*, 14 N.Y. L. FORUM 411 (1968). This has been questioned by some doctors. *See, e.g.*, Ely, *supra* note 3, at 942 n.117.

19. 410 U.S. at 162-166.

20. *Id.* at 156. Even appellant conceded that a holding that the foetus was a person would dictate state protection of its life. *Cf.* Epstein, *supra* note 4, at 171-185.

21. 410 U.S. at 150-152. *Contrast* Means, *supra* note 18 *with* Byrn, *supra* note 6, at 827-835.

22. How this could have any significance is unclear. Purposes can change without requiring symbolic reenactment of laws which already achieve the new purpose, McGowan v. Maryland, 366 U.S. 420 (1961); Braunfield v. Brown, 366 U.S. 599 (1961) (both deal with Sunday closing laws). This reasoning was explicitly endorsed in Doe v. Bolton, 410 U.S. at 190-191. Still this appears to be the principal focus of Means' argument. Means, *supra* note 18; the Court cited Means six times. *See also* his statement in response to a question from the floor *in Symposium, National Population Programs and Policies: Social and Legal Implications*, 15 VILLANOVA L. REV. 785, 876 (1970). How neutral is the application of principle when the Court relies on an argument which depends on a concept which the Court expressly rejects in a companion case? *Cf.* Wechsler, *Toward Neutral Principles of Constitutional Law*, 73 HARV. L. REV. 1 (1959).

23. 410 U.S. at 160. Inability to decide usually supports deference to a not unreasonable legislative determination. No reason is given for the contrary conclusion here, *id.* at 162. This is the major thrust of the two dissents, *id.* at 171-177 (Rehnquist, J., dissenting), 221-223 (White, J., dissenting). *Cf.* Epstein, *supra* note 4, at 175-176.

24. 410 U.S. at 163.

25. *Id.* at 152-156.

26. The Court noted that these rights of privacy might derive from the fourteenth amendment's concept of personal liberty, or the ninth amendment's reservation of rights to the people, *id.* at 153. Griswold v. Connecticut, 381 U.S. 479 (1965), would add the possibility of the due process clause of the fourteenth amendment, while the plaintiff in *Wade* argued the first, fourth, and fifth amendments as well, 410 U.S. at 120.

reasonable regulation by the state. None of this is new. What is new in *Wade* is the Court's identification of the right as fundamental, thereby requiring a compelling state interest to justify regulation.[27] This form of protection in the past has been accorded only a few rights specifically mentioned in the Constitution. Why this special protection should be extended to the right of privacy in the context of abortion is not even suggested. But then, the Court made no effort to explain how a right of abortional privacy grows out of the previous privacy cases,[28] so why should it bother to justify its conclusion that the right is fundamental?

Given the interests as announced by the Court, the striking of the balance is a simple task. No substantial state interest in prohibiting abortions appears before the foetus becomes viable. Even then the foetus must die if the health of the mother is endangered.[29] Before that point, the state can only enact limited regulations to protect maternal health, including limiting the performance of abortions to licensed physicians. Omitted from this balance is any consideration of the father's interest or interests of the state in protecting pregnant minors.[30] The Court also left open the possibility of prosecution of practitioners who abuse the privilege of medical judgment.[31]

Doe v. Bolton[32] dealt with a Georgia statute which sought to limit abortions to certain stated reasons and required, in addition to the medical judgment of the attending physician, written concurrence of at least two other

27. The right can be traced back to Union Pacific R. Co. v. Botsford, 141 U.S. 250 (1891), and finds its best known explication in Griswold v. Connecticut, 381 U.S. 479 (1965). Reasonable regulation of the use of one's body without a compelling state interest is found in Jacobson v. Massachusetts, 197 U.S. 11 (1905) (compulsory vaccination); Buck v. Bell, 274 U.S. 200 (1927) (compulsory sterilization). The fundamental right/compelling interest test does appear in *Griswold*, 381 U.S. at 491-499 (1965) (Goldberg, J., concurring).

28. 410 U.S. at 172-173 (Rehnquist, J., dissenting). One theory has it that up to now "privacy" has meant freedom from search or freedom of expression, not a general freedom to live one's life free from governmental interference—which one supposes is what "liberty" means. *Cf.* Poe v. Ullman, 367 U.S. 497, 548-555 (1961) (Harlan, J., dissenting); Ely, *supra* note 3, at 928-933, 935-937; Epstein, *supra* note 4, at 167-172; Levi, *The Collective Morality of a Maturing Society*, 30 WASH. AND LEE L. REV. 399, 400 (1973); Loewy, *supra* note 6, at 224-225; Tribe 3; Comment, *Roe and Paris: Does Privacy Have a Principle?*, 26 STAN. L. REV. 1161 (1974). Tribe 17 n.83, argues for a traditional, informational privacy basis to link *Wade* to *Griswold*.

29. 410 U.S. at 164-166. Why this must be so is not explained; this balance seems to go quite far towards taking even viable fetal life since the threat to health must include threats to mental health as determined solely by the opinion of the attending physician, United States v. Vuitch, 402 U.S. 62 (1971). Apart from the mental health question, these rules seem to result in the irony that foeti who can live apart from the mother have the "right" to stay in their mother, but those who must die might be expelled. *Cf.* Tribe 4 n.24. LADER II, *supra* note 13, at 164-166, 178, enthusiastically embraces this view. *See also* Viviera, *supra* note 4, at 874-875.

30. 410 U.S. at 165 n.67.

31. 410 U.S. at 166. *Cf.* People v. Nixon, 42 Mich. App. 332, 201 N.W.2d. 635 (1972). One can argue that there are virtually no medical indications for abortions, Callahan, *Abortion: Some Ethical Issues*, in ABORTION, SOCIETY AND THE LAW 89 (D. Walbert & J. Butler eds. 1973) (hereinafter cited as WALBERT); Stone, *Abortion and the Supreme Court: What Now?*, MODERN MEDICINE 37 (Apr. 30, 1973).

32. 410 U.S. 179 (1973).

Georgia licensed doctors and advance approval by an abortion committee at a state accredited hospital.[33] Finding standing and justiciability for both Mary Doe and the physicians,[34] the Court proceeded to invalidate all of the Georgia procedural requirements.[35]

The Court based its conclusion largely on the fact that such procedures were not required for other forms of surgery.[36] As *Wade* had concluded that protection of fetal life was not permitted at least until the last trimester, Georgia could not use this policy as a reason for treating abortions differently from other surgery. Furthermore, there is no connection between these procedures and protection of the mother.[37] Finally, the Court expressed concern that the requirements degraded conscientious physicians by requiring them to prove their conclusions.[38]

These two opinions make strange reading. *Doe v. Bolton* follows rather logically from the premise that abortion is like any other minor surgery. The premise holds if one accepts that the state has no right to protect fetal life throughout most of the pregnancy. Unfortunately the *Wade* opinion (which was supposed to establish that point) is an exceptional example of poor craftsmanship. The opinion is replete with irrelevancies, non-sequiturs, and unsubstantiated assertions. The Court decides matters it disavows any intention of deciding—thereby avoiding any need to defend its conclusions. In the process the opinion simply fails to convince.

II. A MODEL OF ROLES IN THE DUE PROCESS OF LIFE AND LAW

Justice Blackmun speaking for the Court fails to explain persuasively how and why the Constitution commands a detailed scheme of gradually increasing state power to regulate abortions. He approaches the problem as one of deciding when human life begins (or when potential for human life becomes sufficient for independent protection). This approach leads into a quagmire of theological and philosophical disputes which appear unresolvable.[39] Yet these disputes must be resolved if the Constitution is to prescribe

33. GA. CODE ANN. § 26-1202(b) (1970 rev.).

34. 410 U.S. at 187-189.

35. *Id.* at 201. The substantive requirements also fell because of *Wade*, although the Court apparently permitted the requirement of "best medical judgment" to stand even in the first trimester notwithstanding *Wade*. This is not the only apparent contradiction between the two cases. *See, e.g., supra* note 22.

36. The Court adverts to the argument three times, *id.* at 193-194, 197, 199-200.

37. Adverted to twice, *id.* at 195, 199-200. In fact these procedures endanger the mother because of the delays involved—abortion being more risky as the pregnancy progresses, *id.* at 198-199.

38. *Id.* at 196-197. The two opinions display unusual consideration for the sensibilities of the medical profession. *See also id.* at 219 (Douglas, J., concurring).

39. The most quoted passage from the opinions is:

any outcome—unless the problem can be cast into an altogether different mold. Lawrence Tribe[40] has conceived such an original approach.

Tribe's analysis begins from the premise that the Constitution does not often prescribe particular outcomes, but rather assigns roles for an ongoing decision making process.[41] Such "allocations of competences" were the sort of questions addressed by the framers of the Constitution,[42] whether it be between levels or branches of government, public and private authority or even alternate private decisionmakers.[43] Thus in the abortion controversy the Court need not decide when a separate human comes to be. The Court must simply decide which of the several possible decisionmakers should decide this question.

Tribe concludes that the proper person to decide the question is the woman. He has little difficulty dismissing possible alternate private decision-makers.[44] The bulk of the supporting analysis is directed at persuading one that the decision should be private rather than by the state. Tribe suggests that this area involves a "personal question"—much like a "political question"—which is beyond the Court's control.[45] As a basis for this view Tribe argues that when human life begins is inevitably entangled with religion.[46] He even asserts that it is impossible to discuss the question in secular terms at all![47]

To understand and evaluate Tribe's analysis it is important to keep in mind that he not only seeks a definite allocation of decisionmaking to the woman, but that he is also seeking to avoid any governmental commitment to any side of the abortion controversy. Depending on which governmental body Tribe is concerned with, the avoidance problem takes on a slightly altered character. When Tribe discusses the role of the Court in deciding when a separate human comes to be, he sees the problem as one of denying legislative authority to decide without thereby occasioning a judicial usurpation of the authority to decide as occurred in *Lochner v. New York.*[48] When focusing on legislative solutions, Tribe characterizes the problem as one of

---

We need not resolve the difficult question of when life begins. When those trained in the respective disciplines of medicine, philosophy, and theology are unable to arrive at any consensus, the judiciary, at this point in the development of man's knowledge, is not in a position to speculate as to the answer.
410 U.S. at 160.

40. Tribe, *supra* note 3.
41. *Id.* at 10-15.
42. A. BICKEL, THE LEAST DANGEROUS BRANCH 104 (1962).
43. Tribe 13, 38-41.
44. *Id.* at 33-41.
45. *Id.* at 32.
46. *Id.* at 18-25, 28-29, 30-32.
47. *Id.* at 20. But after viability Tribe concludes there is a secular and practical ground for prohibiting abortion since abortion then *is* infanticide. *Id.* at 27-28.
48. 198 U.S. 45 (1905), *overruled in* West Coast Hotel Co. v. Parrish, 300 U.S. 379 (1937). *See* Viviera, *supra* note 4.

avoiding religious entanglement. These difficulties are but different aspects of a single problem: denying authority to the government to have any say in early abortions. Tribe describes this position as placing the Court in "the delightful position . . . of rejecting and assuming power in a single breath"[49]—rejecting the power to decide itself while assuming the power to prevent other governmental agencies from deciding. But he cannot avoid reviving natural law substantive due process and religious entanglement.

Tribe's efforts to distinguish *Lochner* are fairly simple.[50] He concedes that in *Lochner* the freedom of contract upheld against state interference could also be cast in role-allocation terms. He even concedes that the explicit protection of "contract" and "property" by the Constitution bears on role allocation. Nonetheless he concludes that it is transparent that the role allocations derive from no constitutionally defensible scheme because the Court is revising legislative findings about socio-economic conditions and applying supposedly immutable criteria as to proper legislative goals. One is somehow suspicious of the transparency of the impropriety of role allocations under a Constitution whose message is generally Delphic.[51] If the misleading language of the Court in *Lochner* is put aside,[52] and one focuses on role-allocation, it is unclear why the Court needed to substitute its empirical conclusions for legislative findings to conclude that such questions were not confided to legislatures, but rather reserved to private decisionmakers acting through contract. Tribe finds this approach plausible for women contemplating abortion. Why not as to hours of employment for bakers[53] or minimum wages for women?[54] While the scheme advanced in *Lochner* may have been intended as immutable, natural law need not be so treated.[55] And if the *Lochner* scheme is thought to be immutable, how is this different than the prescription of an immutable scheme in *Wade?* In short, if Tribe gives the *Lochner* Court the same indulgences he has given the *Wade* Court, he has offered us no way of distinguishing the cases[56] other than that the values at

49. Tribe 28-29, n.130, *quoting* R. McCLOSKY, THE AMERICAN SUPREME COURT 42 (1960).
50. Tribe 11-15, even though some who applaud the outcome of *Wade* and *Bolton* fear the apparent revival of *Lochner*. See Ely, *supra* note 3, at 937-949. *Cf.* Epstein, *supra* note 4, at 167-168; Tribe 5-10, 52-53.
51. Tribe 14.
52. As Tribe would have us do for *Wade* and *Bolton, id.* at 10.
53. Lochner v. New York, 198 U.S. 45 (1905).
54. Adkins v. Children's Hospital of the District of Columbia, 261 U.S. 525 (1923). Tribe admits that a certain lack of coherence in the role allocations is a minor problem which the Court could easily have corrected if it had been more self-conscious in performing its task, Tribe 11-12.
55. II T. AQUINAS, SUMMA THEOLOGICA, 223-225 (Fathers of Engl. Dom. Prov. trans., Gr. Books ed., 1952); E. BODENHEIMER, JURISPRUDENCE 126-134, 186-193 (1962); B. CÁRDOZO, THE NATURE OF THE JUDICIAL PROCESS 142 (1921); R. STAMMLER, THEORY OF JUSTICE 89-90 (I. Husik trans. 1925); Tribe 13 n.70.
56. Although Tribe describes his paper as "a response to the mounting fear that 'the remainder of this century could be a witness to *Lochner's* ghost in the service of another cause'." Tribe 2 n.11.

stake are fundamentally different. This distinction Tribe takes care to show to be inadequate.[57] Nonetheless his concern over religious entanglement, if well-founded, could work here as well to distinguish *Lochner* through the sort of values at stake.[58]

The crucial contention in Tribe's analysis thus becomes his view that because people decide on a religious basis when a separately valued human life begins, no state organ may take a position on the question.[59] Tribe asserts that because science has exposed the complexities behind what had formerly been thought to be a simple process of conception and fetal development, the inchoate feelings of reverence for life could no longer be framed in secular terms.[60] Claims as to when a separately valuable human comes to be, he asserts, must necessarily be religious affirmations. In the absence of such unanimity as to permit the appearance of secular premises,[61] Tribe sees any position as an establishment of religion. In particular there is an establishment problem because the organized religious groups have come to play a pervasive role in legislative consideration of the entire area of when separately valuable life begins.[62]

Just what "religious" means in this context is not clear. Tribe concludes that it means organized religions are involved. But persons or groups are capable of taking a position regarding abortion or fetal rights without adhering to any doctrine of an organized church.[63] Nor do establishment problems arise only where government favors organized religion.[64] Tribe even concedes

---

57. *Id.* at 8-10. *Cf.* Viviera, *supra* note 4, at 876-877.

58. *Id.* at 31. Tribe also analyzes associational freedom as involved, but essentially to show the woman as primary over other decisionmakers, *id.* at 33-41, or to show a possible requirement of affirmative action by the state to assure minimum access to abortion, *id.* at 42-50. He is quite· correct in concluding that one can resort to associational freedom only with difficulty unless one has independently concluded that the state cannot be said to be protecting the life of a human being, *id.* at 18-19, 35-36 n.159, 50-51. *But see* Thomson, *In Defense of Abortion*, I PHIL. AND PUB. AFF. 47 (1971).

59. Tribe 18-25, 28-32.

60. *Id.* at 20.

61. *Id.* at 23 n.106.

62. *Id.* at 23-24.

63. Although Tribe appears to say just this, *id.* at 20. *Cf.* United States v. Seeger, 380 U.S. 163 (1965), as to the meaning of religious belief or training as a basis for conscientious objection to military service.

64. For clear instances of non-sectarian establishments *see* Engel v. Vitale, 370 U.S. 421 (1962) (invalidating nonsectarian school prayer); Torcaso v. Watkins, 367 U.S. 488 (1961) (overruling requirement of oath of belief in God for Maryland officeholders); *but see* Lewis v. Allen, 14 N.Y.2d 867, 200 N.E.2d 767 (1964), *cert. denied*, 379 U.S. 923 (1965) (sustaining "under God" in Pledge of Allegiance in public schools). *Cf.* Chamberlain v. Dade County Bd. of Public Instruction, 377 U.S. 402 (1964); School Dis. of Arlington Twp. v. Schempp, 374 U.S. 203 (1963); Braunfield v. Brown, 366 U.S. 599 (1961); McGowan v. Maryland, 366 U.S. 420 (1961).

Torcaso, 367 U.S. at 495, reaffirmed the principle that neither a state nor the federal government can constitutionally force a person to profess a belief or disbelief in any religion. Nor can they pass laws or impose requirements which aid all religions based on the existence of God as against those religions founded on different beliefs. However, what constitutes a "religion" for constitutional purposes remains unclear. In *Seeger*, the Court held that language in the Selective

that mere intensive lobbying by organized religions cannot be sufficient to show the necessary entanglement to proscribe government efforts.[65] To adopt such a test would invite manipulations by religious groups who might be lobbying in feigned interest to compel legislative inaction. Rather Tribe describes his test as:

> . . . [E]xcessive entanglement [occurs] only when the involvement of religious groups in the political process surrounding a subject of governmental control is convincingly traceable, as it is in the case of abortion, to an intrinsic aspect of the subject itself in the intellectual and social history of the period. And the theory would in no event support a conclusion that religious entanglement alone requires the invalidation of a legal control for which a compelling need can be plausibly demonstrated by "ways of reasoning acceptable to all" from wholly secular premises, premises resting on "a common knowledge and understanding of the world."[66]

This is a puzzling statement. One is asked to determine that a question is intrinsically religious in view of extrinsic factors![67] By "ways of reasoning acceptable to all" Tribe must mean more than whether the arguments are logically correct. But if he is referring to universally accepted premises, could he provide us with an example from any controversial field of law?[68] As to "wholly secular premises," even Tribe admits there are none.[69] The test suggested must turn on the intensity of involvement by organized religious groups. This alone will measure the "intellectual and social history of the period" sufficiently to permit one to conclude that an issue is "intrinsically" religious. Such an approach has already been dismissed by Tribe as being an unmanageable standard for constitutional litigation.[70]

Tribe has rightly drawn our attention to the difficulties of legislating or adjudicating in areas of vehement religious controversy, such as abortion. Such controversy cannot preclude governmental action, however. First, there are no standards for deciding when such controversy becomes sufficient— Tribe himself failed in his effort to find such a standard. Second, some

---

Service Act of 1940 which exempted conscientious objectors whose opposition to participation in war was based on "religious training or belief" did not cover those who opposed the war from a merely personal moral code whose considerations were essentially political, sociological or economic. *Id.* at 173.

65. Tribe 24.

66. *Id.* at 24-25.

67. Explicitly acknowledged by Tribe, *id.* at 27 n.118.

68. Tribe's apparent example hardly inspires confidence. He asserts that it is impossible to distinguish post-viability abortions from infanticide. *Id.* at 27-28. While I would agree, this is not "reasoning acceptable to all." *Cf.* Schardt, *supra* note 5.

69. Tribe 23 n.106.

70. *See* text accompanying note 65, *supra.*

questions must be answered for legal purposes regardless of the level of controversy. Who is a person is a question without which governmental activity and the resolution of constitutional issues becomes impossible.

Who is a person is not simply a legal question—although one can use law to gain useful insights.[71] Neither is the question purely scientific or medical—although again one can use scientific and medical knowledge to aid understanding. Life can be said to be pure potentiality—or pure actuality, depending on one's point of view. The decision when a separate human being comes to exist is necessarily metaphysical and in this broader sense religious.[72] In society where schools of metaphysical thought are organized into churches, organized religions must play a role in debating such questions. Where important legal questions must turn on the answer, such involvement cannot be an impediment to legal decision. Or should slavery or racial equality be deemed beyond the governmental pale because of the important role churches have played and continue to play in those controversies? Such questions may be termed metalegal. To answer a metalegal question requires a moral judgment based on the application of the traditions of a society to the knowledge available to that society.[73] This in turn requires an appreciation of the broader question—missed by Tribe in his concern over organized religion—of the proper relationship between law and morality under our Constitution.

III. WHAT THE COURT OUGHT TO HAVE DONE

A. *Standards of Critical Morality under the Constitution*

The extent to which law should reflect morality continues to puzzle.[74] Law must reflect moral attitudes to some extent, but the concept of personal liberty requires that some moral choices must be left free for individual

71. *See, e.g.,* Louisell, *Abortion, the Practice of Medicine and Due Process of Law,* 16 U.C.L.A. L. REV. 233, 240-243 (1969). The Court recognized that a purely legal answer would be insufficient, and used that as a reason for supposedly not deciding the question, *Wade,* 410 U.S. at 162. *Cf.* Kelsen, *The Pure Theory of Law—Its Method and Fundamental Concepts,* 50 L. Q. REV. 477 (1934); Perhaps this is a sufficient reason for deferring to legislative judgments as the dissenters would have us do, 410 U.S. at 173-177 (Rehnquist, J., dissenting), 221-223 (White, J., dissenting).

72. Greenawalt, *Criminal Law and Population Control,* 24 VAND. L. REV. 465, 483-484 (1971). *See also,* Byrn, *Abortion on Demand: Whose Morality?,* 46 NOTRE DAME LAWYER 5 (1970). *Cf.* Tribe 19-22.

73. *See generally* D. CALLAHAN, ABORTION: LAW, CHOICE AND MORALITY 349-404 (1970) [hereinafter cited as CALLAHAN].

74. The problem has been developed recently in the debate of two prominent English jurists, P. DEVLIN, THE ENFORCEMENT OF MORALS (1965) [hereinafter cited as DEVLIN]; H. L. A. HART, LAW, LIBERTY, AND MORALITY (1964) [hereinafter cited as HART]. The constitutional context of the debate in the United States is brought out in Henkin, *Morals and the Constitution: the Sin of Obscenity,* 63 COL. L. REV. 391 (1963). *See generally* Comment, *supra* note 28, at 1168-1173.

selection.[75] In part, puzzlement continues because the question is one of a balance which can never be struck for more than a particular time and a particular place. In part the puzzlement is a function of a failure to recognize the variant meanings of law and of morality in analyses of their relationship. The balance is delicate. It changes as the nature of the particular law changes. To make an immoral action criminal is quite different from refusing on the basis of immorality to enforce a contract to do the same act. The interference with personal liberty is much less in the latter case, and thus requires less grievous harm to justify state action.[76] Thus to assert that one cannot legislate morality is meaningless in part because of ambiguity in the word legislate.[77] Furthermore, the word morality is also ambiguous.

Morality has at least two relevant meanings.[78] Whether morality ought to be enforced through law raises questions of positive morality and of critical morality. Positive morality is simply the moral norms in a given society. The question raised is whether certain conduct is deemed immoral according to recognized moral authority in the relevant society. Critical morality is the perspective from which the "rightness" of enforcing positive morality through law is determined. Proponents of the legal enforcement of morality do not simply attempt to prove their case by showing that morality is enforced in a particular society. Rather, they attempt to appeal to general principles of supposed universal validity. These principles are usually considered self-evident, or are asserted to become so after discussion.[79] These principles, once accepted, become the basis for the criticism or evaluation of social institutions generally (hence the term "critical morality"). Both sides of the debate agree on this approach—their differences arise from the selection of differing critical moralities.

Broadly speaking the principles of critical morality can be subsumed within two schools: the utilitarians[80] and those I shall term moralists. Utilitarians adhere to a scheme of "hedonistic calculus" derived from Bentham.[81]

75. Punzo, *Morality and the Law: The Search for Privacy in Community*, 18 ST. L. U. L. J. (1973).

76. Thus the Court's greater willingness to sustain economic regulation compared to regulation of more fundamental rights, most clearly stated in Ferguson v. Skrupa, 372 U.S. 726 (1963). *But see* Lynch v. Household Fin. Corp., 405 U.S. 538, 552 (1972); Tribe 8-10.

77. Usually only criminal prohibitions are considered. *See, e.g.*, HART 30-34; Punzo, *supra* note 75, at 176. *But see* DEVLIN 26-85; Greenawalt, *supra* note 72, at 469-470. For a sociologist's view of the ambiguities, *see* DUSTER, THE LEGISLATION OF MORALITY: LAW, DRUGS AND MORAL JUDGMENT (1970).

78. The following discussion draws heavily on HART 17-24. For other possible meanings of morality not relevant in ths context, *see* L. FULLER, THE MORALITY OF LAW (Rev. ed. 1969); J. RAWLS, A THEORY OF JUSTICE (1971).

79. DEVLIN 13-14; HART 18-19. *But see* Hughes, *Morality and the Criminal Law*, 71 YALE L. J. 672 (1962).

80. Still deriving their arguments from J.S. MILL, ON LIBERTY (1859). *See also* HART 3-6, 22-24. One might better term this school "libertarians." *See* text accompanying notes 88-90, *infra*.

81. J. BENTHAM, AN INTRODUCTION TO THE PRINCIPLES OF MORALS AND LEGISLATION 33-37 (1823).

The scheme is often restated as, "It is the greatest happiness of the greatest number that is the measure of right and wrong."[82] Utilitarians reasoned that compelling one to do what was good for oneself was never sufficient reason to support a law. One could best judge that for oneself. This led to the conclusion that:

> The only purpose for which power can be rightfully exercised over any member of a civilized community, against his will, is to prevent harm to others. His own good, either physical or moral, is not a sufficient warrant.[83]

Some modern utilitarians have backed away from this extreme position by admitting that a limited paternalism is proper.[84] Where one is unable to resist doing an act which nearly all (including the actor, at least if he were rational) agree is harmful, these utilitarians see nothing wrong with helping the individual help himself—if the law otherwise contributes to social good.

Moralists would argue that merely because a standard is part of a society's positive morality, that standard ought to be enacted into law.[85] Now, this position is justified on utilitarian grounds. The acts set a bad example to others, lead to incapacitation of the actor, offend others who know of the acts, bring about a deterioration of taste, of interests, and of social virtues, and foster a breakdown of the community stability necessary for societal survival and other-regarding morality. Only the last argument could not be incorporated into the utilitarian calculus[86]—unless the argument is broken into two parts. If it can be shown that dissensus in private morality leads in fact to such disrespect for others as to lead to the breakdown of public, or other-regarding, morality, no utilitarian would oppose necessary efforts to create consensus in society.[87]

---

82. J. BENTHAM, A FRAGMENT ON GOVERNMENT 93 (F. C. Montague ed. 1891); J. S. MILL, UTILITARIANISM 10 (O. Priest ed. 1957).

83. MILL, *supra* note 80, at 72. This position was adopted virtually without modification in the famous Wolfenden Report, Report of the Committee on Homosexual Offenses and Prostitution (CMD 247) § 13 (1957), but was not adopted here in Paris Adult Theatre I v. Slaton, 413 U.S. 49, 57, 68 (1973). Acts which primarily affect only oneself are generally termed "self-regarding acts" in opposition to "other-regarding acts."

84. HART 30-34; Greenawalt, *supra* note 72, at 470 n.21. Paternalism was accepted in *Wade* without elaborate justification, 410 U.S. at 164-165. Against these one might note those occasional utilitarians who posit freedom of choice as to self-regarding acts as an absolute value about the hedonistic calculus. *E.g.,* Punzo, *supra* note 75, at 181.

85. The discussion of the moralist's position is drawn largely from DEVLIN 8-14.

86. HART 45-48 makes a stinging criticism of the view that offense to others merely because they know of, but need not witness, acts can be a basis for prohibiting an act. Such an argument need not be completely rejected. Personal liberty survives if it is given only slight weight, text *infra* at notes 94-98. What is left of liberty if one accepts the broader argument that society can set its own moral tone? Devlin 86-101.

87. This proposition is so elusive factually as to defy proof, although DEVLIN 13-14 argues this view somewhat unclearly. HART 50-51 raises substantial factual doubt to the view. A more extreme view, also argued by DEVLIN 9, 12-14, is that a society is destroyed by a change in its

The need felt by the moralists to justify their position with essentially utilitarian arguments shows the general acceptance of utilitarianism as the proper critical morality. This conclusion is reinforced in the United States where constitutional separation of church and state, as well as constitutional guarantees of free expression and privacy, strongly argue that there must be some better reason for upholding a law than merely that it coincides with even widely held theological views on morality.[88] Nonetheless, there are no purely self-regarding acts. The closest one can come are acts whose indirect consequences to others are so negligible and whose direct consequences to the actor are so great, that there is a wide consensus that the act is no one else's business.[89]

What emerges is a coalescing of the two opposed views. Their separation for discussion purposes is valid only to highlight what at best are predispositions: utilitarians to discount immorality as evidence of harm to others; moralists to see immorality as evidence of such harm.[90] At the extremes each position is untenable. Neither position can entirely prevail. The question is whether one of these predispositions is proper when interpreting the Constitution.

---

morality. This confuses a change of, with the destruction of, a society. While some lapses might destroy a society (e.g., mass drug addiction), Devlin does not so limit the argument. If change always meant destruction, however, no society could ever change its mores. HART 51-52, 72-75, argued this so persuasively that Lord Devlin retracted this argument, DEVLIN 13 n.1, leaving him with only an obscurely stated moderate version of this thesis. See also Lorenson, Abortion and the Crime-Sin Spectrum, 70 W. VA. L. REV. 20, 28-31 (1967); Punzo, supra note 75, at 193-195.

88. Stanley v. Georgia, 394 U.S. 557 (1969) (upholding one's right to read obscenity in the privacy of one's home); Griswold v. Connecticut, 381 U.S. 479 (1965) (constitutional right of privacy extends to the use of contraceptives by married couples). See generally Henkin, supra note 74, at 407-411; Wechsler, supra note 22. See also Otis v. Parker, 187 U.S. 606, 609 (1903). This secular approach was embraced by the AMERICAN LAW INSTITUTE, MODEL PENAL CODE, Art. 207 (Tent. Draft No. 4, 1955). Rawls, supra note 78, at 60, lists Mills' premise as his first principle of justice, despite his general criticism of utilitarianism. But see Paris Adult Theatre I v. Slaton, 413 U.S. 49, 57, 68 (1973).

89. Cf. the Wolfenden Report, supra note 15, at § 61. Schwartz, Morals Offenses and the Model Penal Code, 63 COL. L. REV. 669, 670 (1963), defines these as offenses which pose no threat to public peace or order, personal security, or economic security. He includes in the category of morals offenses most statutes covering consensual conduct, cruelty to animals, and flag and corpse desecrations. Punzo, supra note 75, at 183-184, argues that there are purely self-regarding acts identifiable because all participants are knowing and willing adults, and because the intrinsic movement of the act is directed only at the cooperating agents themselves. These tests are obscure and uncertain.

90. Hart has expressed the difference thusly:

> . . . [A]s long as the bare fact that conduct contravenes social morality is accepted as a justification for making that conduct a crime, this enables those who defend the laws to say that factual arguments tending to show that the practice does little harm compared with the harm and misery created by its punishment are inconclusive or indeed irrelevant.

H. L. A. HART, THE MORALITY OF THE CRIMINAL LAW 48-49 (1965). This overstates the case as Devlin, at least, finds these factual considerations highly relevant, DEVLIN 14-22. Still, the state can make "unprovable assumptions about what is good for people," Paris Adult Theatre I v. Slaton, 413 U.S. 49, 62 (1973).

Although the Constitution precludes adoption of laws based solely on theologically based morality, it does not follow that legislatures and courts cannot act if there is a social consensus that an act is immoral. All agree that most acts which physically injure others are both immoral and subject to legal prohibition. Prevention of injury is sufficient secular purpose. If the consensus is wide enough in a society, affront to the sensibilities of others through public acts is also generally recognized as sufficient harm to justify legal constraints. Utilitarians would tend to go no further.[91] There is precedent for finding sufficient harm merely from the knowledge that immoral conduct is occurring—if the consensus is extremely broad and the moral values offended are so basic that the affront is truly perceived by many as a great harm. Justice Harlan reflected this view in *Poe v. Ullman*, where he said:

> Yet the very inclusion of the category of morality among state concerns indicates that society is not limited in its objects only to the physical well-being of the community, but has traditionally concerned itself with the moral soundness of its people as well. Indeed to attempt to draw a line between public behavior and that which is purely consensual or solitary would be to withdraw from community concern a range of subjects with which every society in civilized times has found it necessary to deal. The laws regarding marriage . . . adultery, fornication and homosexual practices . . . form a pattern so deeply pressed into the substance of our social life that any constitutional doctrine in this area must build upon that basis.[92]

The vitality of the examples offered by Harlan has never been successfully challenged on constitutional grounds. Morals—meaning the secular morality of an entire people[93]—remain a constitutional purpose for a state's exercise of its "police power."[94] A problem arises only when the tenet has become seriously debatable within a given society, either because there is widespread disregard of the tenet in practice, or because articulate opinion-makers launch an open attack on the old belief. When this occurs even public flouting of the old ethic may become constitutionally protected. Less of a drifting away is necessary before private conduct becomes private freedom.[95] Thus in *Poe v.*

---

91. Hart readily concedes that public indecency can be prohibited, but insists that private immorality never ought to be regulated, HART 46-48.

92. Poe v. Ullman, 367 U.S. 497, 545-546 (1961) (Harlan, J., dissenting) (citations omitted).

93. Henkin, *supra* note 74, at 409.

94. Even federal statutes are upheld, despite the general assumption that there is no federal police power. The most famous example is Caminetti v. United States, 242 U.S. 470 (1917) (sustaining the Mann Act). *See also* Cleveland v. United States, 329 U.S. 14 (1946). One author has obliquely questioned this approach, Skolnick, *Coercion to Virtue: The Enforcement of Morals*, 41 S. CAL. L. REV. 588, 624-626 (1968).

95. *Cf.* Schwartz, *supra* note 92, at 672.

Ullman the majority held nonjusticiable a challenge to the Connecticut statute prohibiting the use of contraceptives by married couples. Justice Harlan not only dissented on the issue of justiciability, he also expressed his view that the statute was an unconstitutional interference with a liberty protected under the fourteenth amendment—notwithstanding his strong views quoted above on the propriety of morals laws.

In controversies such as these one cannot draw neat and clear bounds. The questions remain largely imponderable.[96] The suggested standards and a utilitarian balancing are only somewhat better than guesswork. The law in this area is largely one of deeply felt symbols, with psychic pleasure from the symbolic act of incorporating a moral viewpoint into law to be weighed against the psychic pain to others of this same symbolic act. The weights cannot but reflect the moral judgments of the weighor. It is precisely when the belief in question becomes debatable that these pleasures and pains become greatest and the desire to use law to gain victory most acute.[97] In this area the craft of the judge will remain an art, and not a science. Lord Devlin's summary will probably continue to be accurate for a long time to come:

> The line that divides the criminal law from the moral is not determinable by the application of any clearcut principle. It is like a line that divides land and sea, a coastline of irregularities and indentations. There are gaps and promontories . . .[98]

As if applying the foregoing principles of critical morality were not challenging enough for any judge, our Constitution also embodies certain principles of positive morality which not even a substantial majority can reverse short of a constitutional amendment. A clear instance of this is the

96. *See, e.g.,* Berkowitz & Walker, *Laws and Moral Judgments,* 30 SOCIOMETRY 410 (1967); Walker & Argyle, *Does the Law Affect Moral Judgments?,* 1964 BRIT. J. CRIMINOLOGY 570. There is some evidence that Supreme Court opinions have greater impact than legislation, Muir, *The Impact of Supreme Court Decisions on Moral Attitudes,* 23 J. LEGAL EDUC. 89 (1970); Reich, *Schoolhouse Religion and the Supreme Court: A Report on Attitudes of Teachers and Principals and on School Practices in Wisconsin and Ohio,* 23 J. LEGAL ED. 123 (1970); Zimring & Hawkins, *The Legal Threat as an Instrument of Social Change,* 27 J. SOC. ISSUES 33 (1971). The extent behavior conforms to moral judgments is also not known, Deutscher, *Words and Deeds: Social Science and Social Policy,* 13 SOCIAL PROBLEMS 236 (1966). Behavior also frequently changes less quickly than attitudes after a Supreme Court decision, Dolbaere & Hammond, *Inertia in Midway: Supreme Court Decisions and Local Responses,* 23 J. LEGAL ED. 106 (1970); Shapiro, *The Impact of the Supreme Court,* 23 J. LEGAL ED. 77 (1970); *See generally,* T. BECKER & M. FOOLEY, THE IMPACT OF THE SUPREME COURT (1973).

97. Aubert, *Competition and Dissensus: Two Types of Conflict and Conflict Resolution,* 7 J. CONFLICT RESOLUTION 26 (1963). *See* Gusfield, *Moral Passage: The Symbolic Process in Public Designations of Deviance,* 12 SOCIAL PROBLEMS 175 (1967), for a study of the history of the prohibition movement from the perspective of law as symbol of one subculture's supremacy over another. Where there is agreement in attitude, law is sometimes unnecessary to secure compliance, Romans, *Moral Suasion as an Instrument of Economic Policy,* 56 AMER. ECON. REV. 1220 (1966); Schwartz & Orleans, *On Legal Sanctions,* 34 U. CHI. L. REV. 274 (1971).

98. DEVLIN 21-22.

mandate that races be treated as equal[99]—which is a moral rather than a scientific judgment.[100] The judgment is not simply expressed by the Constitution. The open texture of the language requires the Court to give content to the words used. This content is derived from fundamental contemporary moral precepts. In order for the determination to be constitutional, and not merely personal to the justices, they must be extremely careful to be sure that the tenet is both basic, and fundamentally accepted in the society. To do otherwise with any frequency could bring the court into such disrepute as to undermine its most effective tool—its ability to shape opinion.[101]

Two bases have been advanced for the proposition that a moral principle is entrenched in our Constitution: either the conclusion is inherent in a moral consensus within our society deeper than changing public opinion on a particular issue, or the conclusion derives from a broader consensus transcending national frontiers. In support of the former, one has frequent references in due process cases to traditions of English speaking peoples or to our own specific traditions.[102] This deeper moral consensus is discovered by a careful scrutiny of the "enduring moral structure of our society," or of "shared fundamental values."[103] These fundamental values have been identified as sanctity of life, and basic human equality, decency, and freedom.[104] These are stated at such a high level of abstraction as to be inconclusive as guides to specific decisions in most cases. In order to apply these values to invalidate a law one must discover a specific tradition dictating the use contemplated. This leaves one with the question of how such a custom can be changed, or alternatively, how some usages become entrenched, while others do not? Except where the tradition is rather clearly embraced by the Constitution, or in prior constitutional adjudication,[105] entrenchment ought to be used sparingly. Still one can apply even highly general principles in some instances.

Occasionally, a specific law so clearly offends one or more of these values without advancing another one must conclude that the law is the result of either a great misunderstanding of the values and their application to

99. For clear statements of this basis for upholding racial equality, see Hunter v. Erickson, 393 U.S. 385 (1969); Reitman v. Mulkey, 387 U.S. 369 (1967); Gatreux v. Chicago Housing Authority, 296 F. Supp. 907 (N.D. Ill. 1969), aff'd, 436 F.2d. 306 (7th Cir.), stay denied, 91 S. Ct. 980 (1971). Cf. Dworkin, Lord Devlin and the Enforcement of Morals, 75 YALE L. J. 986, 996-1001 (1966).

100. Jensen, How Much Can We Boost IQ's and Scholastic Achievement?, 37 HARV. ED. REV. 1 (1969); Dobzhansky, Differences are not Deficits, PSYCHOLOGY TODAY 97 (Dec. 1973).

101. See Baker v. Carr, 369 U.S. 186, 266-270 (1961) (Frankfurter, J., dissenting). See also T. BECKER & M. FEELEY, supra note 100.

102. Palko v. Connecticut, 302 U.S. 319 (1937).

103. Gianella, The Difficult Quest for a Truly Humane Abortion Law, 13 VILL. L. REV. 257, 265-266, 301 (1968). Cf. Comment, supra note 28, at 1180-1184.

104. Byrn, supra note 72, at 34-36. These are stated in different terms as survival, justice, welfare, and freedom, in ETHICS, POPULATION, AND THE AMERICAN TRADITION (1972), an unpublished report to the Commission on Population Growth and the American Future.

105. This has been termed the "maturing of collective thought," Hart, The Supreme Court, 1958 Term—Forward: The Time Chart of the Justices, 73 HARV. L. REV. 84, 100 (1959).

specific situations, or an equally serious misapprehension of the facts.[106] Such a determination must be rare given the generality of the principles applied. Rejection of the "separate but equal" doctrine in education is an instance of such a reasoning process.[107] One could accept the doctrine by believing equal education was possible with separation (which the Court found to be a factual impossibility).[108] One could also accept the doctrine by believing that basic human equality did not extend to blacks (a painfully strained interpretation of the value which was not even argued in the case). Since equality for blacks could be found to be an explicitly preferred value in the equal protection clause and in the prohibition of slavery, all that was necessary for the Court to invalidate a law based on such misunderstandings of basic principles would be to find that any gain to other values (e.g. freedom of association) was minimal.[109]

A broader, international moral consensus may be easier to find than a deeper moral consensus within our own nation. Frequently one can find a practice of nations to which there are few exceptions,[110] with deviant nations to some extent chastised for their conduct. International consensus also is found in the pronouncements of emerging international organs. Racial equality is a value to which most nations are committed. This precept is of relatively recent origin, and often is not achieved in practice. Nonetheless, it is generally held in high regard and usually enacted into law. Nations which explicitly reject the precept suffer various international sanctions. The goal of racial equality is also embodied in various multilateral conventions[111] and

106. *Cf.* Dworkin, *Lord Devlin and the Enforcement of Morals*, 75 YALE L. J. 986 (1966).

107. Brown v. Board of Education of Topeka, 347 U.S. 483 (1954).

108. *Id.* at 492-495.

109. Wechsler, *supra* note 22, argues that this was an incorrect approach, apparently because he finds the clash to have been between one person's freedom of association and the like freedom of others. So stated the question is closer.

110. Analogously to "general principles of law recognized by civilized nations" as a source of international law, The Diversion of Water from the Meuse (Netherlands v. Belgium), P.C.I.J. Ser. A/B, No. 70, 76-78 4 Hudson, World Ct. Rep. 172, 231-233 (1937) (J. Hudson concurring); Cayuga Indians (Great Britain v. United States), 6 U.N. Rep. Int'l Arb. Aw. 173 (1910). *See also* C. W. JENKS. THE COMMON LAW OF MANKIND 106 (1958).

111. U.N. CHARTER, Art. 1(3), 55(c), 76(c); the International Covenant on Civil and Political Rights, Art. 2(1), G.A. Res. 2200, 21 U.N. GAOR Supp. 16 at 52, U.N. Doc. A/6316, (*opened for signature* Dec. 19, 1966); the International Covenant on Economic, Social, and Cultural Rights, Art. 2(2). G.A. Res 2200, 21 U.N. GAOR Supp. 16 at 49, (*opened for signature* Dec. 19, 1966); the Genocide Convention, 78 U.N.T.S. 277 (*opened for signature* Dec. 2, 1948); the European Convention for the Protection of Human Rights and Fundamental Freedoms, Art. 14, 213 U.N.T.S. 221 (*opened for signature* Nov. 4, 1950); the American Convention on Human Rights, Art. 1(1), O.A.S. Doc. 65 (English) (*opened for signature* Nov. 22, 1969), *reprinted* 65 AM. J. INT'L LAW 679 (1971).

The United States voted in favor of the International Covenant on Civil and Political Rights and the International Covenant on Economic, Social, and Cultural Rights, both adopted unanimously.

The United States was one of the original 43 signatories of the Genocide Convention. The United States has not signed the American Convention on Human Rights, nor has it ratified any of the other agreements.

resolutions of the United Nations.[112] Whatever may be the direct legal effect of these documents,[113] their consistent pattern and wide (often unanimous) support clearly establish a moral consensus. This broad agreement on moral principles is directly relevant to the resolution of disputes under our Constitution.[114] The consensus delineates what is "implicit in the concept of ordered liberty."[115] Although this method of giving content to due process is not used as frequently as it once was, the technique is still valid.[116]

Law also provides moral standards for society. It teaches by example even where the law cannot be enforced.[117] Thus, it is argued that law should be committed to moral positions in order to set a proper example. That changing laws can be a means for making some changes in society cannot be denied after our experience with race relations. What is sometimes taught, however, is not morality, but rather disrespect for law. This may occur where there is widespread dissensus in the society, with a victorious group seeking to impose its morality on an unpersuaded subculture.[118] If the law is to assume a teaching function in an area where there cannot be enforcement, one must at the very least balance the cost to society in terms of lost respect for law against the gain of the example. A further cost to be considered is the harm to personal perceptions of liberty from symbolic enactments proscribing one's conduct even where it is clear there can be no enforcement. As personal liberty is accorded constitutional protection,[119] extraordinary reasons are necessary to justify laws which are expected to be unenforceable examples. Probably the only reasons one could properly advance for such laws would be

---

112. Most notably in the Universal Declaration of Human Rights, Art. 1, 2, G.A. Res. 217, 3 U.N. GAOR at 71, U.N. Doc. A/810 (*adopted unanimously,* Dec. 2, 1948).

113. *Compare* Sei Fujii v. California, 38 Cal. 2d. 718, 722-725, 242 P. 2d 617, 621-622 (1952), *with* Re Drummond Wren, (1945) Ont. R. 788, 4 D.L.R. 674 (1945).

114. Oyama v. California, 332 U.S. 633, 649-650, 673 (1943) (Black, Douglas, Murphy, & Rutledge, JJ., concurring).

115. Palko v. Connecticut, 302 U.S. 319, 325 (1937).

116. Roe v. Wade, 410 U.S. 113, 152 (1973); Bartkus v. Illinois, 359 U.S. 121, 127-128 (1959). *See also* Pointer v. Texas, 380 U.S. 400, 408-409 (1965) (Harlan, J. concurring).

117. "Our government is the potent, the omnipresent teacher. For good or for ill, it teaches the whole people by its example." Olmstead v. United States, 277 U.S 438, 485 (1928) (Brandeis, J., dissenting).
See also Gianella, *supra* note 107, at 283; Louisell, *supra* note 71, at 250.

118. Gusfield, *supra* note 101, describes the experience with prohibition. *See also* M. EDELMAN, THE SYMBOLIC USES OF POLITICS (1964). Gianella, *supra* note 107, concludes that the same breakdown of respect for law may be occuring through the abortion controversy. *See also* Skolnick, *supra* note 97.

119. . . . (T)he full scope of the liberty guaranteed by the Due Process Clause cannot be found in or limited by the precise terms of the specific guarantees elsewhere provided in the Constitution. This "liberty" is not a series of isolated points pricked out in terms of taking of property; the freedom of speech, press, and religion; the right to keep and bear arms; the freedom from unreasonable searches and seizures; and so on. It is a rational continuum which, broadly speaking, includes a freedom from all substantial arbitrary impositions and purposeless restraints.
Poe v. Ullman, 367 U.S. 497, 543 (1961) (Harlan, J., dissenting). *Cf.* Tribe, *supra* note 3, at 16-17.

a deeper or broader moral consensus in the sense discussed earlier. Law can teach what it cannot compel. If the law is to remain servant rather than master, law can only teach where the society as a whole dictates the lessons.

In summary, the critical morality embedded in our Constitution as the basis for the review of laws, is a complex of several parts. Laws must have a secular purpose. Such a purpose is most easily found where there is injury to another. A secular purpose is also found where there is public flaunting of the secular morality, and even in the rare case where there are private violations of national or local mores. In each of these instances there must be a balancing of the harm sought to be prevented against the harm caused to individuals or to the legal structure by the attempt to control behavior. This balance favors regulation where there is a direct physical injury to another, but becomes progressively more favorable to self-regulation as one moves along the scale to more remote harms. Furthermore, in a few instances, the Constitution embraces certain positive values so basic to our culture that these precepts must be protected and enforced even against the will of a clear majority. The tenets so protected are found either explicitly in the Constitution, or (more often) in a deeper or broader moral consensus transcending the shifting popular opinion on a particular question at a specific moment. In such cases the law may be said to teach by example even where it cannot coerce.[120]

B. Abortion and Constitutional Morality

One could constitutionally analyze the abortion controversy using either critical morality or positive morality. For example, using critical morality to evaluate whether abortion ought to be legal, one could argue that popular opinion—in at least some states—abhors abortion.[121] As abortions are not performed open to public view, one could conclude that only a very broad and deeply felt consensus on the immorality of the act could justify prohibiting it.[122] Legal abortions, however, are not performed in the privacy of one's

---

120. Shapiro, *supra* note 100, at 81-85. Gusfield, *supra* note 101, finds such symbolic gestures to be socially harmonizing. Both subcultures are happy: one because its views are law; the other because it knows the law will not force it to change its conduct. This ignores that such laws are enforced fitfully, resulting in discriminatory and arbitrary justice. *See generally* K. DAVIS, DISCRETIONARY JUSTICE (1971); E. SCHUR, CRIMES WITHOUT VICTIMS (1965). In the abortion context some have argued that this alone should be sufficient basis for legalization, H. PACKER, THE LIMITS OF THE CRIMINAL SANCTION 343-344 (1968); Charles & Alexander, *Abortion for Poor and Nonwhite Women: A Denial of Equal Protection*, 23 HAST. L. J. 147 (1971); Nagan, *Social Perspectives: Abortions and Female Behavior*, 6 VALPARAISO L. REV. 286, 288 (1972) (social fact which law must accept); Zimring, *Of Doctors, Deterrence, and the Dark Figure of Crime—A Note on Abortion in Hawaii*, 39 U. CHI. L. REV. 699, 716-717 (1972). Tribe 30 n.133 recognizes, however, that frequent violation ought not to be the basis of unconstitutionality.

121. *Cf.* Miller v. California, 413 U.S. 15 (1973) (local community standards used to define obscenity). Of Course the analysis would be factually different if a national standard were insisted upon for either abortion or obscenity.

122. *See* text accompanying notes 91-95 *supra*. *See also*, DUSTER, *supra* note 77, at 23-28.

home. As they are performed in places of public accommodation (hospitals, clinics, and doctor's offices), somewhat more latitude for state regulation would generally be permitted.[123] In weighing the claims of the majority to protect its moral sensibilities against the claims of the dissenters to freedom of conscience, the entire range of considerations developed above would be relevant.[124] Would others be led astray? Would respect for life be lessened—even apart from the question of what is the status of the foetus? Would the general level of taste, interests, and morality decline?[125] Along with these one would also balance the cost to society as the dissensus over the law grows deeper and the conflict more acute.[126]

Lengthy analysis of these arguments need not detain us, for the entire scope of the debate changes when one reaches the critical question[127]—the status of the embryo/foetus.[128] Clearly if the foetus is at some point accorded the status of a separately valuable human being, abortion is no longer a self-regarding act.[129] Who is a "person" under the fourteenth amendment is not, however, the sort of question which can be left to individual or local decision. Too many basic rights hinge upon the answer. Are blacks, Jews, or others, "persons"? The questions about foeti, blacks, and others are not merely similar. They are the same questions—how do we define a human being, separately entitled to respect and value? This question is metalegal[130]—which does not excuse answering it. If the conclusions are to be principled rather than arbitrary, one cannot simply decide whether there is a person each time the question arises merely to justify the particular conclusion sought.[131] One should be suspicious of tests which would not be applied at both ends of the lifespan, or to people in general.[132]

---

123. *Compare* Paris Adult Theatre I v. Slaton, 413 U.S. 49 (1973) (right of privacy does not protect showing of obscene films to consenting adults in place of public accommodation), *with* Stanley v. Georgia, 394 U.S. 557 (1969) (state may not prohibit viewing of obscenity in the privacy of one's home).

124. *See* text accompanying notes 74-90 *supra.*

125. This seems to be the basis for restricting pornography, Comment, *supra* note 28, at 1170-1171.

126. As in the prohibition of alcohol, EDELMAN, *supra* note 125, Gusfield, *supra* note 101. For the increasing acrimony of the abortion conflict, *see* LADER I and LADER II, *supra* note 13.

127. Recognized as such by everyone on the Court and by both appellant and appellee *Wade*, 410 U.S. at 156. Failure to decide the question is thus all the more perplexing.

128. Hereafter to simplify discussion I shall use the term foetus to cover the developing child from conception to birth.

129. Analyses which assume that there is no victim thus beg the question as in SCHUR, *supra* note 127, or Heyman & Barzelay, *supra* note 3. Tribe agrees that this is question begging, Tribe 5 n.25.

130. *See* text accompanying notes 71-73 *supra.* In other words, it is a question answered by positive morality.

131. CALLAHAN 392-394. Ramsey, *Abortion,* 37 THE THOMIST 174, 174-176 (1973), points out that advocates of involuntary euthanasia are picking up Callahan's arguments—much to Callahan's discomfort, *id.* at 206.

132. Louisell, *supra* note 71, at 249, characterizes the failure to do so as legal schizophrenia, while Gianella, *supra* note 107, at 264 says:

There is no popular consensus regarding when independent value attaches to human life. Public opinion polls and attitude surveys show no consensus. Laws are contradictory and confusing. Medical opinion is divided.[133] One might conclude that as the question must be answered somewhere, it ought merely to be a question of who can capture the legislature and impose its views on the rest. This assumes that one answer is as good as another. But who would choose to leave the question of whether a racial minority are people to popular vote?[134] One might, then, reason that there being no consensus the state may not adopt any theory of life. The problem with this view (adopted by the majority in *Wade*)[135] is that some theory of life is necessary to any resolution of the constitutional question. The Court generally must decide questions of fact or construction upon which federal constitutional questions rest.[136] If the question cannot be avoided, it should be left to legislative resolution unless constitutional principles direct a result.[137]

The majority correctly observed that no case has held "person" in the fourteenth amendment to include unborns.[138] Of course, no Supreme Court case had held to the contrary either.[139] This is the first time that the constitutionality of abortion laws has been squarely before the Court. It is difficult to visualize another context in which the question of fetal personhood could be presented. One hundred five years without such a question being decided is not surprising when one recalls that minors were first held protected by that amendment in 1967.[140] Other uses of the word "person" in

The double-think hazard here is clear: we will regard the foetus as a human being when it suits us, and not do so when it suits us better.

133. Obstetricians and gynecologists—those in closest contact with the problem—appear least willing to disregard the value of the foetus. Guttmacher, *The Genesis of Legalized Abortion in New York: A Personal Insight*, in WALBERT, *supra* note 31, at 65. *See* notes 171, 186, *infra*.

134. Or delegated to individual choice as Tribe would do for foeti.

135. *Wade*, 410 U.S. at 162. In fact, the majority implicitly decide the question—by consistently referring to the state interest as one of protecting mere "potential life," *id.* at 163: this approach simply avoids having to justify the decision.

136. Napue v. Illinois, 360 U.S. 264, 272 (1959). *See also* Byrn, *supra* note 6, at 813-814.

137. Consider this statement from Miller v. Schoene, 276 U.S. 272, 280 (1928):
. . . (W)here, as here, the choice is unavoidable, we cannot say that its exercise, controlled by considerations of social policy which are not unreasonable, involves any denial of due process.
It should be obvious that the ensuing discussion is relevant to legislatures considering what law to enact—to the extent they have any choice left in the matter.

138. 410 U.S. at 157.

139. *But see* Abele v. Markele, 351 F. Supp. 224, 229 (D. Conn. 1972), *app. vac.* 410 U.S. 951, *rehearing den.* 411 U.S. 940, *aff'd* 369 F. Supp. 807 (D. Conn. 1973):
If the fetus survives the period of gestation, it will be born and then become a person entitled to the legal protections of the Constitution. But its capacity to become such a person does not mean that during gestation it is such a person. The unfertilized ovum also has the capacity to become a living human being, but the constitution does not endow it with rights which the state may protect by interfering with the individual's choice of whether the ovum will be fertilized.

140. *In re* Gault, 387 U.S. 1, 13 (1967).

the Constitution appear to have been postnatal.[141] The most one can infer from this is that there is no explicit determination of the problem in the Constitution. To reason—as the Court does—that this failure to resolve a hitherto moot question casts doubt on one of the possible interpretations seems unfounded.[142]

If the Constitution does not explicitly decide this metalegal question, principles of morality underlying the Constitution might. The proper status of the foetus at various stages of its development cannot be determined by application of the constitutional scheme of critical morality. Critical morality deals with the propriety of regulating self-regarding acts—not with providing specific content to the norms to be enforced, such as those norms defining who is a person in order to determine what is a self-regarding act. For this the positive morality of the Constitution must be used. Lacking a surface consensus, one must therefore search for some broader or deeper agreement on the definition.[143]

C. *Fetal Personhood*

Beyond possession of a human genotype,[144] what defines a "person" is not clear. Within our own cultural traditions, laws, moral philosophies, religious views, literary traditions, and the like could all be examined to seek

---

141. 410 U.S. at 157. *E.g.*, neither foeti nor corporations are counted as "persons" for census purposes.

142. Nor are the three lower court cases any more persuasive. Partly they are based on the same peculiar reasoning—as the question has not been decided before, the answer must be no. For example, one judge reasoned:

"Nor have we been cited authority that the framers of the Constitution contemplated fetal life or thought of unborn children as persons for purposes of constitutional protection or that Congress had fetal life in mind when it drafted the Civil Rights Act. That act adopted after the Civil War was intended to secure to minority races the equal protection of the law, Adickes v. S. H. Kress & Co., 398 U.S. 144, 90 S. Ct. 1598, 26 L. Ed. 2d 142 (1969). We are not aware of any mention in the debates preceding that act which would indicate the intention of Congress to protect unborn children." McGarvey v. Magee-Women's Hospital, 340 F. Supp. 751, 753 (W.D. Pa. 1972), *aff'd without opinion* 474 F.2d 1339 (3d Cir. 1973).

In two of the three cases, the courts also deferred to apparent state legislative judgments that foeti are not people, Byrn v. New York City Health and Hosp. Corp., 31 N.Y. 2d 194, 286 N.E. 2d 887 (1972), *app. dis.* 410 U.S. 949, *reh. den.* 411 U.S. 940 (1973); McGarvey v. Magee-Women's Hosp., 340 F. Supp. 751 (W. D. Pa. 1972), *aff'd without opinion* 474 F.2d 1339 (3d. Cir. 1973). In the third case the court overturned a state statute enacted only four months before explicitly to protect the life of the foetus, Abele v. Markle, 351 F. Supp. 224 (D. Conn. 1972), *app. vac.* 410 U.S. 951, *reh. den.* 411 U.S. 940, *aff'd.* 369 F. Supp. 807 (D. Conn. 1973). *Wade,* 410 U.S. at 158, cited all three of these cases with approval, but made no effort to reconcile their differing postures. Deference to legislative judgment is particularly strange where the possibility of human life is involved. *Cf.* Skinner v. Oklahoma *ex rel.* Williamson, 316 U.S. 535 (1942), where the Court refused to accept the determination by Oklahoma's legislature that chicken stealing is inheritable.

143. *See* text accompanying notes 103-127, *supra.*

144. Disregarding artificial "persons" under the fourteenth amendment.

a deep national moral consensus transcending malleable and unsettled popular opinion. Similar evidence from other nations could be examined in search of a broader consensus. Any moral consensus found must then be applied to the facts of fetal development as now understood to determine whether, or at what point, a foetus becomes a "person."

The abortion laws themselves may be a recognition of foetal personhood, but the penalties for abortion are generally lower than those for homicide. Coupled with the fact that the mother is usually not made a criminal accomplice,[145] this suggests that the crime is against her, not against the foetus. Until 1970, only six state statutes defined the killing of a foetus other than in an abortion as a crime—generally manslaughter.[146] In *Keeler v. Superior Court*[147] the California Supreme Court refused to extend a general homicide statute to cover such killings. This was promptly reversed by the legislature.[148] Thus three years after California liberalized its abortion law, it created the anomalous situation that an accidental killing of a foetus could be criminal homicide, whereas a deliberate killing through abortion was no crime at all. *Wade* placed the other states recognizing this crime in the same quandry. The explanation may be a desire to afford special protection to the mother's desire to have the child. But if that is the case, the states have chosen a peculiar manner of articulating *this* goal.

Most other foetal rights which courts have allegedly recognized are also explainable in terms of according protection to postnatals—either because the rights are conditioned on subsequent live birth of the protected foetus,[149]

145. *But see:* ARIZ. STAT. ANN. § 13-212 (1956); CAL. PENAL CODE § 275 (1968); CONN. GEN. STAT. ANN. § 53-30 (1960); IDAHO CODE ANN. § 18-1506 (Supp. 1971); IND. ANN. STAT. § 10-106 (1956); MINN. STAT. ANN. § 617.19 (1963); N.Y. PENAL LAW §§ 125.50, 125.55 (1967); N.D. CENT. CODE § 12-25-04 (1960); OKLA. STAT. ANN., tit. 21, § 862 (1958); S.C. CODE ANN. § 16-84 (1962); S.D. COMP. LAWS ANN., § 22-17-2 (1967); UTAH CODE ANN., § 76-2-2 (1953); WASH. REV. CODE ANN. § 9.02.020 (1961); WIS. STAT. ANN. § 940.04 (1958); WYO. STAT. ANN. § 6-78 (1957).

Justice Blackmun in Roe v. Wade, 410 U.S. at 157-158, n. 54, used the existence of abortion laws and lower penalties than those imposed for homicide to refute recognition of fetal personhood. In no state are all abortions prohibited. He reasoned that if the foetus is a person not to be deprived of his life without due process of law, and, (in some states) the mother's health was the sole determinant as to whether an abortion could be procured, then this exception would contradict the command of the Amendment. The Court questioned whether the penalties for abortion could be lower than those for murder if the foetus were a person. But a Massachusetts prosecutor recently brought manslaughter charges against a doctor who aborted a 20-28 week old foetus, N.Y. Times, Jan. 12, 1975, at 34, col. 3.

146. ARK. STAT. ANN. § 41-2223 (1964); FLA. STAT. ANN., § 782.09 (1965); MICH. COMP. LAWS, § 750.322 (1948); MISS. CODE ANN., § 2222 (1957); N.D. CENT. CODE ANN., § 12-25-3 (1960); OKLA. STAT. ANN., tit. 21, § 713 (1958). One other state reached the same result through case law, State v. Walters, 199 Wis. 68, 225 N.W. 167 (1929).

147. 2 Cal. 3d. 619, 87 Cal. Rptr. 482, 470 P.2d. 617 (1970). *Accord,* State v. Dickinson, 28 Ohio St. 2d 65, 275 N.E.2d 599 (1971).

148. CAL. STAT. 1970, ch. 1311, § 1 at 567.

149. As for prenatal injuries to one subsequently born malformed, W. PROSSER, HANDBOOK OF THE LAW OF TORTS 335-338 (4th. ed. 1971). *See, e.g.,* Womack v. Buckhorn, 384 Mich. 718, 187 N.W.2d. 218 (1971). Inheritance rights have long been recognized depending on

or because the right is actually designed to protect the interests of the parents.[150] So long as fetal and maternal interests coincide, these explanations fit. There remains only one class of cases, best exemplified by *Raleigh-Fitkin Memorial Hospital v. Anderson*,[151] to which neither explanation applies. Mrs. Anderson was expected to experience severe hemorrhaging in her pregnancy. As a Jehovah's Witness she objected on religious grounds to transfusions of blood. A unanimous court ordered the appointment of a special guardian for the unborn child to consent to any transfusions necessary to protect the child, and ordered Mrs. Anderson to submit to the transfusions. Here no less fundamental a right than religious freedom[152] was overridden on behalf of an unborn child's right to live. *Raleigh-Fitkin* also involved the woman's control of the use of her own body—which was held to be a fundamental right in *Wade*. Perhaps *Raleigh-Fitkin* is implicitly reversed by *Wade*. If not, here is another anomaly created by *Wade*. At the least *Raleigh-Fitkin* shows that courts did in fact act to protect foeti independently of—even adversely

---

subsequent live birth, 1 W. BLACKSTONE, COMMENTARIES 130 (1765). For other rights which have been recognized, *see* Louisell, *supra* note 71, at 235-238; Doe v. Luckhard, 363 F. Supp. 823 (E. D. Va. 1973) (state must provide AFDC for unborns). PROSSER, *id.* at 337, rejects both live birth and viability as being of any relevance—although the Court in *Wade* cites him to the contrary 410 U.S. at 162 n.65. *Cf.* CAL. CIVIL CODE § 29 (1954):

> A child conceived but not yet born, is to be deemed an existing person, so far as may be necessary for its interests in the event of its subsequent birth.

150. As is the case in tort actions for the wrongful death of an unborn child, Verkennes v. Corniea, 229 Minn. 365, 38 N.W.2d. 838, 10 A.L.R.2d. 634 (1949). *See* Annot., 15 A.L.R.3d 992 (1968), for a listing of other cases. As no recovery was allowed for non-pecuniary damages for the wrongful death of any child until recently, it is not surprising that this remedy has only recently been extended to prenatals. *Contrast* Estate of Powers v. Troy, 4 Mich. App. 572, 145 N.W.2d 418 (1966), *with* O'Neill v. Morse, 385 Mich. 130, 188 N.W.2d. 785 (1971). Ziff, *Recent Abortion Law Reforms (or Much Ado About Nothing)*, 60 J. CRIM. L., CRIMINOLOGY & POLI. SCI. 3, 17-19 (1969), argues that protections of the mother's interest explains all of these "rights". No explanation is offered for the peculiar terminology seized by the courts. *See also* Abele v. Markle, 351 F. Supp. 224, 229 (D. Conn. 1972).

> "Of course, the fact that a fetus is not a person entitled to Fourteenth Amendment rights does not mean that government may not confer rights upon it. A wide range of rights has been accorded by statutes and court decisions. These include the right to compensation for tortious injury, the right to parental support, and the right to inherit property. But the granting of these rights was not done at the expense of the constitutional rights of others. A tortfeasor has no constitutional right to inflict injury on a fetus. When government acts through legislation to confer upon a fetus the absolute right to be born contrary to the preference of a pregnant woman, it abridges her constitutional right to marital and sexual privacy. Whether it may do so cannot be established by the fact that other protections can be accorded which do not abridge another's constitutional rights."

151. 42 N.J. 421, 201 A.2d 537, *cert. den.* 377 U.S. 985 (1964). *Cf.* Application of President & Directors of Georgetown College, Inc., 118 D.C. App. 80, 331 F.2d 1000, *reh. den.* 118 D.C. App. 90, 331 F.2d 1010, *cert. den.* 377 U.S. 978 (1964) (mother compelled to submit to blood transfusion to herself over religious objections in interest of seven month old foetus).

152. In re Estate of Brooks, 32 Ill. 2d. 361, 205 N.E.2d. 435 (1965) (upholding adult's right to refuse transfusions on religious grounds). *Cf.* Sherbert v. Verner, 374 U.S. 398 (1963); Abington Township v. Schempp, 374 U.S. 203 (1963); Engel v. Vitale, 370 U.S. 421 (1962); West Virginia State Board of Education v. Barnette, 319 U.S. 624 (1943).

to—the mother. The right cannot be said to have been conditioned on the subsequent live birth of the infant, for without the transfusion, there would have been no live birth.

Western religious traditions, more clearly than legal traditions, support the conclusion that life begins at or near conception. Catholics,[153] most Protestants,[154] and some Jewish theologians[155] can be cited for this proposition, though the conclusion has never been accepted universally within any of these traditions. To the extent there has been change, even the *Wade* Court's rendition of history[156] shows steady progress towards lowering the time after conception at which separate life was said to begin. Only since 1957 has this concept been widely challenged.[157] These challenges have generally attempted to define away the problem[158] rather than provide reasoned discourse on the criteria of human identity.

Two basic theories have been put forward by those who debate the personhood of the foetus. The first is the hylomorphic theory. This theory argues that a prenatal child is not "animated" until it looks human.[159] This argument appeals strongly to the difficulties many have in identifying with someone who looks substantially different. It is particularly strong where there are barriers (distance, or veils,[160] or in this case, mothers) which prevent one from dealing with the individual directly.

This theory would hardly justify most abortions even if it were accepted. The theory's advocates merely display their great misunderstanding of the facts. As early as the third week (about the time a woman may begin to wonder if she is pregnant) rudimentary head, eyes, ears, brain, digestive tract, heart, bloodstream, kidneys and liver have developed.[161] By the eighth week[162] (with tests to verify pregnancy and time to consider whether to abort,

---

153. 3 T. Bouscaren, Canon Law Digest 669-670 (1954); G. Grisez, Abortion: The Myths, the Realities, and the Arguments (1970); Ramsey, *The Morality of Abortion*, in Moral Problems (J. Rachels ed. 1971).

154. D. Bonhoeffer, Ethics 130-131 (N. Smith trans. 1955); H. Thielicke, The Ethics of Sex 226-247 (J. Doberstein trans. 1964). *See also* Time 62 (May 28, 1973) for survey results showing 59% of Protestants opposed to abortions as the taking of life.

155. Jakobovits, *Jewish Views on Abortion*, in Walbert, *supra* note 31, at 103.

156. 410 U.S. at 129-147, *especially* at 141-142.

157. Beginning with G. Williams, The Sanctity of Life and the Criminal Law 208 (1957). *See also* Rosen v. Louisiana State Board of Medical Examiners, 318 F. Supp. 1217, 1223 (1970).

158. *See, e.g.*, Hardin, *Abortion—Or Compulsory Pregnancy?*, 30 J. Marriage & the Family 250 (1968). *See also* The Commission on Population Growth and the American Future, Population and the American Future 101-104, 148-149, 151, 156-157, 160-163 (1972).

159. While this theory can be traced back to Aristotle, it continues to have modern champions, Ziff, *supra* note 149, at 19-22. *See also* Gianella, *supra* note 103, at 272-276.

160. Bordewich, *Where Women Are an Annoyance That Disturbs the Symmetry of Life*, N.Y. Times, Dec. 9, 1973 § 10, p. 1, col. 1.

161. H. M. I. Liley, Modern Motherhood 7 (rev. ed. 1969). *See also* Callahan, *supra* note 73, at 371-373.

162. Liley, *supra* note 160, at 28; Byrn, *supra* note 72, at 7-9; Byrn, *supra* note 5, at

near the time when most women who so choose will be aborted) all the internal organs are developed, the face is completely formed, and the extremities are blunt, but developed. Electroencephalograph (EEG) readings can be taken from its brain. The foetus responds to tickling. The foetus certainly looks human—if that is the relevant criterion.[163]

This appearance may in large part explain the reluctance of many obstetricians and obstetrical nurses to favor unlimited abortions.[164]

In order to avoid the shortcomings of such a superficial criterion, a more sophisticated analysis has been developed. This modern hylomorphic theory is perhaps best stated by Daniel Callahan:

> . . . "(H)uman" cannot be defined in a genetic way *only*, or a psychological way *only*, or a cultural way *only*, it must be defined in such a way as to take account of all three elements in the "human."[165]

An infant is scarcely more human than a foetus. Yet few advocates of abortion now favor infanticide.[166] Callahan was himself driven to concede the personhood of the zygote from conception on.[167]

At the other extreme is the genetic criterion school which would confer personhood on the blastocyst. This school draws strength from the dramatic transformation which occurs at conception. The argument also suffers from serious physiological defects, however. If conception is to mark the point of individuation, how does one deal with segmentation? For up to two weeks

383-391; Hellegers, *Fetal Development*, 31 THEOLOGICAL STUDIES 3, 7-8 (1970); Ramsey, *Reference Points in Deciding about Abortion*, in THE MORALITY.

163. Byrn, *supra* note 72, at 8-9, quotes one physician as describing a foetus as looking even more human (without the expected bluntness) than the dead foeti normally photographed—the difference being that the foetus in question was alive.

164. Guttmacher, *supra* note 133; Mandy, *Reflections of a Gynecologist*, in THERAPEUTIC ABORTIONS: MEDICAL, PSYCHOLOGICAL, LEGAL, ANTHROPOLOGICAL AND RELIGIOUS CONSIDERATIONS 248 (Rosen ed. 1954); TIME 69 (Sept. 27, 1971). For the somewhat similar experience in Soviet medicine, *see* P. GEBHARD, W. POMEROY, C. MARTIN, & C. CHRISTENSON, BIRTH AND ABORTION 217 (1958).

165. CALLAHAN 363.

166. In marked contrast with Japan where infanticide was an accepted form of "birth control" within the memory of some now living. The move away from infanticide in Japan may presage a move away from abortion—at least the question of placing restrictions on abortions has been raised in Japan. ABORTION IN A CHANGING WORLD 260-266 (R. Hall ed. 1970). *See also* L. LEE & A. LARSEN, POPULATION AND LAW 36 (1971). Korea has a similar tradition, *id.*, at 47-49. Where infanticide occurs in the United States it is generally rigorously prosecuted, People v. Chavez, 77 Cal. App. 2d. 621, 176 P.2d. 92 (1947) (infanticide through birth over a toilet). A similar incident occured on a plane over Ohio in March, 1973—the prosecution seems incongruous since under *Wade* the woman could have easily obtained a lawful abortion up to moments before she became a murderess. Dr. James Watson (codiscoverer of DNA) has called for the law to define life as beginning three days *after* birth, in order to permit the elimination of deformed babies, TIME 104 (May 28, 1973). This would allow a choice to all which abortion allows to only a few as most deformities are not discoverable before birth.

167. CALLAHAN 386, 397.

after conception the zygote may split into two or more individuals (which may later recombine). This strongly suggests that an "individual" does not exist until some point later than conception.[168] Our present knowledge suggests no particular development in this stage which could appear to signal the arrival of personhood.

Evidence of a broader, world-wide consensus is even less conclusive. Most countries permit abortions—but generally only for substantial cause.[169] This suggests some valuation of fetal life. The recent trend, however, is towards increasing the availability of abortions. On the other hand, prenatal children are expressly included in various documents protecting basic human rights.[170] At least one hemispheric agreement has prohibited the arbitrary taking of life from the moment of conception.[171] The religious traditions in the United States are paralleled in most other cultures as well.[172]

Neither search can be said to have revealed a direct consensus on when a fetus becomes a "person." Both would place restrictions of various degrees on abortions, frequently articulated in terms of protecting the foetus. Apparently at some point the foetus is to be deemed a person,[173] which is to say

168. Ramsey, *supra* note 138, at 188-194. *See also* CALLAHAN, 379-380.

169. ABORTION IN A CHANGING WORLD, *supra* note 166; LEE & LARSEN, *supra* note 166; Kutner, *Due Process of Abortion*, 53 MINN. L. REV. 1 (1968). The Court's rendition of history shows that abortions have generally been restricted, if not prohibited, 410 U.S. at 130-147. *See also* note 15 *supra*.

170. The Declaration on the Rights of the Child, G.A. Res. 1386, 14 U.N. GAOR Supp. 16 at 19, U.N. Doc. A/4354 (adopted unanimously as supplement to the Universal Declaration of Human Rights, 1959). This document is part of a growing recognition of the rights of children in the United States and around the world. *See, e.g., Symposium, Juvenile Rights*, 4 COL. HUM. RIGHTS L. REV. 303-500 (1972).

171. The American Convention on Human Rights, *supra* note 111, Art. 4(1).

172. *See* notes 160-162 *supra*. Islam has always considered abortion objectionable, LEE & LARSEN, *supra* note 166, at 297-334. At least in Thailand, Buddhist traditions have also condemned abortions (so strongly that they are not as readily obtainable as the law permits), *id.*, at 69-80.

173. That a foetus is deemed a person does not necessarily preclude abortions for sufficiently serious reasons after a due process hearing. *Cf.* Furman v. Georgia, 408 U.S. 238 (1972) (capital punishment upheld only if equally applied without abusable discretion). *See generally* CALLAHAN 307-348; Thomson, *supra* note 58. Friedmann, *Interference with Life: Some Jurisprudential Reflections*, 70 COL. L. REV. 1058, 1067-1070 (1970), and Ramsey *supra* note 131, at 176-182, see the question in terms replacing a "sanctity of life" ethic with a "quality of life ethic," which Kenneth Boulding characterizes as the aristocratization of the middle class, and ". . . aristocrats have always been sons of bitches.", Glasgow, *A Conversation with Kenneth Boulding*, PSYCHOLOGY TODAY 62 (Jan. 1973). For a clear instance of this debate *compare* Katz, *Process Design for Selection of Hemodialysis and Organ Transplant Recipients*, 22 BUFF. L. REV. 373, 404-415 (1973), *with Editorial*, 113 CAL. MEDICINE 67 (1970). Consider also the ludicrous nature of a glowing report by Gordon Chase, New York City Health Services Administrator, that abortions had reduced infant mortality to an all-time low! N.Y. Times, Oct. 8, 1971. The question remains: is it morally superior to cure suffering, or to obliterate sufferers? *Cf.* Kindegran, *Abortion, the Law, and Defective Children: A Legal-Medical Study*, 3 SUFF. L. REV. 225, 272 (1969). *See also* CALLAHAN, *supra* note 73, at 91-120; Bolgen, *There are No Hopeless Children*, THE HUMANIST 14 (July/Aug. 1970); Byrn, *supra* note 5, at 396-399.

As to the difficulties of devising a meaningful due process *see* Kutner, *supra* note 169; Louisell, *supra* note 71, at 251; Comment, *The Hospital Abortion Committee as an Administrative Body of the State*, 10 J. FAM. L. 32 (1970).

accorded value independently of its mother, and even rights against her.[174] In large part the uncertainty arises from a multifaceted biomedical revolution[175] unsettling many cherished, but simple, notions about life upon which our values are based.[176] Emerging responses to other value uncertainties created by these innovations should, then, help settle the problem of when a foetus becomes a "person."

The most directly parallel problem has arisen with regard to death. When is a human being no longer to be valued as such? The question arises because artificial devices can keep heart and lungs operating potentially for years after all other important body functions have ceased. Further, as the heart and lungs can be revived after at least brief interruptions, pulse or breath hardly seem decisive criteria for separating human persons from human corpses.[177] A consensus appears to be emerging that "brain death" is the proper test for death.[178] That the capacity of the brain to function is taken as the test for human life is not surprising. There is general consensus through history that man's brain is what uniquely identifies him from other things—animate as well as inanimate. As the cortical tissue sustains the higher brain functions (both intellectual and artistic), it is the capacity of this portion of the brain which is most critical in determining the presence of a distinct human personality.[179]

---

174. *See* Raleigh-Fitkin Memorial Hospital v. Anderson, 42 N.J. 421, 201 A.2d. 537, *cert. den.* 377 U.S. 985 (1964), discussed in the text accompanying notes 150-151, *supra.*

175. For a simplified overview of these advances, *see* G. TAYLOR, THE BIOLOGICAL TIME BOMB (1968); A. TOFFLER, FUTURE SHOCK 185-218 (1970).

176. Tribe 19-21.

177. *The Day the Cadaver Coughed*, MEDICAL WORLD NEWS (April 12, 1974); Skegg, *Irreversibly Comatose Individuals: "Alive" or "Dead"?*, 33 CAMB. L. J. 130 (1974).

178. CALLAHAN 386-388. *See also A Definition of Irreversible Coma*, J. AM. MED. ASSOC. 205 (Aug. 10, 1968); Comment, *The Criteria for Determining Death in Vital Organ Transplants—A Medico-Legal Dilemma*, 38 MO. L. REV. 220 (1973). The tests for brain death are not entirely settled, generally running along these lines: a flat EEG for 24 hours; unresponsiveness to external stimuli; inability to spontaneously sustain vital functions; and a total lack of reflexes. *Cf.*, Hirsh, *Death: A Medical Status or Legal Definition*, 79, CASE & COMMENT 27, 29 (Oct. 1974). "Recent reports by a group of French investigators and a study at Northwestern University definitely indicate that a flat EEG is not even conclusive evidence of cerebral, 'brain' or 'actual' death. These doctors have shown that resuscitation is still possible under these circumstances in patients—an overdose of sedatives, tranquilizers or narcotics or hypothermia during the first six hours after the appearance of a flat EEG. The French group report that a flat EEG is not absolute evidence of death unless the spinal fluid also shows abnormal elevations of certain chemical enzymes (lactate dehydrogenases-type 5, other transaminases and alkaline phosphatase). Both of these studies cast an indelible shadow on the reliability of a flat EEG as the final and absolute evidence of death and its acceptance as such now appears to have been premature." Nevertheless, support for the flat EEG as a test for death has been growing. A California medical examiner recently allowed the heart of a shooting victim to be removed when the EEG went flat, and a jury in Virginia refused to hold several physicians acting under this test liable for medical negligence. Although most discussion of the problem is among physicians, it is, of course, another metalegal question, Skegg, *supra* note 177, at 132-134.

179. Should we sustain a body which spontaneously supports its vital functions (if it is fed, etc.), responds to tickling and other simple external stimuli, and shows reflexes, but whose cerebral cortex has been completely destroyed?

If the foregoing test is acceptable to determine the end point of a distinct human personality entitled to respect and value as such, it should be adequate to determine the beginning point of a distinct human personality entitled to respect and value as such. A comatose individual does not then interact with his fellow beings. The emerging test centers on the capacity to interact subsisting, though suspended, in the comatose person. A foetus with a functioning brain does not interact much more than the comatose person. But given proper care, fetal capacity to interact blossoms more certainly than the capacity of one in a coma. I therefore propose as a test incorporating these criteria the following:

> A person is an organism endowed with a human genotype and possessing at least a minimal capacity for psychological and cultural interaction as evidenced by a cerebrum capable of functioning.

This test would have several advantages. It combines the contradictory currents directly bearing on abortion in our own and world-wide traditions. The test does not accord recognition as a full person to the unformed conceptus[180] which so many have problems identifying with. At the same time the test accords value to the foetus before birth and at least would substantially restrict the reasons for destroying it after that point. The test comes close to conforming to Callahan's developmental test of humanness,[181] but avoids its dangers. Capacity for interaction, not the quality of interaction, is clearly identified as the measure of humanness. Further, this test, while undoubtedly needing refinement, would be equally applicable at both ends of life continuum. The test embodies the emerging response to the questions of when is there a human being, which has been provoked by the biomedical revolution.

This test has the advantages of the genetic school, without that theory's ambiguities. It is definite and certain. The test relies on an event as dramatic as conception or birth itself—the emergence of the human brain. Finally, the test is administratively feasible. One need only run an EEG on the abdominal wall of the mother to determine if there is cerebral activity.[182] One need not rely on crude guesswork.[183] In short, the test proposed here is sensitive to

---

180. Loewy, *supra* note 6, at 228, calls it a "benign uterine tumor." This test would clearly validate the "morning after" pill.

181. Quoted in the text, *supra* at note 164.

182. This occurs at about the eighth week of pregnancy, LILEY, *supra* note 160; Hellegers, *supra* note 161; Ramsey, *supra* note 161.

183. Guesswork bedevils both conception and viability as tests. Conception is a process, not an event, Brodie, *The New Biology and the Prenatal Child*, 9 J. FAM. L. 391, 397 (1970). Viability varies from 18 to 28 weeks depending on a host of variables, *id.* Similarly, any test which simply selects an arbitrary number of weeks of gestation can only be guesswork, as any prospective parent who has awaited a birth "due date" can testify. The *Wade* Court was bothered by this element of guesswork, and in effect cut the Gordian knot, 410 U.S. at 161; but birth is a process too! If anything, the test proposed here is more certain than any other.

our traditional determinations of humanness, current knowledge of gestational processes, and administrative feasibility.[184]

IV. What Is to Be Done?

By concluding without explanation that the foetus could be no more than potential life, the Court has come up with what appears to be a politically viable compromise. As in 1896[185] the Court has gained support by sacrificing invisible people.[186] A society is judged, however, by its treatment of its least vocal and least powerful members. In our society these invisible people have found in the Court their most reliable champion.[187] For an indefinite future foeti have lost this protector. Will future generations ponder these abortion decisions with the same incredulity with which many have come to view the segregation decisions?

How can one seek to revise the Court's decision? The Court is very unlikely to reverse itself.[188] Nor can one expect to achieve anything by advancing the interests of the unborn child through a guardian ad litem.[189]

---

184. The foregoing obviously does not purport to answer the even more vexing question of when, and for what reasons, fetal humans can be destroyed. Perhaps the desire to avoid the problem led the majority to seek to define away the problem without really exploring the relevant biological and ethical data. Surface consensus is lacking in our society, W. O'Neill, Coming Apart (1971), Toffler, *supra* note 175. This probably accounts for the Court's reluctance to come to grips with the issues, opting for a solution which appears to let each person judge individually without a reasoned elaboration of the basis for its decision. *Cf.* Hart, *supra* note 105, White, *The Evolution of Reasoned Elaboration: Jurisprudential Criticism and Social Change*, 59 Va. L. Rev. 279 (1973).

185. Plessy v. Ferguson, 163 U.S. 537 (1896).

186. R. Ellison, The Invisible Man (1951); Bordewich, *supra* note 159, at 16. If the metaphor describes the plight of blacks or women in some cultures, it is even more apt a description of foeti.

187. Why this should be so is suggested by Justice Stone in United States v. Caroline Products Co., 304 U.S. 144, 152 n.4 (1938). *See generally* Ball, *Judicial Protection of Powerless Minorities*, 59 Ia. L. Rev. 1059 (1974). The argument is developed at some length in the abortion context in Ely, *supra* note 3, at 933-935. Simply put, the argument is that the courts ought to protect groups with no access to the political processes. Rawls, *supra* note 78, bases his theory of justice on how the least advantaged are treated.

188. For those who naively dream of this, perhaps remembering West Virginia State Board of Education v. Barnette, 319 U.S. 624 (1943) and Minersville School District v. Gobitis, 310 U.S. 586 (1940), I can only reply by quoting Fitzgerald's Khayyam:

> The Moving Finger writes; and, having writ,
> Moves on: nor all your Piety nor Wit
>   Shall lure it back to cancel half a Line,
>   Nor all your Tears wash out a Word of it.

The Rubaiyat of Omar Khayyam, Qu. LXXI, p. 19 (E. Fitzgerald trans. 1898 ed.).

189. As supported by Byrn, *supra* note 6, at 851-852. It appears to make no difference whether this issue is raised by a guardian ad litem, as was done in Byrn v. New York City Health and Hospitals Corp., 31 N.Y.2d, 194, 286 N.E.2d 887, 335 N.Y.S.2d 390 (1970), *appeal dismissed* 410 U.S. 949, *reh. den.* 411 U.S. 940 (1973); or through the father under the civil rights acts, 42 U.S.C. § 1983 (1970) (civil action for deprivation of civil rights under color of state law); 42 U.S.C. § 1985(3) (1970) (conspiracy to deprive one of equal protection). A father might try to

Although foeti were not technically parties before the Court, their interests were fully argued by the parties and amici—with the state recognized as representative of foetal interests.[190] Some other avenues of litigation remain which could marginally affect the availability of abortion. Thus, although at the time no state was as permissive as the standards set forth in *Wade*, does this mean the statute in every state is entirely void?[191] If so, there is no law restricting abortions in any fashion pending enactment of a new law by a state incorporating those standards—or even less restrictive ones. Or should one conclude that the statutes ought to be construed as invalid only in so far as necessary to conform to *Wade*?[192] This would leave it to the legislatures to extend permissibility further if they so desire. Thus, differing views could lead to great differences in at least the final trimester of pregnancy.

Wade also raises question about the continuing validity of laws prohibiting the advertising abortion referral services or abortificients.[193] Others have raised the question whether the state must affirmatively provide abortions to those who want them.[194]

---

compel prosecution under 18 U.S.C. § 241 (1970) (conspiracy to deprive one of civil rights); or under 18 U.S.C. § (deprivation of rights under color of law). That a parent is able to proceed under these laws on behalf of the rights of his child, *see* Galindo v. Brownell, 255 F. Supp. 930 (S.D. Cal. 1966) (deceased child); Tyree v. Smith, 289 F. Supp. 174 (E.D. Tenn. 1968) (living child); Armstrong v. Board of Education of Birmingham, 220 F. Supp. 217 (N. D. Ala. 1963), *vac. in part on other grounds*, 353 F.2d 47 (5th Cir. 1964). If repeal of laws is sufficient state action if it results in encouragement to invidious discrimination, Reitman v. Mulkey, 387 U.S. 369, 378 (1967), why not here?

190. A Rhode Island statute declaring foeti people was struck down on the basis of *Wade*, Doe v. Israel, 482 F.2d. 156 (1st. Cir. 1973), *app. pend.*

191. Doe v. Rampton, 366 F. Supp. 189 (D. Utah), *vac.* 410 U.S. 950 (1973); Doe v. Turner, 361 F. Supp. 1288 (S.D. Iowa), *aff'd. as to other matter*, 488 F.2d 1134 (8th Cir. 1973); Doe v. Woodahl, 360 F. Supp. 20 (D. Mont. 1973); Commonwealth v. Page, 451 Pa. 331, 303 A.2d. 215 (1973); Doe v. Burk, 513 P.2d. 643 (Wyo. 1973); State v. Wahlrab, 19 Ariz. App. 552, 509 P.2d 245 (1973); Nelkson v. Planned Parenthood Center of Tucson, Inc., 19 Ariz. App. 142, 502 P.2d. 580 (1973); State v. Lawrence, 261 S.C. 18, 198 S.E.2d. 253 (1973); People v. Frey, 54 Ill. 2d. 28, 294 N.E.2d 257 (1973); State v. Hultgren, 295 Minn. 229, 204 N.W.2d. 197 (1973).

192. Henrie v. Darryberry, 358 F. Supp. 719 (N.D. Okla. 1973); People v. Bricker, 389 Mich. 524, 208 N.W.2d 172 (1973) (allowing prosecution of non-physician); State v. Ingel, 18 Md. App. 514, 308 A.2d 223 (1973); Spears v. State, 278 So. 2d 443 (Miss. 1973); Cheaney v. Indiana, — Ind. —, 285 N.E.2d 265 (1972), *cert. den.* 410 U.S. 991 (1973); State v. Haren, 124 N.J. Super. 475, 307 A.2d 644 (L. Div. 1973); May v. State, 254 Ark. 194, 492 S.W.2d 888 (1973), *cert. den.* 94 S. Ct 448 (1973).

193. State v. New Times, Inc., 20 Ariz. App. 183, 511 P.2d 196 (1973) (unconstitutional as part of an invalid statutory plan to prohibit abortions); *contra* Doe v. Burk, 513 P.2d 643 (Wyo. 1973); Bigelow v. Commonwealth, 214 Va. 341, 200 S.E.2d 680 (1973), *app. pend.* Such statutes also pose freedom of speech problems, Mitchell Family Planning, Inc. v. Royal Oak, 335 F. Supp. 738 (E.D. Mich. 1972); S.P.S. Consultants v. Lefkowitz, 333 F. Supp. 1370 (S.D.N.Y. 1971). *See also* LADER II *supra* note 13, at 163-164.

194. Tribe 42-50; Comment, *Abortion on Demand in a Post-Wade Context—Must the State Pay the Bills?*, 41 FORDHAM L. REV. 921 (1973); Szasz, *Medicine and the State: The First Amendment Violated*, THE HUMANIST 5 (Mar./Apr. 1973). The few cases approaching the issue in the context of abortion are: Doe v. Bellin Mem. Hosp., 479 F.2d 756 (5th Cir. 1973); Doe v. Hale Hosp., 369 F. Supp. 970 (D. Mass. 1974); Nyberg v. City of Virginia, Minnesota, 361 F. Supp. 932 (D. Minn. 1973). *But see* 42 U.S.C. § 300a-7 (1973 Supp.). *See generally*, Carey, A *Constitutional Right to Health Care: An Unlikely Development*, 23 CATH. U.L. REV. 492 (1974).

Interests of other parties might yet be raised. The Court expressly refrained from considering the rights of fathers or of minors.[195] Whether a father has any rights at all in the matter has been hotly debated.[196] Three courts have already concluded that he cannot prevent an abortion.[197] Yet if a father cannot compel a woman to accept the burdens of motherhood, it is arguable that a mother cannot force a man to accept the burdens of fatherhood.

A recent increase in solicitude for the rights even of unwed fathers,[198] can one say that fathers have no rights at any point? The rights of minors also cut both ways.[199] Should the parents control if the minor wants an abortion? If she wants the child? Finally, physicians have interests to be considered. Not only might a doctor refuse to perform abortions on grounds of conscience, but a doctor might still be prosecuted for performing abortions in bad faith—i.e., on some basis other than medical judgment.[200]

---

195. 410 U.S. at 165 n.67.

196. *Summarized in* CALLAHAN 465-467. *See also* Moore, *Abortion and Public Policy: What are the Issues?*, 17 N.Y. L. FORUM 411, 416-422 (1971).

197. Jones v. Smith, 278 So.2d 339 (Fla. App. 1973) (putative father); Coe v. Gerstein, 376 F. Supp. 695 (S.D. Fla. 1973) (husband); Coe v. District of Columbia Gen. Hosp., Ns. 1477-71 (D.D.C. 1972) (husband); only one court—a Canadian trial court—seems to have decided in favor of a father. Tribe 41 n.181. Is this an assertion of emotional immaculate conception? *See,* Roiphe, *Confessions of a Female Chauvinist Sow,* NEW YORK MAGAZINE 52-53 (Oct. 30, 1972).

Tribe, *supra* note 3, at 39-41 opposes any role for the father, as does Means, *supra* note 18 at 428-434. As Means' other arguments were heavily relied on by the Court in *Wade,* they merit some comment here. He cites two cases: O'Beirne v. Superior Court, 1 Civ. 25174 (Cal. Sup'r 1967); and Herko v. Uviler, 203 Misc. 108, 114 N.Y.S.2d 618 (Kings County, Sup. Ct. 1952). Both involved legal abortions, and apparently led to divorce. Neither case was argued on the basis of wrongful death, and both posed standing problems raising constitutional issues which were easily resolved under the circumstances in light of *Wade* and *Bolton.* Both cases rejected the father's right to prevent the abortion, but as a showing of imminent threat of death to the mother was made in each case, their value is limited. As most hospitals have up until now required the husband's consent, the dearth of pre-*Wade* cases should not be surprising, Comment, *The New York Abortion Reform Law—Considerations, Application and Legal Consequences More than We Bargained For?,* 35 ALB. L. REV. 644, 661 (1971). *Wade* itself contributes little of direct relevance. One post-*Wade* article carefully considered the problem at length concluding against paternal rights, Georgies, *Roe v. Wade: What Rights the Biological Father?,* 1 HAST. CONST. L.Q. 251 (1974). Ms. Georgies based her conclusion on the discredited distinction between maternal personal and paternal property rights, *id.* at 272, when the interests of both parents are an amalgam of personal and property rights.

Cf. Murray v. Vandevander, 522 P.2d 302 (Okla. App. 1974) (no action by husband against doctor for hysterectomy without husband's consent).

198. Stanley v. Illinois, 405 U.S. 645 (1972); State *ex rel.* Lewis v. Lutheran Social Services, 89 Wis. 2d 1, 207 N.W.2d 826 (1973).

199. *Compare* Doe v. Planned Parenthood Association, 29 Ut. 2d 356, 510 P.2d 75 (1973); *and in re* Smith, 16 Md. App. 209, 295 A.2d 238 (1972); *with* Pilpel & Zuckerman, *Abortion and the Rights of Minors,* in WALBERT, *supra* note 31, at 275, and Note, *The Minor's Right to Abortion and the Requirement of Parental Consent,* 60 VA. L. REV. 305 (1974).

200. A possibility expressly approved by the Court, 410 U.S. at 166. For an example of such a prosecution, *see* People v. Nixon, 42 Mich. App. 332, 201 N.W.2d 635 (1972). What if a State concludes that there are no medical indications except the imminent threat of maternal death? Apparently this is precluded by *Bolton,* 410 U.S. at 192. But is "best medical judgment," *id.* at 201, a stricter standard than "abuse of medical discretion," *id.* at 166? *See* note 35 *supra.*

Solutions to any of these problems would work no basic change in the way the Court has resolved the clash of interests. The question remains: what is to be done? If the Court will not reverse itself, it is up to the political branches to act. It is unlikely that there will be sufficient support for a consitutional amendment.[201] Nor can it be expected that two-thirds of a Congress comprised largely of the same people who enacted the Equal Rights Amendment (ERA) would approve any modification of *Wade* and *Bolton*. In the event they did, ratification by three-fourths of the states (a majority of which have already ratified the ERA) is inconceivable. Yet Congress could probably achieve a reversal of the decisions simply by enacting a statute defining foeti as persons once higher brain activity is detected. The statute would be an exercise of Congress' power to enforce the fourteenth amendment by appropriate legislation.[202] Such a statute might define both when life begins and when it ends. The Court would probably grant greater deference to Congress than to state legislatures—particularly as Congress is expressly given a major role to play in formulating and enforcing the policy of the fourteenth amendment.

Congressional power to act is not precluded by the Court's finding of no such power in the states. Congress is expressly given a coordinate, if not dominant, role in effectuating the fourteenth amendment. The states are not. Rather they are the objects which the fourteenth amendment sought to limit. *Roe v. Wade* thus should be seen as resting on a holding that states are not free to adopt a theory of personhood.[203] Such a power in the states could defeat the limitations set up by the amendment. This legislation must be corrective of the state action or inaction—it must require states to protect persons within their boundaries.[204] Once a particular understanding of personhood is required of all states,[205] the woman's right of privacy cannot override it—excepting for narrowly defined reasons and following a due process hearing.[206]

---

201. For analyses of legal and policy issues relating to the drafting of an amendment to overturn *Wade* and *Bolton. See* Byrn, *supra* note 5, at 392-406; Rice, *Overruling Roe v. Wade, supra* note 6, at 321-341. Such efforts seem futile under present political realities.

202. U.S. CONST., amend. XIV, § 5. In view of lower court actions, little would be achieved by simply restricting the Court's appellate jurisdiction, art. III, § 2—except as part of a larger enactment such as suggested here. *Cf.* Rice, *Overruling Roe v. Wade, supra* note 6, at 320. Tribe 10-15, is quite correct that proper role-allocation is critical in this case. Perhaps between the states and women, women should win. Congress is quite another matter. *See also* text accompanying notes 41-47, *supra*. And *see* Tribe 33-41.

203. 410 U.S. at 162.

204. United States v. Wheeler, 254 U.S. 281 (1920); Civil Rights Cases, 109 U.S. 3, 13 (1883); United States v. Harris, 106 U.S. 629 (1883).

205. Which would solve the apparent injustices created by variant state laws on abortion which seems to have troubled the Court, Roe v. Wade, 410 U.S. at 139-140; Doe v. Bolton, 410 U.S. at 200. *See also* Charles & Alexander, *supra*, note 120.

206. *Cf.* Furman v. Georgia, 408 U.S. 238 (1972). The right to an individualized impartial hearing has long been deemed essential to due process in both civil, Postal Telegraph Cable Co. v. Newport, 247 U.S. 464, 476 (1918); Baker v. Baker, E. & Co., 242 U.S. 394, 403 (1917);

Congress could not, of course, adopt a definition of persons without a rational foundation. But such a foundation exists here. Even if such a statute failed to pass, however, it would at least fully reopen debate in a proper forum. And debate rather than decision by official fiat[207] is essential to resolve such a basic moral issue as the existence of life.

Louisville & N.R.R. v. Schmidt, 177 U.S. 230, 236 (1900); and criminal proceedings, Cole v. Arkansas, 333 U.S. 196 (1948); Lisenba v. California, 314 U.S. 219, 236 (1941); Tumey v. Ohio, 273 U.S. 510 (1927); Moore v. Dempsey, 261 U.S. 86, 91 (1923).

207. The *Wade* Court's strange deference to the medical profession appears to be an instance of delegating a moral question to technical experts. *Cf.* Callahan, *supra* note 31. As we do not leave teachers to decide the propriety of prayer in public schools, why defer to doctors here over what is essentially a moral, not a medical, issue? *See* Louisell, *supra* note 71, at 246. Technocratic man's tendency to leave difficult questions to experts may work well for technical problems. For moral questions such compartmentalization can lead to disaster.

Capacity, Competence, Consent: Voluntary Sterilization of the Mentally Retarded

Gloria S. Neuwirth,* Phyllis A. Heisler & Kenneth S. Goldrich**

Sterilization is a surgical procedure which renders a person permanently incapable of reproduction. This procedure, requiring at most a short hospital stay, is medically both simple and safe. Neither sexual desire nor performance is affected. For these reasons sterilization is being utilized increasingly by individuals who desire no additional children.[1]

The right to sterilization as a contraceptive means for family planning purposes is now recognized in almost every state.[2] In the case of mentally retarded individuals sterilization has added significance. It can be used simply as a family planning device, an effective contraceptive for one who is incapable of rearing children or, more controversially, as a eugenic tool.

For the competent adult interested in being sterilized for family planning purposes, existing laws present few problems, if any. When the recipient of the sterilization is mentally retarded, however, many legal complications are presented. This paper will attempt to analyze the legal issues involved in sterilization of the mentally retarded individual.

In the absence of specific statutory provisions, legal liability for the performance of any medical treatment, including sterilization, is governed by common law principles. The common law has established that a physician must obtain a consent authorizing any medical treatment.[3] Lack of proper consent will render the physician liable for civil damages in tort.[4]

NOTE: The authors would like to thank Mr. Peter Ames and Ms. Katherine Bier for their valuable contribution to the preparation of this article.

* B.A., Hunter College; LL.B., Yale Law School; Ms. Neuwirth is a practicing attorney with a New York City law firm.

** Staff members, Columbia Human Rights Law Review.

1. Presser & Bumpass, *The Acceptability of Contraceptive Sterilization Among U.S. Couples: 1970*, 4 FAMILY PLANNING PERSPECTIVES 18 (Oct. 1972).

2. *Cf.* discussion on statutory material, *infra*.

3. Such consent is normally obtained directly from the patient, Wall v. Brim, 138 F.2d 478 (5th Cir. 1957). *But cf.* Lester v. Aetna Casualty & Surety Co., 240 F.2d 676 (5th Cir. 1967). There are instances when consent may properly be provided by someone other than the patient, such as substituted consent, Bonner v. Moran, 126 F.2d 121 (D.C. Cir. 1941); Darrah v. Kite, 32 App. Div.2d 208, 301 N.Y.S.2d 286 (1969); Tabor v. Scobee, 254 S.W.2d 474 (Ky. 1952). In an emergency situation consent is implied by law, Barfield v. South Highlands Infirmary, 191 Ala. 553, 68 So. 30 (1915); Jackovach v. Yocum, 212 Iowa 914, 237 N.W. 444 (1931).

4. Schloendorff v. Society of New York Hospitals, 211 N.Y. 125, 105 N.E. 92 (1914). Such

A determination of the essential elements of a proper consent is therefore the threshold issue in any discussion of the legal implications of the sterilization process. There are three elements to a valid consent. First, a consent must be voluntary.[5] A voluntary act "assumes an exercise of free will and clearly precludes the existence of coercion or force."[6] Second, a proper consent "entails a requirement that the individual have at his disposal the information necessary to make his decision."[7] This requirement necessitates a full disclosure by the physician of the purpose and effects of the procedure. In the case of sterilization, for example, the irreversibility of the technique would have to be underscored. In addition, there must be a description of any hazards which may be encountered.[8] Third, it is imperative that the person providing the consent have the mental competence to appreciate precisely what he is consenting to as well as the implications of such consent.[9]

Since the terms "legal capacity to consent" and "legal competence" are used often in this article, it would be helpful to distinguish between them. One is presumed to be legally competent until such time as he is adjudicated incompetent. Legal capacity to consent turns on the ability of a person to understand and appreciate the nature of a transaction at the time of assent. Competence and capacity are concepts which share similarities, but the presence of one need not imply the existence of the other. For example, as will be discussed below, a mentally retarded individual may possess legal competence to enter into a contract or a marriage, yet not have the legal capacity to understand and appreciate the nature of sterilization and will thus be estopped from consenting thereto.

Consent may take one of two forms. The first, "personal consent," requires the recipient himself to make the authorization personally. The second, "substituted consent," allows another party to provide the authorization on behalf of the recipient. Substituted consent is used when the recipient is incapable of providing personal consent.

The first part of this paper will attempt to answer two questions: 1—Under what circumstances, if any, may a mentally retarded individual be capable of providing personal consent authorizing a sterilization? 2—Under what circumstances, if any, can parents, a guardian, a committee of the person, or the courts, provide substituted consent authorizing the sterilization of a mentally retarded individual? The second part of the article presents an analysis of key sections of the Model Voluntary Sterilization Act.

---

liability arises even if the medical treatment is beneficial and is skillfully performed, Zoski v. Gaines, 272 Mich. 1, 260 N.W. 99 (1936); Rogers v. Sells, 178 Okla. 103, 61 P.2d 1018 (1936); Moss v. Rishworth, 222 S.W. 225 (Tex. Comm'n. App. 1920).

5. True v. Older, 227 Minn. 154, 34 N.W.2d 700, 701 (1948).
6. Relf v. Weinberger, 372 F. Supp. 1196, 1202 (D.D.C. 1974).
7. *Id.*
8. *Id.*
9. *Id.*

I.   Consent and the Individual

Whether a mentally retarded person is capable of providing personal consent for a sterilization will depend initially on his ability to comprehend the consequences of the consent. Terms such as "mental retardation" or "mental disability" are imprecise, and therefore no universally applicable statement can be made as to the legal ability of mentally retarded individuals in general to provide consent for a sterilization. Some mentally retarded persons may have such an ability while others may not. The courts are the final arbiters of the legal capacity of an individual. Courts are usually unwilling to consider any person incompetent for all purposes, and therefore any finding of legal competence or incompetence will only be made with respect to matters before the court at the time of adjudication.[10]

There are relatively few cases dealing with consent to sterilization, so it will be necessary to consider precedents in related areas. In *Wyatt v. Stickney*,[11] a class action was initiated on behalf of patients confined in Alabama state mental hospitals. The plaintiffs' major contention was that lack of adequate care for involuntarily hospitalized patients was unconstitutional. The court agreed, holding that:

> The purpose of involuntary hospitalization for treatment purposes is *treatment* and not mere custodial care or punishment. This is the only justification, from a constitutional standpoint that allows civil commitments to mental institutions. . . . To deprive any citizen of his or her liberty upon the altruistic theory that the confinement is for humane therapeutic reasons and then fail to provide adequate treatment violates the very fundamentals of due process.[12]

The institutions were given six months within which to implement a treatment program satisfying minimum medical and constitutional requirements.[13] They failed to do so, and the court, in two related opinions, formulated certain minimum standards for the treatment of institutionalized patients.[14]

The patients confined to the defendant institutions were not "borderline" or "mildly retarded" cases; rather, they were individuals who were functioning at least three standard deviations below the mean on a standardized intelligence test.[15] The patients, according to the court, had "a right not

---

10. *Cf.* Hsu v. Zion Hospital, 259 Cal. App.2d 562, 66 Cal. Rptr. 659 (1968); Swift & Co. v. Smigel, 115 N.J. Super. 391, 279 A.2d 895 (L. Div. 1971)) *In re* Lambert, 33 N.J. Super. 90, 109 A.2d 423 (L. Div. 1954). *But cf.* People *ex rel.* Hrohsahl v. Strosahl, 221 App. Div. 86, 222 N.Y.S. 319 (1927).

11. 325 F. Supp. 781 (M.D. Ala. 1971).

12. *Id.* at 784-785.

13. *Id.* at 785-786.

14. Wyatt v. Stickney, 344 F. Supp. 373, 387 (M.D. Ala. 1972).

15. 344 F. Supp. at 396. The individuals referred to have an I.Q. below 70. The people

to be subjected to experimental research or any unusual or hazardous treatment procedures" without the express and informed consent of the resident, if the resident is able to give such consent, and of his guardian or next of kin, after opportunities for consultation with independent specialists and legal counsel.

With reference to sterilization for an involuntarily hospitalized patient, the implications of *Wyatt v. Stickney* seem to be that if sterilization would contribute to the habilitation of the patient, then he has a right to the operation. Of course, it must be ascertained in such a situation that some less drastic form of contraception is not feasible. If there is an alternative satisfactory contraceptive method, it should be utilized.

In regard to both institutionalized and non-institutionalized mentally retarded individuals, *Wyatt v. Stickney* endorses the view that such persons may have the capacity to consent to unusual or hazardous treatment.[16] Nevertheless, it should be noted that as a protective device, the court required an additional consent by a guardian or next of kin.[17] Furthermore, *Wyatt v. Stickney* declares that in the case of any surgical procedure "which is undertaken for reasons other than therapeutic benefit" to the retarded patient, there must be a court order in addition to personal consent.[18] The *Wyatt* approach permits one to argue that sterilization for the purpose of contraception is therapeutic—i.e., contributive to the rehabilitation and overall health of the mentally retarded patient[19]—and that therefore only a patient's consent is necessary. However usually there are other reasons besides therapy for sterilization of a retarded person. The frequent presence of non-therapeutic reasons appears to limit the precedential value of *Wyatt* in the area of consent by the retarded to sterilization.

In another related area, a mentally retarded mother was found to have the capacity to consent to the surrender of her child for adoption.[20] In this case it was determined that the mother, possessing an I.Q. of sixty, understood precisely what she was doing. She was not in "such a state of insanity" as to render her "incapable of transacting the business."[21] This situation is somewhat analogous to a sterilization, which is a surrender of the opportunity to have children. However, sterilization is of course more serious in that it forecloses future conception.

Mentally retarded persons have been found capable of possessing sufficient intelligence and comprehension to provide informed and legally

---

comprising this group represent approximately the lowest two or three per cent of the general population.

16. *Id.* at 401-402.

17. *Id.*

18. *Id.* at 407.

19. *Cf. In re* Cavitt, 182 Neb. 712, 717, 157 N.W.2d 171, 175-176 (1968), *aff'd. on rehearing*, 183 Neb. 243, 159 N.W.2d 566, *appeal dismissed*, 396 U.S. 996 (1970).

20. *In re* Surrender of Minor Children, 344 Mass. 230, 181 N.E.2d 836 (1962).

21. *Id.*

binding consent to marriage,[22] sexual intercourse (which in the absence of such consent would be rape),[23] and contracts.[24]

The rights of marriage and sexual intercourse are closely related to the right to sterilization. In slightly different contexts each has an effect on the basic human right to procreate or not to procreate. The fact that a mentally retarded person may have the capacity to consent to marriage or sexual intercourse suggests that he understands the implications of those relationships, including procreation. It follows that an individual who comprehends and appreciates the act of procreation and has the capacity to consent thereto can comprehend, appreciate and knowingly consent to sterilization.

Sterilization is an exercise of the right not to procreate. In *Griswold v. Connecticut* the Supreme Court held that married persons had a right to receive contraceptives and contraceptive information.[25] This was an exercise of the right not to procreate which falls within the protected area of privacy surrounding the marital relationship.[26]

Griswold and other Supreme Court decisions in the area of privacy lend strong support to the view that if a mentally retarded person has the capacity to understand and appreciate the act of sterilization, he should be allowed to exercise his right not to procreate. However, the irreversibility of sterilization distinguishes it from choices such as marriage or contraception, and ascertaining whether the requisite capacity to understand exists is more complicated. For it must be clear that an individual comprehends not only that sterilization involves a decision not to procreate, but also that this decision is one from which there is no retreat.

In addition to the issue of comprehension, the issue of voluntariness is also of crucial importance when dealing with personal consent by a mentally retarded individual to sterilization. Both relatives and the state may have an interest in persuading a mentally retarded individual to undergo a sterilization, particularly in the case of a mentally retarded woman. Quite possibly such a person will be subjected to undue influence, coercion or force, by interested parties. In *Relf v. Weinberger*,[27] Federal District Judge Gerhard Gesell found that threats ·were made against mentally retarded women to

22. Mere weakness of intellect is not sufficient to invalidate a marriage if the parties are capable of comprehending the subject of the contract, its nature and probable consequence, Wilson v. Mitchell, 10 Misc.2d 559, 169 N.Y.S.2d 249 (Sup. Ct. 1957); Ertel v. Ertel, 313 Ill. App. 326, 40 N.E.2d 85 (1942); Naylor v. Naylor, 109 N.J. Eq. 603, 158 A. 432 (Chanc. 1932).

23. The court held that "the degree of intelligence necessary to give legal consent may exist with an impaired and feeble intellect . . . ," Hacker v. State, 73 Okla. 119, 120, 118 P.2d 408, 412 (1941).

24. Peterson v. Ellebrecht, 205 Cal. App.2d 718, 23 Cal. Rptr. 349 (1962); Hsu v. Mt. Zion Hospital, 259 Cal. App.2d 562, 66 Cal. Rptr. 659 (1968); In re Lambert, 33 N.J. Super. 90, 109 A.2d 423 (L. Div. 1954); Jewish Child Care Ass'n. of New York v. Mattfolk, 36 App. Div.2d 122, 318 N.Y.S.2d 947 (1971); Casebier v. Casebier, 193 Ky. 490, 236 S.W. 966 (1921).

25. 381 U.S. 479 (1965).

26. *Id*. at 485-486.

27. 372 F. Supp. 1196, 1202 (D.D.C. 1974).

induce them to consent to sterilization. These threats included the removal of benefits from federally funded poverty programs—benefits to which the individuals concerned had a legal right.[28] The existence of coercion and force precludes the exercise of the free will (i.e., voluntariness) necessary for proper consent.

In the above discussion it has been assumed that the mentally retarded individual is an adult. A minor, merely because of age, legally may be incompetent to provide consent to medical treatment. However, a minor in some states may be competent legally to consent to medical care without parental knowledge or approval. If "emancipated" a minor may be competent to consent to a vasectomy,[29] birth control services,[30] or other medical care.[31] Some courts follow this "mature minor doctrine," i.e., that a minor can effectively consent to medical treatment if it is for his benefit.[32] When the minor is mentally deficient, the situation is complicated by the dual incompetence of age and mental disability.

However, it is clear that mental retardation does not necessarily prevent a person from providing competent consent to a sterilization. There are mentally deficient persons who can and do comprehend the act of sterilization, including its consequences and effects. To determine whether such comprehension exists, physicians often use the "functional test," which indicates the extent to which a given individual functions within society. Factors considered include work experience as well as family and peer group relationships. If an individual, though retarded, can function within society, he is assumed to understand the implications of his acts and would not have his competence questioned by a physician.[33] Others, whose competence is questioned initially, may later be found capable of providing consent after review by a committee in a procedure such as that described below. Such individuals should not be deprived of the opportunity to exercise or withold their consent, either by the use of substituted consent, or by the removal of the opportunity to be sterilized. However, the realization that sterilization is permanent, that it involves a fundamental human right, and that the retarded

---

28. *Id.*

29. Smith v. Seibly, 72 Wash.2d 16, 431 P.2d 719 (1967).

30. *In re* P.J., 101 Daily Wash. Law Rptr. 613 (D.C. Super. Ct. 1973). The court ordered an abortion to be performed on a seventeen year-old girl who had been previously adjudicated a person in need of supervision. Respondent girl wanted the abortion, but her mother opposed it on religious grounds. The decision is based on several grounds, the most important being the constitutional right to abortion, and the respondent's status of "quasi-emancipation."

31. Bach v. Long Island Jewish Hospital, 49 Misc.2d 207, 267 N.Y.S.2d 289 (Sup. Ct. 1966).

32. Younts v. St. Francis Hospital, 205 Kan. 292, 469 P.2d 330 (1970); Lacey v. Laird, 166 Ohio 12, 139 N.E.2d 25 (1956).

33. This information was provided to the authors in the course of an interview conducted in November 1974 with Dr. Linda D. Lewis, Chief, Neurology Clinic, Columbia-Presbyterian Medical Center. The authors wish to express their appreciation to Dr. Lewis for her invaluable time and assistance.

potential recipient is highly susceptible to undue influence compels the conclusion that adequate protection for the rights of those incapable of consent can only be preserved and protected by requiring a court order, or at least committee review, in addition to personal consent.

II. SUBSTITUTED CONSENT

A. *The Parent*

The general rule is that parental consent is sufficient to authorize medical treatment for a minor child because the treatment is presumed to be potentially beneficial to the child. Although this rule does not apply to a normal adult child, the cases are split as to whether this rule can apply to parental consent for a mentally retarded adult child. In 1963, the New York Appellate Division held that a father was authorized to consent to the use of shock therapy for a mentally ill child who had reached majority age.[34] This finding was made despite the fact that the recipient of the treatment had not been adjudicated an incompetent.[35] The New York court reasoned that since a parent may consent to the performance of an operation on a minor child, the parent may also "speak on behalf of a mentally ill adult child for whom no committee of the person has been appointed."[36] In 1968, the Kentucky Court of Appeals held that a lower court had no power to authorize sterilization of a mentally retarded adult.[37] The court reasoned, "[n]or, at her age, does the law give her parents any control of her person or property," thereby depriving her parents of the power to provide substituted consent.[38]

If the New York decision is adhered to, the law regarding parental consent in the case of a minor child (discussed below) will be applicable to the mentally retarded adult as well. If, however, the Kentucky decision is followed, parents who wish to have their mentally retarded adult sons and daughters sterilized will have to petition proper authorities.

Parental capacity to consent to medical treatment for a normal child is broad, but not unlimited. A parent may not prevent medical treatment necessary to save the life or protect the health of a child by witholding consent.[39] In such cases courts have ordered medical treatment over the objections of the parent,[40] though if there is an honest question as to the

---

34. Anonymous v. State, 17 App. Div.2d 495, 497, 236 N.Y.S.2d 88, 90 (1963).
35. *Id.*
36. *Id.*
37. Holmes v. Powers, 439 S.W.2d 579 (Ky. 1968).
38. *Id.* at 580.
39. *In re* Vasko, 238 App. Div. 128, 129, 263 N.Y.S. 552, 553-554 (1934); Mitchell v. Davis, 205 S.W.2d 812 (Tex. Civ. App. 1947); Morrison v. State, 252 S.W.2d 97, 100 (Mo. Ct. App. 1952).
40. Morrison v. State, 252 S.W.2d 97, 100 (Mo. Ct. App. 1952).

efficacy of a proposed treatment and the exercise of discretion is called for, "the opinion of the parents shall not be lightly overridden."[41]

Another limit is that a parent may not consent to hazardous or unusual medical treatment for a child, unless there is a clear benefit to the child.[42] This situation arises most often where there are two siblings in a family, one ill and the other healthy, and the ill child can be aided by a transplant or skin graft from the healthy child. In these cases the courts attempt to balance the potential benefits to the ill child against the potential danger to the healthy child,[43] as well as the latter's attitude, ability to comprehend and potential capacity to consent to the procedure.[44]

The above rules were formulated with regard to a normal child. In the case of a retarded minor child, there arises the issue of dual incompetence. Logic compels that a parent may consent to medical care for a retarded child if such consent would be sufficient for treatment of a normal child. In the case of a normal child, it appears that parental consent to sterilization would not be sufficient to authorize the procedure. There is no benefit conferred upon the child, and the child would be deprived of a basic human right. In the case of a retarded child, however, sterilization may be beneficial both physically and emotionally.

No case has been found where a parent's informed consent to sterilization of a retarded minor has been challenged. There is dicta in a 1968 Kentucky decision which implies that parents of a retarded minor might furnish a legally effective consent to a mentally retarded minor child's sterilization.[45] However, a 1943 opinion by the New York Attorney General reaches the opposite conclusion.[46] The opinion states that a mentally deficient minor may not be legally sterilized on the application of the parents unless the operation is "for the health of the individual," although the particularly tender age of the child involved (twelve) may have influenced the decision.[47] It is unclear whether the opinion referred solely to physical health, not mental health, but there is language in the opinion which suggests such an inference,[48] thus reflecting New York's long-standing disapprobation of eugenic sterilization.[49] New York courts have yet to consider whether sterilization of mentally retarded individuals for the purpose of family planning is permissible.

---

41. *Id.* at 102.

42. Masden v. Harrison, No. 68651 Eq. (Mass. Sup. Jud. Ct. 1957).

43. *Id.*

44. *Id.*

45. Holmes v. Powers, 439 S.W.2d 579 (Ky. 1968).

46. 1943 Opinion New York Attorney General 336.

47. *Id.*

48. The opinion states that the sterilization "should be approached with extreme caution and permitted only when it clearly appears that sterilization is indicated as a *proper medical measure* for the protection of the health of the individual" (emphasis added).

49. *Cf.* Osborn v. Thompson, 103 Misc. 23, 169 N.Y.S. 638 (Sup. Ct. 1917), *aff'd*, 185 App. Div. 902, 171 N.Y.S. 1094 (1918).

There does appear to be one major problem in granting to parents the capacity to provide a substituted consent for the sterilization of a mentally retarded child, whether minor or adult. The interests of the parent and child vis-a-vis sterilization may not be congruent. In fact, it is likely that their interests may be directly opposed. A parent may genuinely believe that the mentally retarded individual cannot bear the emotional and physical strain of raising children. There may be concern, rational or irrational, that uncontrolled promiscuity will lead to an unwanted pregnancy. However, more self-interested concerns might prompt parental consent, such as fear that any offspring born to a mentally retarded child will eventually become the responsibility of the retarded person's parents. In order to "simplify" everyone's life, especially their own, parents may consent to a sterilization for the mentally retarded child. A human right as basic as procreation cannot be taken from a person because of another's selfish interests. For this reason, it is recommended that a parent's substituted consent to authorize a sterilization for a mentally retarded child be supplemented by a court order granted on the basis of committee recommendation following a hearing in which the child is represented by legal counsel. This will help insure that the decision has been made solely for the benefit of the mentally retarded child.

B.   *The Guardian*

In every state statutory system, a guardian may be appointed to manage the person and/or property of judicially determined incompetents. The appointment of a guardian with full legal power to deal with the incompetent's property insures the validity of the incompetent's otherwise void or voidable transactions,[50] but it also carries with it the stigma of legal incompetence which may lead to the conclusive determination of incapacity to contract, convey property,[51] make wills,[52] institute suit,[53] vote and hold public office.[54]

The emphasis given to the commercial aspects of guardianship may be contrasted with the absence of any substantial body of data concerning guardianship of the person.[55] There are no specifications in any jurisdiction as to the duties of such guardians and little supervision of them following their appointment.[56] Decisions concerning the ward's capacity to enter into noncommercial transactions such as marriage, divorce, adoption, medical treatment, sterilization and abortion remain unclear.

---

50. R. ALLEN, E. FERSTER & H. WEIHOFEN, MENTAL IMPAIRMENT AND LEGAL INCOMPETENCY 71 (1961) [hereinafter cited as ALLEN].
51. *Id.* at 260.
52. *Id.* at 283.
53. *Id.* at 295.
54. *Id.* at 365.
55. *Id.* at 367.
56. *Id.* at 247.

In the absence of statutory authority, a guardian may not consent to the adoption of his ward's children[57] nor may he institute divorce proceedings on behalf of an incompetent ward.[58] Consistent with this limited view of a guardian's authority is *Frazier v. Levi*,[59] which held that, absent statutory authorization by either the Texas Constitution or the Probate Code, the court had no power to approve or order the sterilization of a retarded woman on the application of her guardian. The rationale of this view seems to be that the general authority conferred upon the guardian to conduct the ward's commercial transactions does not extend to the nebulous realm of inherently personal consensual acts.

C.   *Court-Ordered Substitute Consent*

Generally, only where sizable property or substantial sums of money are involved do interested parties have enough incentive to go to court to have a person adjudged incompetent and a guardian appointed. Thus, those mentally retarded individuals without appointed guardians live in a kind of legal limbo; the issue of their capacity to consent arises only when challenged in a particular circumstance—as, for example, when a private physician questions the validity of consent to a prospective sterilization by either the retarded individual or his or her parents. In this situation, courts have authorized medical or rehabilitative care for incompetents under the doctrine of "parens patriae" which asserts the state's sovereign power of guardianship over persons possessing a disability.[60] However, recent decisions have questioned the authority of a court, acting as guardian of a retarded adult, to order or approve sterilization in the absence of express statutory provision. That such authorization must be explicit was affirmed in a 1971 Ohio case, *Wade v. Bethesda Hospital*,[61] in which the federal district court ruled that statutes giving a probate judge power to provide for the "supervision, care and maintenance" of a retarded person did not establish jurisdiction to order sterilization. The court held the probate judge civilly liable for a sterilization he had ordered, noting that he had acted "wholly without jurisdiction in this matter."[62]

To insure greater protection of the retarded individual's rights in court-ordered sterilization proceedings, such experts in the field as the

---

57. Baker v. Thomas, 272 Ky. 695, 114 S.W.2d 1113 (1938).

58. ALLEN, *supra* note 50, at 297.

59. 440 S.W.2d 393 (Tex. Civ. App. 1969).

60. Strunk v. Strunk, 445 S.W.2d 145 (Ky. App. 1969). It should be noted that New York, among other states, has enacted legislation providing for the appointment of a type of guardian to manage the affairs of a retarded without requiring that the retarded be adjudicated an incompetent. Called a "conservator," the appointment of this individual is preferred by New York law to the naming of a guardian. MENTAL HYGIENE LAW § 77 (McKinney Supp. 1974).

61. 337 F. Supp. 671 (S.D. Ohio, 1971).

62. *Id.* at 674.

International Project of the Association for Voluntary Sterilization (AVS) have suggested the appointment of a disinterested committee to review and supply substituted consent to applications for sterilization of the mentally incompetent. The AVS's suggested board would be composed of five persons, including lay and professional members of both sexes as well as a representative of the ethnic, religious or philosophical group of the prospective recipient.[63]

A review committee device similar to that suggested by AVS is incorporated in the detailed guidelines designed to insure the voluntariness of consent to sterilization by residents of Alabama state mental institutions. However, these guidelines, as enunciated by Federal District Court Judge Frank M. Johnson in *Wyatt v. Aderholt*,[64] further stipulate that the committee may not approve the proposed sterilization unless it can affirmatively determine that the inmate "has formed, without coercion, a genuine desire to be sterilized."[65]

The necessity of securing the uncoerced consent of the prospective patient has been emphasized in a 1974 District of Columbia case, *Relf v. Weinberger*,[66] which held that federal funds could not be authorized for sterilization procedures under guidelines which allowed a review committee to sanction the operation without requiring the personal consent of the incompetent. Judge Gerhard Gesell found that the notion of voluntary consent, "at least when important human rights are at stake, entails a requirement that the individual have at his disposal the information necessary to make his decision and the mental competence to appreciate the significance of that information. . . .No person who is mentally incompetent can meet these standards, nor can the consent of a representative, however sufficient under state law, impute voluntariness to the individual actually undergoing irreversible sterilization."[67]

D. *State Legislation Dealing with Substitute Consent*

From the above discussion it should be clear that, absent express statutory authorization, the retarded individual and his parents or legal guardian face great difficulty in securing sterilization from hesitant doctors and hospitals. A requirement of "voluntariness," while admirable as a means of protecting the retarded individual from a coerced sterilization, frequently has the effect of frustrating a legitimate desire of the parents or patient to

63. ADVANCES IN VOLUNTARY STERILIZATION-PROCEEDINGS OF THE SECOND INTERNATIONAL CONFERENCE ON VOLUNTARY STERILIZATION 275 (M. Schima, I. Lubell, J. Davis & E. Connell ed. 1974).
64. Civ. No. 3195-N (B) (M.D. Ala., Dec. 20, 1973).
65. Civ. No. 3195-N (B) (M.D. Ala., Jan. 8, 1974).
66. 372 F. Supp. 1196 (D.D.C. 1974).
67. *Id.* at 1202.

consent to an operation which would improve the retarded individual's chances of functioning within the community.

At present the need for suitable statutes and guidelines to make sterilization available to those mentally retarded capable of requesting it has not been met. The great majority of the state statutes dealing with sterilization focus not on providing guidelines to protect the adequacy of consent by retarded individuals to contraceptive sterilization but rather establish procedures whereby the institutionalized incompetent can be eugenically sterilized upon the fulfillment of minimal substituted consent requirements.

Twenty-one states presently have statutes which either require or permit involuntary sterilization of mental incompetents.[68] These laws were products of the late nineteenth century interest in the new sciences of eugenics and genetics and were based on the premise that mental illness was an inherited deficiency or weakness;[69] the statutes provided for sterilization of the mentally deficient, the mentally ill, habitual criminals, epileptics and other so-called social misfits, all of whom were grouped into broad, ill-defined categories.[70] Prior to the 1927 Supreme Court ruling in *Buck v. Bell*,[71] all statutes which had applied eugenic sterilization laws to the institutionalized incompetent had been declared unconstitutional.[72]

In *Buck v. Bell* the Court found adequate procedural safeguards in a Virginia statute requiring notice, hearing and appeal to uphold the constitutionality of the involuntary sterilization thereunder of an eighteen-year-old inmate of a mental institution. Justice Holmes found such regulation within the police power of the state, noting that "the principle that sustains compulsory vaccination is broad enough to cover cutting the Fallopian tubes."[73]

Since the decision in *Buck*, three state sterilization statutes have been

---

68. ARK. STAT. ANN. §§ 59-101 to 502 (1947); CAL. WELFARE & INST. CODE § 7254 (West 1966); CONN. GEN. STAT. ANN. §§ 17-19 (1958); DEL. CODE ANN. tit. 16 §§ 5701 to 5705 (1953); GA. CODE ANN. §§ 84-931 to 936 (Supp. 1974); IOWA CODE ANN. §§ 145.1 to 145.22 (1966); ME. REV. STAT. ANN. tit. 34 §§ 2461 to 2468 (1964); MICH. COMP. LAWS. §§ 720.301 to 10 (1948); MINN. STAT. ANN. §§ 256.07 to .08 (1965); MISS. CODE ANN. 41-45-1 to 19 (1972); MONT. REV. CODE ANN. §§ 69-6401 to 6 (1947), *as amended* (Supp. 1974); N.H. REV. STAT. ANN. §§ 174.1 to 14 (1970); N.C. GEN. STAT. §§ 35-36 to 57 (1966), *as amended* (Supp. 1973); OKLA. STAT. tit. 43A § 341-6 (1967); ORE. REV. STAT. §§ 436.025 to 110 (1971); S.C. CODE ANN. §§ 32-671 to 680 (1962); UTAH CODE ANN. 64-10-1 to 14 (1953); VT. STAT. ANN. tit. 18 §§ 8701 to 4 (1957); VA. CODE ANN. §§ 37.1-156 to 171 (1950), W. VA. CODE ANN. §§ 16-10-1 to 7 (1966); WIS. STAT. ANN. tit. 7 § 46.12 (1963).

69. Pate & Plant, *Sterilization of Mental Defectives*, 3 CUMBERLAND-SAMFORD L. REV. 458 (1972).

70. Paul, *State Eugenic Sterilization History*, in EUGENIC STERILIZATION (J. Robitscher ed. 1973).

71. 274 U.S. 200 (1927).

72. Williams v. Smith, 190 Ind. 526, 131 N.E. 2 (1921); Haynes v. Lapeer, 201 Mich. 138, 166 N.W. 938 (1918); Smith v. Bd. of Examiners, 85 N.J.L. 46, 88 A. 963 (1913); Osborn v. Thompson, 103 Misc. 23, 169 N.Y.S. 638 (Sup. Ct. 1918).

73. 274 U.S. 200, 207 (1927).

struck down, but the unconstitutionality of these laws was based on procedural deficiencies rather than the substantive issues determined.[74]

The only sterilization case considered by the Supreme Court subsequent to *Buck* involved an Oklahoma statute which provided for sterilization of habitual criminals. This law was held unconstitutional on the grounds that its exclusion of persons convicted for violations of prohibition laws, revenue acts, embezzlement or political offenses violated the constitutional prohibition against class legislation.[75]

Thus, the precise issue involved in *Buck v. Bell* has not been reargued. This has led some writers to suggest the possibility of a Supreme Court reversal were the question to be raised with respect to another eugenic sterilization law.[76]

E.   *Statutory Provisions*

All the sterilization laws provide for sterilization of institutionalized persons, but only nine of the statutes deal with the non-institutionalized mentally deficient as well.[77] Sterilization proceedings may be initiated by application of the superintendent of the institution in which the incompetent is confined,[78] by report from a member of a eugenics board[79] or on the petition of a physician, guardian, relative or public agency.[80] Grounds for a sterilization order vary from state to state, but typically they are vague and include the following requirements: "that according to the law of heredity the subject is the potential parent of socially inadequate children who would be likewise afflicted,"[81] that "procreation of the subject is deemed inadvisable,"[82]

74. *In re* Opinion of the Justices, 230 Ala. 543, 162 So. 123 (1935); Brewer v. Valk, 204 N.C. 186, 167 S.E. 638 (1933); *In re* Hendrickson, 12 Wash. 2d 600, 123 P.2d 322 (1942).

75. Skinner v. Oklahoma, 316 U.S. 535 (1942).

76. Ferster, *Eliminating the Unfit—Is Sterilization the Answer?*, 27 OHIO ST. L.J. 591, 596 (1966) [hereinafter cited as Ferster].

77. ARK. STAT. ANN. § 59-502 (1947); DEL. CODE ANN. tit. 16 § 5702 (1953); GA. CODE ANN. § 84-933 (Supp. 1974); IOWA CODE ANN. § 145.2 (1966); ME. REV. STAT. ANN. tit. 34 § 2461 (1964); MONT. REV. CODE ANN. § 69-6403 (Supp. 1974); N.C. GEN. STAT. § 35-37 (Supp. 1973); ORE. REV. STAT. § 436.025 (1971); VT. STAT. ANN. tit. 18 § 8702 (1957).

78. CAL. WELFARE & INST. CODE § 7254 (West 1966); CONN. GEN. STAT. ANN. § 17-19 (1958); ME. REV. STAT. ANN. tit. 34 § 2461 (1964); MICH. COMP. LAWS § 720.305 (1948); MINN. STAT. ANN. § 256.07 (1965); N.H. REV. STAT. ANN. § 174.1 (1970); N.C. GEN. STAT. § 35-36 (Supp. 1973); OKLA. STAT. tit. 43A § 341 (1967); S.C. CODE ANN. § 32-67; (1962); UTAH CODE ANN. § 64-10-1 (1953); VA. CODE ANN. § 37.1-156 (1950); W. VA. CODE ANN. § 16-10-1 (1966).

79. IOWA CODE ANN. § 145.2 (1966).

80. ARK. STAT. ANN. § 59-501 (1947); DEL. CODE ANN. tit. 16 § 5701 (1953); GA. CODE ANN. § 84-933 (c) (i) (Supp. 1974); ORE. REV. STAT. § 436.025 (1971); VT. STAT. ANN. tit. 18 § 8702 (1957); WIS. STAT. ANN. tit. 7 § 46.12 (1963).

81. MISS. CODE ANN. § 41-45-1 (1972); N.H. REV. STAT. ANN. § 174.1 (1970); OKLA. STAT. tit. 43A § 341 (1967); S.C. CODE ANN. § 32-671 (1962); UTAH CODE ANN. § 64-10-1 (1953); VA. CODE ANN. § 37.1-156 (1950); W. VA. CODE ANN. § 16-10-1 (1966).

82. DEL. CODE ANN. tit. 16 § 5701 (1953); WIS. STAT. ANN. tit. 7 § 46.12 (1963).

that procreation would produce children with an inherited tendency to certain named conditions or that the physical and/or mental condition of the patient would be improved by the operation,[83] that the subject "is afflicted with a mental disease which is likely to be inherited,"[84] that sterilization is "in the best interest of the mental, moral and physical improvement of the patient or the public good,"[85] or that the subject cannot provide care or support for prospective children.[86]

All the statutes require that notice be given to the person who is to be sterilized as well as to his or her relatives or guardian. Most provide for a pre-sterilization hearing before an administrative agency or court from which an appeal can be taken;[87] all require some form of consensual validation before the operation may be performed.[88]

The consent mechanism takes various forms in different states; in Minnesota, the Commissioner of Public Welfare, as the "legal guardian" of feebleminded persons may give his consent to a sterilization if no spouse or close relative of the patient can be found.[89] Connecticut law permits consent by the trustees of the institution where the mental patient is confined if the patient has no next of kin or guardian.[90] In Georgia, mental incompetents may be sterilized after an adjudication that the individual's condition is "irreversible and incurable" with the written consent of parents or a court-appointed guardian ad litem and approval by a committee of the hospital where the operation is to be performed.[91]

Several statutes which allow consent by patient, parent, guardian or next of kin also provide for administrative or judicial proceedings to override

83. CONN. GEN. STAT. ANN. § 17-19 (1958); IOWA CODE ANN. § 145.9 (1966); ME. REV. STAT. ANN. tit 34 § 2463 (1964); MICH. COMP. LAWS. § 720.306 (1948); ORE. REV. STAT. § 436.070 (1971); VT. STAT. ANN. tit 18 § 8702 (1957).
84. CAL. WELFARE & INST. CODE § 7254 (West, 1966).
85. N.C. GEN. STAT. § 35-39 (Supp. 1973).
86. GA. CODE ANN. § 84-933 (b) (Supp. 1974).
87. For example, the Maine law provides that "Within 30 days of the issuance of any order of sterilization an appeal may be taken to the Superior Court by the inmate or his or her representative. Such appeal shall be filed and heard in the county where the inmate was domiciled when committed. The proceedings in such appeals shall be governed by the rules provided for probate appeals. In this appeal the person for whom an order of sterilization has been issued shall be designated as the plaintiff and the superintendent of the institution in which said inmate is under care or custody shall be designated as the defendant. The finding of the court shall be certified to the department. Such finding may affirm, revise or reverse." ME. REV. STAT. ANN. tit. 34 § 2465 (1964).
88. Typical is the Minnesota consent provision for sterilization of feebleminded individuals: "When any person has lawfully been committed as feebleminded to the guardianship of the commissioner of public welfare the commissioner may, with the written consent of the spouse or nearest kin of such feebleminded person, cause such person to be sterilized. . . . If no spouse or near relative can be found, the commissioner of public welfare, as the legal guardian of such feebleminded person, may give his consent." MINN. STAT. ANN. § 256.07 (1965).
89. MINN. STAT. ANN. § 256.07 (1965).
90. CONN. GEN. STAT. ANN. § 17-19 (1958).
91. GA. CODE ANN. § 84-933 (c) (Supp. 1974).

either objection to sterilization or failure to secure consent. In Oregon, if parental consent is not obtained but no request is made for a rehearing of board approval, the failure to request such hearing is "conclusively deemed" equivalent to consent to the operation.[92] Similarly, while the North Carolina eugenics board may order sterilization of a mental defective on consent of the individual, next of kin, legal guardian or solicitor of the county and a court-appointed guardian, an appeal from the court order may be taken by any of these individuals—thus giving the court-appointed guardian or solicitor great discretion in the absence of parental involvement.[93]

F. Criticism of the Statutes

The eugenic nature of most state sterilization statutes is reminiscent of Nazi racist practices and raises serious genocidal questions. Can it be coincidence that 75% of the mentally retarded come from low income groups which are disproportionately non-white?[94] Though the sterilization laws were advocated as a means of saving society from the dangers of supposedly inherited mental illness, mental retardation, epilepsy and criminality, the laws have proved a striking failure as a means of eliminating the unfit.[95]

According to the American Medical Association's Committee to Study Contraceptive Practices and Related Problems, "Our present knowledge regarding human heredity is so limited that there appears to very little scientific basis to justify limitation of conception for eugenic reasons. . .there is conflicting evidence regarding the transmissibility of epilepsy and mental disorders."[96] The skepticism of the scientific community as to the inheritability of mental disorders was expressed by the Mental Health Committee of the South Dakota Medical Association in explaining the proposed South Dakota Mental Health Act:

Medical Science has by no means established that heredity is a factor in the development of mental disease with the possible exception of a very few and rare disorders. The committee holds that the decision to sterilize for whatever reason should be left up to the free decision reached by patient and family physician mutually and that the state has no good reason to trespass in this area.[97]

92. ORE. REV. STAT. § 436.110 (1971).
93. N.C. GEN. STAT. § 35-48 (Supp. 1973).
94. Frothingham, The Concept of Social Competence as Applied to Marriage and Child Care in Those Classified as Mentally Retarded, 104 C.M.A. J. (1971).
95. Ferster, supra note 76 at 619.
96. AMERICAN MEDICAL ASSOCIATION, PROCEEDINGS 54 (1937).
97. MENTAL HEALTH COMMITTEE, SOUTH DAKOTA MEDICAL ASSOCIATION, EXPLANATION OF PROPOSED SOUTH DAKOTA MENTAL HEALTH ACT (1959).

Thus, if we assume that eugenic sterilization laws are based on erroneous scientific presumptions about the inheritability of mental illness, such laws satisfy no compelling state interest and require a finding of arbitrary and unreasonable deprivation of liberty.[98]

Further, the adequacy of the procedural safeguards which the statutes purport to provide the institutionalized patient is open to question. As pointed out more than thirty years ago by the American Neurological Association,

> the word voluntary is frequently a mere subterfuge, in that it is often a condition of discharge from the institution that the patient be sterilized and consequently the individual involved is in the position of being confined or confinable until he gives his consent for sterilization, which hardly makes the bargain free and equal and nullifies the real meaning of the word voluntary.[99]

The majority of compulsory sterilization statutes also fail to clarify the gray area of the law dealing with the retarded non-institutionalized individual. Doctors and hospitals remain reluctant to perform sterilization operations on the retarded for fear of liability in tort; courts will not order sterilization in the absence of statutory authority; and since the majority of state statutes do not provide for the non-institutionalized person, the hopeless cycle of inefficacy and obsolescence is perpetuated.

A few states have attempted to legislate in this nebulous area; the Montana sterilization law has as its self-declared purpose, "to provide a method through proper hearing whereby certain persons whose sterilization would benefit themselves and the state may voluntarily consent to such sterilization under adequate safeguards protecting them against involuntary or unnecessary sterilization."[100] The act applies to persons "who would be diagnosed as capable of consent to sterilization but whose capacity to consent has been questioned by a licensed physician."[101] Thus the act allows the private physician to conduct the first screening of the patient in determining capacity; if he is satisfied with the patient's comprehension of and consent to the operation, he is not required to seek further authorization.

If the doctor does question the patient's ability to consent, the Montana act establishes a state board of eugenics empowered to conduct hearings to determine whether the individual might be expected to transmit mental deficiencies to offspring or be unable to care for and rear such offspring, and to ascertain whether the applicant is "capable of understanding and does

---

98. Ferster, *supra* note 76, at 616.
99. COMMITTEE OF THE AMERICAN NEUROLOGICAL ASSOCIATION, EUGENICAL STERILIZATION 7-8 (1935).
100. MONT. REV. CODE ANN. § 69-6401 (1947), *as amended* (Supp. 1974).
101. *Id.* § 69-6401.

understand the nature and consequences of the medical treatment he or she will undergo and with such understanding voluntarily consents thereto."[102] At this hearing a written consent to the sterilization must be signed by the patient and his parents or guardian; if the board finds the individual incapable of *voluntary* consent, however, thereafter it is unlawful for any person to perform or procure a sterilization for the applicant.[103] Thus the Montana statute is unique among the state laws in mandating the personal and voluntary consent of mentally disabled persons to their sterilization.

While no other state statute sets up as comprehensive an administrative scheme for dealing with sterilization of non-institutionalized retarded persons as does Montana, the Maine, Vermont, North Carolina and Oregon sterilization laws all make some provision for sterilization of non-institutionalized incompetents. The Maine statute allows sterilization by private physicians on application of the patient unless the physician questions the patient's capacity to consent; in such cases consent of a relative or guardian is required.[104] Vermont law provides for sterilization of non-institutionalized incompetents upon the application of two physicians and the written request of the patient or the patient's natural or legal guardian (if the patient is deemed incapable of understanding the irreversible nature of the operation) and the voluntary and comprehending submission of the patient.[105] The Oregon sterilization statute goes even further in attempting to ensure the voluntariness of the consent to sterilization by the non-institutionalized retarded; not only must the written consent of the patient and his guardian, spouse or next of kin be secured before the operation may be performed, but no consent is deemed valid unless the patient has been represented by counsel at a hearing before the state board of social protection.[106] Finally, the Arkansas compulsory sterilization law[107] expressly stipulates that none of its provisions interferes with the right of the patient and/or his parents or legal guardian to seek sterilization through direct medical channels. Thus this state at least recognizes the classification of mental incompetency by which the non-institutionalized retarded are identified, although the law in no way provides legislative guidance in this area for confused and uncertain doctors, parents and patients.

III. PROPOSED LEGISLATIVE SOLUTIONS

In an attempt to resolve the problems left unanswered by the law with respect to the capacity of non-judicially declared incompetents or their

102. *Id.* § 69-6403(d).
103. *Id.* § 69-6406.
104. ME. REV. STAT. ANN. tit. 34 § 2461 (1964).
105. VT. STAT. ANN. tit. 18 § 8702 (1957).
106. ORE. REV. STAT. § 436.056 (1971).
107. ARK. STAT. ANN. § 59-502 (1947).

representatives to consent to sterilization proceedings, the following Model Voluntary Sterilization Act has been formulated. Its purpose is to insure the availability of contraceptive sterilization for the mentally retarded within procedural guidelines adequate to safeguard the voluntariness of the consent so obtained. The following provisions of law are recommended to effectuate the principles enunciated by the 1968 Proclamation of Teheran as adopted by the International Conference on Human Rights which provides that ". . . parents have a basic human right to determine freely and responsibly the number and spacing of their children."[108]

A. Model Voluntary Sterilization Act

Sec. 1. Purpose of the Act.

This legislature recognizes that any legally competent person as provided herein may consent to voluntary sterilization. Further, the legislature intends to provide a method through proper hearing whereby mentally retarded persons, who would be diagnosed as capable of consent to sterilization but whose legal competence to consent has been questioned by a licensed physician, may voluntarily consent to sterilization.

Sec. 2. Voluntary Sterilization for Competent Persons.

a. A licensed physician may perform a sterilization upon any person over twenty-one (21) years of age, or over eighteen (18) years of age and married, [or otherwise emancipated under state law] who is mentally competent to consent and who does in fact consent to be sterilized.

b. Consent shall be freely and intelligently given in writing. Free and intelligent consent shall require that a [physician] [appropriate expert] inform such person as to
>   1. Method of sterilization;
>   2. Nature and consequences of such sterilization;
>   3. Likelihood of success;
>   4. Alternative methods of sterilization;
>   5. Alternative methods of birth control;
and be satisfied that such consent has been given after full and fair deliberation of these matters.

[If an individual is a member of a particular ethnic, religious or philosophical group, he or she shall be afforded the opportunity to confer with a representative of the group concerned, if the individual so desires.]

---

108. *Supra* note 63. The Model Voluntary Sterilization Act which follows in the text was drafted by Association for Voluntary Sterilization staff members based on proceedings of the Second International Conference held in 1973.

Sec. 3. *Voluntary Sterilization for Retarded Persons.*

a. The persons to whom this section is applicable are those mentally retarded persons of any age who have the capacity to understand and appreciate the nature of the medical treatment they are to undergo and the consequences thereof and to manifest assent or dissent thereto.

b. Any person to whom this section is applicable and whose legal competence to consent has been questioned by a licensed physician or might be so questioned, may consent to voluntarily sterilization after application to and approval by the Review Committee as hereinafter provided and, if an appeal is taken, by the [   ] Court.

Sec. 4. *Review Committees Established.*

To carry out the purposes and provisions of this act, there is hereby created and established for each [federal judicial district] in the state of [   ] a Review Committee which shall consist of the following:

a. One (1) physician licensed to practice psychiatry in the state to be appointed for a term of three (3) years by the governor after considering the recommendation of the state medical association;
b. One (1) lawyer licensed to practice law in the state to be appointed for a term of three (3) years by the governor after considering the recommendation of the state bar association;
c. One (1) lay member to be appointed for a term of three (3) years by the governor after recommendations by qualified organizations in the field of mental retardation;
d. A consulting physician, either a licensed specialist in urology or in gynecology and obstetrics as appropriate, to be selected by the members of the committee appointed as provided in a, b, and c;
e. A representative of the particular ethnic, religious, or philosophical group of the applicant to be selected by the members of the committee appointed in a, b, and c;
[f. An ex officio member who shall act as the committee's secretary and the keeper of its books and records,]

provided that no committee member, except as appointed in f, shall be otherwise employed by the state. Nor shall a member engaged in the custodial or professional care of an individual applicant, or previously engaged in the [professional] care of such applicant, or personally related to him or her, participate in the committee's consideration of that individual's application.

Sec. 5. *Application for Sterilization.*

It shall be the duty of the Review Committee to receive applications for voluntary sterilization by or on behalf of persons claiming eligibility under Sec. 3 of this act. The applicant himself, or a parent or legal guardian or custodian of the applicant, may file papers in any form calculated to apprise the committee of the desire of the applicant to be sterilized.

Upon receipt of such application, the Review Committee shall appoint a patient advocate for the individual requesting sterilization, unless the individual has already obtained counsel, and shall schedule a hearing not less than [20] days nor more than [45] days after such appointment, or, if no appointment, after receipt of the application.

Further, the committee shall notify any parent(s), legal guardian, and/or custodian of the applicant of the nature, location, date, and time of such hearing [by registered mail.]

Sec. 6. *Patient Advocate.*

If an applicant cannot afford or otherwise obtain counsel, he shall be furnished with a patient advocate. Counsel, or such patient advocate as designated herein, shall represent the expressed wishes of the applicant regardless of who may initiate the proceedings or pay the attorney's fee. The committee shall have discretion to appoint a patient advocate for any applicant, regardless or whether a parent or legal guardian or custodian has provided counsel for applicant.

The patient advocate shall be an attorney licensed by the state and qualified to protect the rights and legal interests of the applicant.

Sec. 7. *Hearing—Showing Required—Designation of Surgeon—Written Consent.*

The Review Committee shall conduct a hearing at which the applicant must be present in person for examination by the board and evidence must be presented to establish:

a. Whether the applicant is one of the group covered by Sec. 3.a of this act;

b. Whether the applicant, whether or not a minor, has been counselled as to the nature and consequences of sterilization as defined in Sec. 2.b of this act and whether the applicant understands and appreciates such information and voluntarily assents thereto;

c. If the applicant is under twenty-one (21) years of age, whether his or her parent(s), if living and competent, or, if not, his or her legal guardian understands and consents to the sterilization;
d. If the applicant is over twenty-one (21) years of age, whether any parent(s) or legal guardian who is in custody of the applicant understands and consents to the sterilization;
e. Whether any undue coercion or promise of release from an institution has induced the applicant's consent;
f. Whether sterilization is otherwise ill-advised or whether an applicant is unable or unlikely to procreate;
g. Whether such treatment can be carried out without unreasonable risk to the life and health of the applicant;
h. The method and manner in which sterilization is to be accomplished.

Further, at such hearing the applicant shall designate the person to perform such sterilization who may be any physician and surgeon licensed to practice medicine in the state.

At such hearing, the applicant shall sign a written consent to sterilization in the form to be provided by the committee.

Sec. 8.   *Notification of Findings—Appeal of Right to*
        [   ] *Court—Certificate.*

Within [three (3)] weeks after the hearing, the Review Committee shall make its findings in writing. It shall be the duty of the committee to supply a copy of the findings to the applicant, counsel or patient advocate, and any parents(s) or legal guardian or the applicant. Within [two (2)] weeks of receipt of the findings, any party so notified shall have an appeal of right to the [   ] Court for review of any of the findings made. Notice of the appeal shall be served on the committee and all parties notified of the findings. Such appeal will automatically stay the effect of the findings until court review has been completed.

If no appeal is taken within the designated period, the committee shall make a certificate reciting its findings and signed by all members of the committee. The certificate shall conspicuously state the committee's "Approval of Sterilization" or "Disapproval of Sterilization." The original of such certificate shall be sent to the physician designated by the applicant to perform the sterilization; copies thereof shall be sent to the applicant, counsel or patient advocate, and any parent(s), legal guardian or custodian, and one copy to remain in the permanent files of the committee.

Sec. 9.   *Findings Prerequisite to Approval of*
           Sterilization—Operation Arranged.

If the Review Committee finds and certifies

a. That the applicant is one of the group covered by Sec. 3.a of this act;

b. That the applicant, whether or not a minor, has been counselled as to the nature and consequences of sterilization as defined in Sec. 2.b of this act and that he or she understands and appreciates this information and voluntarily assents thereto;

c. That any parent(s) or legal guardian of a minor applicant, or any parent(s) or legal guardian who is in custody of an applicant over the age of twenty-one (21) has understood and consented to the sterilization in writing;

d. That no undue coercion or promise of release from an institution has induced the applicant's consent;

e. That sterilization is not otherwise ill-advised;

f. That the method and manner in which such sterilization is to be accomplished is medically approved according to the standards for such procedures in the state;

g. That such medical treatment can be carried out without unreasonable risk to the life or health of the applicant;

h. That the person designated to perform such sterilization is one qualified under this act,

the physician designated to perform the sterilization, upon receipt of the certificate issued by the Review Committee, may proceed with treatment in accordance with the certificate. Arrangements for such medical treatment shall be made between the physician designated in the certificate and the applicant or his or her parent, guardian or custodian. Provided nothing in this act shall be deemed to prohibit payment in whole or in part for the treatment by any federal or state program, agency or department.

Sec. 10.   *No Civil Liability Arises from*
             Sterilization—Exception.

Neither the members of the Review Committee nor any physician and surgeon or assistant concerned nor any other person participating in the execution of the provisions of this act in conformity with the board's certificate shall be thereafter liable either civilly or criminally to anyone having performed or authorizing the performance of such sterilization; provided, that such physician or surgeon or assistant concerned will nevertheless be liable for any damage caused by the negligent performance of such sterilization in accordance with the general law of the state covering such negligence.

B.   Comments and Criticism of the Act

Section 1.   Purpose of the Act

This section sets forth a limited purpose for the Act, namely, it provides for a procedure by which a person of questionable legal competence may be declared capable of providing a voluntary consent for sterilization. The Act is not aimed specifically at either: (a) the situation wherein a person is to be sterilized on the application and consent of another (e.g., parent, guardian, state) and therefore denied the opportunity to provide personal consent, or (b) the situation wherein a person is adjudged an incompetent, i.e., incapable of providing consent, but exhibits a clear need, either emotional or physical, to be sterilized.

The Act can provide some guidance for situation (a). As a matter of public policy, no person should be sterilized on the application and consent of another unless he has been adjudged an incompetent under the provisions of this Act. This presents situation (b). There is a clear need for legislation which reaches beyond the scope of this Act to provide for the sterilization of an incompetent on the application and consent of another person. This suggestion should not be confused with the various eugenic sterilization laws presently in effect in some states. In keeping with the basic policy of this Act, the proposed sterilization procedures would only be permitted in instances where it was in the best interests of the person to be sterilized. Some situations warrant permitting substitute consent for sterilization, such as where the individual is incapable of even the most basic motor coordination, or incapable of the simple logic required for daily functioning in society. It should appear that these impairments are permanent and that a less drastic method of contraception is unavailable or infeasible. Only in such extreme cases should sterilization be permitted for persons not adjudicated incompetent.

Section 3.   Voluntary Sterilization for Retarded Persons

a.   This section merely sets forth the requirements which any person must meet under the common law to be legally capable of providing consent. It reflects two of the three factors necessary for a valid consent—mental competence and full disclosure—but omits the requirement of voluntariness. However, this should not be construed as an elimination of that requirement. The section serves the limited purpose of defining the qualities which an individual must possess to be capable of providing consent, not the requirements by which a final authoritative consent to sterilization is to be judged.

b.   The use of the phrase, "or might be so questioned" creates certain difficulties in the application of this section of the Act. If one's competence is not questioned by his physician but "might [have been] so questioned" by a different physician in the same situation, is the individual required to appear before a review committee and be "approved" before providing valid consent? This result would fly in the face of the rest of the Act and would make administration of this section of the Act impossible. The "could" standard is too vague. A preferable word is "should." The phrase, "or should be so questioned" indicates that if the prospective sterilization recipient fails to meet certain standards, questioning by the physician would be required, and the failure of the physician to do so would permit the committee to intercede. Certain guidelines should accompany this section as a guide to which a physician can turn in attempting to decide whether or not questioning of a particular individual's competence is necessary.

Section 4.   Review Committee Established

To insure the disinterestedness of court-authorized sterilization and to protect the patient from possible coercion, a review committee composed of independent members is an important safeguard. While it has long been recognized that a parent or legal guardian's consent to the sterilization of a retarded ward may serve the selfish interests of the parent alone, it should also be remembered that a select panel composed of professionals (doctors and hospital officials, mental health commissioners, public welfare officials etc.), in providing consent, may have an "institutional" interest in rendering the retarded individual "manageable" that is adverse to the protection of the patient's personal rights. The inclusion of lay members on the proposed review committee helps to insure non-institutional representation. Further, the provision in section 4.e for a representative of the applicant's particular ethnic, religious or philosophical group hopefully would guarantee that sterilization proceedings for the retarded are not in fact blind approvals for eugenic sterilizations.

The provision in f barring participation in the committee's decision to those who have either cared for or are related to the retarded individual is necessary to insure the disinterestedness of the committee's decision.

Section 6.   Patient Advocate

Assuming, as we do, that substituted consent to sterilization supplied by a review committee is justifiable only when predicated on a finding of benefit to the retarded individual concerned, accountability for committee decisions must not be restricted to peer review and autonomous committee action must be avoided. To insure that the interests of the retarded individual himself are paramount in the committee's decision, the retarded individual, operating at a clear disadvantage within the review committee proceeding, must be guaranteed independent legal counsel. As pointed out by one expert in the field, "the advocate for the retarded should not be the institution in which he is confined or anyone subject to its influence . . . by the very way in which our system works the interest of the client must be expected occasionally to be at variance with the interest of the agency."[109]

The statute requires that the patient be represented by counsel, but the provision that counsel must represent the wishes of the patient regardless of who pays the attorney's fees seems an inadequate protection against the potential conflict of interest that may arise when parents fund the legal fees. Although there is committee discretion to appoint a substitute advocate (apparently in the event of such a conflict), a provision establishing an outside fund for such fees might better eliminate this potential conflict of interest problem.

*Section 7.   Hearing—Showing Required—Designation
of Surgeon—Written Consent*

The proposed statute, while safeguarding the patient's right to be present at the sterilization hearing, is silent as to the patient's right to cross-examine witnesses, to present witnesses on his or her behalf or to introduce evidence—rights which should be guaranteed in a sterilization statute. Furthermore, while the section stresses the preeminence of voluntary consent by the patient himself, the requirement of parental consent as well seems superfluous where the subject is either an emancipated minor or one who has reached majority age. Finally, the hearing should establish as a prerequisite to sterilization that no less restrictive alternative means of contraception is available and that sterilization would benefit the retarded individual's ability to function in the community.

* * * *

The above Model Act together with the suggested modifications represents an effective means of dealing with the gray area of the retarded but legally competent non-institutionalized individual whose capacity to consent to sterilization has been questioned. It provides adequate procedural and substantive safeguards to insure that all of the elements required for a valid consent—competence, full disclosure and voluntariness—have been met and at the same time allows the individual the right to choose his or her method of family planning, if desired.

As with the Montana statute, but in a more comprehensive manner, the Model Act intentionally provides only for personal consent, not substitute

---

109. Murdock, *Civil Rights of the Mentally Retarded*, 48 N.D. LAWYER 133, 145 (1972).

consent. In the case of persons for whom substitute consent is necessary, either because of an adjudication of incompetence or determined incapacity to consent (in each instance accompanied by compelling circumstances warranting substitute consent), careful consideration must be given to drafting separate additional statutory provisions which give broad protection to the individuals involved.

For the mentally retarded who have the capacity to consent, however, the statutory provisions suggested in the Act provide an established procedure which prevents imposition of the wishes of others while at the same time allowing the retarded to exercise their right to elect to have children or not, as they choose. It is certainly in the interest of public policy to allow the individual, wherever possible, to make such fundamental private decisions himself.

Toward Creating a Philosophy of Fundamental Human Rights

By
Theodore H. Lackland*

I. General Introduction

The Supreme Court has shown a tendency to conceptualize constitutional standards more broadly in recent years to protect certain classes of personal activity from state regulation. As a standard for analysis the Court has found a convenient category it calls "fundamental rights," or more recently "rights to privacy." This standard was applied first in due process cases and more recently in equal protection cases as well. A view of the relevant cases dealing with human reproduction, as it will be undertaken here, will indicate that the concept is fairly well entrenched in the Court's thinking. This view will also reveal, however, that the Court has not made a concerted effort to articulate what standards are used to determine whether a right is fundamental nor to explain how these standards are determined.

In a search for appropriate standards, this article will not focus on the cases or the legislative history of the constitutional convention. It is the intention here to suggest that perhaps it would be more fruitful to analyze the philosophical underpinnings of the American view of law and government to determine what foundation for our concept of law and government would support a conclusion that there are fundamental or basic human rights which are not stated in the Constitution. This analysis will suggest that the answer goes beyond an interpretation of our Constitution and rests upon the same foundation that supports the Constitution itself. It goes to the basic considerations of a concept of law and how that law must relate to man if he is to be a free individual. It is in analyzing what is required to insure a democratic government that we arrive at the proper conceptual context in which the problem can be best analyzed.

The analysis will be in two parts. In the first part an attempt will be made to formulate a concept of fundamental rights which is consistent with

---

* Associate Editor, Columbia Human Rights Law Review.

the point of view put forth by Justice Goldberg in *Griswold v. Connecticut.* The emphasis in this section will be on articulating a concept which is in accordance with the language and theory of the United States Constitution. The second part will examine general philosophical theories which would put the concept into an historical and intellectual perspective. For the purposes of this section it will be assumed that the American view of democracy and individual liberty is the model against which this concept of fundamental human rights must be judged. Three general philosophical points of view will be examined to determine if any one of them would support the double burden of the American view of law and democracy as well as a concept of fundamental human rights. They are: natural law—which will be rejected for philosophical reasons; skepticism-utilitarianism—which will also be rejected for the same reasons; and finally incipient phenomenology as articulated by Immanuel Kant—which will be put forth as the most useful alternative.

The purpose of the inquiry is not to suggest that the Supreme Court adopt the difficult and controversial position of Kant, or indeed any position. It is merely to suggest that the Kantian method of analysis and concept of man may be helpful in defining the concept of fundamental rights. The Kantian method of analysis is characterized by a refocusing of the classical philosophical inquiry from an investigation and explanation of experience to an investigation and analysis of the individual. It will be suggested that the Court make a similar reorientation in its search for a foundation for a concept of fundamental rights. Instead of attempting to determine whether a right is fundamental by investigating either the contemporary standards of a *majority of society* or a contemporary view of the proper role of government, the Court should attempt to determine which rights are essential to a contemporary concept of the free individual. The Court should, in effect, discuss law and government in terms of the free *individual* and not attempt to make individual freedom follow from a concept of government.

II.   CASE LAW

A.   *Perspective*

The basic concern here is to analyze that class of cases having to do with human reproduction and to analyze the language of each opinion to determine what logically can be inferred from what each Justice has written. The basic problem inherent in an attempt to discover and to articulate those premises which undergird the point of view of a Supreme Court Justice lies in the very real possibility that logical consistency may not be, for each of them, a concern or conscious aim. Nonetheless, an attempt will be made to find these premises, to articulate them, and to place them against the background of the

historical and intellectual warp and woof from which the cloth of jurisprudence is woven.

The cases, therefore, will be used not as tenets regarding a particular
point of law but as a starting point for an inquiry into what general conclusions
can be drawn from the language of each opinion to arrive at that point which
best expresses each Justice's view of the origin of fundamental rights. To that
extent therefore, this analysis will distort the emphasis of the Court. Whereas
a court is normally concerned with settling a dispute and determining legal
obligations, the concern here is to determine what the Court assumes is the
origin of individual liberty. One should be cognizant of the purpose here and
understand that what is sought is not an *explication* of standards but an
understanding of the premises upon which those standards may be based.

B.   *Sterilization*

1.   Buck v. Bell[1]

In an opinion written by Mr. Justice Holmes the Court concluded that
sterilization *per se* was not a threat to any constitutionally protected human
right. It was an act that to be performed legitimately required only that there
be a rational connection between the act and the legislatively stated reason for
it.[2] In this case the state was free to sterilize feeble-minded persons as long as
the procedural amenities were followed—notice, a hearing, written evidence,
and the right to appeal.

As to the basic question of substantive law, that is, whether sterilization
is itself a valid social tool, Justice Holmes accepted the proposition that an

---

1. 274 U.S. 200 (1927).

2. The Court has, through its decisional process, evolved a test which is triggered by a
determination that a right is "fundamental" or equivalent to those enumerated by the Bill of
Rights. If the right is fundamental a state legislature may infringe upon it only if it has an interest
so compelling as to make the infringement necessary: such interest is said to be "compelling." If
the right is found not to be fundamental, the Court will uphold the state action if it is found to be
reasonable. The act is reasonable if the Court can find a rational connection between the effect of
the act and a legitimate state purpose.

Implicitly resolved in the determination that a right is fundamental is the question of
whether or not it is proper for the Supreme Court to ever review a state act which does not
infringe upon a right enumerated in the Bill of Rights. This area is one of the many ancillary
issues inherent in this discussion. For a statement of the attitude which has been adopted by the
Court, *see* Justice Holmes' dissent in Lochner v. New York, 198 U.S. 45, 74 (1905). Justice
Holmes argued that the Court should not act as a super-legislature in economic and social
matters. If a right is not enumerated in the Constitution, the Court should not look to the
abridgement of a right as a denial of a constitutionally protected freedom. In the area of individual
rights the Court often utilized a contrary standard. For a very good discussion of this area, *see*
Lacy, *The Bill of Rights and the Fourteenth Amendment: The Evolution of the Absorption
Doctrine*, 23 WASH. & LEE L. REV. 37 (1966). The author traces the development of the
Supreme Court's method of analysis wherein the Bill of Rights has been applied to the states by
the first section of the fourteenth amendment.

individual's ability to procreate is subject to the power of the state (through an act of its legislature) and that such an ability can be destroyed upon a showing that the needs of the state are served better by its destruction. As stated by Justice Holmes:

> We have seen more than once that the public welfare may call upon the best citizens for their lives. It would be strange if it could not call upon those who already sap the strength of the state for those lesser sacrifices, often not felt to be such by those concerned in order to prevent our being swamped with incompetence. It is better for all the world, if instead of waiting to execute degenerate offspring for crime, or to let them starve for their imbecility, society can prevent those who are manifestly unfit from continuing their kind. The principle that sustains compulsory vaccination is broad enough to cover cutting the fallopian tubes [citations omitted] . . . . Three generations of imbeciles are enough.[3]

When discussing the fact that the state law operates only against those who are confined in institutions and not against others, regardless of where they might be, Justice Holmes also rejected the idea that such a procedure was a denial of equal protection.[4]

In finding that the standards of due process of law are satisfied by the proper procedure and refusing to question the power of the state, Holmes implicitly rejected the argument of the plaintiff that such action violated her constitutional right of bodily integrity.[5] At the same time he also rejected any claim that the right to bear children, in this context, is constitutionally protected, in and of itself.

2. Skinner v. Oklahoma ex rel. Williams[6]

The Court had before it in *Skinner* an Oklahoma statute which provided for the sterilization of certain criminals. The statute provided for many (but not all) of the same procedural safeguards as did the statute in *Buck*.[7] Section 195 of the statute excluded "offenses arising out of the violation of the prohibitory laws, revenue acts, embezzlement, or political offenses . . . ."[8]

The statute provided that one who had been convicted three times for

---

3. 274 U.S. at 207.
4. *Id.* at 208.
5. *Id.* at 201.
6. 316 U.S. 535 (1942).
7. The statute considered in *Buck* provided for the opportunity to be heard on the issue of whether one is probably a potential parent of a socially undesirable offspring. The Oklahoma statute did not provide for such an opportunity.
8. 316 U.S. at 537.

the commission of certain felonies could be sterilized. Justice Douglas found that the statute was unconstitutional in that it violated the equal protection clause of the fourteenth amendment. The language of the statute excluded felonies effectuated by embezzlement which could have an effect on society of equal or greater harm than a felony effectuated by larceny. For example a chicken thief convicted three times could be sterilized whereas an employee who three times embezzles thousands from his employer would not be. There would seem to be an implicit distinction between a crime which may characteristically involve violence and one which characteristically does not. Justice Douglas was not willing to search for a rationale to explain the difference.

Although throughout the opinion Justice Douglas paid due deference to *Buck* the disagreement finally surfaced when the rationale was stated. Douglas wrote:

> We are dealing here with legislation which involves one of the basic civil rights of man. Marriage and procreation are fundamental to the very existence and survival of the race. . . . We advert to them [these fundamental rights] merely in emphasis of our view that strict scrutiny of the classification which a State makes in a sterilization law is essential, lest unwillingly, or otherwise, invidious discriminations are made against groups or types of individuals in violation of the constitutional guaranty of just and equal laws. . . . When the law lays an unequal hand on those who have committed intrinsically the same quality of offense and sterilizes one and not the other, it has made as invidious a discrimination as if it had selected a particular race or nationality for oppressive treatment.[9]

The viewpoint of Justice Douglas when compared with that of Justice Holmes is both fundamentally different and at once the same. They are different in that Justice Douglas assumed, *a priori*, that there are fundamental rights of man which can be infringed upon only after showing that that the law is both fair and essential.[10] Justice Holmes in *Buck* made no such assumption; the test for him was whether the law rationally related to its purpose and was rationally applied. They are similar in that neither viewed this right, no matter how "fundamental," as absolute. At no point did Justice Douglas say the law itself was unreasonable; only that the factors which are to be employed in deciding who is to be sterilized are in part arbitrary. Like Justice

---

9. *Id.* at 541.
10. Although Justice Douglas indicated that the Virginia statute in *Buck* was not based on such a meaningless distinction and was not used with such an invidious effect, 316 U.S. at 542, there is no indication as to how he would have viewed that case were it before the Court again.

Holmes, it would appear that Justice Douglas burked a substantive, indeed the real, issue, that is whether sterilization is ever a permissible tool.

Justice Douglas' view was not wholly accepted, although there was none who took exception to his conclusion. Mr. Chief Justice Stone took exception to the inference permitted by an analysis of Douglas' view; that is, that ". . . Oklahoma may resort generally to the sterilization of criminals on the assumption that their propensities are transmissible to future generations by inheritance. . . ."[11] Justice Stone stated further:

> . . . I think the real question we have to consider is not one of equal protection, but whether the wholesale condemnation of a class to such an evasion of personal liberty, without opportunity to any individual to show that he is not the type of case which would justify resort to it, satisfies the demands of due process.[12]

Mr. Justice Stone concluded his opinion, which argued for a due process (as opposed to an equal protection) argument, by stating that to require a state to use an objective and reasonable standard for sterilization was not unreasonable.[13]

The problem presented by this view is the same as that presented by Justice Douglas' view. If some rights are indeed "fundamental," which are they, where are they articulated, and how does one know they are constitutionally protected when the language of the Constitution is silent? Mr. Justice Jackson came closest to seeing the broader issue in his concurring opinion when he stated:

> There are limits to the extent to which a legislatively represented majority may conduct biological experiments at the expense of the dignity and personality and natural powers of a minority—even those who have been guilty of what the majority defines as crimes. But this Act falls down before reaching this problem which I mention only to avoid the implication that such a question may not exist because not discussed.[14]

C.   Birth Control

Griswold v. Connecticut[15] is significant not only for its holding but also for the numerous concurring and dissenting opinions which vividly illuminate

---

11. 316 U.S. at 543 (concurring opinion).
12. *Id.* at 544.
13. *Id.* at 545.
14. *Id.* at 546-47.
15. 381 U.S. 479 (1964).

the competing views with regard to personal freedom and the power of the state to control it. The Court struck down a Connecticut statute that made it a crime for any person to use any drug or article to prevent conception. Mr. Justice Douglas writing for a plurality of the Court developed a rationale that appears to be unique. He found emanating from the Bill of Rights and its specific guarantees penumbras which guarantee various zones of privacy.[16] Married persons have a privacy right which was unnecessarily violated by the overbroad Connecticut statute. Douglas ended his opinion by stating:

> We deal with a right of privacy older than the Bill of Rights—older than our political parties, older than our school system. Marriage is a coming together for better or for worse, hopefully enduring, and intimate to the degree of being sacred. It is an association that promotes a way of life, not cause; a harmony in living, not political faiths; a bilateral loyalty, not commercial or social projects. Yet it is an association for as noble a purpose as any involved in our prior decisions.[17]

Justice Douglas seems to recognize that rights must be articulated in some document or by some system of justice. They must exist in some frame of reference or context; they cannot exist in a void.[18] Justice Douglas found that the fourteenth amendment due process clause incorporated the Bill of Rights and that within the penumbra created by the Bill of Rights was the right of marital privacy. The right was elevated to the same plane as those explicitly enumerated in the Bill of Rights and by the fourteenth amendment, state action, when affecting it, was made subject to a higher standard. The intrusion by the state must be necessary and unavoidable in the execution of a legitimate state interest.

The language of Justice Douglas succeeds in stating the test against which the law is to be judged. It does not explain why the right is of the kind which should be accorded a higher standard. As a practical matter the test to be applied is precisely the test that is applicable when a right is deemed "fundamental."[19] Justice Douglas apparently concluded that the right is deemed fundamental because it is central to one's concept of society and proper social order. However, if a right is found in one's concept of social

---

16. *Id.* at 484.
17. *Id.* at 486.
18. Logic alone would seem to dictate as much. If there is no context or basis, the standard is, arguably, without meaning.
19. *See* Karst, *Invidious Discrimination: Justice Douglas and the Return of the Natural-Law-Due-Process Formula,* 16 U.C.L.A.L. REV. 716 (1969). This article traces Justice Douglas' articulation of his standard for due process through a series of cases which cover his life on the Court up until 1969 and contrasts it with the point of view of Justice Black.

order it does not seem to follow, *a priori*, that it must be found in the penumbra to the Bill of Rights.[20] The process by which Justice Douglas comes to know that this right is somehow special is not articulated.[21]

Mr. Justice Goldberg concurred in the result although he refused to accept Justice Douglas' contention that the fourteenth amendment due process clause incorporated only the first eight amendments of the Bill of Rights. In his view the due process clause goes to any right deemed fundamental, whether or not it is explicit in the Bill of Rights or found in its penumbra. Marital privacy is just such a right. The fundamental rights not found in the first eight amendments were, for Justice Goldberg, in the ninth amendment. He stated:

> The language and history of the Ninth Amendment reveal that the Framers of the Constitution believed that there are additional fundamental rights, protected from governmental infringement, which exist alongside those fundamental rights especially mentioned in the first eight constitutional amendments.[22]

Although the ninth amendment as written is a restriction only upon federal action (as opposed to state action), Justice Goldberg viewed the effect of the fourteenth amendment on the ninth to be the same as it was upon the first eight amendments of the Bill of Rights: a restriction on state action with regard to fundamental rights.[23] The ninth amendment serves in this context to show that fundamental personal rights were not meant to be enumerated totally by the first eight amendments of the Bill of Rights.[24]

Justice Goldberg anticipated how these fundamental rights are to be determined by quoting several earlier cases:

> In determining which rights are fundamental, judges are not left at

---

20. *See* note 29 *infra.*
21. The Court used an equal protection argument in Eisenstadt v. Baird, 405 U.S. 438 (1972), to strike down a statute which made it illegal to provide contraceptive devices and materials to *unmarried* couples. The decision rested on *Griswold's* assumption that sexual privacy was constitutionally protected. The decision expands the holding of *Griswold* without illuminating any of the reasons for it.
22. 381 U.S. at 488.
23. The point remains, however, that the Bill of Rights as written restricts federal power, and the fourteenth amendment applies similar limitations on state action. That is altogether different from saying, as Justice Goldberg suggested, that:
[while] the ninth amendment—and indeed the entire Bill of Rights—originally concerned restrictions upon *federal power*, the subsequently enacted Fourteenth Amendment prohibits the States as well from abridging fundamental personal liberties. And, the Ninth Amendment, in indicating that not all such liberties are specifically mentioned in the first eight amendments, is surely relevant in showing the existence of other fundamental personal rights, now protected from state, as well as federal, infringement. 381 U.S. at 493.
24. 381 U.S. at 493.

large to decide cases in light of their personal and private notions. Rather, they must look to the traditions and (collective) conscience of our people to determine whether a principle is 'so rooted (there) as to be ranked as fundamental. . . .' (citations omitted). The inquiry is whether a right involved 'is of such a character that it cannot be denied without violating those fundamental principles of liberty and justice which lie at the base of all our civil and political institutions , . . .' (citations omitted). 'Liberty also gains content from the emanations . . .' (citations omitted) of specific (constitutional) guarantees and 'from experience with the requirements of a free society.'[25]

The basic questions remain: Where specifically does one look to find these "fundamental principles"? What test does one employ to determine their priority? Who decides their relevance? Justice Goldberg does not answer, but he focused our attention on the need to make an attempt. Also Justice Goldberg made it clear that by whatever means these rights are to be determined they are not to be tampered with or the subject of experimentation by the states.[26] To this writer, however, Justice Goldberg's greatest contribution to this area was his articulation of the great fear of what may be the consequence of loosely conceived "fundamental" rights:

> While it may shock some of my brethren [reference to Justice Stewart] that the Court today holds that the Constitution protects the right of marital privacy, in my view it is far more shocking to believe that the personal liberty guaranteed by the Constitution does not include protection against such totalitarian limitation of family size, which is at complete variance with our constitutional concepts. Yet, if upon a showing of a slender basis of rationality, a law outlawing voluntary birth control by married persons is valid, then, by the same reasoning, *a law requiring compulsory birth control also would be valid.* In my view, however, both types of law would unjustifiably intrude upon rights of privacy which are constitutionally protected.[27]

However, Justice Goldberg does not deny that the states have a legitimate interest in curbing premarital sex. His argument, rather, is that the statute was unnecessarily broad and encroached upon a constitutionally protected area; accordingly the invasion is unnecessary and not based upon a rightly perceived need to protect a legitimate state interest.

---

25. *Id.*
26. *Id.* at 496.
27. *Id.* at 497 (emphasis added).

Mr. Justice Harlan's concurrence centered on his belief that the due process clause of the fourteenth amendment does not necessarily bring within the purview of state action the limiting language of the Bill of Rights. In his view the concern should be whether a particular state statute violates the basic values implicit in the concept of ordered liberty.[28] How these values are to be determined remains an unresolved problem.[29]

Mr. Justice White was concerned not with privacy but with the application of what he believed to be the pertinent test for a determination of due process in fourteenth amendment terms. The right "to marry, establish a home and bring up children" are among "the basic civil rights of man."[30] Justice White said further: "These decisions affirm that there is a 'realm of family life which the state cannot enter' without substantial justification."[31] The concern chiefly is with medical assistance in birth control matters for those who may not otherwise be able to afford it. The effect of the statute goes beyond the scope of the activity the state can arguably and legitimately circumscribe; that is, all forms of promiscuous or illicit sexual conduct. The problem of how one determines the full content of "basic civil rights of man" remains unstated.

Justices Black and Stewart dissented. In Justice Black's view the issue was not whether the state law was wise or that the policy was good, but simply whether the Constitution speaks to make this statute unconstitutional. Justice Black stated:

---

28. *Id.* at 500.

29. It would not seem to be an adequate explanation to say that one intuitively knows what is fundamental and what is not. If this were the case it would not be an argument for an expansive reading of the Bill of Rights; rather, it would be a strong argument for the proposition that written constitutions are unnecessary, at least insofar as the written document speaks to the individual rights the people are presumed to enjoy. Therefore, either the standard must be articulated and a written constitution is necessary, or these standards can be known intuitively and no written constitution is necessary.

It seems illogical to argue that rights generally must be written to be guaranteed but that some are intuitively "knowable" and can remain unwritten (all these rights being of the same degree of importance). The word "knowable" is in quotes because its use raises the epistemological problem of whether rights derived through this process of intuition are in fact *known*, or more generally if this is the kind of mind content one would want to call knowledge. The language used by Justice Douglas would suggest that unwritten rights are inferable from those that are written (penumbras from the Bill of Rights). But many rights can be inferred. One must ask, are they all fundamental?

The best explanation is suggested by Professor Wechsler, that the Bill of Rights represents, in part, those rights thought to be important at a given moment in history. Wechsler, *Toward Neutral Principles of Constitutional Law*, 73 Harv. L. Rev. 1 (1959). The Bill of Rights is not an exhaustive list but rather represents the kind of fundamental rights and principles, which because of history and the political situation, were thought important enough to articulate. Such a point of view implies that other rights exist to be articulated as the need arises. The written Constitution in this context places no special emphasis on those rights contained in the Bill of Rights. It is not necessary therefore to speak of emanations or penumbras.

30. 381 U.S. at 502 (concurring opinion).

31. *Id.*

The Court talks about a constitutional "right of privacy" as though there is some constitutional provision or provisions forbidding any law ever to be passed which might abridge the "privacy" of individuals. But there is not. There are, of course, guarantees in certain specific constitutional provisions which are designed in part to protect privacy at certain activities.[32]

Justice Black's primary concern was to preserve those rights enumerated and not to shrink them by a use of language substituted for that found in the Constitution.[33]

In condemning the majority's implicit use of a "natural law due process" theory (Justice Black's language) Black stated:

If these formulas based on "natural justices," or others which mean the same thing, are to prevail, they require judges to determine what is or is not constitutional on the basis of their own appraisal of what laws are unwise or unnecessary. The power to make such decisions is of course that of a legislative body.[34]

Justice Black did not consider Justice Goldberg's statement of a standard adequate as a safeguard against the use of "their private and personal notions" by judges to solve constitutional problems.[35]

D. *Abortion*

Roe v. Wade[36] raises many issues which do not concern us here.[37] The basic concern is with the determination by the Court that the relationship between a pregnant woman and her doctor is within a constitutionally

---

32. *Id.* at 508 (dissenting opinion).
33. *Id.* at 509.
34. *Id.* at 511, 512.
35. *Id.* at 519.
36. 410 U.S. 113 (1973).
37. *See* Vieira, *Roe and Doe: Substantive Due Process and the Right of Abortion,* 25 Hast. L.J. 867 (1974). The author views *Roe* and *Doe* as a return to the discredited substantive due process doctrine and argues that the new fascination may be unwise. The author makes a point by point refutation of *Roe. See also* Note, *Roe v. Wade and Doe v. Bolton: The Compelling State Interest Test in Substantive Due Process,* 30 Wash. & Lee L. Rev. 628 (1973). The article traces the concept of substantive due process from Justice Holmes' dissent in Lochner v. New York, 198 U.S. 45 (1905), and asserts that it is an attempt to give substantive content to the term "liberty" in the fourteenth amendment's due process clause in order to protect values not specified in the Bill of Rights. *Roe and Doe* in the author's view represent a continued attempt to apply the substantive due process standard. *See also* Note, *Roe & Paris: Does Privacy Have a Principle?* 26 Stan. L. Rev. 1161 (1974). The article discusses the concept of privacy and attempts to set the context in which the term could possibly have meaning. The author reviews the John Stuart Mill principle on the need to justify an infringement of freedom by harm to others and recounts the Hart-Devlin debate.

protected zone of privacy which permits no state interference during the first three months of pregnancy.

Before arriving at that point the Court considered: first, whether the fetus is a "person" in constitutional terms;[38] second, where the legitimate interest of a state begins; third, the mother's right to privacy. Although we are concerned primarily with the third, it is so interwoven in the first two as to be inseparable.

Mr. Justice Blackmun, writing for a majority of the Court, recognized that the Court had never held that the term "person" applied to a prenatal situation.[39] But from the language of the Constitution itself and relevant cases, the Court inferred that the term did not include the unborn.[40] At once, however, Justice Blackmun recognized that his analysis and conclusions were not totally dispositive of the issue.[41]

The fact which saved the Court from the need for further analysis was that the State of Texas did not itself treat the fetus as though it were a person in other than the abortion situation. Even in the abortion context, the Texas law did not treat abortion the same as murder insofar as the penalties were concerned.[42] As to the related issue of when life begins, the Court merely recognized the fact that there is substantial dispute on the subject.[43] Justice Blackmun stated that whenever fetal life may in fact begin, the State of Texas could not override the rights of the woman by choosing one view over many others.[44] The life of the fetus, whatever its significance, is a recognized factor to be viewed in conjunction with the other operative considerations.[45]

As to the second factor the state is recognized to have a legitimate interest in preserving the life and health of the mother and, at some point, in

---

38. For a discussion of the Court's treatment whether the fetus is a "person" in constitutional terms, *see* Comment, *Roe v. Wade: Its Impact on Rights of Choice in Human Reproduction*, 5 COLUM. HUM. RIGHTS. L. REV. 497, 509 (1973).

39. 410 U.S. at 157.

40. *Id.* at 158.

41. The Court attempted to answer the contention of the State of Texas that fetal life began with conception and from that point the life of the fetus could be protected by the state. Justice Blackmun stated:

Indeed, our decision in *United States v. Vuitch*, 402 U.S. 62 (1971), inferentially is to the same effect [that is, an unborn child is not a person], for we there would not have indulged in statutory interpretation favorable to abortion in specified circumstances if the necessary consequence was the termination of life entitled to Fourteenth Amendment protection.

This conclusion, does not of itself fully answer the contentions raised by Texas, and we pass on to other considerations.

410 U.S. at 159.

42. Justice Blackmun recognized that it was inconsistent for Texas to argue that the fetus is a person and entitled to fourteenth amendment protection but fail, *inter alia*, to treat the destruction of a fetus as though it were murder. 410 U.S. at 157, n.54.

43. 410 U.S. at 160.

44. *Id.* at 162.

45. *Id.*

the life and health of the fetus as well.[46] The Court found that at the point when the fetus is capable of an independent existence the state has a valid interest in its survival.[47] The state can therefore regulate abortion to protect its interest in the fetus' existence *after a certain period of time* and *to protect the health and life* of the mother.

The entire discussion thus far presumes that the right the mother has is fundamental or constitutionally protected. Justice Blackmun stated:

> This right of privacy, whether it be founded in the Fourteenth Amendment's concept of personal liberty and restrictions upon state action, as we feel it is, or, as the District Court determined, in the Ninth Amendment's reservation of rights to the people, is broad enough to encompass a woman's decision whether or not to terminate her pregnancy. The detriment that the state would impose upon the pregnant woman by denying this choice altogether is apparent.[48]

The effect of this determination was a requirement that the state have a compelling interest before interference with this right could be permitted. The Court found the right to be qualified three months after pregnancy began. The Court stated:

> We, therefore, conclude that the right of personal privacy includes the abortion decision, but that this right is not unqualified and must be considered against important state interests in regulation.[49]

That is to say that the right of privacy found herein is not absolute throughout and the woman is not isolated in her privacy.[50] The result is that the health of

---

46. *Id.* at 163.

47. The Court finds this conclusion acceptable because the mortality rate for mothers before the three month point is lower for abortions than for unterminated pregnancies. Therefore, the state cannot regulate abortions during this prior period on the supposition of protecting maternal health.

The state has an interest in the fetus after the "compelling" point has been reached because it has a capacity for independent life. Thus from the point of viability the state can regulate abortions to protect the fetus, if the procedure does not at the same time endanger the woman. The Court assumes, quite improperly, that viability is the point when state interest in fetal life is engaged. To say that merely because the fetus will more than likely survive the state has an interest in protecting it is to assume that viability is the most important single factor (perhaps the only factor) relevant to a determination of the point at which the state has an interest. It is with this naked assumption that one has difficulties, not with any underlying truth it may in fact represent. For a discussion of the tests which can be used to determine at which point life begins, *see* Dellapenna, *Nor Piety, Nor Wit: The Supreme Court on Abortion*, 6 COLUM. HUM. RIGHTS L. REV. — (1974).

48. 410 U.S. at 159.

49. *Id.* at 154.

50. *Id.* at 155 where the Court states:

the woman as a mother and the interest of the state in the fetus act (after a certain point) to counter-balance her right and to operate as a competing interest. For the first three months the woman remains *absolutely* free to have an abortion as she so desires.

Mr. Justice Douglas concurred. He recognized three forms of fundamental rights: first, the absolute first amendment right of expression, intellect, tastes, interest and personality; second, the qualifiable rights with regard to the "freedom of choice in the basic decisions of one's life respecting marriage, divorce, procreation, contraception, and the upbringing of children;"[51] third, the qualifiable freedom to care for one's health and person.[52] But as to the basic conclusions of Justice Blackmun, both Justices Douglas and Stewart (who also concurred) had little to add.

Mr. Justice Rehnquist argued in his dissent that the test should be one of mere rationality, inferring from prior case law that the right to an abortion was not fundamental. He stated:

> The test traditionally applied in this area of social and economic legislation is whether or not a law such as that challenged has a rational relation to a valid state objective. *Williamson v. Lee Optical Co.*, 348 U.S. 483, 491 (1955). The Due Process Clause of the Fourteenth Amendment undoubtedly does place a limit, albeit a broad one, on legislative power to enact laws such as this. If the Texas statute were to prohibit an abortion even where the mother's life is in jeopardy, I have little doubt that such a statute would lack a rational relation to a state objective under the test in *Williamson, supra.* But the Courts' sweeping invalidation of any restrictions on abortion during the first trimester is impossible to justify under that standard, and the conscious weighing of competing factors that the Court's opinion apparently substitutes for the established test is far more appropriate to a legislative judgment than to a judicial one.[53]

II.   ARTICULATION OF A THEORY OF FUNDAMENTAL RIGHTS

When the examination of the cases was undertaken it was not anticipated that one would find that an opinion written by a Justice would rest on a

---

Although the results are divided, most of the courts have agreed that the right of privacy, however based, is broad enough to cover the abortion decision; that the right, nonetheless, is not absolute and is subject to some limitations; and that at some point the state interests as to protection of health, medical standards, and prenatal life, become dominant. We agree with this approach.

51. 410 U.S. at 216. Justice Douglas did not discuss why it was more important to be able to talk about sterilization (for instance) than it would be to limit such acts when done to those who are not able to articulate an objection (*Skinner* would not make all sterilization illegal).

52. 410 U.S. at 213.

53. *Id.* at 171.

clearly articulated philosophical theory; nor was it anticipated that a group of opinions by the same Justice in the area of human reproduction would reveal, when read together, reliance on such a theory. What was hoped for was that a basic definition of fundamental human rights would emerge from which an inference could be drawn as to what philosophical theory would support such a definition and conclusion of law What was found instead was a general reliance on an unspoken theory or premise broad enough to support the dual conclusion that there are fundamental human rights and that these rights are deserving of the same protection given those rights enunciated in the Bill of Rights. The desire here is to provide a foundation for the concept of fundamental human rights that has a philosophical foundation which is consistent with the theory of the American Constitution.

The search for a basic definition or principle is not a plea for a rigid imposition of a full blown theory of law or philosophy upon a dispute without regard to the equities of the case. It is merely a search for a single principle, a point of orientation, from which one can view the concept of fundamental rights and understand the assumptions which underlie it as well as the conclusions which follow from it. We seek not to *impose* philosophical attitudes on the Court but to *recognize* the intellectual "baggage" which accompanies a concept the Court has chosen to use and to determine if the concept and "baggage" are consistent with the generally accepted view of American government as it relates to individual freedom.

The fact that the Court has failed to articulate a basis for the concept of individual rights can be viewed in one of two ways. One can say on the one hand that because the Justices have stated no theory or provided no basis, the people are not burdened with a philosophical theory loosed within their midst that may be abhorrent to their own point of view. Philosophical theories are, after all, much like religions; each of us is most comfortable with our own view and resents others needlessly imposing theirs upon us. But, at the same time, if a result is reached which perhaps can only be explained by a philosophical concept as it relates to a problem, it would seem that a failure to state the point adds to one's confusion and in no way serves to placate his desire to remain free from this kind of imposition. In these circumstances the imposition is an accomplished fact. What we seek is the justification for it.

One can, on the other hand, recognize immediately that a stated premise provides not only a context for understanding a conclusion but also a springboard for disagreement with it. In this view as well, a statement of the premise is necessary. The conclusion, in fact, appears to be the same regardless of the initial attitude one may have. If the premise is necessary to the conclusion it should be explained, even if the premise is philosophical in nature.

By applying this standard to the Supreme Court—this demand for total articulation of all premises—one is doing no more than demanding that the

Court provide the perspective from which it sees the problem and thereby furnish the limitation on its power which is inherent to that perspective. To say that the context limits the exercise of power is to say no more than that if one determines the concepts which must be considered to solve a problem, one is also implicitly asserting that if one goes outside those concepts which form the context, that excursion will not be productive in the solution of the problem. Therefore, if one can find a context for the concept of fundamental or basic human rights with which the Court would agree, one would be saying to the Court that its actions ought to be limited to this context when it is dealing with the issue. The Court need not address the philosophical theory which explains the concept, but it should be cognizant of the limits of the concept which can be inferred by an appeal to a philosophical theory. Because a philosophical theory provides a context for a concept of fundamental rights it is essential to our inquiry. One should be cognizant of the function of the theory as a limitation on judicial action as well as a justification for it.[54]

The first task then is to state a concept or definition of fundamental rights, the second task is to juxtapose it with the Constitution. In determining what ought to be the content of the concept of fundamental rights one must first recognize its present usage. The attempt will be to go beyond the bare statement of the phrase, "fundamental right," as though no explanation were needed and to state both the concept behind the phrase and the context in which the phrase has meaning. There is considerably more behind the phrase than the Court seems willing to concede. By "fundamental right," as it is used here, the writer means a right which is essential and necessary for the freedom of the individual—each individual regardless of status, class, race, or occupation. We anticipate the discussion of Kant in the next section by stating that the power of the majority, and indeed the state (government generally), is to be defined and viewed in terms of the individual. A democracy in this view is not a government in which people are *allowed* to be free; it is a government created and controlled by a free people. The people defined the

---

54. Haigh, *Defining Due Process of Law: The Case of Mr. Justice Hugo L. Black*, 17 S.D.L. Rev. 1 (1972). This article presents a view of Justice Black as one concerned with limiting judicial discretion and thereby rendering judicial review more compatible with democratic values. Due process for Justice Black is viewed here as the written law of the land. The common law is not viewed at all as an operative standard. Despite Justice Frankfurter's contrary view he wrote to Justice Black:

> I appreciate the frailties of men, but the war is for me meaningless and Hitler becomes the true prophet if there is no such thing as Law different from and beyond the individuals who give it expression. And what I am talking about is that if each temporary majority on this Court—and none is very long—in fact merely regards its presence on this Court as an opportunity for translating its own private notions of policy into decisions, the sooner an educated public opinion becomes aware of the fact the better not only for truth but also in the true interest of democracy.

Letter from Justice Frankfurter to Justice Black, Nov. 13, 1943 cited by Haigh at 36.

government. The government does not define the basic rights of the people; the government can only protect those rights.

This subtle reorientation has startling ramifications. By simply redefining the relationship of a government to a people one can bring into focus more clearly the nature of those rights thought to be fundamental or basic. If a right is arguably necessary to the freedom of an individual, it is fundamental. If it is not necessary, it is not fundamental. Of course, not all rights are fundamental. For instance the right to own a gun, one could argue, is not fundamental; whereas the right to marry or to have children is. The test for determining whether a given right is fundamental is a determination of whether the right is essential for the freedom of *an* individual in society. The determination is not of what is appropriate for one of wealth or status, but simply what is appropriate for everyone. This approach hopefully would alleviate the concern for a particular minority or political group. The right, if fundamental, is held by everyone. If it is fundamental, an individual can be denied it only under the most extreme circumstances such that its denial would be tolerated universally. It would have to be an occasion wherein each one would be denied exercise of the right. No right in this view is absolute and no one is above the restrictions which could be placed on the exercise of a fundamental right. Further elucidation can be done best in the context of the Constitution.

The first problem in the area of constitutional law is that historically the rights deemed fundamental have not been treated, *as a matter of principle,* differently from "economic or social rights."[55] Under the applicable constitutional test unless a right can be found in, or implied by, the language of the Constitution, states are allowed to restrict its exercise upon a showing that there is a reasonable connection between the effect of such a law and a legitimate state interest. If it can be determined that the category, "fundamental rights," is one that is constitutionally protected, then no explicit constitutional language need be found nor language which implies the existence of a particular right. All that one need show is that the right is fundamental and that fundamental rights are protected.

The second problem is finding language in the Constitution which would support this thesis. One could argue that the right is protected by the due

---

55. *See* Goodpaster, *The Constitution and Fundamental Rights,* 15 ARIZ. L. REV. 479 (1973). The author accepts the premise operative here, that is that the Court has failed to develop an underlying principle in the handling of the problem of fundamental rights. He tied this problem to the unresolved issue of the scope of judicial review. Until this point this writer is in complete accord. But the author of this article went no further than to distinguish between rights which embody substantive social and economic views and those which theoretically act to limit possible abuses of governmental power. Even though the distinction is helpful it does not appear to create mutually exclusive categories. Arguably an abuse of government power may embody a substantive social or economic view. His distinction is helpful principally because it serves to put the inquiry into proper perspective by distinguishing fundamental rights from the problem of judicial review.

process clause of the fourteenth amendment or the language of the ninth amendment. Justice Harlan argued that the due process clause protects fundamental rights,[56] but he did not explain, as we have seen, how he determined that a given right is fundamental. We have provided content for the concept and, arguably, an appropriate test and if one adds the general theory of Justice Harlan, the argument seems complete. The right is fundamental if it is essential to the freedom of the individual and it is constitutionally protected by the due process clause of the fourteenth amendment.

If one were to argue that the right is found in the ninth amendment one would necessarily accept the view expressed by Justice Goldberg in *Griswold*.[57] The ninth amendment states that the enumeration of rights in the Constitution is not exclusive as to those rights retained by the people. Because the Bill of Rights operates in part to give special treatment to certain rights, it does not necessarily follow that there are not other rights equally deserving of the same special treatment. If the fourteenth amendment is written to protect individual and personal rights from excessive state interference, it would seem that the rights guaranteed to the individual by the ninth amendment are necessarily further immune from state interference by the operation of the fourteenth amendment on the ninth.

If the same test articulated above were applied to Justice Goldberg's argument, the result would be to give a foundation to the principle of fundamental rights as he discussed it.[58] It would provide a context and a test which would act as a self-limiting concept and restrict the Court's activities to those areas it could reasonably articulate with a principled and well-reasoned argument.

The final task remaining is to provide a philosophical justification for this concept of fundamental rights which is consistent with American constitutional principles. Three philosophies will be discussed which state a form of limited government. They are in order of historical development: natural law, skepticism—utilitarianism, and Kant or incipient phenomenology.

III.   A Philosophical Justification

A.   *Natural Law*

Natural law provided a basis for a view of government and rights at the time the Declaration of Independence was written. If intellectual history had not turned its face against this view, one could argue that no explanation is necessary because natural law is still the universal assumption which under-

---

56. *See* quote cited at notes 28 and 48 *supra* and accompanying text.
57. 386 U.S. at 484.
58. *See* quote cited at notes 22-27 *supra* and accompanying text.

lies any theory of law. It would, therefore, be beneficial to investigate the content of natural law and its eventual demise.

If one assumes that the Declaration of Independence represents an articulation of the original or incipient American position on the source of fundamental rights as they relate to governmental power, then an examination of its language may be helpful in discovering what this source was thought to be.[59] The document itself refers to the "laws of nature and of nature's God," to "inalienable rights" and to "self-evident truths." It also speaks of the power which flows to the government from the consent of the people and the right of the people to change the form of government: a right to revolution as it were.

One could look to John Locke[60] as the philosopher from whom these concepts were borrowed. One could also look farther back in time to Thomas Aquinas.[61] Both philosophers reflect a natural law point of view. The Supreme Court in devising a test for determining whether a particular right was fundamental has looked on occasion to the common law of England.[62] If one is to believe Justice Black, a majority of the Court has also looked to the natural law.[63] If one assumes, *arguendo*, the truth of this conclusion, it would be advantageous to examine a source which attempted to reconcile the common law with natural law, and that source would be William Blackstone. In maintaining that the common law does, or should, rest on a natural law foundation, he provided a uniquely Anglo-American perspective from which all the elements of such a judicial view of fundamental rights can be regarded.[64]

---

59. The influence of natural law through Locke and Aquinas upon our founding fathers seems to be conceded without question. For instance, *see* 5 F. COPLESTON, A HISTORY OF PHILOSOPHY 151 (1964).

60. J. LOCKE, SECOND TREATISE ON CIVIL GOVERNMENT (T. P. Peardon ed. 1952). Locke proposed a system of government in which all elements, legislative, executive, and judicial are answerable to the people.

61. ST. THOMAS AQUINAS, SUMMA THEOLOGIAE (Pegis ed. 1945). Aquinas developed a system in which law was divided into two categories, natural law which was eternal and reflected the law of God and positive law which was created and controlled by man.

62. For an example of the Supreme Court's use of the common law, *see* Murray's Lessee v. Hoboken Land and Improvement Co., 59 U.S. (18 How.) 272 (1856). Justice Curtis devised a test for the Court in determining due process questions. He asked two questions:

1) Is the process forbidden by the Constitution; and
2) Is the process forbidden by those English customs and practices which are held compatible with our system of government.

See generally the cases in which the Court was asked to determine whether the Constitution required a following of the common law jury system which required a 12 man jury (Williams v. Florida, 399 U.S. 78 (1970)) or a unanimous verdict (Apodaca v. Oregon, 406 U.S. 404 (1972)).

63. *See* quote cited at note 34 *supra*. The Court has, however, never explicitly adopted the natural law as a test for determining whether a claimed right is fundamental.

64. *See generally*, W. BLACKSTONE, COMMENTARIES ON THE COMMON LAW (G. Chase ed., 3d ed. 1899). Blackstone attempted to put the common law of England into a natural law context. The question with regard to his efforts is whether the common law was within a natural law context or whether Blackstone was trying to restructure the common law to place it there. If one reads the history of the development of the common law, the argument can be made that

If the Supreme Court does indeed use a Blackstonian view of the common law as a basis for its concept of fundamental rights, it is instructive to consider how it proceeds or might proceed under such an orientation. When the Supreme Court has referred to the common law it has been basically a view to history[65] and the place the proposed right was said to have in the common law. If the Court were to refer to natural law it would be a reference to how the proposed right fits into the universal law of God as it is reflected in the social relationships of men. One could gain insight into this body of law by the proper application of reason to the facts.[66] Therefore, if the common law is related to the natural law, the test for whether a right is fundamental would be either a view to the common law of England or the natural law which arguably Blackstone thought undergirded it. A given right would be fundamental if it was recognized by the common law or by the natural law if the common law did not speak to the point. Because the common law is grounded, in this view, in the natural law the inquiry is not an investigation of alternative sources but of separate layers of a common source.

Using this approach, if the right is viewed as recognized by the common law, history is totally dispositive of whether the right is fundamental (although an extrapolation may be necessary when the circumstances reflect a uniquely contemporary situation)—a problem of how the facts of history are to be interpreted remains a possible source of controversy, but it is nonetheless within the context of history that the problem is to be analyzed. If the asserted right is thought to be a natural right and was not found in the common law, reason and logical analysis would allow one to view the facts against the ordered universe which reflects the will of God and God's determination of how man fits in that universe.

The natural law system is characterized by the assumption that the world and the universe are an organized and orderly system. The system can be known to an inquiring individual by appealing to experience. One looks to how the right is said to be central to the human condition. One then looks to see if the claimed right is in fact central. Reason and logic are guaranteed by God to not lead one to a wrong result so that if one is logical and gathers

history does not reflect a conscious growth of the respect for individual liberty but rather traces the development and decline of the royal prerogative. In this view many of Lord Coke's decisions which held that the common law protected such rights appealed to precedents which historically did not support that conclusion. Examples of such decisions are Smith v. Smith Co. Eliz. 741, 78 Eng. Rep. 974 (C.B., 1600), Sir Anthony Roper's Case 12 Co. Rep. 45, 77 Eng. Rep. 1326 (C.B., 1607), Prohibitions Del Roy 12 Co. Rep. 31, 77 Eng. Rep. 1312 (1607), Case of Prohibitions 13 Co. Rep. 30, 77 Eng. Rep. 1440 (1609), and the Case of the Marshalsea 10 Co. Rep. 68b, 76a, 77 Eng. Rep. 1027, 1038 (K.B. 1613). Therefore the natural law may not be directly relevant to the common law at all and the common law may not in fact demonstrate a concern for individual rights.

65. *See* note 62 *supra.*

66. In this regard Justice Black's fear that a judge using a natural law analysis would act on his own emotion or own view of reality arguably is not well founded. *See* note 34, *supra.*

sufficient fact the conclusion will be a proper one which all reasonable men will see as the only valid one. Natural law analysis is, therefore, an application of reason to fact and the comparing of the results to the natural order of things which is known through reason and which reflect the will of God.[67] This view of natural law is reflective of Aquinas and Blackstone.

The utility of the natural law view as a context for fundamental rights lay in its assumption that truth and reality are universal and necessary constants which make the world and its content available to us all with the proper application of reason to the facts. The process by which one comes to know the truth is a process in which, by the acquisition of facts through experience, the content of the mind is brought up to the level of reality.[68] One's ideas, judgments, and conclusions are thus brought to a level which is shared by all who understand the world: one reality, and one true view of it. If people disagree regarding the truth of a particular matter, it is because one or the other has either failed to be logical or has not ascertained all the facts.

In Blackstone's view[69] (and natural law theorists generally) the natural law coupled with a consent theory of government created a concept of democracy. In this general theory one does not find basic human freedom and the total of all rights in the government. One is not free because one is an American: one is free because one is human. The legislative branch of government may ascertain and change with minimal reason only a part of the rights and privileges said to exist. There are other secondary or positive rights which are granted by society and are a result of an individual's consent to remain within a societal context. These rights can be taken when it is both appropriate and necessary. Men are free to recognize these rights and to negate them without a view to God or nature. The government need only gain the consent of a majority of the people or their elected representatives. It need be shown to a court upon review only that the action was reasonable and appropriate to achieve a socially desirable end. The Supreme Court decided finally in *Ferguson v. Skrupa*[70] that it would not review laws and judgments from state legislatures and courts which were economic or social in their concern. If the Court were in a natural law context it would be asserting merely that economic and social rights were positive rights and not natural rights.[71]

---

67. The natural law assumption which allows such general and universal conclusions is that the mind is a passive agent and adds nothing to what comes to it through experience.

68. T. AQUINAS, DE VERITATAE, Art I, of 9 (translated by W. Mulligan 1952).

69. W. BLACKSTONE, I COMM. 133 and I COMM. 135.

70. 372 U.S. 726 (1963). The Court stated that it would turn its face against the substantive due process principle and not apply the strict scrutiny test to cases dealing with social and economic issues.

71. *See* Goodpaster, note 55 *supra*. The author there attempted to distinguish economic and social issues from fundamental rights problems and thereby sought to apply the standard of judicial review which gave deference to state action to the former and not the latter.

Those rights called "fundamental" or "natural" would be excluded from this standard of review. To them one could then arguably apply the "compelling state interest" test[72] to determine if the individual can be denied the freedom to exercise that right.

If one attempts to put this natural rights concept into the context of the Constitution, one is immediately confronted with the problem of where it can be placed. As stated earlier in an articulation of this writer's definition of fundamental rights, one can find the due process clause of the fourteenth amendment or the ninth amendment appropriate for this purpose. A natural law theory would be consistent with the majority of the Supreme Court's use of the phrase "fundamental right" and as we have seen the language is close enough for Justice Black to conclude that such is the case.[73] Since *Griswold*[74] the Court has found privacy to be a convenient concept which for all practical purposes has replaced fundamental rights.[75] The language used to express the concept is the same in content as that which was used to express the concept of fundamental rights.[76] The Court has been equally remiss in explaining the premises and test which would both explain why a given right is a privacy right and how one is to know it. Again natural law provides a basis which is not inconsistent with what the Court has articulated as its concern. Given the similarity in language and possible philosophical foundation, it appears that privacy is the old wine in new bottles.

To accept this concept of privacy or fundamental rights one must somehow deal with the Bill of Rights. Is one saying that the Bill of Rights is without import as a classification of fundamental rights? Basically, yes. In the words of Professor Wechsler:

> . . . I argue that we should prefer to see the other clauses of the Bill of Rights [excluding "due process" and "equal protection" for purposes not relevant here] read as an affirmation of the special values they embody rather than as statements of a finite rule of law, its limits fixed by the consensus of a century long past, with problems very different from our own.[77]

They stand not so much as a forever closed concept (as Justice Black would have it[78]) but as examples of the kinds of concerns the Republic once thought

---

72. *See* Justice Douglas' opinion in *Skinner* note 9 and accompanying text, *supra*.

73. *See quote cited at note 34 supra* and Haigh, note 54 *supra*.

74. 381 U.S. 479 (1964).

75. *See*, Kauper, *Penumbras, Peripheries, Emanations, Things Forgotten: The Griswold Case*, 64 MICH. L. REV. 235 (1963). The author discusses how the theory of fundamental rights or privacy enunciated in *Griswold* has "accordian-like qualities," capable of embracing any asserted right that might appeal to a majority of the Court.

76. *Compare* the language in *Griswold with* that in *Skinner*.

77. Wechsler, *Toward Neutral Principles of Constitutional Law*, 73 HARV. L. REV. 1, 19 (1959).

78. *See* Haigh note 54 *supra*.

important or as expressions of basic attitudes about the relationship of government to the rights of the individual.

The felt need to seek a new concept of rights manifest in *Griswold* is a result of the decision by the Court to abandon the use of substantive due process as a basis for extensive review of actions by states.[79] It is unclear how the Court determined which rights were fundamental. But, in arguing against substantive due process, Justices Black[80] and Rehnquist[81] stated that without the substantive due process standard the Court has no justification for using fundamental rights as a basis for extensive review. If this be so, then there is also no need for basing fundamental rights on a natural law theory. The result is the death of not only substantive due process but fundamental rights and natural law as well. If the Court has, indeed, abandoned natural law (assuming it was ever adopted), then it has arrived at a point reached in the philosophical community after it considered and understood David Hume.[82]

B. *Skepticism—Utilitarianism*

David Hume questioned the basic premise of natural law and thereby brought under question all that had been built upon its foundation. This included, of course, the concept of human rights and individual freedom found in the idea of natural rights. Hume began by asserting that there was nothing which would qualify as knowledge that could not be traced to a sense experience. Sense experience is datum taken from the everyday world. One must be able to say he saw it, touched it, tasted it, heard it, or smelled it before he can be said to have experienced it, and without having experienced it one cannot be said to have *knowledge* of it. One must review the content of one's mind and expel that which was based on sense experience. One is skeptical about any general statements made about the world. The concern, for Hume, was with understanding experience—experience was the sole source of knowledge.[83]

Hume noted quite properly that one cannot experience God, necessity, universality, or a cause and effect principle. These are concepts which are essential to a concept of separate human rights (separate from government). Following the analysis of Hume, they must be stricken from that which one could properly call knowledge. The effect upon natural law was devastating. God was important to natural law because although one may want to argue that these rights are found in the nature of man, God acts as the creator and guarantor of not only the rights of man but of the general freedom as well.

79. *See* Ferguson v. Skrupa 372 U.S. 726 (1926) and text accompanying note to *supra*.
80. *See* quote cited at note 34 *supra*.
81. *See* quote cited at note 53 *supra*.
82. D. HUME, A TREATISE ON HUMAN NATURE (C. W. Hendel ed. 1927).
83. Hume was concerned with countering the assumptions of natural law. Chief among them was the belief that what could be inferred from experience must be necessarily true.

Necessity is an important concept because it allows one to use logical relationship to explain and relate events. At the core of the science of logic is the premise that conclusions which follow from its use are necessary. The concept of universality allows one to make general (as opposed to particular singular) statements about the world which are true. The cause—effect principle allows one to connect events and predict results.

Hume denied that any of these concepts were traceable to experience. He denied that human freedom could be based on any concept other than custom which grew out of a concern by the majority for ends most useful for the general good.[84] As Hume stated in programmatic terms:

> That Justice is useful to society, and consequently that *part* of its merit, at least, must arise from that consideration, it would be a superfluous undertaking to prove. That public utility is the *sole* origin of justice, and that reflections on the beneficial consequences of this virtue are the *sole* foundation of its merits; this proposition, being more curious and important will better serve our examination and inquiry.[85]

As a consequence of the Humean critique many points of view in the form of jurisprudence have developed which attempt to limit governmental power by appeal to general utility or majority will.[86] The emphasis in this view is upon the effectuation of the will of the majority after determining what is best for the general society. What one is saying if he were to adopt this view is that the will of the majority is sufficient to both limit government action and protect individual rights. Since the concern here is with individual rights, the first portion of the preceding sentence will be accepted as valid and only the second half will be examined.

The point to be emphasized is that a government normally represents the will of the majority[87] and that if the majority is to limit the power of the government, one is in effect requiring the majority to limit itself.[88] History

---

84. *See generally* D. HUME, AN ENQUIRY CONCERNING THE PRINCIPLES OF MORALS (C. W. Hendel ed. 1927). Section III (*of Justice*) and Section IV (*Why Utility Pleases*).

85. *Id*. Part I at 9.

86. This general category is intended to cover the very broad area of jurisprudence that is traceable to Hume, Bentham, or J. S. Mill. This view is generally given the name utilitarianism.

87. As apartheid in South Africa and the status of women in America indicate, majority rule can represent a concept of power as well as numbers; *i.e.*, a minority of the people may have a majority of the power. To say it another way, majority will is most reasonable when the government is a representative democracy wherein the distribution of power reflects the various interest groups affected, but neither majority rule nor democracy demand it. They would seem to only require that the majority's will be done. A minority can, in fact, control. Does it become wrong because the minority rules? Or is it only wrong when the minority operates to further its own end at the sacrifice of the majority's interest? When right and wrong are reduced to a question of numbers they seem to lose their majesty.

88. It seems unreasonable to argue that the majority of the people decide both the

has shown that this self-limitation has not been enough to protect minority rights. Something more in the form of limitation is needed. One could reasonably argue that such a limitation can be provided within the context of utilitarianism. To this writer's view, however, the fault lies in the basic assumption that limitations on governmental power can be sufficiently effected by looking to limit the power of the government without a view to individual freedom as the source of the limitation. If one takes the individual into account as a limiting principle, it would seem to go beyond the basic premise of Hume that *general utility* was the sole basis for limiting governmental power.[89]

If one looks only to history the philosophy of Hume has not proven adequate. If the history of slavery in America were not sufficient to warn the most benevolent of men that minority rights are not sufficiently safeguarded by majority rule, then certainly Nazi Germany stands like a colossus to bear witness to the inadequacy of such a position.[90] It seems hardly credible to assert that slavery becomes socially justifiable because the majority wills it, or that the slaughter and imprisonment of innocent people by the Nazis was proper because the government that decreed it was freely elected. The arbitrary imprisonment called slavery does not become meritorious because only the slaves complain or the wanton slaughter that typified the Nazi regime become justifiable because a government can demonstrate the benefits. These are not hypothetical situations or logical constructs to be discussed and obscured by counter-productive polemics; they are *reality* and a failure to deal with them by one who defends utilitarianism is a failure to be relevant.

By way of conclusion this writer asserts that if one is to discuss and ultimately to discover a basis of individual rights which is transcendental to a government of free men, it is necessary to recognize at first that the form of government cannot at once be both the guarantor *and* the source of all rights and freedoms. There must be clearly identifiable rights, for the safeguarding of which the society must be held accountable to each and every individual. For if the state is not constrained to protect rights it did not grant and the state can formulate rights as it believes them necessary, it can effectively control all individual freedoms without regard to any concepts but those it formulated.

---

justification of law and law itself. Upon reflection asking one to make this distinction is much like asking one to discuss "a night in which all cows are black."

89. *See* quote cited at note 85 *supra*.

90. If one finds no difficulty with the excesses of Nazi Germany, then one would be at a loss to explain the assumption which underlay the Nüremberg trials; that is, that some acts are legally (in the broadest sense) indefensible regardless of the formal or procedural legality of the acts themselves. To say Nüremberg was based on a moral premise is perhaps to cast a false light on the proceedings. Morals may be thought to underlie some laws, but it hardly seems just to thrust one's sense of morals on another and to punish him because he does not accept the moral conclusions now, nor did he accept them when the act was committed, *unless* by morals one means that rationale which is the basic underpinning of law and makes a legislative enactment a legal obligation.

D. *Immanuel Kant*

Immanuel Kant saw quite clearly the impact of the Humean critique upon what he considered to be indispensable concepts. He sought to explain these natural law conclusions about universality, necessity, God, and the cause-effect principle from another perspective. Kant conceded the legitimacy of Hume's critique of natural law but in his concern to guarantee human freedom from arbitrary and unnecessary state action he chose a new orientation and concept. The new orientation was the "Copernican Revolution" and the new concept was human self-consciousness.

The Kantian system is valuable in the discussion not for its overall content or the logical force which may or may not accompany its exposition. It is important for our purposes here because it is premised on the belief that individual freedom would be explained best in terms of the individual and not the form of government. If individual freedom was the motivating force behind the founding fathers' choice of our constitutional government, the assumption by the Supreme Court of this premise would not be inconsistent with history. It would also allow the Court to ground its concept of fundamental rights in a philosophically defendable context.

The detailed discussion of the Kantian position is presented here to allow the reader to see the context in which this concept of freedom was discussed by Kant. It is not presented as a guide to how the Court ought to reason. It would be no more appropriate for the Supreme Court to cite Kant or any other thinker who generally held this view than it would be for the Court to cite Blackstone or natural law. The adoption of this context would allow the Court to say merely that the question of what a fundamental right is or ought to be is a question of whether the right is essential to one's idea of a free individual. This new orientation is the perspective provided by Kant and Kantianism is useful for this purpose alone.

The burden of explaining the Kantian epistemology is not a burden one accepts lightly. It is necessary here because only by a careful examination of the Kantian epistemology can we understand his belief that human freedom and human rights which we find at its core are the touchstone from which his view of the world can be explained. It is this concept of human freedom we present as a basis for a theory of law which accepts it as a premise and protects it through a judicial system.

No attempt will be made to provide a definitive statement of the Kantian world-view. The limits of space and the nature of our inquiry demand more of an overview than an exposition. Immanuel Kant's point of view presents a great challenge to one's ability to articulate for two basic reasons: first, the subject matter and the scope of his inquiry cover the entire range of human understanding; and second, he found a unique point of orientation which continues to cause difficulties for those not initiated in the rigors of philosophical analysis.

Also the view presented here is not intended to be a definitive statement on the nature of man. Many important developments since Kant call into question some of his assumptions.[91] But given that Hume dealt a death blow to natural law, the basic Kantian approach serves to indicate that there is an alternative to a general consent theory of government which rests solely on majority rule.[92] The alternative is an attempt to discover a basis of law in what is called "morals." By morality is meant a general relationship between men which requires the creation of neutral principles.[93] In determining these neutral principles Kant began with an analysis of the nature and scope of knowledge.

Kant began with his famous "Copernican Revolution." In the preface of the second edition of the *Critique of Pure Reason* Kant explained his intention. What Copernicus had done, of course, was to hypothesize that the sun was in fact the center of the universe and not the earth. Even though this assertion appeared to contradict sense experience, it allowed him to explain better planetary movement and to formulate thereby laws which were descriptive of their orbits. Kant attempted a similar revolution in philosophy. He sought to explain reality not as had been the case heretofore, in terms of laws implicit in nature, but rather in terms of laws implicit in man. Whereas Hume had questioned the origin of thought and the relation of ideas to experience, Kant questioned experience and tried to relate it to the *a priori* structures of the mind. We will go no further into the Kantian philosophy than this and attempt to explain why this distinction is crucial to our discussion.

Kant recognized that if the philosophy of Hume could not be explained so as to preserve the basic tenets of natural law (freedom, universality, necessity, and the cause and effect principle), then freedom from arbitrary majority action could not be justified in philosophical terms.

There is no empirical datum which can be found which would verify that men are free and essentially equal. There are no empirical data available which would justify the assertion that positive law (that is, legislative enactments and judicial opinions) must respect this freedom and individuality. Kant reasoned that the natural law concepts, among them universality, necessity (the tools of logic as well as metaphysics), cause, effect, and God

---

91. Chief among the assaults on Kant was the one led by Hegel (PHENOMENOLOGY OF MIND (translated by J. B. Baille 1910)). Hegel attacked the Kantian assumption that experience could never, through reason, bring one into direct connection with the world of things-in-themselves.

92. Arguably there are three basic approaches: natural law, which is philosophically antiquated and never really adopted by the Supreme Court, at least overtly; general consent theory or utilitarianism, which makes no allowance for basic human rights; and Kantianism or phenomenology, which presents an attempt to save human rights as a concept and to explain them in terms of *a priori* principles.

93. Morality is one of those terms which has religious as well as broad philosophical meaning. The term is used here to indicate a basis for law and not to imply any religious significance.

were the concepts in terms of which this freedom of man could be explained.[94]

The explanation chosen by Kant was revolutionary because he posited some of these elements beyond the capacity of man to learn through experience and he put some of them into the structure by which man in fact understands the world. They become the apparatus, the categories, which allow man to assimilate and organize those bits of reality which come through experience. The observation by Hume, that experience can never give man a view of reality but only a view of how reality appears to man, was never questioned by Kant. He stated:

> There can be no doubt that all our knowledge begins with experience. . . . But though all our knowledge begins with experience, it does not follow that it all arises out of experience.[95]

In fact Kant divided reality into two spheres: that which could be experienced by man—the phenomenon, and that which could not be explained through an analysis of sense experience but which nonetheless serves as a substratum that made those sense experiences understandable—the noumena. In a word, the world of experience, the phenomena, presented aspects of things as they appear from an individual's perspective; the noumena, world of things-in-themselves, was the reality. Since man cannot see all sides of an object at once, or understand all the reality there is in any concept, he can never "know" a thing in its entirety. He seeks only to understand that aspect of the thing which is presented to him. He then infers from these phenomena the basic underlying reality of the world. If one analyzes the matter properly, he will see that there is much which cannot be known through experience but must be inferred from what one has experienced. This inferred reality is that of which Hume spoke as being beyond the experience and outside the realm of knowledge.[96] This noumenal world of things-in-themselves was, for Kant, the world in which God remained a valid entity.[97]

Our primary concern is with those aspects of the Kantian system which he explained in terms of the individual. By "individual" it is clear from the

94. From this point of view the central question for Kant was a moral one. To answer the moral question Kant had to create a philosophy which explained both reality and man. His exposition is so tightly reasoned that it is difficult to explain a portion of it without appearing to leave a part out which appears relevant or including material which does not appear to be relevant. *See* E. CASSIRER, ROUSSEAU, KANT AND GOETHE (translated by J. Gutman, P. O. Kristeller & J. H. Randall 1955).

95. I. KANT, CRITIQUE OF PURE REASON 25 (N. K. Smith ed. 1958).

96. This is the reality Hume assumed to be beyond experience. He stated at 1 of the ENQUIRY CONCERNING HUMAN UNDERSTANDING: "All the perceptions of the human mind resolve themselves into two distinct kinds, which I shall call Impressions and Ideas." Hume here was speaking of experience and thoughts about experience.

97. *See generally,* the preface of the second edition of the CRITIQUE OF PURE REASON (N. K. Smith ed. 1958).

general tone of his work that he did not mean a representative one of many or a nameless, faceless everyman. By "individual" Kant meant each singular person as a human being who represents and stands for no more than his own self (it is a distinction which is crucial to the discussion). This Kantian individual is viewed in a phenomenal world, a world of appearances. In Hume's view this was sufficient to conclude that universally true propositions did not exist. Not so for Kant. This was sufficient to conclude merely that they did not exist *in the phenomenal world*. Kant found them in the structures of the mind—in how man *thought* about the world.[98]

Kant is best understood if one views the individual's coming to know the world as a process. The outer world, the world perceived phenomenally, exists in space and stands at one end of the process. The inner world, the inner structure of the reasoning faculties of man, is comprised of categories into which the bits of the outer world that come through experience are placed in an act of understanding. An experience is without meaning until the mind categorizes it. The categorization is the putting into context, the generalizing of an experience so that it is seen, for example, as a cause-effect relation. As Kant stated:

> Without sensibility no object would be given to us, without understanding no object would be thought. . . . It is, therefore, just as necessary to make our concepts sensible, that is to add the objects to them in intuition, as to make our intuitions intelligible, that is to bring them under concepts.[99]

A primary difficulty here presents itself. The term intuition can be construed to mean several things.[100] For our purposes it is sufficient to say that intuition is a form of the inner sense in which one looks into himself and the structures of his mind. This looking into one's self, this self-reflection, is the other end of the process. The process itself is called consciousness. One can through consciousness look outward, through experience, and see the phenomenal world; or one can look inward into himself through intuition, and see himself and infer from these two views the existence of the noumenal world.

In the moment of self-reflection, when one views himself as a conscious subject, the final piece of the puzzle is fitted into place. It is when one grasps the method by which the mind understands and sees that method as the key to making experience meaningful, sees the world *as the world*, and sees himself as the subject of consciousness, it is only then can one say he *understands*.

98. *Id.* at 17.
99. *Id.* at 91.
100. *See,* THE PHILOSPHY OF KANT; IMMANUEL KANT'S MORAL & POLITICAL WRITINGS (C. J. Friedrich ed. 1949).

It is in this light that the Kantian moral philosophy can be understood. One does not reach the categorical imperative—the rule that an action is right if it is one that each individual would like to see made the appropriate action for everyone—by viewing the world or positive law. One looks inward to establish the *a priori*, the purely rational, basis for law.

The nature of law, for Kant, is to express the notion of freedom in the external relations of men.[101] The legitimacy of law, as law, lies in its recognizing and safeguarding the freedom of a people. Just as in the natural law, a denial of rights by the state and a consequent curtailment of freedom is justifiable only if the greater collective freedom is served by it.

But to determine a standard against which law itself must be judged, one must look to the purely rational; that is, to the *a priori* rule which is created by a rational consideration of existing factors. One must determine how one would want everyone in the world to act were he confronted with the need to decide. Kant stated:

> In order to give laws, reason should necessarily only have to presuppose *itself* because rules are objectively and universally valid only when they are without any of the contingent subjective conditions by which one rational being is differentiated from another.[102]

It is in a consideration of freedom and the creation of universal obligation that morality must be viewed, and it is in terms of this morality that law itself must be judged.[103] Not being a Kantian scholar this writer does not presume to be qualified to indicate how he would react to our present concern or how the Kantian approach ought to be applied. There does, however, seem to be three distinct areas of inquiry. One must first determine why the right is asserted. This requires that the Court determine how the right is said to affect the concept of individual human freedom and why that right is essential to that concept. Next, the Court should create a neutral context in which the right asserted is put into perspective. This context should be such that it applies universally to everyone who is in a like situation. Finally, the Court must view the legal problem and these principles against the particular issue with which the Court is concerned.

If the Court were to approach the cases with which we began using

---

101. *See* GREGOR, LAWS OF FREEDOM (1963). A very good exposition of the Kantian view of freedom.

102. FRIEDRICH. THE PHILOSOPHY OF KANT at 213.

103. This language of Kant anticipates the discussion by Jean Paul Sartre in BEING AND NOTHINGNESS (translated by H. Barnes 1964). The Sartrean concern was to discuss morals and freedom in terms of human self-consciousness. The point is worth noting because the concept at its core was the seed for several philosophical points of view.

these steps, the result would not necessarily change. The effect would be to give the people a view of what the Court is doing and why. It would result in a peace of mind and intellectual contentment that is not possible given the approach the Court presently uses.

IV. CONCLUSION

The problem which faces the Court is two-tiered. On one level the Court is often asked to make legal decisions about controversies which are only partly legal in nature. It must first somehow answer questions and resolve disputes with regard to matters about which it has no expertise. *Roe* and abortion is an example of this. The argument can be made that *Roe* is also an example of how poorly the Court has dealt with this kind of problem—that judgment is not relevant to what we are about and need not be made here.

On the other level the Court may be asked to formulate or develop a sense of what is, or ought to be, the nature of law as it relates to individual human freedom. *Griswold* is an example of this problem. As we have seen, the Court has not shouldered this burden well. In fact it has all but ignored the problem by not looking to the philosophical underpinning which such a view, if held, would require. This failure seems odd given that the Court has shown a sharp and sophisticated sense of the probable social ramification of a particular decision and dealt with it quite well.

If the Court is to gain respect for its ability to handle all the relevant aspects of its decisions, it must deal with the philosophical, as well as it has with the social, ramifications of those decisions. If not, it must at some point recognize that if it is unwilling or unable to provide principled reasons for its decisions, then one may see on the horizon a developing sentiment that if the Court cannot be intellectually honest with America, perhaps Americans will come to ignore it. Although this eventuality would be a blow to the respect for the rule of law, it would also be an implicit recognition that the rule of law is most effective when people not only understand the rule but the reason for it as well. A mature democracy should demand no less.

PART II

A WORLD VIEW

The symposium on Law and Population was
held in Tunis and sponsored by the UN Fund
for Population Activities and the UN, in
cooperation with ILO, UNESCO, WHO, the
Tunisian government, the International
Planned Parenthood Federation, and the
International Advisory Committee on
Population and Law. Fifty nations and
fifteen organizations participated.

Foreword

Mohamed Mzali
Minister of Public Health and Vice President
of the High Council of Population, Tunisia

In all eras, man has aspired to improve his condition, struggling against everything which blocks his progress. Through his intellect and thought, through culture, science and technology, he has been able to rise above nature, to become the master of matter, and to overcome myriad obstacles in order to live a life worthy of his condition as a man.

The progress which has been made up to the present time has been considerable,—I would even say spectacular. Man is today protected against a great number of scourges which, only a few years ago, menaced him with awesome threats.

But a new danger, even more menacing, lies in wait for him: it is the demographic explosion which threatens to sink our whole planet into misery, hunger and even into decay.

It is time for man to become aware of this problem and of the steps he must take to deal with it.

May not his experience, his resources, even his power be used now to control his own growth?

Seven years ago,—to be exact, in May 1968, at the International Conference on Human Rights at Teheran, fifty-six countries* proclaimed the fundamental human right of man freely to decide on the size of his family, and to have the benefit of the information and instruction required to make it possible to enjoy this right. The same year, the whole international community, speaking through the United Nations General Assembly confirmed that proclamation.

Now, the population problem is taking on a judicial nature. A new human right has been born which needs legal support. All Governments are called on today to adopt the laws and measures necessary to guarantee to their people the full exercise of their right to family planning.

---

* The voting on Resolution XVIII of this Conference was fifty-six to none, with seven abstentions.

209

Is it, indeed, necessary to stress that this is a question of a better quality of life, of well-being and of progress? Is it necessary to recall the close interaction between population and economic and social development?

The Symposium on Law and Population organized at Tunis in June 1974 represents the first milestone on the road of law and population. It is to be hoped that all countries will put the recommendations of this symposium into effect, and will concert their efforts to establish an International Population Code which will certainly contribute to the betterment of humanity's lot. The United Nations, and particularly the UNFPA, has a very important role to play in this field.

Tunisia, which can today pride itself on its accomplishments in the field of population law, will continue to make its contribution to this international effort for the well-being of man.

The series of legislative measures which have been taken from the first months of independence until the present to benefit women, the family, and family planning, and the enthusiasm with which they have been greeted by the Tunisian people, may perhaps lead the way in the search for a solution to demographic problems. Is not the Tunis Symposium on Law and Population a tribute to the bold and courageous experience of our young country?

Introduction

During June 17-21, 1974 a Symposium on Law and Population was held in Tunis, sponsored by the United Nations Fund for Population Activities and the United Nations, in cooperation with the International Labour Organization, the United Nations Educational, Scientific and Cultural Organization, the World Health Organization, the Tunisian Government, the International Planned Parenthood Federation and the International Advisory Committee on Population and Law. In addition, financial contributions were made by the Organization for Economic Cooperation and Development and the International Development Research Center of Canada toward meeting the travel and per diem expenses of some of the participants. Over a hundred experts in the fields of law, medicine and the social sciences from fifty countries participated in the Symposium in their individual capacities to exchange views and experiences and to explore the existence of common features in their countries' legal systems related to population.

Under the patronage of President Habib Bourguiba, the Symposium served as a "follow-up" to a major study on Law and Population undertaken by some twenty-five Law and Population Projects around the world (funded mostly by the United Nations Fund for Population Activities). The study was "designed to clarify the impact of certain laws on population trends and to identify inconsistencies between existing legislation and Government policy with regard to population" in light of human rights principles. These projects aimed at providing "the basis for the development of guidelines for the revision and adaptation of legislation as required in support of population action programmes in the countries concerned."

In preparation for the Symposium, a series of background papers were commissioned, the texts of which are reproduced in this volume. In addition, following the model of the United Nations International Law Commission whose rapporteurs prepare Draft Articles and Commentaries as bases for discussion, the rapporteurs of the Symposium prepared Draft Recommendations on each of the topics, based on:

(a) relevant United Nations declarations, proclamations or conventions;

(b) proposals of the background papers commissioned by the Symposium;

and

(c)   results of studies undertaken by the various Law and Population
       Projects around the world.

The resultant Recommendations reflect the thorough deliberation which
went into the Workshop and Plenary Sessions. It may be of interest to note
that the relevancy and applicability of these Recommendations in the various
country and regional settings form the themes of the various Regional Seminars on Law and Population in 1974-75: In Nairobi on 24-30 November
1974 for anglophone Africa; in Lome, Togo on 10-14 March 1975 for francophone Africa; in Jakarta on 21-24 July 1975 for South and Southeast Asia;
and in Beirut on 4-6 December 1975 for the Middle East and North Africa.
All of these seminars plan to publish their proceedings, background papers
and recommendations. In addition, the Symposium's recommendations
served as bases for discussion in the Inter-Hemispheric Conference on Law,
Population and the Status of Women held in Airlie, Virginia, 11-15 May
1975, as well as the National Seminar on Law and Population held in Jogjakarta, Indonesia 26-29 May 1975. All of these testify to the high quality of
the Symposium's Recommendations which may lend themselves to regional
as well as national adaptation for action.

The need to relate law and human rights to population—the *raison d'etre*
for, as well as the most important single message from, the Tunis
Symposium— has received strong endorsements from both the World Population Conference and the World Conference of International Women's
Year. The World Population Plan of Action adopted in Bucharest in August
1974 specifically accords "high priority" to:

> The review and analysis of national and international laws which
> bear directly or indirectly on population factors (paragraph 78 (h));
> and
> Collection, analysis and dissemination of information concerning
> human rights in relation to population matter, and the preparation
> of studies designed to clarify, systematize and more effectively im-
> plement these human rights (paragraph 78 (g)).

Similarly, the World Plan of Action adopted by the World Conference
of the International Women's Year in Mexico City in July 1975 stresses the
following:

> 38. Governments should review their legislation affecting the
> status of women in the light of human rights principles and interna-
> tionally accepted standards. Wherever necessary legislation should
> be enacted or updated to bring national laws into conformity with
> the relevant international instruments. Adequate provision should
> also be made for the enforcement of such legislation. . . Where they
> have not already done so, Governments should take steps to ratify

the relevant international conventions and fully implement their provisions. . . .

39. Appropriate bodies should be specifically entrusted with the responsibility of modernizing, changing or repealing the outdated national laws and regulations, keeping them under constant review, and ensuring that their provisions are applied without discrimination. . . .

Publication of this volume is thus timely and fills an urgent, immediate need.

It cannot be over-emphasized, however, that the Recommendations adopted in Tunis were those of individual participants attending the Symposium and do not necessarily reflect the views of their respective Governments or the United Nations Fund for Population Activities, the United Nations, or any of the cooperating agencies.

SECTION 1

Welcoming Addresses

Address

Mezri Chekir
Director-General of the National Office of Family Planning and Population
Republic of Tunisia

It is well known that population problems have worried Governments for quite some time. The result of this concern is that many nations have undertaken experiments designed to affect the variables which influence population growth and movement. Each nation has followed what seemed to it to be the best direction, taking into account its own problems and its own economic and social development needs. Similarly, on the international level, organizations and experts have long been interested in the problems involving the various aspects of population. But we must recognize that examination of the legal aspects of this important issue is of recent origin.

We all welcomed with great satisfaction the international declarations made in 1966, 1968 and 1969 which have become landmarks in the development of international legislation in the area of population, but which, in reality, merely express a general willingness on the part of the world community to agree on broad principles. The road we are left to travel in terms of making these principles a facet of reality is long. We need only to review the impressive list of issues set forth in this Symposium's programme to become aware of the distance we have yet to go.

Allow me to call your attention to the experiment we have been conducting in this country which, as you well know, grants considerable importance to the problem of population. Our efforts are the product of a fight for progress which is the design of President Habib Bourguiba, an eminent jurist and avant-garde thinker. This has resulted in the promulgation of innovative legislation which serves as a foundation for our entire family planning policy. We have gathered these texts together in a special collection which we are pleased to present to you, along with documentation relating to Tunisian action in the area of population.

The National Office of Family Planning and Population is entrusted with the task of carrying out research aimed at achieving the harmonious growth of the Tunisian population. To this end, we submit to the Government all proposals of a legislative or regulatory nature and administer all programmes and plans for action whose main goal is to maintain the stability of the family and to protect the health of the citizens.

I assure you that the Tunisian experts and officials are pleased to have the opportunity to be in contact with the eminent individuals who make up this assembly. We look forward to assisting you and exchanging ideas. In closing, I would like to express the wish that the results of our work in Tunisia may live up to the principles which have governed the organization of this meeting. I also hope that the conclusions we reach at this Symposium will constitute an appreciable contribution to the development of a World Plan for Action in the area of population.

Statement

By
Rafael M. Salas
Executive Director, United Nations Fund for Population Activities

Many countries today acknowledge the increasing role which law and human rights play in the field of population. That these are not mere rhetorics may be seen by the fact that a substantial number of legal reforms have in fact taken place, many of which are directly attributable to the endeavors of the various Law and Population Projects. The Fund wishes to congratulate you for your achievements, and is convinced that the present Symposium will serve not only as a "follow-up" to your work, but also as a cornerstone for future population activities based upon human rights. As a lawyer myself, I am keenly aware of how important it is not only to look at the law as it is, but also to work for its improvement toward what it ought to be. In this light, the Symposium may adopt recommendations of interest to the World Population Conference.

We are gratified by the fact that the Symposium is co-sponsored by the United Nations. Furthermore, we are blessed by the cooperation of ILO, UNESCO, WHO, IPPF and the International Advisory Committee on Population and Law—a non-governmental organization accredited to ECOSOC. This fact in itself shows that we are marshalling all the interdisciplinary resources to tackle the multi-dimensional problem of population —an approach long over-due.

Population law may be defined as "that body of the law which relates directly or indirectly to the population growth, distribution and those aspects of well-being affecting, as well as affected by, population size and distribution"—a definition accepted at the UNESCO Workshop on the Teaching of Population Dynamics in Law Schools, held in February 1974. As such, population law is concerned not only with the problems posed by population size and distribution, but ultimately with human rights. Family planning, for example, should not be viewed as a goal in itself, but rather as a means to an end—opportunities for adequate food, health, clothing, shelter, education, work, recreation, old-age security, etc.—all of them basic human rights which family planning affects.

But "right" and "duty" are two sides of the same coin. Acceptance of human rights necessarily entails a corresponding duty not only to refrain from activities which would impede the exercise of the right but, positively, to undertake the necessary measures for the realization and safeguarding of such a right. Furthermore, inherent in the concept of "right" is the discharge of it with "responsibility"—whether explicitly provided as in the Teheran Proclamation on Human Rights with respect to family planning as a basic human right, or implicit as in the right to the freedom of speech, either in time of peace (*e.g.*, libel, defamation, nuisance, obscenity) or during war or emergency (*e.g.*, treason, sedition, censorship). Continuing the family planning right as an example, "responsible" parenthood must seek to balance the "individual" with the "collective" right—*i.e.*, from the right of children to that of the society at large. The question of when exactly does the "individual" right give way to the "collective" is always difficult to answer—even in the case of freedom of speech notwithstanding its centuries-old development and refinement. However, it is equally clear that inability to define with exactness the relationship between the individual and collective rights does not negate their existence. Problems such as these will remain to test the inventiveness and ingenuity of lawyers.

It is encouraging to note that the United Nations Symposium on Population and Human Rights, held in Amsterdam in January 1974, unanimously adopted a recommendation calling upon all international organizations to render assistance to Governments in the compilation, review and reform of their laws in the light of both population policy and human rights. We also welcome the decision of the IPPF's Management and Planning Committee in October 1973 to establish a panel of experts on the matter of "Law and Planned Parenthood," which will work with all of the IPPF's constituent national associations in bringing about revisions in legislation. As far as the Fund is concerned, the degree of importance we attach to the Law and Population Projects may be gleaned from the fact that it was the first project directly executed by the Fund. The project is conducted not merely as an academic study, but a dynamic project which will have long-felt effects on the behavior of countries that respect the "rule of law." We would like to see the population factor formulated into policies and executed as operationally feasible programmes in all countries if possible, but never losing sight of the ultimate goal of human rights.

When the World Population Conference and Year are over, our tasks as lawyers are just beginning. For the World Population Plan of Action remains to be implemented, which means the removal of conflicting laws which frustrate such implementation and the adoption of new laws to further the objectives of the plan. To us lawyers, every year is the World Population Year.

This Symposium would not have been possible but for the gracious invitation and generous assistance extended by the Government of Tunisia.

It is fitting that this Symposium should be held in Tunisia, the first country to adopt a deliberate legal approach to population. It has in recent years raised the minimum age of marriage, abolished polygamy, permitted voluntary sterilization by distinguishing it from castration, and liberalized the law—at first to allow abortion to women with five or more children, at request. While we may or may not agree with all of these legal reforms, we are grateful for the wealth of experience gained from these pioneering efforts and they should prove invaluable to all of us. We are particularly indebted to His Excellency Habib Bourguiba, President of Tunisia, under whose patronage this Symposium is being held.

I note the comprehensiveness of the subject matters in your agenda and the difficult task ahead of you in reaching consensus on all these matters. However, the very fact that you have taken so much trouble in coming from away places to attend this Symposium is itself a hopeful sign. It shows shared determination that the Symposium shall not fail. On this optimistic note, I wish you a successful and fruitful meeting.

Speech of Greeting

Dr. Jean de Moerloose
Chief of Health Legislation
World Health Organization

Mr. Minister, Ladies and Gentlemen:

I am happy to be the representative here of the World Health Organization, and to convey to you the wishes of the Director General for the success of the Symposium.

I should like to sketch for you the role which the WHO plays in the population field and to set forth at this time the ties which bind us to the Law and Population Programme whose spark plug you know in the person of Dr. Lee.

Of course you are aware that our International Parliament—the World Health Assembly—gave us an important mandate in 1965, only a few years ago, to deal with the problems of family planning, population dynamics and research into the questions of human reproduction.

WHO is therefore authorized, on the request of its member states, to stimulate, promote and coordinate research on the physiological, clinical, epidemiological and psychological aspects of human reproduction and to undertake the study of population dynamics and family planning.

WHO fully understands that the planning of the family constitutes an essential element for family health—which is the building block of each nation—and particularly for the health of mothers and children. The integration of family planning services into the regular health services, and particularly into the framework of mother and child protection services, is the element which is most effective in producing the desired results.

For this purpose, it is necessary to train personnel at all levels, and certainly at the operational level so that they can respond more effectively to local, and particularly rural, problems.

All evidence shows that these activities require a close collaboration with the United Nations, and especially with the UN Fund for Population

Activities, as well as with the various UN specialized agencies represented here. For the success of the enterprise, there is the same requirement of close collaboration with the various international non-governmental and charitable organizations—in particular with the Law and Population Programme.

We all know that there are close relationships—no doubt very complex—between demographic changes and the health of the individual, of the family and of the general community.

WHO has no official policy on the question of population matters. Our policy depends on the sovereign decision of each member Government. WHO merely offers assistance, on request, to those Governments which have previously determined what their own policy shall be.

We know that national policies must be derived from a number of factors—religious, moral, ethical and others—and in particular this applies in such fields as contraceptives, sterilization and abortion, where it would be dangerous for an inter-governmental organization like WHO to suggest any policy whatever. However, the interest which WHO has in the success of this symposium is clear. In effect, without adequate legislative measures, no programme of family planning can be carried out effectively.

It is moreover because of this legislative aspect that the majority of our participants here come from a legal background.

Doctors and public health specialists are nonetheless invited to participate in the debates. This collaboration between doctors, lawyers and the representatives of other disciplines is in fact essential for the working out of acceptable rules and thus to respond to the Proclamation of Teheran on the rights of man—and in particular to the objective of giving to couples the right to decide freely and responsibly on the number of their children and on the timing of their births.

The fusion of legal and medical disciplines in this situation is essential. It is moreover an event of capital importance for us doctors to be able to count on the help of lawyers, economists, demographers and other specialists in order to resolve successfully one of the most important problems of our epoch.

Therefore, WHO wishes all success to this symposium.

Statement

By
Riad B. Tabbarah
Chief, Population Policy Section, Population Division
United Nations

On behalf of the Secretary-General of the World Population Conference, Mr. Antonio Carrillo-Flores, and the Director of the Population Division, Mr. Leon Tabah, I thank your excellency and the Tunisian Government for hosting this Symposium and for the great hospitality you have already shown us. Arab hospitality is of world renown, and the Tunisian version of it is certainly an outstanding example. We hope to spend in your country a most memorable week.

May I also on behalf of the United Nations as a co-sponsor of this Symposium, welcome the distinguished delegates to this Symposium. This is indeed a distinguished group. I am sure that this meeting will prove to be a most interesting and useful one.

This meeting is one of the major events of the World Population Year. As you all know, the culmination of the Year's activities will be the World Population Conference which will take place in August in Bucharest. World Population Conference is the first world-wide *political* conference on population, it is the third World Population Conference except that the first two were conferences of technicians and not of political leaders and policy-makers. The decision to hold a world-wide political conference on population is a recognition of the international community that population matters have become in the public domain and that it should now break away from the narrow confines of demography into the open field of population policy. The increasing interest of jurists in population questions and their relationship to the legal system, as is proven again by the broad and distinguished attendance at this Symposium, is in consonance with this new international approach to population.

The World Population Conference has been preceded by two years of substantive preparations. Perhaps the most important activities in this regard were the four symposia which were organized by the United Nations during the last year and early this year. The symposia dealt with four major themes of the Conference, namely, Population and Development, Population, Resources and the Environment, Population and the Family, and Population and Human Rights.

The Conference itself will consist of a plenary, three committees of the whole and a working group of the whole. The three Committees will deal with the first three themes I just mentioned; the fourth, population and human rights, is expected to be at the base of all the discussions in the Conference. The working group will deal with perhaps the most important single document that will come out of the Conference—the World Population Plan of Action. While all committees may propose recommendations and resolutions to the plenary, as well as to the working group, we expect that the main body of recommendations will be in the World Population Plan of Action.

At the request of the Economic and Social Council, the Secretary-General of the United Nations is placing before the World Population Conference a draft of the World Population Plan of Action. This draft has been prepared over the past two years by the Secretary-General of the Conference, Mr. Carrillo-Flores. The result of these consultations is a draft containing some eighty recommendations which we hope will be a good basis for discussion and consensus at Bucharest.

The recommendations contained in the draft World Population Plan of Action do not deal only with questions of family planning; in fact, they deal with six categories of variables, namely, population growth, morbidity and mortality, reproduction and family formation, population distribution and internal migration, international migration, and demographic structure. In addition, some recommendations are made on statistics, research, training and other supportive activities. The draft World Population Plan of Action, therefore, views population policy very broadly, in a way that reflects the varied population problems in the world. We hope that your recommendations will take a similar broad approach to the population questions.

May I again wish you a most successful meeting and a happy stay in Tunisia.

Address

By
Mohamed Mzali
Minister of Public Health and Vice-President of the Higher Council
on Population
Republic of Tunisia

At the outset, let me express what a pleasure it is for me to preside over the opening session of this important international meeting. The selection of Tunis as the meeting place for the eminent officials present here is undoubtedly a tribute paid to Tunisia for the efforts it has continued to make in the area of population, since its independence, under the enlightened guidance of President Habib Bourguiba.

A quarter of a century has passed since the Universal Declaration of Human Rights was adopted, thus guaranteeing the fundamental rights, the dignity and the worth of the human person. However, the weight of poverty still bears down on a large part of mankind today: almost 300 million children suffer from malnutrition, 50 million men do not have jobs and some 200 million other men are underemployed, and countless millions of human beings still live in destitute, infamous and intolerable conditions. Even in certain developed countries, the number of social misfits, "excluded" people, and (according to the title of Mr. René Lenoir's book which just appeared 4 months ago), the number of victims of physical and moral pollution has not stopped increasing.

So much poverty and injustice, so many emotional deprivations, can only portend a dark tomorrow, explosions, and confrontations of unforeseeable dimensions and incalculable consequences.

Becoming aware of these dangers by merely analyzing their causes is not enough, because every awakening implies a responsibility and the international community's responsibility is to work things out so that all nations, all Governments can combine their efforts in a spirit of active solidarity and of lucid generosity and mobilize their human and socio-economic resources to ensure dignity for all the men and women on this earth.

In this, the end of the twentieth century, when technology dominates, when suffering, hunger and sickness pollute everything, we should fight

all these plagues and be able to overcome them. The human spirit which
has many times proven its capacity to master matter, which has conquered
space and reached the moon—something which was merely looked upon
as a poet's dream or as Caligula's simple exclamation: "I want the moon!"
—should today once again take up the challenge, propose a reason for being, for hoping, for striving, and devise a strategy for integral development.
After asking so much of science or demanding so much of nature, it is time
for man to ask a little more of himself; that is the secret to success for this
new challenge.

Meetings such as this which propose precisely to put law in the service of development by acting on the demographic problems, clearly show
that the human mind has not abdicated its responsibility, that man is resolved to fight in order to live in dignity.

As for Tunisia, it has thrown itself into the fight for development from
the dawn of its independence. In our eyes, political liberation actually made
no sense at all unless it was followed by the liberation of Tunisian men from
the agony of underdevelopment. For us, independence was only a means
to carrying on the real fight for dignity. Thus, our policies have aimed directly through integral development and the advancement of man at ensuring for our citizens (male and female) the right to a worthwhile, happy life,
free of restrictions and alienation. But it had become evident that this objective could not be attained as long as the demographic growth continued
along its reckless, anarchic and dangerous rhythm, dangerous for the stability of the family and, therefore, of society. For it would have re-enacted
the drama of Sisyphus. It would be tantamount to making efforts for growth
and, just when we accumulate our wealth, realizing that the number of
mouths to be fed, of young people who need employment, of students to
be enrolled in school, has increased much more than the country's new
economic conditions will allow. This is the plight of developing countries.
What should be done is to demystify Sisyphus and, in particular, adopt a
Family Planning policy so that, once one has reached the top, one isn't then
obliged to redescend and take up the boulder which created the drama of
Sisyphus. We want to make our family planning policy not into a tragedy
in the Greek sense of the word, but into an epic which can be won, which
must be won.

This is our goal. That is why we have resolutely taken the direction
of family planning which, we are convinced, leads surely to a better education for the coming generation, to a healthier population and, therefore,
ultimately, to national prosperity. For one should not speak of the problem of family planning merely in economic terms. There is a qualitative
respect for life which must be taken into consideration as a first priority
objective. Regardless of the family's economic level, if the couple is not
happy, if the mother and father are not healthy, if they cannot decide on

the number of children to have, if the mother cannot offer her children comfort, not just with milk or food, but also with affection, tenderness and love, then the family, the basic unit of a society, cannot be alive and shining. No matter what the collective or "per capita"—as the economists say—income may be, the society will not be happy, it will not be free and dignity will not exist. One can have a million tons of oil, one can have accounts in banks in a good number of civilized countries, one can have air-conditioned Cadillacs, but, despite all this, one will still remain underdeveloped and poor in the human sense of the word. The problem does not present itself in the economic terms of income per inhabitant (this is important), but for us, the problem is one of the quality of life, of the liberation of women, of the liberation of the couple, of the happiness of the family, of the psychological stability of the children. Everything must work towards this. The texts, habits, laws, everything must be bent towards the human advancement of the family.

Sometimes, for example, people do not even dare speak of the family (but, it is not the only concept which people do not dare speak of nowadays). Even adults who are "respectable" who, during their early youth, had much intellectual courage, who have written a lot, who have given many lectures, now that the times are what they are, they no longer dare —especially not in front of the children or the audio-visual media—to speak of the family for fear of being accused of being middle-class, even though the word "rétro" ("backward") is fashionable; but, ultimately, one is afraid of being rather conservative, of not being "with it." At the risk of seeming "rétro" or conservative, I continue to believe that the family (and we will come back to this) is the foundation of society. There is no progress, no happiness, no dignity, no liberation, no freedom, no psychological-social stability without a harmonious and happy family. From this perspective, family planning becomes the corner-stone of this family policy which is the introduction of society to happiness and of man to dignity.

To return to the Tunisian experience, I believe that today we can speak of an identifiable Tunisian policy concerning family planning, of a particularly Tunisian action which aims first of all at liberating the individual, as I have just stated, at pulling him out from under the yoke of fatalism, of prejudice and of carelessness, in order to bring him to an appreciation of his power over himself and of the power he holds over his life and his condition. This self-determination and liberation offer sure economic and educational advantages. A stabilized family is free on the social, economic and cultural level because promulgating texts is not enough. We have known certain countries which copied constitutions, plagiarized laws, so they could say that their legislation was modern. But what of their people? If the population, or a good portion of the population, continues to believe that it can do nothing more than have children, or live in a hovel or stagnate in poverty, that it is the will of God, and the nature of things, then these laws and these texts are like showy clothing. What is needed along with these laws is a continuous effort to educate, which requires great courage in order to defatalize the demographic growth, so that fathers and mothers might understand cause and effect, so that they might take on their destiny and existentially enjoy freedom of choice. It is a long effort which is not easy because, from the very start one runs the risk of shocking people. I have known many of those in charge in certain countries who agree with me, who tell me: Obviously it would be great to bring that about in our countries, but here, in our countries, in our villages, we cannot talk about it because people would not listen to us anymore, they would turn their backs on us. What then is the role of the elite, what is the mission of those in charge? Is it enough to promulgate texts, to write articles, to analyze the problem in specialized magazines? Shouldn't one rather go before the people first, thrust oneself upon them by means of a moral and human glow, place oneself on their level, by virtue of a modesty of which only great souls are capable, and initiate a dialogue with them? Should one not try while respecting their beliefs, their credo, to bring them to reflect, to interpret the texts differently, as a function of and in light of scientific data, of psychology, of the requirements of morality, of the constraints of modern times, of their own aspirations?

Likewise, giving women their rights is good, but if one does not also carry out a parallel educational action with the masses of women, how can one expect them to assume their rights and carry out their duties?

Slaves did not feel alienated either, they considered it normal to live as slaves, and one would have astounded a slave if, a few centuries ago, one had said to him: Sir, you are suffering in your dignity, free yourself. He would have told you: but, ultimately, we are made this way because there are the free men and the others, the slaves. About 25 centuries ago, Plato considered it normal that there were the free men and the others, that is, the slaves. This is shocking today, but 25 centuries ago it was normal. Thus, it is a matter of educating, of demystifying, of raising people from one level to another. This is the role of the elite, of the leaders, of the militants, of those in charge: Go into the villages, to the countryside, into the neighborhoods outside the big cities which swarm with poor people and explain to them, open their eyes, without demagogy, or so-called revolutionary slogans, teaching them to think, starting from certain unchallengeable and irrefutable facts, help them become accustomed to analyzing correctly, in those areas where they used to submit and accept. This is the work we still have not ceased.

Since we intended to remain faithful to the spirit of the Declaration by the Heads of State on family planning, since Tunisian policy, on the whole, is based on the respect and the defense of man's rights, since, for us, man is the supreme value, we did not hesitate one single instant to follow this policy which will allow the Tunisian man to fully use his right to family planning, with complete awareness and knowledge.

In complete agreement with the spirit which governed the organization of today's meeting, the Tunisian Government has always been convinced that all policies must rely on the law and that it is not by chance that, from the time of its independence, the Tunisian legislature has promulgated a large number of legislative texts having a direct or indirect effect on family planning. Such is the case with the Code of Personal Status, promulgated on August 13, 1956, only four months after the establishment of the first Government of independent Tunisia, formed by President Bourguiba. This status is actually the "code of the liberation of women" and the point of departure for the social revolution undertaken in this country.

Until then the woman was chained to the home where her main role was to procreate and to take charge of household chores. Today, the Tunisian woman is a full and separate citizen, enjoying the rights of all citizens and also assuming, I hope, her duties.

We must also stress that the abolition of polygamy, and the regulation of divorce and marriage were actually the precursors of family planning, since such measures could only bring about a decrease in fertility and a regulation of births.

Other no less important legislative measures have followed in the same direction: to protect, enrich and promote the Tunisian people. Public health, maternal and child care, nutrition and hygiene, are only factors, all of which were the object of special attention by the Government, and areas in which considerable progress has been achieved, a progress which is not without its effect on family planning.

At the same time, the advancement of employment and greater access to employment by women have been the objects of many legislative measures, and they also have produced a definite form of progress. I am convinced that other legislative measures in favor of women working will have to be taken in the years to come.

We have also made gigantic efforts in the areas of teaching and elementary education. Both are keystones to development and off-shoots of the demographic problem, since we consider it a truism that there are no underdeveloped countries, only underdeveloped people. The promotional action relating to education manifests itself in all corners of Tunisia, touching countryside and cities, children and adults, men and women. Today, more than one-third of the operating budget is allotted to education and one-fifth of the population is in school.

All of these measures and accomplishments have had an indirect but certain effect on family planning. However, the family planning programme has benefited from legislation which, in some sense, is its alone. Since 1960, the Tunisian Government has promulgated six laws and decrees concerning family planning. These texts concern contraceptive products and devices, and family allotments. We have limited allotment benefits to the first four children only. It is a sort of discouragement.

We have raised the minimum age for marriage and liberalized abortion (Law of September 1973). Furthermore, two important independent institutions have been created: the National Office of Family Planning and Population (Law of March 23, 1973) and the Higher Council on Population (Law of January 4, 1974).

I must point out, however, that the success recorded in this area is not due only to the legislative, administrative or budgetary measures which the Government had to take. Without the intellectual courage, the conviction and the perseverance of President Bourguiba who, for fifteen years, has not ceased to demystify the taboos, to conquer resignation, carelessness, to educate the masses by explaining to them the relationship of cause and effect, to free the minds, to break the social and metaphysical yokes inherited from the decadent period, without the direct contacts with the peasants, the workers, the women in the villages, the countryside, without all this, the "demographic conscience," if I may call it that, would not have emerged and the texts would not have been as effective as they are today.

By so doing, President Bourguiba is actually only continuing the work begun almost half a century ago to bring about a change in mentality and the elevation of man on the cultural and moral level so that he can be the architect of his own liberation.

Thus, we have not stopped at formulating options, analyzing problems, indeed we have striven to put our plans into a systematic form of action. We have set up throughout the country, in the countryside and the cities, an infrastructure which, today, is capable of providing free family planning services to our citizens. We have continued to conduct informational and educational campaigns to motivate couples. Today, family planning has become part of our lifestyle. An irreversible dynamic has been created. Sterilization, as well as recourse to abortion, are following an ascending curve.

Ladies and Gentlemen:

Tunisia has resolutely set in motion a lucid and effective population policy. Such meetings as this will allow responsible Tunisians on all levels not only to profit from the contacts and the discussions which will take place during one week in Tunis but also to expose you to our experience and to point out its originality.

I wish you complete success in your work which, I am sure, will contribute to the advancement of international cooperation in the area of population to the benefit of all mankind.

And, to conclude, I declare the Symposium on Law and Population now open. Thank you.

Socio-Economic Laws Affecting Population

Status of Women,
Family Planning and
Population Dynamics

By
Vida Tomsic*

For some time now it has been obvious to those who have worked in this field that a great degree of interrelationship exists between the status of women, the practice of family planning and population dynamics. In the past few years scientific studies have surfaced which substantiate this notion.[1] This paper will attempt to explore some of the current thinking on the nature and legal aspects of this interrelationship with a view to reaching some conclusions that will give rise to recommendations for future reform.

The subjects of status of women and family planning are usually treated as human rights issues in which the legal approach seems to be predominant. Population dynamics, on the other hand, are generally viewed as a part of the vast problem of socio-economic development. However, a clear-cut differentiation between the legal and the socio-economic approach to these three subjects is not possible as in reality they are linked to the level of development and the socio-political system of each country. Legislation can undoubtedly be a very strong factor in influencing change; it can, of course, also obstruct change. But we can also observe many changes—especially in the sphere of the status of women and fertility—that have occurred before the laws were altered, and even in spite of them. For example, practically all of Europe moved from high to low rates of fertility even though abortion and contraception were strictly forbidden and before modern oral contraceptives

* Member, Council of Federation of the Socialist Republic of Yugoslavia.

1. For the purposes of discussing this relationship, and more specifically, its legal aspects, we have as background papers an in-depth *Study on the Interrelationship of the Status of Women and Family Planning*, U.N. Doc. E/CN.6/575 and E/CN.6/575/Add. 1, and several studies on the role of women in development and on the socio-economic implications of the population trends as elaborated in the past year by various United Nations agencies. *See*, among others, *Report of the Interregional Meeting of Experts on the Integration of Women in Development*, U.N. Doc. ST/SOA/120 (1973).

235

had been discovered. It has been argued that such reductions in fertility were the result of industrial development. Nevertheless, the role of legislation, especially in the sphere of human rights, cannot be ignored as it is an important factor in the humanization and democratization of relationships.

I. The Nature of Human Rights with Special Reference to the Status of Women and Family Planning

A. *Human Rights*

One has to accept two basic principles as to the creation and implementation of human rights. First, human rights are not rights which are merely created *for* the people, they are rights which are to be exercised *by* the people themselves. Every individual, man or woman, has to be in the position to use these rights. Second, it is not possible to exercise *one* of these rights without necessarily referring to other basic human rights. These basic human rights are so interconnected that it is impossible to practice one of them without affecting other rights and individuals in a society. Therefore, we are justified in speaking about the complex, multi-sided struggle for the affirmation of human rights, which at the same time entails recognizing certain duties and responsibilities towards other people and the larger social community.

It has not been by chance that the elaboration of human rights by the United Nations has not only followed the course of establishing these rights as the rights of individuals but also has placed them in the context of a country's economic growth and social change. The struggle for human rights is the real essence of social change. The product of this struggle goes beyond mere solemn declarations to encompass the possibility of exercising these rights in day-to-day life. The prerequisites for the real enjoyment of human rights include more than the creation of laws which abolish all forms of discrimination, thus ensuring the realization of democratic human rights. The "political will" to support the concerted interaction of progressive social forces is also essential in order to overcome economic underdevelopment, the old traditions which are part of it, and the unconscious or conscious resistance to new, more democratic relations between individuals within a given country. Because it is well recognized that resistance to badly needed social changes arises not only within a country but also from foreign conditions, the establishment of new political and economic relations between countries and the abolition of colonialism, imperialism and other kinds of foreign pressures are also fundamental prerequisites to the realization of human rights.

In discussing this subject, I think it is also important to distinguish between what we declare to be human rights and what are merely methods, the means for realizing these rights. In this context perhaps we should speak of human rights as being capable of realization only when a person is absolutely free to decide between alternatives, that is, when he has the necessary knowledge, when the means are accessible to him and when he is conscious of every consequence of his decision.

B. *Status of Women*

1. Introduction

The principle of the equality of men and women has been established in the Charter of the United Nations and elaborated in all its fundamental documents. That is not to say, however, that the subject is a simple one which can be treated in a few words. It is an immensely complicated subject which is affected by a number of factors which are not legal in nature.

By definition the status of women is measured in relation to the status which men enjoy in a given society. In a general way, it can be stated that discrimination by sex from a strictly legal point of view has greatly diminished. In a majority of countries the principal laws which discriminate against women have been abolished. But obviously the very essence of the issue of social affirmation of the status of women lies beyond the legal framework. Once the legal basis for equality is established, the focus broadens to include a concern for the status of every citizen in the society. With the achievement of the legal equality of women comes the revelation that broad masses of men, especially in the developing world, have no more control over their own lives and conditions than women have and that now the struggle for human rights is not primarily delineated by sex.

By this I do not wish to ignore the observable quantitative and qualitative lack of participation of women in various fields of the economic, social and political life which occurs despite legal equality. The question of what hinders the more complete integration of women into the development process requires analysis. This should be done with a view toward proposing strategies for overcoming these barriers.

2. Status of Women and Development

Experiences from all over the world tend to indicate that social change cannot occur in a country without accelerated development. Put simply, change cannot occur in the absence of economic growth. On one hand, it is not possible to improve the status either of women or of all citizens through legal means alone. On the other, the acceleration of the development depends in large measure on the adherence to the international obligations spoken of in the United Nations as part of the International Development Strategy for the Second United Nations Development Decade as well as by the Declaration and the Action Programme of the Special Session of the General Assembly on Raw Materials and Development. Numerous United Nations discussions have also referred to the fact that mere material investments do not in themselves constitute development; investment must be systematically accompanied by deep economic-social changes in the production relationships and in relationships between people within the society.

The abolition by law of all forms of discrimination (discrimination based on sex included), the inclusion of people from all classes of the society in the development process, and the redistribution of the fruits of development among the broad masses of people are important prerequisites for accelerating development and some fundamental social changes. A history of programmes instituted for the purpose of eradicating centuries-old forms of discrimination against women has taught us that discrimination based on sex is premised on ideas and practices which, at first glance, seem to be "normal" and "natural." In reality these practices and ideas are the very essence of the present problem of the secondary status of women. To many it is inconceivable that women can maintain their traditional role in the family and in the household and simultaneously fully enjoy their status as productive, full-fledged citizens in contemporary society. Attempts to secure an improved status for women by changing the ethical-political attitudes have led only to failure. Despite high-flown rhetoric, women are, in practice, frequently left to perform only the most difficult, unrewarding and disagreeable forms of work. The actual level of their social treatment has remained very low.

This is not surprising. Programmes for improving the status of women, oriented as they are toward attaining equality with men, have produced poor results. Because of their deficiencies, it is desirable to reconsider the goals and standards around which such programmes are organized. The question also arises as to whether we should start with a critical examination of those social institutions which fail to ensure that women play a role in formulating their countries' policies. In large measure, the problem of the status of women centers on the question of the extent of their participation in the production of national wealth, in decision-making, in the management of social-political matters, and in new ways of dealing with their hitherto predominant roles as mothers and housewives.

That the direct participation of women in the economic life of their countries is the essential condition for enhancing their status is obvious. It must not be forgotten, however, that women have played some role in economic life since the beginning of the human race. In the traditional agricultural economy, women take an active part in production, but their contribution generally remains anonymous as it is often noticed only by the owner of the property or the head of the family. All development plans should stress the need to move away from traditional roles for women and toward giving them access to schools, so they can better their qualifications and work under equal conditions.

To a certain degree existing protections afforded employed women in most countries should be criticized because often more thought is given to how the woman is to be relieved at her working post in order to fulfill her traditional obligations as mother and housewife than is given to accelerating the process of taking part of the domestic work and part of the child care out of the individual household. It is, however, interesting to note that some of these tendencies are being rejected, notably so where jobs have been increasingly occupied by younger and more qualified women, who seek to achieve full success in their work rather than be relieved of work. While a small number of enterprises are hiring women on a part-time basis, attempts at giving working women a day off in the course of the work week to devote to domestic duties have been rendered irrelevant because of the general shortening of the work week itself.

But the fact that the work week has been shortened for individual workers does not necessarily mean that the machines lay idle. The work often goes on around the clock.

In this connection, such measures as the prohibition of the employment of women at night give the impression of being a two-edged sword. On one hand, it reduces the possibilities of women getting employment in modern industry, where the income is generally higher, but where three or four shifts work around the clock. On the other hand, there is an increase in the number of women who work night shifts, especially in health institutions and in industries which can show that they cannot function without them (some textile factories). However, those industries, particularly health services, which have been exempted from the decree against the night-time employment of women, have not devoted themselves sufficiently to alleviating the problem of their daily household and family duties when working night shifts. The efforts being made to have child care centers conform their working hours to the needs of the employed mothers do not properly solve the problem. Thus, perhaps it is necessary to reconsider the whole approach to the problem of the protection of the woman at work, especially when the rapid development of technology and the application of scientific methods in production are taken into account. It would seem that the future road to re-affirmation of the role of women as producers and equal participants in the labour force can hardly lead to the desired destination if the organized action of the society does not aim at providing services and institutions devoted to child care. It is not just the matter of unburdening the woman but also of providing real social care for children.

Problems of population should be dealt with as one of the preeminent problems of the society, and all citizens should have a voice in the process of determining economic-social policies and actions related to population. Equality in work and in political life must be accompanied by specific measures to assure the right to freely and responsibly decide questions related to child-bearing and by measures for the socialization of the care for children. In this regard the laws which determine and regulate the woman's position in society are important, although they alone cannot solve the problems which arise because of her biological function. In the past this function was responsible for a division of work between the sexes which in a sense expropriated the woman and put her under the supervision of her father, her husband, or her brother. She was allotted the care of children and household, *i.e.*, the needs of the everyday life of the family members. The gaining of "equal rights" for women within the society runs counter to their playing the traditional role within the household and the family. We see this tension when we set about to divide the household duties and chores "equally" among all the family members. It carries over into attempts to describe a woman's life-span as being made up of three successive but distinct periods of time: education, motherhood, later outside work. Her life-time orientation should be one of equal participation in the economic production of the society, and the greatest part of the domestic work should be taken over by social services. Social processes, supported by the contemporary development of technology, have already started moving in this direction. The use of technology depends not only on the overall development, but also on the direction which social forces are given in the struggle so as to insure that work, not property or sex, is the measure of an individual's position. This type of development can be aided considerably by the legislator. But all this only opens possibilities; the full assertion of status depends on increased economic development. This can be seen in Yugoslavia where progressive legislation and efforts for an accelerated abolition of the vestiges of discrimination are nevertheless limited by the level of economic development. There is evidence of a strong correlation between the regional per capita income, the level of the employment of women, the levels of literacy, fertility, infant mortality, abortion, and the numbers of women who use contraceptives. For example, the more developed regions, *i.e.*, those with the highest per capita income, have the largest share of women in the non-agricultural labour force. The birth rate in the Republic of Slovenia, where 41 per cent of the women are in the labour force, is one third of the birth rate of the underdeveloped Kosovo autonomous region, where only 19 per cent of the women are in the labour force. And the proportion of women using contraceptives in regions of the highest female employment is six times higher than in those of the lowest.

C. *Family Planning*

In contrast to the long-range commitment of the United Nations to equal status of women, its elaboration of the right of individuals and couples to decide freely and responsibly questions related to child-bearing (the human right to family planning) is of rather recent origin. The limits of this right are still being explored.

It is no coincidence that women's movements in many countries led the struggle for greater access to the knowledge and means necessary for practicing family planning. In such struggles women saw the possibilities of balancing their sexual lives and motherhood with their potential for participating in economic and social life—without being forced to sacrifice one part of their vocation for another. One of the important ways of realizing the objectives of family planning is to provide for the full emancipation of women—their emancipation in the intimate sphere of life included—and, thereby, the full development of their personalities. The spread of knowledge about, and the use of, "female" contraceptives for the prevention of unwanted pregnancy are undoubtedly of great significance to women, their health, their sexual life, and the harmonization of their biological function with their schooling and work.

In elaborating the legal and social substance of the concept of family planning as a human right, we must recognize the role of the individual in the society as the vehicle for social reproduction, of which biological reproduction is a part. The creation of economic and social processes which enable individuals to master their social position and to establish conditions for a free social as well as individual and family life, is a prerequisite for the emancipation of the individual in all spheres of social and private life. Thus, as with the economic, legal and political equality of women, family planning is an element of revolutionary social change, which calls for a deliberate effort on the part of the community to upgrade the status of women by discarding views and moral values concerning the status of women which have emerged in the class society. Generally speaking, history has shown that the changes in material living conditions which result from rapid industrialization, increased employment of women, urbanization as well as decreases in child mortality have tended to cause a spontaneous reduction in fertility. However, old concepts and moral values continue to persist in society even though new values should be fostered because of new conditions.

Social action designed to provide information about family planning and aimed at promoting a responsible attitude in parents towards their offspring should enable people to master their fertility while at the same time dissociating harmonious sexual life from procreation. One of the desired results of such programmes is to enhance the responsibility which parents feel for their offspring.

Just how a child is viewed by his parents often differs depending on the type of society. In societies which are structured around subsistence agricultural production, the child represents an additional source of labour and a guarantee for the old age security of the parents. In industrial societies, the birth of a child signals a long-term obligation for parents to provide for his education, and, ultimately, the child will find employment outside of the family circle. As societies shift from one form to another the immediate material "interest" of the family in the child tends to disappear and the child becomes "wanted" for primarily non-material reasons. It is more commonplace now for parents to be entitled to health services and pensions as a result of their own work. Certainly, if the broader community continues to consider child care as being a private matter, leaving it entirely to the family, it is possible to understand the concern that such a tendency might result in people deciding to have the least possible number of "wanted children." On the other hand, some of the people who deal with population problems are preoccupied by the fact that leaving the decision-making power entirely in the hands of parents would result in the birth of too many "wanted" children. Both concerns fail to take into account economic causes that influence the parents' desires for offspring.

When we say that the child has the right to be "wanted," we are saying that parents should realize the birth of a child carries with it serious responsibilities. We reject the idea of the complete irresponsibility of the individual with regard to his biological reproduction, which is nonchalantly disseminated by some churches ("He who takes care of the birds in the forest and of the fish in the water will also take care of the child"). Today, in the era of ecological problems, mankind is already taking care of the birds and the fishes; therefore, it is all the more the duty of parents not to surrender their natural capabilities for procreation to forces outside themselves. It is also the duty of parents to exercise their parenthood in a responsible manner, to be prepared to raise their children in the family and to create for them, through work and action in the society, the best possible conditions for their psycho-physical development within the framework of socially-organized health, educational, recreational, day-care and other institutions.

The Resolution on Family Planning was adopted in Yugoslavia for the purpose of elaborating the relationship between rights and duties, realizing women's equality and providing the best possible health protection for the family. It was adopted in 1969 by the Federal Assembly at the behest of the Federal Council for Family Planning and the Conference for Societal Activities of the Women of Yugoslavia. The resolution has stressed that:

> The changed position of women in society has affected the structure and relationships within the family and has, consequently, decisively influenced the fulfillment of their role as mothers. A lower birth rate and a reduction in infant mortality are some of the results of these changes. On the other hand, the size of a family is being increasingly influenced by the fulfillment of the desire for a better life and a higher standard of living. Deliberate family planning is in the common interest of both parents and society. The creation of conditions ensuring the birth of a wanted child is of particular importance to women, to their psychological and physical integrity, and to the proper exercise of their parental responsibilities, all of which contribute to the raising of a healthy younger generation. As a continuous human and social effort, family planning in its modern application has many significant social, medical, economic, political and other advantages.

The Resolution on Family Planning proceeds from the assumption that the realization of the right of parents to decide on the number and spacing of their children is not only one of their human *rights* but also one of their *duties*. Several years have passed since the adoption of this resolution by the highest legislative body. In the meantime, a number of new problems—of a medical, legal, educational, moral, ethical and demographic character—have emerged in our country. In the new Constitution of the Socialist Federal Republic of Yugoslavia, adopted in February 1974, a special article of the chapter on the freedoms, rights and duties of man and the citizen states: "It is a human right freely to decide on the birth of children. This right may only be restricted for reasons of health."[2] At the time of the public discussion of the draft of the Constitution there was much debate concerning the meaning of the formulation of the right of "individuals and families to make decisions regarding conception and birth of children." It was argued that such a declaration gave the individual, *vis-à-vis* the state, the right to avail himself of *all* means and service leading to that end, regardless of their harmful effect on human health, and irrespective of general medical, social, ethical and moral norms. However, the federal Resolution has already provided a sufficiently clear framework for this human right and for the general social actions required for its implementation. This right—as is the case with all other recognized human rights—presupposes the existence of certain socially-determined responsibilities and actions for its realization. When Marxists speak of the freedom of the individual, they do so conditionally. They recognize the existence and action of objective laws governing the development of the society as well as the limits of the freedom of the individual as related to the freedoms and rights of other individuals.

Responsible parenthood as we understand it in Yugoslavia is not restricted within the bounds of an individual family but is realized—on the basis of the democratic self-managerial position of the individual—through actions of solidarity in the work organization, in the local community and community of interest, in the commune and in the broader socio-political communities. Participation in the self-management of the country, that is, assuming responsibility for the decisions on over-all economic and social development by the masses, enables the individual to build into his social actions a component which takes into account the interests of his children, as these interests coincide with those of all people in the society. The process of planning socio-economic development, as a form of democratic self-managerial action, becomes, at the same time, a process of acquainting every individual producer and citizen with the conditions and prospects of the

---

2. CONSTITUTION OF THE SOCIALIST FEDERAL REPUBLIC OF YUGOSLAVIA, art. 191 (1974).

development of both his narrower and broader community and with the conditions in which his children will be born and live. In this regard, they are not mere observers but are actively involved in the creation of better living conditions for their families.

Within the framework of a complex socio-economic development policy, the following conditions are necessary in order to secure the realization of the human right concerning decisions about the number and spacing of children:

1. Sex information and education regarding human reproduction should be introduced into the regular school curricula and other forms of out-of-school education, as well as the establishment of pre-marital and marital counselling centres;

2. The medical and socio-medical aspects of family planning should be incorporated into the general medical service and particularly into the work of the general practitioners and the service for the protection of the health of women, mothers and children.

In Yugoslavia, the availability of medical *advice* is ensured to all, without restrictions as to age or marital status by the law on health protection. As regards accessibility to *contraceptives*, restrictions can be justified only for health reasons—for instance, by special procedures for administering oral or other contraceptives. As for *sterilization*, which is being intensively propagated in some countries as a means of family planning, we reject it as a means to be used massively because it is irreversible. In Yugoslavia sterilization is performed only on the basis of medical indication.

Within the whole complex of medical questions involving family planning, *abortion* occupies a special place. In our country we have never identified the right to planned parenthood with the right of abortion. We feel that this medical interference with a healthy and normal course of pregnancy is not desirable, but that it should, nevertheless, be made available to women, regardless of their marital status or material situation, in all those cases in which for various reasons, including non-medical, the birth of the child would be undesirable. In this context then, abortion is a legalized means of family planning and it is available in accordance with a fixed procedure within a determined period of time after conception.[3] Because of the increased accessibility of contraceptives and improved abortion techniques, it is increasingly important to ascertain prior to approving an application for abortion whether the prospective child is genuinely unwanted. If, in their request for abortion, the woman or both parents are not guided by the fact that the child is unwanted but by some other reasons, which could be possibly taken care of through social assistance, then the social services

---

3. Decree No. 33 of 16 February 1960, *Sluzbeni List Federativne Republike Jugoslavije*, 2 March 1960, No. 9, at 221-222.

should mobilize the competent social factors with the view to eliminating, if possible, the obstacles barring the way to the birth of a wanted child. Within the framework of efforts to ensure the birth of wanted children, medical and legal aid should also be extended to an increasing extent to parents who are unable to have children, a concept which encompasses also *the treatment of sterility* and *artificial insemination*.

3. The social services should increasingly integrate family planning into their preventive and curative plans for families and children. In this context, together with all social factors, an atmosphere of parental responsibility could be fostered, and parents could be helped to obtain medical advice when needed at the earliest possible moment. By analyzing the reasons for which people have fewer or greater numbers of children than they would desire, the social service could greatly promote the orientation of social policy toward ensuring the happiness of each child. In this connection, it is particularly necessary to draw attention to the importance of *adoption*. More modern legal provisions and a more flexible operation of social and legal services related to adoption proceedings could become a component of efforts aimed at enabling every child to feel the warmth of individual parental love and to enjoy a happy family life, while at the same time enabling many people to realize their desire to have children.[4]

II. POPULATION DYNAMICS AND POPULATION POLICIES

The Study on the Interrelationship of the Status of Women and Family Planning by the Special Rapporteur gives rather convincing data on the influence that the status of women exerts on fertility. Paragraph 67 states that:

> [T]he study establishes clearly that there is a vital link between the condition of women, population questions and over-all development.

Paragraph 68(b) goes on to state that:

> The status of women and, more especially, their educational level, the extent to which they are employed and the nature of their employment or occupation, their position in the family and their participation in community and national life have a marked, and

---

4. The constitutional right to decide freely questions related to the birth of children has been stated in the new Constitution of every Yugoslav republic. The Constitution of the Socialist Republic of Slovenia states further that: "In connection with the realization of this right the social community guarantees the necessary education and appropriate social protection and medical help, according to the law." Some of the problems mentioned above are regulated by special laws and other laws are in the process of being completed on the basis of new constitutional stipulations. The republic of Slovenia has adopted a special Resolution on Family Planning. Policies adopted by political and social forums are also of great importance, especially regarding education to responsible parenthood.

even decisive, influence both on family size and on the success of family planning programmes. Constant childbearing, in which the woman has little say or freedom of choice, leads to high fertility patterns that in themselves are not desired by the majority of countries where they are prevalent. This report reveals that, more often than not, high fertility is not a matter of free choice of the individual. It usually goes hand in hand with low status of women, lack of educational and employment opportunities for them, and conditions of poverty, over-work and drudgery. It prevails especially in many of the world's rural areas and urban slums. It is both the *result* and the *cause* of under-development, setting in motion a vicious circle, especially where resources are limited.

At the outset, it is important to clear up a certain amount of definitional and conceptual confusion which exists regarding the relationship of family planning to population policy. *Family planning*,[5] is often erroneously identified with a population policy oriented toward decreasing population through the propagation of the means for the prevention of unwanted pregnancy, as well as prevention of unwanted birth through abortion. The use of the term "birth control" construed in the sense of "population control" has contributed to this confusion. Efforts to prevent the identification of family planning with anti-natalist policy through the adoption of the terms like "family planning" and "planned parenthood" have not yet succeeded in wiping out the present erroneous conceptions. This is particularly caused by the yet prevailing tendency in the world to treat population policy separately from socio-economic development and to treat it as one, or predominantly one, aspect only, namely, as an intensive attempt at influencing natality through "family planning" actions. Against the view and practice of considering family planning primarily as an anti-natalist population policy, some efforts have been made in governmental (UN) and in non-governmental (IPPF) organizations to define the concepts more precisely and to identify the successes or failures of family planning actions conceived as population policy measures. Some United Nations seminars and expert group meetings have contributed towards clarifying the substance and scope of family planning as it leads to the realization of one of the fundamental human rights.

Population policy, on the other hand, is a component of a broader socio-economic policy aimed at implementing complex developmental measures, and not merely measures oriented directly or indirectly towards fertility. United Nations documents have been constantly emphasizing the principle

5. The term "family planning" is not the most adequate one, and, therefore, it introduces some misconceptions into our social endeavours. While searching for a more adequate term in Yugoslavia, we nevertheless use the term "family planning" as the nearest to the substance of free, responsible and socially-active parenthood.

that the formulation of population policy is the sovereign right of every state, while family planning is a fundamental human right. In fact, population policy proceeds from the socio-economic and political system of a given country and reflects the position of the individual in the society as well as the aims of leading social forces. For this reason the principles underlying policy differ in various states. These differences are in turn influenced to a considerable extent by the stand taken by certain circles, especially in western countries, that the "population explosion" is responsible for the poverty and underdevelopment of the majority of mankind, rather than visa versa. The known mutual relationship between demographic conditions, levels of national income, distribution of income, status of women, infant mortality and other indices of socio-economic development make possible the adoption of a scientific approach with regard to the formulation and implementation of population policies.

We should not endorse views and actions aimed at reforming or "emancipating" women (or men) only in one sphere, for example, in the sphere of biological reproduction and sexual life. If the conditions of production and social relations remain on the level of the individual family, a production community, entailing a patriarchal subordination of women and their subjection to economic, legal and social discrimination, then attempts at changing the behaviour of people in the family will surely end in failure. In such conditions "emancipation" in the sexual sphere would lead only to new alienations in the form of various "sexual revolutions" or would have as a consequence negative results from so-called family planning actions in developing countries which are conducted with populationist intentions. Therefore, we must strongly condemn proposals offering family planning as a technique for offering contraception, sterilization or abortion as a substitute for development through the stimulation of complex socio-economic processes. Action for free and responsible parenthood can be conducted successfully only as a *component of general socio-economic development.*

In planning development, a country has to study demographic trends and identify optimal demographic development within the context of general progress with a view to attaining a balance between economic development, resources and population trends. However, the demographically desirable average statistical figures cannot be considered as enunciating an "ideal size of family." Actually, it could hardly be said that there is an ideal size of family. The ideal size varies from one particular family to another owing to differences in actual conditions (including subjective ones). As shown by numerous surveys and research papers, there prevail among people in certain social environments views concerning the "ideal" number of children they wish to have. In some countries attempts are made to present—for populationist propaganda purposes—as "ideal" the size of a family that is usually smaller, but in some cases also larger, than the one people have actually accepted in their living practice. It appears that stress should be placed on emphasizing ideals and values concerned with *relations in the family* and with an *appropriate attitude regarding the care of all children in the narrower and broader community.* We strive for relationships where the individual is the *subject* and not the *object* of the spontaneous play of natural laws governing reproduction and is also not subjected to a state that either limits or allows planned behaviour in biological reproduction. Individuals will continue to decide, as they have done in the past, to have a larger or smaller number of children or to remain childless. Consequently, one should not create psychological traumas either among women and parents or among children by proclaiming certain possibly statistically desirable quantities as "ideal."

Views according to which the dissemination or prohibition of contraceptives should be the main instrument of population policy are not acceptable, not only because of the complex character of the conditions influencing demographic development, but also for reasons of principle. In implementing demographic objectives, neither coercion nor restriction should be placed on the accessibility of contraceptives. Contraception should be restricted only for medical reasons. Special attention should be devoted to abortion as an individually and socially undesirable means of ensuring a desired size of family. But restrictions on abortion should be allowed only for medical reasons, with a view to creating certain conditions in which abortion is least harmful. All this means that family planning can be successful only after a certain level of development has been attained.

Many of the necessary conditions for successful family planning are already being realized as a result of the development of productive forces, the progress of science and technology—medical science in particular—and the spread of democracy and of the concept of human rights. However, I should like to reiterate here that this process can lead to the full implementation of the human right to family planning only when there is a constant harmonization between the individual and the general interest of the society. The right to self-decision in biological reproduction has to be wrenched from the hands of natural spontaneity, from "divine" decision-making. On the other hand, scientific discoveries in themselves do not mean that they have become a means for enabling the individual to liberate himself from the impact of spontaneous laws of nature and from social laws and taboos. Numerous conflicts between the individual and the state as well as certain representatives of the medical profession concerning, for instance, the accessibility of contraceptives and abortion on the one hand, and, on the other, intensive actions in some countries for the promotion of certain methods of family planning indicate that this is an area of potential for manipulation. Sometimes "God" has been replaced by the technocratic forces of the modern state or by outside factors.

The differences in demographic situations do not warrant changes in the basic principles concerning family planning as a human right. Consequently, we should not accept change in principles governing population policy. Selective and regionally differentiated measures can be taken, *e.g.*, with regard to favouring schooling and employment of women, stimulation or discouragement of migratory trends, channeling of investments, especially into housing. In this context, various measures of social policy in favour of families and children have, for example, been taken in Yugoslavia, particularly in regions where birth rates are low. Actually, in these regions because of social reasons people have a smaller number of children than they would normally desire. It is quite understandable that because of this people opt for socio-economic measures which are likely to enable them to fulfill their desire to have children. Therefore, a pre-determined social policy adopted by common agreement concerning the needs of children, and implemented by citizens in their socio-political organizations, can have the effect of contributing to the strengthening of the responsibility of parents with regard to their active involvement in the creation of better living conditions for their children, and, consequently, to the birth of wanted children only.

At the birth of the child the intimate sexual relation between two partners ceases to be exclusively their own private affair. In the Declaration on the Rights of the Child, the United Nations has elaborated the minimal standards that should be assured to all children of the world. The child enjoys the protection of the whole society, including protection from the possibility of legal deprivation of parents of their parental right. Consequently, it is not only in the interest of the mother and the father but also in the interest of the entire social community that the child should not be born unwanted and should not be deprived, from the very outset, of parental care when it is in the greatest need of it. Therefore, it is in the interest of the individual and of the society as a whole that matters in such an important sphere of life should not remain subject to ancient traditions, prejudices and fortuitous circumstances. On the basis that all parents have an interest in the well-being of their children and on the basis of the interest all people have in a development of the younger generation that will guarantee a better life for all, the action for planned responsible parenthood should be linked to the population policy and thus to the entire social and economic policy of every country. In this manner the intensified conflict between the individual interests of parents and the broader interests of the society can be overcome. Naturally, this means that the individual citizen will be better able to enjoy his democratic freedom because, in executing the socio-economic development policy, the governing forces consider the interest and the activity of people and through laws and statutes, as well as in practice, continually remove the obstacles to the direct participation of all citizens and especially of women in the development and the management of the country. In this sense I regard family planning as free, responsible and socially-active parenthood.

III. Conclusions and Recommendations

1. In the course of realizing the goals of the United Nations Strategy for the Second Development Decade and of the Declaration and Action Programme of the Special Session of the General Assembly on Raw Materials and Development such international, political and economic conditions must be created as to enable countries to formulate independently their population policy and to provide individuals with the ability to exercise their human right to family planning.

2. It is in the interest of the society and its members in each country that:

(i) men and women exercise their parental function in a responsible manner;

(ii) families be able and willing to provide the necessary conditions for healthy psycho-physical development of their children, in the sense of integrating and sharing the functions between the family and the society—for which socially-active parenthood is required;

(iii) that, by multi-sided active participation of citizens in forming and realizing decisions, permanent and dynamic coordination of national resources, consumption and population is made possible—which should be the goal of the population policy as part of the policy of development.

3. It is to the benefit of the citizens, men and women alike, to decide for themselves the number and spacing of children. In order to acquire this benefit they must have the right to unimpeded access to the necessary education, information, means and medical help related to family planning.

4. In the interest of their children and of other family members, as well as in the interest of the national development, women should be persuaded to accept their professional work as a life-time orientation. Therefore, legislation must open new ways for changes that must take place within the family and the society related to their employment, their participation in politics and their motherhood. Women should not be made to choose between the family and the profession, but should be helped towards becoming an active factor in the society through the active co-creation of new social conditions for their children and through evolution of domestic chores from the individual family to public service.

5. It is the right of the child to be born wanted. This means that a child has the right to be born into an environment within the family and the society that will meet its biological and emotional needs.

6. Laws can either promote or impede the development. But it must be remembered that laws have different effects on people in different socio-economic conditions. It is the purpose of this symposium to contribute to the efforts to analyze different laws and the impact they have in practical life and to develop laws in this field which will help progress. Therefore, the sym-

posium should support all laws and statutes that serve the purpose of making possible the practice of the human right of family planning.

7. In discussing human rights it should be kept in mind that means ought not to be substituted for goals, and should also not be in opposition to them. It is important to distinguish between the conception of what we declare are human rights and what is just a method, a means towards realizing these rights. The test for whether a right is really fully enjoyed should be when a person is absolutely free to decide between alternatives, that is, when he has the necessary knowledge, the means are accessible to him, and when he is conscious of every consequence of his decision.

8. Every national legislative scheme should demonstrate a concern for far-reaching improvement in the status of women in the following areas:

(i) *Economic sphere*: Women should be treated as equal participants at every level of development in the agricultural and industrial production. All practices which discriminate by sex should be eliminated. Equal pay for equal work and contribution should be guaranteed. All work should be accessible to women under equal conditions, and they should have equal opportunities for education and qualification. Lastly, the labour legislation should be revised to include the language of some of the ILO conventions on the protection of the working woman.

(ii) *Political sphere*: The mere abolition of limitations on woman's electoral rights is not enough. Leading social forces should be used to muster the political will by permitting expanded participation of women in the management of the political life in each country.

(iii) *Family sphere*: Naturally, motherhood is of considerable social importance. Legislation must be designed to see the woman not as an instrument of bearing a larger or a smaller number of children, but as a responsible subject of her biological function. Concerns for the protection of the mother must not result either in making motherhood so private that it concerns only the individual family or in negating the father's rights and duties. It is the duty of both parents to exercise their parenthood in a responsible manner, to be prepared to raise their children within the family and to create, through their work and their activity in the society, the best possible conditions for their children's psycho-physical development.

(iv) *Household sphere*: Within the trend toward an increasingly diversified division of labour within the society there is the possibility that many everyday household needs and duties can be covered by industry and social services. This trend should be speeded up by legislation, tax policies, etc., as it means new job possibilities, especially for women, and better life for families.

9. In order to ensure that the human right to decide on the number and spacing of children is fully realized, the following is necessary: the in-

troduction of sex information and of education as related to human sexuality and responsibility for childbirth into school curricula and into other forms of non-school education; the establishment of pre-marital and marital counselling centres; the introduction of the medical and socio-medical elements of family planning into the general scheme of medical services, particularly into the work of general practitioners and maternal child health care services. The means by which this human right can be practised are contraception, sterilization, treatment of sterility including artificial insemination, abortions and adoption.

Legislation should contribute the implementation of family planning as a human right and should within this framework define medical, psychological and ethical contra-indications that could arise in connection with certain medical methods of family planning (abortion, oral contraception and sterilization).

REFERENCES

A Questionnaire on the Fertility of Married Women and on Family Planning, STANOVISTVO, July-December, 1971 (Belgrade: Institute of Social Science).

D. BREZNILE, A. MOJIĆ, M. RASEVIĆ, and M. RANCIC, FERTILITY OF INHABITANTS IN YUGOSLAVIA (Belgrade: Demographic Research Center, Institute of Social Science 1972).

CONSTITUTION OF THE SOCIALIST FEDERAL REPUBLIC OF YUGOSLAVIA, art. 191 (1974). Declaration on the Rights of the Child, General Assembly Res. 1386, 14 U.N.-GAOR, Supp. 16, p. 19, Doc. No. A/4354 (1959).

Decree No. 33 of 16 February 1960 (Termination of Pregnancy) Sluzbeni List Federatione Republike Jugoslavije, 2 March 1960, No. 9, at 221-222.

Report of the VII Congress of the Gynecologists and Obstetricians of Yugoslavia, Belgrade, 1972 (the main theme of the meeting was Medical Aspects of Induced Abortion).

Resolution on Family Planning, Sluzbeni List SFRJ 1969/20, No. 307, at 612.

S. Simoneti and F. Novak, Decline of Birth Rate and its Influence on the Decline of Infant Mortality (paper presented to the IPPF Conference, Ottawa, May 1972).

V. Tomsic, The Status of Women and Family Planning in the Socialist Federal Republic of Yugoslavia (working paper WP/13 for the United Nations Seminar on the Status of Women and Family Planning, Istanbul, July 11-24, 1972).

V. Tomsic, Women of Yugoslavia in the Social Development of their Country (information supplied to the Social Development Commission of ECOSOC, August, 1971).

U.N. ECOSOC, Study on the Interrelationship of the Status of Women and Family Planning, Report of the Special Rapporteur, Doc. No. E/CN.6/575 (1973).

United Nations, Seminar on Family Planning and Social Policy in Europe, Doc. No. SOA/ESPD/1971/2, Keljava, Finland, May 16-25, 1971.

United Nations, International Forum on the Role of Women in Population and Development, Doc. No. ST/ESA/SER.B/4, New York and Airlie House, Virginia, February 25-March 1, 1974.

United Nations, Report of Interregional Meeting of Experts on the Integration of Women in Development, Doc. No. ST/SOA/120 (1973).

G. Zarkovic, *Natural Increase and Population Planning in Yugoslavia*, 28 *Narodno-zdravlje*, No. 2 (1972).

Report of Workshop on Status of Women

After a brief opening statement by Dean Irene Cortes of the University of the Philippines College of Law, Mrs. Vida Tomsic reviewed the salient points of her paper presented at the morning plenary session and framed the role of the workshop as she viewed it: to not only reiterate the generalities of earlier United Nations resolutions and documents, which call for equality of women with men, but also to push for further improvement in the realm of the status of women by using the tool of law. Of particular importance to her were the issues of women's employment and political activity.

With regard to the former, Mrs. Tomsic felt that any recommendations from the workshop should tackle head on the issue of development *vis-a-vis* the status of women, as it relates to the recent clamor in the United Nations for a new economic order. While the laws in most countries theoretically proscribe any form of discrimination based on sex, she noted that in practice there is generally a great disparity between the status of men and women and expressed a preference for expanding the role of women in the economic sector as a means of enhancing the status of women. Attempts in the past to do this have been hampered by so-called "protective legislation," which has placed women in a special category for employment purposes. In her view, it is essential that women be allowed all the opportunities given to male workers. Rather than having women absent themselves from employment for long periods of time for child-bearing, as is now the case almost everywhere, women should be given the power to decide whether and when to have children without being forced to forego a working career. While recognizing that it would involve a long-range, slowly developing change, she suggested that the traditional division of labor between men and women be re-evaluated and ultimately changed.

As for the political implications related to the subject, she opined that in order to enhance the role of women in the political arena there would have to be some fundamental changes in the political systems now functioning in the world. In most cases this would mean shifting from the male-dominated governmental systems to ones which permitted the participation of all the citizenry.

The discussion topics for the workshop then centered on four subjects:

(1) education, (2) employment, (3) political and civil status of women, and (4) property rights.

Education

The inter-relationship between the status of women, the practice of family planning and levels of education was recognized as a source of many of the problems that nations now face with regard to women's employment and fertility. Several recent studies have underscored the inverse relationship which exists between a woman's education and training, on one hand, and family size on the other. The subordinate status of women in many cultures similarly affects their participation in the life of the society. This fact has been recognized and various nations are beginning to offer training for women. Programmes of this type in Africa include the offering of: (1) a short compulsory programme of education for women; (2) training opportunities for women at the village levels in vocational skills; (3) schooling which would include the teaching of the skills required for marketing, bookkeeping, etc.; (4) reforms in the school curriculum; and (5) revisions in educational material to meet women's needs in vocational education and counselling.

Several of the participants drew attention to the fact that other variables affect the level and quality of education and thus fertility. For example, socio-economic factors play a role in determining whether women have access to education and the ability to make decisions which control the size of the family. Fleeting reference was made to the fact that because of the existence of patriarchal systems in many countries, which traditionally vest in men the authority to make high-level decisions, perhaps efforts should be made to more adequately educate the policy-makers so that the proper policy decisions would be made regarding the education of women and the availability of family planning. In a larger sense this would mean that men must also be educated to a mind which could sponsor the attitude that women should not be oppressed. It was also observed that the goal of providing education for women would be meaningless if it were not accompanied by other reforms.

Because of their inherent nature, many educational materials convey messages which emphasize rather than break down disparity between the traditional roles of men and women in a society. It was suggested, therefore, that governments undertake programmes bent on eradicating passages in those materials which convey misconceptions relating to the status and role of women in society.

Note was also taken of the fact that the traditional culture and social values in many countries perpetuate the subordinate status of women and that where women's rights have been made equal through legislation, women are largely unaware of their legal rights. Therefore, there was a need expressed for programmes to educate women as to their legal rights.

Considerable time was spent discussing the tremendous barrier which illiteracy poses to the status of women, especially where the subject of women's fertility is concerned. It was observed that if fertility habits are to be changed, women must be taught to read at the earliest age and therefore be able to assimilate information in order to apprise themselves of the family planning choices available to them. But concern was also expressed over the fact that formal and primary education will not reach all women, particularly those who are now in the reproductive years, so that non-formal education of women regarding family planning matters and educational opportunities should be considered in any recommendation to be presented by the workshop.

Some attention was given to the fact that an overly rapid population growth has an impact on the possibility of providing education to women, as well as men, and that some consideration should be given to this phenomenon. A spiralling population growth carries with it the potential for outstripping the ability of a country to apportion its resources so as to provide education for all. It was also felt that as far as possible the content of education given to women should include sex education, and that social and economic impediments to the education of women should be removed. This could be accomplished by governments adopting educational policies and programmes which would provide education for women toward the end that they attain equality with men. It was suggested that these types of policies should be adopted by governments with the least possible delay.

The types of educational reforms discussed during the workshop are not made without cost. The more affluent nations seem to be able to find the financial resources to develop strong educational systems. But what of the countries whose resources are limited? Though there has been a tendency in the past for international organizations to stress economic development to the exclusion of developing other social priorities, reference was made to the possibility of using international assistance programmes as a practical way to stimulate the development of adequate educational facilities in countries that have traditionally lacked the resources to do so on their own.

Employment

The workshop then turned to consider the relationship which economics has to the overall status of women. The subject of employment is necessarily intertwined with that of education, for a woman who is uneducated will not have adequate access to employment opportunities. Education, then, is the precursor of employment. And employment in some measure appears to be the precursor of lower fertility. Recent studies have shown that the fact that a woman is employed outside the home affects the decision not only as to when to have children, but also as to the quantity. In a study made of 50 countries where at least 35 percent of the women were employed outside the home, the annual growth rate was shown to be less than 2%. This is in contrast to countries where the women were not employed outside the home and fertility rates were as a rule much higher. Among employed women in some areas of the world there are noticeable differences in the rates of fertility. In Latin America, professional women have a higher fertility rate than those employed in clerical jobs. This is likely due to the fact that professionals can hire others to care for the children while they work.

Reference was again made to the desirability of allowing women to play a more active role in the developmental process, particularly in the areas of employment, by removing the barriers which presently frustrate this goal. Any attempt to institute such changes may involve more than just legal reform. Laws may already exist which give women the rights to full participation in the economy of a country. Whether they can take advantage of those rights is another question. Where there is an absence of child care centers, the decision must be made between the parents as to who will care for the children and who will work. The decision is traditionally made in favor of the woman remaining in the home and the man taking on the role of the breadwinner. Therefore, the question exists as to what can be done to allow women to take advantage of their economic potential. The creation of adequate child care centers may permit the woman to continue to work. And other work security arrangements such as guaranteeing return to a job after maternity leave may go far toward making it possible for women to participate fully in the economy as wage earners.

Political and Civil Status

It was emphasized that one of the major problems related to the political and civil status of women is that women do not know their rights. Therefore, a suggestion was made that some type of legal aid, perhaps of the ombudsman type, be made available to women so as to inform them of their legal protections, rights and capacities relating to marriage and its dissolution, education, employment, migration, and property. A question was raised as to whether stressing legal aid to women would tend to discriminate against men. In the final analysis, it was felt that while legal aid should be made available to men and women alike, emphasis should be placed on educating women as to their political and civil rights.

The importance of women playing an active role in policy-making was stressed. It was noted that one of the most formidable barriers to allowing women to play a more active role in the political system are the inherent negative societal attitudes toward women who are involved in public life. Though a few notable exceptions exist, most political systems simply do not allow women to actively participate at a high level. A suggestion that a pro-rata number of places be guaranteed for women in the policy-making body of governments, including the legislative branches, while uniquely forward looking, was deemed to be self-defeating.

Nevertheless, a consensus existed among the workshop participants to the effect that women should be allowed to take a greater part in the policy decision-making process.

Property Rights

In some societies there exist either cultural or legal barriers which adversely affect women's property rights. Some of these practices thwart the woman's ability to inherit, acquire, and dispose of property in her own name. Such practices run counter to the overriding desire for equality of the sexes. The workshop recommended that such practices be abandoned.

Some Considerations of Incentives and Disincentives in the Promotion of Family Planning: India's Experience

By
V. I. Chacko*

INTRODUCTION

The feasibility of offering cash or other substitute incentives as a means of establishing the motivation to practice family planning may be considered largely from the viewpoint of indigent populations. The role of incentives, disincentives, or a combination of both in family planning has been attracting more serious interest than it did ten or twenty years ago, especially in the poorer countries where high rates of population growth have outstripped development. Since India is typical of the countries where the rapid growth of population threatens to affect all aspects of life, the considerations which apply to incentives and disincentives, and the experience gained there, may be of wider application.

I. EMERGENCE OF A NATIONAL POPULATION POLICY

A. *Initial Assumptions*

The Government of India recognized the need for a population policy fairly early after the country's independence. An active anti-natalist policy was adopted as part of the First Five-Year Plan in 1952. However, the successful implementation of that policy was based on the assumptions that the people of India were aware of the consequences of high rates of population growth and that the expression of national concern would result in a general adoption of measures appropriate to check it. Neither was necessarily the case. As in many other countries, the net gain in population increase in India has resulted more from a fall in the high mortality rate than

---

* Chief Executive and Advisor, United Tea Planters' Association of Southern India.

from a new phenomenon of excessive fecundity. But levels of fecundity have failed to trail off as mortality rates decreased.

Some time passed before there was official recognition of the fact that an active promotion of family planning, involving a massive national campaign, was needed. Since the campaign had to be addressed to the individual couple in order to promote a decision-making process of sustained concern and effectiveness, it became apparent that such a programme would involve conceptual, organizational and operational problems of intractable complexity and magnitude, all of which are reflections of the situation in India. Apart from the vertical social, educational and economic divisions in Indian society, there are sharply marked horizontal divisions based on language, community, religion, states, regions and distance. Education and motivation on the subject of population problems related to family behaviour would require an adequate machinery for campaign management. It also would require the rendering of services beyond the means available to a developing country, even if it is assumed that a sufficient level of promotional input would have the desired effect.

B. *The Effect of Inaccurate Assumptions Related to Population Programmes*

Many of the assumptions which grew out of the experience of the first decade after India had formally adopted an anti-natalist policy and a national programme in support of it proved to be false. It proved impossible to base a population programme on the simple premise that individuals in India would of themselves adopt measures to limit fertility.

It became evident that general awareness about population growth and the complementary individual commitment to check it were products of a quality of life which widespread illiteracy and poverty do not provide. Cultural factors also served to frustrate the programme. The strong tradition of large families and the direct evidence of their usefulness in primary rural labour are factors which run contrary to the acceptance of the concept of smaller individual families. The traditional value attached to the demonstrable existence of male virility and the parallel sanctification of the woman's role as mother both tend to provide approval and support for large rather than small family norms. The adoption of any practice contrary to long established value systems was further complicated by the fear of using modern contraceptive methods. In addition ridicule from fellow villagers was usually attached to any overt acceptance of such methods. All of these cultural barriers inhibited the effectiveness of the campaign. Popular leaders drawn from the same rural society tended to exhibit these same prejudices, and in any case would not advocate a cause which could produce an unpredictable reaction among their followers. Very often there was a conflict in their minds between the objective of population control and the political and communal interests of their own group.

II. The Role of Government in Incentive Programmes

The introduction of any form of incentive related to bringing about a decline in fertility must perforce depend, in the first place, upon a general sense of approval and also on the unambiguous articulation of a national policy in favour of birth control. This basic position was reached during the third and fourth Plan periods spanning the "sixties" in India. Since that time, the question of the use of cash incentives as a part of the plan to promote acceptance of family planning has been caught between two arguments. One point of view has it that the offering of any incentive, and particularly cash incentives, as a reward for accepting birth control measures was at best a crude device for obtaining consent and that in reality it amounted to an act which exploited the acceptor's impoverished condition. After all, it has been argued that incentives are not being offered to the rich or accepted by them. The opposite argument has been that the time required for a lengthy educational programme was not available to the countries most hard-pressed by excessive population and that if the use of incentives would pave the way for wider acceptance of some forms of family planning, they should be offered. But use of incentives raised questions concerning cost not only of the incentives but also of the elaborate administrative machinery required to supervise their distribution.

A. *Government Experiments and Incentive Policy*

The first tentative experiment in the use of fertility-related incentives in India was set up by the State Government in Tamil Nadu. The incentives offered took the form of cash compensation for the loss of earnings which might occur due to incapacitation following the operation for sterilisation. Though the scheme stimulated many inquiries, response in terms of acceptance was limited. The next step taken by the State was to contact the people and to question them about why they did not accept the offer of service and care. This stimulated a wider exchange of views on a matter which was not usually considered a proper subject for open discussion. But, in reality, the provision of a substantial cash incentive for accepting family planning methods would have been beyond the capacity of any one State, and the success of such measures is still in doubt.

The national population policy of itself does not include a cash incentive scheme. Rather, it relies on information, education, promotion and service. It does, however, encourage employers to establish and support family planning facilities, the cost of which is treated as a deductible revenue charge under the income-tax law. In some States, like Maharashtra, certain disincentives to high fertility have been introduced for government employees. Such benefits as housing, education and access to welfare are restricted where the number of children exceeds three.

The formulation of a national population policy which includes the use of incentives has suffered both from the scarcity of resources in relation to the vast population and from the ethical consideration as to whether a cash incentive is not a form of "bribe" to the poor to accept something which they would not or might not otherwise accept. The possibility of being accused of exploiting the poor, which cash incentives would seem strongly to suggest, has prevented the government from taking a formal position on incentives. Yet, in the general context of a national policy which favours all activities supportive of family planning, the use of incentives as a means to promote it, such as the compensatory cash payment in Tamil Nadu for incapacitation, could not be included in the same suspect category as a cash reward for sterilisation. National policy on incentives has been apparently neutral, displaying a slight willingness to tolerate the use of incentives where somebody else is willing to meet the cost. For example, neither the Union Government nor the State Governments stand in the way of cash incentives for sterilisations being paid by private employers. Understandably, the onus of bearing the cost of a cash benefit cannot be put anywhere else.

B. *Tax Benefits for Family Planning Activities of Employers*

The tax deductibility of the cost of cash incentives as a legitimate welfare expenditure has been recommended by all official committees which have studied the problem, including the Central Labour Welfare Committee of which this writer was a member. But the fact that such expenditures, including the cost of promotion, education and service, have been made deductible has not led to any noteworthy expansion of interest in family planning activities in India. Much of the present level of interest and activity has been achieved as a result of the concern of individual employers on the national scene. The fact remains that if in theory the tax deductibility of such expenditures, coupled with the possible lowering of welfare costs for employers, were designed to instantly attract profit-motivated employers into undertaking massive family planning drives, in practice it has failed to do so. Because the use of cash incentives and the establishment of related family planning services can be organized presently only through business enterprises, we must examine more closely and re-evaluate the motivations of the employers if the most economically active section in the community, namely the industrialists, are to be persuaded to undertake a family planning campaign supported by cash incentives.

III. THE INVOLVEMENT OF EMPLOYERS IN INCENTIVES

There is no need to make any distinction between private employers and employers in the public sector for present purposes. Although public sector management is more likely to carry out the orders of the government in regard both to population activities and incentives, and although their costs and benefits would not be a matter of motivation to the extent that they might be in the case of private employers, the ultimate legal and ethical considerations would not differ.

A. *Some More Faulty Assumptions*

When a private employer is viewed as an instrument for furthering family planning activities, it is assumed that what motivates his role in business extends to his interests and relationship with his employees. If his profit-making motive can be stimulated by demonstrating how much he could gain by persuading his employees to accept the idea of limiting the size of their family, it is assumed that he will find adequate motivation for involving himself in population activities. This chain of reasoning is obviously based on the notion that employers are motivated by a crude commercialism, which may not, in fact, be the case among all the employers as a class. A more valid assumption probably would be that employers are likely to be reluctant to undertake an activity which may entail more cost to them than would tangibly benefit their business. In other words, business motivation may be derived more from a desire to avoid incurring unbeneficial costs rather than from a desire to make a profit out of family planning activities. It is unlikely that the sole possibility of gaining from family planning activities will induce employers as a class to undertake population activities. The more dominant factor seems to be a fear of incurring additional costs rather than any expectation of saving costs. This explains one of the reasons for the general lack of active participation by the business community in family planning programmes.

When incentives are considered in terms of the impact they might have on acceptor response, there is as much an element of crudity in the reasoning as there is in the idea of employers being drawn into family planning activities in the hope of increasing their profit. In developing countries, with relatively limited organised industrial activity, the number of people which may be reached through employers is small, even though over time it is capable of generating a widespread effect.

Private employers have the same rights and obligations as private citizens within the general community. Because involvement in family planning is not obligatory, the tax deductibility of expenditures incurred on family planning activities, even where it is written into labour welfare laws, is a right which the employer may exercise. Through added education, motivation and persuasion more employers may be induced to undertake family planning programmes for their workers. To what extent employers will benefit by reducing their welfare costs is yet uncertain. They cannot, however, be compelled to undertake family planning activities by statutory compulsion when the extent of acceptor response is still uncertain, and in any case cannot be enforced.

B. *The Moral Question*

The question that becomes important in regard to the idea of a cash incentive is whether it is moral to take advantage of the poverty of the acceptors as a means to achieve an objective which is recognised as nationally desirable—that of reducing the rate of population growth. This doubt about the ethical basis of the incentive is compounded by the limited number of people to whom such an incentive can be made available, the reluctance of certain sections of the population to bear the cost of the incentive, and the tenuous evidence so far available regarding the effectiveness of the cash incentive.

C. *Variations of the Cash Incentive Scheme: Deferred Incentives*

The "no-birth bonus scheme," introduced on a selected group of plantations in Southern India, is an innovative variant of the cash incentive scheme. It has the same final objective as a direct incentive. However, it has a conceptual origin which takes into account the major points of criticism directed against cash incentives. The bonus, which the participating plantations pay into the individual account of each woman worker who joins the scheme, operates in the same manner as other deferred payment end-of-service programmes, such as the provident fund and gratuity. When Dr. Ronald G. Ridker, then of the Agency for International Development in India, first proposed this scheme as a deferred incentive, its attraction lay in the fact that it catered to a desire for the long-term welfare of the working family rather than to the desire for immediate gain of a cash award for undergoing sterilisation. As a result, the "no-birth bonus scheme" was then embedded into a comprehensive labour welfare programme which included environmental hygiene, preventive medicine, nutritional support and development of the young on the selected tea plantations.

If it is argued that limiting the family has as its primary objective improving the well-being of the family, since the worker could take better care of his family within the means available to him, then a long-term concern about the family's welfare is implicit, and this concern can be strengthened by a superannuation benefit of long-term expectation. The scheme has the added advantage of assuring the worker's old age security—an anxiety which people traditionally assuaged by having large numbers of children. Recent experience has shown that family planning motivation is more apt to be successful if the incentive tends to reassure the recipient that its purpose is not to lure the acceptor onto the operating table or into adopting family planning techniques with the promise of an immediate cash payment but rather to demonstrate a continuing concern for the entire family's welfare during its working life and thereafter.

In the developing countries where intense population activities are urgently needed, the question of any form of incentive being offered is likely to be raised only in regard to labour employed in industrial under-takings. As for the rest of the population, governments are likely to confine their activities to family planning promotion and services rather than to incentives except for specific occasions of short duration and limited cover-age, as in the case of the various sterilisation camps held in India. However, there has been a move toward the introduction of certain disincentives which involve the withdrawal of some of the concessions and privileges traditionally granted Government servants.

D. *The Case for a Sharing of Benefits*

An important issue raised in the last few years concerns the benefit flowing from the acceptance of family planning. This obviously refers to workers engaged in industrial undertakings, where the involvement of em-ployers in the furtherance of family planning is assumed to benefit those same employers. If such benefits do accrue, it is argued that it is only fair and reasonable that such benefits be shared. The industrial community in any society represents the most active segment of the population and the effect of any success achieved in the industrial community could have dif-fuse and tremendous impact on the rest of the population. If industrial em-ployers tend to gain from their workers' acceptance of family limitation, it would seem that a case can be made out for the sharing of that gain.

Workers are as much a part of the total population as employers or any other section of the community, including self-employed persons. In the family planning context, an employer's gain is derived from the fact that he is statutorily obliged to provide certain facilities or make certain payments at his cost to a worker employed by him. If the worker accepts a limitation on the size of his family and, as a result, the employer is saved the cost which he would otherwise have incurred, it is assumed that the employer has benefitted to the extent of that saving. The next gain could be arrived at by deducting the cost incurred by him. When a self-employed citizen limits his family, the cost to the country of the various facilities which the State maintains at public cost is correspondingly saved. But would the sharing of the gain be applicable in this case?

In the case of industrial employers, it is assumed that only the em-ployers gain from the workers' acceptance of family limitation. This as-sumption requires examination. It would seem that there are three bene-ficiaries in this situation: the State, the worker and the employer. In terms of computable benefits the largest beneficiary is the worker himself, fol-lowed by the State and the employer.

The demographic problems of a country may require national policies of regulation and promotion in conformity with its interests, population policies and goals. Obviously, legislation ought to be designed to further the national policy. The obligations laid on employers of labour under the

demands of such a policy can only extend to the provision of certain facilities, but they cannot force labour to accept the services. An effective family
planning programme may lead to a reduction of maternity and other costs
in an industrial enterprise. As a result, the benefits payable to workers
under the maternity benefits statute may diminish. There is also, possibly,
a saving from the avoidance of absenteeism which occurs when either the
workers or their children are ill. However, to quantify such benefits ac-
cruing to the employer presents a serious problem. If the gain cannot be
quantified, it makes it difficult to allocate the benefits of such gain between
the employer and the worker.

In the contentious area of industrial relations, the right of the workers
to better wages and conditions rests upon established customs, agreements
and statutes. In an area where the larger national and international issue
of population growth is concerned, the priority seems to be clearly in favour
of getting every viable agency to support the campaign for population limitation rather than of opening up new areas of conflict by the introduction of
a tenuous concept, such as attempting to quantify economic gains through
family planning to industry and workers alike.

IV.   Disincentives as a Population Measure

Disincentives have a positive role to play, provided the informational
input and service arrangements are adequate. Countries like Singapore
have limited the claims to maternity benefits, discriminated in favour of
small families in the allocation of housing flats, reduced tax allowances for
children beyond two and charged steeply increased accouchement fees
as the number of children exceeds two. Certain states in India like Maharashtra, apply some of these disincentives to government servants, but not
to industrial labour or to the general population. An active anti-natalist
policy should be more explicit, particularly in regard to benefits associated
with marriage or maternity. For instance, the Indian Central Provident
Fund Act and the Rules thereunder specifically provide for loans and advances for meeting expenses connected with the marriage of the children
of beneficiaries. An amendment to the Rules to restrict such advances to
cases where the sons and daughters marry at a later age than is prevalent
at present could have some impact.

Limiting maternity benefits to two children or a progressively reduced
rate of benefits for subsequent children would require an amendment to
legislation on maternity benefits in many countries. Where such reduced
benefits apply, the difference between the original rates and the reduced
rates should be payable by the employers into a common welfare fund for
employees. Whereas, the computation of benefits arising from general family planning activities would be difficult, where there is a specific amount
prescribed as maternity benefits, any reduction of that amount is easy both
to determine and to pay into a welfare fund.

V. CONCLUSIONS AND RECOMMENDATIONS

Any attempt at promoting family planning through cash or other incentives will always involve an organizational network capable of rendering the informational and supportive services, as well as one capable of systematising the cash incentive payments so that they will have the greatest impact on the target group. Since the opportunity to decide the number and spacing of the children a family should have is considered a basic human right, that right becomes illusory if the information necessary to make the decision is not available. If it is a national policy to subscribe to the Universal Declaration of Human Rights, the Teheran Proclamation on Human Rights and the U.N. Declaration on Social Progress and Development, and if the availability of information and services are decisive in making those rights meaningful in individual family decisions, the responsibility cast on the Governments of the subscribing countries are of such a magnitude that they are beyond the capacity of any one of them to bear.

In such circumstances, the utilization of all organised sections of the community in extending these services to the wider population becomes an important element of planning and administration. If the national goal of population limitation is to be achieved, the cost of undertaking such incidental tasks should be a legitimate charge on the State. That would mean the full reimbursement to the business sector of the costs it incurs in providing family planning information, services and incentives through the use of an equivalent tax deduction, or of a compensatory payment where tax deductions are not possible. Tax deductions admissible under the income tax laws of most countries do not fully reimburse the employer who incurs expenditures which help to further the national population programme. By charging such costs to the revenue account of a business or industrial undertaking, only a part of the costs are in fact reimbursed. A revision of the tax laws so as to fully reimburse the costs incurred would be more in keeping with the purposes of the national policy and would make a significant contribution to the promotion of active participation by employers in the national campaign.

If voluntary organisations of social workers were to expand their area of effective coverage, some of the incentives made available through employers to their employees could be extended to self-employed village populations through such voluntary organisations—provided the costs of the incentives and services are met by the Government under suitable laws. The strengthening of the activities of such voluntary agencies in this area of family planning would provide for dispersed initiative with greater local adaptability and broader acceptance than a more centrally bureaucratised family planning organization.

Since most of the least developed countries have a strong rural orientation in their population, a dispersed service and incentive system would have a far greater net impact than centralised government schemes. Since concessions through tax laws are restrictive in their effect, alternative schemes for meeting the cost should be legally provided. If the government policy towards family planning is positive and dynamic, and if it rests on voluntary efforts at the local level, social security bonds, educational bonds and a no-birth bonus could be devised and operated through a variety of local institutional media.

In the developing art of social action to discourage large families and to encourage small families, both incentives and disincentives should be considered as part of an integrated national policy operable under the circumstances of each country.

REFERENCES

GOVERNMENT OF INDIA, FIRST FIVE YEAR PLAN 18 (1952).

GOVERNMENT OF INDIA, REPORTS OF THE COMMITTEE ON LABOUR WELFARE AND NATIONAL COMMISSION ON LABOUR (1969).

P. HALL, LAW AND POPULATION GROWTH IN SINGAPORE (Law and Population Monograph No. 9, 1973).

INCENTIVE APPROACHES IN POPULATION PLANNING PROGRAMS: READINGS AND ANNOTATIONS (O. Finnigan ed. Manila: Agency for International Development 1972).

Nine Point Programme in UPASI Scheme (1972).

E. POHLMAN, INCENTIVES AND COMPENSATIONS IN BIRTH PLANNING (Chapel Hill, N.C.: Carolina Population Center 1971).

R. Ridker, *Savings Accounts for Family Planning, An Illustration from the Tea Estates of India*, 3 *Studies in Family Planning*, No. 7, at 150-152 (New York: The Population Council 1972).

E. Rogers, *Incentives in the Diffusion of Family Planning Innovations*, 2 *Studies in Family Planning*, No. 12, at 241-247 (New York: The Population Council 1971).

UNITED NATIONS, MEASURES, POLICIES AND PROGRAMMES AFFECTING FERTILITY, WITH PARTICULAR REFERENCE TO NATIONAL FAMILY PLANNING PROGRAMMES, U.N. Doc. ST/SOA/SER.A/51 (1972).

Report of Workshop
on Incentives and Disincentives

The use of incentives and disincentives in the context of family planning programmes was discussed on the basis of the background paper written by V.I. Chacko, Chief Executive and Advisor, United Tea Planters' Association of Southern India. In introducing his paper, Mr. Chacko described the Indian experience with a deferred incentive system called the "no-birth bonus scheme," recently initiated on plantations in Southern India. Under this scheme, women were credited with a cash bonus for every month in which no child was born. The bonus was to be payable at the end of their service in the same way as the gratuity and provident or retirement fund. The scheme had covered increasing numbers of women over the previous three years, but although the results thus far were spectacular in terms of reducing fertility among the women participating in the programme, it was still too early to say to what extent the success was due to the deferred incentive feature.

The workshop heard other examples of national experience with monetary incentives and disincentives, such as limiting family allowances or tax exemptions to a small number of children, but recognized that such programmes would not necessarily be relevant in all countries. It was noted that in some countries only a small percentage of the people paid income taxes and thus reductions in tax exemptions would have little impact. Some participants also pointed out that in fact family planning services in many parts of the world were not yet freely available to all people, and that without access to family planning services, incentives and disincentives would unfairly discriminate against those who lacked the knowledge and means to limit the size of their families. In such areas, therefore, the first priority must be to make the full range of family planning services freely and effectively available to all persons.

Finally, as to monetary disincentives such as increases in delivery charges at government hospitals or limits on income tax exemptions, it was noted that such measures affect the financial position of the family as a whole and thus may endanger the interests of children. The view was expressed that the interests of children must be paramount, and that therefore care must be taken to ensure that monetary incentives and disincentives do not injure the innocent children who are already members of the family.

As to non-monetary incentives, it was noted that the provision of incentives was an important means of displaying the attitude of the government and of bringing home to the people the necessity for family planning. One example was a "mother of the year" award, which emphasized the quality of life in the family rather than the quantity of children. The publicity attendant to the award helped to motivate people to utilize available family planning services.

The question of the effectiveness of incentives and disincentives in varying social and cultural conditions was considered at length. Although many programmes of incentives and disincentives were under way in some countries, there had not yet been sufficient experience to draw firm conclusions as to their value. Experience in some countries showed that there was no problem of incentives to family planning: when the full range of family planning methods was made effectively available, people would use them. In other countries it had been found that incentives and disincentives were necessary to motivate people to use the services that were available. It was noted in particular that children were frequently relied upon to provide security in old age, and that in this context it would be important to couple incentives both with health programmes to ensure the survival of children and with old age security programmes to reduce the reliance upon children.

In the light of the extensive discussion, and bearing in mind the differences in national social and cultural traditions, a consensus was reached in the workshop to recommend that countries planning to utilize incentives or disincentives should design their programmes to take into account the value systems and mores prevailing in the society, and to counteract the practical obstacles confronting family planning programmes.

In considering the human rights aspects of incentives and disincentives, the workshop recognized that care must be taken to ensure that benefits or services provided as incentives to family planning be in addition to the benefits and services to which all persons are entitled as basic human rights. Similarly, any benefits or services withheld or withdrawn as disincentives against large families should not diminish the enjoyment of basic human rights.

Legislation and Demographic Changes

By
Alexandre Paraiso*

Over the millenia, man has always done his procreating as though it were a matter of fate; generations of human beings have received life from their parents and have in their turn, inflicted it upon their children through sexual intercourse, without considering whether it was necessary that the children be born and in what number they were needed.

"Go forth and multiply," said the Creator.[1] From that time on, no matter what the vicissitudes, man has obeyed the divine injunction without daring to disregard it.

Nevertheless, for reasons of personal convenience—most frequently because of necessity—man has made certain slight changes in his way of carrying out the Divine order. In other words, without absolutely disobeying his natural instincts, man has been led to modify the rhythm of his procreation for reasons which vary from country to country and from period to period, all of which lead to the same result of changing his original procreative behaviour.

This modification of procreation in the light of life's pressures has been given several names, such as "birth control," "regulation of births," or "family planning"—all of which expressions put the accent on only one aspect of behavioural modification, namely, limitation of fertility. However, as we shall see, man has not only sought to *limit* the number of births in order to adapt himself to the needs of society, but, as history has taught us about certain peoples in the past, also adopted techniques of *favoring the increase* in the population in order to take into account the necessities of the moment after a heavy loss of life through war, disease or famine.

Moreover, the above-mentioned expressions which are employed far too frequently by the Neo-Malthusians have the ring of genocide, sometimes frightening the people who are not fully aware of the basic reasons on which they are based. It is for this reason that we prefer to use the word

---

* Justice of the Supreme Court, Dahomey.
1. Genesis 1:28.

271

"orthogenesis"[2]—an expression used in medical circles and which has recently been given a legislative status by the creation of "orthogenic centers" in France. As far as I am concerned, and in view of the above, I suggest the following definition of orthogenesis:

> The group of corrective techniques whose purpose is the improved adaptation of human procreation to the requirements of family, national and world existence.

Conceived in this manner, the modification of fertility will have, on the one hand, a pro-natalist effect for sterile couples or for regions which are demographically deficient but which nevertheless have a high potentiality to sustain life, and, on the other hand, a limiting effect on expanding families or for regions which are economically underdeveloped but afflicted with overpopulation.

Historically, the means used to achieve the above ends have been "old wives' methods" or taboos and prohibitions decreed by tribal magistrates or chiefs. We can cite, for example, from our own memory the insertion of small objects into the uterus to slow down fertility, or the use of postnatal restraint observed by many peoples in Africa where young mothers would live with their parents between delivery and the weaning of the child. This period may last as long as two or three years. An example of the opposite type—favoring demographic growth—would be the custom among the Yorubas of lower Dahomey under which a young girl reaching puberty and receiving an offer of marriage must be married off immediately. Otherwise, her father, when going to heaven, would suffer a very disagreeable penalty. As a result, there are very precocious marriages in that racial group.

From the same point of view, the Code of Henry II of France (1556) imposed a death penalty upon the crime of concealing a pregnancy, the purpose of which was to prevent the child from being deprived of baptism.[3] According to Jousse[4] abortion was punished with the same penalty. The prevention of abortion and infanticide can only have as a result the growth in the number of children who are born.

At the present time, the techniques of demographic modification which are best known are mechanical or chemical contraceptives. Since other papers will deal with the effects of these contraceptives and the rules governing their use, I will merely point out that:

(a) These are matters for individual action, of a personal character and with an effect only upon the individual's well-being.

(b) They are techniques about which there are many disputes.

---

2. R. GERAUD, LA LIMITATION MÉDICALE DES NAISSANCES.
3. H. BERGUES, LA LIMITATION DES NAISSANCES DANS LA FAMILLE 43.
4. JOUSSE, TRAITÉ DE LA JUSTICE CRIMINELLE EN FRANCE (1771).

Abortion and sterilization, when used for contraceptive purposes, are also not of an obligatory nature, as pointed out by Harriet B. Presser. These techniques are not only not obligatory, but, on the contrary, they are criticized and contested. May I cite as examples two declarations on the subject of abortion as a means of checking the demographic explosion; one comes from the West and the other comes from the Communist countries.

The first statement is by Leon Heritier, Mayor of Frejus and member of the majority in the French Parliament:

> The liberalization of abortion is genocide and a plot against the white race. . . . France has already three million Moslem workers which cannot be assimilated into our society. A falling off of the birth rate caused by egotism and made possible by abortion will bring with it a greater influx of Moslem workmen. The white race will be submerged and will be altogether extinguished.[5]

The second quotation is taken from the Soviet newspaper, *Voprossy Filozofii*:

> Abortion is an anachronism. . . . The policy of a Socialist State favoring family planning is in the sense of increasing the number of children as well as limiting the number of births. In the U.S.S.R. abortion has been free since 1920, but it is a barbarous method, harmful to the health of the mother. . . . There are good reasons that it occurs at a low level of the population. A woman who has been freed from her centuries-old passivity, and who has become a cultivated and free being, should not in our cosmic century have recourse to methods of her grandmother.[6]

Fortunately, among the methods used under the theory of orthogenesis, we are not confined to traumatic methods which are solely dependent on one's own accord. There is a technique of which one of the results is to modify the procreative behavior of the whole population. It is an impersonal and obligatory mass technique. This technique is the law. The law as a technique for demographic change and as an instrument of a population policy—that is the subject which I shall attempt to discuss with you. This theme is not new, even though it is not well known, and other voices more competent than my own have already developed it.

The influences of laws on the demographic development of one country were first analyzed by Mr. Doublet who was Conseiller d'Etat before becoming Prefect of the Paris region. Principally, it was Professor Luke T. Lee, Director of the Law and Population Programme of the Fletcher School of

5. CANARD ENCHAINE, No. 2775 (Jan. 2, 1974).
6. In Express, No. 1171 (Dec. 13, 1973).

Law and Diplomacy at Tufts University, in Massachusetts, who was the first to make a systematic analysis of the matter, and who pointed out its various elements.[7]

When one considers the relationship between law and demographic evolution, the first thing that strikes him is the inconsistency between the law and present day conditions and, at the same time, the failure to adapt present laws to the existing situation as a means of positive action in the field of demographic evolution.

I. THE INCONSISTENCY OF THE LAW

As pointed out by Professor Luke T. Lee,[8] "Low priority accorded to law codification in many emergent countries means retention of archaic laws inherited wholesale from former colonial powers, which often defeats the official policy favoring family planning." Thus, the majority of African countries which encourage family planning, although they do not subsidize it, have in their legislative arsenal the old French law of 1920 which forbids anti-conceptive propaganda. Among the twelve francophone states, only Mali repealed (in 1972) the old law of 1920, and has authorized "practices for the purpose of regulating births."

Gabon is an interesting case in that it has retained the old law of July 31, 1920, for the obvious reason that it feels itself to be underpopulated. What one finds more difficult to understand is the law of October 4, 1969, which permits the use of contraceptives only for therapeutic purposes. The difficulty is to find the distinction between therapeutic purposes and personal purposes. We find the same incoherence in the French law of 1967 which repealed the old law of 1920. Anti-conceptive propaganda is still forbidden, but it is now permitted to use contraceptive methods. Nevertheless, abortion remains formally forbidden. It must be stressed that there is a mistaken belief which is widespread among the public, and even among some experienced jurists, that therapeutic abortion is authorized in France. All we need to do is to take another look at the law of December 28, 1967, to see that this is not the case. The law merely authorizes a surgical intervention—the "employment of a therapy which might bring on the interruption of a pregnancy, as a secondary effect."

II. THE INAPPROPRIATENESS OF THE LAWS

A law is not well adapted as to the achievement of its purpose when it does not bring about all the effects which the legislature desires. As far as population is concerned, this inappropriateness springs from the fact that, in

---

7. Lee, *Legislation and Family Planning*, 2 STUDIES IN FAMILY PLANNING, No. 4 (The Population Council 1971).

8. *Id.*

most of the cases, the legislature was not expressly concerned with producing an effect upon demographic evolution when it drafted this or that law. Demographic policies which are both intentional and well organized exist in only a very small number of states, and even in these states, the legislative measures were taken without an in-depth study of what would be the most adequate method of affecting the population of the country. The case of Gabon which, although underpopulated, nevertheless authorizes the use of the Pill (admittedly in a restrictive manner) and that of Pakistan, which started a sterilization campaign without being concerned beforehand about the psychological effects of such a decision, demonstrate the inadequacy or inappropriateness of many laws in the demographic field.

III.   CLASSIFICATION OF THE LAWS

Why do we bother with a classification? We have defined orthogenesis as a group of scientific techniques. If orthogenesis is a science, we feel that it should be able to be studied scientifically. Some of the methods of orthogenesis have been explained to you by other speakers. They deal with contraceptive methods, and we have already expressed our views as to them.

The law, from our point of view, is a different method. Thus, if the law is an art, it is also a science,[9] and if it is a science, it should be subject to the requirements of classification. This is not a mere exercise in style, but I am proposing to the practitioners herewith tools labelled and classified in accordance with the use to which they are to be put.

A.   *Distinction Based on Effects Produced*

One can classify laws into two major categories in accordance with their effect: *i.e.*, laws which have a direct effect and laws which have an indirect effect.

The laws which have a direct effect are those adopted by the Government after taking into consideration the demographic data in the country. For example, there are the laws encouraging sterilization in Pakistan, India and in Puerto Rico. These laws were intended at first to stabilize the population and thereafter to reduce the fertility rate of the population once it had been stabilized.

The laws having an indirect effect are those whose purpose is not to produce a modifying effect on population growth, but which nevertheless do produce such an effect in an indirect manner. These laws were adopted with an original intent frequently far removed from any consideration of demographic phenomena. For example, in the colonial period, there was a law promulgated which was known as the Mandel Decree of June 15, 1930. It

9.   1 COLIN & CAPITANT, DROIT CIVIL 110.

fixed at 14 the minimum age of marriage for girls and at 16 the age of marriage for men. At the beginning, this law was intended to bring under control the existing practice of child marriage of girls so as to protect their health as recommended by physicians. Pregnancy is particularly unhealthy for a mother if it starts too early and is too frequent. According to statistics,[10] in 1975 there will be in Dahomey 164,000 girls between 10 and 14 years old. If you take into consideration the fact that the average girl reaches puberty at about 12, this gives you about 100,000 persons who will be potential brides and who would have been able to have children in 1976 except for the Mandel Decree. We shall see later other examples of the indirect effects of law.

B.   *Distinction Based on the Form of the Law*

To the above distinction based on the direct or indirect effect, we must add another distinction based on the *form* of the law. That is to say, a distinction based upon the way in which the law is drafted. The principal distinction is between laws which prohibit actions and laws which authorize actions. Thus, the old French law of 1920 on anti-contraceptive propaganda is in prohibitive form, as is true of the French law of December 28, 1967, in regard to abortion. In contrast, the laws on voluntary sterilization are in a positive form.

C.   *Distinction Based Upon the Purpose of the Law*

Finally, there is a third form of suggested classification which is based upon the *purpose* of the law. Among these one can distinguish:

i.   Incentive Laws
ii.   Preventive Laws
iii.   Restrictive Laws.

1. Incentive Laws

As to laws which generate or produce initiative, these, as the name implies, are those which stimulate fertility. These are usually laws which have an indirect effect, whether they are in a positive form (such as laws giving subsidies to births or allowing tax deductions to large families), or in prohibitive form (like the Chad law of December 29, 1965, which provides for a six-month imprisonment for the mere offer of a contraceptive).

In the history of the countries of francophone Africa, the classic example of incentive laws is the famous Law No. 50-772 of June 30, 1950, known as the "Lamine N'Gueye Law"—named after the well-known parliamentarian

---

10. National Institute of Economic and Statistical Studies (I.N.S.E.E.), Perspectives de Population dans les pays Africaines & Malgâches d'Expression Française (1963).

from Senegal in the Fourth French Republic who was responsible for the adoption of the law. Article 6 of this law provides the basis for the granting of allowances to officials belonging to the Ministry of Overseas France. In the application of this law, a decree of May 5, 1951, and then an *arrêté* of January 14, 1952, spelled out in more detail the different payments available to the functionaries of that time.

The provisions of the *arrêté* of January 14, 1952, offer to all civil personnel belonging to the various ranks of the Overseas France Ministry, as well as to its contractual personnel, the following scale of allowances:

1) An allowance for setting up a household—a contractual sum of 6,000 francs for each grantee for the first two years following the marriage.
2) Family allowances after the second dependent child without any limitation, provided that the children are recognized and registered as such with the civil authorities.
3) A grant for the early years of each of the children entitled to receive a family allowance. This is only provided when a child reaches the age of one and two. The maximum amount is 3,000 francs.
4) Allowances for a household receiving only one salary. These are given to those families, households or persons who only have the benefit of one professional income coming from salaried activities. This sum is paid from the time of the birth of the first dependent child in the following amounts:
   4,800 francs a year for a single dependent child under five years;
   2,400 francs for a single dependent child over five years of age;
   4,800 francs a child in a family of two or more children, who remain dependent;
   7,250 francs for three or more dependent children.
5) Taking into consideration the family situation, an additional family supplement was allowed to the people referred to above, containing both a fixed amount and an additional sum based upon the salary withheld for pension purposes.

These were the essential elements of the famous law which greatly affected the lives of the officials of the old colonial system which most of them now remember with nostalgia. We have not had the time needed to carry out a statistical study of the effect of this incentive law. Suffice it to say that we have discovered the case of a male nurse who had thirty-one children and who earned more than a doctor with the rank of colonel in charge of a military hospital.

There are other examples of laws which serve as incentives to procreation. One such law provides for an allowance, encouraging mothers of families to take care of their children themselves by remaining at home, at a sum equivalent to the payment which she would have received for working outside the home. For a rich country which, nevertheless, has a demographic deficit like Gabon, such a rule would be very useful.

Another law provides for housing facilities for young married couples. Since young couples lack financial security, they hesitate to have their first child and, even more so, to have further children. Thus, a policy which systematically favors the provision of housing to young households in proportion to the number of their children would have an incentive effect, particularly when it is combined with other welfare provisions.

Certain tax laws also fall under this incentive category. The part of his income which is deductible from his income tax by a man who has family burdens is called his "family quotient." In almost all countries, bachelors are more heavily taxed than married persons, and among these, those who have children pay less than others.

It is clear at once that any system which gives an important financial allowance to a mother who raises her own children, which offers comfortable housing to big families and which provides a considerable tax reduction to these families would necessarily have the effect of encouraging births and of replenishing the population deficits which have been recognized in certain regions of Africa south of the Equator.

Finally, there is another example of an incentive law with indirect effect and in positive form. It involves the field of migration. This means the movement of an individual from his habitual domicile to another domicile for a considerable period. The migration which concerns us here is international migration and particularly from the point of view of emigration. Emigration does not have as its only purpose the reduction of the population of the country from which emigration took place and the increase in the population of the country of immigration. Emigration, in fact, does not affect all the levels of the population. It is selective and involves the departure of young adults, and among these, men rather than women. Thus, it does have an effect on the population of the country by sex and by age. The departure of young adults contributes to the aging of the population, and the number of women tends to become greater than that of men. Thus, distortions occur in the marriage structure, and aging is a factor which adds to mortality and diminished births over the long run.[11]

2. Preventive Laws

These are laws intended to persuade populations to moderate the rhythm of their procreation on the basis of self-regulation. For example, the law of Dahomey of August 31, 1959, limits to six the number of dependent

---

11.   J. Beaujeu-Garnier, Trois Milliards d'Hommes (Hachette edit).

children for whom the head of the family may claim family allowances. (The earlier "Lamine N'Gueye Law" of June 30, 1950, did not limit the number of dependent children who could benefit, provided that they were recognized and registered with the civil authorities). On the whole, these laws are less resorted to in comparison with other means such as the provision of contraceptives. The comparative results are difficult to determine since there are no statistics showing the moderating effect of contraceptives in those countries which have supplied them on a large scale.

3. Restrictive Laws

The purpose of these laws is to prevent the population from passing a certain ceiling; in other words, to obtain a weakening in the rate of fertility and to compress natality.

As to direct laws in this category, we are not aware of any with the exception of the famous Nazi racial laws and their effects on the lives of six million innocent people. The objection to this type of law is the risk that it may be genocidal in purpose or effect because it can be so applied as to affect only a racial, ethnic, or religious minority.

As for laws of indirect effect, they are relatively numerous despite the fact that the legislature is never aware of their secondary effects—with the clear exception of the Chinese Government which adopted the policy of setting as the average ages of marriage 25 for women and 30 for men.

Laws on compulsory education and the minimum age of child labor fall also into this category. In many countries there are laws on the minimum age for leaving school. This is generally fifteen years, and corresponds with the age for entering apprenticeship. This minimum school age or minimum apprenticeship age can have the same limiting effect as the minimum marriage age. In fact, if a girl is kept in school until fifteen and is certain that she cannot marry at fourteen (although this is otherwise legal), and if she enters at once into an apprenticeship of some kind which can last three years, it means that eighteen is the age at which she can expect to marry and have children. As far as the boy is concerned, at eighteen, after completing his school and apprenticeship, he knows that he has to do his military service when he reaches the age of 21 for a period of two years. This has the effect of pushing back to 23 his chances of earning a living and getting married.

Thus, we see that, even if the child does not continue with higher education, there are great possibilities in delaying his or her marriage through a combination of laws on military service, compulsory education and the minimum age of apprenticeship. Moreover, we know that a large proportion of children—approximately a third of the children who receive any education at all—continue their studies beyond the primary education, thus further delaying their marriage.

CONCLUSIONS

On the basis of the above, we can draw the following conclusions:

1. *The potential of the law to modify fertility patterns is poorly understood* for the following reasons:

(a) Lawyers are not yet interested in this field, which is far removed from their usual professional concerns; and

(b) The statistical data on which it would be possible to base firm conclusions do not exist, since research has not yet been undertaken on a systematic basis. We are also dealing with human beings, and it is necessary to base our findings on a minimum period of more than one generation, which is the time necessary to see how the average child, born after the enactment of new laws, himself would react to this law.

2. *With a few exceptions, and despite the Teheran Proclamation, Governments still do not have population policies, which are either responsible or coherent.*

International organizations, both public and private, which could have helped their members, have hitherto tended to deal with the problem on the medical basis. Since contraceptive supplies are generally offered only to the countries of Latin America, Africa, and Asia, accompanied by rather clumsy declarations,[12] the accusation that we are dealing with genocide and racism begins to spread, and an organization as respectable as the International Planned Parenthood Federation is viewed as suspect, despite the fact that its purpose is the balancing between procreation and the moral and intellectual welfare of the family.

Nevertheless, despite these difficulties, it is possible to foresee a growing role for the law in establishing and maintaining a balance between procreation and the requirements of life. Medical procedures are, of course, necessary because historically they are the first steps to be taken, and also because their primary effects are immediate and tangible. In addition, they have benefited, and are still benefiting, from large financial contributions. Despite this, we have seen a growing objection to medical techniques, particularly sterilization, the irreversible effect of which can create, in the case of the male, an inferiority complex and a harmful frustration in his mental health and social life.[13] In contrast, a law which is adopted in an appropriate manner can have many advantages. It can have a bearing on the population of an entire region, and can be involved with the total condition of a society, particularly if its enactment can be preceded by public education and mass support.

---

12. Pradervand, *Critique de l'Approche Néomalthusienne des Problemes de Population* (unpublished).

13. H. Presser, BULLETIN DE DÉMOGRAPHIE, No. 5 (1971).

Finally, it is to be hoped that, in one way or another, a general compilation of population law will be undertaken in each country under the auspices of the United Nations or of some other organization and that, thanks to the collaboration of demography and the law, a world policy of population, maturely considered and on a non-discriminatory basis, can open a new era for humanity.

Report of Workshop on Legislation and Demographic Changes

In reviewing his paper, Judge Paraiso spoke briefly of the history of human population growth which showed that man has consciously taken steps to alter his growth rates in the past, in accordance with the requirements of the situation. He cited various traditional methods of limiting or of increasing fertility and various historical cases. He added that, at present, the making available of contraceptives appeared to be the method most under consideration. However, he felt that this only affects individuals. If the whole population of a country is to be reached, it would be necessary to consider ways to use the law to reach all the people and affect their behavior.

There was disagreement among members of the workshop as to the significance of the word "means" in the United Nations Declaration on Social Progress and Development, which declares that families should have access to the means necessary to practice the human right of family planning. Some participants felt that means should be defined to include access to voluntary sterilization and abortion, while others felt this interpretation would not be acceptable in their countries, thus preferring to interpret the word narrowly to mean access to contraceptives only. In light of the lack of agreement, it was felt to be unwise to attempt to define the word in any way which might limit its scope.

Some participants asked whether a direct relationship between education for women and fertility could be proven. It was pointed out that upper class women in some countries do have better education and low fertility, but that the low fertility is the result of better access to contraceptives and to information about them. It was explained, on the other hand, that a United Nations questionnaire had clearly shown that there is a relationship between female education and fertility. It was recognized that much depends on the type and amount of education a woman receives and on her opportunity to use her education in outside employment. Nevertheless, the relationship often does exist.

The subject of family planning education was touched on briefly. Some participants felt it would be difficult to get the idea accepted in their countries because of the cultural and religious constraints. However, it was agreed that education on human reproduction, family planning techniques, and population awareness should be provided by utilizing all available means in a manner consistent with the national culture.

There was considerable discussion on the relationship between elementary education and child labor. While it seemed to many to be futile to require children to attend school, or forbid them from working where schools do not exist, in the final analysis it was agreed that countries should strive to provide free and compulsory education until the age of thirteen and that the minimum working age also should be thirteen.

Whether child allowances affect fertility was also discussed. Many nations, France among them, have elaborate allowance schemes. It was pointed out that they seem to have little effect unless they more than offset the actual cost of having increased numbers of children. At present, the International Labour Organisation takes the position that the use or withholding of these allowances, as incentives for pro- or anti-natalism, should not be allowed to interfere with basic welfare rights. In short, it was felt that if the population depends on the allowances for its well-being, they should not be used as a tool of population policy.

Finally, the participants agreed to recommend a number of principles with regard to national and international migration. Among other things, it was pointed out that the problem of the so-called "brain drain" has considerable importance for developing countries and therefore policies should be sought which would limit this effect of migration.

SECTION 3

Laws on Reproduction and Family Formation

Family Relations Laws

Nani Soewondo*

The kind of laws that can be used to implement population policies and to solve population problems can be divided into the following categories: laws directly affecting fertility by intervening at some point in the procreation process (contraception, abortion and sterilization); laws indirectly affecting fertility through regulation of social relationships related to fertility (marriage, divorce, child support, inheritance, etc.); and laws indirectly affecting fertility through economic effects (tax, child allowances, maternity benefits, etc.).

This paper deals with the second category of laws. The importance of this subject lies in the fact that in all societies people live within a network of family rights and responsibilities regulated by the laws concerning family relations. I would like to approach the subject from three different, though complementary, points of view.

I. INTERNATIONAL EFFORTS TO STRENGTHEN FAMILY RELATIONS LAWS

Any reference to family relations law leads necessarily into the subject of the status of women. At the *international* level, it is appropriate to acknowledge the valuable contribution of the United Nations and its specialized agencies, in spotlighting the areas of discrimination affecting women and formulating guidelines to be followed by Governments at the national level, as well as the efforts of various interested non-governmental organizations to bring about legal reform. Special mention should be made of the Commission on the Status of Women, established in 1946, which has been working for equal rights of men and women in the political, civil, social, economic and educational fields, and was, in 1965, one of the first United Nations bodies to endorse family planning.

The Declaration on the Elimination of Discrimination against Women, adopted by the United Nations General Assembly in 1967, represents a

---

* Director, Law and Population Project and Chairperson, Indonesian Planned Parenthood Association Law and Population Committee.

milestone in the work of the United Nations to promote equal rights for men and women. Article 6 of the Declaration deals with the rights and obligations of husband and wife at marriage, during marriage and at the dissolution of marriage, and stresses particularly that "appropriate measures" be taken to ensure that:

(a) Women shall have the same right as men to free choice of a spouse and to enter into marriage only with their free will and consent;

(b) Women shall have equal rights with men during marriage and at its dissolution. . . .

At the last session of the Commission on the Status of Women, held in January 1974, a resolution, which drew its inspiration from the Declaration, was adopted on the legal capacity of married women reiterating the importance of ensuring that the legal capacity of married women be equal to that of men insofar as it affected: (a) gainful employment outside the home, (b) the capacity to administer the property and revenues of their work, (c) the administration of the joint property of the spouses, (d) the parental authority over their children and their interests and (e) the dissolution of marriage and its legal effects.

The U.N. Seminars, held at a world-wide as well as regional level, have also had an important influence in arousing the interest of Governments, non-governmental organizations and individuals in the various problems related to the status of women and, in turn, its relationship with family planning and population.

The patterns of family life, and the rights and responsibilities of family members, were extensively discussed in the Interregional Seminar on "The Family in a Changing Society," organized by the United Nations in London, 18-31 July 1973. As this seminar involved a world-wide representation of people of different cultures, we may assume that its conclusions and recommendations reflect universally held points of view regarding the family and the relationships of its members. Therefore, I would like to stress some of the findings of the Seminar connected with family relations law. They are as follows:

The participants of the Seminar agreed that, whatever its form or pattern, the family fulfilled various basic biological, sociological and psychological needs of the individual and performed various functions which were regarded as essential to the stability of society. It should therefore be preserved and receive the full support that society could give in fulfilling these fundamental functions.

Participants agreed that there was a discernible trend towards the recognition of equal rights and responsibilities of men and women in matters affecting marriage and the family.

Despite the progress achieved, it was still felt that much remained to be done in order for men and women to be recognized in law as equal partners in marriage and to eliminate glaring forms of discrimination against women. Various participants stressed the importance of enacting legislation which would be in conformity with the principle of equality of rights of men and women, and in particular with the relevant provisions of the Declaration on the Elimination of Discrimination against Women, especially its Article 6. For without adequate legislation the position of women would be threatened and insecure.

Participants discussed the question whether the law should precede the readiness of the population to accept new norms, and thus orient or influence social change, but at the same time, running the risk that if adopted prematurely, it would not be observed. On the one hand, various examples were cited on the positive effects of the enactment of liberal legislation on the status of women which, as a result, had been improved not only in law but also in fact. On the other hand, reference was made, in some instances, to the fact that century-old laws and customs which had provided women substantial rights had been almost totally ignored and that cultural barriers and social pressures, particularly in patriarchal societies, inhibited women and prevented them from availing themselves of their rights.

Participants agreed that legislation alone was therefore not enough to bring about an actual equitable allocation of rights and responsibilities within the home among the various members of the family and that it ought to be supplemented by a variety of measures aimed at enforcing it, such as family courts, family counsellors, etc.

The need was also stressed for widespread information on laws and regulations in force at the national level and on standards adopted at the international level so that women would be made aware of their rights and obligations, together with the need for education from early childhood, both at home and at school, for a cooperative and joint approach of all members of the family to the allocation of tasks within the home.

The Seminar recognized that:

(a) In many countries wide discrepancies existed between law and practice, especially in the area of family law, where traditions and customs often played an important part in influencing or delaying the implementation of the law;

(b) Legislation, nevertheless, could be a significant instrument for change and constituted an important step towards the achievement of equal rights and responsibilities for women and men;

(c) Widespread educational campaigns were required to create public awareness and understanding of existing rights as well as of the need for legislative reforms, especially in family law;

(d) The United Nations and the specialized agencies had accomplished important work in setting international standards through the elaboration of conventions, declarations and other recommendations, which required implementation at the national level;

(e) The United Nations Commission on the Status of Women would consider, early in 1974, the need for a new instrument or instruments of international law on the elimination of discrimination against women, taking into account the views expressed by Governments on that question.

The Seminar concluded that every effort be made to encourage Governments which had not already done so;

(a) To accede to, or to ratify, and fully implement international instruments aimed at establishing the principle of equal rights of men and women;

(b) To enact or review national legislation, especially in the area of family law and employment, and ensure that it was in conformity with the relevant international instruments, and in particular, with Articles 6 and 10 of the Declaration on the Elimination of Discrimination against Women.

The Seminar also endorsed the United Nations Convention and Recommendation on Consent to Marriage, Minimum Age for Marriage and Registration of Marriages and the Supplementary Convention on the Abolition of Slavery, the Slave Trade and Institutions and Practices similar to Slavery, and urged that effective measures be taken to prohibit child marriages and the inheritance of widows wherever these practices still existed.

In the international context it is important to stress also the work of the United Nations Seminars on the Status of Women and Family Planning, particularly in connection with family relations law. A world-wide Seminar on the Status of Women and Family Planning was held in Istanbul, Turkey, in July 1972. Two Regional Seminars on the same subject were held for the countries of the Western Hemisphere in Santo Domingo, Dominican Republic, in May 1973, and for the ECAFE Region in Jogjakarta, Indonesia, in June 1973.

II. Regional Activities Related to Family Relations Law

Some of the key findings of the Jogjakarta Seminar on the Status of Women and Family Planning may be reproduced bearing upon relationship between the status of women and family planning. The Seminar considered:

that the status of women is a significant factor influencing family size, and that family planning offers an important means of raising the status of women, and of enabling them to participate actively in the creation of the conditions necessary to enable both women and men to enjoy the rights to which they are entitled as human beings;

. . .

The Seminar recommended that Governments:

ratify, accede to, and implement the provisions of United Nations conventions, declarations and other recommendations aimed at establishing the principle of equal rights of men and women;

review or enact national legislation that may have a bearing on the status of women and family planning, such as laws concerning age of marriage, inheritance, divorce, taxation, education, employment and immigration in order to ensure that such legislation is in accordance with the relevant United Nations instruments, including the Declaration on the Elimination of Discrimination against Women.

Furthermore, the Seminar, taking into account:

that there is a close relationship between the low status of women, early and universal marriage of girls, and a high fertility;

that, in order for the age of marriage to have a marked effect on family size, educational and employment opportunities must be made available to women;

that the unilateral right of husbands to divorce their wives at will, or on grounds of failure to bear children or to bear a child of a particular sex, lowers the status of women and may also encourage high fertility;

that polygamy may tend to increase the birth rate because of the larger number of women who are married at any one time;

Recommended:

that Governments, which have not already done so, ensure that the laws provide for a minimum age of marriage for women of not less than 16 years, for the registration of all marriages, and for the contracting of marriage only with the full and free consent of intending spouses;

that women's organizations and other civic and educational bodies actively promote and support the acceptance of a later age at marriage for girls, of the free choice of spouse, of the right to enter marriage only with free and full consent, and, where appropriate, create awareness of the right not to marry, with the goal of improving the status of women and reducing existing social pressures toward early and universal marriage;

that Governments enact or review legislation to ensure that women and men have equal legal rights at marital dissolution, and that the interests of children shall be fully protected;

that adoption might be encouraged as a further measure to reduce divorce on grounds of childlessness, or failure to bear a desired son or daughter;

that Governments enact or review existing legislation so as to restrict polygamy by specifying conditions and obligations which should be proved in court;

that, in order to ensure the personal status and dignity of women in the marriage relationship, national legislation should accord to women, on the basis of equality with men, the right to acquire, administer, enjoy, dispose of and inherit property, including property acquired during marriage;

that Governments, with the help of non-governmental organizations, ensure that all women, and especially the less-educated women at the lower economic levels, should know their legal rights and be given legal aid to enable them to exercise them equally with men.

III. FAMILY LAW AND NATIONAL LEGAL REFORM

I will now discuss the subject of family relations law at the *national* level, using the Indonesian experience as a focal point for discussion. Family relations law in Indonesia includes basically two types of law: Marriage Law and Inheritance Law.

A. *Marriage Law*

The legal status of women within the family is of importance to the family as an institution as well as to efforts to achieve other rights for women, such as rights affecting their political, social and economic activities.

Until recently different groups of Indonesian citizens were subject to different marriage laws. For example, there were codified laws governing the marriage of Indonesians of foreign extraction (the Civil Code) and of the Indonesian Christians (the Marriage Regulation for Indonesian Christians). But there was no codified law on marriage for the majority of the Indonesian people who are adherents to the Islamic faith. Only customary (*adat*) law and Islamic law were applicable to them. With regard to customary law, the three types of family structures to be found in Indonesia, namely, the patrilineal, matrilineal and bilateral (or parental), have a special influence on the marriage law and practice. Since the First Indonesian Women's National Congress in 1928, women's organizations have worked for improvement in the status of women, especially as it is affected by marriage law. The basic issues on which efforts to reform concentrated were, among others, child marriage, forced marriage, easy arbitrary divorce by the husband, unrestricted practices of polygamy and lack of proper alimony for the divorced wife. Because of the lack of a codified marriage law, the majority of the population suffered from the unsatisfactory conditions which were a product of the absence of legislation on the subject. Out of this milieu grew the struggle for a codified marriage law to protect the family and its members, particularly the wife and children.

The Indonesian Constitution has guaranteed fundamental rights and freedoms to men and women equally since the Proclamation of Independence in 1945. Under the law, Indonesian women have equal political rights, equal opportunities for education, equal pay for equal work with some special protections for women workers, and equal position in social life. But until recently the woman's position in the field of marriage law was still unfavourable.

Beginning in the 1950s many attempts have been made to have a marriage law enacted. Marriage bills were discussed in Parliament in 1958-59 and again in 1967-70, but the discussion ended before any results could be produced. In July 1973, the Government submitted a new Marriage Bill aimed at unifying the marriage law. This latest Marriage Bill has recognized the principle of the equality of rights for both men and women in marriage and divorce. But several Moslem leaders considered some of the proposed articles to be contrary to aspects of the Islamic religion. This concern gave rise to heated debates in and outside of Parliament. In the end a compromise was reached and the Bill, along with several amendments, was adopted by Parliament in late December, and subsequently enacted into law on January 2, 1974. At last Indonesia has a codified and unified Marriage Law.

The only drawback resulting from the compromise mentioned above was the fact that some of the basic principles of the law were left to be dealt with by implementing regulations, which are not yet completed and which, when promulgated, may still differentiate between the various religious groups. In general the new Marriage Law is thought to have improved the status of women in marriage but the extent of the improvement will not be known until the implementing regulations are announced.

The basic points of the Marriage Law are as follows:

1. *Minimum age of marriage*

Article 7 sets the minimum age at 19 for men and 16 for women. Exceptions to this requirement may be granted by the Court at the request of the parents. (The Marriage Bill originally proposed that the minimum age be 21 for men and 18 for women, but the article was amended in Parliament.) The Minister of Justice, in clarifying the Marriage Bill before Parliament, made special reference to the age of marriage and how it relates to population.

2. *Consent requirements*

Article 6 requires that a marriage be based on consent of the future spouses. A person who has not yet reached the age of 21 years must obtain the consent of both parents.

3. *Registration*

Article 2 stipulates that a marriage is legal if it is performed according to the laws of the respective religions and beliefs of the parties concerned. It requires that every marriage be registered according to the regulations in force. (This article is referring to the forthcoming implementing regulations.)

4. *Polygamy*

Polygamy has always tended to raise controversial issues. It has been generally acknowledged that it threatens the happiness and the welfare of the family, and may also aggravate the population problem. But inasmuch as polygamy is allowed according to the precepts of the Islamic religion, even the most progressive of women's organizations have thought it wise not to advocate its total abolition. Efforts have, however, been made to adopt legislation to restrict the practice of polygamy by specifying requirements which must be ruled on by a court. In practice polygamy has been accepted sometimes as an alternative to divorce, based on the opinion that it is better to share a husband than not to have one at all.

Articles 3, 4 and 5 place the following limitations on the practice of polygamy. Though marriage is generally based on the principle of monogamy, polygamy may be permitted by decision of a Court, if so desired by the parties concerned. At the request of the husband, the Court may give permission for polygamy in cases where:

(i)   the wife cannot fulfil her duties as a wife;
(ii) the wife is physically disabled or contracts an incurable disease;
(iii) the wife is infertile.

Before a request can be submitted to the Court, the husband must show that he has the consent of the wife (wives), demonstrates to a certainty that he is able to support his other wives and children, and guarantee that he will behave justly towards all his wives and children.

5. *Rights and responsibilities of husband and wife*

Article 31 of the new law states that the rights and obligations of the wife in the family as well as in society are proportionate to those of the husband. Both have the capacity to take legal actions. The husband is the head of the family, and his spouse is the housewife. Article 34 states that the husband has the obligation to protect and support his wife to the best of his ability, while the wife has the obligation to take care of the household.

6. *Marital property*

Goods acquired during marriage shall become joint property under the provisions of Article 35. Property brought into marriage by the husband or the wife, or acquired by either one of them as a gift or inheritance, remain the property of the party concerned, unless the parties decide otherwise. Article 36 gives to both husband and wife the legal capacity to dispose of their joint property, as long as both parties agree. The husband and wife naturally have legal capacity to dispose of their own property.

7. *Divorce*

The new law has been devised to avoid the practice of arbitrary divorce. Article 39 requires that a divorce must be obtained by a decision of a Court, after the Court has tried unsuccessfully to reconcile the parties. The decision to grant the divorce must be based on proof of the inability of husband and wife to live together. The procedural aspects of the divorce proceedings before a Court will be a subject for a separate regulation. The Marriage Bill originally set forth both the grounds for divorce and the procedure for obtaining it, but that provision was amended by Parliament and, under the present scheme of things, these basic points will be taken care of by implementing regulations.

Article 41 stipulates the following consequences of divorce:

(i) The mother, as well as the father, shall both remain responsible for the care and education of the children, as dictated by the best interests of the children. In case of dispute on the custody of the children, the Court shall decide.

(ii) The father is responsible for the expenses for the care and education of the children. If the father is unable to assume these responsibilities, the Court may decide that the mother is also responsible.

(iii) The Court may decide that the husband has the obligation to pay alimony to his ex-wife or has other obligations towards her.

8. *Status of the children*

Article 42 declares that a child is legitimate if born in or as a result of a legal marriage. Article 43 notes that a child born out of wedlock has only a civil relationship to its mother and her relatives. The status of these children will further be regulated by government regulations.

9. *Obligations of parents and children*

Article 45 requires that both parents are responsible for the care and education of their children. This they must do to the best of their abilities. This obligation continues irrespective of divorce either until the children get married or are able to support themselves. Under Article 46 children are required to respect their parents and obey their just wishes. In their turn, when the children are grown, they are obliged to take care of their parents and relatives, in a straight ascending line, who are in need of assistance.

10. *Court of Justice*

Article 63 provides that all cases arising under the Marriage Law shall be judged by: (1) the Religious Courts (for those people who profess the Islamic religion); (2) the General Courts (for those of other religions). Decisions of the Religious Courts shall be confirmed by the General Courts. The Marriage Law has increased the jurisdiction of the Religious Courts, which formerly were only competent to judge limited cases of marriage and divorce. This has raised the question about whether the Religious Courts will be able to handle the cases connected with the Marriage Law, as their judges for the most part are only experts on Islamic law and lack any formal legal education.

B.   *Law and Population Seminar*

It is hoped that the basic principles of the new Marriage Law will have a positive effect on the results of the Government Family Planning Programme and will help to solve the population problem in Indonesia. To complete the picture relating to the Marriage Law, I would like to review the results of the Seminar on Law and Population, which was attended by 34 participants from different law faculties, ministries, institutes and private organizations involved in law or family planning. The Seminar on Law and Population, held in Jakarta January 28–February 2, 1974, discussed the new Marriage Law extensively. Its Conclusions and Recommendations included the following:

1. *Minimum age of marriage*

When considered from the point of view of family welfare, as well as the family planning and population programme, the minimum age of 19 for the man and 16 for the woman is too low. Exceptions should be restricted. The implementing regulation on marriage procedure should include the requirement of a certificate stating the age of the future spouses, to be provided by the Civil Registration Office concerned.

2. *Polygamy*

Polygamy will result in a larger number of children. The consent of the wife required for polygamy should be stated in writing or by appearing in person before the officer concerned. The required permission for polygamy should be granted by the Court infrequently. When infertility of the wife is used as a reason for polygamy, the husband should be required to prove it with a doctor's certificate.

3. *Divorce*

As the grounds for divorce are not mentioned in the Marriage Law, this will still facilitate divorce, unless this is prevented in the implementing regulations. The grounds for divorce should be stated specifically. If there is no definite obligation of the husband to pay alimony, recourse to divorce will be made more often. With regard to alimony, the Court should be able to order the husband to provide cost of living expenses for his ex-wife.

4. *Status of the children*

There is no clear definition concerning legitimate and illegitimate children, and therefore the position of the child is not yet fully protected. This has yet to be regulated by the appropriate implementing regulations.

5. *Court of Justice*

The Marriage Law has stipulated that cases involving people of Islamic faith should be judged by the Religious Courts, while those involving people of other religions should be judged by the General Court of justice. In the context of the new duties assigned to the Religious Courts, it is necessary to improve and standardize their qualifications with regard to personnel, facilities, administration and procedure.

6. *The extended family*

In the unilateral (patrilineal and matrilineal) social structure, the extended family is also responsible for the care of the children. This may result in a larger number of children as they are not the sole responsibility of the parents. Therefore, the continuation of these systems may have a negative effect on the results of the family planning programme. Formal and non-formal education, a parental-individual inheritance law as well as a law on social welfare could have positive consequences for the success of the programme.

7. *Inheritance law*

The law concerning inheritance now in force in Indonesia is derived from two sources, customary (*adat*) law and the Civil Code.

The types of family structures mentioned above, namely, the unilateral (patrilineal and matrilineal) and the bilateral (parental) systems, exercise considerable influence on inheritance law. According to the patrilineal system, sons are important for the continuation of the family. Thus, only sons will inherit their father's property. They do, however, have the obligation to support their sisters and other relatives still staying with the extended family. Under the matrilineal system, sons and daughters inherit only from their mother's property, while the children of their father's sisters will inherit their father's property. According to the parental system sons and daughters will get an equal share of the property of both parents.

It is common practice, however, that in patrilineal communities daughters will get valuable goods at the time of their marriage, and that in matrilineal communities the children will get valuable goods from their father on various occasions. In practice, where the influence of the family unit has been weakened by married couples leaving the extended family, all children will get a more or less equal share of the property of both parents. According to Islamic law, sons and daughters inherit from both parents, but women receive only half the share given to men.

The problem of whether customary law or Islamic law should be applied arises often. In regions where the provisions of Islamic law are generally accepted, Islamic law will be applied to questions involving inheritance.

Since 1968, the Institute for Development of National Law, working under the Ministry of Justice, was given the task of drafting a bill on the basic principles of Inheritance Law. A Working Committee on Inheritance Law was established to conduct surveys and seminars on inheritance law in different regions in Indonesia, usually in cooperation with a faculty of law. Subsequently, the Committee drafted a document containing the basic principles of inheritance law. In January 1974, a discussion on inheritance law was organized by the Institute, which was attended by 22 participants from different law faculties, ministries, institutions and organizations. Among the basic principles adopted by the Working Committee and supported in the discussion was the principle of individual parental inheritance, which includes the principle of equal rights of inheritance. At the moment the draft Bill on Inheritance Law has not yet been finished, so there is still diversity among the laws governing inheritance.

IV.   CONCLUSION

I hope that I have adequately stressed the main issues of family relations law, particularly marriage law, as it relates to family planning and population in my country. As can be seen, there is need for further reform.

With regard to the problem of how to improve existing laws in the field of family relations, I would like to suggest that the recommendations of the

U.N. Seminars mentioned above be used as bases for discussion at this Symposium.

BIBLIOGRAPHY

Declaration on the Elimination of Discrimination Against Women, General Assembly Res. 2263, 22 U.N. GAOR, Supp. 16, p. 35, Doc. No. A/6716 (1967).

S. GAUTAMA & R.N. HORNICK, AN INTRODUCTION TO INDONESIAN LAW: UNITY AND DIVERSITY (Jakarta: Alumni Print 1972).

INDONESIAN LAW AND POPULATION PROJECT, COMPILATION OF LAWS ON POPULATION (1974).

R. SUBEKTI, S.H., LAW IN INDONESIA (Jakarta: Gunung Agung 1973).

United Nations, Seminar on the Family in a Changing Society: Problems and Responsibilities of Its Members (Preliminary text of Report dated September 21, 1973) (London, July 1973).

United Nations, Seminar on the Status of Women and Family Planning, Doc. No. ESA/SDHA/AC.2/21 (Jogjakarta, Indonesia, June 1973).

Undang-Undang Perkawinan (Marriage Law), No. 1, 1974.

Report of Workshop
on Family Relations Laws

The relationship between family relations laws and the formulation of national population policies was discussed on the basis of a background paper written by Mrs. Nani Soewondo, Director of the Legal Committee of the Indonesian Planned Parenthood Association. Family relations laws are defined in Mrs. Soewondo's paper as laws that indirectly affect fertility "through regulation of social relationships related to fertility" such as marriage, divorce, child support and inheritance, as distinguished from laws that indirectly affect fertility "through economic effects" such as taxation, child allowances and maternity benefits.

There was wide recognition in the workshop that perhaps more than any other national laws, family relations laws reflect deeply held religious beliefs and practices, as well as national social and cultural traditions. Efforts to utilize family relations laws to accomplish the goals of national population policies thus raise basic questions about the relationship between national laws and religious laws, and as to the extent to which the legal process should be used to bring about, or merely to reflect, social change. Although divergent views were expressed on these basic questions as they are presented in different national settings, it was agreed that national family relations laws do significantly affect the achievement of national population policies, and that therefore such laws should be reviewed by governments and clarified so as to be consistent with declared national population policies and with the relevant United Nations declarations.

In this light, the workshop explored a number of questions relating to marriage and divorce, the position of divorced women, inheritance laws, the registration of births and the rights of the child.

With regard to the minimum age for marriage, it was noted that in 1965 the General Assembly had recommended that governments establish a minimum marriage age of not less than 15 years, and that more recently the 1973 United Nations Regional Seminar on the Status of Women and Family Planning (Jogjakarta) had recommended that the minimum marriage age for women be 16. Although some participants considered that for various reasons a higher minimum would not be feasible in their countries, there was substantial agreement at the workshop that the Symposium should take a step forward in recommending 18 as the minimum marriage age for both

300

men and women. A significant minority would have preferred to exempt pregnant women from the 18-year minimum, but the majority of the workshop considered that such an exemption would provide too ready a means for avoiding the effect of the minimum marriage age and thus substantially impair its effectiveness as a means of controlling fertility.

Divorce, the position of divorced women, and national inheritance laws, were discussed at length, with many examples of the types of laws which prevail on these subjects being drawn from the national laws and practices of the participants. Although the discussion bore witness to the diversity of national cultures and traditions on such questions, it was evident that change was underway in many countries. Several speakers pointed to the leading role that the revision of national laws had played in bringing about change in their countries, while others expressed the view that the marriage and divorce laws in their countries had fallen behind the pace of social change and were ripe for revision. The unilateral right of men in some countries to divorce their wives at will was criticized by some speakers as incompatible with equality between the sexes and detrimental to the status of women. It was suggested by some speakers that such inequalities were matters of cultural tradition, and were not part of the basic beliefs of any religion, so that there was room for change that might well be accomplished through the revision by governments of their national laws. A consensus supported recommendations that governments ratify the United Nations Convention on Consent to Marriage, Minimum Age for Marriage and Registration of Marriages, and that governments take the necessary steps to bring into effect both the principles of the Convention and the principle of equal rights for men and women during marriage and at its dissolution.

With regard to the registration of births and the rights of the child, a consensus at the workshop agreed upon the importance of effective systems for the registration of births as a means of providing accurate information for the formulation and implementation by governments of their national population policies. Noting the provisions of the United Nations Declaration of the Rights of the Child, which applies to every child "without distinction or discrimination," the workshop also agreed upon the necessity for implementing legislation adopted by governments to ensure that every child is wanted by the parents and protected by society in terms of adequate education, medical care, nutrition, housing and recreation.

Laws Regulating the Manufacture and Distribution of Contraceptives

By
Dr. Malcolm Potts*

INTRODUCTION

Family planning has only recently been recognised as a basic human right. It is, nevertheless, an ideal well buttressed by the older, more universal, notions of the right to privacy and the inviability of the domicile. It is gratifying that attention is being given to the legal restraints on the distribution of contraceptives, for their removal is an important factor in the equation for improving present family planning services.

In the contemporary world, demographic factors, while philosophically secondary to broad concepts of human rights, have assumed immediate, practical significance. These factors goad us into attempting to expand access to modern family planning techniques. Yet, it is no secret that family planning faces an uphill task in many countries. Resources are often in short supply. And the elimination of existing legal barriers to the distribution of contraceptives can often prove a significant variable in an activity where a small investment in human effort can yield a high return.

Laws and regulations controlling the manufacture and distribution of contraceptives are various, and thus difficult to catalogue. Nevertheless, the total range of controlling factors needs to be understood. The purpose of this paper is to give illustrative examples of the types of laws which frustrate family planning activities. No attempt is made to provide a comprehensive review. The important problem of contraceptive use by minors is discussed elsewhere in this symposium.

I. THE BIOLOGY OF THE REVERSIBLE METHODS OF CONTRACEPTION

The word contraception, for a series of reasons, is sometimes misused. It will be used in this paper to describe the reversible methods of contraception which act before implantation of the fertilised egg. This definition allows the

---

* Consultant, International Planned Parenthood Federation.

inclusion of coitally related methods (*e.g.*, hormones which act within 24 to 48 hours of sexual intercourse), but excludes menstrually related methods (*e.g.*, the use of prostaglandins or the surgical techniques of "menstrual regulation"). The definition also includes intrauterine devices (IUD) which may act before *or* after fertilisation, or before *and* after fertilisation.

Whenever contraceptive methods are reviewed, it is important to understand the biological function of a contraceptive. Semantically, and in the perception of the lay public, a contraceptive is often regarded as a tap which turns fertility off and on. Unfortunately, all methods have a measurable failure rate. None are adequate for the community as a whole to control fertility over a fertile lifetime within the goals set by modern industrial societies, or sought after by many developing countries. Therefore, abortion and sterilisation are a necessary complementary part of any scheme for fertility regulation.

In biological terms, a contraceptive is an agent which extends the length of time it takes a woman to become pregnant. A woman who has regular intercourse, but does not use a contraceptive, requires approximately three to six menstrual cycles to conceive. Even the most simple method of contraception greatly extends this time. The most effective methods will reduce the probability of conception to such an extent that there may be less than one pregnancy in a decade of exposure.

II. METHODS

A. *Coitus Interruptus (Withdrawal).*

This remains the most frequently used technique for much of continental Europe. It is significant in Latin America, the Philippines and most Moslem countries, but seems genuinely less common in Hindu and Oriental societies. Many couples achieve low pregnancy rates with its use. In historical terms it has been a significant variable in demographic change.

B. *Prolonged Lactation.*

Calculations from at least one developing country show that more people are protected against pregnancy by lactation than by the very extensive family planning programme. While lactation does have an inherent contraceptive effect, and is often prolonged for this reason, it is difficult to predict when the first ovulation will occur. The woman is generally vulnerable if she uses no other method towards the expected end of lactation.

C. *The Rhythm Method (Periodic Abstinence).*

Like oral contraceptives and intrauterine devices, there are several varieties of the rhythm method. Those varieties which attempt to identify when ovulation has occurred and restrict coitus to the days following proven ovulation can achieve a high degree of effectiveness. However, a significant number of women have menstrual cycles of such irregularity that many versions of the method are unsatisfactory. It is also difficult to use during lactation and near puberty and the menopause.

D. *Condoms.*

Consistently used, condoms are an effective method of contraception and have the added advantage of not requiring medical supervision. Their use is increasing rapidly, especially in the developing world, to the extent that demand is outstripping present production.

E. *Spermicides.*

A variety of spermicides are available, including tablets, jellies, creams, foams and water soluble plastic films. Some are used alone, others in combination with a mechanical barrier, such as the *diaphragm* or *cervical cap*, which acts as a vehicle to hold the spermicide in relation to the cervix.

F. *Intrauterine Devices.*

There are two principal types: inert plastic devices and those which have an active chemical or metallic addition to them. They all require a trained person to insert them. Therefore, in addition to any regulation of distribution, they raise issues relating to medico-legal responsibility.

G. *Steroidal Contraceptives.*

A variety of hormone agents will control fertility. They are mostly given by mouth, but some are available as injections, and experiments are taking place to test the effectiveness of subcutaneous contraceptive implants.

The orally effective agents mostly consist of combinations of oestrogens and progestins, but some progestin only preparations ("mini-pills") have been developed. The combined pills, properly taken, have the lowest failure rate of any of the reversible contraceptives. Both oestrogen and progestins, in isolation, can prevent embryonic development and implantation when given post-coitally.

When relatively little was known about oral contraceptives, their use was always supervised by medical practitioners. Today it is thought that 45 million women use this method of contraception. Experience extends over a decade and a half and good side effects (*e.g.*, lessening of breast disease), as well as bad side effects (*e.g.*, increasing tendencies towards thromboembolic disease), have been discovered. It is difficult to predict those women who may suffer side effects, and the role of medical prescription of oral contraceptives is under review. It has been withdrawn or modified in some countries (*e.g.*, Chile, Jamaica, Pakistan, the Philippines and Thailand). Both manufacturers and the dispensers have obligations in tort, as well as statutory law, in relation to oral contraceptives. Moreover, the introduction of new pharmacologically active compounds is regulated by drug registration committees in many countries.

H. *Manufacture.*

Spermicides can be made in small quantities with relative ease. Most IUDs are moulded in plastic and, given adequate quality control, relatively small scale local production is possible.

Oral contraceptives and condoms are manufactured by capital intensive processes, requiring a minimum of labour, much of which must be highly skilled. Great economies of scale are possible. Conversely, low volume production tends to be associated with moderate to poor quality, especially in the case of condoms. A single condom machine can often more than meet the market potential of a country of tens of millions of inhabitants.

Packaging costs represent a large proportion of pill and condom manufacturing costs in the case of condoms (often over 50 percent). But packaging is amenable to local, relatively small scale production, which may also have the advantage of meeting local marketing needs.

III. CURRENT LEGAL RESTRICTIONS

A. *Manufacture.*

The manufacture of contraceptives is only rarely prohibited. Spain[1] and the Gabon do forbid manufacture,[2] but several countries which are equally, or more conservative, as far as the use of contraceptives is concerned, such as Eire, Portugal and Argentina, permit local production.[3]

The manufacture of oral contraceptives is usually controlled under the appropriate medicines act and, in the case of Japan the authorities who possess the powers delegated under Section 12 of the Pharmacy Law do not permit the manufacture of steroidal products for contraceptive purposes because of their potential risks to health of the consumers. Until recently, certain European countries (*e.g.*, Austria) had specific legislation forbidding IUD manufacture.

Sometimes contraceptive manufacture falls under blanket legislation controlling industrial development, as in Iran and Mexico, where there must be a 51 per cent state ownership of any industry.[4]

---

1. CODIGO PENAL, § 416(2).
2. The prohibition against manufacture of contraceptives in Gabon is a function of an amendment which tightened the former French Law of 1920 and prohibited their importation. P. PRADERVAND, FAMILY PLANNING PROGRAMMES IN AFRICA 23 (Paris: Organisation for Economic Cooperation and Development 1970).
3. J. STEPAN AND E. KELLOGG, THE WORLD'S LAWS ON CONTRACEPTIVES, at 36, 45, 81 (Law and Population Monograph Series No. 17, 1974). This monograph is an excellent source of material on laws relating to contraception.
4. *Id.* at 56, 88.

In addition, there are less obvious, but possibly more important places where the processes of the law influence contraceptive manufacture, especially in relation to steroidal contraceptives. It requires a large investment of money and many years to produce a new, pharmacologically active contraceptive. It can take ten years to conclude all the toxicological tests required before a new product is released for use. Once in widespread use, rare adverse side effects may arise and tort liability can prove costly to the manufacturer.[5] One fact and two questions may help illuminate this important and still evolving area of medico-legal thinking:

i. It is impossible to discover all possible side effects of a new therapy until it has been widely used for many years and until at least one generation of children has been born to users.

ii. What, if any, responsibility does a manufacturer have for an adverse side effect—such as thrombosis—which could not have been predicted when the drug was first used?

iii. What, if any, liability does a manufacturer have for known side effects when the user has been warned and made an informed decision to select the method in question (*e.g.*, the pill rather than the diaphragm)?

The law has an important task to perform in sharpening the distinction between negligence and mishap and in protecting the rights of the consumer, without pressing extreme cases which would slow contraceptive development leaving the community using the second best, because the investment for necessary improvement had become unrealistically high.

B.   *Tariffs and Taxes.*

Price is an important factor affecting the accessibility of a community to contraceptives—whether sold to the individual or in bulk to a government or international agency. In instances where contraceptives are imported commercially, the taxes and tariffs levied on them can obviously affect the price.

Even countries with overt family planning policies, such as Thailand, Iran and the Philippines, levy tariffs on the importation of contraceptives and/or raw materials used to produce them. Most developing countries treat contraceptives like any other imported commodity, although the logistics of manufacture and the modest turnovers relative to the social significance of the end product suggest that a special case might be made out. Indonesia

---

5. The United States and some Scandinavian countries are developing case laws on this subject. One of the more notable cases involved a suit brought by the heirs of Margaretha Andersson against the Astra-Syntex Company in the Trolhätlen District Court as the result of a pill-related death. The case was settled out of court.

took a forward looking step when it abolished the duty on contraceptives in 1971.[6]

It should be noted, however, that contraceptives which are donated by international agencies for local family planning use are generally exempted from the tariff and duty schemes.

C. *Distribution, Prescription and Display.*

This is an area where attention to detail is essential, for relatively minor restrictions can have a major effect on the consumer. The man who buys a tube of toothpaste because he is too shy to ask the girl in the pharmacy for a condom is a reality. Regulations, such as those until recently enforced by the Pharmaceutical Society in Britain, which literally made the condom an under the counter item, must have caused many unwanted pregnancies. Those most hurt by relatively trivial barriers are often those most in need of help.

A few countries forbid the sale of contraceptives. In Indonesia it is largely that no one has yet repealed an anachronistic, colonial law (Chapter XIV of the Penal Code: Crimes Against Morals) which forbids the unsolicited dissemination and display of contraceptives. Nevertheless, the Government employs approximately 5,000 family planning field workers, each one of whom is theoretically eligible for nine months' imprisonment for violation of Article 283 of the Penal Code. In Ireland the law relating to contraception remains the subject of intense political concern. Contraceptives and contraceptive information cannot be sold or promoted under the Criminal Law Amendment Act of 1935 and the Censorship Acts of 1929 and 1946. In 1973 the Irish Supreme Court upheld the individual's right to use contraceptives in the Mary McGee case, but did not strike down the laws relating to sale.[7] In February 1974 the Irish Family Planning Association and Family Planning Services were prosecuted by the Attorney General. The suit arose after the two organisations sent contraceptives and family planning information to two young school children whose parents were acting as agents provocateurs. The family planning groups were acquitted when the Dublin District Court found the mailings were not "sales" within the meaning of the 1935 law and that the booklets were not illegal as they "did not advocate the unnatural prevention of conception."[8] A private member's bill aimed at

6. The old duty under Postal Tariff 167 (11)(a) was abolished under the Ministry of Finance Decision No. Kep 396/MK/111/7/71.
7. In the McGee case, the Supreme Court ruled that the ban on importation of contraceptives for private use was unconstitutional. The Court based its decision on an interpretation of Article 41 of the Constitution which relates to the protection of the "family, in its constitution and authority." The decision invalidated *pro tanto* Section 17(3) of the Criminal Law Amendment Act, 1935. The Times (London), Dec. 20, 1973, at 4, col. 1.
8. The Times (London), Feb. 20, 1974, at 2, col. 3.

partially reforming the anti-contraceptive laws failed to pass in the Dublin Senate in March 1974.[9] Currently, the coalition government has introduced a very limited reform which would permit the supply of contraceptives to married couples over 18 through a limited number of licensed places.

At least one country has recently taken steps to restrict the distribution of contraceptives. In March 1974 Argentina, by executive decree, forbade the promotion of any contraceptive measure and limited the use of steroidal preparations to strictly medical indications.[10]

Often the display of contraceptives is forbidden, even when sale is legal. This is the case in Belgium.[11] In France, several other countries, and in the State of New York, condom sales are limited to pharmacies. In Britain, Sweden, the German Federal Republic, and some other countries, national or local statutes regulate the siting of public condom vending machines. In Sweden, "the presence of contraceptives in the vending machine must not be indicated in such a way that special attention is drawn to the fact"[12]—hardly a regulation devised to please a salesman.

Oral contraceptives can fall under the same restrictions as condoms and spermicides, but the major barrier to their wider use is usually the prescription requirement. Often, even in developing countries, this bottleneck is made tighter by a limitation of sales to pharmacies. In Botswana, which has 600,000 people, there are but two pharmacies. In practice, oral contraceptives will not be available to the bulk of the world's population who live in villages until the prescription requirements are reviewed and revised.[13] The People's Republic of China, Chile, Bangladesh, the Philippines, Pakistan, Thailand, Jamaica and Fiji are countries which have removed or modified the requirement.

The pharmacist and/or prescribing physician have liabilities in tort which might arise upon the issuance of contraceptives. In the case of *Troppi v. Scarf*[14] a Michigan pharmacist was found negligent for filling a prescription for oral contraceptives with a tranquilizer.

Obscenity and postal laws are other areas of statute law which may impinge on contraceptive distribution, as they did in the United States until the early 1970s.[15]

---

9. The Times (London), Mar. 28, 1974, at 4, col. 7. The bill would have allowed chemists to sell contraceptives.

10. *Law and Policy* POPULATION REPORT, series E, No. 1, at E-3 (July 1974).

11. PENAL CODE, § 383.

12. Royal Order No. 326 (June 5, 1959).

13. The consequences of prescription regulations and current medical opinion were well summarized in the statement of the IPPF Central Medical Committee in 1973 titled *The Distribution and Supervision of Oral Contraceptives*.

14. 31 Mich. App. 240, 187 N.W.2d 511 (1971).

15. For a brief review of the various types of laws which frustrated contraceptive distribution in the United States, *see* Pilpel, *Legal Impediments to Voluntarism*, in THE WORLD

D. *Advertising.*

In all existing family planning programmes, personnel costs greatly exceed commodity costs. Proven techniques of advertising are only beginning to find their way into private and governmental family planning services, but they have the potential of being relatively cost effective in both developed and developing countries. Advertising has been widely used in India, both to get across broad family planning messages and to promote brands of contraceptives. In the West, state and local family planning services have been advertised in several countries, but brand name advertising has often been restricted by law or by codes of practice. For example, in Britain state subsidised family planning services have been advertised on Independent Television, but brand name advertisements are refused. The code of advertising practice for London transportation specifically excludes contraceptive advertising, although abortion clinics are often advertised in thinly veiled ways.

Almost invariably, prescription drugs are not advertised to the lay public. However, this rule is not necessarily in the health interests of the community, especially when applied to oral contraceptives in developing countries. In the Philippines, artifical milk for infant feeding is widely advertised. Bottle feeding provides an inferior diet, is dangerous where water supplies are often dirty, and costs many poor women more money than they can sensibly afford. Yet, its promotion goes unregulated. In the same country it is illegal to advertise oral contraceptives, although their use nearly always benefits the health of the mother by relieving her of the burden of repeated pregnancy and, at the national level, population grows at 3.4 per cent a year, greatly straining the economy.

IV.   THE NEED FOR CHANGE

Coitus interruptus, prolonged lactation and the rhythm method do not require any material aid (other than a clinical thermometer for one version of the last procedure). Therefore, they have never been, and never will be, regulated by any aspect of the law. They are all widely used and can be tolerably effective. Their practice immediately discredits and invalidates any legal effort to restrict public access to the other means of fertility regulation. Laws attempting to restrict the alternative methods might be considered analogous to a penal system which punishes murder if it is committed with a pistol or a knife, but not if it involves strangling or drowning.

If it is assumed that family planning is a basic human right and if it is accepted that fertility regulation has beneficial social and medical consequences, then it is appropriate to consider altering restrictive legislation in

POPULATION CRISIS: POLICY IMPLICATIONS AND THE ROLE OF LAW 76-83, (J. Paxman ed., Charlottesville: John Bassett Moore Society 1971).

the area of contraceptive manufacture, distribution and promotion. But the question remains: How much effort should be put into this field?

Oral contraceptive pills can be obtained in Ireland, providing they are *not* labelled as such on the packet; the Swedish regulations on vending machines are not enforced; Indonesian field workers for family planning are not being imprisoned. Nevertheless, change would be welcome. Family planning practices appear to diffuse down social networks from the socially privileged to the most disadvantaged. In Europe this process has taken a century and is still incomplete. The developing world cannot, and must not wait so long, either to meet the demands of social justice or to tackle demographic problems. Legal changes are a prerequisite for what has been called the "democratization of birth control." The amount of effort to be expended in changing anti-contraceptive legislation should not be judged on the basis that many individuals can circumvent almost any barrier to obtain contraceptives, but by the fact that the socially most disadvantaged are usually most hurt by restrictions, however trivial, that increase the social, economic, cultural and geographical distance between them and the service they need.

In many countries that have adopted family planning (and population policies) the spread of family planning has been slow and relatively costly. It is regrettable that many of these governments, often individually spending millions of dollars on family planning, have still not tidied up the ledger of contraceptive legislation. It is paradoxical that in developed areas, such as New York State, restrictions make it almost more difficult to obtain a condom than an abortion, while in Dublin a man may go to prison or be fined for selling a contraceptive, although it is perfectly legal to perform a vasectomy regardless of age or marital status.

Changes in legislation have proved to be potent instruments for achieving improved family planning services. Further changes will be welcome. For example, the ability of manufacturers to mount advertising campaigns may prove more useful than training another group of field workers—and would cost the state nothing. The removal of prescription requirements for oral contraceptives could well achieve more for family planning in a developing country than negotiating a loan from an international agency to build several thousand more family planning clinics.

V. WAYS AND MEANS OF CHANGE

In a field like contraception, which is still subject to change and development, economy of legislative action seems wise. Over the past few years, the United States has seen a rash of legislation designed to ease the distribution of contraceptives. In some cases, the words "prevention of pregnancy" were simply deleted from a statute regulating obscene literature.[16]

---

16. Senate Bill No. 1076 amending the Iowa obscenity law.

However, in other cases, such as California (SB 567) and Massachusetts (HB 3250), restrictive clauses were replaced by explicitly liberal wordings:

> Prescriptive devices shall be dispensed by prescription through physicians and pharmacies to all, regardless of age, marital status, religion and without spouse or parental consent.
>
> Non-prescriptive contraceptive devices such as condoms, foams, creams, jellies, suppositories may be distributed in all retail outlets and by all social agencies, public health nurses, physicians, etc., to anyone, regardless of age or marital status, religion and without spouse or parental consent.[17]

In situations where opinions on birth control are sharply polarised, such legislation may give encouragement to ardent family planners and act as a deterrent to those who would further their own beliefs by prosecuting others. However, in a philosophical sense, straightforward repeal of restrictive legislation would seem simpler.

The California legislation to "amend . . . and repeal sections 4306 and 4323 of the Business and Professional Code relating to prophylactics," while constructive, verges on the meddlesome and redundant in specifying that condoms must be "hermetically sealed in a manner approved by the [State] Board [of Pharmacy]."[18] An injunction which would be out of place, for example, if plastic instead of rubber condoms were to be marketed. In short, in the case of restrictions on contraceptive distribution, repeal is almost always preferable to reform. Adequate control of many aspects will always remain under various trade description, obscenity laws and other statutes and regulations applying to condoms as well as other commodities.

VI. Recommendations

1. Laws regulating the manufacture, sale, display, advertising and importation of contraceptives should be repealed, permitting these items to be treated like any other common, high volume, low price commodity. It is to be noted that contraceptives would remain subject to a reasonable application of the obscenity laws, trade description acts, as well as the normal responsibilities of manufacturer and distributor under the law, for adequate standards of production, accurate labelling and honest advertising.

2. Tariffs and taxes should take into account the logistics of contraceptive manufacture and the needs of the community for cheap, high quality products. In many countries a special case can be made out for excluding contraceptives from normal tariff and tax policies.

---

17. Massachusetts House Bill No. 3250.
18. CAL. BUS. & PROFESSIONS CODE § 4323.5 (West 1974) *repealing* § 4306.

3. Local and indirect regulations concerning contraceptive display, advertising and distribution should be reviewed and, where necessary, harmonised with national laws.

4. The need for medical supervision of IUDs and steroidal contraceptives should be reviewed nationally, rather than internationally, taking into account such factors as maternal mortality, incidence of induced abortion, cultural appropriateness of possible channels of distribution and potential financial and personnel resources, both as available, and as related to the competing needs of other aspects of health care.

Report of Workshop on the
Manufacture and Distribution
of Contraceptives

Dr. Malcolm Potts, in summarizing his paper, stressed a few of the most pressing problems in the contraceptives field for which he felt it was particularly important to find solutions. First, of particular concern to the search for a perfect contraceptive is the problem of the liability of manufacturers of new contraceptives found subsequently to have undesirable side effects. Since it is impossible to prove a contraceptive to be totally safe in less than one generation's time, it will be necessary to find a solution to this problem so that new and better contraceptives can be promptly developed and placed on the market. Second, in dealing with the problem of manufacturing contraceptives in the developing countries, the question of the economy of scale would have to be considered. In the case of the condom industry, which is capital intensive, one factory can supply the need of several small countries. Therefore, it may be important to try to lower import barriers and to concentrate on local packaging activities. Similar considerations apply to other contraceptives. Third, Dr. Potts argued that the ban on the display of contraceptives in stores should be ended. Such a policy is harmful since the people who need them most are frequently embarassed by having to ask for contraceptives specifically.

In conclusion, Dr. Potts took note of the lack of logic in many countries' policies on the subject since they accept contraception by coitus interruptus as legal, while declaring that the use of a pharmaceutical product to accomplish the same result is illegal and unacceptable. Therefore, he suggested that contraceptives be treated like any other medical product, and not discouraged by any special set of discriminatory rules.

In the general discussion, five points drew particular attention.

1. A question arose as to the wisdom of confining sales of contraceptives (particularly pills) to pharmacies in countries where there are but few pharmacies. This raised the general question of medical supervision of pill taking. The physicians present at the Symposium were of divided opinions as to the dangers of the pill, on one hand, and on the other, as to the benefits to be gained by permitting liberal distribution of the pill, presently the most effective contraceptive available. It was agreed that in the light of the chang-

ing status of medical science, governments would have to decide the issue on the basis of public health conditions in their own countries.

2. On the question of the relationship of contraceptive services to the general public health services, all agreed that the former must be regarded as a normal and regular aspect of the latter. These services, however, would have to be concerned with providing the technique most desirable for a particular patient.

3. Warnings were given by several participants as to the obstructive nature of administrative practices. In cases where the law is silent, hostile administration can effectively block free access to contraception. So ways must be sought to ensure that the intent of the United Nations declarations be made a reality.

4. On the moral, practical and medical side, there was general agreement that contraception is far more desirable than abortion. From the standpoint of the comparative cost, the case was cited of one country where there had been a period of scare as to the pill. The result was a far greater recourse to abortion, with the attendant strain on the medical services, since abortion services cost four times more than contraceptive services.

5. Finally, there was a strong feeling that the act of conceiving must be regarded as a deliberate and responsible act. To accomplish this end, the means for contraception must be made widely available and its use encouraged.

Laws Relating to Professional Paramedical Role in Contraception

By
Allan G. Rosenfield*

INTRODUCTION

In an increasing number of countries, there is an interest in utilizing the various categories of paramedical health workers to deliver health and family planning services. Generally, there are no specific laws regulating the roles such personnel can assume. In most countries, however, there are laws relating to the practice of medicine and to the prescription of drugs. Such laws may define activities to be conducted by physicians, but rarely the types of activities to be conducted by other personnel. For example, the prescription of "dangerous" drugs is limited to the physician, most often under the direction of a food and drug authority.

There also may be laws which establish different categories of drug stores, some of which may only carry proprietary drugs, while others, usually with a pharmacist in residence, can carry prescription drugs, theoretically to be prescribed only with a doctor's prescription. But in practice, in a large number of countries most drugs are available over the counter.[1] The distribution of proprietary drugs, of course, is not limited to physicians and these can be bought over the counter in various categories of drug stores.

In most countries legislation plays a less important role in governing paramedicals' activities than regulations established by the Ministries of Health, Food and Drug Administrations (FDA) and/or medical societies. There is, nevertheless, great variation as to the enforcement of the regulations promulgated by these agencies. In most of the industrialized nations of the West, rather strict enforcement of the regulations is in effect, i.e., most drugs, particularly those under the dangerous drug acts, are only available

---

* Associate Director, Technical Assistance Division, The Population Council.
  1. WESTINGHOUSE POPULATION CENTER, DISTRIBUTION OF CONTRACEPTIVES IN THE COMMERCIAL SECTOR OF SELECTED DEVELOPING COUNTRIES: SUMMARY REPORT (1974).

with a doctor's prescription in licensed pharmacies or drug stores. Similarly, most procedures, particularly those of a surgical nature, are limited to qualified physicians, and in more recent times, often limited to specialists. Usually, the practices and standards are established by medical agencies or societies rather than by specific legislation.

For a variety of reasons these established practices are being criticized and reviewed both in the industrialized and the "developing" nations because of serious inadequacies in the health care and family planning delivery systems. In most cases, the steps being taken to liberalize practices do not involve changes in legislation *per se*, but rather changes in regulations by the appropriate agency, which, in the case of many "developing" countries, is often the Ministry of Health.

At the same time, because so little has been written in the literature concerning the actual legal status of the utilization of various categories of personnel, reviews of such laws are most appropriate at this time so that there will be a better understanding by those involved in attempting to bring about change. Most countries do have drug acts, although they often give the authority for specific actions within the act to the Ministry of Health, and the local FDA usually acts as part of this Ministry. These laws may include definitions of who may sell drugs of different categories and when a physician's prescription is (theoretically) required.

I. THE EVOLVING ROLE OF PARAMEDICAL PERSONNEL IN HEALTH CARE

Despite the rather strict medical conservatism which usually underlies existing restrictive regulations, specific exceptions to the norms of medical practice have been made by the medical profession over the years. In many European countries, for example, trained nurse midwives have long been allowed to deliver babies, and often to give necessary medications. In a number of Western countries nurses have been trained to administer general anaesthesia, an admittedly hazardous activity in which potential complications, including death, exist when anaesthesia is administered by ill-trained personnel. Nurses also are often allowed to administer intravenous solutions and, after a physician's prescription, to give drugs intramuscularly, and occasionally intravenously.

These are all technical activities which at one time were probably carried out only by physicians. But, for practical purposes, the medical profession simply changed the procedure manuals to allow their personnel to conduct these activities. To my knowledge, actual legal change has been uncommon in these areas.

In a number of countries in the so-called developing world, increased utilization of paramedical personnel has been undertaken because of the very serious limitations on the number of available medical personnel.[2] In many of these countries the vast majority of physicians live and practice in urban areas, with the result that in rural areas there are often 100,000 or more people per practicing physician (and many of these physicians are in fact administrators rather than practitioners).[3] For a number of years innovative approaches in several African countries were carried out in which assistant doctors or medical assistants and auxiliaries were given specific training in order to carry out a variety of simple medical activities. Some of them were taught to diagnose and treat simple ailments, providing patients with appropriate medications. For example, they were trained to care for children with conditions such as diarrhea and respiratory diseases. In order to be able to handle emergency situations, they were often taught simple surgical techniques, including the suturing of lacerations and the setting of bone fractures. In most of these cases, the legislation governing medical practice was not changed; the Ministry of Health in the individual countries simply modified its regulations to allow these necessary practices to be followed.

Some paramedicals have even received specialized training in such surgical techniques as hernia repair and appendectomy. Both of these can be complicated procedures, and yet, with appropriate specialized training, persons with less than a full medical education have been successfully taught to carry out the procedures.

In recent years, some of the most innovative activities in the health field have been reported from the People's Republic of China.[4] Various levels of paramedical personnel have been trained to carry out a variety of medical activities. The concept that developed was to provide the best care possible for the most people, rather than the highest quality care possible, which could only be achieved for a small minority of the population. Unfortunately, in a good part of the world the latter is the case, with the majority of the people receiving little or no medical care because of inappropriate regulations, most of which are formulated by the medical profession, and not by the lawmakers. The reports from China have been most impressive, suggesting a far more appropriate model than the Western system for the delivery of health care services in areas in which medical manpower is in short supply.

To illustrate the problems which confront us as a result of medical procedure adopted wholesale in developing countries, I would refer to the standards now used in most countries. Medical standards generally hold that

---

2. N.R.E. FENDALL, AUXILIARIES IN HEALTH CARE, PROGRAMS IN DEVELOPING COUNTRIES (Baltimore: Johns Hopkins Press 1972).

3. J. BRYANT, HEALTH AND THE DEVELOPING WORLD 74 (Ithaca: Cornell University Press 1969).

4. Chen, *China's Population Program at the Grass-Roots Level*, 4 STUDIES IN FAMILY PLANNING, No. 8, at 219 (1973); Rifkin, *Public Health in China: Is the Experience Relevant to Other Less Developed Countries?* 7 SOCIAL SCIENCE AND MEDICINE 249 (1973).

doctors must record a medical history and perform a physical and pelvic examination. In discussing the importance of a pelvic examination it is worth reviewing the general benefits of such an examination. Unquestionably, there are significant benefits to be gained from screening for cancer of the cervix, assuming facilities and personnel exist to conduct such screening programs. Such programs are extremely beneficial, but the major limiting factor, in most areas of the world, is the lack of sufficient facilities and personnel to handle these smears in a large-scale programme, with most such services presently limited to the larger urban medical centers. The introduction of a widespread screening programme is quite costly, and it has been suggested that compared to other pressing health needs, the priority of developing such a programme is quite low.[5]

Routine pelvic examination also is recommended as a possible means of detecting early cancer of the ovaries. Preventive measures for ovarian cancer, however, have been most unsuccessful, even in those areas of the world where routine pelvic examinations are performed regularly. Several studies in the United States have shown that between 70-90 per cent of all patients with ovarian cancer seek advice late, in spite of regular check-ups.[6] It has been reported that even semi-annual examinations by gynecologists have not been found effective in lowering the death rates of this disease.[7] Finally, routine pelvic examination also adds little to the detection of endometrial cancer, since patients generally present abnormal vaginal bleeding before significant changes are noted on the examination.

Thus, while routine pelvic examination is beneficial, such a requirement would drastically limit the number of patients who would be able to receive services because of the severe shortage of medical personnel available to perform the examination. There is a need to seek new models for health care which can provide the best care possible by better utilizing the time of medical personnel and by providing the services which are most needed.

II. Paramedical Personnel and the Distribution of Contraceptives

A. *Oral Contraceptives*

In most countries oral contraceptives have been classified as a dangerous drug, and usually require a physician's prescription for their use. In actual practice, however, particularly in the developing world, these drugs are available over the counter in various categories of drug stores. The policies concerning such drugs are usually set, as mentioned earlier, by the food and drug

5. Rosenfield, *Family Planning: An Expanded Role for Paramedical Personnel*, 110 Am. J. Obstetrics and Gynecology 1030 (1971).
6. Moore and Lambley, 98 Am. J. Obstetrics and Gynecology 624 (1967).
7. Textbook of Obstetrics and Gynecology 1000 (D.M. Danford ed. 1966).

authorities of the various countries. These FDAs often follow the policies established in the United Kingdom or the United States. This is true in Jamaica where before a new drug can be sold it must be demonstrated that the drug has been approved for sale in the country of origin. But it must be asked if the United States FDA (USFDA), for example, is the appropriate model to follow.

The USFDA is a highly regarded agency throughout the world, but its policies are based on standards established primarily for urban areas, in which there are usually less than 1,000 people per physician. Thus, the majority of people can receive medical attention, although admittedly there are many problems related to the delivery of health care in urban areas, too, particularly in the urban slums. As mentioned earlier, in many rural areas there are more than 100,000 people per physician. It does not appear rational to expect that similar prescription standards and criteria can be established for these two very different types of localities.

In setting regulations concerning the utilization of drugs, the risk versus the benefit of the drug must be taken into consideration, not in the abstract, but in relation to the actual conditions in the setting in which it is to be used. The literature concerning known and potential complications of oral contraceptives is voluminous. Of particular importance have been reports from England[8] and the United States[9] on deaths due to pill-related thromboembolic (or blood clot) disease. These studies, which were based on the use of a higher dose of steroids than are presently in common use, suggested that for every 100,000 women using the pill three would die due to complications related to blood clots. More recent data suggest that this rate may indeed be somewhat lower.[10]

Other complications reported include various metabolic and vascular changes, as well as jaundice. Extensive reviews, however, of the overall risks of oral contraception have been carried out by the USFDA Obstetrics and Gynecology Advisory Committee,[11] by the World Health Organization[12] and by other agencies. They have all concluded that, from the evidence available at the time of the reports, the benefits of oral contraception outweigh the risks in properly screened patients.

---

8. Vessey and Doll, *Investigation of the Relation Between Use of Oral Contraceptives and Thromboembolic Disease: A Further Report*, 2 BRITISH MED. J. 661 (1969).

9. Sartwell, *et. al.*, *Thromboembolism and Oral Contraceptives: An Epidemiologic Case Control Study*, 90 AM. J. EPIDEMIOLOGY 365 (1969).

10. Drill, *Oral Contraceptives and Thromboembolic Disease: In Perspective and Retrospective Studies*, 219 J. AM. MED. ASS'N 583 (1972).

11. ADVISORY COMMITTEE ON OBSTETRICS AND GYNECOLOGY, SECOND REPORT ON ORAL CONTRACEPTIVES (U.S. Food and Drug Administration 1968).

12. WORLD HEALTH ORGANIZATION SCIENTIFIC GROUP, METHODS OF FERTILITY REGULATION: ADVANCES IN RESEARCH AND CLINICAL EXPERIENCE, Technical Report Series No. 473 (Geneva: World Health Org. 1971).

In the West, thromboembolic disease, the most important complication, is also a common complication seen in the immediate postpartum period, and also after surgical procedures. Although not yet statistically documented, it is the clear impression of many well-trained physicians that thromboembolic disease is extremely uncommon in developing nations, particularly in rural areas, both after delivery and after surgical procedures. The explanation for this phenomenon is not yet available, but it is probably related to differences in dietary habits and in style of life (walking and physical activity versus a more sedentary style in the West) rather than to some genetic differences. Thromboembolic disease postpartum and post pill use is probably related in both cases to changes in hormonal levels (of estrogen and/or progesterone). It has been hypothesized, therefore, without any means of proof at the present moment, that if blood clots are uncommon in the postpartum period in rural areas, that they will also be uncommon in women from these areas who are on the pill.

Even assuming the rate of death due to the pill found in the United States and the United Kingdom applies in the developing world, it is necessary to compare this to the risk of death due to pregnancy. In many rural areas of the world, as many as 500 to 1,000 women will die per 100,000 pregnancies. This figure is undoubtedly highest in those rural areas where women deliver at home with little or no trained care. Furthermore, maternal mortality rates are highest among women of high parity and of older age.[13]

It has been suggested by some that if all pregnancies above parity four and in women over the age of 35 could be prevented by contraception, this would have a more positive effect on maternal and infant health than any other single step that could be taken in the field of health. This suggests the potential impact of widespread contraception on maternal and child health, not to mention the impact in terms of alleviating population pressures.

A number of countries have begun to allow paramedicals to prescribe the pill. In none of these countries, to the knowledge of the author, has legislation been specifically changed; rather, Ministries of Health or other such agencies have simply changed the regulations concerning the utilization of such personnel. A simple checklist such as that attached in Table 1 (Appendix) has been utilized by paramedics in which a series of short questions is asked and a simple examination performed. If there is a positive answer to any of these questions, the pill may not be prescribed but the patient is instead referred to a physician for further evaluation.

Actually, there is little a physician can do that the paramedic cannot do in terms of this initial screening. Physicians, for example, are not able yet to

13. G.W. Perkin, *Pregnancy Preventives in "High-Risk" Women: A Strategy for New National Family Planning Programs* (paper presented at the IPPF Conf. on Family Planning and Nat'l Devel., Indonesia 1969).

predict which patient is likely to develop blood clots. The best that can be done is to check for varicose veins or phlebitis and ask about any pertinent history. This can be done as well by a trained paramedic.

In Thailand, in 1970, a research project was developed to study the safety and practicality of the utilization of auxiliary midwives to prescribe the pill.[14] These personnel had received basic training in the field of family planning during training courses of the National Family Planning Program run by the Ministry of Public Health. Included in the training program had been lectures and discussions on oral contraceptives, including indications, contraindications, side effects and complications. Auxiliary midwives in four provinces, using the checklist mentioned above, were allowed to prescribe the pill. As a result, there was approximately a 400 per cent increase in the number of acceptors in the first six months of the study, as compared to the previous six-month period. A follow-up study was conducted in which continuation rates were shown to be higher in the study area than in control provinces where doctors prescribed the pill (76 per cent and 67 per cent respectively). There was no statistical increase in side effects and complications noted at the time of the follow-up survey, although the time period was perhaps too short to draw a definite conclusion.

Because the results of the pilot programme were so encouraging, the Ministry of Health ruled that all auxiliary midwives in Thailand could prescribe the pill. This, in effect, increased the number of clinics offering the pill from 350 (those with a physician) to close to 4,000 (those in which there was at least one auxiliary midwife in residence). Following the ruling, there was a dramatic increase in the numbers of pill acceptors in the National Family Planning Program, from approximately 8,000 new acceptors per month prior to the new regulation, to over 30,000 acceptors per month at its peak. This was a dramatic demonstration in that particular country of the effectiveness of the utilization of paramedical personnel to prescribe the pill. It allowed the national programme to exceed its targets by as many as 100,000 acceptors, reaching an annual total in 1972 of 450,000 new acceptors of contraception, of which 75 per cent received the pill. The majority of this latter group received them from the auxiliary midwives. A number of other countries are making use of such personnel to prescribe the pill, such as Malaysia, South Korea, and, most notably, the People's Republic of China.

1. Community-based Distribution of Oral Contraceptives

While not the specific topic of this paper, there have been a number of recommendations that the pill should not be considered as a dangerous drug, at least under circumstances existing in most rural areas, and that widespread

14. Rosenfield and Limcharoen, *Auxiliary Midwife Prescription of Oral Contraceptives*, 114 AM. J. OBSTETRICS AND GYNECOLOGY 942 (1972).

distribution, through a variety of commercial channels, is more than justified, using the risk-benefit rationale described above. After extensive review of the field, and of the literature, it is the opinion of the author that the benefits to be gained in terms of family planning and maternal and child health improvements, by extending the distribution points to the village level, significantly outweigh the possible risks. Studies of this approach seem in order.[15] While it is possible that women will not take the pill reliably, because of inadequate instructions through such an approach, preliminary data from Colombia and elsewhere suggest that this may not be the case. Suffice it to say that FDA regulations in a number of countries should be reviewed, looking specifically at the risk-benefit ratio within a particular country, in relation to such an approach.

B. *IUD Insertion*

The question of the utilization of paramedical personnel to insert intrauterine devices, while subject to much debate, should not actually be as controversial as it first appears because it already has been carried out in a number of places with success. Again, in most of these areas legislation was not changed, Ministry regulations were simply revised. It has been suggested that the procedure for inserting an IUD is easier and less hazardous than the delivery of a baby, which auxiliary midwives already are allowed to do in many countries throughout the world.

In order to test the practicability of permitting paramedics to insert IUDs, an interesting project was conducted in Korea in which three groups were observed. In the first group an IUD insertion was performed by an obstetrician; in the second, by a nurse/midwife, supervised by the same physician; and in the third, by a specially trained nurse/midwife without direct supervision. There were no differences between the groups in terms of perforation, expulsion or incidence of other complications. The only difference found was that the unsupervised nurse rejected more patients than the others, referring patients about whom she had any reservations to a physician for a check prior to insertion.[16] In Pakistan (prior to partition) female lay personnel were given an intensive training course and allowed to insert the IUDs without direct supervision. During 1967 and 1968, 600,000 IUDs were inserted by these personnel, accounting for approximately 75 per cent of all insertions in that country. Utilization of such personnel was attempted because of the cultural demand that pelvic examinations be performed by females in a country with an inadequate supply of female physicians. One of the conclusions of the Pakistan experience was that "IUD performance of

---

15. Atkinson, Castadot, Cuadros and Rosenfield, *Oral Contraceptives: Considerations of Safety in Non-Clinical Distribution*, 5 STUDIES IN FAMILY PLANNING, No. 8, at 242 (1974).

16. Yang, Bang, Song and Choi, *Improving Access to the IUD: Experiments in Koyang, Korea*, 1 STUDIES IN FAMILY PLANNING, No. 27, at 4 (1968).

paramedical personnel is reasonably comparable to that of medical personnel.
. . . [F]ull-time family planning personnel, whether medical or paramedical,
generally give better services as far as sterile technique, clinic organization,
record keeping, and follow-up procedures are concerned, than do those personnel, medical or paramedical, who do family planning on a part-time
basis."[17]

The use of paraprofessionals has been tried in many other settings,
including the Kentucky Frontier Nursing Service, Barbados, New York City,
People's Republic of China, Thailand and elsewhere. The key to the success
of a paramedical IUD insertion programme is an effective training course,
which must be geared to the needs of the job and to those of the trainee.
While there are many aspects of the training, the most important is the actual
technique of IUD insertion. The first step is to learn how to perform a pelvic
examination, which entails a good deal of practice, rather than didactic lectures. A pelvic examination is not a difficult procedure. It simply requires
practice under observation. Oftentimes paramedical personnel may receive
better training than the average physician because the paramedic's training is
both more specific and more closely supervised. It is often assumed by
trainers that the physician already knows how to carry out a pelvic examination and, thus, little time may be spent supervising physicians during their
training.

Again, given the tremendous shortages of medical personnel, the development of practical training courses for various categories of health personnel, particularly nurse/midwives and auxiliary midwives, is of key importance in expanding the outlets providing intrauterine devices. While there
have been disappointments with this method of contraception, as with all
methods of contraception, continuation rates in general, particularly for
higher parity women, are higher than with oral contraceptives. The method
does not require daily pill taking, failure rates are low, and its separation
from the act of coitus all suggest that the IUD still can play a major role in
national programmes, particularly if they are made more readily available. It
must be stressed, again, that training is of key importance, not only as to the
technique of insertion but also as to how to handle the complaints and
complications that patients may have.

C. *Injectable Hormonal Contraception*

In many cultures, treatment by injection is very popular. Thus, there has
been interest in developing an injectable contraceptive. At present, the
widely used agent of this type is Depoprovera (DMPA). There is increasing
evidence that this is a safe drug, although, as with the pill and IUD, there are

---

17. Kaul, *A Comparison of Field Performance of Medical vs. Paramedical Personnel in the IUD Programme in Mymensingh and Lahore (Pakistan)*, 3 PAKISTAN J. FAMILY PLANNING 75 (1968).

side effects and possible long-term complications. The risk-benefit ratio is such that, after extensive review of the literature, it has been recommended that the preparation be approved for national family planning programmes.[18] The same rationale which supports the use of paramedics to prescribe the pill applies here, and such personnel have been so used safely. This method, prescribed and delivered by paramedical personnel, would be another development of importance in the expanding of family planning coverage.

III.   CONCLUSIONS

There have been many debates as to whether or not the family planning programmes can be successful in bringing about fertility reduction as well as improvements in maternal and child health. Some of those concerned about the rapid rates of population growth, and the need to bring about fertility reduction, believe that steps "beyond family planning" are necessary. Many of these steps may well have great importance in relation to fertility reduction and some of them are being discussed during this symposium.

At the same time, however, it is fair to suggest that family planning programmes could be far more effective than they have been to date. A recent paper by this author has suggested a number of areas in which family planning programmes could be made more effective, and one of the most important relates to far more effective and practical utilization of paramedical personnel.[19] We have covered their utilization in terms of the prescription of hormonal contraception and the insertion of the intrauterine device. Another paper at this symposium will cover the utilization of paramedics to carry out sterilization and abortion procedures. Suffice it to say, it appears most appropriate given proper training, to consider that paramedical personnel could be trained to perform the following procedures: vasectomy, which is a relatively uncomplicated repetitive procedure; immediate postpartum tubal ligation, also a very simple and repetitive procedure; and perhaps early suction curettage, particularly during the first few weeks of pregnancy, when the procedure is relatively safe. As with IUD insertion, the key again is appropriate training. It is probable that, in many countries medical regulations could be changed to allow this, although in some, actual legislation may have to be changed.

One concern always raised is the problem of malpractice responsibility. This is more of a problem in the West, but its importance in developing countries cannot be overlooked. In general, Ministry of Health regulations

---

18.   Rosenfield, *Injectable Long-Acting Progestogen Contraception: A Neglected Modality*, AM. J. OBSTETRICS AND GYNECOLOGY (in press).

19.   Rosenfield, *Family Planning Programs: Can More Be Done?* 5 STUDIES IN FAMILY PLANNING, No. 4, at 115 (1974).

carry great weight even if lawsuits are brought. While review of the law is very important, the conservative attitudes of the medical profession are perhaps even more important. There is a need for physicians to be more realistic and practical in setting standards of good medical practice. The aim, as in the People's Republic of China, should be towards the provision of the best quality of care possible for the most people. By following Western medical practices, we have in effect denied care to a substantial portion of the population of many of the countries, and this is a practice which needs review and change if we are to improve health care and family planning practices in these countries.

RECOMMENDATIONS

1. Each country should make an effort to review the laws relating to the prescription of drugs, specifically oral and injectable hormonal preparations. In terms of changes discussed in this paper, attention should be paid to an understanding of the breadth of responsibilities of various agencies (Ministries of Health, FDAs, etc.) under existing laws.

2. Each country should review the laws relating to practices such as pelvic examination and IUD insertion. In most, the procedure will not be specifically mentioned, but the law may well relate generally to the carrying out of procedures by personnel other than physicians. Regulations of Ministries of Health, FDAs and other appropriate agencies should be reviewed as well.

3. Efforts should be made, within the medical profession, and particularly within food and drug authorities, to review the risks versus benefits of specific medications and procedures in relation to circumstances within the given country, rather than utilizing practices adopted from Western nations.

4. Policies established by specialists in highly recognized medical schools in each individual country should be reviewed, and, where appropriate, national seminars should be held, involving the key medical and legal authorities in discussions of these issues. Such national meetings may well have more impact among people who are not yet knowledgeable and concerned about such issues, than do international meetings which generally attract the committed.

Appendix

TABLE I

QUESTIONNAIRE FOR MIDWIVES PRESCRIBING ORAL
CONTRACEPTIVES

	Yes	No
History: ask if the patient has had a history of any of the following:		
Yellow skin or yellow eyes		
Mass in the breast		
Discharge from the nipple		
Excessive menstrual periods		
Increased frequency of menstrual periods		
Bleeding after sexual intercourse		
Swelling or severe pains in the legs		
Severe chest pains		
Unusual shortness of breath after exertion		
Severe headaches		
Examination: Check the following:		
Yellow skin and yellow eye color		
Mass in the breast		
Nipple discharge		
Varicose veins		
Blood pressure (yes=above 160)		
Pulse (yes=above 120)		
Sugar in urine		
Protein in urine		

Instructions: If all the above are answered in the negative, the patient may receive oral contraceptives. If any of the above are answered in the positive, the patient must be seen by a physician before oral contraceptives may be prescribed.

Report of Workshop on
Laws Relating to Paramedical Role
in Contraception

Rather than hear a summary of the paper presented at the plenary session by Dr. Allan G. Rosenfield, the workshop launched directly into the discussion of the legal and customary constraints regarding the use of professional paramedicals in the distribution of contraceptives.

The need for exploiting this source of manpower was underscored at the outset. This need is premised on the fact that there is a general world-wide lack of medical and paramedical personnel specifically trained to deliver family planning related health services. Where laws and medical regulations reserve to medical doctors the types of activities which are related to contraceptive distribution, the effectiveness of the distribution system is limited. This is particularly true in the less developed nations where doctors are customarily concentrated in the urban centers, leaving the numerous rural populations—sometimes representing 80% of a country's population—without access to effective contraceptive services. Many of the developed countries, most notably the United States, are also experiencing similar problems because there are insufficient numbers of doctors who possess expertise in family planning related health care.

A short interchange was devoted to the terminology being used. Questions arose as to what the term "paramedicals" meant. What are they? What types of health personnel does or should the categorization include? Is the use of the word "paramedicals" designed to encompass only traditional midwives, auxiliary health workers and medical assistants? Or is it meant to include all types of health personnel except doctors? The classification of types of health workers appeared to create problems for several of the participants. For example, in many countries midwifery is a profession governed by special legislation as is the case with the nursing profession. Some participants felt that classifying these types of health workers as paramedicals would be to downgrade the professions. As a consequence, it was obvious that more thought will have to be devoted to working out acceptable definitions and classifications.

The discussion then focused on four aspects of the problem: (1) legal barriers to the use of paramedicals; (2) training for paramedicals; (3) redefining the functions of paramedicals; and (4) paramedical liability.

Legal Barriers to the Use of Paramedicals in Contraception

Of the laws and regulations which determine the extent to which paramedicals can play a role in contraceptive distribution attention focused on three types which are important: those which require that a prescription for oral contraceptives be obtained from a doctor; those which require that oral contraceptives be sold solely in a pharmacy; and, those which require that IUD's be inserted by doctors. It was pointed out, for example, that to insist that only doctors insert IUD's is to deny access to this type of contraception to vast numbers of people. For example, in Nigeria where there are only a handful of gynecologists, a provision that IUD's be inserted only by them runs counter to the desire to make contraceptives available to all who desire them. In light of the need for widespread distribution of family planning methods, several countries have either abolished the types of restrictions mentioned above or have expanded the types of personnel who can be qualified to perform the tasks. Among those mentioned as having authorized paramedicals to prescribe and distribute the pill are Thailand, the Philippines and South Korea. Pakistan, Mexico, the Philippines, South Korea and Indonesia have authorized paramedicals—principally nurses or midwives—to insert the IUD. Perhaps the most famous model for utilization of paramedicals in family planning is that now functioning in the People's Republic of China, where several classes of paramedicals—from the renowned "barefoot" doctors to health auxiliaries—are performing a number of tasks which in the Western-type health system are characteristically reserved for doctors.

Training for Paramedicals

Though the several country experiences with paramedicals cited above seemed to provide a basis for recommending expanded use of this type of personnel, questions arose as to whether they could be effectively trained and if so whether the quality of their performance was comparable to that of qualified medical practitioners. The answer given by the medical experts present in the workshop to the former question was in the affirmative. Paramedicals can be trained to prescribe pills, check for contraindications and insert IUD's. As a point of fact a recent study in South Korea concerning the proficiency of paramedicals inserting the IUD showed that the incidence of perforations was no greater than when inserted by trained physicians. Similarly, studies in Thailand, where paramedicals are authorized to distribute the pill, indicate no increases in the incidence of contraindications or complications. On the other hand, some of the participants expressed the opinion that there is some truth to the observation that many paramedicals will not or do not have the ability to know the real medical indicators which signal complications. However, on the whole, it was felt that they could be trained to observe such signals and then refer cases to doctors.

One of the problems present is that there is no uniform standard for the training of paramedicals. Would it be advisable to set such standards? Medical experts were of the opinion that the struggle to establish universal standards has in the past hindered medical training. It simply does not make sense to insist that the same training standards be applied in Bolivia, Cameroon and Malaysia as are in force in the United States, Germany and Japan. Many of the participants were of the opinion that guidelines would be established but they should be adapted to the level of medical care and needs presently in existence in each country. The models for training should likewise be adapted to the appropriate local situation, and where possible the training should take place in a local setting.

It was apparent from the drift of the discussion that the training element should be considered a key factor in any attempt to use paramedicals. Paramedicals should be given training on the manual functions which they are to perform; they should be taught how to use the pill screening checklist to determine the recipient's propensity for side-effects and contraindications; and some form of continuing supervision should be maintained over them, either by doctors or other highly experienced paramedicals.

Redefining the Functions of a Paramedical

Any attempt to increase the bailiwick of paramedicals necessarily involves a recasting of the present definition of roles. These roles can and should be outlined sharply. Despite the importance of doing this, it was recognized that in practice the paramedical in the field is called upon to perform many medical functions for which he may or may not be properly trained. Likewise, the possibility of effectively supervising their activities, especially in the rural areas, is minimal. Nevertheless, it is essential that ways be sought to expand their functions and improve their training. To facilitate this expansion of roles it was noted that many of the medical regulations will have to be changed.

Several other contradictory themes ran through the discussion. On one hand, it was asserted that doctors in general are woefully lacking in family planning expertise. This gave rise to the suggestion that the first priority be to see to it that doctors presently practicing medicine also receive proper training in this area. On the other hand, it was argued that while it is important that doctors have family planning training, it is more essential that doctors delegate routine functions to paramedical personnel, for not to do so would be to waste a scarce resource. There are obviously a number of tasks for which only doctors are skilled and suited; it has been demonstrated that the distribution of pills and the insertion of IUD's are not in that category.

Another aspect related to the rationale for supporting an increase in the use of paramedicals is one of numbers and time. It is basically unrealistic to think that doctors can provide all of the manpower needed to make contraceptives available to all who want them. Many people in developing countries go their whole lifetime without seeing a doctor. Paramedical personnel are presently available in greater numbers than are doctors, and it takes less time to train them and get them into activity. Moreover, cultural preferences make it possible to use certain types of paramedicals. For example, in Pakistan, because of the intimate nature of the functions performed, tradition permits only women doctors to work in family planning programmes and do such things as insert IUD's. Because there was a dearth of women doctors in Pakistan, authorities sought other ways of getting this type of health service to the populace. This gave rise to the widespread use of Lady Family Planning Visitors (LFPV) to insert IUD's and give other contraceptive advice.

Midwives, several participants emphasized, have not been trained in contraceptive services; their task traditionally has been to deliver babies. In fact, midwives are trained to perform a number of functions—pre-natal, maternal and child care, vaccination, etc.—and family planning services can be an important part of that expertise. It is simply a matter of giving refresher courses. One participant pointed out that if a midwife is authorized to deliver a baby—a task which involves potentially dangerous complications—she can certainly be trained to deliver contraceptive services. Indeed, many countries train midwives to function as a link in the contraceptive distribution chain.

Paramedical Liability

Lastly, the legal rules covering liability arising from medical treatment were a point of concern. Many of the malpractice statutes cover only doctors. Where paramedicals are given authority to do tasks which have traditionally been within the domain of doctors, provisions should be made for their being held responsible if they are negligent. Such changes would protect the individual consumer. Mention was also made of possibly getting insurance for paramedicals, a problem which seemed to be endemic solely to the developed nations.

Voluntary Sterilization: A Human Right

By
Harriet F. Pilpel*

INTRODUCTION

"To be or not to be" was a question Shakespeare's Hamlet found difficult to answer. It is equally difficult to answer the question "to sterilize" or "not to sterilize." For if by "to sterilize" is meant the right of every competent adult voluntarily to choose, on the basis of an informed consent, sterilization for whatever reason—family planning or otherwise—then the answer to the question is "yes." If, on the other hand, the question is raised whether sterilization should ever be the result of coercion or compulsion, then the answer is "not to sterilize" in such circumstances. Because any reference to sterilization involves these two aspects of the question we should carefully draw a number of distinctions.

First, I shall distinguish throughout this paper between voluntary and compulsory sterilization. In the United States today—1974—there are no laws limiting the grounds on which voluntary sterilization may be obtained. A few states impose procedural requirements such as a waiting period, such as requiring that the procedure be done in a hospital, such as (rarely) specifying that the spouse's consent must be obtained before the procedure is done, etc. Until recently, low income groups in many parts of the country were denied access to voluntary sterilization due to its high cost, while those who could afford private physicians had little difficulty in gaining access to the procedure. But at the same time that *voluntary* sterilization as a matter of free choice was often difficult for poor people to get, compulsory sterilization laws which remained on the books of twenty odd states were all too often invoked against the poor who were being denied the procedure as a matter of free choice. Under our constitutional law, it is now reasonably well established (although the United States Supreme Court has not yet passed on the question) that at least public facilities must make available voluntary sterilization as a patient's option if it makes available gynecological procedures of the same general type (a D and C or a hysterectomy, for example). Conversely,

---

* The author is a senior partner in a New York City law firm.

and again while the United States Supreme Court has not directly passed upon the subject, it would seem that *compulsory* sterilization whether on grounds of lack of legal capacity, dependency, criminality or anything else is unconstitutional in the United States under the declared constitutional right of privacy in matters relating to marriage, family and sex recently declared by the United States Supreme Court.[1]

When it comes to voluntary sterilization, however, difficult questions arise in connection with minors and incompetent adults. For if a person lacks the actual and/or legal capacity to consent to a sterilization, how can the procedure be "voluntary"? The United States Department of Health, Education and Welfare has given this problem considerable attention and promulgated within the past months a set of Guidelines for voluntary sterilization in federally financed projects. A copy of the most recent "Guidelines for Sterilization of Minors and other Legally Incompetent Individuals" appears as Appendix A to this paper. In March 1974, the prior Guidelines were declared invalid by a federal court in the nation's capital on the ground that the legislation setting up the program did not permit under any circumstances the sterilization of minors or of feebleminded or other mentally incompetent persons who do not have the legal capacity to give informed consent.[2] At the same time, the same prior guidelines were also declared invalid with respect to competent adults on the ground they made insufficient provision to assure that neither sterilization—nor refusal to be sterilized—could be made the basis for any reward or penalty. In other words, the Court ruled that there must be more explicit statements in these regards to avoid any possibility of coercion, no matter in what degree. Attention is directed to Section II of this paper where draft provisions designed to make voluntary sterilization available to those who want it and to rule out the possibility of compulsory sterilization, are set forth.

Another distinction to be borne in mind in connection with sterilization is a distinction equally applicable to many other medical matters, that is the distinction between what is supposed to be done, *i.e.*, the "law on the books," and what is actually done, *i.e.*, the "law in fact." For regardless of constitutional rights, in the United States at least, but probably also in other countries, some people entitled to sterilization are denied it despite their informed request for it and some others who do not wish to be sterilized are undoubtedly coerced to be by all sorts of means, from the subtle to the obvious. Similarly, it must be remembered that practices of doctors and hospitals may exist as to both voluntary and compulsory sterilization inde-

---

1. Griswold v. Connecticut, 381 U.S. 475 (1965); Eisenstadt v. Baird, 405 U.S. 438 (1972); Roe v. Wade, 410 U.S. 113 (1973).

2. Relf v. Weinberger, Civil Action No. 73-1557 and National Welfare Rights Organization v. Weinberger, Civil Action No. 74-243 (Decision dated March 15, 1974, Gesell, J., United States District Court for the District of Columbia).

pendent of specific statutory and constitutional requirements which affect how the operation is carried out and to whom it is available.

Finally, a distinction must always be drawn between castration, *i.e.*, the removal of a person's (almost always a male's) sex organs, and sterilization which as a surgical procedure has no effect on a person's sexual performance but which if successful destroys his ability to procreate. (For an apparent example of a law which seems to treat castration and sterilization as if they were the same thing, see the Nicaraguan law quoted below.)

I.   A Bird's Eye View of the Laws of the World Relating to Voluntary Sterilization[3]

A review of national legislation bearing on voluntary sterilization in different countries reveals the existence of three basic types of law, each of which will be briefly discussed.

A.   *Laws Authorizing Voluntary Sterilization*

Where laws specifically authorize voluntary sterilization, they sometimes prescribe certain procedures or conditions for the operation.

1. Waiting Period

Many laws require a waiting period between the request for a voluntary sterilization operation and the actual operation in order to assure that the operation is truly voluntary and to permit possible reconsideration. Thus, the 1962 statute on sterilization of the State of Virginia provides:

> . . . no vasectomy shall be performed pursuant to the provision of this section prior to thirty days from the date of consent or request therefor; provided further that no salpingectomy or other irrevocable surgical sexual sterilization procedure shall be performed prior to thirty days from the date of consent or request therefor on any female who has not theretofore given birth to a child.[4]

A 1972 amendment of the Singapore Voluntary Sterilization Act of 1969 reduced the waiting period from thirty to seven days.[5] Denmark re-

3. This section of the paper is adapted from a paper delivered at the Seminar on Voluntary Sterilization and Post-Conceptive Regulation, sponsored by the IPPF's South East Asia and Oceania Regional Office, in Bangkok, 30 January-2 February, 1974, by Dr. Luke T. Lee, Director, Law and Population Programme, Fletcher School of Law and Diplomacy (administered with the cooperation of Harvard University) Tufts University. Dr. Lee's paper was based in large part on a study done by Jan Stepan and Edmund Kellogg titled *The World's Laws on Voluntary Sterilization for Family Planning Purposes*, which appeared as Law and Population Monograph Series No. 8 (1973).

4. VA. CODE ANN., tit. 32, Ch. 27, § 423 (1972).

5. Voluntary Sterilization Act No. 26 of 1969, *as amended by* Act of 2 May 1972, § 5 (4).

quires that an operation may not be performed later than six months after its authorization, presumably because of possible changes of mind or circumstances.

2. Minimum Age

The imposition of a minimum age requirement on applicants for voluntary sterilization is to protect them from reaching a rash decision with irreversible consequences, only to regret it later in life. The minimum age for voluntary sterilization is 18 in Denmark (with careful screening of applicants under 21 years of age),[6] 21 in Singapore,[7] and 25 in Austria.

3. Spouse's Consent

Apparently on the ground that the number of children is a matter of concern to both of the spouses, some laws require that prior to voluntary sterilization, evidence must be submitted showing the spouse's consent to the operation. Such laws exist in Denmark, Singapore and Japan. Japan requires also consent from one "who, not legally married, possesses marital status" with the applicant.[8] However, the better view would be to allow each spouse to make up his or her own mind as to whether to have a voluntary sterilization. Where one so decides against the opposition of the other, it may well be that such a unilateral step of the other spouse should give the opposing spouse a basis for an action for divorce or legal separation.

4. Facilities

Several countries require that voluntary sterilization operations be performed in hospitals managed or supervised by the government. Examples are Czechoslovakia, Denmark, Singapore and a few states in the United States.

5. Sex Discrimination

The laws of a few countries authorize voluntary sterilization for one of the sexes, but not for the other. For example, a 1941 statute of Panama allows voluntary sterilization to be performed on women only, in contradistinction to an earlier law which permitted voluntary sterilization for persons of both sexes.[9]

6. Minimum Number of Living Children

Some countries' laws require that before an applicant can be given authorization for voluntary sterilization, evidence must be shown that he or she

---

6. Law No. 234 of 3 June 1967.
7. *See* note 5 *supra*, § 5 (2).
8. Law No. 156 of 13 July 1948, § 8, para. 1. Full text of the law, as amended, appears in English in 16 INT'L DIGEST OF HEALTH LEGISLATION, 690 (1965).
9. Law No. 48 of 13 May 1941.

already has a certain number of living children—5 for Panama, 4 (or 3 if the woman concerned is over 35 years of age) in Czechoslovakia, 3 in India, and 1 in Singapore.[10]

7. Social and Economic Hardship

While a large number of children may indicate the presence of socio-economic hardship, other factors may also contribute to such hardship. Hence, the laws of some countries provide explicitly for socio-economic hardship to be a ground for authorizing voluntary sterilization, e.g., the laws of Denmark[11] and Sweden.

8. Authorization by an Official Board

The laws of several countries require the establishment of an official board to receive, review and decide on applications for voluntary sterilization, whether in all or selected (e.g., if the applicant is under age) cases. There is no consensus, however, with respect to the size or professional composition of the board, or for the method for reaching a decision (by majority or unanimity rule).

B. *Laws Prohibiting Voluntary Sterilization*

A number of countries prohibit voluntary sterilization under any circumstance. Section 471 of the Turkish Criminal Code of March, 1926, for example, provides:

> Whoever, by his acts, causes a man or woman to become sterile, and any person giving consent to the performance of such acts on himself, shall be punished by imprisonment for six months to two years and by a heavy fine of 100 to 500 liras.

It may be noted that although sterilization on eugenic and preventive medical grounds was allowed by decision No. 6/8305 of 11 June 1967 of the Turkish Council of Ministers, no mention was made regarding voluntary sterilization on family planning grounds—this despite the fact that the decision was issued pursuant to Sections 3 and 4 of Law No. 557 of 1 April 1965 concerning family planning.

Section 552 of the Italian Penal Code of 19 October 1930 provides:

> Whoever performs acts on persons of either sex, with their consent, intended to render them incapable of procreating, will be punished by imprisonment from six months to two years and with a fine from eight to forty thousand lira.

---

10. Stepan and Kellogg, *supra* note 3, at 8.
11. Note 6 *supra*, § 4, para. 2 (23).

Whoever gives consent to those acts being performed on himself shall suffer the same punishment.

In South Vietnam, Section 8 of Law No. 12 of 22 May 1962 concerning the protection of morality states:

> It is forbidden to conduct propaganda for, or to encourage . . . the unnatural prevention of pregnancy[12] . . . except where the doctor decides otherwise on the basis of clear evidence that the life of the woman will be endangered by delivery.
> If found in violation of this article, the main defendant and his accomplices will be subject to a fine from 10,000 to 1,000,000 piastres, or to a confinement of from 1 month to 5 years, or both of these two penalties. As to the crime of pregnancy prevention only one of these penalties is applied.

In a few jurisdictions, only the persons performing the sterilization operations are punishable. Section 360 of the Penal Code of Nicaragua is an example of this and provides:

> The following shall be punishable for grave bodily injury: 1) whoever, without causing death, maliciously (*maliciosamente*) castrates or renders the reproductive organs (*organos generadores*) of another person useless, without his consent; 2) whoever commits the same offense against an adult person with his consent.

A few Latin American laws reduce the severity of the punishment for the person performing the sterilization operation if the operation takes place with the consent of the person operated upon, *e.g.*, the laws of Guatemala and Nicaragua. Since voluntary sterilization is, by definition, performed always with the consent of the person, it thus falls under the lesser degree of crime.

C.   *Lacuna in Statutory Laws*

Confusion arises in a great many countries and states where statutes do not specifically prohibit or permit voluntary sterilization. In some countries it is thought that a sterilization operation may be considered a criminal offense as a form of intentional infliction of "grievous bodily harm," "assault," or "mayhem,"[13] (as expressed in Common Law jurisdictions), or of *"coups et blessures volontaires"* (intentional wounds and injuries), etc.

However, in many countries, the consent of the "victim" exculpates the person inflicting any "injury." Thus, Article 24 of the Penal Code of South Korea provides:

---

12.   Apparently by contraception or voluntary sterilization.
13.   Mayhem was defined at common law as deliberately inflicting injury on oneself or another in such a manner as to interfere with that person's service to the king.

Conduct which infringes a legal interest with the consent of someone who is authorized to dispose of such interest shall not be
punishable, except as otherwise provided by law.

Likewise, Section 44 of the Uraguayan Penal Code of 1 July 1934 with
the heading of "Consent to Injuries" provides:

Causing bodily injury with the consent of the injured (paciente) is
not punishable, except where the object is to elude compliance with
the law, or to inflict damage to a third person.

Similar provisions are found in the penal codes of Ethiopia and Greece,
as well as those of India, Pakistan, and Sri Lanka.

In certain African countries with an English Common Law background,
e.g., Ghana, Nigeria, Tanzania and Zambia, voluntary sterilization may be
subsumed under "surgical operation" with the result that the intended benefit to the patient in good faith excludes criminal liability for the surgeon.[14]

On the other hand, in France, Belgium and some other Civil Law countries, consent of the "victim" of "grave bodily injury" does not exculpate the
surgeon in performing sterilization operations. In the celebrated *"Bordeaux
sterilisateurs"* case of 1937, the last known case found in these countries, a
group of people were accused of advocating and practicing voluntary sterilization on ideological grounds. Although the accused were not authorized
physicians, and could have been punished on that ground, the decision was
based rather on the principle that the consent of the sterilized persons was
irrelevant to the criminal responsibility of the accused, pursuant to the doctrine that the patients "could not authorize anybody to violate, on their
persons, the rules governing the public order (*l'ordre public*)."[15]

In Austria, before 1974, non-therapeutic sterilization was considered a
crime in spite of consent.

The degree of confusion which exists in many countries is indicated by
the fact that the laws ostensibly applicable to sterilization are the criminal
laws on assault and serious bodily injury which equate the benign work of a
skilled physician on a willing patient under clinical conditions with a brutal
criminal assault.

It should be noted, however, that whether voluntary sterilization is prohibited *per se* or by analogy to infliction of "grievous bodily harm," actual
prosecution or conviction of doctors or patients is rare (*e.g.*, the last known
case in France occurred in 1937, that in Austria in 1934, and no cases can be
recalled in such countries as Chile, Indonesia, Sweden, and Colombia).[16]

---

14. Criminal Code of Ghana, Act No. 29 of 1960, § 42 (c); Penal Code of Tanzania of
1945, § 230; Laws of Republic of Zambia, Penal Code, Ch. 6, § 210 (1965).
15. La Cour de Cassation (Crim.), 1 July 1937, *Gaz. Pal.*, 28 Sept. 1937, *Recueil Sirey*;
1938-1-193.
16. Stepan and Kellogg, *supra* note 3, at 18-19.

In still another group of countries, lack of specific provision in criminal codes concerning the legality or illegality of voluntary sterilization brings forth the application of the doctrine, *Nullum crimen, nulla poena sine lege.* Pursuant to this criminal law principle which underlies virtually all the legal systems of the world, an act is considered "criminal" only if so specified in a criminal code, and therefore voluntary sterilization is generally considered legal in these countries whose laws do not expressly forbid it. For example, Article 172 of the Penal Code of Iran of 1928 provides:

> He who intentionally inflicts an injury or blow to another which causes cutting, breaking, damaging, or disfunctioning of a limb, or ends in permanent sickness or loss of one of the senses, shall be subject to 2-10 years of solitary confinement . . .

Since voluntary sterilization does not "squarely fit" the above statute, it is permitted in Iran.

Article 262 of the Revised Penal Code of the Philippines states:

> *Mutilation*—The penalty of *reclusion temporal* to *reclusion perpetua* shall be imposed upon any person who shall intentionally mutilate another by depriving him, either totally or partially, of some essential organ for reproduction.

In his opinion rendered 17 September 1973, Secretary of Justice Vicente Abad Santos interpreted this Article 262 to permit tubal ligation and vasectomy on the grounds, among others, that these methods "do not involve looping or clipping off of the organs of reproduction of both sexes," as in the case of castration, but "are effected by the closing of a pair of small tubes in either the man or the woman so that the sperm and ovum cannot meet." Accordingly, they should not be regarded as "mutilation within the contemplation of Article 262."

On the whole, there is a general trend toward liberalizing the laws and toward permitting voluntary sterilization. Thus, President Bourguiba of Tunisia, in a speech on the eve of the *"Mouled,"* in April 1973, stated that there are no Moslem objections to sterilization, in contradistinction to castration, and the operation is occurring frequently in Lebanon. Denmark is reportedly considering liberalizing its law and the American Bar Association voted in 1973 to recommend to all the states that they eliminate whatever present restrictions they may have.[17]

II. Proposals for Legislative Reform

In view of the uncertainty surrounding the legal status of voluntary sterilization in many countries, the Association for Voluntary Sterilization

---

17. As pointed out in the Introduction few states of the United States impose any restriction on voluntary sterilization.

convened a Second International Conference on Voluntary Sterilization on 25 February-1 March 1973 in Geneva. An important part of the Conference was the conducting of a legal workshop under the chairmanship of Mme. Anne-Marie Dourlen-Rollier of France. This author acted as the Rapporteur. The workshop recommended the adoption of the legislative proposal which emerged as the result of its deliberations. The proposal was also transmitted to the appropriate officials of several nations (including the United States) and to the World Health Organization. It reads:

PREAMBLE

In 1968, the Proclamation of Teheran was adopted by the International Conference on Human Rights. Paragraph 16 provides that:
. . . Parents have a basic human right to determine freely and responsibly the number and spacing of their children.
Any law which imposed compulsory sterilization on any individual is inconsistent with the principles of the Teheran Proclamation.

The following provisions of law are recommended to effectuate those principles and provide for freedom of choice in the matter of voluntary infertility.

I. *Generally applicable*

Every individual of either sex has the right to obtain a procedure that will establish voluntary permanent or temporary infertility, and the government has an obligation to make available appropriate service, subject to the following:

1) The individual is over the age of local consent and furnishes evidence of his or her voluntary consent;
2) The individual is fully informed by an appropriate person of the immediate and possible and probable long term consequences of the procedure, and informed of the various methods of family planning. When appropriate the individual shall also be encouraged to consider carefully, over an interval of time, the consequences of the different courses of action available.
3) If an individual is a member of a particular ethnic, religious or philosophical group, he or she, shall be offered the option of receiving such information, as set out in 2) above jointly from the person giving the information and a representative of the group concerned, unless the person giving the information belongs to that group.

II. *Applicable to incompetents*

The following shall apply with respect to any person who does not have legal capacity to consent: if the parents or guardian of such a person, and a physician have decided that temporary measures will be ineffective, they may apply for a procedure to render that person permanently infertile to a Board, duly appointed by the appropriate authority, which may after full consideration, grant their application . . .

The Board shall consist of at least 5 persons, both lay and professional of both sexes, which shall act by a vote.

The Board shall also include a person or persons, representative of the particular ethnic, religious or philosophical group of which the person who is the subject of the application is a member.

III. *Performance by individuals*

Nothing in these provisions of law shall compel any individual to participate in a voluntary infertility procedure, but any individual declining to participate shall have the obligation to inform the individual requesting the procedure, of another person or facility which offers such procedures. However, every government supported facility shall be obliged to make such procedures available.

IV. *No effect on marriage and divorce laws*

Nothing in these provisions of law shall be interpreted to modify the laws on marriage and divorce.

V. *No liability for non-negligent voluntary infertility procedure*

No physician or other person or health facility shall be held civilly or criminally liable for proceeding in accordance with the foregoing provisions.

Clearly there are other aspects of voluntary sterilization which may well be included along with the Workshop recommendations. To mention only a few:

(1) A person undergoing a voluntary sterilization operation should always be told—and should acknowledge in writing that he or she has been told—that a cessation of fertility will probably occur but is not guaranteed.

(2) To the extent that there are any adverse consequences which may follow from a voluntary sterilization operation, the patient should be told in advance what these are—and this advice should also be reflected in a writing signed by the patient which will along with the written statement referred to in 1 above establish that the patient did in fact give an "informed consent."

(3) Although sterilization is sometimes reversible, no person should seek the procedure except on the assumption that it will be irreversible.

(4) A voluntary sterilization should not be performed on any patient unless that patient is fully competent to give a legal consent *and* has no doubts that he wishes to be rendered incapable of future procreation.

(5) Perhaps the most difficult questions to grapple with in connection with voluntary sterilization are those which are addressed to the competency of the patient to give a legally binding informed consent. It is in this context that problems occur as to whether a given sterilization procedure was in fact truly "voluntary." Actually, this type of issue is implicit with reference to all medical and surgical procedures. However, other medical and surgical procedures are less likely to be used against defenseless minority groups which may fall victim to persons or groups which advocate their "voluntary" sterilization on grounds which may reflect more the advocate's social and economic concerns than they do the best interests of the patient.

To avoid this, the personnel doing sterilization operations must be especially vigilant to assure that the procedure is not performed unless there is *no doubt* concerning the person's legal competence and the fact that he or she really wants to be sterilized. Exactly how this can be accomplished seems to me not yet to have been adequately faced or thought through by any of the disciplines involved, *i.e.*, the obstetrician-gynecologists, the urologists, the psychiatrists, the social workers or, indeed, the lawyers and legislators. This Symposium could make a major contribution and one that is badly needed in this field if it at least considered the problem and began to develop criteria. Actually, an antecedent determination of competence to consent to a voluntary sterilization is not different in kind from determinations with respect to other surgical procedures. It should be possible by submitting the question to all the professional groups involved (including groups which are especially sensitive to this issue) to begin to formulate ways of reaching criteria as to whether a patient does have the legal capacity to consent. If there is such capacity, the next question, namely whether the patient is sufficiently "informed," should be relatively easy to resolve. Where such capacity does not exist either the more or less extreme position reflected in the attached guidelines can be adopted or a less prohibitive course followed which would permit sterilization of incompetents by fully protecting the incompetent such as is done by the draft proposal set forth above—to which perhaps should be added a requirement of court approval.

In this connection, it has additionally been suggested that possibly all facilities and programs which make voluntary sterilization available should be required to have at least one expert "patient advocate" on their staffs whose job it would be to make certain that the person requesting the sterilization is competent and really understands and wants it.

III. Conclusion

The word "sterilization," in English at least, has unfortunate connotations and too often calls to mind the inhuman genocidal practices of the German Nazis. It has been suggested that the technique be referred to instead as "voluntary infertility" which seems to me far preferable. In any event, whatever it is called, voluntary sterilization is a contraceptive method (often referred to as "surgical birth control") which should be available to all who understand and really want it and which in no circumstances should be used where there is any doubt whatever as to comprehension or freedom of choice of the person requesting it. It should always be borne in mind that refusing this method to someone who understands and wants it is a violation of that person's human rights as is, of course, the coerced application of the method to one who either doesn't understand it or doesn't positively and without doubt want it. Freedom of choice as to voluntary sterilization is part of the "basic human right to determine freely and responsibly the number and spacing of their children" as proclaimed at Teheran by the International Conference on Human Rights in 1968.

APPENDIX   A

Title 42—Public Health

CHAPTER I—PUBLIC HEALTH SERVICE, DEPARTMENT OF HEALTH, EDUCATION, AND WELFARE

SUBCHAPTER D—GRANTS

PART 50—POLICIES OF GENERAL APPLICABILITY

Restrictions Applicable to Sterilization Procedures in Federally Assisted Family Planning Projects

On February 6, 1974, the Department adopted regulations on sterilization restrictions in Federally funded programs and projects (39 FR 4730, 4733). Thereafter the effective date of the regulations was delayed to permit resolution by the United States District Court for the District of Columbia of legal issues raised in Relf v. Weinberger, Civil Action No. 1557-73 and in National Welfare Rights Organization v. Weinberger, Civil Action No. 74-243 (39 FR 5315, 9178).

On March 15, 1974, the United States District Court entered its judgment and order in the two lawsuits referred to above, declaring that the family planning sections of the Public Health Service Act (42 U.S.C. 300 et seq., 708(a)(3)) and of the Social Security Act (42 U.S.C. 602(a)(15), 1396d(a)(4)(C)) do not authorize the provision of Federal funds for the sterilization of any person who (1) has been judicially declared mentally incompetent, or (2) is in fact legally incompetent under applicable State laws to give informed and binding consent to the performance of such an operation because of age or mental capacity. The court ordered that the Department's regulations be amended to conform with the directive just described and that they further be amended to state that Federal funds will not be provided under the aforesaid family planning sections for the sterilization of a legally competent person without requiring that such person be advised that no benefits provided by programs or projects receiving Federal funds may be withdrawn or withheld by reason of his or her decision not to be sterilized and without requiring that such advice also appear prominently at the top of the consent document mentioned in such regulations.

On March 20, 1974, to permit the Department to consider what action must be taken to amend its regulations and other matters, a notice was published delaying the effective date of the regulations (39 FR 10431) and continuing in effect the previous notice of the Department with respect to sterilization guidelines (38 FR 20930).

This previous notice provided that pending the effective date of the final regulations Federal financial participation should be withheld from any sterilization procedure performed on an individual who is under the age of 21 or who is himself legally incapable of consenting to the sterilization.

The purpose of this document is to adopt regulations in accordance with the Court Order with respect to persons legally capable of consenting to a sterilization while continuing in effect the moratorium set forth in the previous notice of the Department with respect to sterilization of individuals under the age of 21 or legally incapable of consenting to the sterilization. The continuance of the moratorium, together with the adoption of these regulations, brings the Department into compliance with the Order of the District Court while the Department considers its options, including appeal of that portion of the Court Order relating to persons legally incapable of consenting to a sterilization.

The regulations published at 39 FR 4730 and 4733 whose effective date was delayed by notice published at 39 FR 10431 are hereby replaced by the regulations contained herein. Accordingly, the above referred to moratorium is continued until further notice published in the FEDERAL REGISTER and a new Subpart B is added to Part 50, as set forth below, effective on April 18, 1974, applicable to existing programs and projects as well as to programs or projects approved for Federal support on or after that date.

Dated: April 16, 1974.

CASPAR W. WEINBERGER,
Secretary.

Subpart B—Sterilization of Persons in Federally
Assisted Family Planning Projects

Sec.
50.201 Applicability.
50.202 Definitions.
50.203 Restrictions on sterilization.
50.204 Reports.

AUTHORITY: Sec. 215, 58 Stat. 690, as amended (42 U.S.C. 216).

§ 50.201 Applicability.

The provisions of this subpart are applicable to programs or projects for health services which are supported in whole or in part by Federal financial assistance, whether by grant or contract, administered by the Public Health Service.

§ 50.202 Definitions.

(a) "Public Health Service" means the Health Services Administration, Health Resources Administration, National Institutes of Health, Center for Disease Control, Alcohol, Drug Abuse and Mental Health Administration, Food and Drug Administration and all of their constituent agencies.

(b) "Nontherapeutic sterilization" means any procedure or operation, the purpose of which is to render an individual permanently incapable of reproducing and which is not either (1) a necessary part of the treatment of an existing illness or injury, or (2) medically indicated as an accompaniment of an operation on the female genitourinary tract. For purposes of this paragraph mental incapacity is not considered an illness or injury.

(c) "Secretary" means the Secretary of Health, Education, and Welfare and any other officer or employee of the Department of Health, Education, and Welfare to whom the authority involved has been delegated.

(d) "Informed consent" means the voluntary, knowing assent from the individual on whom any sterilization is to be performed after he has been given (as evidenced by a document executed by such individual):

(1) A fair explanation of the procedures to be followed;

(2) A description of the attendant discomforts and risks;

(3) A description of the benefits to be expected;

(4) An explanation concerning appropriate alternative methods of family planning and the effect and impact of the proposed sterilization including the fact that it must be considered to be an irreversible procedure;

(5) An offer to answer any inquiries concerning the procedures; and

(6) An instruction that the individual is free to withhold or withdraw his or her consent to the procedure at any time prior to the sterilization without prejudicing his or her future care and without loss of other project or program benefits to which the patient might otherwise be entitled.

(7) The documentation referred to in this section shall be provided by one of the following methods:

(i) Provision of a written consent document detailing all of the basic elements of informed consent (paragraphs (d)(1) through (d)(6) of this section).

(ii) Provision of a short form written consent document indicating that the basic elements of informed consent have been presented orally to the patient. The short form document must be supplemented by a written summary of the oral presentation. The short form document must be signed by the patient and by an auditor-witness to the oral presentation. The written summary shall be signed by the person obtaining the consent and by the auditor-witness. The auditor-witness shall be designated by the patient.

(iii) Each consent document shall display the following legend printed prominently at the top:

NOTICE: Your decision at any time not to be sterilized will not result in the withdrawal or withholding of any benefits provided by programs or projects.

§ 50.203 General Policies.

(a) In addition to any other requirement of this subpart, programs or projects to which this subpart applies shall not perform nor arrange for the performance of any non-emergency sterilization unless: (1) Such sterilization is performed pursuant to a voluntary request for such services made by the person on whom the sterilization is to be performed; and (2) such person is advised at the outset and prior to the solicitation or receipt of his or her consent to such sterilization, that no benefits provided by programs or projects may be withdrawn or withheld by reason of his or her decision not to be sterilized.

(b) A program or project to which this subpart applies shall not perform nor arrange for the performance of any non-emergency sterilization unless such program or project has obtained legally effective informed consent from the individual on whom the sterilization is to be performed.

(c) Programs or projects to which this subpart applies shall not perform nor arrange for the performance of a non-therapeutic sterilization sooner than 72 hours following the giving of informed consent.

§ 50.204 Reports.

In addition to such other reports specifically required by the Secretary, the program or project shall report to the Secretary at least annually, the number and nature of the sterilizations subject to the procedures set forth in this subpart, and such other relevant information regarding such procedures as the Secretary may request.

[FR Doc. 74-9078 Filed 4-17-74; 10:23 am]

Report of Workshop on Voluntary Sterilization

The question of national laws bearing upon voluntary sterilization was discussed on the basis of a background paper written by Mrs. Harriet F. Pilpel, Counsel to the Planned Parenthood Federation of the United States. Mrs. Pilpel's paper reviews the national laws of many countries and concludes that the law regarding voluntary sterilization is unclear in most countries and needs clarification.

Following a brief discussion of the contexts within which involuntary sterilization has been resorted to in some countries, and of the grave issues that would be raised by any suggestion that involuntary sterilization be utilized as part of national efforts to limit population growth, the workshop decided to confine its attention to the use of voluntary sterilization as a contraceptive method in family planning.

Voluntary sterilization for contraceptive purposes was seen to raise a number of basic questions that must be dealt with by Governments in adopting or revising national laws on the subject. These include the question of informed consent, including such issues as inducements or incentives, minimum age for sterilization, adequate counselling and a waiting period; the question of requiring the consent of the spouse; and the question of procedures and standards governing sterilization, including the scope of the liability of persons performing the sterilization.

The workshop devoted special attention to the question of the need for the spouse's consent and the effect of voluntary sterilization upon the marriage relationship in differing social and cultural conditions. Some participants considered that a requirement that the spousal consent to the sterilization amounted to a veto that would keep one spouse, most often the woman, in bondage to the other. It was suggested that the proper remedy in such cases would be to dissolve the marriage, rather than to prevent the desired sterilization. Other participants expressed the view that divorce was not the answer since in many societies divorce is not freely available, and even where available, divorce would destroy the family and leave the woman and children without adequate support. Furthermore, some participants viewed the family planning right as the joint right of both spouses to determine the number and spacing of their children; as such the joint right should not be destroyed by the unilateral decision of one spouse to become sterilized.

Mindful of the sharply differing views and the diversity of national cultures and traditions bearing on the question, the workshop drew no conclusion as to the need for the spouse's consent. A consensus in the workshop meeting supported the recommendation that, having regard to legal and cultural traditions and mores, Governments should adopt such legislation as may be required to make voluntary sterilization available for contraceptive purposes.

On the question of informed consent, the workshop endorsed a requirement of full freedom of choice, based upon legally competent and fully informed consent. Such consent could not, in the view of some participants, be guaranteed by a simple minimum age requirement. In addition, several participants questioned whether cash inducements to sterilization vitiated the voluntary nature of the consent, especially in the case of the poor. In view of the separate treatment given at the Symposium to the subject of incentives and disincentives, however, the question of the relationship between incentives and free consent was not pursued in drafting the workshop's recommendation on voluntary sterilization.

On the question of medical procedures and requirements, there was agreement that national sterilization laws must ensure conformity to proper medical practices, including the licensing of personnel. It was further agreed that, except in cases of negligence, Governments should ensure that neither criminal nor civil penalties or liabilities are imposed upon persons performing voluntary sterilizations for contraceptive purposes. The latter recommendation had general support as a necessary measure to clarify the position of the medical personnel involved in voluntary sterilizations, as it was felt to be a pressing problem in countries that had not sought to regulate voluntary sterilization by comprehensive legislation. Some participants raised broader questions, however, suggesting a need for Governments to consider assuming responsibility for longer range problems that might befall persons who had become sterilized, such as the need to provide for their old age. These questions were considered to fall more appropriately within the general subject of providing adequate social services in connection with national population programs, dealt with elsewhere at the Symposium, and therefore not included in the recommendation on voluntary sterilization.

Legal Problems Related to Abortion and Menstrual Regulation

By
Anne-Marie Dourlen-Rollier*

Abortion has always been used as an *a posteriori* method of birth control which makes it possible to terminate an unwanted pregnancy. It has become a sociological phenomenon which has spread over the entire world. Societies differ, however, in their attitudes toward this problem, in their frankness in recognizing it and in their understanding for those women who choose to terminate a pregnancy.

During recent years, the legal problems with regard to abortion have become much greater in scope, as much because of a change in attitudes as because of scientific and technical progress. The development of modern methods of regulating fertility has been so great that humanity is on the verge of acquiring the complete mastery over its reproductive function. These new discoveries present legal problems which could not previously have been envisaged, but which now must be resolved. Hence, the necessity to consider first the present situation before we contemplate the future.

I. The Present Situation Relating to Abortion

The principal religions of the world and the majority of societies accept the practice of contraception, but reference to abortion is often greeted with disapproval and in some cases with active opposition. Thus, under the laws in many countries, abortion is considered a crime—either a felony or a misdemeanor—and is permitted only in exceptional cases such as where the life of the mother is threatened by the pregnancy. A few countries have legislation which forbids abortion in all circumstances. In countries where legal abortion is very rare, the resulting resort to clandestine and illegal

---

* Secretary-General, Association Nationale pour l'Etude de l'Avortement (France).

procedures has assumed the proportions of a genuine scourge. For example, in Egypt it is estimated that there is one abortion for every two live births. In Turkey, it was estimated that during the 1960s there were about 500,000 abortions performed each year and that 10,000 deaths resulted from botched abortions. In France, where the official figure released by the National Institute of Demographic Studies for illegal abortions is between 250,000 and 300,000 a year, the majority of medical practitioners estimate the number of clandestine abortions at between 500,000 and 800,000 abortions. In Belgium, the minimum estimate is that 30,000 abortions are done each year while the number of births is in the neighborhood of 130,000.[1] Latin American specialists believe that at least 50 per cent of all pregnancies are terminated by illegal abortion and that there are four times as many abortion-related deaths among young women as there are in countries where abortion is legal.[2] A recent study carried out in the United States shows that 10 per cent of the girls between 13 and 19 have been pregnant at least once.[3]

A. The Evil and Uselessness of Repressing Abortions

If there is one fact that comes to light as a result of studies of the world-wide practice of illegal abortion, it is that the fear of punishment does not check resort to abortion. Every year millions of women defy the laws of their countries by having secret abortions and bearing humiliation at the risk of compromising both their health and their lives. Both the police and the judiciary are increasingly hesitant to apply repressive laws and fewer convictions are obtained against abortionists and the women who have had themselves aborted. Thus, there arises an obvious dichotomy between the actual situation and what the law allows or prohibits.

According to Casamayor:

When the daily practice within a country becomes remote from the law applicable to that practice, a major danger is created for the stability and for the general mental health of the society.

Prohibitions which are no longer regarded by the society as the expression of a relevant religious, moral or economic reality usually arrive at a point where they are held in disrepute. The result is that such prohibitions are no longer tolerated, either by the population or by those who are responsible for their application. At that moment the repressive practice becomes meaningless.

1. N. Y. Times, Jan. 25, 1973, at 5, col. 4.
2. Centro Nacional de Familia, 2 ESTUDIO SOBRE ABORTO INDUCIDO, No. 5, at 2, Table 1 (La Paz 1970).
3. Sorensen and Hendin, *Adolescent Sexuality in Contemporary America; A Survey of Teenage Attitudes and Practices*, Boston Globe, Feb. 18, 1973, at 4-9 (Magazine).

Public opinion gladly accepts the practice of levying punishments, even heavy punishments, against violations of many criminal laws. At times such punishments are even deemed inadequate because there is a genuine need for this type of legislation. In contrast, however, the repression of abortion appears to have become anachronistic and even useless, especially insofar as it affects the women who have chosen to have abortions.[4] As a result, the population cultivates the habit of ignoring the law and adopts illegal practices to circumvent the prohibitions. In a sense, one can say that the non-application of severe criminal legislation, which does not accord with the views of the majority, corrupts that society.

The ineffectiveness of repression also gives rise to a feeling of inequality, since the unhappy women who are brought before the courts are fully aware that women in a higher income bracket are able to escape the trauma of having a secret abortion and being subject to all the penal sanctions because the latter can travel to one of the many countries where laws are more liberal to secure an abortion. In view of this, an argument can be made that the repressive laws on abortion discriminate in favor of one class to the detriment of others and create an unacceptable form of social inequality. Under present conditions, the hypocrisy connected with clandestine abortion is generally repudiated, and a vigorous reform movement is underway to eliminate punitive attitudes toward the interruption of pregnancy.

B. *Rights of the Fetus Versus Rights of the Woman*

These reform efforts pose the question: Would it not be better to face the practice of abortion squarely and recognize that women have the right to interrupt their pregnancies if they see no other way to prevent an undesired birth? The acceptance of this right is in conflict with the traditional position under which man and society have an absolute obligation to respect the life of the embryo. This view is derived in part from conventional wisdom under which the embryo is considered as a human being from the moment of conception. By this, the interruption of the process of gestation at any point in time is regarded as being tantamount to murder, and thus should be forbidden by law. This position, which is that of the Catholic Church, has had a noticeable influence on abortion legislation in many countries.

This perception is, however, of relatively recent origin. From the time of St. Thomas Aquinas until the end of the nineteenth century, the religionists did not consider abortion to be murder until the soul had "animated" the body—sometime during the fourth or fifth month of pregnancy. It was only in 1869 that Pope Pius IX suppressed the distinction between abortion

---

4. In recognition of this fact, President Giscard d'Estaing has recently instructed prosecutors not to prosecute women who have "had themselves aborted in a way contrary to the French law of 1920." Boston Globe, July 26, 1974, at 31, col. 5.

during the first phase of embryo development and that which takes place later. In English law the same evolution took place. In 1861, British legislation making the interruption of pregnancy at any time from the moment of conception a crime was first promulgated.[5]

All religions are not so Draconian in their views. The traditional tenets of Islam only forbid abortion after the animation of the fetus. As far as Judaism is concerned, it is not believed that the embryo is a human being independent of its mother until it is on the point of birth, at which time it is called "nefesh," or a living soul.

The recently developed Catholic doctrine, which calls for the complete prohibition of abortion from the moment of conception, is being contested by increasing numbers of theologians, who believe that it is possible to carry out interruptions of pregnancy when the circumstances of the birth make the new life a calamity rather than a blessing.

Eminent scientists are now speaking out against the confusion between abortion and infanticide. They argue that man is a sociological concept before he becomes a biological concept. Therefore, a pregnant woman should not become the prisoner of an embryo which has no sociological meaning for her since she has not accepted it. The logical conclusion is that she should be able to choose whether or not to bear a child.

Moreover, due to the new scientific discoveries which permit contraception on a non-empirical basis, for the first time in history, procreation and sexuality are not necessarily linked. This basic change has brought about a new attitude toward the transmission of life from generation to generation. Fertility was traditionally considered to be the natural destiny of woman, who had no sure way to escape it except through continence. Nowadays, when dissociation between sex life and the function of reproduction is possible, women who still feel the need for motherhood as profoundly as their grandmothers did, have a chance to regard a birth as a matter of choice and to limit the transmission of life to those children who are desired. Better able to be aware of their responsibilities, the majority of women wish to master their own destiny and believe that it is up to them and their partners to make the decisions about bringing a child into the world. It is not the right of society to impose the birth of a child upon them against their will.

Thus, the principle of personal responsibility has been substituted, or is in the process of being substituted, for the notion of leaving matters to chance. It is significant that the United States Supreme Court, as the basis for its famous decision of January 22, 1973, took into consideration "the right of privacy."[6] According to the court's opinion, the decision of the woman to continue or discontinue her pregnancy is an integral part of that right.

The traditional conflict between the rights and interests of society con-

5. Offences Against the Person Act, 24 and 25 Vic., c. 100, 58, at 438 (1861).
6. Roe v. Wade, 410 U.S. 113 (1973).

cerned with the protection of the development of the fetus, on one hand, and those of the woman and possibly of her family, hitherto neglected, on the other, is being resolved in a number of countries in favor of the latter. The purely ethical criterion concerning early abortion is becoming blurred. In its place a new criterion is being substituted: that of knowing whether a woman is qualified or unqualified to bring up a child, that is, whether she can "give it life" instead of merely "letting it live."

While attempting to solve the dilemma of competing rights, certain questions surface. If it is felt that society has the duty of protecting the rights of the embryo, must it not equally be admitted that society must also help the pregnant woman and her family in difficulty? If the interruption of pregnancy is the only issue, should not society also recognize the duty of having the operation carried out under conditions which will enhance the psychological and physical health of the woman, rather than ruining it by exposing her to the risks of dangerous, traumatic and clandestine procedures?

C. The Freedom of Choice

The freedom of men and women to control their fertility has been recognized as a fundamental right by the international community since the adoption of the Teheran Proclamation in 1968. The following year the United Nations General Assembly gave its endorsement to the precepts of the Proclamation relating to this freedom by stating that parents have the exclusive right "to determine freely and responsibly the number and spacing of their children."[7] It also was stipulated that the right of family planning includes not only information, but equally the accessibility to the means necessary to put the right into effect. A number of countries now recognize this possibility of choice in the field of procreation, since laws are rare which totally forbid information on modern methods of contraception.[8] However, three factors may interfere with the exercise of this new liberty. These are:

— the still-frequent ignorance of scientific contraception among girls and women;
— the medical contraindications and psychological resistance toward use of these methods; and
— the failure of the method used.

A recent study carried out in the United States on the sexual experience of unmarried adolescents showed that less than 20 per cent of the sexually

7. Declaration on Social Progress and Development, General Assembly Res. 2542, art. 22(b), 24 GAOR, Supp. 30 at 49-50, Doc. No. A/7630 (1969).
8. See generally, Stepan and Kellogg, The World's Laws on Contraceptives, Law and Population Monograph Series No. 17 (1974).

active girls between the ages of 15 and 19 stated that they had used contraceptive methods.[9] The *Rapport sur le Comportement Sexuel des Français*[10]
tells us that two-thirds of the people interviewed stated that they lacked
access to any contraceptive method at the time of their first sexual relationship. It also revealed that even though 94 per cent had heard of the pill, only
one-half of them considered it to be either very effective or effective
enough. Should we not, therefore, agree with Dr. Christopher Tietze "that
the most rational way of controlling fertility is to use a good contraceptive
method, even if it is not 100 per cent effective, and, when pregnancies result
from a failure of the method, to interrupt them with the best possible
conditions—that is, in the hospital?"

D. *Progress in Techniques of Interruption of Pregnancy*

Religious difficulties have not been the only reasons for the promulgation of restrictive laws and for interference with the recognition of the right
of a woman to decide upon the number and spacing of her births. In fact, at
the time when these laws were put into effect in the nineteenth century, the
interruption of pregnancy, even when accomplished by a doctor, was a high
risk medical procedure. Until the early 1960s, the techniques of abortion
used in most hospitals were fifty years old. The aspiration method which was
developed in China was first used on a mass scale in Europe by the socialist
countries. It is now used in all countries where abortion is legal and represents considerable progress both from the point of view of safety and effectiveness. For late abortions, the intra-amniotic injection, if used with great
care, permits the operation to take place under conditions which produce a
very low number of accidents and few minor complications.

In countries where abortion is legal and carried out in accordance with
these new methods, the number of post-abortive deaths is extremely low. In
Hungary and Czechoslovakia, the figure between 1957 and 1967 was 2.8 per
100,000 abortions. During the first three months of legalized abortion in
New York State, the figure was two per 100,000 abortions (as contrasted
with 20 per 100,000 for pregnancies carried to term). On the other hand, in
places where clandestine abortion is frequent because of restrictive laws, the
average mortality rate is 50 to 100 per 100,000 illegal operations. Thus,
legislation on abortion has become a crucial issue in public health.

---

9. Study made by John and Melvin Zelnick of John Hopkins University, Department of
Population, Hygiene and Public Health sampling 4,240 unmarried people of those ages as
reported in *Contraception and Pregnancy: Experience of Young Unmarried Women in the United
States*, 5 FAMILY PLANNING PERSPECTIVES, No. 1, at 21-35 (1973).
10. P. SIMON, A.M. DOURLEN ROLLIER, J. GONDONNEAU AND L. MIROMER, RAPPORT
SUR LE COMPORTEMENT SEXUEL DES FRANCAIS (Paris: Editions Julliard 1973).

II. CONSEQUENCES OF THE DEVELOPMENT OF CONTEMPORARY ABORTION ATTITUDES AND TECHNIQUES

A. *Repressive Laws and Non-Enforcement*

Though rather restrictive laws on abortion exist in the Philippines, Thailand and in parts of the Middle East, there are very few prosecutions against either the aborter or the woman. In Europe, the situation is the same, but the enforcement of the law varies depending on the country and the circumstances. In the Netherlands, although a very strict law is in force, a factual situation has arisen which seems to be irreversible. In fact, specialized clinics have been functioning since 1970 under the sponsorship of family planning associations. Numerous Dutch women, and women from nearby countries, have made use of the services of these eleven establishments. In Belgium, although the prosecutions are very rare, in January 1973, Dr. Willy Peers was arrested because he interrupted the pregnancy of a young mentally defective woman who had been raped by her father. In fact, Dr. Peers, a gynecologist from Namur and professor at the Free University of Brussels, made no further effort to hide the fact that he was carrying out abortions free, under hospital conditions, where his conscience required that he offer help due to situations of distress and injustice. The imprisonment of this doctor lasted almost a month and it gave rise to an enormous amount of emotion both in Belgium and in neighboring countries. In Italy, there are about 150 to 200 prosecutions each year.

In France, over the past ten years prosecutions have averaged about 500 a year. The number is low in comparison with the number of secret abortions, but despite the acquittal of the young Marie-Claire by the tribunal of Bobigny in November 1972, prosecutions are continuing and convictions are still taking place. We can cite the examples of Dr. Ferrey-Martin, a gynecologist at Grenoble, and of several staff members of the Hospital of the Cité Universitaire in Paris who, during the month of February 1974, were prosecuted for having carried out an abortion of a young woman who was severely ill.*

Thus, the notion that abortion is a criminal act, which gives rise to guilt feelings, persists. In many cases, doctors and patients find themselves at the mercy of the whims of the prosecuting attorneys. The idea that abortion is a penal offense should be erased. We must decriminalize abortion and regard it as merely a necessary medical procedure. Otherwise, a hypocritical, discriminatory and guilt-producing atmosphere will remain.

---

* Editor's note: Since this paper was delivered, the French National Assembly has voted by a surprisingly wide margin to legalize abortion during the first ten weeks of pregnancy. The new law will allow any permanent resident of the country who is "distressed" by a pregnancy to acquire an abortion during that time. The operation must, however, be carried out by a doctor in

TABLE I

COUNTRIES WHICH STILL HAVE A RESTRICTIVE ABORTION LAW[11]

Countries in which there is a total legal prohibition without any exception for therapeutic abortion:

EUROPE	*CENTRAL AND SOUTH AMERICA*	*AFRICA*	*ASIA*
Ireland	Barbados	Mauritius	Hong Kong
Malta	Bolivia	Zaire	Indonesia
Portugal	Colombia		Philippines
	Dominican Republic		Taiwan
	Guatemala		
	Panama		
	Trinidad and Tobago		

Countries in which there is a legal prohibition but an exception is provided only where abortion is necessary to safeguard the life of the mother:

EUROPE	*AFRICA*
Albania	Algeria
Belgium (in practice)	Egypt
France	Ivory Coast
Germany, Federal Republic of	Liberia
Italy	Nigeria
Luxembourg	Senegal
Netherlands (in practice)	South Africa
Spain	

ASIA	*CENTRAL AND SOUTH AMERICA*
Banglade	Chile
Cambodia	El Salvador
Iran	Guatemala
Iraq	Mexico
Kuwait	Nicaragua
Lebanon	Paraguay
Malaysia	Peru
Pakistan	Venezuela
South Vietnam	
Sri Lanka	
Syria	

It is clear from the above that the majority of the countries with prohibitive laws:

1. *have a majority of Catholics in the population (Europe and Latin America)*
   Only Uruguay accepts the possibility of legal abortion; Argentina and

an established hospital or clinic. The new law awaits approval of the Senate and is designed to go into effect early in 1975. N.Y. Times, Nov. 28, 1974, at 1, col. 2.

11. For an excellent classification of abortion laws, *see* Kalis and David, *Abortion Legislation: A Summary International Classification, 1974*, in ABORTION RESEARCH: INTERNATIONAL EXPERIENCE 13-34 (H.P. David ed.) (Lexington, Mass: D.C. Heath and Co. 1974).

Brazil make an exception in the case of rape or incest; Costa Rica on the basis of the *health* of the mother; Cuba on both the above bases;

2. *and/or were under French or Belgian influence (Africa)* The laws of Cameroon, Ghana, Kenya, and Morocco are a little more liberal, accepting abortion as an exception to save the *health* of the future mother;

3. *and/or have not yet emerged from religious or customary influences, or the idea that fertility is associated with virility, etc. (Asia, Middle East, etc.)*

B.   *Growing Trend Toward Abortion Liberalization*

Increasing numbers of countries are adopting laws which permit abortion during the early stages of pregnancy, justifying their decision principally on concerns for the physical, social, and mental welfare of the women requesting the procedure. This evolution is taking place in a number of different ways, depending upon the particular characteristics of the legal system of each country.

1. Existing Laws Interpreted in a More Liberal Manner

This is the case in Japan. The Eugenic Protection Law of 1948 has been amended a number of times, and now authorizes the physician to proceed with an abortion in the case of a woman "whose health might be seriously compromised by the prolongation of the pregnancy or by giving birth, both for physical and economic reasons."[12] In fact, the interpretation of this text by the doctors is extremely liberal so that any woman in good health, rich or poor, can obtain an abortion if she desires it.

2. Broadening of the Grounds for Legal Abortion Through Legislative Action

The Abortion Act of 1967 in the United Kingdom (in force since April 26, 1968) provides that interruptions of pregnancy may be carried out free of charge by the doctors of the National Health Service, provided that two of them consider the operation necessary either:

— to preserve the life or prevent damage to the physical or mental health of the future mother;

— to prevent harm to the children already born to the family; or

— if there is a serious risk that the future child would suffer from serious physical or mental defects.[13]

It is made clear that in judging the harm which the pregnancy might cause to the health of the pregnant woman, it is proper to take into consideration the circumstances she will face at the time of the birth and, if possible, in the future.

---

12.   Art. 14, para 1(4).

13.   Laws of Great Britain, 2 Eliz., c.87, 1, para 1(a) (1967).

A 1961 amendment to the Czechoslovak law of 1967 permits abortion where there are at least three living children. In addition, other socio-economic grounds may be considered.

Since February 1970, the law in Finland has been made very flexible. Since that date, women under 17 or over 40, as well as mothers of four children, are given the right to terminate their pregnancies. In other cases, the same right is given when family conditions (income, housing, etc.) would make the education and upbringing of the expected child difficult.

Amendments to the Swedish law in 1946 and 1963 have considerably enlarged the grounds for abortion established by the law of 1938. According to these amendments, "prevention of the exhaustion of the pregnant woman" may be taken into consideration. Despite the relatively liberal stance of the Swedish law, a law was adopted by the Parliament on July 9, 1974 providing for abortion on request until the twelfth week of pregnancy. In essence, the woman herself is the sole judge of whether she should have an abortion during that time. Between the twelfth and the eighteenth weeks, she must consult with a social worker because the operation involves a greater risk, but the social worker will not be able to prevent the interruption of the pregnancy unless there are serious contraindications. Beyond the eighteenth week, the case must be submitted to the Public Health and Welfare Service.[14]

3. Establishment of a Legislative System which Permits Abortion in the Earlier Stages of Pregnancy Without Qualification

Since 1920, the policy of the Soviet Union with respect to abortion has been changed a number of times. A decree of the Presidium of the Supreme Soviet dated November 23, 1955, provides that abortions are authorized if they are carried out by competent people in hospitals, "so as to give to women the chance to decide for themselves if they wish to give birth to a child."[15] The Ministry of Health sets forth a rather extensive list of contraindications and the gynecologist involved is required to warn each woman of the possible consequences of the operation. Nevertheless, if she persists in her intention, her request must be agreed to. The cost of the abortion is approximately US $6, but if her reasons are therapeutic, it is done without cost.

4. Liberalization Resulting from a Judicial Decision

This has been the method used in the United States for liberalizing the abortion law there. In its landmark decision of January 22, 1973, the Supreme Court decided that:[16]

---

14. SFS 595 (1974).
15. *Lovtidende A*, 1973-NR.XXXII, No. 350, June 13, 1973.
16. Note 6 *supra*.

> — during the first three months of pregnancy the decision to have an abortion falls entirely upon the interested woman with the agreement of a doctor;
> — during the last six months the legislation of each state may provide reasonable regulations governing abortion which are related to protecting the woman's health; and
> — during the last six weeks of the pregnancy, when the fetus may have become viable, each state is authorized to regulate or even forbid the abortion provided that the abortion is not necessary to safeguard the life or the health of the mother.

Prior to the *Roe v. Wade* decision, four states had already permitted abortion based on the request of the woman alone: Alaska, Hawaii, Maryland, and New York (the last since July 1, 1970). As a result of the Supreme Court decision, thirty-one states have been obliged to repeal their restrictive abortion laws which were in force at the time. Moreover, the Supreme Court declared that rules which imposed a residence requirement on the woman desiring the abortion were unconstitutional, and as a result of this, sixteen other states have had to modify their existing legislation. Thus, the court recognized that, in the absence of overwhelming grounds of public interest, the Government may not limit the woman's fundamental "right of privacy" by forbidding abortion.

The Democratic Republic of Germany, whose law has been liberal since an amendment in 1965, promulgated, on March 9, 1972, a new law providing for abortion on request until the twelfth week of pregnancy. The interruption must be carried out by a gynecologist in a hospital.

In Denmark, a law which authorizes free abortion until the twelfth week of gestation was adopted in June 1973.[17] As with some of the other recently adopted laws, the decision whether to have an abortion is solely the woman's. The consent of the father of the child is not required. Neither is the consent of the parents, even if the mother is less than 18 years old. The Austrian Parliament also adopted at the beginning of 1974 a law authorizing abortion during the first ninety days of pregnancy, despite the vigorous opposition of the Catholics.

In Tunisia, a decree authorizes interruption of pregnancy during the first three months of gestation so long as it is carried out by a physician in a hospital or in an authorized clinic. Previously, abortion was only legally possible for mothers with more than four children. The Indian penal law which only authorized abortion to save the life of the mother was repealed in 1971. In effect, since January 1972, the new law provides a number of

---

17. This section is adapted from a study prepared by Luke T. Lee and John M. Paxman titled *Legal Aspects of Menstrual Regulation* which appears as Law and Population Monograph Series No. 19 (1974).

grounds for abortion. But these are expressed in such a way that abortion on request is available as a practical matter. One of the grounds provided is the failure of a contraceptive method, and it is virtually impossible to prove that a pregnancy was not caused by a contraceptive failure. The operation must, however, take place in a hospital or in an authorized establishment.

5. Law Modification Resulting from Political Action

The People's Republic of China not only authorizes abortion on the request of the woman, but it is also carried out free of charge as a part of the public health service. Thus, this country has applied in their totality the provisions of the United Nations Declaration of 1969 on Social Progress and Development. The integration of abortion in family planning services was probably the result of a decision by the Communist Party, and taken more as an aspect of its concept of the new society than on the basis of legislative texts or judicial decisions. Abortion is thus freely available in that country as much in the urban as in the rural areas, and it is said that abortion is often to be encouraged after the birth of the first child. It should also be pointed out that the technique for the interruption of pregnancy has been greatly simplified.

The system of requiring the consent of a commission has often been abandoned. Even when it still exists, the interpretation of the law is becoming increasingly liberal. Such is the case in Sweden, Poland, Czechoslovakia, and Switzerland, in the Cantons of Geneva and Vaud.

TABLE II

COUNTRIES WHICH HAVE LIBERAL ABORTION LAWS

EUROPE	ASIA	AFRICA	NORTH AMERICA
Austria	China	Sierra Leone	United States
Bulgaria	India	Tunisia	
Cyprus	Japan	Uganda	
Czechoslovakia	North Vietnam	Zambia	SOUTH AMERICA
Denmark	Singapore		Uruguay
Fed. Republic			
of Germany			
German Democratic Rep.			
Hungary			
Iceland			
Norway			
Poland			
Romania			
Sweden			
U.S.S.R.			
United Kingdom			
Yugoslavia			

Those people who are still subject to restrictive laws are struggling to obtain liberalization, and it is certain that many will obtain satisfaction in the near future. Nevertheless, the problem of the interruption of pregnancy has already been profoundly modified and will be more so during the next ten years.

III. ABORTION LAWS, MEDICAL SCIENCE AND THE FUTURE

Due to the progress of science, the interruption of a pregnancy will soon no longer require surgical intervention during the first part of the period of gestation. The discovery of new chemical substances and endometrial aspiration make it possible to proceed toward menstrual regulation at a time even before the woman knows whether she is or is not pregnant. Thus, the distinction between contraception and abortion is becoming more and more tenuous. The question is whether the use of prostaglandins or the technique of uterine aspiration constitute a post-coital contraceptive in the legal sense of the term, or whether they constitute abortion.

These methods, in effect, permit a woman to eliminate an ovum and to regulate her menstrual cycle before she herself is certain whether that ovum has been fertilized. Similar problems have already been raised by the discovery of the IUD (sterilet) and the "morning-after pill." Certain authors have already contended that their use is an abortive act.[18] Nevertheless, these methods are generally considered as contraceptive despite the fact that the IUD does not prevent the fertilization of the egg by the sperm. It merely prevents nidation of the egg within the uterus.

It is possible that the new methods of post-coital regulation will be classified as having a contraceptive function, unless a special intermediate category is created between contraception and abortion. This legal problem is not of great interest in those countries which have adopted liberal legislation on abortion, but it is of capital importance in those countries where repressive laws still exist.

To carry out a legal analysis of the problem we must distinguish between two categories of repressive laws, namely:

— those which make abortion a penal offense regardless of whether the woman is pregnant or not; and

— those which expressly or implicitly require pregnancy as a necessary element of the offense.

---

18. Meloy, *Pre-Implantation Fertility Control and Abortion Law*, 41 CHICAGO-KENT L. REV. 183 (1964). Voices in the French Parliament hostile to the IUD were heard in 1967 calling it a "permanent abortifacient." JOURNAL OFFICIEL, *Assemblée Nationale*, July 1, 1967, at 2566; *Sénat*, Dec. 5, 1967, at 2036.

A. *Laws Requiring Proof of Intent*

The first category is represented by the laws in force in France and Jamaica, which make abortion a *matter of intent*. As a consequence, the offense occurs as soon as a woman procures or tries to procure an abortion *regardless of whether she is pregnant or whether she considers herself to be pregnant.* Because the early British and French laws were identical in this regard, the majority of the countries which were former British and French colonies have among their statutes abortion laws of the intent variety. If the new techniques and substances used for menstrual regulation are employed with the intention of bringing about an abortion, it is likely that an offense exists. The difficulty, of course, lies in the definition of the offense and in the proof of the intention.

In fact, there exist a number of other purposes for the use of the methods involved, other than the possible interruption of pregnancy. Here an analogy to other contraceptive methods is useful. The condom has always been freely sold in France because it provides protection against venereal disease, while the other contraceptive methods and materials were, until 1967, strictly prohibited. In Italy and in Latin America, the "pill" can be obtained in a pharmacy because it is useful for certain therapeutic reasons other than contraception. Prostaglandins, as well as the technique of uterine aspiration, also offer a duality of uses. They may be used for diagnostic purposes or therapeutic purposes, as well as for the regulation of the menstrual cycle. Thus, one has good grounds to argue that their use does not, in itself, constitute the proof of an intention to commit an abortion.

B. *Laws Requiring Proof of Pregnancy*

The second category of law is represented by many statutes in Latin America which provide in effect that the carrying out of an abortion on a pregnant woman is a penal offense. In order to prove that this offense has been committed, it is therefore necessary to prove the actual existence of the pregnancy. In Argentina, Brazil, and Mexico the law considers that if this is not clearly shown, there is no offense.[19] In Egypt, Pakistan, Korea, and the Federal Republic of Germany, legal texts require either a miscarriage or a destruction of the fetus. It is up to the prosecutor to prove this destruction, something which will be virtually impossible to do where the new techniques are used.

C. *Distribution of the New Methods*

The problem is raised from another point of view: namely, whether the importation and distribution of these new products and substances violates

---

19. Argentina Case of F., C., 79 *La Ley* 30 (C.A.N.P., July 4, 1955); Brazil: 228 *Revista dos Tribunales* 354 (No. 4,436) (1954).

the law. In a number of countries, the manufacture, importation and distribution of abortive products and articles is forbidden (France, francophone Africa, Belgium and the Philippines). It is thus necessary to provide a precise definition of what one means by an "abortive product." This is something which seems not to have been done either officially or satisfactorily. Specialists have tried such definitions as "a product or article which when it is used with the avowed intention of provoking abortion actually has an abortive effect,"[20] or "an abortifacient is a product or article whose only function and purpose is to terminate a pregnancy."[21] Under this last interpretation, articles and substances which can be used for different purposes would not be classified as abortifacients.

The American Law Institute takes the position that none of the provisions of its section on abortion are applicable to the prescription, administration or distribution of medicines or other substances designed to prevent a pregnancy, whether it be by preventing the nidation of the fertilized egg or to assist in some other method which has its effect before, during, or immediately after fertilization.

Thus, there is a developing line of thinking under which prostaglandins can be used as a menstrual contraceptive pill. If this interpretation is accepted, the distinction between abortion and contraception will become more blurred. Therefore, why not utilize these methods to prevent pregnancy without specifying whether it is a matter of contraception or abortion?

The laws of the nineteenth century and the beginning of the twentieth century were drafted without any idea of what future technology would have to offer in this field. That is why they do not deal with the ambiguity caused by the progress of medical procedures. The majority of the laws in the field of abortion were based on the assumption that pregnancy begins at the moment of conception, but present thought indicates that it is possible to speak of pregnancy only at some point after nidation. It is only natural that the legal approach to the problem should be changed. In this respect, it is significant to point out that all of the draft abortion laws before the *Bundestag* in the Federal Republic of Germany[22] were based upon the principle that whatever the type of abortion law, it would not be applicable until after the fourteenth day following conception, *i.e.*, after the moment when one is certain that the fertilized egg has been implanted in the uterus.

---

20. Proposed by Dr. Mary Calderone of SIECUS and Harriet F. Pilpel.
21. Proposed by Dr. Russell de Alvarez of the Temple University Medical School.
22. At the beginning of June, 1974, the *Bundestag* adopted in final form a law providing that abortion should be granted through the third month of pregnancy, with the decision left solely to the woman, after consulting with a physician. The Constitutional Court at Karlsruhr decided on June 21, 1974, to suspend the application of the new law at the request of the *Land* of Baden-Württemberg, which was supported by three other *Länder* The request was based on Article 2 of the Constitution which provides that: "Every person has the right to life and to physical integrity."

The introduction of new techniques gives us every reason to modify old laws. These amendments will perhaps have the result of returning us to the rule in effect until the nineteenth century; namely, the legal definition of abortion did not apply until the "quickening" of the fetus.

REFERENCES

ABORTION—A WORLD SURVEY, Supplement to the International Planned Parenthood NEWS (March 1972).

H. P. DAVID, Z. ALAM AND M. KALIS, ABORTION LEGISLATION: A SUMMARY INTERNATIONAL CLASSIFICATION (Wash., D.C.: Transnational Family Research Institute 1972).

A.M. Dourlen Rollier, *Le Problème de l'Avortement dans les pays de la Communauté Europeenne*, 26 REVUE INTERNATIONAL DE CRIMINOLOGIE ET DE POLICE TECHNIQUE, No. 3 (Geneva 1973).

L.T. Lee, *Law and Family Planning*, 2 STUDIES IN FAMILY PLANNING, No. 4 (1971).

L.T. Lee, *Brief Survey of Abortion Laws of Five Largest Countries*, POPULATION REPORT, Series F. No. 1 (Wash., D.C.: The George Wash. U. Med. Center 1973).

L.T. Lee, *International Status of Abortion Legislation* in THE ABORTION EXPERIENCE (H. Osofsky and J. Osofsky eds.) (New York: Harper and Row 1973).

L.T. Lee and J. Paxman, *Legal Aspects of Menstrual Regulation*, Law and Population Monograph Series No. 19 (Medford, Mass: Law and Population Programme 1974).

C. Tietze and D.A. Dawson, *Induced Abortion: A Factbook* in REPORTS ON POPULATION/FAMILY PLANNING, No. 14 (New York: The Population Council 1973).

T. van der Vlugt and P.T. Piotros, *What is Menstrual Regulation?* POPULATION REPORTS, Series F, No. 2 (Wash., D.C.: The George Wash. U. Med. Center 1973).

H. de Watteville, *L'avortement Tardif*, 24 LA REVUE DU PRACTICIEN, No. 9 (Paris 1974).

Report of Workshop on Legal Problems Related to Abortion and Menstrual Regulation

In summarizing her paper, Mme. Dourlen-Rollier stressed five principal points.

First, the practical effect of very restrictive laws against abortion is not to stop it, but to force those who desire one to participate in illegal, secret and dangerous operations, and to discriminate against the poor who cannot travel abroad. Second, there is a good possibility to include the right to early abortion as a human right under the United Nations Declaration on Social Progress and Development. Abortion constitutes a "means" of family planning if it is regarded as a necessary back-up to contraception. In view of the general ignorance about contraception and of the number of contraceptive failures, abortion should be regarded as necessary to prevent unwanted births. Third, because of recent medical advances, abortion has become far safer than it was, particularly in the early stages. There is some evidence which indicates that early abortion is safer than carrying a baby to full term. These changes should be reflected in the law which was originally based in part on the medical danger of abortion during the nineteenth century. Fourth, laws are changing fast in many countries to allow abortion, and over half of the world's people now have legal access to it. Fifth, the new techniques of menstrual regulation and the "morning-after" pill must be kept legally distinct from abortion, but in order to do that, the law may need clarification. In conclusion, Mme. Dourlen-Rollier called for the "decriminalization" of abortion, for abortion to be made available on request during the first twelve weeks of pregnancy, and for greater information and education in the field.

Professor Mabrouk spoke on the same subject, basing his presentation on the 1973 revision of the Tunisian law. He pointed out that the new law, which is strongly supported by Tunisian women, is very flexible and is based partly on the fact that a severe law does not dissuade people from seeking abortion, as well as the fact that Tunisia cannot afford to have its population grow at its present rate. Abortion is available on request during the first three months, and after that it is permitted on eugenic or therapeutic grounds.

In the rather lively discussion of the subject which followed the presentation, the following points were explored:

First, the issue of whether the husband's consent should be required before a woman can have an abortion was raised. A number of speakers felt that the lack of the consent requirement might weaken the family structure. Others felt that abortion should be treated like any other medical matter, with the decision being left to the woman and the physician. No consensus was reached, but it was recognized that the issue of spousal consent would have to be resolved in each country according to local family law.

Whether abortion is a human right under the Tehran proclamation and the Declaration on Social Progress and Development was again discussed in this workshop. It was argued that modern medical techniques and contemporary thinking call for a reconsideration of the question, which can no longer be regarded as it was in the mid-19th century when the anti-abortion laws were adopted. But no consensus was reached.

The idea of decriminalizing abortion, at least in the early stages, received general support. It was pointed out that the women who seek abortions are not criminals. They are victims of circumstance and thus should be given dignified and humane treatment without discrimination. Moreover, on the understanding that abortion was generally undesirable, and taking note of the experience in East European countries which showed that repeated abortions might cause the danger of miscarriage during later desired pregnancies, members of the workshop insisted that women receiving abortions should be given full instruction about contraceptives.

As to the safety of first trimester abortion under present conditions in developed countries, there was no general agreement. On one hand, it was pointed out that the statistics in New York State showed that it involves less risk than childbirth itself. On the other hand, it was argued that since experience in some countries shows that repeated abortions may do harm, nothing should be stated from the point of view of health that might in any way encourage resort to abortion. In any event, abortion is not without dangers and education is needed to make all women understand this. It was finally agreed to leave the matter out of the recommendations.

A number of participants spoke about the effect which old colonial laws or attitudes had in some of the newly independent countries. It was pointed out that some outmoded laws of former metropolitan countries, which have since liberalized their own laws, had been left in effect in some of their former dependencies. On the other hand, some African participants felt that Africa had always been opposed to abortion and that the laws of the metropolitan countries had merely reinforced this view. After a long discussion, the matter was left out of the recommendation.

The new techniques of menstrual regulation, the IUD and the "morning after" pill raise some perplexing problems. It was agreed that there might be a danger that their use could be covered by restrictive abortion laws where the "intent to abort" is the essence of the "crime." There was general agreement that these matters should be kept fully separate from those of abortion, no matter what a country's definition of abortion might be.

Lastly, the right of medical personnel to refuse to participate in abortion procedures on grounds of conscience was recognized, and it was suggested that a clause to this effect be added to the recommendation, along with the provision that where this occurs the woman be referred to some other facility which does provide the service.

Development of the Right to Abortion in Tunisia

By
Mohieddine Mabrouk*

INTRODUCTION

A right to abortion. Some people may think that to speak of a right to abortion is to invoke a paradox. They would recognize the right to life of the fetus but not the mother's right to artificially interrupt an untimely or unwanted pregnancy. Quite apart from this ethical issue, a society (such as Tunisia's) can approach the abortion problem from the viewpoint of demographic expansion or reduction. It may choose either to encourage demographic growth or to restrict it. The route chosen depends in large measure on the resources which a society has at its disposal and on the "quality" of life it can assure its citizens. Thus, it seems to me that right is in service to the demographic policy of a nation. This explains why the abortion law in Tunisia has progressively passed from one that is prohibitory to a liberalized form.

At the present time our country is experiencing a "race between demography and development." We are aware of the urgency to stop the demographic flow, which now threatens to compromise the development process. At the time of our independence, in 1956, the death rate was 20 per thousand and the birth rate was 50 per thousand, thus the population growth rate was 3 percent. In 1970, the birth rate decreased, descending to less than 40 per thousand. By 1971, the natural population growth rate decreased to 2.3 percent, and emigration brought the figure below 2 percent.

Nevertheless, there are other measures designed to limit fertility which must be taken because, if the decrease in the death rate should become stable at a lower figure, it has been predicted that our situation would be the following: 1) the birth rate would rise again above 40 per thousand; and 2) the natural growth rate would reach 3 percent in 1981 and 3.4 percent by the end of the century. As a result, the population of Tunisia, presently number-

---

* Maitre-Assistant, Faculty of Law, Tunis, Tunisia.

ing 5,500,000, would reach 13,500,000 in the year 2,000. Only one generation separates us from the end of the century. The year 2,000 is tomorrow.

In terms of development, Tunisia already must triple the number of jobs created during the 1960s in order to absorb those who are presently in the labor force. A further decrease of 1 percent in the fertility rate between now and 1980 would save the country an expenditure of over 50,000,000 dinars on primary and secondary education during the next 20 years. Tunisia owes it to itself to decrease its population growth rate. In order to accommodate the development plans for the country our population must be 10,000,000 inhabitants (and not 13,500,000) at the end of the century. This is the goal the Government has set for itself.

According to the design of the Fourth Plan (1973-1976), for economic and social development, efforts in family planning are being made to avoid 30,000 births in 1976 and 50,000 in 1981. The "liberalization" of the abortion laws is among the means placed at the disposal of the family planning programs.

I. The Essence of the Abortion Law Reform

Abortion is presently subject to Article 214 of the Penal Code in its revised form. (Decret-loi No. 73-2 of September 26, 1973, as ratified by Law No. 73-57 of November 19, 1973). Under the new law "the artificial interruption of a pregnancy will be allowed when it occurs during the first three months." No justification for the abortion need be presented during that time, and it is to be considered a "social abortion" or an abortion "for personal convenience." However, the abortion must be performed "in a hospital or health facility or in a licensed clinic, by a doctor who is legally practicing his profession."[1] After the first three months of pregnancy, on the other hand, recourse to abortion must be justified in cases where:

—the health of the mother or her emotional balance runs the risk of being compromised by the continuation of the pregnancy; or

—there is the possibility that the child will be born with a rather serious illness.[2] In the cases above cited, interruption of the pregnancy must occur in an approved establishment and upon presentation of a report by the treating physician to the doctor who will perform the abortion.[3]

Since at least one of these justifications must be present, the abortion is termed "therapeutic." The reasons for artificially interrupting the pregnancy at this stage are medical or eugenic. The medical reasons are designed to cover both a physical or emotional rationale. Among the prominent indications for interrupting a pregnancy are: acute hydramnion; hypertension; toxemia due to pregnancy during a permanent hypertension with Bright's dis-

---

1. Art. 214, para. 3, *as amended* 1973.
2. *Id.*, para. 4.
3. *Id.*, para. 5.

ease; arterial sclerosis; heart disease; and cancer of the breast or of the pelvic organs. To these medical reasons of a physical nature can be added those medical reasons of an emotional or psychological nature such as evidence of the danger of suicide. Among the eugenic reasons for interrupting pregnancy are: lesions caused, in utero, to the fetus by medication (thalidomide), x-ray and viral infections (rubella, for example); and hereditary transmittal of mental retardation.

II. A HISTORY OF ABORTION LAW REFORM

It should be noted that "therapeutic abortion" was permitted in Tunisia as early as 1940.[4] Abrogating the 1940 text, Law No. 65-24 of July 1, 1965 revised paragraph 4 of Article 214 of the Penal Code to read as follows:

Interruption may also take place when the mother's health could be endangered by the continuation of the pregnancy.

It is only as a result of the latest reform of the abortion law that the risk of illness or deformity of the conceived infant was considered to be a justification for interrupting a pregnancy. Thus, the Tunisian legislator has shown concern for the child's future as well as that of the mother.

As a result of these gradual shifts in thinking, abortion is no longer justified merely in strict medical terms—even if they have been broadened—it is performed after consideration of medical and social indications.

The World Health Organization has defined health as "a complex state of physical, mental and social well-being and it does not involve merely the absence of disease or infirmity."

"Social" abortion was upheld in these terms by Law No. 65-24 of July 1, 1965, new paragraph 3:

However, interruption of a pregnancy is authorized when performed during the first three months and when the two spouses have at least five children.

This text was criticized because:

—it did not allow abortion until after the fifth child—therefore, too late; thus, it is not important that the spouses freely decide on the number of

---

4. AMR of April 25, 1940, following the French decree of July 29, 1939:
When safeguarding the mother's life requires either surgery or the use of medication which may induce interruption of the pregnancy, the doctor treating the patient or the surgeon will be obliged to seek the advice of two consulting physicians, one of whom chosen from the list of experts at the Cicil or Regional Tribunal who, after examination or discussion, will verify in writing that the mother's life can only be safeguarded by means of such a therapeutic intervention. A copy of the consultation form will be remitted to the patient, the other two will be kept by the two consulting physicians.

their children (before the fifth, that is);

—it made abortion subject to agreement of both spouses while, in a non-marital situation, the consent of the father is not required since he is either unknown, absent or indifferent to the mother's condition.

These criticisms and others were at the heart of the 1973 reform.

In a statement to the press, published on September 19, 1973, the National Union of Tunisian Women declared rather emphatically that "at some time in her life, each woman may pressingly need to interrupt, once or several times, a pregnancy she could not avoid. The woman bearing the child in her womb during nine months is the first one who is concerned with this pregnancy."

In the same document, it is also pointed out that "[a]ny woman in such a situation will ultimately use whatever means are available to interrupt her pregnancy without worrying about the risks involved."

What is most remarkable about the reform of the law is its "liberalization" of what may be called social abortion. The new law will signal an "improvement in the quality of life" and will make it possible for the unborn child to be truly wanted. This newly approved form of abortion will allow our society to win the "race between demography and development."

The texts regarding abortion are based on reality and adapted to the urgent needs of the national policy on family planning.

At the beginning of our independence, it was necessary to review the texts of laws derived from the colonial period and to rid them of what was contrary to our demographic policy.

Article 214 of the Penal Code has undergone several revisions, inspired by the evolution in thinking about the subject of abortion, in 1913 (July 9), 1940 (April 25), 1965 (July 1), and 1973 (September 26).

To this list of legal reforms we must also add another equally repressive text from the colonial period: AMR of September 18, 1920 (almost an exact replica of the French law of July 31, 1920) which penalized incitement to abortion and contraceptive propaganda. This text was abrogated by Law No. 61-7 of January 9, 1961, regarding contraceptive products and devices.

III. Conclusion

Great strides have been made in the abortion law since 1913. Although the abortion law in Tunisia has evolved from a position of being considered a crime in all cases to one of being permitted under certain circumstances, it is no longer considered a violation of the law unless it is performed after the first three months of pregnancy without justification, or if it is performed by someone other than a doctor.

Nonetheless, since there is now an established "right to abortion," it would be more in keeping with the spirit of our times to deal with the subject of abortion in some manner other than in the Penal Code.

The Role of the Paramedical in Voluntary Male Sterilization and Menstrual Regulation

By

F.M. Shattock* and N.R.E. Fendall**

Abstract

The paramedical worker can take an active role in vasectomy and menstrual regulation. The procedures are effective, safe and easy to perform. The authors propose a plan for the training, use and supervision of paramedicals as a source of manpower to deliver family planning services especially in developing nations with a shortage of medical doctors.

I. INTRODUCTION

The use of the prefix "para" in discussing this topic is an unfortunate one, as it connotes "having an ancillary status of function."[1] "Ancillary" itself is defined as "subservient, subordinate."[2] It is also, unfortunately, becoming common to describe this cadre of medical workers as "physician surrogates." None of these terms adequately describes the primary health care role that can and should be taken by these medical workers in the areas of birth control and voluntary sterilization.

Two names are most commonly applied to non-physician medical workers today:

(1) *The paramedical*—examples of this type are Registered Nurses, Health Visitors, etc., who have completed secondary school training and, in addition, have received a university education or comparable technical training; and

---

* Professor, Department of Tropical Medicine, Liverpool School of Tropical Medicine, University of Liverpool, Liverpool, England.

** Professor, Department of Tropical Community Health, Liverpool School of Tropical Medicine, University of Liverpool, Liverpool, England.

1. VII OXFORD ENGLISH DICTIONARY 443 (1961).
2. "Ancillary" is derived from the Latin word *ancilla* or "handmaiden." I OXFORD ENGLISH DICTIONARY 315 (1971).

(2) *The auxiliary*—examples of this class are the Medical Assistants of Africa, the Mantri of the Far East, the Enrolled Midwives, etc., who have received a full or partial middle school education followed by a technical education of limited breadth, depth and duration.[3]

In a number of developing countries the entry requirements for auxiliary training consist of either a Form II or Form III secondary school education, which is then followed by two or three years of technical training. Such personnel form the large bulk of the manpower available to the medical service in many developing countries. After further training, on a postgraduate basis, many of the members of this cadre are perfectly capable of undertaking on their own specific tasks. However, in view of their lesser schooling and technical education, a greater degree of selectivity is required in their selection for post-graduate training than is the case with the paramedical cadre.

The difference between the two categories, therefore, is based on the amount of school education and technical training which the workers receive. With the rapidly increasing educational possibilities being offered in the developing countries, this difference is becoming increasingly blurred. For example, the Zambian Medical Assistant (an auxiliary) was originally required to have a Form II education. This was later raised to Form III, and today many entrants have completed their secondary school education. It is also difficult to differentiate between the breadth, depth and duration of the Zambian Registered Nurse's three-year vocational training which creates a paramedical, and those of the three-year Medical Assistant training which creates the auxiliary.

In most developing countries physicians are mainly located in the cities and larger towns, usually practicing in hospitals. This also applies to the paramedical cadres such as the Registered Nurses who, at a peripheral level, are mainly based in District Hospitals. The auxiliary cadres, such as the Medical Assistant, are the grass-roots workers, based in the Rural Health Centers. Therefore, the latter cadres are, in most developing countries, required to provide medical help to the majority of the rural population —which in some countries is as high as 80% of the total population. As things would have it, these cadres are also the least supervised.

II.   Vasectomy and Menstrual Regulation: A Brief History

A.   *Vasectomy*

In 1830 Sir Astley Cooper discovered that by tying the vas in a dog the sperms would only survive as far as the ligation. Sixty years later surgeons

---

3. N. Fendall, Auxiliaries in Health Care: Programs in Developing Countries (Baltimore: John Hopkins Press 1972).

began to tie the vas as part of the operation of prostatectomy, but this procedure was only undertaken to prevent any subsequent infection travelling from the bladder to the testes via the vas. Vasectomy as a specific sterilization operation was not undertaken until about 1895 when Dr. H. Sharp, the institutional physician at the Indiana State Reformitory, sterilized several hundred imprisoned "degenerates" on eugenic grounds.[4]

During the past few decades surgical male sterilization has come to be recognized as a prime method of fertility control in many areas of the world. It has been estimated that some ten million surgical sterilizations have been undertaken in the developing world and some fifteen million in the developed world. However, these figures are probably low since Datta-Ray[5] reports that in India alone fourteen million sterilizations, the majority being vasectomies, have been undertaken since 1965.

Vasectomy is becoming increasingly popular in many countries. In the Netherlands a sample survey of a 700,000-member insurance group showed that in 1969 only 10 males requested vasectomy, whereas three years later 1,136 requested it.[6] In the United States a minor boom in vasectomies resulted from adverse publicity connected with oral contraceptives coinciding with the feminist movement, which argued that men should shoulder a greater responsibility in the field of pregnancy control. The number of vasectomies rose from 250,000 in 1969 to 750,000 in 1971 and has since levelled off to about half a million annually. In Runcorn, England, a free contraceptive service was commenced two years ago and a local general practitioner has recently stated that he regarded free vasectomy as having been the biggest breakthrough of the campaign.[7]

In most Latin American countries it appears that the laws do not allow voluntary contraceptive sterilization. However, these laws are generally not enforced.[8] Vasectomy is now gaining acceptance by a wide spectrum of the people and the religious and social constraints which had traditionally caused it to be regarded as unacceptable are gradually becoming more lax.[9]

In Asia vasectomy forms a very significant part of the programmes of India and Bangladesh. It is fairly common in Thailand and Japan, less com-

4.   Guttmacher, in MATERNAL AND CHILD HEALTH PRACTICES, PROBLEMS, RESOURCES AND METHODS OF DELIVERY 453 (H. Wallace, E. Gold & E. Lis eds.) (Springfield, Ill.: Charles C. Thomas 1973).

5.   Datta-Ray, *Family Planning in India: A Crisis in Confidence*, 1 PEOPLE 2, 3-7 (1974).

6.   MEDICAL NEWS (London), 6:13, at 5 (1974).

7.   London Daily Mail, April 22, 1974, at 7.

8.   Goldberg, Goldsmith & Echeverria, *Vasectomy as a Contraceptive Choice in Latin America* in ADVANCES IN PLANNED PARENTHOOD: PROCEEDINGS OF THE ELEVENTH MEETING OF THE ASSOCIATION OF PLANNED PARENTHOOD PHYSICIANS (Amsterdam: Excerpta Medica 1974) [hereinafter cited as PROCEEDINGS].

9.   Wortman and Piotrow, *Vasectomy, Old and New Techniques* in POPULATION REPORT, Series D, No. 1 (1973).

mon in South Korea and the People's Republic of China and is rarely used in the rest of Asia, although West Malaysia and Singapore have included it in their national programmes and it is undertaken in Sri Lanka and Hong Kong. The Indian Government adopted a sterilization policy in 1959 and India's success in this field is attributable to intensive publicity drives and such techniques as the mass vasectomy camps and mobile clinics. The overwhelming proportion of males undergoing vasectomy in India are now illiterate or have received less than a full primary education.[10] The success of East Pakistan's (now Bangladesh) programme became apparent in the early part of 1967-68 when sterilization figures rose dramatically from the hundreds to the thousands in a single month. Both East and West Pakistan started vasectomies in 1965.

Relatively few vasectomies are undertaken in Africa and the Middle East.

B. *Menstrual Regulation*

A review of the contraception field over the past few years reveals the following four problems: limited supply remains the principal barrier of oral contraceptives; a continuing unmet demand for condoms; infrequent resort to male vasectomy; and a lack of improvement in intra-uterine devices. There has been a marked improvement in female sterilization through the use of the laparoscope and with the "mini-laparotomy"—which, indeed, holds out hope of also becoming an operation capable of being undertaken by suitably-trained paramedicals. But the most powerful single development in the past five years has been in the field of menstrual regulation.

In the late 1960s the plastics industry developed a flexible polyethylene tubing which was modified by Dr. Karman and attached to a syringe. With this apparatus, Dr. Karman was able to undertake abortions in the early weeks of the first trimester of pregnancy, the suction being induced by withdrawing the plunger of the syringe to strip off the uterine endometrium which in a non-pregnant woman normally would be lost at menstruation.

At that time, so few legal abortions were being undertaken that, even with its introduction, this technique was little used. It was still customary to hospitalize the patient for a few days and to undertake a dilatation and curettage under a general anesthetic, which meant incurring a blood loss of up to one pint.

As various countries began to liberalize their abortion laws and abortions were performed in increasing numbers, it became necessary to devise a

---

10. Bhatia, *The Role of Sterilization Operations* in FAMILY PLANNING IN POPULATION CONTROL: IMPLICATIONS, TRENDS AND PROSPECTS: PROCEEDINGS OF THE PAKISTAN INTERNATIONAL FAMILY PLANNING CONFERENCE, Dacca 1969 (N. Sadik, J. Anderson, K. Siddaqui, *et. al.*, eds.) (Lahore: Sweden Pakistan Family Welfare Project 1969) [hereinafter cited as POPULATION CONTROL].

routine for an early abortion which was both quicker and safer than a dilatation and curettage. Today vacuum aspiration has become the widely accepted technique for undertaking an abortion during the first trimester.

Early in 1971 at a symposium on abortion held at the University of California, Los Angeles, Dr. Karman and Dr. Pion discussed the possibility of using the vacuum aspiration technique at an even earlier stage of pregnancy. At that time, the technique was not usually undertaken before the sixth week of pregnancy—the time pregnancy could be diagnosed. At the end of 1971, Dr. Pion and his colleagues published the first scientific paper[11] on the induction of the menstrual period within one or two weeks of a missed menstrual period, i.e., prior to the clinical diagnosis of pregnancy.[12]

There is no reliable pregnancy test which can be performed in the doctor's office, i.e., without a laboratory, before the twelfth day after a missed menstrual period. By that time the woman is either already three to four weeks pregnant, depending on the day of ovulation and of fertilisation, or has had 40 days of amenorrhoea from her previous menstruation. The immunologic slide test is not reliable during the first two weeks following a missed menstruation because at that time the level of human chorionic gonadotropin produced by the early implanation site causes an excessive number of false positives. In 1,204 women up to two weeks after a delayed menstrual period the Pregnosticon Dri-Dot test in one series[13] ranged from 0%-24% false positives and 2.2%-66% false negatives. A newer technique developed by Saxena and Landesman[14] at Cornell Medical Center is the radio-receptor assay. This method uses finger tip blood and is reliable from the sixth day after ovulation with no false negative results in a series of 250 women. This test therefore enables the diagnosis of pregnancy even before the woman has missed her menstruation.

Most studies have indicated that when menstrual regulation is undertaken within 7 days of a missed menstrual period only about 50% of the women concerned were pregnant and if undertaken within 7-14 days of the missed menstruation about 85% were pregnant. As the ideal time for undertaking menstrual regulation lies between the ninth and fourteenth days after a missed menstruation, by using the immunologic slide test some 40% will be performed unnecessarily.

It must, however, be realised that in the context of the developing countries the Cornell radio-receptor test will not be possible as it requires

11.   Pion, Wabrek and Wilson, *Innovative Methods in Prevention of the Need for Abortion*, 14 CLIN. OBSTET. GYNEC. 1313 (1971).
12.   Pregnancy or non-pregnancy could be determined by microscopically examining the evacuated material.
13.   van der Vlugt & Piotrow (eds.), *Pregnancy Termination* in POPULATION REPORT, Series F, No. 4 (1974).
14.   MEDICAL NEWS (London), 6:24, at 1 (1974).

both special equipment and an operator with technical skills. This is also true for the immunologic slide test. Thus, in those countries, even in the hospitals, reliance will still have to be placed on pregnancy tests which are only conclusive two weeks after the missed menstrual period while, without the availability of these tests, as in some District hospitals and all Rural Health Centers, reliance has to be placed on a physician's ability to diagnose pregnancy six weeks after the missed menstruation or a midwife's ability (without a vaginal examination) to diagnose pregnancy in its tenth week.

The suction necessary for menstrual regulation may be produced in a number of ways. Feng[15] reviewed 600 induced abortions undertaken by a catheter and suction in Peking between January 1958 and June 1959. In 1964 Mu Hsia-po and his colleagues[16] discussed the use of a 1/4 horsepower motor to induce the suction for use in pregnancies of under ten weeks duration and in the same year two other Chinese articles were published on the use of electro-suction. In the following year an article appeared on the use of a negative pressure bottle with the negative pressure being produced by a hand-pump and P'an recommended the use of a hand-pump by the rural medical corps. In 1966 Ch'eng Pang-chung and colleagues[17] described the use of a fire-cup type of suction bottle which had been used successfully in over 700 cases and was an adaptation of the traditional fire-cup used for the extraction of pus.

The procedure of menstrual regulation is relatively so new that, as yet, it has no definitive name. Various names have been used by various authors, such as: menstrual regulation (M.R.), menstrual planning, endometrial aspiration, pre-emptive abortion, minisuction and atraumatic termination of pregnancy. The U.S. Supreme Court in its January 1973 decision legalising early abortion called it "menstrual extraction."[18] Nor, as yet, is there a universally accepted definition of the procedure clearly differentiating it from a definitive abortion. The 1974 Sri Lanka International Conference of the Family Planning Associations defined it as "any treatment administered within fourteen days of a missed menstrual period to ensure that a woman is not pregnant or does not remain pregnant." This definition was aimed to cover a procedure undertaken before the routine pregnancy tests would be positive with any degree of accuracy—except for those advanced institutions where the Saxena-Landesman radio-receptor assay technique will reveal a pregnancy even before the next menstruation is due.

15. *Cited by* Orleans, *Family Planning Developments in China, 1960-1966: Abstracts from Medical Journals*, 4 STUDIES IN FAMILY PLANNING 8 (1973).

16. Mu Hsia-po, Jih Pi-ta and Chih Yuan-chieh-chih, Shansi Med. J., *cited in* Orleans, *supra* note 15.

17. P'an Jun-min, *cited in* Orleans, *supra* note 15.

18. Roe v. Wade, 410 U.S. 113 (1973).

Segal and Tietze do not mention the method in their 1971 review of current and prospective methods of contraceptive technology.[19] Van der Vlugt and Piotrow[20] stated in April 1973 there had been only eleven scientific reports published and, in their 1974 report, stated that the number of documented cases had increased to 5,338.[21]

By early in 1973 only a few clinics in the United States and the United Kingdom were offering the procedure on a regular basis and it was available to an even lesser extent in Singapore and Calcutta. It is now being used on a wider basis and by the end of 1973 over ten thousand menstrual regulation kits (a 50cc syringe, multiple size cannulae, a plastic speculum and instructions) had been supplied all over the world by one American agency.[22]

III. The Use of Paramedicals in Family Planning

As has been noted, in a developing country the rural population (some 80% of the inhabitants) will be very largely served by the auxiliary medical worker, and in the urban areas in some countries the population attending clinics will be served by paramedical or auxiliary workers. In the field of family planning, paramedical and auxiliary health staff are already heavily involved in the delivery of hormonal and IUD contraceptives.

Yang and Bang[23] studied the results of IUD insertions in South Korea by three types of workers—obstetricians, nurse-midwives supervised by obstetricians, and specially trained midwives working without supervision. Judging by uterine perforations, expulsions and other complications, there was no difference among the three groups. The only exception was that the unsupervised nurse midwives rejected slightly more patients, *i.e.*, referred them to a physician, apparently because they were being ultra-cautious.

Paramedical personnel are also inserting IUDs in India, especially in the Punjab and Haryana.[24] In West and East (now Bangladesh) Pakistan a cadre of Lady Family Planning Visitors was created in 1966[25] and their training and practice includes the insertion and removal of IUDs. In Pakistan, during 1967-68, where there is no direct supervision of the insertions, nonprofessional personnel inserted 75% of the country's total insertions of

19. Segal & Tietze, *Contraceptive Technology: Current and Prospective Methods* in Reports on Population/Family Planning 1 (1971).
20. van der Vlugt & Piotrow, *Menstrual Regulation: What is It?* in Population Report, Series F, No. 2 (1973).
21. *Id.*
22. Information presented to International Conference on the Physician and Population Change, Stockholm, 1974.
23. Yang & Bang, 4 Studies in Family Planning 27 (1968).
24. Narain, *India, the Family Planning Program Since 1965*, 4 Studies in Family Planning 35 (1968).
25. Fendall, *supra* note 3.

600,000 IUDs.[26] Berggren, Vaillant and Garnier[27] state that IUDs are inserted by midwives, under medical supervision, in rural Haiti. Paramedical personnel are also inserting IUDs in a number of other countries including Barbados, Thailand and the People's Republic of China.

Ostergard[28] states that family planning programmes in the United States are already using paramedicals as primary providers of patient care services. The 12-24 week training period, which is both didactic and clinical, enables them to fit both diaphragms and IUDs. Ostergard also shows that there is no difference in the capacity of various paramedical and auxiliary grades in learning the necessary didactic or manual skills to function effectively in this area.

Ostergard, Broen and Marshall[29] tested the patients' acceptance of staff members in a federally-funded clinic and found that only 0.6% of the clients preferred the care of a physician and that 43.8% of the 10,582 clients specifically preferred the care of the paramedical family planning specialists, with 55.6% stating that they had no preference.

It is useful to consider the paramedicals' role in the insertion of IUDs because, as van der Vlugt and Piotrow[30] have rightly pointed out, the procedure for menstrual regulation is not unlike that used for the insertion of an IUD. In both a small tube is inserted through the cervix and into the uterus. During the insertion of an IUD a small plunger is depressed inserting the IUD into the uterus. During menstrual regulation the plunger is withdrawn creating the negative pressure necessary to strip off the endometrium which is normally shed at menstruation.

The physicians' principal role should be to devise a safe procedure, and to aid in the selection and training of paramedicals and in the preparation of their training courses. They should act as a back-up referral system and undertake the field supervision of the medical workers. Prior to the delegation of a task to the paramedicals the physicians must ensure that the method being used is *effective*, *safe* and *easy to perform*. In the context of vasectomy and menstrual regulation this means that the procedures are effective in terminating fertility or have a very low incidence of continuing pregnancies. Safe means that there should be only a low incidence of complications. Easy to perform implies a standard procedure, using standard equipment and on an out-patient basis, which precludes a general anesthesia.

---

26. Rosenfield, *Family Planning: An Expanded Role for Paramedical Personnel*, 110 AM. J. OBSTETRICS AND GYNECOLOGY 1030 (1971).

27. Berggren, Vaillant and Garnier, *Lippes Loop Insertion by Midwives in Healthy and Chronically Ill Women in Rural Haiti*, 64 AM. J. PUB. HEALTH 719 (1974).

28. Ostergard, *The Potential for Paramedical Personnel in Family Planning: An Analysis Based on the Department of Health, Education and Welfare Five Year Plan for Family Planning Services*, 64 AM. J. PUB. HEALTH 27 (1974).

29. Ostergard, Broen and Marshall, *The Family Planning Specialist as a Provider of Health Care Services*, 23 FERTILITY AND STERILIZATION 505 (1972).

30. van der Vlugt & Piotrow, *supra* note 20.

A.   *Does Vasectomy Meet These Requirements?*

1. Effectiveness

Vasectomy is a very effective procedure if undertaken properly. With adequate training there are only two types of cases which could give rise to difficulty, *i.e.*, operative failure. The first, the presence of a double vas, is rare, and the second, the congenital absence of a vas, is very common. Hanley,[31] who has had considerable experience with vasectomy, stated that in twenty years he had only found a congenital absence of the vas in about 100 cases. The vas may not be palpable due to an undescended testicle and the surgical dissection may be difficult in the presence of a hernia or other abnormality so that the paramedical would need to be instructed that vasectomy must only be undertaken in men who are perfectly normal on clinical examination.

Effectiveness will be judged by sterility. In a few cases a recanalisation of the vas may occur at a later date. This may be guarded against by removing a sufficient length of the vas. It must also be realised that immediately following vasectomy a man is not sterile, since living sperms are stored beyond the site of operation. It is therefore necessary to use another form of contraception for the first three post-operative months. To ascertain that the man is sterile, the semen must be microscopically examined at intervals. However, many patients do not return for examination and failures of conception prevention from this cause are not operative-technique failures. Wickramasuriya[32] issues twenty condoms to all men undergoing vasectomy on the tea estates in Sri Lanka for use in the first three post-operative months. After three months the men are expected to return for examination but only 50% do so. Sinha, Jain and Prased[33] interviewed 337 men who had undergone vasectomy in urban Lucknow and state that only seven returned to have their semen tested.

In many cases a reversal operation is technically possible—though the effect of such reversals is difficult to assess due to differing criteria, such as reappearance of sperm, sperm viability or actual pregnancy. In developing countries, with their deficiencies of surgeons and facilities, it is necessary to regard the procedure as irreversible and to so instruct the patients. The few available surgeons and facilities should be reserved for greater surgical priorities.

2. Safety

Is there a low incidence of complications?

---

31.   Hanley, *Vasectomy for Voluntary Male Sterilization*, LANCET, Feb., 1968, at 207.

32.   Staff, Margaret Pyke Center, *One Thousand Vasectomies*, 4 BRITISH MED. J. 216 (1973).

33.   Aluwihare, *Male Sterilization*, 8 IPPF MED. BULL., No. 1, at 3 (1974).

Many million vasectomies have been undertaken and to date only one death has been reported from anaphylactic shock. A few deaths have also been recorded due to tetanus, occurring in the mass vasectomy camps. The IPPF *Handbook for Doctors*, 1974, states that the operation has a mortality of 1 in 100,000 or less, even when performed under difficult circumstances in developing countries.

The most recent major review of vasectomy in a single clinic is that of the Margaret Pyke Center in London reviewing 1,000 vasectomies.[34] In that series twelve men (1.2%) developed a minor infection, a further twelve developed a haematoma and one developed an abscess, an overall morbidity rate of under 2.5%.

3. Ease of Performance

The operation has been undertaken on many millions of men as out-patients and under a local anaesthetic. It requires a minimum of surgical instruments.

Vasectomy therefore answers the three criteria of effectiveness, safety and ease of performance required prior to delegation to paramedical staff.

Have they actually undertaken it? It is believed that they have done so in some countries, though the authors have been unable to find any reference to it. Two recent major reviews of vasectomy, the last in 1973, do not mention the undertaking of vasectomy by paramedicals, although the remark is made in one: "Whether assistant physicians can be so trained will depend on acceptability to the medical profession and successful experimentation in some centers," Dr. Aluwihare,[35] a general surgeon at the University of Ceylon, suggested at the 1974 Sri Lanka Congress that vasectomy training should be extended to every Ayurvedic doctor, the indigenous medical practitioners. Marzuki,[36] when questioned as to why only a few vasectomies were being undertaken in Malaysia, replied that it was due to "a lack of medical and paramedical personnel needed for the job." It is not, however, clear if the paramedicals were to operate in their own right or act only as hand-maidens to the physicians.

B. *Does Menstrual Regulation Meet These Requirements?*

1. Effectiveness

In the case of menstrual regulation effectiveness is judged by the continuation of pregnancy following regulation, but this concept is affected by

---

34. Marzuki, in POPULATION CONTROL, *supra* note 10.

35. Brenner, Edelman, Davis, *et. al.*, *Suction Curettage for Menstrual Regulation* in PROCEEDINGS, *supra* note 8.

36. Newman & Murphy, *Menstrual Induction: Psycho-Social Aspects* in PROCEEDINGS 15, *supra* note 8.

the fact that in various series from 20% to 60% of the women have not been pregnant at the time, depending on the period of amenorrhoea prior to regulation being undertaken. At the conference on menstrual regulation held in Honolulu in 1973[37] the failure-to-terminate rate was defined as the number of continuing pregnancies divided by the number identified as being pregnant after regulation, this factor multiplied by 100. Using this formula the failure-to-terminate rate for menstrual regulation in 1,854 women who were diagnosed as being pregnant immediately after aspiration was 1.1 per 100. Factors associated with a failure-to-terminate included cannula size, source of suction, type of anesthesia, length of amenorrhoea and inexperience with the technique.

2. Safety

Van der Vlugt and Piotrow[38] have listed the immediate and delayed complications of menstrual regulation from six studies involving 3,490 women. In the six studies the immediate complication rate (those occurring before 24 hours) varied from 0 to 3.9 per 100 women and included one case of uterine perforation, and others of fainting, vomiting, severe uterine cramps and cervical trauma. Delayed complications (24 hours to six weeks after operation) included post-operative infection, bleeding, spotting, cramps, retained products of conception and continuing pregnancies. Post-operative infection requiring antibiotic treatment ranged from 1.4 to 2.3 per 100 women and the rates for bleeding, cramping and spotting from 0.3 to 3.8 per 100 women. Rates for incomplete procedures resulting in retained products of conception ranged from 0.2 to 1.5 per 100 women and rates for continuing pregnancy from 0.1 to 3.7 per 100 women. This study of 3,490 women in six series covered reports from 22 countries including Bangladesh, England, India, Korea, Singapore, Egypt, Iran and the United States.

Complication rates which have been reported appear to be affected by the length of amenorrhoea and the pregnancy status and diminish with increasing experience of the procedure. A higher rate of complications may be expected if a general anaesthesia is employed. The overall immediate complication rate in a combined study in 598 women in North Carolina and London[39] was 9.6 per 100 women, but of these 8.2 per 100 women were due to the anaesthesia.

Pain is a subjective interpretation, and Newman and Murphy[40] asked 43 women who had undergone menstrual regulation in San Francisco to compare the pain they had endured to that of their normal menstruation. Sixteen women said that the pain experienced was less than with their menstrual

---

37. van der Vlugt & Piotrow, *supra* note 13.
38. *Id.*
39. Brenner, Edelman, Davis, *et. al.*, *supra* note 35.
40. Newman & Murphy, *supra* note 36.

period and seven said that it was about the same. Fifteen found the operation more painful and five had found it "much more painful." In that series the procedure was undertaken with the administration of aspirin and codein thirty minutes before and a paracervical block three minutes before regulation. Suction was provided by a foot-operated pump.

No death has been directly attributable to menstrual regulation. Tietze and Lewit in their report on the Joint Program for the Study of Abortion[41] mention a death from a suction evacuation procedure, but it is not stated if the death occurred in the first six weeks (putative) of pregnancy and so falling within the menstrual regulation category or later in the first trimester. Most probably it occurred in an early putative pregnancy as the victim was a girl of 18 who committed suicide three days after the procedure and ". . . before she could be informed that she had not been pregnant."

3. Ease of Performance

Technically, the procedure is straightforward and presents no difficulties to a properly trained person. The equipment required consists only of a 50cc syringe and cannula and a speculum, and indeed menstrual regulation kits are available. The procedure has been undertaken in many areas in out-patients and under no anaesthesia.

Have paramedicals actually undertaken menstrual regulation? Again, no reference can be found to it. Pi-chao Chen[42] in his study of China's population program mentions that a paramedicals' training book, *An Instruction Manual for Retraining Barefoot Doctors*, was compiled by the Kilin Medical University for a pilot project in Kilin province. The project was for the advanced training of barefoot doctors and the *Manual* provides detailed instructions on the suction termination of pregnancy, tubal ligation and vasectomy. However, Pi-chao Chen was unable to ascertain how many, if any, barefoot doctors had been so instructed.

As in the case of vasectomy, some physicians are already expressing their opinion that this is a procedure which could be undertaken by properly taught paramedicals—albeit with some reservations on the part of some physicians.[43]

Hall[44] while considering the volume of the abortion demand in New York following the liberalization of New York's abortion law, predicts that the same physicians who are presently forecasting a scarcity of medical personnel to meet the demand will be the most vigorous in combating any threat

---

41.   Tietze & Lewit, *Joint Program for the Study of Abortion: Early Medical Complications of Legal Abortion*, 3 STUDIES IN FAMILY PLANNING, No. 6, at 99 (1972).

42.   Pi-chao Chen, *China's Population Program at the Grass-Roots Level*, 4 STUDIES IN FAMILY PLANNING, No. 8, at 219 (1973).

43.   LANCET, Jan. 19, 1974, at 48.

44.   ABORTION IN A CHANGING WORLD, ch. 19 (R. Hall, ed. 1971).

by paramedical personnel to take over this work and its income. However, he states: "Whereas there is little doubt that nurse-midwives could be trained to do abortions, I doubt that this will come to pass in the near future."[45] Karman himself states: "In a supervised clinic setting they [paramedicals] are capable of performing safe abortions on carefully selected patients."[46] He also points out that traditionally midwives and paramedicals have performed abortions even before the procedure was legal. Currently, Dr. L. Laufe, Chief of Obstetrics and Gynecology at Western Pennsylvania Hospital, Pittsburgh, in conjunction with the Pittsburgh Graduate School in Public Health, is training nurses to perform menstrual regulation and hopes that he will be able to establish an international training center to teach menstrual regulation and other basic family planning techniques.[47] Dr. Sadik stated at the Honolulu Menstrual Regulation Conference: "To reach rural areas or places where physicians are not available, auxiliary nurse-midwives, who have already been taught to insert IUDs, can be taught to perform menstrual regulation. . . . [O]ne of the advantages of menstrual regulation is its simplicity and the possibility of rapid application in different settings."[48]

Van der Vlugt and Piotrow in their 1973 paper on pregnancy termination raise two questions.[49] First, they ask, "Can paramedical personnel be trained to perform the procedure as effectively as obstetricians, gynecologists or other physicians?" They believe that, as yet, this cannot be answered with certainty without further research and experience, as the technique is relatively so new.

Personally, we believe there is a more fundamental question. Is it necessary to expect a paramedical auxiliary in a developing country (whose populations, excluding China, form 72% of the world's population) to achieve a standard expected from an obstetrician gynecologist? In one large African country, to take but one example, there are only four obstetricians, based at three main hospitals, to serve a country of 290,000 square miles and a population of over four million. Therefore, should paramedicals there be expected to achieve the standard of "other physicians?" To this our answer would be "No," as we would expect them to surpass that standard. In a developing country the "other physicians" are usually general duty medical officers practising the whole gamut of medicine. Even if they had been trained in this technique, it would not often be used due to the demands of all their other medical work. On the other hand, if a specially-trained paramedical/auxiliary is carefully selected before training and then attached to a maternal and child health unit, she would rapidly acquire a large experi-

45. *Id.*
46. Karman, *The Paramedic Abortionist*, 15 CLIN. OBSTET. GYNEC. 379 (1972).
47. van der Vlugt & Piotrow, *supra* note 20.
48. Sadik, *Menstrual Regulation Update*, POPULATION REPORT, Series F, No. 4 (1974).
49. van der Vlugt & Piotrow, *supra* note 20.

ence of the technique. It has been shown that (among other factors) the incidence of complications diminishes with increasing experience.

Van der Vlugt and Piotrow's second question is to wonder if women could be taught the technique of regulating their own menses and to use the technique in their homes as some feminists originally suggested. It is doubtful if women, even though specially trained would undertake to regulate their own menses in this manner. Experience has shown that women are loathe to examine their own breasts regularly for "lumps" and even more reluctant to undertake a routine vaginal examination to ascertain if the "tail" of their IUD is still in place. Furthermore, if the service were brought nearer to the client, as could be done by the use of paramedicals, such self-regulation would not be necessary.

IV. THE UNTAPPED POOL OF MANPOWER

The IPPF's survey of the unmet needs in family planning[50] revealed that less than one third of the 500 million women at risk of pregnancy are presently protected by regular contraceptive practice and that only one half of the world's population has access to an organised family planning service. The non-users are heavily concentrated in the rural areas of developing countries and abortion is still the most common method of birth control. Nearly one in three pregnancies are deliberately terminated, legally or illegally, and in some areas the proportion exceeds two in three pregnancies.

Logically, we are therefore faced with two problems in the delivery of family planning services. First, until the advent of a better contraceptive method and its general acceptance we must offer either male sterilization or a form of abortion as early as possible in pregnancy (since later abortions carry a greater morbidity and mortality risk) as a backup service to the contraceptive program. Second, we must ensure that these services are offered where they are most needed—in the rural areas of the developing countries, the very areas where there are the minimum number of medical professionals and the maximum number of paramedicals and auxiliaries.

That there is a plethora of paramedical/auxiliary workers already available in national family planning programmes is seen in the Population Council's 1973 *Factbook*.[51] This *Factbook* states the personnel and facilities specifically allocated to family planning services in 37 countries, among which are:

Bangladesh, 1972   Physicians certified for IUDs and vasectomies, 1,000. Other personnel, 20,823 of whom 8,000 are part-time *dais* (village midwives) and 10,000 are distributors of conventional contraceptives.

---

50. INTERNATIONAL PLANNED PARENTHOOD NEWS 1 (1974).

51. D. Nortman, *Population and Family Planning Programs: A Factbook*, 2 REPORTS ON POPULATION/FAMILY PLANNING (5th ed. 1973).

Pakistan, 1972   Physicians certified for IUDs or vasectomy, 1,363.
                     Others, 24,548 of whom 2,246 are full-time and
                     6,896 part-time Field Motivators. 13,662 are dis-
                     tributors of conventional contraceptives.

India, 1972   Physicians, 5,107. Others, 46,338 of whom 18,983
                     are auxiliary midwives, 3,125 are public health
                     nurses and lady home visitors and 12,880 are fam-
                     ily planning health assistants.

Thailand, 1972   Physicians, 599. Others, 7,213 of whom 1,060 are
                     nurse-midwives, 3,968 are auxiliary midwives and
                     1,985 are male health workers.

South Korea, 1973   Physicians certified for IUDs and/or sterilizations,
                     1,614. Others, 2,393 of whom 706 are Health
                     Center nurses and 1,473 are Field Workers
                     (licensed nurse aids).

Egypt, 1972   Physicians, 3,850. Others, 7,800 of whom 6,000
                     are nurses and midwives and 1,800 are social
                     workers.

If a great number of these nurses and midwives could be trained in IUD
insertion and in menstrual regulation and suitable male paramedicals in vasectomy then in these six countries alone the 13,533 physicians could be
joined by some 40,000 nurses and midwives in oral contraceptive prescription, IUD insertion and menstrual regulation.

V.   REQUIREMENTS PRIOR TO ENABLING PARAMEDICALS AND AUXILIARIES TO UNDERTAKE VASECTOMY AND MENSTRUAL REGULATION

A.   *Training of Paramedicals and Auxiliaries*

It has become apparent from the foregoing that the degree to which
paramedicals can be utilized in performing vasectomies and menstrual regulation is directly proportional to the type, quality and amount of training they
receive. In attempting to formulate guidelines for training, I suggest that the
following elements be considered.

1. Section of Standard Techniques

Presently there are a number of slightly differing techniques in use for
vasectomy, *e.g.*, the amount of vas excised and the method of dealing with
the severed ends. A standard technique for use by paramedicals must be
selected, as well as a standard post-operative dressing and suspensory ban-
dage. Consideration must also be given to the advisability of the routine use
of a post-operative chemotherapeutic, such as a sulphonamide. The equipment to be issued must also be standardised. There is, presently, a much

greater standardisation in menstrual regulation and the menstrual regulation kits include a 50cc syringe which ensures that the necessary vacuum will be created by the syringe and not by a hand-, or foot- or electric pump which can cause a higher complication rate.

It is necessary to lay down guidelines on a national level, as paramedical staff are mobile and may easily be posted. Differing standard techniques in differing provinces would place too much of an unnecessary burden on the paramedicals.

2. Guidelines on the Selection of Patients

This involves both medical and legal considerations. The medical considerations consist of ensuring that the patient is fit. As far as vasectomy is concerned, it is never an emergency procedure so that a temporarily unfit patient may justifiably be told to wait until he is better. However, in the case of menstrual regulation it is not so much an elective procedure since the mortality and morbidity of an abortion increases with increasing delay. Furthermore, menstrual regulation, at least by one definition, must occur in the first six weeks of amenorrhoea. After that time, the procedure remains the same but the terminology changes to an induced abortion by suction evacuation. Therefore, the "degree of fitness" of a woman asking for menstrual regulation must be carefully defined for paraprofessional performance.

Specific contraindications to vasectomy by a paramedical would include *any* divergence of the anatomy from the normal, *i.e.*, an undescended testicle, a hernia, etc.

Legal considerations must also be identified and carefully explained to all paramedicals during their training. Examples of these concerns are those provisions in the legal codes which set an age minimum or a minimal number of children required before vasectomy may be undertaken, whether one or both partners have to give consent, etc. Similar requirements exist where menstrual regulation is to be undertaken.

3. Identification of Operative and Post-Operative Problems

These must be identified and the teaching oriented to cover them, their treatment or referral to a physician. Examples concerning vasectomy would be hypersensitivity of the vas causing pain or fainting; loss of the vas after sectioning; haemorrhage ranging from skin bruising to haematoma formation; infection and post-operative discomfort. In the case of menstrual regulation they would include faintness; haemorrhage; sudden abdominal pain; retained products of conception and a continuing pregnancy.

4. Formation of the Teaching Course

It would be unwise to include the teaching of vasectomy and menstrual regulation in the basic paramedical teaching courses. It would be wiser to restrict such teaching to selected field personnel after they have already served at least one year in the field in a polyfunctional capacity. Such selected personnel could then be taught in annual or biannual courses held at a central or provincial level. In the case of decentralised courses, it is essential that the techniques taught be identical.

The course content and duration would be decided centrally. The decision would be reached by a central committee consisting of representatives from the Ministry of Health, the Obstetric Unit of the teaching hospital, if any, representatives of the obstetricians working in the rural areas and senior members of the cadres of paramedicals which would be actually involved in the delivery of the service. If there are no "rural" obstetricians, they would be well represented by the general duties medical officers who staff the District Hospitals and number the functions of District Obstetrician amongst their many other duties. These physicians would add their practical knowledge of the rural areas to the professional knowledge of the teaching hospital obstetricians.

Teaching would be both didactic and participatory. Prior to certification each paramedical will have undertaken a stipulated number of vasectomies or menstrual regulations under personal supervision. The duration of the course will depend on the caliber of the staff being trained, auxiliary staff probably requiring a slightly longer training than paramedical staff. A basic minimum would be one month.

It is essential that each course should teach the whole spectrum of pregnancy spacing since vasectomy and menstrual regulation form but small parts of a whole. The personnel will be expected to advise on all aspects of family planning and to participate in as many areas as they can within the existing culture.

5. Selection of Teaching Personnel

The result of all paramedical and auxiliary basic and post-graduate teaching stands or falls on two variables—the caliber of the teaching and continuing field supervision. Originally, the post-graduate courses in family planning, vasectomy and menstrual regulation will be undertaken only by professional personnel. At a later date, after students have graduated and have had a considerable field experience, they will be reassessed and selected persons given further training so that they may largely undertake the teaching courses. Thus, the fate of the whole school will stand or fall on the initial professional teachers who must be selected with the utmost care.

They need not be obstetricians, but since obstetricians have a large say in the formulation of the course content they must possess two essentials. First, they must be properly motivated, motivated to believe that the paramedical is undertaking a proper job in his own right and not as a second-best until such time as sufficient physicians can be trained. Second they must have had a wide rural experience as the majority of the work will be undertaken in the rural areas and outside hospitals.

6. Supervision

It is widely agreed that the work of the paramedical cadres is directly related to the amount of supervision they receive. Such supervision must not be purely negative, *i.e.*, critical. Supervisory visits are as much to raise the morale of the paramedicals as to supervise their work. Where praise is due it must be given and where criticism is due it must be done in such a way that an element of praise can also be included.

In many of the developing countries supervision is minimal and is largely undertaken at a Provincial level by the Provincial Medical Officer or the Provincial paramedical, etc. Such men have vast territories to cover and a minimum of time available. In theory, supervision should be undertaken by the District Medical Officers, but these men are often the only physician at a District Hospital for which they are responsible as well as being responsible for a district of some hundreds or thousands of square miles.

It cannot be gainsaid that in many of the developing countries the only medical service to the mass of the people is that provided by the medical cadres. Nor can it be gainsaid that in very many of those countries the supervision of such personnel is woefully lacking. Since their performance is directly related to the supervision they receive, it would appear that the whole concept of supervision must be re-examined. There appears to be a very good case indeed for special supervisory teams consisting of professional and paramedical members. A place on a supervisory team should be included in the career ladder of the personnel concerned and will certainly endow them with a deeper insight into the various medical problems in the country concerned.

It would also be beneficial if the few obstetricians such countries possess could undertake regular supervisory tours of the rural areas as an essential part of their duties. It could be argued that if they feel their fulltime services are required at their central hospitals then they have failed in their teaching programs, since one of their tasks is to teach their juniors in their team. Too often one finds the few obstetricians and pediatricians in a developing country fully absorbed in teaching medical students and in abstruse research whilst the country as a whole is struggling, rudderless, to provide direction to an elementary maternal and child health service, which includes family planning.

7. Selection of Paramedical and Auxiliary Personnel

In this connection there are three vital points, two of which have already been mentioned—that such teaching should be restricted to post-graduate teaching of specially selected paramedicals and that the teaching should encompass the whole field of maternal and child health including all aspects of family planning. The third point is that the developing countries, and also developed countries, need multipurpose workers, not unipotential workers.

It is a waste of slender finances and resources to train unipotential workers in numerous fields.

B. *Legislation in Support of Paramedical Participation*

Public legislation has been essential for the development of the health services and disease prevention and is as vital for the success of family planning programmes. The legal protection of all persons engaged in it must be ensured, particularly if they are not already covered under the umbrella of medical and health legislation. All of the legal aspects and implications of using paramedical staff must be considered and model legislation drawn up. The effectiveness of the paramedical cadres on numerous occasions has been hampered because their legal status has not been explicitly established. And as the "licensing" of all medical practitioners is becoming a more common practice, it is essential that the paraprofessional (paramedical and auxiliary) cadres be established in law as well as in fact.

In general, legislation must be designed to:
1. Enable a procedure to be undertaken;
2. Provide the client with an assurance that the procedure will only be undertaken by an approved person; and
3. Provide legal protection for the approved person.

Dean and Piotrow[52] have shown that during 1973 and the first half of 1974 nearly 30 countries have revised some aspect of their national law and policy relating to family planning. Furthermore, under the sponsorship of the International Advisory Committee on Population and Law twenty-four developing countries have established Law and Population Projects to compile, review and revise laws which are outdated or inconsistent with United Nations declarations. Five countries have eased their restrictions on voluntary sterilization,[53] and ten countries have changed their laws or policies to make pregnancy termination more available on various health grounds.[54] Lee and Paxman[55] have pointed out that the use of menstrual regulation may be legally possible in many other countries which have so-called restrictive abortion laws. This is due to the way in which those laws define the crime of abortion.[56]

---

52. Dean & Piotrow, eds., *Eighteen Months of Legal Change*, POPULATION REPORT, Series E, No. 1 (1974).

53. Austria, Denmark, Iran, the Philippines, and Tunisia.

54. Austria, El Salvador, Guatemala, Iran, Korea, Sweden, Tunisia, United States, and West Germany.

55. L. Lee & J. Paxman, *Legal Aspects of Menstrual Regulation*, Law and Population Monograph Series No. 19 (1974).

56. The United States Supreme Court seemed to include menstrual regulation as a means of abortion that could not constitutionally be prohibited during the first trimester of pregnancy. Roe v. Wade, 410 U.S. 113 (1973). Most American state laws would not seem to differentiate between methods.

Within the past two years explicit legal recognition has been given to the role of paramedical personnel, especially in connection with oral contraceptives. But increasingly more paramedicals are being trained and authorised to insert IUDs. Midwives and nurses who have received two months training in government-designated institutions were authorised to distribute oral contraceptives and to insert IUDs in the Philippines by a decree issued in January 1973. In September 1973 the Philippines also reinterpreted their law on "mutilation" to exclude tubal ligation and vasectomy. There is thus a growing trend of legislation to enable menstrual regulations and abortion and voluntary sterilization to be undertaken, to recognise the role that should be played by the paramedical cadre and to protect the client—as demonstrated by the Philippine law enabling paramedicals to undertake IUD insertion *if* they have received two months training in a government-designated institution. More specifically, the law should deal with the seven areas discussed next.

1. Legal Protection for the Client

The client must have the assurance that vasectomy and menstrual regulation will only be undertaken by a properly trained and recognised paramedical and this requires restrictive legislation defining a "properly trained" person. The client's dignity must be maintained. This is lost not only in the massive vasectomy camps in India, but also in the United States, the United Kingdom and elsewhere where paramedicals have manifested hostility towards women undergoing abortion and some hospital administrators have been uncooperative in administering the new laws.[57]

One consequence of development has been an increasing transfer of decision-making from the community to the individual, such as in the liberalisation of the abortion laws. Social evolution, sexual equality and increasing standards of education are producing individuals who are more likely to question or contradict imposed solutions. Thus, changes in social attitudes can result in new laws. When new mores have become accepted by the majority, legislators must carefully reconsider existing legislation. One consideration being whether the newly "accepted" mores are those of a vocal minority or of the so-called silent majority. It may also be that the vocal minority are giving expression to a human right which has been ignored in a policy of *laissez faire*, the few individuals striving against the social forces, the former demanding and the latter resisting change.

In the context of vasectomy, the principle of guarding the rights of the individual must include the setting of a minimal age at which the operation may be performed since, at least in the developing countries, the operation must be regarded as irreversible. It is therefore essential that the individual

---

57. ABORTION IN A CHANGING WORLD 466 (R. Hall, ed. 1971).

concerned should be of a sufficiently mature age to consider the full implications. In the context of menstrual regulation the lower age at which this may be undertaken must also be stipulated. Not infrequently it has been undertaken below the age of consent so that the operator, if not informing the authorities, becomes an accessory to a crime. Such considerations will affect a paramedical operator as much as a professional one.

2. Legal Protection for the Practitioner

The practitioner, professional or paramedical, also requires legal protection. The effectiveness of the paramedical on numerous occasions has been hampered as his or her legal status has not been explicitly established. The most recently published illustration of this is Rudolph, Zalar and Goldstein's review of the University of California Family Planning Nurse Specialist programme.[58] These authors state that legal considerations influenced the utilisation of the trained FPNSs, with nurses, physicians and administrators all agreeing that the undetermined legal status of the FPNSs caused them great concern. Although all students had been trained in IUD insertion, only five of the first 28 graduates were inserting them due to legal questions. It is also of the greatest importance that the authors state that the paramedicals experienced various degrees of role confusion, as in some clinics guidelines on their employment were absent or vague.

Although the doctrine of "custom and usage" establishes the authority of a physician to delegate tasks, it has been found in practice in the United States that it does not readily apply to either new types of personnel nor to innovations in the use of existing personnel.[59] In 1971 in the United States at least 14 states adopted some form of delegation amendments to their existing medical practice acts.[60]

A necessary prerequisite to the recognition of the paramedical in law and their acceptance by the general public is the proper accreditation of their training programme, as is presently being undertaken in the United States.

58. Rudolph, Zalar & Goldstein, *Factors Influencing the Use of Family Planning Nurse Specialists*, in PROCEEDINGS 81, *supra* note 8.

59. Sadler, *Licensure for the Physician's Assistant*, in INTERMEDIATE-LEVEL HEALTH PRACTITIONERS 180 (V. Lippard & E. Purcell, eds.) (New York: Josiah Macy, Jr. Foundation 1973).

60. *See, e.g.*, N.Y. PUB. HEALTH LAW § 3701 (McKinney Supp. 1972) ("physician's associate" or "specialist's assistant"); CAL. BUS. & PROF. CODE § 2511(d) (West Supp. 1971) ("physician's assistant"); N.C. GEN. STAT. § 90-18(13) (1971) ("assistant to the physician"); and CONN. GEN. STAT. ANN. § 20-9 (1971). The other states are Alaska, (ALASKA STAT. §§ 68.64.170, .360 (1973)); Florida (FLA. STAT. ANN. § 458.135(2)(d) (Supp. 1971)); Iowa (IOWA CODE ANN. § 148B (1972)); New Hampshire (N.H. REV. STAT. ANN. § 329.21 (Supp. 1971)); Oregon (ORE. REV. STAT. § 677.065 (1971)); Utah, (UTAH CODE ANN. § 58-12-40 (Supp. 1971)); Washington (WASH. REV. CODE ANN. Ch. 18.71A (Supp. 1971)); and West Virginia (W. VA. CODE Ch. 30-3A (1971)).

Abrahamson has stated that such accreditation involves six major components:

— Some form of statement or approval
— Issued by some predesignated agency or institution
— Informing interested and/or concerned parties
— That the training programme is satisfactory and/or adequate
— That the aim of the programme is to produce practitioners; and
— That such practitioners should have certain performance capabilities.[61]

These six points would form the basis of the accreditation of a paramedical training programme. Following their training, the paramedicals should undergo a qualifying examination set by a legally recognised authority and on qualification would have their names entered on a register which would be kept by a legally recognised body. This body, the equivalent of the Medical Council,[62] would also have the powers of peer judgment and erasure or revocation.

This register would be solely concerned with post-graduate achievements, a separate register being kept of those having passed the qualifying examinations to enter the general paramedical ranks. The public's assurance that a paramedical was qualified in a post-graduate field such as in family planning, including menstrual regulation and/or vasectomy, would be that his or her name appears in both registers. The entry of their name in the post-graduate register would also qualify the paramedical for legal protection.

For general acceptance by the public, as well as for an easier legal recognition, the paramedicals should also create a national body which should be legally recognized. Nurses already have a national body in many countries—the General Nursing Council or its equivalent. This body could also represent the newer types of nursing personnel such as the Nurse Practitioner, the Child Health Associate, the Family Planning Nurse Specialist, etc., if such groups are either represented by members of their own specialty on the Council or on a subcommittee immediately below it. It is impossible for the interests of one group to be safely guarded by another.

In the developing countries where a General Nursing Council is not yet established, one should be legislated for as well as equivalent Councils for other medical workers such as the Medical Assistants. It is only by the establishment of such Councils that peer judgment can be undertaken and Council members can have a say, or indeed control, of training programs and examinations. It is doubtful if the paramedicals in the developing countries

---

61. Sai, *The 1973 IPPF Regional Conference on the Medical and Social Aspects of Abortion in Africa*, ABORTION RESEARCH NOTES, Supp. 8 (1974).

62. The Medical Council is the English counterpart to an American State Licensing Board.

will receive a wholehearted acceptance by the general public until they are firmly established in fact and in legislation.

3. Supervision

As has been stated, the ultimate performance of a paramedical in the field will depend on the degree and quality of supervision under which he is placed. Legislation or regulations are required to define supervision, and these must be realistic for the country concerned. Whereas it is possible in a developed country for a paramedical undertaking menstrual regulation or vasectomy to be under fairly close supervision of a professional, such is far from the case in a developing country.

4. Enabling Legislation in Respect of Menstrual Regulation

As with enabling legislation concerned with the termination of pregnancy, this must also be oriented to the country concerned. If a developing country passes legislation enabling pregnancy termination to be undertaken when certified as necessary by three medical practitioners, one of whom must be a specialist (except in the case of an immediate medical necessity —which will not arise in menstrual regulation) as has recently been passed by one developing country, such legislation is completely unrealistic where the required "specialist" does not exist except in a few larger urban areas, and in the great mass of the country many whole districts would be hard-pressed to ensure that a woman meets two general physicians. Moreover, discrimination must not exist against the unmarried woman. The Accra Conference on Medical and Social Aspects of Abortion in Africa[63] called for extensive legal reform to end what was felt to be a discrimination against the poor, the unmarried and the woman in the rural areas of Africa.

5. Conscience Clauses

Abortion legislation concerning professionals when liberalised usually includes an escape clause whereby those physicians whose conscience is unalterably against abortion may refuse to undertake the procedure. It is doubtful if such a clause would be necessary for paramedicals who are given post-graduate training in menstrual regulation and vasectomy, as such persons if selected for such training would doubtlessly reveal their objections at their first interview.

6. The Period During Which Menstrual Regulation Is Permitted

The main difference between menstrual regulation and a suction evacuation abortion in the first trimester of pregnancy is the duration of the pregnancy prior to performing the operation. In general, the term menstrual regulation is limited to the first fourteen days after a missed menstruation (a

---

63.   Sai, *supra* note 64.

pregnancy of up to one month's duration and a period of six weeks from the last menstrual period). This time interval appears to be chosen since it is the interval during which pregnancy cannot be confidently diagnosed by the routine laboratory tests. However, a paramedical working in a Rural Health Center and even in many District Hospitals will not have the facilities for undertaking such tests and without undertaking a vaginal examination will be unable to diagnose a pregnancy before the tenth week—only two weeks before the end of the first trimester. Therefore, it may well be that in framing legislation enabling paramedicals in the developing countries to undertake suction evacuation this fourteen-day period after the first missed menstruation could be extended. This is even more necessary considering the long distances many patients have to travel to reach a Rural Health Center.

7. Site of the Operation

In enabling legislation it is not uncommon for strict requirements to be laid down as to the site and required amenities where abortion, menstrual regulation or vasectomy may be undertaken. Thus, in the United Kingdom, Hungary, Tunisia and Singapore, pregnancy terminations may only be undertaken in an approved or designated hospital or on an approved premises. In New York City, shortly after the liberalisation of the abortion law, terminations were being performed in physicians' surgeries and small clinics. Three months after the liberalising legislation was passed new municipal regulations became effective and virtually prevented such operations outside large clinics or hospitals due to the various equipment requirements. Requirements enacted supposedly to safeguard a woman's health have also required that the woman must be admitted as an in-patient.

Legislation in developing countries must not be oriented towards the single teaching hospital or the three or four central hospitals but must take into account the facilities available in the considerably poorer District Hospitals and in the Rural Health Centers which care for the majority of the population.

VI. MATERNAL AND CHILD HEALTH RELATED TO
PREGNANCY PREVENTION AND TERMINATION

Menstrual regulation and vasectomy are secondary preventive methods necessitated by the absence of the ideal primary preventive method, an ideal contraceptive. As secondary preventive methods, their use should be reserved to that of a back-up system for the conventional contraceptives. Legislation enabling or liberalising their use must be aimed equally at encouraging the use of the more conventional contraceptive methods.

Liberalisation of abortion laws will of itself produce health benefits. Tietze[64] states that in New York City two years after the liberalisation of the

---

64. Tietze, *Two Years Experience with a Liberal Abortion Law: Its Impact on Fertility Trends in New York City*, 5 POPULATION PLANNING PERSPECTIVES 36 (1973).

abortion laws there had been a decline of about 19,000 births above what would otherwise have been expected. In the United Kingdom it has been estimated that since the liberalisation of the abortion law in 1968 the number of deaths from abortion has fallen by half. It has also been suggested that on a worldwide basis there are probably four abortions for every ten term deliveries so that without abortion the world birth rate would rise from 35 to close on 50 per 1,000. This would produce a doubling of the world's population in fourteen years instead of the presently estimated twenty.

The mortality and morbidity associated with abortion increases with the length of the pregnancy concerned, and it is therefore essential for the health of the mother to enable her to seek an early abortion in an unobstructive way. Research has also shown that mortality is lower with menstrual regulation, before a pregnancy can be diagnosed, than with an early abortion. Liberalisation of the abortion laws is therefore not enough and putative pregnancies should be terminated, when desired, prior to the stage at which pregnancy may be diagnosed—which may be a late stage indeed in the rural areas of the developing countries.

Table I

Abortion mortality: The estimated number of legal abortions, number of deaths (all cases) and mortality ratio per 100,000 abortions in New York City[65]

Length of gestation & method of termination	Number of Terminations	Number of Deaths	Mortality ratio per 100,000 abortions
12 weeks or less	321,500	6	1.9
13 weeks or more	80,500	14	17.4
Suction	261,700	3	1.1
D&C	84,600	2	2.4
Saline	53,300	10	18.8
Hysterotomy	2,400	5	208.3

Table I shows that the mortality rate is less for abortions undertaken in the first trimester of pregnancy and is least when suction is used. Stim[66] also compared the complication rates in two series of first trimester abortions using the methods of dilatation and curettage and of minisuction:

Table II

Complications	Standard abortion (D&C)		Minisuction	
	Number	%	Number	%
Immediate	11	4.9%	10	3.2%
Early, within 45 days	33	15.0%	26	8.4%
Late	1	0.4%	—	
Total:	223		310	

---

65. Stim, *Minisuction: An Office Procedure*, in PROCEEDINGS, *supra* note 8.
66. *Id.*

No accurate figures can be established for the mortality and morbidity rates of abortion undertaken outside the medical setting (presumably illegal) but in some communities the mortality rate is about 1,000 per 100,000—which is in contrast to a figure of from 3 to 5 per 100,000 for legal abortions in the first trimester.

Lanman, Kohl and Bedell[67] have shown how infant health was also improved by a liberal abortion policy in New York, one year after the law had become effective. In six Brooklyn hospitals elective abortions increased from 1% to 54% of the deliveries and the number of spontaneous abortions (probably induced illegally) decreased by 20%. Immature infant births dropped by 36%, for the previous ten years they had been relatively constant at 19 per 1,000 deliveries but fell to 9 per 1,000 deliveries after the law was liberalised. The number of unwanted and abandoned babies fell by 56% from the period commencing six months after liberalisation.

If liberalised termination of pregnancy legislation, including menstrual regulation and vasectomy being undertaken by suitably qualified paramedicals, could be included with liberalisation of all contraceptive laws (*i.e.*, deprescription of the pill and the use of commercial outlets) and included in an overall Maternal and Child Health Law, very great benefits could be expected. It is noteworthy that such a law was enacted in South Korea in January 1973. The law not only eased the conditions under which legal abortion could be undertaken but in specific clauses placed an onus on all provincial authorities to promote the health of mothers and children through *improved medical care and family planning*. This law included the setting aside of a certain sum of money to enable the lower socio-economic groups to obtain an abortion.

VII.   Conclusion: A New Approach

It is a common practice in discussing the work of the paramedical and auxiliary cadres to introduce the subject by "explaining" or "defending" their employment. In general, three such "excuses" are given:

(1) They are cheaper to train and require less training time than physicians;

(2) They are cheaper to maintain in the field; and

(3) They are a "second best" until such time as enough physicians can be trained.

In view of the difficulty created by the terminology used to describe these workers, their vital role in providing medical care to the vast majority of the population, and the existing rigid barriers separating the professional, paramedical and auxiliary, it is necessary to completely re-evaluate the medical care delivery system. The whole medical care delivery system must be

---

67.   Lanman, Kohl & Bedell, reported in *Pediatric News*, May 1970, at 60.

reviewed and redefined so that we may evaluate precisely what is "doctors' work" and what is "non-doctors' work." Thus, by detailed job descriptions on which training will be founded, we will be able to deliver medical care not through a conglomerate of "second-bests" but through the best man or woman available to provide the specific function required.

Secondly, the team approach to medical care must be developed with no team member being required to work in isolation. Two types of teams are required: the Primary Health Care team and the Referral Health Care team. The former would consist mainly of "auxiliaries" with a few "paramedicals" and a very few physicians, whereas the latter would consist largely of physicians and paramedicals with a very few auxiliaries. The Primary Health Care team will provide medical care on an out-patient basis—both preventive and curative care—and will be reinforced with the other necessary components of health care such as sociological care and, where necessary, educational and agricultural advice. This team will care for the great majority of the "sick" and will operate from Rural and Urban Health Centers, clinics, surgeries and hospital out-patient departments. The Referral Health Care Team will only be concerned with patients admitted to hospitals but will also act as a backup and consultation service to the Primary Health Care Team.

Responsibility for matters concerning pregnancy planning would be placed on the Primary Health Care Team and would include vasectomy and menstrual regulation. The Referral Health Care Team would be concerned with abortions after the first trimester of pregnancy and, at present, with female sterilization. Such a system would not preclude the widespread distribution of contraceptives such as the condom and the non-prescription oral contraceptives through commercial and other outlets.

In summary, it may be said that the existing medical system creates hurdles so that we have to whip people to jump over them—we call this "motivation."[68] The two primary objectives of physicians in relation to the provision of medical care should be first, to strike down all barriers to medical care delivery; and second, to put together teams to provide efficient, effective medical care and to learn to delegate.[69]

---

68.   Potts, The Future Role of Physicians in Population Change (paper delivered at the International Conference on the Physician and Population Change, Stockholm, August, 1974).
   69.   *Id.*

Report of Workshop on Role of Professional Paramedical Personnel in Menstrual Regulation and Vasectomy

The feasibility and implications of using professional paramedical personnel to perform menstrual regulation and vasectomy were rather fully discussed by Dr. F.M. Shattock in his paper. The upshot of it all was that Dr. Shattock was of the opinion that paramedicals could be used to perform the procedures if they were properly trained and supervised. His conclusion was based in large part on years of working with paramedicals in the African setting. The workshop sought to add some dimension to the issues raised in the paper. In an attempt to further define the role of the paramedical in this area, the workshop's discussion centered on three facets of the subject: (1) the paramedicals' role in the delivery of health services; (2) paramedical training and supervision; and (3) barriers to paramedical use. At the outset it was acknowledged that it would be impossible to adequately meet the family planning needs of the population without utilizing the services of paramedicals.

Delivery of Health Services

Emphasis was placed on the fact that before paramedicals can assume responsibilities with respect to menstrual regulation and vasectomy, they must be functioning within organizational structure of a health service system. While all countries have health care delivery systems, it was pointed out that in most cases the paramedicals are not permitted to undertake the performance of procedures under discussion here. Several participants stressed the importance of creating health care teams and of redefining which duties must or should be handled by a doctor and which can be assumed by a paramedical. In this context it was felt that family planning should be integrated into the basic health care service system. At least one of the participants cautioned that the best way of improving health care in general is to ensure that the paramedicals in the health care team are adequately trained in all aspects of health care, rather than have them do only family planning-related duties. The point was made that it is a dreadful waste of resources to have a paramedical go into the family setting to instruct a woman on the use of the IUD, if the health worker cannot also note during the visit that the husband is tubercular and one of the children is deathly ill. Thus, it was suggested that a whole hierarchy of health care personnel be created, with some of the members of the team specializing in the family planning aspects of health.

Training and Supervision of Paramedicals

Much of the discussion was devoted to what most of the participants felt was the key issue in this field—the training and supervision of paramedicals. The consensus of the people present was that paramedicals could be trained to perform menstrual regulation and vasectomy, though the former is a relatively new technique and not a great deal of information is available about it. It was also noted that many paramedicals, such as the midwives in Indonesia, were already using traditional methods for abortion. The essential elements of any training programme in this area were felt to be the method of selection of trainees, the content of training courses and the manner in which supervision is maintained. As to the selection of trainees, it was concluded that because of the nature of the procedures which would be taught, candidates for training must be carefully screened. Participation in the training programme should be restricted to paramedicals who have already been trained in other areas of health care and have had considerable field experience. It was also concluded that the content of the training should include instruction on recognizing contraindications and evaluating and screening out of patients who are not healthy enough to undergo the procedures. Likewise, uniform methods of providing supervision by and consultation with medical doctors or highly skilled paramedical personnel should be created, and those authorized to perform menstrual regulation and vasectomy should be placed on a registry. Lastly, the issue was raised about who should set standards. Put another way, should the World Health Organisation be called upon to establish international guidelines? It was the opinion of the group that assistance in establishing standards at the international level could be useful, but the opinion was qualified because it was recognized that medical practices and standards vary from nation to nation depending on a number of factors. Therefore, it was suggested that the standards would be more acceptable and realistic if they were tailored to the needs in the local setting.

Barriers to Wider Use of Paramedicals

The discussion was interspersed with brief references to the barriers which exist to implementing a health programme calling for the increased use of paramedicals. The following questions were raised: What cultural preferences are there which would frustrate the use of paramedicals? How do doctors feel about letting paramedicals carry more of the work load? Will the laws which are presently in force bar the paramedicals from doing these tasks? With regard to the first, some concern was expressed that the people might not accept in confidence a paramedical who is trained to do what a doctor has normally done for them. But this concern seemed to diminish in light of the fact that the majority of the world's population, particularly in the less developed world, already receive medical care from paramedicals. It was noted also that in many countries local customs require that women treat women and men treat men, especially where procedures such as menstrual regulation and vasectomy are concerned. The opposition of doctors to delegating duties to paramedicals was cited as one of the major barriers to fully utilizing the services of the paramedicals. It was also noted that legislation and health regulations have a role to play in this area. In order for paramedicals to be able to perform the duties under discussion, it will be necessary to revise many of the laws. These laws, it was added, must be adapted to the local setting.

SECTION 4

Coordination of Population Laws and Policies

Coordination of Population Laws and Policies: National Governments

By
Elizabeth Odio*

INTRODUCTION

In the search for a better understanding of the demographic phenomena, the legal aspect—*i.e.*, the relationship between these phenomena and the rules of law—is both relevant and important. The association between the demographic situation and the processes of economic and social development have been evident for some time. Traditionally, population has been regarded as a vital element of the total development of peoples. The difference of opinion between knowledgeable persons has generally centered upon whether a given country's problem is one of population or of development. If it is the former, the solution would be demographic; if the latter, economic.[1] Despite the fact that there are people, at least in Latin America, who believe that the relationship between population growth and economic development is not clear,[2] it is generally agreed "that population must be taken into consideration as a basic element in formulating policies on employment, redistribution of income, education, the increase of savings, industrialization, energy, the supply of basic needs, and the creation of poles of development."[3]

Nevertheless, during all these years of analysis, consideration has not been given to the *legal* aspects of demography. The idea of quantifying the effects of the different types of legal rules on the demographic behaviour of a specific population has, up to now, been totally disregarded, despite the fact that the law always has an influence—be it positive or negative, direct or indirect—on population growth and movement.

* Professor, Law Faculty, University of Costa Rica. Director, Law and Population Project.

1. Carmen A. Miro, *La influencia de los cambio de población*, ACTS OF THE EIGHTH INTERNATIONAL CONFERENCE OF IPPF, Santiago, Chile, 9-15 April, 1967, at 17.

2. Octavio Cabello, *Vivienda, crecimiento de población y desarrollo económico*, in EL DILEMA DE LA POBLACIÓN EN AMÉRICA LATINA, 152 (Bogota 1968).

3. Initiative on the General Population Law of Mexico presented to the Congress by President Luis Echeverría, Sept. 13, 1973, at 1.

When the United Nations Conference on Human Rights proclaimed in Teheran in 1968 that family planning is a basic human right, it placed upon the international community, and upon each country in particular, a responsibility of a legal nature. This responsibility is not only one of international law, but also—and more basically—one which involves the domestic legislation of each state. From the moment that the Teheran Proclamation was adopted, there arose an inescapable duty to investigate specifically how, and in what manner, demographic phenomena and the rules of law relate to and influence each other. The obvious result of the past lack of understanding of this relationship is that population growth and movement as such have been the object of conscious, direct legal regulation in only a few countries. One of the exceptions to the rule has been the Philippines where a recent amendment to the constitution states that:

It shall be the responsibility of the State to achieve and maintain levels most conducive to the national welfare.[4]

We can, however, state that in a number of cases, laws have been put into effect which do directly affect the demographic structure of a country.

The impact which certain laws may have on the size and structure of a population is clear. Such laws as those governing family relations, abortion, sterilization, taxes, land tenancy, etc., are closely allied with demographic phenomena. From a strictly juridical point of view, this fact stresses the obvious, and may therefore be easily dismissed. But the law, we must remember, is a composite of mandatory rules which regulate the conduct of the individual in society. Put simply, the law regulates human life. Thus, all juridical regulations maintain a more or less direct link to demographic developments. It is from that point of view that we must frame our search for a more precise definition of the relationship between law and population developments.

I. Strengthening the Nexus Between Law and Population: A Modest Proposal

This immediate relationship can perhaps be viewed most clearly through the establishment of rules which in their distinctive shadings directly regulate demographic phenomena. There are rules which could well be integrated into a General Population Law. We could reach a clearer understanding of the relationship between law and demography by making maximum use of the power of law as a catalyst for social change. After all, legislation and the processes of constitutional reform can be defined as "certain processes of change which have been given formal legitimacy."[5]

---

4. Constitution of the Philippines, art. XV, § 10 (1973).
5. T. Parsons, Ensayos de Teortia Sociológica 319-332 (Buenos Aires: Editorial Paidós 1967).

Recognition of the fact that law regulates certain facets of human behaviour may make the direct relationship between law and demographic phenomena more apparent. For example, if one were to set up mandatory rules for the specific purpose of regulating fertility, it would undoubtedly be found that these rules have a more direct impact on population than rules designed to regulate migration of foreigners into a country. Nevertheless, one cannot avoid the fact that compulsory rules cannot be dictated in countries whose legal systems are based on general principles of inviolable respect for human beings and their basic liberties.

At this point it is apparent that the role which national governments can play in the regulation of the demographic phenomena is singularly important. At the outset, I should make clear that the analysis of this question should be regarded from its practical point of view under which State and Law are the two complementary focal points of the same phenomena. From this point of view, State activity, seen in the form of action on the part of the organizations which we call "Government," should be regarded as the "Law in Action," or, the "Law in Motion."

Within this framework, I shall provide a sample outline for the discussion of the following suggestions:

A.   *The Formulation of a General Policy Regarding Population*

From what has been said above, I believe that it is the basic task of the Government of each country to develop a general policy which is both adequate and appropriate to the subject of population. The demographic problem is, in essence, a political one. The economic, statistical and juridical aspects of this delicate question are no more than partial approaches to, or at the most, special viewpoints on, the matter. Thus, one cannot fail to recognise that the decision which must be taken in this matter is a political one. It is the task of the State to fix its own goals for economic growth through integrated national development plans. And, as President Echeverría of Mexico made clear in the message which accompanied his proposed revisions of the Mexican General Population Law, in the formulation of these plans population plays a fundamental role.

The United Nations has stressed in various instruments that family planning is a basic human right and that it includes the right to information, education and access to the means for its practice.[6] Despite the unquestionable importance of these declarations, and the superior position which they hold in the internal juridical order of each country, I do not believe that the State should confine its action in this field solely to the essence of the

---

6.   Teheran Proclamation on Human Rights and Resolution XVIII titled "Human Rights Aspects of Family Planning;" Declaration on Social Progress and Development, Articles 4, 22(b) General Assembly Res. 2542, 24 U.N. GAOR, Supp. 30, pp. 49, 50, Doc. No. A/7630 (1969).

declarations themselves, for the question of population involves more than family planning.

Demographic aspects must, of necessity, be included in the objectives for economic and social development which each State establishes for itself. Each State must define in its own political terms what it should do with regard to its population and how the dynamics involved are to be managed. It may well be that the specific needs of a State require a fundamental policy in favor of population growth in order to increase its human resources. On the other hand, it may be necessary to stabilize population so that its uncontrolled growth will not destroy the framework of a balanced and equitable development. But these decisions are for the State to make, and they will vary according to national circumstances. It should be clear in any case, that a population policy cannot be considered as a substitute for economic development. It is not sufficient merely to reduce or increase fertility. The basic task of the State must be to provide adequate food, employment, education, health, and housing to all its citizens, and as should be obvious to all, these are not accomplished simply through the application of measures which stem the demographic growth.

On the basis of the above principles, I would propose that each State should establish through its Government an adequate and appropriate demographic policy, and this policy should take the form of a General Population Law. (See Appendix A).

B. *The Promulgation of a General Population Law*

Although I have stated earlier that the basis for decisions on demographic matters is essentially political, we cannot forget for a moment that the transformation of a population can and must be regulated by law. The action taken by the State in this field should be framed in the juridical context of a general law which, in its turn, is founded upon constitutional precepts.

In the case of Costa Rica, the Constitution proclaims absolute respect for fundamental human rights. So any action in Costa Rica must perforce comport with the precept. The General Population Law, the promulgation of which should be a concern of each Government, necessarily will have to embody and reflect the political and juridical situation of each State. It should, therefore, be a reflection of a State's own particular ideology. In other words, in a field as vital and sensitive as this, external influences which reflect realities and necessities foreign to the particular State in question are not acceptable.

The General Population Law should be based on an over-all demographic policy which is designed to improve the life of the citizens by achieving a more equitable distribution of income. The legal instrument should establish the purposes and limitations of State action in the field. It should create the appropriate organizations to oversee the activities of the State, and grant to them the authority and means necessary to act. In sum the law should include basic provisions on:

(1) general demographic objectives;
(2) family planning programmes, offered as public health and education services;
(3) direct regulation of existing private activities in the field;
(4) international and internal migration;
(5) creation of an organization to coordinate and implement the Government's policies in this field;
(6) amendments to those laws which are opposed to or which militate against the basic objectives of the General Population Law; and,
(7) enforcement provisions.

The experience from the research carried out by the Law and Population Project in Costa Rica indicates that the lack of a clear over-all demographic policy, and basically of a General Population Law, has resulted in many contradictions among important laws, and also between the laws and important governmental activities. For example, the age of legal capacity in Costa Rica—including the minimum legal age of marriage—has just been reduced from 21 to 18 years for both sexes. There are laws that offer family subsidies and allowances to families based on the number of children. And abortion is a crime, as is sterilization when used as means for family planning. On the other hand, the Government is enthusiastically supporting a National Programme of Family Planning and Sex Education. The confusion and contradictions are clear.

Therefore, in Costa Rica, we are proposing the enactment of a General Population Law as a method of coordinating the existing population-related laws and eliminating the contradictions between the official attitudes of the Legislature (which can be classified as unknowingly pro-natalist) and the activities of the Executive Branch, which seek to reduce the present levels of fertility.

C. *Creation of a Competent Public Organization*

Since demographic problems are found in all the areas of governmental activity, the new organization or mechanism which will be set up under the General Population Law will probably tend to impinge on the activities of existing government bodies. Thus, to the end that the population activities of the State be coordinated rather than isolated and incoherent, the General Population Law must provide for a competent public organization charged with carrying out the policy established by the State. This new organization must be composed of high level representatives from the offices whose activities are most directly related to population questions. Similarly, there must be representatives from those branches of the Government charged with the formulation and implementation of economic development plans.

With the creation and integration into the Government of this new organization, the concept that demographic problems are not merely problems of health or education but rather are basically political problems will take concrete shape. It will come to be understood that they affect the very existence of the State in all its activities.

Thus, the plan to include the creation of a National Population Council in the new Mexican law, referred to above, seems logical. The Council is the key provision of the system for integrated action on the part of the Mexican State in the population field, and this is evidenced by the fact that the Secretary of the Government serves as its Chairman.

To draw further from the Mexican precedent, let me point out that the Council will include, in addition, representatives of the Ministries of Public Education, Health and Welfare, Development and Public Credit, and Labour and Social Security, as well as a representative from the Office of the President. Without doubt, we have in the Mexican law an example not only important for America in particular, but also for all the member States of the United Nations.

II. Conclusion

To summarize, we cannot overemphasize the vital role which national Governments can play in coordinating laws and policies related to population. We must see to it that this role draws its real significance from the fact that demographic problems are accepted as being political in nature. Problems arising from the proper growth, decrease or distribution of a population will never be solved so long as they are only regarded as economic, demographic or juridical in nature. In short, the problem is multifaceted. Its solution must be multifaceted also.

Any decision reached by the State should be reflected by the establishment of a general policy. This policy must, in turn, be incorporated into a law which gives to the State the legal authority and the organizational ability to successfully implement the policy. Where possible, it is desirable that the actions of each particular State be consistent with world standards, thus facilitating equitable and balanced development the world over.

Perhaps this should be one of the objectives which the United Nations should establish during its World Population Year.

General Law on Population*
Chapter 1. Objectives and Attributions

ARTICLE 1—The dispositions of this law are of a public nature and for general observance in the Republic. Their objective is to regulate the phenomena that affect population in regard to size, structure, dynamics, and distribution in the national territory with the goal of achieving just and equitable participation in the benefits of economic and social development;

ARTICLE 2—The Executive Branch, through the Secretariat of the Interior, will direct, promote and coordinate when necessary adequate measures to resolve national demographic problems.

ARTICLE 3—To this end, the Secretariat of the Interior will direct and execute or when necessary foster with qualified agencies or corresponding bodies the means necessary to:

I. Adjust programs of economic and social development to the necessities posed by the size, structure, dynamics and distribution of population;

II. Carry out family planning programs through the public health and education services run by the public sector and see that these programs and those realized by private organizations are executed with absolute respect for the fundamental rights of man and that they preserve the dignity of families with the aim of rationally regulating and stabilizing the growth of population as well as achieving better utilization of the human and natural resources of the country;

III. Reduce mortality;

IV. Influence population dynamics through the systems for education, public health, professional and technical training and child welfare and obtain collective participation in the solution of their problems;

V. Promote the full integration of marginal groups in national development;

VI. Subject the immigration of foreigners to the course of action judged pertinent and procure their better assimilation in national life and their adequate distribution throughout the territory;

VII. Restrict emigration of nationals as demanded by national interest;

VIII. Procure the planning of urban population centers to assure the effective provision of required public services;

IX. Stimulate the establishment of strong concentrations of national population on frontiers that are sparsely populated;

X. Procure the mobilization of the population between different regions of the Republic with the object of adjusting geographic distribution to the possibilities of regional development, based on special settlement programs for the said population;

XI. Promote the creation of towns with the aim of consolidating settlements that are geographically isolated;

* This is an unofficial translation of Chapter I of the General Law on Population published in Mexico's *Diario Oficial*. January 7, 1974. The other six chapters of the law deal with immigration, emigration, migration and population registration.

SOURCE: IPPF/WHR News Service 2(1): 9, February 1974.

XII. Coordinate the activities of the agencies of the public sector at the federal, state and municipal levels, as well as those of private organizations in order to aid the population in areas where disaster is foreseen or occurs; and

XIII. Other objectives that this law and other legal dispositions make necessary.

ARTICLE 4—To achieve the previous article, it is the job of the agencies of the Executive Branch and the other bodies of the public sector, according to the attribution conferred by the law, to apply and execute the necessary procedures to carry out each of the aims of the national demographic policy; but the definition of norms, group initiative and the coordination of the programs of said agencies in demographic matters falls exclusively to the Secretariat of the Interior.

ARTICLE 5—A National Population Council will be created that will be in charge of the country's demographic planning with the object of including population in social and economic development programs that are formulated within the government sector and relating their goals to the needs posed by demographic phenomena.

ARTICLE 6—The National Population Council will be composed of a representative of the Secretariat of the Interior who will be its head and who will act as president of the same, a representative from the Secretariat of Public Education, Health and Welfare, Housing and Public Credit, Foreign Relations, Labour and Social Welfare, one representative of the Presidency and one representative from the Department of Agricultural Affairs and Colonization; the representatives will be heads of these agencies or the subsecretaries and secretary general that they designate. For each representative, a deputy who must be at the same administrative level or that immediately below will be appointed.

When there is a question of matters in the jurisdiction of other agencies or bodies of the public sector, the Council president can request that the members attend the corresponding session or sessions or name a representative to relieve them.

The Council may have the help of technical consultants and may integrate interdisciplinary advisory units that it deems necessary with specialists in demographic and development problems.

Report of Workshop on Coordination of Population Laws and Policies: The Role of National Governments

Though many countries have expressly adopted population policies, their efficacy has been questioned because there is no government-wide attempt to coordinate all the activities which bear on population. This results in disjuncted population programmes which more often than not either duplicate or contradict each other.

In her paper, Professor Elizabeth Odio stressed that the adoption of a population policy was essentially a political decision. As such, each Government must set its population policy on the basis of the country's needs, without foreign pressures and interference.

The policy itself must be made up of various elements, among them: a statement of objectives, the provisions of family planning services by the Ministry of Public Health, coordination of the efforts of private organizations, a migration policy, amendment of obsolete laws, enforcement provisions, and an organization to implement the programme.

In the discussion of the paper, the following points were stressed:

The workshop agreed with Professor Odio that Governments have a duty to establish a population policy for their countries. But inasmuch as this is a political matter, the workshop was of the opinion that it should not attempt to deal with the substantive nature of what a policy should be.

There was also agreement that population policy is composed of many elements in addition to family planning. For example, such subjects as population distribution, migration, public health, mortality, economic development and demography must be taken into account. Therefore, the policy must be drawn up by an interdisciplinary team so that it will be comprehensive.

Professor Odio pointed out that population policy is not a substitute for economic development. Governments must provide for the basic needs of their citizens, and this includes achieving a better distribution of income.

In order to successfully execute population policy, Professor Odio advised that the policy, having been decided upon, must be made part of a general population law which in turn would be reinforced by appropriate new or amended laws on specific points. It would also be necessary for the Government to establish a high level inter-Ministerial Council to coordinate activities under the new law.

The Local Government as a Direct Participant in Population Activities

By
Reuben R. Canoy*

The conclusions arrived at by the Cagayan de Oro Population Planning Commission after nearly a year of work on a "Model City Project" present a very strong case for making the local government a direct participant in population control programs.

As is too well known by those who are involved in it, the population problem is a complex one. While it is obviously sociological in nature, it is the result of the interaction of forces that are also economic, political, religious and geographical. The experience gained by the Model City Population Project in this typically Philippine urban community of 150,000 points to at least one indisputable conclusion: that the local government, as a political entity, has the means to effectively carry out national population policies and programmes at the grassroots level.

This is nothing new. It is new only in the sense that until recently, local governments in the Philippines lacked the initiative to coordinate the various population agencies and organizations operating within their jurisdiction, despite the fact that they have been the political units or subdivisions which functioned since Spanish times as implementing arms of the central government and as initiators of any endeavor or project that would promote or enhance the general welfare of the citizens in the locality.

Under the American regime, President McKinley issued instructions to the Second Philippine Commission of 7 April 1900 in which he urged and directed that body

to devote their attention in the first instance to the establishment of municipal government in which the natives of the Islands, both in the cities and rural communities, shall be afforded the oppor-

---

* Mayor, Cagayan de Oro, The Philippines.

tunity to manage their own local affairs, to the fullest extent of which they are capable and subject to the least degree of supervision and control which a careful study of their capacities and observations of the workings of the native controls show to be consistent with the maintenance of law, order and loyalty.

Today, local governments in the Philippines have metamorphosed into four major categories: the government of Provinces, the government of Cities, the government of Municipalities and the government of Barrios (villages). The provinces consist of municipalities, and barrios within the municipality, while the cities consist of the urban centers of population (known as poblacion) and barrios or villages within their territorial boundaries.

Since this report concerns the Model City Project on Population Planning in Cagayan de Oro, it is pertinent at this point to examine the composition of a typical government of cities in the Philippines. There is, first of all, the Office of the Mayor who, as chief executive officer, is responsible for the conduct of public business and services and the enforcement of all laws, decrees, policies and programmes emanating from the central authority as well as ordinances enacted by the local legislative body (City Board, City Council or Municipal Board).

Assisting him in the task of running the city government are: the Vice Mayor, the Secretary to the Mayor, the City Administrator, the Secretary to the City Council or Board, the City Department Heads, the City Treasurer, the City Engineer, the City Public Works Supervisor, the General Services Officer, the City Health Officer, the City Agriculturist, the Chief of Police, the Chief of the Fire Department, the City Fiscal (Prosecuting Attorney), the City Legal Officer, the City Assessor, the City Auditor, the Superintendent of City Schools, the City Development Council, the City Architect, the Parks Superintendent, the City Librarian, the City Forester, the City Veterinarian, the City Hospital Administrator, the City Judge, and other National Offices (Officials) in the City.

Philippine cities are created by charter, and as no uniform charter has been evolved the number of officials as well as the size of the local legislative body may vary from place to place. But whatever their size, it is clear from the above enumeration of offices that the local governments have the administrative apparatus and the manpower to carry out a total and coordinated approach to family planning. Not only that, as political subdivisions, they have certain powers and local funds that could be used for the promotion of population programmes.

For some reason, however, their potential has been overlooked by the national government and international agencies. One unfortunate result of this is that the different family planning organizations within the City which draw support from the central government or international agencies operate independently of each other. This lack of coordination and, in certain cases, the desire of some family planning representatives to achieve local prominence even at the expense of others in order to merit the continued support of funding institutions, hinder the maximum utilization of facilities, personnel and commodities.

What is even worse, in the absence of a centralized management and records system, the same local acceptors are often listed several times by various family planning groups, thereby resulting in a distortion of the population picture at the national and international levels.

It was with a view to correcting such a situation and testing the effectiveness of the local government as a direct participant in the population programme, that the Model City Project came into being. It was initiated on 16 May 1972 by this writer and Dr. Luke T. Lee, Visiting Professor of the University of the Philippines College of Law, and Director of the Law and Population Programme, Fletcher School of Law and Diplomacy, Tufts University, U.S.A.

The original proposal which contained a number of projects-within-a-project underwent, as it were, a process of evolution at the hands of citizens' committees that were created by Executive Order of the Mayor. The idea behind this move was to secure the total involvement of the local people themselves by enlisting their support at the planning stage, thereby ensuring the successful implementation of the projects.

A modest grant from the Ford Foundation enabled the citizen-planners, who included lawyers, doctors, educators, businessmen, leaders of civic, religious, labour, women and youth organizations, to articulate their thoughts and aspirations in an impressive Model City Project proposal.

To our mind, the fact alone that people representing a real cross-section of the community could get together and seriously address themselves to the population problem constituted a major breakthrough in creating a genuine awareness of the problem as it applied to their own city. Every step that the City Government has taken, since then, has received the unqualified approval and support of the community and the agencies and organizations engaged in population activities.

Thus, Cagayan de Oro owns the distinction of being the first city in the Philippines to have incorporated in its annual budget an appropriation for the creation of a purely local Population Planning Office, manned by a Population Planning Officer and a capable technical staff. It is also the first city to have organized, through an Executive Order of the City Mayor, a local Population Planning Commission composed of the heads of agencies and organizations, both governmental and private, involved in population work.

As can be gleaned from the above list, quite a number of family planning agencies and organizations exist in Cagayan de Oro City. Considering the extent of population activities in the Philippines and other countries, it may be presumed that the same situation obtains in many cities around the world. The experience of Cagayan de Oro would seem to indicate that where several population groups operate within the same area, the leadership and initiative of the city government can serve to unify and give a central direction to their efforts.

More than that, such leadership and initiative can give full meaning at the local level to the principle adopted by the United Nations Conference on Human Rights in Teheran that "parents have a basic human right to determine freely and responsibly the number and spacing of their children"—a principle which Governments have the moral as well as legal duty to implement.

It was precisely with this principle in mind that the proponents of the Model City Project on Population Planning sought the direct participation of the City Government of Cagayan de Oro, to tap not only the available funds and resources of the City but also its powers as a political entity. The results, by local standards, have so far been encouraging.

Through the Population Planning Office, which serves as a secretariat for the Commission, the recording system has been centralized, thereby minimizing if not eliminating the possibility of errors and distortions in the listing of acceptors. A wider coverage of the City has been attained, and family planning services made available to more people through the designation of specific areas of operation. With the cooperation and assistance of all organizations, public and private, a baseline survey on media reception and family planning knowledge, attitudes and practices (KAP) has been completed.

As a result of this survey, a local strategy for securing public acceptance of family planning and a massive information drive have been formulated. The ability of the City Government to coordinate this particular activity will be put to an acid test very soon, when the various population agencies in Cagayan de Oro will join hands to saturate the urban center and the villages with family planning information through the local media (newspapers, radio and television), lecture groups and speakers' bureaus.

There is no doubt that the local government can effectively provide incentives for and the directions of population activities within its jurisdiction. On the other hand, the opportunity to use its powers to legislate on population matters remains constricted, in view of the fact that, in the Philippines at least, laws relating to persons and family relations (reproduction and family formation) are enacted and promulgated by the national government.

One of the proposals advanced in the Cagayan de Oro Model City Project was the possible enactment of a law or ordinance requiring applicants for a marriage license to submit proof of attendance at a seminar conducted by a duly recognized family planning organization, before the City Government would issue the license. When the Chairman of the Legal Committee

of the Project communicated with the national Population Commission in
Manila, the proposal was referred to the Law Center of the University of the
Philippines for comment.

The Law Center took the position that the proposed measure "fails to
meet constitutional standards which must be satisfied by any restriction on
intellectual and personal liberties."[1] It pointed out further that the measure
"will take so much for so little, and so in this sense also will probably do more
harm than good. Its exactions in the delicate sphere of individual liberties
are out of proportion to what good it can be expected to accomplish . . ."[2]

There, for the time being, the matter rests. The lesson that may be
gained from this attempt by one Philippine city to initiate legislation in the
new field of population is that more impetus can be given to population activities through the involvement of local governments.

A city can always invoke the general welfare clause of its charter or the
police powers inherent in any government in promoting family planning
and responsible parenthood. But if its charter were to contain specific
provisions or grant of powers to legislate or enact measures implementing the generally accepted family planning principles, and if the national government and international agencies were to harness and utilize the
existing machinery and resources of the local government to realize
population objectives, a new and greater dimension would be added to
the present effort which ignores or disregards the capabilities of the political unit and all that such a unit can offer in terms of additional logistics and management.

Instead of relying too heavily on scattered and independent groups of
medical practitioners and social workers whose work is often directed and
funded by a central authority or mother organization located far outside the
area of operation, national and international population experts should give
serious consideration to the untapped potential of local governments which,
after all, are in close daily contact with the people and can provide the two
elements essential to the effective motivation of people: *communications* and
leadership.

Recently, President Ferdinand E. Marcos sounded the danger that overpopulation poses to our national existence. "Today," he said, "we face such
pressures and tensions and if we look around it is quite obvious that the conflicts that we see which may explode into possibly a world conflict, arise out
of pressures of population. If this is true, all countries, all nations and all
leaders should devote all resources, all energies and all talents to only one
thing, and that is: reduce or at least lessen the increase in population in the
world today."

---

1. Memorandum from the University of Philippines Law Center to Mr. Florentino
G. Dumlao, Jr., Chairman, Legal Committee of the Model City Project for Family Planning,
Cagayan de Oro City, December 28, 1973. *See* Appendix *infra* at 437.
    2. *Id.*

In making this statement of concern, the President was surely thinking of the Philippines' own galloping birth rate of 3.1 per cent annually. The Philippine Population Center Foundation believes, however, that there is a good chance that this national birth rate can be successfully lowered to 2.5 per cent within five years.

A former director of the United National Population Division, Frank W. Notestein, thinks that there are reasons for hope in the worldwide population crisis. In the Philippines, that hope lies in the success of efforts to co-ordinate and therefore strengthen the activities of the various population control agencies and family planning organizations operating in the country. In what ways can local governments contribute to the national goal of lowering the birth rate to within manageable level?

The answer to this question is what the Model City Project of Cagayan de Oro seeks to find.

I. *Background of Project*

  1. *Origin and Objectives*

   1.1 The Model City Project on Population Planning in the City of Cagayan de Oro was initiated on May 16, 1972 by Mayor Reuben R. Canoy and Dr. Luke T. Lee, Visiting Professor, College of Law, UP and Director of the Law and Population Programme, Fletcher School of Law and Diplomacy, Tufts University, Massachusetts, U.S.A.

   1.2 It is the first attempt by a Philippine, or, indeed, any local government to take initiative to coordinate population policy and family planning activities.

   1.3 The Model City Project is conceived as:

   a) A vehicle to promote, at the local level, the principle adopted by the U.N. that the opportunity to decide the number and spacing of children is a basic human right, and therefore government has a moral and legal duty to enhance it;

   b) A local effort to implement the national objectives on family planning and population control, and to coordinate the efforts of international, national and local Family Planning Agencies and organizations;

   c) A laboratory for testing projects on a small scale whose results would help determine their nationwide applicability.

  2. *Cagayan de Oro Profile*

   2.1 The City has a total land area of 46,278 hectares, with the urban center located within 1,425 hectares or 3.07 per cent of the area. The rest is rural in character, with lands classified either as forest or agricultural.

   2.2 The economic growth of Cagayan de Oro as reflected by its annual revenue, has been more dramatic during the past two years than in the preceding four-year period. In Fiscal Year 1967, income was approximately P3,000,000. By 1971, this reached P4,000,000. In Fiscal Year 1973, revenue shot up to P6,990,877.10. Expected income for the Fiscal Year ending June 30, 1974 is P7,000,000.

   2.3 From 117,078 in 1967, the population of Cagayan de Oro rose to 139,920 in 1972. This represented a growth rate of 3.65%. By 1975, the population is projected to reach 171,000 or an increase of 23.7% from 1972.

II. *Population Related Problems*

   3.1 Along with problems resulting from rural to urban migration, as well as from population shifts caused by civil disorder in certain parts of Mindanao, the changes in human fertility, mortality or distribution of population are bound to create a wide range of problems for local government and administrations. These are:

   a) Overcrowding of the city proper (poblacion) with its accompanying squatter problem;

   b) Irreversible increases in the price of real estate;

   c) Inflation of food prices and cost of personal services caused by increased demand;

   d) Upsurge in the incidence of crime;

e) Unemployment and lower per capita income.

3.2 How to fund the inexorable demand for developmental projects and essential public utilities and services becomes a grave local concern in the face of an exploding population problem. When a too-rapid population growth overtakes the city's capability to raise public revenue adequate to support such demand, then development and public services suffer to the point of making the city unlivable.

3.3 Assuming a sustained growth rate, the population of Cagayan de Oro would reach 538,400 by year 2000, or an increase of 213.2% over the 172,000 projected population for 1975. The implications, in terms of basic community services, are grave. Cagayan de Oro's urban planners and city managers would be called upon to cope with the following:

i) *Housing*

a) An American-sponsored survey in 1968 revealed a housing shortage in the Philippines of about one (1) million units. To minimize this, it was recommended by the survey party that a total of five houses be constructed for every 1,000 people. Present facts, however, reveal only two houses built for every 1,000 people.

b) From the projected population and dwelling unit requirements, in the City of Cagayan de Oro, 15,242 would have been needed in 1970 and 17,963 by 1975. In the year 2000, some 20,000 more units would be required.

ii) *Rice/Corn and Other Food Requirements*

With the City Population forecast to reach some 172,000 by the end of 1975, the total requirements of rice and corn would amount to 270,040 and 103,200 cavans respectively. The projected rice and corn requirements are presented in schematic form below:

	Projected	Projected Food Requirements			
Year	Population	Rice		Corn	
1975	172,000	270,040	cavans	103,200	cavans
1980	226,900	356,233	"	136,140	"
1985	291,400	457,498	"	174,840	"
2000	538,400	845,288	"	323,040	"

The relative smaller volume of corn required shows residents' preference for rice as the basic staple food. Being the basic staple foods, these requirements will continue to increase. (See Table 2 for other projected major food requirements of the city).

iii) *Water*

a) *Future Water Consumption* in the City of Cagayan de Oro is estimated to increase from approximately 800 million gallons in 1975 to about 7,500 million by the year 2000. (Values of annual consumption and population served that were used to calculate the same are shown in Table 3).

b) *Future Water Production*: Annual water production represents the total supply that a water system must produce to meet all of the delivered water requirements of its service area, i.e., consumption and unaccounted for production. (Knowledge of a system's total annual water production is a valuable tool to future system planning. Future production required by the Cagayan de Oro system is shown in Table 4).

c) *Future Water Demands*: Basic factors of water system design normally are based upon short-term periods of water demand rather than upon average annual amount. Particularly critical are average water demands—as expressed by water production required for a maximum-day demand and a peak-hour period. The design of certain elements of domestic water system normally is based upon water demands projected for the two latter periods. (Design flows considered appropriate for the Cagayan de Oro system are shown in Table 5).

iv) *Electricity*

In 1973 the total electric consumption in the City of Cagayan de Oro was 11,963,073 KWH. It was reported that from 1970 to 1974 it had an average annual increase of 13.2%. Based on the average 13.2% annual growth in KWH consumption by residential customers by the year 1980 some 28,494,936 KWH will be provided. By the year 2000 some 40,470,580 KWH will be required.

v) *Education*

In the City of Cagayan de Oro, the public school system, which had a total enrollment of 22,092 in school year 1971-72, comprises forty-three (43) elementary schools, two (2) secondary schools and a school of arts and trades. The City offers free public elementary education which covers tuition and books.

Complementing the public schools are fifteen (15) private schools, five (5) on collegiate level, three (3) on secondary level, one (1) on the elementary level, and six (6) special vocational schools.

With the population of Cagayan de Oro doubling every twenty (20) years, this implies that an additional of 552 classrooms will be needed, 552 new teachers hired and 22,092 new desk chairs to be provided by the year 2000.

vi) *Refuse Collection and Disposal System*

The estimated volume of refuse in Cagayan de Oro City from 9,232 households currently being serviced is an average of 3,000 cubic meters per month or 6.2 kilos of refuse per capita per day.

With the ultimate aim to service the projected population of 538,400 (or roughly 89,733 households) by the year 2000 the estimated refuse will rise to about 1,000 cubic meters per day or 125 tons daily. If ordinarily, a garbage truck makes eight (8) cubic meters per route and each truck will make two (2) routes per day, the city will require at least sixty-three (63) trucks to haul the daily bulk of refuse—if the present system prevails.

Provisions or specific plans may be necessary within the proximate future to diversify the methods of refuse disposal such as installation of kitchen grinders directly connected through the sewerage systems, etc., or the reduction of family refuse output by improved preparation of food, etc.

vii) *Environmental Aspect*

In recent years, concern for the environment has become widespread. As population grows, the extent of pollution also increases unless additional facilities are provided to keep pace with the waste products of this increased population. The City of Cagayan de Oro has set up a Local Environmental Planning Commission to look into the potential environment problems and take precautionary measures that will affect the development of the city by the year 2000.

III. *Coordination of Family Planning Efforts*

The Model City Project on Population Planning envisions the total and coordinated approach to family planning in order that maximum use of locally available resources, manpower and facilities might be achieved. Thus, practically all aspects of population management within the city—educational, social, economic, medical, legal and administrative—are involved in the Project.

4.1 In July 1973, upon approval by the City Council of the budget for FY 1973-74, the Model City Population Planning Office was established under the Office of the City Mayor. The City government provides for a Director, and several aides, interviewers and researchers. The Office operates as the:

    a) Secretariat and Technical Staff of Cagayan de Oro Population Planning Commission;

    b) Central Coordinating headquarters of various agencies and organizations engaged in family planning in Cagayan de Oro;

    c) Clearing house of population information, and

    d) Implementing arm' of the measures introduced in the Model City Project.

4.2 Some of the important projects so far accomplished by the City Population Planning Office are:

    a) A master list of all acceptors registered with the different Family Planning clinics and a system of counter-checks to avoid duplication and erroneous reporting of the number of acceptors in Cagayan de Oro;

    b) A baseline survey on Media and Family Planning—Knowledge, Attitudes and Practices (KAP)—which shall be the basis of an information campaign and a local strategy for securing public acceptance of family planning;

    c) Start of a massive information, education and communications campaign using the local dialect for radio spots and programs, T. V., local newspapers and inserts, film clips in movie houses, and

    d) Use of Audio Visual units for film showings in rural areas, and Information/Education/Communication campaign on family planning.

4.3 In September 1973, the Cagayan de Oro Population Planning Commission was created by Executive Order of the City Mayor, and charged with the following functions and duties:

    a) To act as the policy-making body of the Model City Population Project;

    b) To coordinate all activities of the different private and public agencies engaged in family planning within the city;

c) To undertake studies and make recommendations for the purpose of evolving population planning policies and guidelines.

4.4 As a central coordinating and policy-making body, it is composed of heads or presidents of organizations actively involved in family planning.

4.5 The Commission elects its own Chairman and Vice-Chairman, and such other officers as it may deem necessary. It is empowered to require the assistance of any Department or Office of the City Government for the purpose of carrying out its functions and duties.

4.6 The Project Director of the Population Planning Office, automatically serves as the Executive Secretary, and his Office Staff also composes the Commission Secretariat.

The Commission meets regularly at least once a month, or as often as called by the Chairman.

IV. *The Model City Program of Activities*

Whereas past family planning efforts have focused on the provisions of services and supplies, the Model City Project stresses the stimulation of effective demand. The programme of activities may be divided into four broad categories:

a) Administrative and Community Development;

b) Incentive Programs;

c) Medical and Public Health Measures; and

d) Information and Education.

5.1 Under the Administrative and Community Development Program, the following projects are considered:

a) *Free Marriage License*, to be issued to applicants who attend family planning lectures by the City Health Office or any recognized family planning agency.

Financial Implications: 1,156 licenses were issued in 1973. Since the license fee is fixed at P2.00, the annual subsidy required would amount to P2,312.00 which may be borne by the City Government or by a funding agency.

b) *Paternity Leave with Pay*, to be granted male employees of the City Government if they are enrolled in family planning lectures. A two-week leave shall be allowed (one week before delivery, and one week after up to and including the third child). The Model City Project seeks to persuade major private employers in Cagayan de Oro to adopt a similar policy.

Financial Implications: None. The Project will utilize existing resources.

c) *Public Housing*, to be made available preferably to families with three children or less. Because of the visibility value of the proposed housing projects (to be carried out as part of a slum clearance move in two areas in Cagayan de Oro), the preference for small-size families in the interest of health and safety, would emphasize the importance and desirability of family planning.

Financial Implications: The Model City Project would secure soft, long-term loans for the housing scheme, either from banking institutions or a foundation like Philippine Business for Social Progress. Appropriate administrative and monitoring apparatus would have to be set up by the Project.

d) *Legal Aid*, to be extended to enrolled acceptors with three children or less for support in paternity suits. N. B. The Legal Aid Clinic of the Model City Project will also provide unwed mothers and children born out of wedlock counsel on their rights under the law.

Financial Implications: None. The Project will coordinate existing private and public resources.

5.2 *The Proposed Incentive Programs are as follows*:

a) *Incentives for Family Planning motivators and doctors*, possibly under a "piece rate" system and to be closely supervised and monitored to prevent double reporting of acceptors.

Financial Implications: The cost of this incentive program would be about P3.00 per recruitment above target levels, for a total of P9,000 per year. Funds to be sought from national or international funding agencies or organizations.

b) Free Marriage Application Fee to be granted to applicants who have attended family planning lectures either by the City Health Office or by a recognized family planning agency.

N.B. The Cagayan de Oro Tax Code of 1974 requires a fee of P10.00 in addition to the P2.00 imposed by the national law. The local fee may be waived by the City Government.

Financial Implications: The amount involved under this scheme may reach P10,000 which the city can well bear.

c) *Free Education at City High School*, to be awarded to any one of three children, whose parents have been married 12 years and have three children or less.

Financial Implications: Very nominal, may cover cost of tuition fee.

5.3 *Medical and Public Health Measures include*:

a) *Free contraceptive supplies and services*, to be distributed through the various FP Clinics coordinated by the City Population Planning Office.

Financial Implications: Supplies and devices to be procured from the FPOP, IMCH, MCH (UP) and the Commission on Population. A mobile clinic for rural areas is being sought from POPCOM.

(N. B. The Population Planning Office will serve as a "broker" to tap local, national and international agencies and organizations for technical and commodity assistance normally extended by them to family planning groups).

b) *Free Delivery Services up to the Third Child* to be made available initially and until arrangements are made with other hospitals at the City Government Hospital to registered acceptors, provided, however, that such acceptors submit to postpartum family planning programs to be administered by the City Health Office.

Financial Implications: Mothers with two children or less may participate in this programme. When funding arrangements are made with other hospi-

tals, they may choose to deliver at any registered hospital. Private physicians would be reimbursed for their services at the current rate of P50-P70 per delivery.
- c) Integration of family planning in factory health clinics, with family planning services to be supplied by the City Health Office and other FP agencies and organizations operating in Cagayan de Oro.
  Financial Implications: None. The City will coordinate existing resources and facilities.

5.4 *Information and Education*:

This program envisions the saturation of Cagayan de Oro with FP information, to make the people totally aware of the importance of family planning. A two-pronged approach is considered:
- a) Media
- b) Special Information Teams

The City Population Planning Office under the City Mayor has already conducted a baseline survey to determine:
- a) The most effective media and content to be used in the City;
- b) Knowledge, Attitudes and Practices (KAP) concerning family planning in Cagayan de Oro.

N. B. This is the first survey of its kind ever to be undertaken by any local government unit, and in view of the significance of the results, some highlights are included in the appendix.

V. *Nationwide Implications of the Model City Population Planning Project*

As previously stated, one of the underlying objectives of the Model City Project is to test projects on a small scale whose results would help determine their nationwide applicability.

For this reason, there has been no effort on the part of the Project implementors to lean heavily on outside funding and commodity support. Whenever possible, local resources are to be tapped and local expertise enlisted. Otherwise, the Project would be difficult, if not impossible, to duplicate in other chartered cities of the Philippines.

Even at this early stage, it is obvious that local governments can assume a greater share of the family planning effort through:
- a) Information and education programmes;
- b) Coordination of activities of various family planning agencies and organizations and the distribution of supplies and commodities;
- c) Total involvement of the people of the community in the family planning effort, especially in the educational aspect;
- d) The passage of local legislation such as the Model City Planning Ordinance, which would give legal status to all family planning programmes within the city and thus promote the lowest political level, *the principle that the decision to plan the size of one's family is indeed a basic human right.*

The response of the citizens of Cagayan de Oro to the Model City idea has been most heartening. The feasibility study on the Project is, in fact, the work not of a few individuals but of a large number of concerned citizens representing the different sectors of the community. Some of the project proposals may be difficult to carry out, considering the financial capability of the city. But the fact that local leaders have spent a great deal of time and effort on the formulation of these proposals indicates a genuine interest in population planning not evident in the same degree in other Philippine cities. It is to be hoped that the experience of Cagayan de Oro City will serve as a model which the country can adopt.

VI. *Tables and Appendices*

TABLE I

CAGAYAN DE ORO CITY POPULATION,
ACTUAL PROJECTED, 1967-2000

YEAR	POPULATION	INDEX
1967	117,078	100
1968	120,711	103
1969	124,437	106
1970	128,319	109
1971	132,181	112
1972	139,920	119
1975	172,000	146
1980	226,900	193
1985	291,400	248
1990	368,100	314
1995	448,700	383
2000	538,400	459

Source: Bureau of Census and Statistics
Cagayan de Oro City Office

TABLE II

PROJECTED MAJOR FOOD REQUIREMENTS OF CAGAYAN DE ORO CITY BY COMMODITY, 1972 to 1975, 1980, 1985, 1990, 1995, 2000

YEAR	PROJECTED POPULATION [1]	PROJECTED FOOD REQUIREMENTS [2]						
		RICE (a)	CORN (b)	BEEF (c)	PORK (d)	POULTRY (e)	EGG (f)	VEGETABLES (g)
1972	139,920	219,674	83,952	769,560	1,203,312	419,760	475,728	1,413,192
1973	148,315	232,854	88,189	815,732	1,275,509	444,945	504,271	1,497,982
1974	157,214	246,826	94,328	864,677	1,352,040	471,641	534,527	1,587,861
1975	172,000	270,040	103,200	946,600	1,479,200	516,000	584,500	1,737,200
1980	226,900	356,233	136,140	1,247,950	1,951,340	680,700	771,460	2,291,690
1985	291,400	457,498	174,840	1,602,700	2,506,040	874,200	990,700	2,943,140
1990	368,100	577,917	220,860	2,024,550	3,165,660	1,104,300	1,251,540	3,717,810
1995	478,700	704,459	269,220	2,467,850	3,858,820	1,346,100	1,525,580	4,531,870
2000	538,400	845,288	323,040	2,961,200	4,630,240	1,615,200	1,830,560	5,437,840

[1] Based on the population projections of the Bureau of Census and Statistics
[2] Based on the 1969 NEC Statistical Reported per capita disappearance food requirement, as follows:

(a) 1.57 cavans   (c) 5.5 kilograms   (e) 3.0 kilograms
(b) 0.60 cavans   (d) 8.6 kilograms   (f) 3.4 kilograms
                                            (g) 10.0 kilograms (4 pieces/kilo)

TABLE III

PROJECTED FUTURE WATER CONSUMPTION[1]
CAGAYAN DE ORO CITY

Year	Per Capita Consumption, gpcd* Domestic	Industrial	Total	Population Served	Annual Consumption (mg)
1975	24.0	8.0	32	67,200	785
1980	31.6	9.4	41	108,700	1,627
1982	33.0	10.0	43	126,500	1,988
1985	36.0	11.0	47	153,100	2,627
1990	39.0	12.0	51	207,400	3,861
1995	43.8	13.2	57	268,100	5,578
2000	48.0	14.0	62	332,900	7,534

Source:

[1]Wilson, A., Montgomery, J. Report of Feasibility Improvement and Expansion of Urban Water System, Cagayan de Oro City Area, James M. Montgomery, C.E., Inc., Makati, Rizal, June, 1973
*gallons per capita per day

TABLE IV

PROJECTED FUTURE WATER PRODUCTION[2]
CAGAYAN DE ORO CITY
(Millions Gallons)

Year	Annual Consumptions	Unaccounted for Water Production (1) %	Annual Production
1975	785	25.0	1,046
1980	1,627	20.0	2,034
1982	1,988	19.0	2,455
1985	2,627	17.5	3,184
1990	3,861	15.0	4,542
1995	5,578	15.0	6,562
2000	7,534	15.0	8,864

(1) Sum of system losses and unmetered deliveries
Source: Ibid.

TABLE V

PROJECTED FUTURE WATER CONSUMPTION[1]
CAGAYAN DE ORO CITY

| Year | Required Annual Production (mg) | Future Water Demands, mgd | | |
		Average Day	Maximum Day (1)	Peak Hour (2)
1975	1,046	2.87	3.59	5.74
1980	2,034	5.57	6.96	11.14
1982	2,455	6.73	8.41	13.46
1985	3,184	8.72	10.92	17.44
1990	4,542	12.44	15.55	24.88
1995	6,562	17.98	22.48	35.96
2000	8,864	24.28	30.35	48.56

NOTES:
    1. 125% of average day demand;
    2. 200% of average day demand.
Source: [1]Wilson, A., Montgomery, J. *Report of Feasibility Improvement* and Expansion of Urban Water System, Cagayan de Oro City Area, James W. Montgomery, C.E., Inc., Makati, Rizal, June, 1973.

MASS MEDIA SURVEY PROJECT ON FAMILY PLANNING

The Model City Project Survey Team interviewed 410 households in Cagayan de Oro City by means of systematic sampling. Our estimate of the sample of households was approximately 2% of the eligible family planning acceptors of the city which included barrios Carmen, Canitoan, Pagatpat, Bulua, Iponan, Puntod, Lapasan and Nazareth. Of the respondents, 297 (72.7%) were married and 113 (27.3%) were unmarried.

The questions asked were grouped into four categories:
a) *Radio*
    More than half of the respondents, 236 (57%) have radios, 174 (43%) do not have. Of the four radio stations, DXCC ranked first as their favorite station. DXOR ranked second, followed by DXMO and DXKO.
    Radio time cited as the mst convenient time for listening, according to order of preference is as follows:

    6:00 a. m.
    1:00 p. m.
    5:00 a. m.
    7:00 a. m.
    7:00 p. m.

Only 43% heard the message on any of the following family planning radio spots:

— need to plan families
— contraceptive methods
— drama on family planning
— news on family planning
— effects of large/small family

More than 57% of the respondents did not hear any of the family planning messages over the radio. Of those who heard the message, 27% could remember and 16% could not remember what the message was.

b) *Television*
Only twenty-six respondents have TV sets. The fact that most respondents are residents of the rural areas and many of them belong to the low income group explains why the majority do not have TV sets.

In addition to this, electrification in several of these sample areas has just been recently introduced. However, of the twenty-six respondents who have TV sets, 18 (68%) saw the family planning film on TV; and 32% did not see it. Half of those who saw the film remembered the message.

c) *FP in Cinema Houses*
Seventy-four per cent (74%) did not see any family planning film inside the movie houses. Of the twenty six per cent (26%) who saw the film only 18% could remember the message shown.

d) *Other Media on Family Planning*
Responses to the questions related to other media revealed that the health center is an important source of information for family planning. Friends, neighbors, and relatives were also found to be almost equal in importance as sources of information for family planning.

Conclusion:

The survey on MASS MEDIA indicated that:
i) The use of radio as medium of information and education about FP would be very feasible to eligible acceptors both in the rural and urban areas.
ii) The best times to be utilized for radio spots and programs are 6:00 a.m.; 5:00 a. m.; 1:00 p. m.; 7:00 a. m. and 7:00 p. m. according to order of preference.
iii) Radio spots have to be reinforced with an information and education campaign through individual and group approaches by the medical and health teams.
iv) Radio drama about family planning gives more meaningful and effective learning experience especially to the rural folk.

KAP SURVEY ON FAMILY PLANNING

In order to have some baseline data, the Model City Population Planning Office conducted a KAP (Knowledge, Attitudes and Practices) survey on family planning with a random sampling of 1,200 eligible acceptors (married couples, unmarried persons and community leaders). The sample barrios included Bulua, Canitoan, Carmen, Iponan, Lapasan, Nazareth, Pagatpat and Puntod.

The objective of the survey was to assess what the subjects know, how they feel and what they do about family planning.

1. *KAP Married Persons*

   1.1 Attitudes on Family Planning

     Of the married respondents, ninety-seven point four per cent (97.4%) favored other couples in doing something to prevent or delay pregnancy. Seventy-six per cent (76%) said they do not want to have more children than they now have. The respondents seem to be motivated to limit their family size.

     Sixty-one per cent (61%) favored 3 to 4 children, which was the most popular family size; twenty per cent (20%) answered 1 to 2 children; sixteeen per cent (16%) favored 5 to 6 children; three per cent (3%) thought 7 to 8 children was the ideal completed family size.

   1.2 Knowledge and Use of Family Planning

     Eighty-seven per cent (87%) know the different methods of family planning and the thirteen per cent (13%) who have no knowledge at all expressed desire to learn about family planning. Although the majority are aware of the different methods of contraception, only 278 (43%) are at present using methods of contraception. Of this 43%, sixty per cent (60%) are rhythm users; thirty-two point five per cent (32.5%) use the pill; four per cent (4%) use the condom, foam and withdrawal methods; two point five per cent (2.5%) favor IUD and one per cent (1%) favor the tubal ligation.

     Of the 278 users, 18% found the methods they are using to be ineffective; while 82% are satisfied with the methods.

     At the time of the interview, previous users gave the following reasons for no longer continuing with family planning methods:

side effects	80%
expense	10%
husband's objections	7%
inconvenience of the method used	3%

2. *Community Leaders*

   2.1 Attitudes and Use of Family Planning

     Eighty-three per cent (83%) responded that the number of people in their community is increasing rapidly and eighty-five per cent (85%) think this increase is a problem in the community for reasons of economy, and because living conditions have become more difficult.

     Majority of the community leaders cited as "large" a family having seven or more children, and as "small" a family with only one or two children. These respondents believe that financial problems, education and health are the most common problems related to large families.

2.2 Knowledge and Use of Family Planning

The community leaders understand family planning as spacing (60%) and limitation (40%). The sources of this knowledge are the radio (70%), lectures during seminars (20%) and relatives, friends, and neighbors (10%).

Ninety per cent (90%) of the respondents know the pills, sixty per cent (60%) know withdrawal, thirty per cent (30%) know IUD, twenty per cent (20%) know the foam and other spermicidals, and fifty-seven per cent (57%) know the rhythm and condom as methods of contraception.

Fourteen per cent (14%) are at present using a method while a large proportion do not use any method at all to prevent or delay pregnancy. Of the users:

40% use the pill;
38% practise the rhythm;
15% practise the withdrawal method, and
 7% use the condom.

The purpose of practising family planning is for economic reasons (45%); care of children (30%) and family happiness (25%).

As community leaders, it is expected that they have participated in family planning activities in their community. However, it was found out that only a few (30%) had attended family planning seminars. Their participation is more on counselling their neighbors, relatives and friends.

When asked about their willingness to actively participate in the family planning program in their respective community, ninety per cent (90%) said YES.

3. *Unmarried persons*

3.1 Attitudes on Family Planning

On the question as to the right age for a girl and a boy to get married, 50% of the girls answered 25 to 29 years old, while 60% of the boys answered 25 to 29 years old.

These responses seem to point out that these unmarried respondents are aware of the hardships and responsibilities of parenthood. They believe that marriage at an early age will result in an increase in the number of children.

When asked about their attitude, as to when should the first baby be born after marriage, 50% responded one year after marriage; 37%, two years after marriage; 13%, three to five years after.

As to the ideal number of children they expect to have when they get married:

60% said three to four children;
30% said one to two children, and
10% said five to six children.

To these responses, they cited economic considerations (62%) and family welfare (38%) as reasons why they prefer a small family.

3.2 Knowledge of Family Planning
>   52% understand family planning as limitation;
>   40% as spacing; while
>   8% do not have any knowledge of family planning.
>
>   90% know about the pill;
>   85% about the IUD, and
>   35% about the rhythm.

Conclusion:

The KAP survey revealed that the eligible acceptors (married couples, community leaders and unmarried persons) are aware of the rapid population growth and problems. They have a positive attitude towards family planning and are ready to learn and accept it as a way of life.

The degree of awareness of family planning is extremely high while its practice is in small proportion. The sources of resistance to the practice of contraceptive methods are misconceptions, fears and doubts about the methods, religious beliefs, husband's objections and expenses. Therefore, there is a need to reinforce this awareness by proper education and information on family planning.

REPUBLIC OF THE PHILIPPINES
OFFICE OF THE CITY MAYOR
CITY OF CAGAYAN DE ORO

EXECUTIVE ORDER NO. *9-73*

AN EXECUTIVE ORDER CREATING THE
POPULATION PLANNING COMMISSION FOR THE
CITY OF CAGAYAN DE ORO.

WHEREAS, Cagayan de Oro is a "Model City" for the application of Family Planning Program and which later the experiences in Cagayan de Oro could well be applied to other cities of the Philippines;

WHEREAS, the Municipal Board recognizing the importance of Population Planning has set up a City Population Planning Office;

WHEREAS, quite a number of Family Planning Clinics exist within the City, each operating independently of each other, hence without coordination and with no maximum use of manpower, resources and facilities;

WHEREAS, there is a great need to have a total coordinated approach to Family Planning—educational, social, economic, demographic, medical as well as legal;

WHEREAS, past family planning efforts have focused on the provision of services and supplies while the Model City Population Planning Project stresses the other side of the formula—stimulation and demand;

NOW THEREFORE, I, REUBEN R. CANOY, City Mayor of Cagayan de Oro City, by virtue of the powers vested in me by law, do hereby create the Cagayan de Oro City Population Planning Commission to be composed of the following:

1. Dra. Lourdes Bolongaita—Inst. of Maternal & Child Health (IMCH)
2. Sr. Fabiola Dolalas, F.M.M.—Asian Social Institute (ASI)

3. Dr. Emmanuel Bacas—Dept. of National Defense (DND)
4. Mrs. Elma Lynne Paalam—Officer In-Charge, City Branch Dept. of Social Welfare (DSW)
5. Mr. Zenon Adobas—Community Dev. Officer, Dept. of Local Gov't and Community Development
6. Mr. Romeo Balandra—Regional Director, Population Commission, (POP-COM) Region X
7. Dr. Jacinto Frias—City Health Officer (CHO)
8. Atty. Mordino Cua—President, Southern Phil. Educ'l. Credit Cooperative (SPECC)
9. Mr. Ramon Yap—President, Association of Barrio Councils (ABC)
10. Atty. Fausto Dugenio—President, Association of Barangays (AB)
11. Coun. Berchamans Abejuela—City Councilor
12. Coun. Benjamin L. Vallente—City Councilor
13. Dr. Alex Herrin—Research Institute for Mindanao and Culture (RIMCU)
14. Mr. Jesus Valleser—Officer In-Charge, Nat'l. Media Prod. Center, Region X
15. Mr. Cesario Balintag—City Supt. of Schools, Dept. of Education and Culture
16. Mrs. Solona Canoy—Member, National Board of FPOP; Vice-Pres. for Mindanao Area; Chairman, Dept. of Information, Educ., and Training Program
17. Dr. Jose L. Oceña—President, FPOP, Cagayan de Oro City
18. Dra. Zenaida Floirendo—Phil. Medical Association
19. Chairmen of Working Committee—"Model City" Project
20. Mr. Jose F. Lim, Jr.—Project Director, Population Planning Office

The Commission shall elect its own Chairman and Vice-Chairman and such other officers as it may deem necessary.

The Project Director, Population Planning Office shall automatically become the Executive Secretary to the Commission with all the members of his Office Staff to compose the Secretariat to the Commission.

The Commission shall have the following functions and duties:

1. To coordinate all activities of the different private and public agencies involved in Family Planning within the City in order to maximize the use of manpower, resources and facilities.

2. To act as the policy making body of the Model City Population Planning Project.

3. To undertake studies and make recommendations for the purpose of adopting population planning policies and guidelines.

The Commission shall hold regular monthly meeting, in addition to meetings which are subject to call by the Chairman.

The Commission shall be empowered to request assistance from all Departments of the City Government for the purpose of carrying out its functions and duties.

DONE in the City of Cagayan de Oro, Philippines, this *17th* day of *September*, 1973.

REUBEN R. CANOY
City Mayor

MODEL CITY POPULATION PLANNING
OFFICE OF THE CHIEF EXECUTIVE
CITY OF CAGAYAN DE ORO

September 27, 1973

His Excellency
President Ferdinand E. Marcos
Malacañang Palace
Manila

Dear Mr. President:

A Model City Project for Family Planning in the City of Cagayan de Oro was initiated by Mayor Reuben R. Canoy and Dr. Luke T. Lee, Visiting Professor, College of Law, UP and Director, Law and Population Programme, Fletcher School of Law and Diplomacy, Tufts University.

This Model City Project is conceived as a local effort to share in the implementation of the national objectives for family planning and population control. The project is further envisioned "as a laboratory for testing projects in a small scale whose results would help determine their nationwide applicability."

One of the measures proposed is the requirement that all those who intend to marry should attend a compulsory seminar on responsible parenthood—to instill and inculcate in the minds of the applicants the proper attitude towards family planning. In this regard, it is proposed that a certificate of attendance be required to be presented before a marriage license can be issued.

Of course, we are aware that this matter is beyond the competence of local governments to do so as the matter is specifically treated by the New Civil Code on marriage.

We are therefore proposing that a proper Presidential Decree be issued, amending the pertinent provisions of the New Civil Code, providing that no local civil registrar shall issue a marriage license without a certificate of attendance in a seminar for Responsible Parenthood and Family Planning presented by the applicants.

If this should not be possible, it is earnestly requested that at least for a period of five years, Cagayan de Oro City should be authorized to enact ordinances to put this requirement into effect for purposes of determining the effect of such a measure in reducing fertility rates for possible adoption on a national scale.

It is hoped that with a favorable Presidential certification of this request, we shall have taken a small significant step in the attainment of our national family planning objectives.

Very truly yours,

SGD. FLORENTINO G. DUMLAO, JR.
Chairman, Legal Committee, Model City
Project for Family Planning

January 24, 1974

Honorable Aguinaldo C. Maaba
Cabinet Secretary
Office of the President
Malacañang Palace

Dear Sir:

This refers to your letter dated November 5, 1973, and received by this Commission
on November 19, 1973, requesting for our action on the proposal of Mr. Florentino
G. Dumlao, Jr. of Cagayan de Oro City.

As the proposal seeks to introduce a new requirement on marriage, particularly a
certificate of attendance in a Seminar for Responsible Parenthood and Family Planning by the applicants of marriage licenses, we took the initiative to refer the same to
the U.P. Law Center for an Opinion. On January 3, 1974, we received a Memorandum from the U.P. Law Center wherein an extensive discussion on the possible legal
implications on individual rights of Mr. Dumlao's proposal was made.

While the opinion rendered could truly be construed as an aid to better legislation
like the one proposed, we are taking exception to the position adopted by the
Memorandum for we believe that the proposal is still worth having a second as to its
merits, after which a dissenting view could be strongly maintained upholding its
validity. Thus the objectionable features pointed out could be entirely avoided by
providing alternative safeguards and necessary exceptions.

In compliance with your advice, we are furnishing your Office a copy of the Law
Center's Memorandum. With the highest respect for whatever action you will now
take, we are indorsing the proposal of Mr. Dumlao and requesting that as proposed a
Decree be promulgated with the Memorandum serving as guide.

Very truly yours,

(SGD.) ARTHUR B. CUYUGAN
Associate Director for Administrator
ABC/ROM/vbv

        A CERTIFIED TRUE COPY:

        SGD. MIERCOLITA R. ALLAGA

January 24, 1974

Mr. Florentino G. Dumlao, Jr.
Chairman, Legal Committee
Model City Project for Family Planning
Office of the City Mayor
Cagayan de Oro City

Dear Mr. Dumlao:

Your letter to the President, dated September 27, 1973 was indorsed to us on November 5, 1973 for appropriate action.

Your proposal that an amendatory Decree be issued amending the provisions of the New Civil Code on Marriage by "providing that no local civil registrar shall issue a marriage license without a certificate of attendance in a seminar for Responsible Parenthood and Family Planning first presented by the applicants, truly deserves our appreciation and enthusiasm. For us conceived and if finally carried out, the Decree could surely serve as a continuing measure that could invariably help the earlier realization of the population program of the government.

As the proposed Decree seeks to introduce a new requirement on marriage, the Commission took the view that inasmuch as marriage, its nature, consequences and incidents, involve basic human rights and individual freedom, the possible legal infirmities of the proposed measure was thought of hence we took the initiative to refer your proposal to the U. P. Law Center for an opinion.

On January 3, 1974, we received the opinion requested contained in an extensive Memorandum prepared by the Law Center's Division of Research and Law Reform and we learned that indeed "the proposal may infringe upon basic freedom of every individual concerned."

Without necessarily adhering to the view taken by the U.P. Law Center, and believing that there could be other remedial steps that could be taken to save your proposal, we are sending you a copy of the aforementioned Memorandum for your study and comments. Hopefully the objectionable features raised could be met with other alternatives so that your proposed measure will not be totally disregarded.

In this common endeavor and mutual concern, we assure you that we will do our best to come up, from time to time, with measures to ensure better involvement of all concerned in the National Population Program. Your as suggestion in this regard is not therefore only welcomed but will be acknowledged with appreciation.

Thank you again.
Very truly yours,

(SGD.) ARTHUR B. CUYUGAN
Associate Director for Administration
ABC/ROM/VSV

A CERTIFIED TRUE COPY:

MIERCOLITA R. ALLAGA
Secretary
Dumlao Law Office

MEMORANDUM ON

> THE LEGAL IMPLICATIONS OF
> PROPOSAL PROHIBITING ISSUANCE
> OF MARRIAGE LICENSE WITHOUT A
> CERTIFICATE OF ATTENDANCE IN A
> SEMINAR ON RESPONSIBLE PARENTHOOD
> AND FAMILY PLANNING.

Opinion is requested on the possible legal implications of the proposal made by Mr. Florentino G. Dumlao, Jr., chairman of the Legal Committee of the Model City Project for Family Planning in Cagayan de Oro City, that a presidential decree be issued amending the Civil Code by inserting therein a provision that "no local civil registrar shall issue a marriage license without a certificate of attendance in a seminar for Responsible Parenthood and Family Planning presented by the applicants." The proposal has been made purportedly "to instill and inculcate in the minds of the applicants the proper attitude towards family planning"—and thus as a measure to further the national government's family planning and population control program.

We share the apprehension of the Executive Director of the Commission on Population that the proposal "may infringe upon basic freedoms of every individual concerned." It is in fact certain that it *will* do so. Specifically, the proposal if adopted will clash with the individual's right not to be deprived of his liberty without due process of law, his right to the pursuit of happiness, his right to believe freely. Liberty protected by the due process clause is so broad as to include all the other rights enumerated in the Bill of Rights. So conceived it embraces the freedom to think or believe as one wills and to act or behave as one pleases. (See FERNANDO, THE BILL OF RIGHTS 1-2 [1970].) The Proposal compels the individual to act in a certain way, namely, to attend a seminar. It encroaches on the individual's right to marry when he wants and hence his right to act as he pleases in that it imposes a condition before he can do so. In the same way it interferes with his right to the pursuit of happiness, one of the keys to which is marriage. It impinges on the individual's right to free thought, which includes the right to obtain such knowledge or information as he chooses, by forcing upon him knowledge or information (about family planning or population control) which also infringe on the individual's right to believe as he pleases because the measure contemplated in the proposal may clash with the tenets of the particular individuals' religion.

It is, of course, conceded that these individual rights are not absolute and that they may be subject to certain restrictions in the pursuit of some legitimate and vital social objective. But it must never be forgotten that liberty is the rule and restrictions to it the exception. (FERNANDO, *op. cit. supra*, at 7). And when it is these rights —intellectual and personal rights as distinguished from property rights—that are involved, measures restricting them have to pass through the crucible of utmost caution and the most rigorous and exacting standards to justify their enactment. (Ermita-Malate Motel and Motel Operators Association v. Mayor of Manila, L-24693, July 31, 1967; Mutuc v. Morfe, L-20387, January 31, 1968; West Virginia State Board of Education v. Barnette, 319 U.S. 624.) More legislative preferences or beliefs respecting matters of public convenience will not suffice to justify diminution of these rights, even if the same may well suffice to support regulation of property rights (Schneider v. State of New Jersey, 308 U.S. 147, 161). There must be a clear and present, not merely a doubtful or possible, danger to a compelling and paramount interest which the State has the right to protect; it will not be enough that there is "rational connection between the remedy provided by the statute and the evil to be curbed, which in other contexts might support legislation against attack on due process grounds." (NAACP v. Button, 371 U.S. 415, 83 S. Ct. 328, 9 L. Ed. 405 (1973), citing several cases). More than this, the objectives of the measure must be incapable of being achieved by the adoption of measures less drastic and more narrowly drawn (Elfbrant v. Russel, 384 U.S. 11 (1966)). As always, the standards of reasonableness and fairness must be met. The measure must not be oppressive or work undue hardship on those affected thereby. The means must be proportionate to the end.

Tested against these standards, the proposed measure is patently impermissible as an arbitrary interference of individual freedoms. There is clearly no immediate and compelling necessity for its adoption. The sacrifices and deprivations it will cause are not only manifestly disproportionate to its purpose; the remedy bears only a remote, if any, connection to the achievement of that purpose. Yet its objectives can be achieved by less drastic and less sweeping means.

The proposed measure exacts too much for the accomplishment of so little and, at that, uncertain benefits. Apart from the numerous personal rights it will curtail, in its practical application it is sure to unnecessarily inflict tremendous hardship and frustration upon many people. This becomes manifest when it is realized that, at this moment for many years yet to come, neither the government nor private organizations are and will be ready with facilities and the necessary personnel to conduct nationwide seminars of the kind envisioned in the measure. Do the government and private organizations have adequate facilities and personnel to hold such seminars as often as required throughout the Philippines, including the far-flung provinces, can it have with respect to people who marry at an age when they can no longer expect to be got children?

This is all too insignificant and uncertain a good or benefit for the price that the measure exacts in terms of the intellectual and personal liberties and of the happiness of a great number of people. The means is clearly out of proportion to the end sought or expected to be accomplished. Yet, as already pointed out, the same end can be achieved by less exacting, less drastic and less sweeping means. For instance, it can be accomplished by including in the elementary or high school curriculum the subject contemplated in the proposed measure. Surely this will not entail the compulsion, the deprivations and hardships that the proposed measure, as already demonstrated, will.

It is even possible that the proposed measure if adopted will do more harm than good. Because of the hardships and inconveniences that it sets in the way towards marriage, it could encourage a number of illicit or common law relationships. Whatever good it will do will then be offset by consequent loss or injury to deeply held social values which our Civil Code has enshrined.

We thus submit that the proposed measure fails to meet constitutional standards which must be satisfied by any restriction on intellectual and personal liberties. It will take so much for so little, and so, in this sense also, will probably, do more harm than good. Its exactions in the delicate sphere of individual liberties are out of proportion to what good it can be expected to accomplish. It thus, in Cardozo's phrase, "outruns the bounds of reason" and constitutes an arbitrary interference on individual liberties.

Division of Research
and Law Reform
U.P. Law Center

Dec. 28, 1973
TRUE COPY

1974-02-08

MEMORANDUM CIRCULAR
TO: All Mayors

> SUBJECT: *Family Planning Information and Counselling Service to Applicants for Marriage License*

With the issuance of Presidential Decree No. 79 Revising the Population Act of 1971, it may be superfluous for us to write you for further support of the family planning program. We know that you have already contributed in more ways than just allowing the program to get implemented in your municipality. However, we will risk proposing one more measure which we hope your council would pass. Some mayors in fact initiated the move with the backing of a municipal family planning coordinating council organized by either the community development officer of the Department of Local Governments and Community Development and the Department of Social Welfare social worker. We are referring to the promulgation of the ordinance which requires applicants for marriage license to present a certification that they have been informed about family planning as a prerequisite to the issuance of a marriage license.

We trust that the local civil registrar could cooperate with our representatives or those of other agencies involved in the national family planning program in the carrying out of the provision of your ordinance. We look forward to receiving copies of such ordinance.

<table>
<tr><td>(SGD). JOSE RONO
Secretary of Local Government
and Community Development</td><td>(SGD.) ESTEFANIA ALDABA-LIM
Secretary of Social Welfare</td></tr>
</table>

cc: Regional Directors, DSW Regional Directors, DLGCD
    Prov. Social Welfare Officers, DSW
    Prov. Development Officers, DLGCD

A true copy:
sla/Technical Staff
CMO—Cag. de Oro
3 March '74

February 26, 1974

Mr. Arthur B. Cuyugan
Associate Director of Administration
Commission on Population
ABI Bldg. 136 Ayala Avenue
Makati, Rizal

Dear Mr. Cuyugan:

Thank you for your letter of January 24, 1974.

The favorable recommendation of the measure we have proposed and the encouragement and support of our local effort and initiative to make family planning an accepted and living reality is most rewarding.

In presenting our proposal, we were aware of the possible constitutional questions that may be raised against it. We believe however that the objections are not constitutionally unsurmountable to preclude achieving the objectives we have established. We hope that with your continued support, we may find a proper solution along the line we have suggested eliminating the objectionable aspects thereof.

Although this is not the time to make an extensive comment on the Memorandum of the U.P. Law Center, we would like to believe that solutions to new and novel problems brought about by an adoption of national policy on family planning cannot be determined by a myopic and close adherence to purely academic standards on constitutional law theory. All the more the alleged "infirmities" pointed out by the "Memorandum" brings to sharper focus the felt need of a pilot area where ideas about family planning may be adopted, applied and tested locally before adoption as a continuing measure in the national level. This is the alternative that we have suggested in our letter to the President, in the event that an amendatory decree is not possible.

Very truly yours,

(SGD) FLORENTINO G. DUMLAO, JR.
Chairman, Legal Committee
Cagayan de Oro City

A True copy:
/vmb

Report of Workshop on Local Government and Population Policy

In his paper, Reuben R. Canoy reviewed the role of local governments in implementing population policy. As an example of what could be done, he referred to the "Model City Project" of Cagayan de Oro, the Philippines, of which he is Mayor. The Project was established to explore the possible ways in which local governments could use their resources to the end of implementing family planning as a human right. As a chartered city, Cagayan de Oro was granted certain specific powers. The question was how could these powers be used to stress family planning. It became apparent that the city could not change laws, such as those governing the minimum age of marriage. But it could pay the marriage fees, set up family planning consultations with prospective couples, establish media campaigns, etc., in an effort to make the citizens of the municipality conscious of their responsibilities with regard to population.

Dr. Walter Rodrigues also discussed the importance of the role of local governments based on his experience in Brazil. Because Brazil has a federal form of government, the state governments have independent powers in the population field. Therefore, the "community problem" has a special significance in Brazil. The main problem at present is to get contraceptives into the hands of the people. Brazil does not use voluntary sterilization or abortion as family planning methods, not so much because they may be illegal, but because they are too expensive and the means are not widely available. Of late, the emphasis has been to utilize local political leaders in an effort to increase the effectiveness of family planning programmes. The responsibility for motivation has been assumed by some of the local governments. In some cases, local leaders have withdrawn family allowances where they felt that the allowances were encouraging large families. At times local governments have also taken charge of contraceptives delivery by using personnel and methods which have local appeal and do not offend any local sensitivities. This system has proven to be very successful. In one case, results that had taken six years to produce elsewhere were achieved in six months. Here, the contraceptive acceptance rate reached 58%, with a continuation rate of 83%.

Finally, the support of local leaders, city mayors, and state governments has been an important factor in changing the attitude of the federal government to the extent that it is now considering amendments to present restrictive laws.

At least one participant took issue with the "Model City" approach and urged that it be looked at closely before it was accepted as a model with universal potential. He noted that revenues in Cagayan de Oro had quadrupled in a few short years but that if population growth were slowed, the city might not have the revenues available to continue its incentives and programmes relating to family planning. Many cities in the world simply do not have the financial resources to do what Cagayan de Oro was proposing to do. In many cities there are other urgent priorities which will take precedent over family planning.

But it was agreed that local governments can contribute to the solution of population problems.

Population in the UN System: Developing the Legal Capacity and Programs of UN Agencies

By
Daniel G. Partan*

OUTLINE

---

* Professor of Law, Boston University.

This paper briefly summarizes the results of a study of the mandates and programs of UN agencies in the population field made for the Law and Population Programme at the Fletcher School of Law and Diplomacy. The study analyzes the legal basis supporting UN system action on population questions, and offers a concept of UN competence in the population field upon which future UN action might be founded. The study reviews the population program resolutions and decisions of the General Assembly, the Economic and Social Council, the Population Commission and other UN bodies, and comments upon some of the functions and activities of the two central UN population agencies, that is, the Population Division of the UN Secretariat and the United Nations Fund for Population Activities (UNFPA). The study also reviews the current population programs of major UN agencies in terms of the mandates under which they were adopted and the constitutional authority of the agency concerned. This review includes the World Health Organization (WHO), the United Nations Children's Fund (UNICEF), the Food and Agriculture Organization (FAO), the International Labour Organization (ILO), the United Nations Educational, Scientific and Cultural Organization (UNESCO), the International Bank for Reconstruction and Development (World Bank), and the Regional Economic Commissions, that is, the Economic Commission for Africa (ECA), the Economic Commission for Asia and the Far East (ECAFE), the Economic Commission for Europe (ECE), the Economic Commission for Latin America (ECLA), and the UN Economic and Social Office in Beirut (UNESOB).

The conclusions reached and the recommendations made in the study are described here. The full report of the study appears under the title, POPULATION IN THE UN SYSTEM: DEVELOPING THE LEGAL CAPACITY AND PROGRAMS OF UN AGENCIES, published in 1972 by A.W. Sijthoff, Leyden, The Netherlands, and the Rule of Law Press, Durham, North Carolina.

I. THE LEGAL CAPACITY OF THE UN SYSTEM:
GENERAL CONCLUSIONS

In designating 1974 as "World Population Year," the General Assembly has called for the development of a detailed program of action to be undertaken by the UN system during that year. The Assembly considered that UN system assistance "should continue to be available upon request for evolving and implementing a dynamic population policy" meeting the needs of Member States. It stated as its basic premise that the "formulation and implementation of population policies and programmes are matters falling under the internal competence of each country," and that, consequently, UN system action in the population sphere "should be responsive to the varied needs and requests of individual Member States."[1]

Within this framework, UN system action in the population field can be traced to three distinct grounds for United Nations concern: first, the human rights aspects of family planning; second, the interrelationships between population growth and economic development; and, third, the potential impact on the environment of population growth rates, and of population size and distribution, in relation to levels and forms of production and consumption.

In common with general United Nations practice, however, most UN action on population questions has not rested squarely on any single ground; most action can be seen as founded upon a combination of the three. For example, the draft resolution recommended by the Population Commission at its 16th Session for adoption by the Economic and Social Council makes use of all three grounds for UN action. The draft resolution urges Member States "to co-operate in achieving a substantial reduction of the rate of population growth in those countries which consider that their present rate of growth is too high," and "in accordance with their national population policies and needs, to ensure that information and education about family planning, as well as the means to effectively practice family planning, are made available to all individuals by the end of the Second United Nations Development Decade." It also calls upon the Secretary-General "to study the possibilities of developing a global population strategy, including population movements, for promoting and co-ordinating population policies in Member States with the objective of achieving a balance between population and other natural resources."[2]

A. *UN System Recommendations to Governments*

The UN system as a whole has the legal authority to study, to discuss and to adopt recommendations on population questions based upon each of

---

1. General Assembly Res. 2683 (XXV), 25 GAOR Supp. 28, p. 55 (A/8028) (1970).
2. Population Commission, Report of the 16th Session, 1971, 52 ESCOR Supp. 3, at 44-48, paras. A(1)(b) and (c), p. 45, and para. D(4)(a), at 47 (E/5090)(E/CN.9/263) (1972).

the three grounds mentioned, that is, human rights, economic development and environmental impact. UN policy recommendations in each area have two chief functions. First, they develop world community policy for the guidance of Member States; and, second, they provide guidelines for UN action programs in areas in which UN action programs may be undertaken. In addition, UN policy declarations in the human rights area contribute to the development of international law human rights standards, and thus may ultimately become binding both upon UN agencies and upon governments.

The legal competence of the United Nations system to function in the population field derives fundamentally from UN Charter Article 55, and from the conception of the UN system as the vehicle for developing community standards on world problems over the field indicated in Article 1, paragraph 3, of the UN Charter.[3] The UN system, headed for this purpose by the General Assembly, articulates and coalesces United Nations policy on population questions through its debates and resolutions. The Assembly and the other organs of the UN system have no legislative authority to establish legally binding obligations for Member States in the population field, but the great contribution of the UN system can be to provide a means through which a consensus on world community policy can be developed, and through which that policy can be implemented on the basis of co-operative action voluntarily undertaken by Member States.

With regard to the human rights basis for UN system action in the population field, the work of the UN system might result in the adoption of a General Assembly declaration on the human rights aspects of family planning. If such a declaration were adopted in circumstances that indicate both an intention to frame world community policy and the acceptance of that policy by a consensus of Member States, it would be an important step in the establishment of a binding international law obligation to observe the human right in question. Whether at any given point the rights embodied in the declaration could be characterized as binding in international law would be a function of at least three factors: the degree to which the right is supported by a consensus expressed through the UN process; the degree to which the right had been carefully and consciously developed in the UN process as

---

3. UN Charter Article 1, paragraph 3, states as a basic UN Purpose the achievement through the UN system of "international cooperation in solving international problems of an economic, social, cultural, or humanitarian character, and in promoting and encouraging respect for human rights and for fundamental freedoms." Article 55 elaborates this basic UN Purpose in calling upon the United Nations to promote:
   a. higher standards of living, full employment, and conditions of economic and social progress and development;
   b. solutions of international economic, social, health, and related problems; and international cultural and educational cooperation; and
   c. universal respect for, and observance of, human rights and fundamental freedoms for all without distinction as to race, sex, language, or religion.

involving the legal obligations of states; and the degree to which state practice, in addition to the UN process, appeared to support the concept of obligation with regard to the human right in question. The UN contribution to the generation of customary international law can accelerate the process and provide instant evidence of the "sense of obligation" through expressions of intent to regard the standard as binding, but the UN process does not function in a vacuum, and would not replace reference to the actual practice of states.[4]

A General Assembly declaration may thus "make" the international law of human rights as part of a UN-centered customary law process. In this sense, then, the adoption of an Assembly declaration may result in customary international law obligations for Member States that would be equally as binding as they would have been had the obligations stated in the declaration been incorporated in a ratified treaty.

B. *UN System Population Program Assistance Requested by Governments*

The UN system as a whole has the legal authority to provide all forms of population program assistance that may be requested by governments. This conclusion may not apply to each branch of the UN system as a result of specific constitutional or functional limitations observed by some UN agencies, but no such limitations apply to the UN system considered as a whole. As indicated earlier, however, UN system action is always guided by the policy developed through the UN process, and UN system action is subject to the standards laid down in international law.

Each of the several largely autonomous agencies in the UN system active in the population field determines its own program aims and limitations in relation to its functions and powers as set forth in its constitutional document. In such a system of autonomous agencies, it is understandable that the interests and programs of the agencies may not entirely match the needs and desires of all Member States. For example, UNICEF has only recently been willing to include contraceptives among the supplies made available to family planning programs at the request of Member States, and both UNICEF and WHO have placed great emphasis in their population programs on integrating family planning with maternal and child health services.[5]

Although particular agency policies of this character may limit the role of the agency involved in relation to the family planning needs of some states, the limitations need not affect the capacity of other UN agencies to supply the needed assistance. The chief agent for change in this regard would

---

4. The role of the UN system in the development of the customary international law of human rights is discussed in PARTAN, POPULATION IN THE UN SYSTEM, chapter 3.

5. *See id.*, chapters 11 and 12.

be the United Nations Fund for Population Activities (UNFPA), which has authority to turn to agencies outside the UN system when required for the execution of its programs.[6]

II. POPULATION AND HUMAN RIGHTS

A. *Human Rights Aspects of Family Planning*

As developed through the UN system, the human right to free choice in determining family size leads to two basic rights. First, the family planning right includes a right to access to adequate education and information on questions of family planning. Second, it includes a right to free access to the means needed to exercise the right to free choice in determining family size.

The Teheran International Conference on Human Rights declared in 1968 that: "Parents have a basic human right to determine freely and responsibly the number and the spacing of their children." A resolution adopted at the Teheran Conference added to this basic right a "right to adequate education and information in this respect."[7] Furthermore, in 1969, in its "Declaration on Social Progress and Development," the General Assembly stated that the implementation of the family planning right required "the provision to families of the knowledge and means necessary to enable them to exercise their right to determine freely and responsibly the number and spacing of their children."[8]

The general formulations of the family planning right presently drawn from General Assembly resolutions and from the Proclamation of Teheran might be further developed through a General Assembly Declaration on the Human Rights Aspects of Family Planning. Such a declaration would have the status of a General Assembly recommendation, and would not in itself be binding upon governments. It would establish UN policy, however, and would contribute to the development of the international law of human rights. An Assembly declaration might therefore ultimately result in an international law obligation of governments to provide the knowledge and means necessary to exercise the right to free choice in determining family size.[9]

B. *Scope and Content of the Family Planning Right*

The human right to free choice in determining family size implies both a right to be free from compulsory pro-natalist measures, and a right to be free

---

6. *See id.*, chapters 5 and 7.

7. Final Act of the International Conference on Human Rights, UN Sales No. E.68.XIV.2, pp. 2 and 14 (1968).

8. General Assembly Res. 2542 (XXIV), Art. 22(b), 24 GAOR Supp. 30, pp. 49, 52 (A/7630) (1969).

9. *See* PARTAN, POPULATION IN THE UN SYSTEM, chapters 2 and 3.

from compulsory anti-natalist measures. The precise scope of the right remains to be clarified in terms of the international law obligations of governments, but it is clear that governments would be permitted to continue to take action that may affect fertility over a wide range of subjects. Examples include marriage and divorce laws, the provision of maternity and child-care benefits, and the adoption of incomes and social security policies. A more precise definition of the limits of government action should be developed through the General Assembly Declaration on the Human Rights Aspects of Family Planning proposed above.

At base, a right to determine freely and responsibly the number and spacing of children would seem to embrace both a right to purchase and to use all medically approved forms of contraception, and a right to be free of compulsory anti-natalist policies involving compulsory contraception, sterilization or abortion. Except as required by reasonable public health standards, the "right" would seem to mean that governments may not forbid the sale or use of contraceptives, or forbid the operation of birth control clinics, or the use of birth control practices extending to and perhaps including voluntary sterilization. Similarly subject to reasonable regulation, the "right" would seem to mean that governments may not forbid sex education in the schools or ban public information programs designed to influence the exercise of the free choice guaranteed by the family planning right.

Abortion presents a difficult problem. Discussions leading to family planning statements have sometimes noted that voluntary abortion is common even where unlawful, and may be the leading "birth control" method in some countries.[10] No government representative appears to have characterized voluntary abortion as a "human right" however, and many appear to hold the view that abortion at any stage of pregnancy is to be sharply distinguished from contraception.[11] Given these views, it is unlikely to be fruitful to take up the issue in the early stages of developing the family planning right.

Outside of the areas of prohibitions on government conduct implied from the family planning right, it would seem that the right of governments to pursue their national population policies is qualified only by the unclear and unquantifiable obligation of governments to make available the knowl-

---

10. The study entitled *Human Fertility and National Development*, UN Doc. ST/ECA/138, UN Sales No. E.71.II.A.12 (1971), and prepared for the UN Advisory Committee on the Application of Science and Technology to Development (ACASTD), states at 49 that: "Induced abortion is probably the single most widely used method of fertility control in the world today and has been associated with declining birth rates in many countries."

11. *See, e.g.*, the provisional report of the Secretary-General to the Population Commission at its Fifteenth Session entitled MEASURES, POLICIES AND PROGRAMMES AFFECTING FERTILITY, WITH PARTICULAR REFERENCE TO NATIONAL FAMILY PLANNING PROGRAMMES, UN Doc. E/CN.9/232, at Part II, section D, *Laws relevant to abortion, contraception and sterilization*, pp. 62-77 (1969).

edge and means needed to exercise the family planning right. The government's "knowledge and means" obligation may, for example, be interpreted as placing limits on government pro-natalist propaganda, and as obligating the government to support birth control clinics and family planning public education programs. The "knowledge and means" standard of the Assembly's Social Progress Declaration quoted above certainly calls for some efforts in this direction, and cannot be satisfied by an official "hands-off" policy.

Government policies in other areas that may affect fertility appear to be untouched by the human rights standard. For example, governments appear to retain freedom of choice concerning such subjects as marriage and divorce laws, and child care and benefit programs, as well as income and tax policies including social security and inheritance policies. A substantial range of government action that may in fact influence family planning choices, and hence fertility and population growth, may nevertheless be regarded as non-compulsory, and hence as not violative of the free choice in family planning reserved to individuals as a human right.[12]

C.   *UN Action to Give Effect to the Family Planning Right*

Turning to actions that the United Nations might take to give effect to a United Nations view of the scope and content of the family planning right, two points should be made. First, as indicated earlier, the international law obligation of governments to respect the family planning right would apply to the United Nations with equal force. The UN system could not support government programs or take direct action that did not fully respect the right of free choice of family size. Second, the UN system might choose to use its resources to stimulate and to support population programs that promote the effective realization of the human right to determine family size. Considering that the promotion of respect for fundamental human rights is a basic Purpose of the United Nations set forth in Article 1, paragraph 3, of the Charter, it is natural to expect UN system action to be geared to the accomplishment of this Purpose whenever possible. Lacking the means for authoritative determination of such issues as the scope and content of the family planning right, the UN system is nevertheless compelled to resolve such questions for itself in the human rights area, and, having taken a view that can be characterized as the UN view, the UN system should then adhere to that view in its dealings with Member States.

The UN system may thus seek to promote the observance of the family planning right through the support of government programs that are designed affirmatively to give effect to the family planning right. The UN system may choose to concentrate its resources in support of such programs,

---

12.   *See* PARTAN, POPULATION IN THE UN SYSTEM, chapters 2 and 5.

but the UN system has no authority to use development assistance funds, or other UN programs, as a means of coercing governments to take action to give effect to UN population policies or to human rights standards. The most that can be done in this regard is to establish programs that will assist governments and non-governmental institutions in taking the action needed to give effect to UN policies and to UN-developed human rights standards.[13]

III.   POPULATION AND DEVELOPMENT

A.   *Population Growth and Economic Development*

The United Nations has the legal authority to adopt a UN policy on the relationship between rapid population growth and economic development. In so doing, the United Nations might recommend a maximum growth rate, or a set of growth rates adjusted to varying conditions, that could be used as a guide in UN development assistance programs. The UN may also choose to concentrate its resources in assisting governments that wish to moderate their population growth rates, taking UN policy recommendations into account in this regard. As with UN action to give effect to human rights standards, however, the UN system has no authority to use UN development assistance funds as a means of coercing governments to conform to UN population growth rate policies.[14]

Although the work of the UN system has shown clearly the link between rapid population growth and economic development, the General Assembly has failed to "decide" that such a link in fact exists, and to consider and adopt a UN policy that UN development assistance should be tied to progress towards reducing the rate of population growth.

The closest that the UN system has come to setting standards for population growth in this context appears to have been the 2.5 per cent annual population growth rate figure used in the General Assembly's definition of goals and objectives for the Second Development Decade in its 1970 resolution entitled "International Development Strategy for the Second United Nations Development Decade." That resolution states in paragraph 15 that:

> The target for growth in average income per head is calculated on the basis of an average annual increase of 2.5 per cent in the population of developing countries, which is less than the average rate at present forecast for the 1970s. In this context, each developing country should formulate its own demographic objectives within the framework of its national development plan.

---

13. *See id.*, chapter 4.
14. *See id.*, chapter 6.

Paragraph 65 of the Assembly resolution goes on to state that: "Those developing countries which consider that their rate of population growth hampers their development will adopt measures which they deem necessary in accordance with their concept of development."[15]

In using the 2.5 per cent population growth rate figure as the basis for establishing the Second Development Decade income growth rate targets, the Assembly acknowledged that the 2.5 per cent figure for average annual increase in the population of developing countries "is less than the average rate at present forecast for the 1970s." The Assembly therefore appears to have based its Second Development Decade planning on the assumption that the developing countries will implement population policies designed to reduce their population growth rates to the 2.5 per cent standard, but at the same time the Assembly has taken no steps to structure the UN development assistance machinery around the 2.5 per cent figure.

From the legal point of view, it seems clear that the authority of the United Nations to operate development assistance programs should carry with it the authority to determine the conditions under which UN assistance will be granted. Given the limited resources at the disposal of the United Nations, some choices must be made, and a choice founded on a judgment as to the likelihood of success of classes of development assistance programs could not be condemned as arbitrary or discriminatory.

Thus, although as indicated above, it would be improper for the United Nations to use UN development assistance funds as a means of coercing governments to accept UN development assistance policies, the United Nations might legitimately decide to give preference to development assistance plans that attempt to moderate population growth rates. The distinction drawn in this regard would be between UN economic aid decisions that distinguish between governments in terms of their conformity to UN policy, which would be regarded as beyond UN authority, and UN decisions that distinguish between development plans in terms of their probability of success, which would be regarded as legitimate choices in the allocation of UN funds.[16]

IV. POPULATION AND THE ENVIRONMENT

A. *Population at the Stockholm Conference*

United Nations concern with rapid population growth has centered on the relationship between population growth rates and economic development. In terms of the ultimate total size of world population, or the rapid

---

15. General Assembly Res. 2626 (XXV), 25 GAOR Supp. 28, pp. 39, 40-41 and 47 (A/8028) (1970).

16. *See* PARTAN, POPULATION IN THE UN SYSTEM, chapters 6 and 7.

increase in size of segments of world population, the problem has generally been seen as raising the possibility that the growth of the world's population might outstrip world food production, resulting in mass famine on a scale never before experienced.

As pressing and as difficult as the problems of economic development and food production may appear, this may be too narrow a view of the impact of population growth. Coupled with rising expectations in living standards, a more immediate and more threatening problem may be presented by the relationship between total world population size and total available natural resources. As stated by the General Assembly resolution that convened the 1972 Stockholm Conference on the Human Environment, the chief problem may be the "continuing and accelerating impairment of the quality of the human environment caused by such factors as air and water pollution, erosion and other forms of soil deterioration, waste, noise and the secondary effects of biocides, which are accentuated by rapidly increasing population and accelerating urbanization."[17]

The Stockholm Conference took population growth and distribution into account within the framework of its consideration of "The Planning and Management of Human Settlements for Environmental Quality." Within this framework, the Conference recommended that UN agencies provide increased assistance in family planning to countries which request it, and asked WHO to promote and to intensify research into human reproduction. The Conference declared that:

> Demographic policies, which are without prejudice to basic human rights and which are deemed appropriate by Governments concerned, should be applied in those regions where the rate of population growth or excessive population concentrations are likely to have adverse effects on the environment or development, or where low population density may prevent improvement of the human environment and impede development.[18]

The Conference also declared that the "natural growth of population continuously presents problems on the preservation of the environment,"[19] and asked the Secretary-General to ensure that, during the observance in 1974 of

---

17. General Assembly Res. 2398 (XXIII), *Problems of the Human Environment*, 23 GAOR Supp. 18, p.2 (A/7218) (1968).

18. Declaration of the United Nations Conference on the Human Environment, UN Doc. A/CONF.48/14, Principle 16, p. 6 (1972).

19. *Id.*, para. 5, at 2. The paragraph calls for "adequate policies and measures" to face the problems caused by population growth. It also states that: "Of all things in the world, people are the most precious. It is the people that propel social progress, create social wealth, develop science and technology and, through their hard work, continuously transform the human environment." *Id.*, at 2-3.

World Population Year, special attention is given to population concerns as they relate to the environment.

B.   *Environmental Impact Questions*

The Stockholm Conference on the Human Environment thus did not consider the following questions that might have been thought to fall within the scope of its mandate: What is the relationship between total world population size and the quality of the human environment? Is there a maximum or an optimum population size for a country or for a particular area, given the available natural resources and the stage of economic development? If so, how should the maximum or optimum population size be determined? Finally, would the sum of the maximum or optimum population sizes determined for each country yield a world maximum or optimum population size?

The questions just posed have not yet received systematic consideration in the UN system, which has only recently begun to consider the implications for the environment of population growth rates and of total population size. With regard to the "environmental impact" basis for United Nations action on population questions, so little is known at present about the relationships between population growth rates, structure, distribution and total size, on the one hand, and production, consumption and environmental impact on the other, that the United Nations is not now able to formulate UN policy in this area. The UN role is therefore at present confined to research, study and discussion, looking to the development of the knowledge upon which future action might be based.[20]

V.   UN POPULATION PROGRAMS

A.   *Population in UN Development Assistance*

Turning to the administration of UN development assistance programs, the shift in the UN system to country programming provides an opportunity for promoting the integration of demographic and development planning. As each country formulates its development program in the context of UN development assistance, the UN system can provide the technical assistance needed for demographic planning, and can help in formulating and carrying out population programs integrated with overall country development programs.[21]

The Secretary-General's 1971 report to the Population Commission entitled "Population and the Second United Nations Development Decade" stresses the interrelationship between demographic and development planning, but acknowledges the difficulties of carrying out "elaborate analysis and

---

20.   *See* PARTAN, POPULATION IN THE UN SYSTEM, chapter 8.
21.   *See id.*, chapter 7, for a description of the UN Development Co-operation Cycle.

planning procedures" with the limited facilities commonly available in developing countries. The report suggests that, at a minimum, the following facilities are needed:

- (a) reliable statistics, including population census and vital statistics;
- (b) adequate demographic and related research facilities;
- (c) comprehensive demographic projections with the necessary number of alternative variants;
- (d) demographic staff in the planning agency; and
- (e) direct contacts between the policy-making body and technical staff.[22]

Considering the urgent need for such facilities, the Secretary-General's 1972-1976 population program proposals give high priority to assisting governments in developing the facilities needed to formulate demographic objectives that are co-ordinated with development objectives. UN technical co-operation will have a fundamental goal of helping governments to acquire a "capacity to deal with demographic aspects of development in accordance with their respective needs and circumstances."[23]

In developing countries that recognize the need to moderate population growth rates and undertake to integrate demographic and development planning, the present need appears to be to consolidate UN population program assistance into a co-ordinated program that meshes with the country's development plan. The assistance thus rendered by the United Nations system should be tailored to fit and to fulfill the needs of the recipient country. It should not, as may often have been true in the past, be designed to make the fullest, or the most convenient use, of the resources of the agency that renders assistance. The aid given should also be sequenced, or phased, in the fashion required by the recipient; it should not be delivered on a schedule that suits only the convenience or the programming of the UN agency concerned.[24]

The desiderata just outlined for UN population program assistance are not easy to fulfill in a system of autonomous executing agents. Each UN agency tends to take its own view of the priorities in population programming, and each develops its own "packages" or population programs geared to the individual agency's special area of interest and self-developed mandate in the population field. The primary need, therefore, is to bring the development assistance agencies of the UN system together in support of comprehensive national population programs.

---

22. UN Doc. E/CN.9/243, paras. 18 and 20, pp. 8-10 (1971).
23. UN Doc. E/CN.9/246, para. 18, p. 7 (1971).
24. *See* PARTAN, POPULATION IN THE UN SYSTEM, chapter 7.

B.   *The Role of Non-Governmental Agencies*

The normal role of the UN system in the population field is to provide population program assistance at the request of governments, and the UN system would not be expected to become involved in activities within Member States that are opposed by the governments of those states. There is no barrier, however, to UN system action at the request of non-governmental agencies, where the government expresses no opposition to the activities in question, even though it will not officially sponsor them. Thus, in the case of family planning programs undertaken to give effect to the family planning right, the UN system may assist such programs at the request of non-governmental agencies, so long as the programs are tolerated by the government concerned.[25]

Both where UN family planning activities are undertaken at the request of governments, and where such activities do not have official government sponsorship, the UN system may function either through UN agencies or through other governmental and non-governmental institutions acting as executing agents. Both the United Nations Development Programme (UNDP) and the United Nations Fund for Population Activities (UNFPA) have the authority to turn to institutions outside the UN system to act as executing agents in filling the needs of UN and country programs that cannot be met through UN agencies.[26]

The UNFPA terms of reference authorize UNFPA to respond to requests for assistance from non-governmental sources, and to select non-governmental agencies as executing agents for Fund projects. The UNFPA terms of reference are also open to the interpretation that UNFPA may fund projects in countries that have not officially sanctioned family planning programs. This broad view has apparently been adopted by the Fund. In 1970, Rafael M. Salas, Director of the Fund, stated that in some instances UNFPA intends to fund projects through the International Planned Parenthood Federation, and that this "will be particularly true in areas, as in Latin America, where the governments wish family planning activities to take place but sometimes do not wish to have official policies or programmes supporting such activities."[27]

The UNFPA "Tentative Work Plan" for 1972-1975 announces that "the Fund will support, upon request and where the government does not object, the development of family planning delivery systems through non-governmental agencies in countries without an official programme."[28] The Work Plan takes the view that:

---

25.   *See id.,* chapter 5.
26.   *See id.,* chapter 7.
27.   UNFPA, Statement by Rafael M. Salas, Director, at the Regional Conference of the International Planned Parenthood Federation, Tokyo, Oct. 16, 1970 (mimeographed).
28.   UN Doc. UNFPA/PCC/IV/4, para. 122, p. 48 (1972).

The UNFPA is not limited to acting upon specific requests from Governments or organizations, but may take the initiative to promote additional activities in accordance with its terms of reference and priorities in order to shape an integrated and comprehensive population programme of assistance to meet the urgent needs of dealing with population problems.[29]

VI.   RECOMMENDATIONS: HUMAN RIGHTS

A.   *General Assembly Declaration on the Human Rights Aspects of Family Planning*

The human right to free choice in determining family size should be developed through a General Assembly Declaration on the Human Rights Aspects of Family Planning. Such a declaration might be drafted in the first instance by an *ad hoc* joint committee of experts appointed by the three relevant Economic and Social Council Commissions: the Population Commission, the Commission on Human Rights and the Commission on the Status of Women. The resulting draft could be submitted to the 1974 World Population Conference for consideration and then transmitted through the Economic and Social Council to the General Assembly for adoption in 1975.[30]

B.   *Annual Population Reports by UN Member States*

In addition to adopting a Declaration on the Human Rights Aspects of Family Planning, the General Assembly should request UN Member States to submit annual reports on the development by each state of its population policy, and on measures taken to give effect to the family planning right. The style and content of the general report on population policies might be left largely to the discretion of each Member State, but specific information should be requested as to the family planning right. The report should include both measures taken to protect the free exercise of the family planning right, and measures taken to provide the knowledge and means needed for the free exercise of the family planning right.[31]

In calling upon Member States to submit annual population reports, the Assembly would be exercising its power to study, debate and recommend on population questions, and invoking the pledge undertaken in UN Charter Article 56 "to take joint and separate action in cooperation with the Organization" to achieve the purposes set out in Article 55.[32] There is thus some basis to characterize an Assembly decision to call for population reports as

---

29.   *Id.*, at para. 14, p. 10.
30.   *See* PARTAN, POPULATION IN THE UN SYSTEM, chapter 2.
31.   *See id.*, chapter 4.
32.   UN Charter Article 55 is quoted in note 3 *supra*.

obligatory, but there would be no means of ensuring compliance. Even if compliance were wholly voluntary, however, the suggested annual population reports might produce much useful information that would aid in the process of further defining the family planning right, and might serve as the basis for an "Annual Population Status Report" to be issued by the Secretary-General.

C.   *Review by a Committee of Experts*

The annual population policy and family planning reports should be given for review and comment to a new standing committee of experts appointed jointly by the three Economic and Social Council Commissions concerned, that is, the Population Commission, the Commission on Human Rights and the Commission on the Status of Women. The reports and comments of the proposed committee of experts should be submitted to the Economic and Social Council for transmission to the General Assembly.[33]

The proposed committee of experts could be empowered to request clarifications of information submitted by governments, and to ask questions about the conformity of particular government practices with UN human rights policy as developed in the proposed UN Declaration on Human Rights Aspects of Family Planning and in other Assembly resolutions. The expert committee's observations and conclusions would help to give the Assembly the information it needs to further develop the human rights aspects of family planning.

D.   *A UN Family Planning "Knowledge and Means" Program*

In order to give effect to the family planning right as defined in the proposed General Assembly Declaration on the Human Rights Aspects of Family Planning, the United Nations should adopt a family planning "knowledge and means" action program. The proposed program should bring together some of the scattered family planning activities within the UN system and endeavor to fill the gaps so as to be able to offer a cohesive program within all Member States.[34]

The proposed UN family planning "knowledge and means" program should elaborate and give specific meaning to the family planning right in different regional and national contexts through expert seminars, model family planning laws, and technical assistance in the development of family planning laws and of national family planning programs. The program should stimulate research on all aspects of the population problem including, for example, research on family planning education and motivation, and studies of the effect of national laws on fertility in differing social and cultural

33. *See* PARTAN, POPULATION IN THE UN SYSTEM, chapter 4.
34. *See id.*, chapter 5.

settings. The program should collect and publish on a regular basis laws affecting fertility and national family planning laws and regulations. It should study the effectiveness of family planning laws and programs in varying national contexts, and operate a clearing-house for legal and sociological research in this field. Finally, the program should be in a position to develop "packages" of family planning program assistance to be made available within Member States. The new program might culminate in a UN Declaration on the Right to Family Planning Knowledge and Means that would render more definite and specific the family planning right first articulated in the proposed Declaration on the Human Rights Aspects of Family Planning.

E.   *Administration of the UN Family Planning*
     "Knowledge and Means" Program

The proposed UN family planning "knowledge and means" program would normally be made available on request by governments, but it should also be made available on request by non-governmental organizations in countries in which the government will tolerate, but not sponsor, family planning programs. In such countries UN assistance could be made available either directly to national non-governmental agencies, or, where appropriate, indirectly through international non-governmental organizations active in the countries concerned.[35]

Turning to the organization and the place within the UN system of the proposed UN family planning "knowledge and means" program, the UN agencies that have acted as executing agents for UN population assistance programs might be utilized for parts of the "packages" to be developed within the family planning program, but no single agency has taken a broad enough approach to be made responsible for the program as a whole. It might therefore be appropriate to give the program over to the administration of the United Nations Fund for Population Activities (UNFPA), functioning through a special family planning program unit established within the UNFPA staff.

The administration by UNFPA of a UN family planning "knowledge and means" program would bring to a head three questions that have plagued UNFPA since its creation. First, should the UNFPA acquire a more solid constitutional basis than the present decision of the Secretary-General and agreement between the Secretary-General and the Administrator of the United Nations Development Programme (UNDP)? Second, should UNFPA be given policy guidance through a council of government representatives, rather than the present Advisory Board and Inter-Agency Consultative Committee? And, third, should UNFPA develop its own field staff for contacts with governments and non-governmental organizations in the countries in which UNFPA programs are operated?

---

35. *See* the conclusion stated in the text at notes 25-29 *supra*.

If UNFPA were to acquire major operational responsibilities in a UN family planning "knowledge and means" program, it would most likely be considered necessary to give UNFPA both a constitutional document and a governing council. Both might be supplied through a General Assembly resolution tying UNFPA in some degree to the United Nations Development Programme. Three alternatives are possible. Responsibility for UNFPA might be given to the UNDP Governing Council, to a separate committee of that Council, or to an entirely new body. Whichever method is chosen, the special needs of UNFPA should be recognized, excluding full merger with UNDP.[36] Consideration might also be given to establishing a separate family planning program advisory committee, whose members might be drawn from among individuals prominently associated with UN human rights, status of women and population programs.

As to UNFPA field representation, the present system utilizing Population Programme Officers directly responsible to the UN Secretariat Population Division, and acting through regional and country offices of UNDP, may need revision as UNFPA becomes involved in operational tasks. UNFPA may require its own staff in countries in which large-scale family planning programs are undertaken.[37]

VII.   RECOMMENDATIONS:
POPULATION AND ECONOMIC DEVELOPMENT

A.   *General Assembly Recommendation on the Interrelationship between Population Growth Rates and Economic Development*

The General Assembly should adopt a recommendation on the interrelationship between population growth rates and economic development. The Assembly might recommend an overall population growth rate ceiling, beginning with the 2.5 per cent annual population growth rate used in planning the Second United Nations Development Decade. Based on the results of various studies now in progress, the Assembly might in addition recommend a series of growth rate ceilings, taking into account the stage of economic and social development reached by the country concerned, and its overall development objectives. In both cases, the recommendations would be made for the guidance of UN Member States, and would in no way be binding either on UN agencies or on the states concerned.[38]

Although it is apparent from General Assembly resolutions relating to the Second United Nations Development Decade that population growth rates are of central importance in achieving the goals set for the decade, it is

36. *See* PARTAN, POPULATION IN THE UN SYSTEM, chapters 5 and 7.
37. *See id.*, chapter 18.
38. *See id.*, chapter 6.

equally clear that the Assembly has not sought to adopt an explicit UN policy on the link between population growth rates and development. The reluctance of the United Nations to articulate a population growth rate policy has been based both upon the "internal competence" concept and upon the belief that the "diversity of demographic, economic and social conditions affecting population requires that objectives and goals for population policies be formulated for and by societies themselves."[39]

Considering that the proposed UN population growth rate policy would be a recommendation adopted by the General Assembly, and that no coercive action would be taken to implement the policy, the "internal competence" of countries in matters of population policy would be preserved. As to the "diversity of demographic, economic and social conditions" affecting population questions, recent United Nations studies acknowledge the gaps and inadequacies of data in the population field, but do not treat rapid population growth as such as within the class of subjects on which knowledge of demographic and economic interrelationships is inadequate.[40]

B. *Integration of Demographic and Development Planning*

The General Assembly should urge governments to improve their facilities for demographic planning, and to take steps to integrate their demographic and development planning. Special funds for this purpose might be made available through the UN Fund for Population Activities (UNFPA), both as a separate category of UNFPA assistance and as part of comprehensive national population programs.[41]

In line with the Pearson Commission's conclusion that "there can be no serious social and economic planning unless the ominous implications of uncontrolled population growth are understood and acted upon,"[42] it would be appropriate for the Assembly to recommend that developing countries take into account the need for moderating population growth rates in formulating country programs within the framework of the UN Development Programme. It would also be appropriate for the Assembly to stress the need to integrate demographic and development planning, and to make special funds available for the acquisition of the necessary planning facilities.

Beyond this point, since the bulk of UNDP funds are tied to country programming and to the indicative planning figure concept,[43] it is necessary

---

39. UN Doc. E/CN.9/245, Annex, *Proposed Measures and Activities for World Population Year, 1974*, para. 34, at 16 (1971).

40. *See, e.g.*, the report of the Lyon Expert Working Group on Population Research in National Institutions, UN Doc. E/CN.9/242, paras. 87-96, pp. 26-29 (1971).

41. *See* PARTAN, POPULATION IN THE UN SYSTEM, chapter 7.

42. PEARSON, REPORT OF THE COMMISSION ON INTERNATIONAL DEVELOPMENT SUBMITTED TO THE INTERNATIONAL BANK FOR RECONSTRUCTION AND DEVELOPMENT 58 (1969).

43. *See* PARTAN, POPULATION IN THE UN SYSTEM, chapters 6 and 7.

to turn to the special funds distributed through the United Nations Fund for Population Activities (UNFPA). Although UNFPA is administered through UNDP, UNFPA funds are not part of the UNDP indicative planning figure structure, and can be concentrated where they will do the most good from the standpoint of population policies. Thus, a modest degree of preference might be expressed in UN development assistance through allocation of UNFPA funds to activities designed to integrate population factors into development planning, and to moderate population growth rates.

C. *Country Programming and the Role of UNDP*

Country programming, as envisaged in the United Nations Development Co-operation Cycle, should proceed from the definition of the development needs of each country outwards to the UN agencies capable of providing portions of the assistance required. Planning for each country should take account of UN policy recommendations, particularly as regards the integration of demographic and development planning, but should result in a comprehensive UN assistance program designed according to the needs of the country program, rather than a program responsive to the interests or strengths available in UN agencies. When country programming proceeds as intended, the task of UNDP and UNFPA is to fill the needs of the country program, using in the first instance UN agencies as executing agents, but going beyond UN agencies where a country program calls for assistance that cannot be found within the UN system.

The Resident Representatives of the United Nations Development Programme (UNDP) should be directed to raise in their country programming consultations with governments both the question of improving facilities for demographic planning, and the question of moderating population growth rates as recommended by the General Assembly. The UNDP role would be limited to persuasion, as UNDP is not in a position to give preference to country development programs that seek to integrate demographic and development planning and to moderate population growth rates.[44] As recommended above, however, special funds might be made available through UNFPA to assist governments in taking these steps.

VIII. RECOMMENDATIONS: POPULATION RESEARCH AND TRAINING

A. *Co-ordination of Population Research*

The UN system should endeavor to co-ordinate population research through recommending research priorities, and through directing the flow of research funds towards the most pressing problems and towards the institu-

---

44. *See id.*, chapters 6 and 7.

tions most capable of contributing to the solution of those problems. This might be accomplished through a new joint UN Committee on Population Research Priorities, established with the participation of the UN Fund for Population Activities (UNFPA), the Population Division of the UN Secretariat, and other UN agencies and governmental and non-governmental organizations substantially involved in population research.[45]

The proposed joint Committee on Population Research Priorities might keep the entire field of population research under continuous review through a small working group, and hold periodic conferences to ensure the participation of all major agencies and organizations. The proposed committee could also serve as a focal point for the stimulation and the organization of parallel and comparative studies of appropriate aspects of the population problem.

B.   *A Clearing-House for Population Research*

The United Nations should establish a clearing-house for population research in connection with the proposed joint Committee on Population Research Priorities and in co-operation with CICRED, the newly established Committee for International Co-ordination of National Research in Demography.

The proposed clearing-house should maintain a register of population research planned and in progress, and set up systems for the effective distribution of the results of population research. In establishing the clearing-house, care should be taken to avoid duplication of existing services, and to cover the entire field on a regional or world-wide basis as appropriate. The clearing-house for national population laws, and for legal and sociological research, proposed as part of the UN family planning "knowledge and means" program should be established in close co-operation with the proposed more general clearing-house for population research.[46]

C.   *Environmental Impact Research*

In addition to the continuing work of the UN system in the design and co-ordination of research on the interrelationships between population and economic development, and on other major questions in the population field, the UN system should design and co-ordinate research on the impact of population size and growth rates on the environment.[47]

Three points seem clear at this stage. First, the interrelationships between population size, economic development and environmental impact are not understood well enough to formulate environmental protection goals for use in planning population and economic development policies and objec-

---

45. *See id.*, chapter 9.
46. *See id.*, chapters 5 and 9.
47. *See id.*, chapter 8, and the conclusions stated in the text at notes 17-20 *supra*.

tives. Second, although man's understanding of these interrelationships may not be adequate to form policy, the fact of a relationship between environmental impact and gross population size and level of economic development is plain enough to call for serious and immediate study through the UN system. Third, unlike the question of the relationship between population growth and economic development, the question of the environmental impact of total population size coupled with level of economic development does not apply solely to the developing countries. The environmental impact question applies with equal if not greater force to the policies of the economically developed countries.

A United Nations environmental impact research program should attempt to generate the data necessary for formulating environmental protection goals for use in planning population and economic development objectives and policies. To do so, it must take into account both population size, growth and distribution factors, and patterns of production and consumption.

The design and co-ordination of UN environmental impact research might be entrusted to an appropriate UN agency, such as UNESCO, UNFPA, or the Economic and Social Council's Advisory Committee on the Application of Science and Technology to Development (ACASTD). The research design might be submitted to the 1974 World Population Conference in the form of a preliminary environmental impact report to be considered at the Conference and transmitted to the Economic and Social Council for adoption in 1975.

D. *Training for Population Programs*

Considering the large number of personnel, and the wide variety of skills needed in population programs, the question of training for population programs calls for a number of different approaches at a variety of levels. The first step in developing co-ordinated UN system assistance over this broad field should be a systematic survey to find out just what skills will be needed at what time and in what parts of the world. Such a survey might be undertaken through a special committee on training for population programs, that brings together all UN and non-UN agencies active in this field.[48]

Although much of the required training will necessarily occur at the local level, there will undoubtedly be a need for regional and sub-regional training of high-level personnel, and for the training of "trainers" who will ultimately train field personnel. In this connection, there is a need for the development of a "multidisciplinary" approach to the training of "trainers" and of high-level personnel that should be explored through experimental and demonstration training projects.[49]

---

48. *See id.*, chapter 10.
49. *See* the Report of a United Nations/UNESCO/WHO Mission, *The Feasibility of Establishing a World Population Institute*, UN Doc. ST/SOA/SER.R/12 (1971), and Population Com-

The proposed special committee on training for population programs might be established within the framework of the UNFPA Inter-Agency Consultative Committee, re-structured to include all agencies substantially involved in population training programs. The proposed committee should keep the situation under continuous review, and should recommend measures for the systematic planning of a UN system role in population training programs.[50]

---

mission, Report of the 16th Session, 1971, 52 ESCOR Supp. 3, paras. 168-77 at 41-42 (E/5090) (E/CN.9/263) (1972).

50. *See* PARTAN, POPULATION IN THE UN SYSTEM, chapters 10 and 18.

Report of Workshop on the Role
of International Organizations

The role of international organizations was introduced by Professor John Humphrey of McGill University, formerly Director of the Human Rights Division of the United Nations, and by Professor Daniel G. Partan of Boston University School of Law, the author of the background paper circulated as a basis for discussion.

Professor Humphrey spoke of the adoption of the Universal Declaration of Human Rights by resolution of the General Assembly in 1948, and of its gradual transformation through state practice into customary international law increasingly recognized as binding upon Governments. A similar analysis can be applied to the population field, in which human rights standards, such as the right to determine the number and spacing of children, are beginning to emerge through a combination of resolutions of international meetings and the practice of Governments. The repetition of positions both by international organizations and by Governments thus contributes to the development of a new field of law. He also pointed out that even if a right is not regarded as legally binding or enforceable, the doctrine of estoppel would prevent Governments which voted for the right in the United Nations from enacting a domestic law which is contrary to that right.

Professor Partan described the legal capacity of United Nations agencies to contribute to the further development of the human rights aspects of family planning. Consideration might be given to utilizing the United Nations process to clarify the scope and content of the obligations of Governments with respect, for example, to the provision of the knowledge and means required for family planning. This might be accomplished through the development of a General Assembly Declaration on the Human Rights Aspects of Family Planning, which could provide guidance to Governments on some of the difficult issues involved and, if acted upon by Governments, might lead to a new customary international law of family planning.

The workshop session considered and approved specific recommendations in three areas related to the efforts of national Governments to compile, review and revise their national laws relating to population. First, it was recommended that international organizations encourage and assist such efforts, aimed at review and revision of national laws in the light of both population policy and human rights. Second, noting the designation of 1975 as International Women's Year, and the bearing of the status of women on population policies, it was recommended that international organizations assist Governments in compiling, reviewing and revising national laws affecting the status of women. Third, the session recommended the publication on a regular basis of a world legislative series on population, similar to the series on health law published by the World Health Organization.

Considering the potential role of regional organizations in the population field and the desirability of close collaboration between countries in the same region, the workshop session recommended that regional organizations sponsor law and population research and seminars on a regional basis. The session also recommended that a regular law component be incorporated into the programmes of the United Nations regional demographic training and research centres.

The session next discussed the status of the Symposium itself and its authority to make recommendations to intergovernmental organizations and to Governments. It was made clear that the Symposium consisted of individual experts in a number of fields. Most were lawyers, but there were a number of physicians, sociologists, political scientists, theologians, and demographers present as well. Many of these experts were involved with the Law and Population Projects of their own countries, and were in a position to exchange experiences and draw conclusions for the benefit of experts involved with the problem in other countries.

It was recognized that the Symposium was not authorized to "resolve" as to its conclusions, but that, as experts, the participants could make recommendations on the basis of their expertise.

SECTION 5

Text of Recommendations

Symposium on Law and Population
Text of Recommendations
June 17-21, 1974

Tunis

OUTLINE

INTRODUCTION

The Symposium on Law and Population adopted the following recommendations which reflect the discussions at the meeting.

It was recognized that the recommendations were not necessarily representative of the views or policies of the United Nations specialized agencies concerned, or of Governments and non-governmental organizations. The Symposium dealt with a number of issues on which relevant and reliable scientific information is incomplete or inconclusive. The meeting requested that the International Advisory Committee on Population and Law review the recommendations of the Symposium and decide to what extent they should, within the Committee's mandate, be adopted and submitted in an appropriate form for the consideration of Governments and organizations at the World Population Conference.

In making the following recommendations, the Symposium was guided in its deliberation by a number of United Nations instruments; foremost among these were: the Teheran Proclamation on Human Rights which declares that couples have the right to "determine freely and responsibly the number and spacing of their children," and the United Nations Declaration on Social Progress and Development which calls upon Governments to make available to couples the "knowledge and means necessary to enable them to exercise" this right.

The Symposium was aware of the fact that a free decision to make use of family planning requires that individuals have a meaningful existence and a high degree of self respect which will lead them to plan their lives and the size of their families. The Symposium was also aware that the mere provision of means and services will be ineffective unless free and informed individuals are provided with the proper motivation.

RECOMMENDATIONS OF SYMPOSIUM

I. THE STATUS OF WOMEN

[Original English]

The Symposium on Law and Population,

Recalling that the equal rights of all human beings, without distinction based on sex, are set forth in the United Nations Charter, the Universal Declaration of Human Rights, the International Covenants of Human Rights, the Declaration on the Elimination of Discrimination Against Women, the Declaration on Social Development and in various Conventions and Recommendations of the United Nations and its Specialized Agencies, particularly in the United Nations Conventions on the Political Rights of Women, on the Consent to Marriage, Minimum Age for Marriage and Registration of Marriages, and in the United Nations Recommendation on the same subject; in the UNESCO Convention on the Elimination of Discrimination in the Field of Education, in the ILO Conventions on the Elimination of Discrimination in Employment and Occupations, on Equal Remuneration for Work of Equal Value, and in ILO Recommendations concerning working women with family responsibilities;

Realizing that the preparations made for the World Population Conference, including the documentation and deliberations of the symposia on the relationship between population on one hand and development, family, environment and natural resources and human rights, on the other, the regional conferences on population, the International Forum on the Role of Women in Population and Development, and the regional intergovernmental consultations and seminars in the ECAFE and ECA regions have considerably increased the general awarenesss of the interrelationship between development, population, the status of women and other issues, and that pragmatic measures for the improvement of the status of women and for their full integration in development with special reference to the population factor are suggested by the before mentioned gatherings;

Recalling that the full integration of women in the development effort is one of the goals of the Second Development Decade's International Development Strategy and that a Programme for Concerted International Action for the Advancement of Women was adopted by the same United Nations General Assembly in 1970;

Considering that the human right to determine freely and responsibly the number and spacing of their children is of particular importance for women, who play the most crucial role in the human reproduction and that it is a prerequisite for their equal access with men to other human rights as well;

Bearing in mind the interrelationship between the status of women, especially their education and training, their economic opportunities, their status in civil law and their participation in the life of the society, including political decision-making and administration, on one hand, and the composition and size of their families, on the other;

Taking into account the direct effect of the mental and physical condition of the mother on the health and development of the child and therefore on the quality of the population;

Deploring that despite the adopted international standards for equality and non-discrimination, between men and women, discrimination against women still continues, due to the lack of general development, caused by the slow implementation of the goals and objectives of the International Development Strategy and within the national framework and the low priority, given by the Governments to the implementation of the internationally adopted requirements, and the low number of States, who have ratified the above-mentioned Conventions;

Considering that current and future trends in population size, growth, composition and distribution are inexorably linked to and affected by the status of women throughout the world;

Recognizing the vital relationship between the status of women and the overall social and economic development;

Realizing that the existing discrimination against women significantly limits their opportunity for free choice as to the number and spacing of their children, restricts their exercise of other human rights and prevents their full participation in the social and economic development in their own countries and in the international community;

Considering also that the discrimination against women works to the detriment not only of women but also directly or indirectly affects their children, their entire family, as well as the society at large, and obstructs the implementation of population policies and the total development effort; and,

Taking into account that the World Population Year 1974, the International Women's Year 1975, the adoption of the Declaration and Action Programme by the Special Session of the General Assembly on Raw Materials and Development and the mid-term review and appraisal of the Second Development Decade's International Development Strategy in 1975, offer a most opportune time for assessment of the current status of women and its consequences in relation to the population trends and policies and in the total development effort, in addition to the promotion of the basic principles of human rights;

Recommends that:

1. Governments give highest priority to the ratification of the above-mentioned Conventions and to the implementation of the international stan-

dards," contained in the international instruments, strategies and programmes, referred to above;

2. All people, men and women alike, be included in planning and policy-making in all questions concerning the entire development of a country, including questions of population, so that the exercise of individual rights may be harmonized with corresponding civic rights and responsibilities;

3. Governments and intergovernmental organizations pay full attention to the importance of technical and financial assistance through international cooperation to carry out local, national, regional and international plans, programmes and policies designed for the advancement of women and their full integration in the development process;

4. More concerted action be taken at local, national, regional, and international levels taking into account the assistance that can be offered by national and international non-governmental organizations in cooperation with the Governments and inter-governmental organizations; and,

5. Governments examine their laws, regulations and customs affecting the status of women with a view to bringing about their conformity with the basic principals of equality between men and women without discrimination as to sex.

II.   INCENTIVES AND DISINCENTIVES

[Original English]

A.   *Basic Principles*

The Symposium on Law and Population,

Recognizing the obligations of Governments to take steps to secure for all their people the full realization of the economic, social and cultural rights expressed in the Universal Declaration of Human Rights;

Noting that as stated in Article 25 of the Universal Declaration of Human Rights such rights include the right of every person to "a standard of living adequate for the health and well-being of himself and of his family, including food, clothing, housing and medical care and necessary social services;"

Noting further, as recognized in General Assembly Resolution 2542 (XXIV), the necessity of assuring that family planning services are freely available in order to provide families with the knowledge and means required for the free exercise of the right to determine freely and responsibly the number and spacing of their children; and,

Taking into account that changes in family size may in some circumstances have an impact on the economic resources of the family and on security in old age which Governments may wish to redress by offering benefits or services in the context of family planning;

Recommends that:

1. Any benefits or services provided or withheld as incentives or disincentives take into account the value system and mores prevailing in any given society and be planned so as to counteract the practical obstacles facing family planning programmes;

2. Governments adopting programmes of incentives relating to family planning ensure that any benefits or services provided as incentives to family planning be in addition to the benefits and services to which all persons are entitled as basic human rights; and,

3. Governments ensure that any benefits or services withheld or withdrawn as disincentives in the context of family planning do not conflict with the enjoyment of basic human rights.

B. *Old-Age Benefits*

The Symposium on Law and Population,

Considering that one of the fundamental goals of family planning is to enhance the well-being of all members of the family and to enable parents to provide more adequately for their children while at home and in school;

Recognizing that in many societies children have traditionally served as a major source of support during the old age of their parents; and,

Taking into account that many parents may choose to practice family planning if they could be assured of adequate support in their old age through other means;

Recommends that Governments desiring to provide incentives to family planning undertake programmes through which persons limiting the size of their families can be assured of adequate income in their old age; such programmes might take the form of bonuses or benefits payable to persons in their old age.

C. *Role of Non-Governmental Organizations*

The Symposium on Law and Population,

Considering the urgent need for family planning education and services in many countries that lack adequate national public health and social welfare services;

Taking into account that in many such countries basic health and welfare services are customarily provided by non-governmental organizations, including employers, labor unions and community centers; and,

Noting that in many such countries family planning education and services might appropriately form a part of the basic health and welfare services provided by such non-governmental organizations;

Recommends that:

1. Governments in such countries encourage the relevant non-governmental organizations to include family planning education and services in the basic health and welfare services made available through such organizations; and,

2. Costs of family planning education and services made available through non-governmental organizations be supported to the maximum extent possible through subsidies to such organizations or, as appropriate in the circumstances, through credits against the taxes paid by the organization, pending their integration into the national public health and social welfare services.

III. LEGISLATION AND DEMOGRAPHIC EVOLUTION

[Original French]

A. *Right to Information on Family Planning*

The Symposium on Law and Population,

Recalling that the United Nations Symposium on Population and Human Rights, held in January 1974 in Amsterdam, expressed the hope that international organizations would assist Governments in "providing family planning information . . . to all persons who want" it, and that this should include "material on family life and population dynamics at all levels of the educational system;" and,

Recalling further that there is often a close relationship between a low level of education and high fertility, as there is between fertility and other social and cultural variables, in particular, the way of life;

Recommends that Governments should not only repeal present legal restrictions on the dissemination of family planning information, but also take positive steps to provide it in a manner consistent with their national culture, using all available channels of information, and taking advantage of such assistance as may be offered by international organizations in this field; it being understood that such information includes material on human reproduction, health aspects of reproduction, family planning techniques, and population awareness.

B. *Education and Child Labor*

The Symposium on Law and Population,

Noting that the Declaration on the Rights of the Child states that the child is entitled to free and compulsory education at least in the elementary stage;

Bearing in mind that under the same Declaration the child should not "be admitted to employment before an appropriate minimum age;"

Noting the close relation which exists between compulsory education and laws on child labor, since without such education, it is difficult to enforce or to justify a minimum working age, and at the same time, unless there is such a minimum age, parents will be tempted to take advantage as soon as possible of the income which their children would produce; and,

Noting further the obligation of Governments to introduce compulsory elementary education, which usually means keeping children in school until they reach the age of 13;

Recommends that Governments, if they have not already done so, institute a system of free and compulsory elementary education as a matter of first priority, and, at the same time, establish a minimum working age which should not be less than 13 years.

C. *Social Security*

The Symposium on Law and Population,

Recalling that the Universal Declaration of Human Rights states that "everyone, as a member of society, has the right to social security," and that the United Nations Declaration on Social Progress and Development calls for the use, as a common basis for development policies, of "means and methods" which include the implementation of comprehensive social security schemes and social welfare services;

Bearing in mind the direct effect which the provision of such services, and particularly of illness protection, has on population dynamics, and the possible effect on fertility which would result from the economic security for older persons which a social security system would guarantee; and,

Recognizing that, at least in some countries, parents would rather depend for their economic support on official social security schemes for sickness and old age protection than rely on their children for this purpose;

Recommends that Governments adopt a system of social security appropriate to the conditions of their respective countries, taking into consideration the demographic effects of this system.

D.   *Maternal and Child Protection*

The Symposium on Law and Population,

Bearing in mind that the fear of infant mortality is one of the important factors in the motivation of parents to have many children, and that an awareness of improved chances of child survival might have an important effect in weakening this motivation considerably; and,

Recalling the United Nations Declaration of the Rights of the Child which provides that "special care and protection shall be provided both to him and his mother, including adequate pre-natal and post-natal care;"

Recommends that Governments strengthen their pre- and post-natal care services as well as their general public health services so as to better protect child health and reduce infant mortality.

E.   *Internal Migration*

The Symposium on Law and Population,

Recognizing that while in some countries the size and the rate of growth of population may not be considered to pose serious problems but that in most countries the unplanned growth of the urban population, especially in metropolitan areas, strains the labour market, social services, etc., and that many migrants have to live in conditions of deprivation, misery and squalor;

Recommends that:

1. Development programmes attempt, wherever feasible, to create employment and income opportunities, social services and other amenities in rural areas, or in areas accessible to the rural population, with a view to holding to manageable proportions the exodus from country to town;

2. Arrangements be made to better inform potential rural migrants of the economic and social conditions, especially employment and income prospects, in urban areas; and,

3. Measures which infringe upon the right of freedom of movement and residence within national boundaries enunciated in the Universal Declaration of Human Rights and other international instruments be avoided.

F.   *International Migration*

The Symposium on Law and Population,

Recognizing that migration across national boundaries can contribute to achieving a better balance between labour and other factors of population in both the countries of immigration and emigration;

Noting that in this regard, the freedom of movement for employment has generally tended to contract; and,

Bearing in mind that the scope and conditions of international migration can be effectively regulated by legal provisions;

Recommends that:

1. Migrant workers should be provided proper treatment and that necessary social welfare measures be extended to them and their families in receiving countries in conformity with the provisions of the relevant ILO conventions and recommendations as well as other international instruments; and,

2. Governments adopt policies in regard to migrant workers aimed at preventing discrimination against migrants in the labour market, preserving their human rights, combatting prejudice against them and facilitating reunion of families.

IV. FAMILY RELATIONS LAWS

[Original English]

A. *Minimum Marriage Age*

The Symposium on Law and Population,

Bearing in mind the Convention on Consent to Marriage, Minimum Age for Marriage and Registration of Marriages, which specifically requires states to "take legislative action to specify a minimum age for marriages;"

Recalling the General Assembly Recommendation on Consent to Marriage, Minimum Age for Marriage and Registration of Marriages that the minimum age for marriage shall not, in any case, be less than fifteen years of age; and,

Recalling further that the United Nations Regional Seminar on the Status of Women and Family Planning held in Jogjakarta, in June 1973, recommended that in view of the "close relationship between the low status of women, early and universal marriage of girls, and high fertility . . . Governments, which have not already done so, ensure that the laws provide for a minimum age of marriage for women of not less than 16 years;"

Recommends that:

1. Governments review the existing laws on the minimum marriage age with a view to specifying it at no less than eighteen years of age; and,

2. Governments establish effective systems for enforcing such laws.

B. *Consent to, and Registration of Marriages*

The Symposium on Law and Population,

Bearing in mind that the Convention on Consent to Marriage, Minimum Age for Marriage and Registration provides that "no marriage shall be legally entered into without the full and free consent of both parties, such consent to be expressed by them in person after due publicity . . . ," in view of the need for "complete freedom in the choice of a spouse;"

Bearing in mind that the same convention provides that "all marriages shall be registered in an appropriate official register;" and,

Recalling that the United Nations Regional Seminar on the Status of Women and Family Planning in 1973 recommended "the registration of all marriages," the "contracting of marriage only with the full and free consent of intending spouses," and the need to create awareness of the "right not to marry;"

Recommends that:

1. Governments ratify the Convention on Consent to Marriage, Minimum Age for Marriage and Registration of Marriages; and,

2. Governments take the steps necessary to enact laws which are consistent with the principles mentioned above and that the competent organs concerned be instructed to implement such laws.

C. *Marriage and Divorce*

The Symposium on Law and Population,

Bearing in mind that the Universal Declaration of Human Rights and the Declaration on the Elimination of Discrimination against Women provide that men and women are "entitled to equal rights as to marriage, during marriage and at its dissolution;" and,

Recalling that the United Nations Seminar on the Status of Women and Family Planning in 1973 recommended that "women and men have equal rights at marital dissolution" and that the "unilateral right of husbands to divorce their wives at will lowers the status of women;"

Recommends that Governments take the steps necessary to enact laws which are consistent with the principles mentioned above and that the competent organs concerned be instructed to implement such laws.

D. *Registration of Births*

The Symposium on Law and Population,

Recognizing that a fool-proof system for the registration of all births is essential for the effective implementation and enforcement of many laws, including those governing the minimum age of marriage, child labor, compulsory education, social security and old age protection;

Bearing in mind that the Draft World Population Plan of Action, prepared by the Secretary-General, calls for the establishment of "vital registration systems and, in the interim, for the development of sample registration data;" and,

Conscious of the fact that the implementation of population policies by Governments will require dependable demographic data;

Recommends that Governments take steps to establish effective systems for the registration of births.

E. *The Rights of the Child*

The Symposium on Law and Population,

Recalling the Declaration of the Rights of the Child, which affirms that "mankind owes to the child the best it has to give;"

Noting that under the above-mentioned Declaration, the child is entitled to special protection, opportunities and facilities "to enable him to develop physically, mentally, morally, spiritually and socially in a healthy and normal manner and in conditions of freedom and dignity," as well as to free and compulsory education, at least in the elementary stages, and to the right to adequate nutrition, housing, recreation and medical services;

Noting further that the child, as stated in the Declaration, needs "love and understanding" for the full and harmonious development of his personality, and requires affection, moral and material security from his parents;

Considering that the Declaration applies to every child, "without distinction or discrimination on account of race, color, sex, language, religion, political or other opinion, national or social origin, property, birth or other status," and that these requirements, for humanitarian reasons, apply urgently to refugee children caught in the circumstances of war and emergencies, no matter where they live, as is now the case of the Palestine refugee children;

Recommends that Governments adopt the necessary implementing legislation to ensure that every child is a wanted and protected child, whose best interests shall be the paramount consideration; in particular, that he shall be wanted by the parents and protected by the society in terms of adequate education, medical care, nutrition, housing and recreation.

V. CONTRACEPTION

[Original English]

The Symposium on Law and Population,

Bearing in mind that family planning has now become a basic aspect of health and socio-economic welfare;

Considering that in many countries access to contraceptives, which is an important aspect of the basic human right of family planning, may be available only to a fraction of the population, particularly under present medical requirements;

Taking into account the fact that a number of countries in various regions have successfully established training programmes in family planning for professional para-medical and auxiliary health personnel;

Recognizing that the experience in several countries has shown that such procedures as the prescription of oral contraceptives and the insertion of IUD's can be safely and effectively performed by appropriately trained and supervised professional para-medical and auxiliary health personnel; and,

Recognizing that the pattern of supervision of the distribution of contraceptives depends upon expert medical advice, which itself changes with time, and which divides contraceptives into those that are safe for widespread distribution and those for which it is desirable to retain some degree of medical supervision;

Recommends that:

1. Governments remove legal and administrative obstacles to manufacture, display, advertisement, sale and widespread distribution of contraceptives, and enact such provisions as may be necessary to make contraceptives readily available;

2. Contraceptives be treated in the same manner as other products requiring broad and regular distribution and that limitations be imposed only to the extent that they are absolutely necessary on health grounds;

3. Sale of contraceptives not be restricted to pharmacies or medical facilities, unless necessary on health grounds;

4. Import as well as duty restrictions on contraceptives be removed or kept to a minimum, and that local packaging be encouraged, seeking assistance from UNIDO and UNCTAD as appropriate;

5. Governments review their regulatory provisions relating to the prescription of hormonal contraceptives, insertion of IUD's, and other family planning procedures, weighing the risks and benefits under national conditions, with a view to maximizing the role of professional para-medical and auxiliary health personnel in providing these services;

6. The World Health Organization and other organizations continue

and intensify efforts to develop flexible and realistic international guidelines for the training and qualification of physicians and other categories of professionally qualified personnel in family planning, and that Governments take steps to follow these guidelines;

7. Governments of countries with official health insurance schemes ensure that the cost of contraceptives is covered by those schemes; and,

8. In situations where the price of contraceptives is beyond the reach of the community, due to manufacturing costs or to additional costs which may arise due to the manufacturer's liability at law from possible adverse effects, Governments (or international bodies) consider subsidizing the price.

VI. VOLUNTARY STERILIZATION

[Original English]

The Symposium on Law and Population,

Bearing in mind the recommendation of the Second International Conference on Voluntary Sterilization, held in Geneva in 1973, that each individual should be recognized as having "freedom of choice in the matter of voluntary infertility;"

Recommends that:

1. With due regard to the legal and cultural traditions and mores, and the economic needs, of the respective countries, Governments adopt such legislation as may be required to make voluntary sterilization available for contraceptive purposes;

2. In adopting such legislation Governments ensure freedom of choice based upon legally competent and fully informed consent, and subject to proper medical procedures and requirements; and,

3. Governments further ensure that neither criminal nor civil penalties or liabilities be imposed upon persons undergoing voluntary sterilization for contraceptive purposes or, except in cases of negligence, upon persons performing such sterilizations.

VII. ABORTION

[Original both French
and English]

The Symposium on Law and Population,

Mindful of the fact that an increasing number of countries have recognized the right of women to decide for themselves the number and spacing of their children;

Conscious that restrictive abortion laws do not prevent women from resorting to clandestine and dangerous measures, which result in high rates of injury and mortality;

Recognizing that restrictive abortion laws result in discrimination between rich and poor, since the former can either travel abroad for safe abortions in more liberal countries or obtain safe but illegal abortions at home;

Recognizing that all countries prefer contraception to abortion, but that some countries interpret abortion as a family planning method, while others do not, and that this judgment depends on religious, cultural and medical insights which are still evolving;

Taking into consideration that recent medical progress has perfected the techniques for the interruption of pregnancy, thus considerably reducing the danger of abortion during the early stages of pregnancy;

Taking into consideration that the majority of the world's population now live under legal systems which enable women to have access to abortion;

Noting further that a 100 percent effective contraceptive method has not yet been developed, and that contraceptive failures may also result from the ignorance of the couple concerned and from the misuse of these methods; and,

Bearing in mind that menstrual regulation, if performed prior to the time at which a possible pregnancy could have been determined, would not violate the anti-abortion laws of many countries;

Recommends that:

1. A woman having an abortion in the early stages of pregnancy not be dealt with under the penal codes, but be accorded humane treatment and effective contraceptive advice;

2. Abortion in the early stages of pregnancy be treated in the same manner as any other health act;

3. Abortion after the early stages of pregnancy be permitted at least to protect the life and health of the woman, and particularly to prevent the birth of defective offspring, and in cases of rape and incest;

4. Abortion legislation be so drafted as to be part of maternal and child health care legislation, with emphasis on the fact that women who have recently had abortions be given full information regarding available family planning services;

5. No individual be compelled to participate in an abortion procedure against his or her conscience, but in cases where such objections are made, the woman requesting the abortion be referred to a person or institution which does offer such procedures; and,

6. Menstrual regulation be treated as falling outside the scope of restrictive abortion laws.

VIII. ROLE OF PROFESSIONAL PARAMEDICAL PERSONNEL IN MENSTRUAL REGULATION, EARLY ABORTION AND VASECTOMY

[Original English]

The Symposium on Law and Population,

Mindful of the growing importance of menstrual regulation, early abortion and vasectomy as family planning techniques in the context of the right to access to the knowledge and means necessary to exercise freedom of choice in determining the number and spacing of children;

Bearing in mind that there is a need for the speedy expansion of the technical, medical and other categories of professionally qualified personnel in the field of maternal and child health care services, of which family planning is an essential component; and,

Recognizing that certain surgical techniques of fertility regulation are being simplified, that vasectomy, menstrual regulation and early abortion already have been successfully performed by professional para-medical and auxiliary health workers and that expert opinion, in the light of local circumstances, has in some countries and may in the future in others, delegate appropriate procedures to such personnel when they are specially trained and supervised;

Recommends that:

1. Governments expand the facilities and develop guidelines for the training of professional para-medical and auxiliary health personnel in this field as to be acceptable to the local community;

2. International organizations take positive supportive action to assist Governments in the establishment of integrated maternal and child care health services in which medical workers play a role;

3. Governments review their national policies, laws and regulations in these matters taking into account the urgent need for the rapid increase in the number of technical, medical and other categories of professionally qualified personnel working in the field of maternal child care services;

4. Nothing in these recommendations shall compel any individual to participate in such procedures, but any individual shall have an obligation to inform the individual requesting such procedures of another person or facility which offers such procedures as legally available, it being understood that every Government-supported facility shall be obliged to make available such procedures as are lawful.

IX.   ROLE OF NATIONAL GOVERNMENTS IN THE FORMULATION AND IMPLEMENTATION OF POPULATION POLICY

[Original English]

The Symposium on Law and Population,

Recalling that the United Nations Declaration on Social Progress and Development calls for the "formulation and establishment, as needed, of programmes in the field of population, within the framework of national demographic policies . . . ;" and,

Recognizing that law, as an instrument of policy, has an important role to play in implementing national population policy, as well as human rights;

Recommends that:

1. Governments establish, if they have not already done so, population commissions or other bodies to formulate national population policies and coordinate the activities of the various Ministries in the field of population, and that they consider the adoption of a general population law which clearly sets forth these policies;

2. As an aid in the performance of this task, Government commissions undertake or encourage the undertaking of the compilation, review and revision of the laws of their countries in the light both of national policies and of human rights, taking advantage of assistance from international organizations in this regard; and,

3. Governments consider the recommendations of this Symposium in formulating their national population policies and laws.

X.   ROLE OF LOCAL GOVERNMENT IN THE IMPLEMENTATION OF POPULATION POLICY

[Original English]

The Symposium on Law and Population,

Recognizing the potential of local Governments in bringing their personnel, resources and unique knowledge of local conditions and requirements to bear on the implementation of national population policies;

Conscious of the need for a total and coordinated approach to population; and,

Recalling the inauguration of a "Model City Project" in Cagayan de Oro in the Philippines in 1973, which seeks to implement the principle of family planning as a basic human right of the population in that city primarily through the coordination of local initiatives and resources;

Recommends that:

1. Local Governments be actively involved in the population field;

2. The utilization of local personnel and resources be maximized in the fulfillment of national population policies, including the use of educational, social, economic, mass media, medical, as well as legal components;

3. Such local governments as face particularly great demographic pressures establish a special body to provide leadership and coordination of local activities; and,

4. Local governments provide for the full participation of the citizenry in the formulation and implementation of the policies mentioned above.

XI. ROLE OF INTERNATIONAL ORGANIZATIONS IN REGARD TO
POPULATION POLICY

[Original English]

A. *Compilation, Review and Revision of National Laws*

The Symposium on Law and Population,

Bearing in mind that the national laws, regulations and decisions, including customary law, of all countries should be consistent with fundamental principles of human rights in the population field;

Recognizing that archaic or out-dated laws continue to hamper the full implementation of human rights in many countries;

Taking into account the difficulties encountered by Governments in revising their laws to reflect the development of human rights in the population field; and,

Noting that the United Nations Symposium on Population and Human Rights held in Amsterdam in January 1974 specifically called upon international organizations to render assistance to Governments in "reviewing national legislation in the light of both population policy and human rights;"

Recommends that:

1. International organizations—both governmental and non-governmental—concerned with the population field encourage Governments seeking assistance in this field to include the compilation, review and revision of national laws in the light of both population policy and human rights as part of their population programmes; and,

2. Appropriate measures, including in-depth studies on law and behavior, be undertaken in each country with a view to an effective implementation of such laws.

B. *International Women's Year*

The Symposium on Law and Population,

Bearing in mind that discrimination against women is often rooted in legislation which in turn reinforces discriminatory practices;

Considering the close relationship between such discriminating laws and demographic phenomena;

Recognizing the need for the compilation, review and revision of laws affecting the status of women; and,

Noting the designation of 1975 as the International Women's Year;

Recommends that:

1. All international organizations, both governmental and non-governmental, include in their programmes for the International Women's Year assistance to national governments or organizations in the compilation, review and revision of laws affecting the status of women; and,

2. Compilation of the laws bearing on the status of women of all countries be undertaken and published by a United Nations organ on a periodic basis.

C. *Legislative Series*

The Symposium on Law and Population,

Considering that an increasing number of countries in all parts of the world are establishing projects for the compilation, review and revision of their national population laws in the light of both population policy and human rights;

Recognizing the desirability of coordinating such projects so that each may profit from the experience of the others; and,

Noting the usefulness of the *International Digest of Health Legislation*, published by the World Health Organization, and of the *Legislative Series*, published by the International Labour Organization;

Recommends the publication, on a regular basis, under the auspices of an appropriate international organization, of a "Legislative Series on Population" or "Population Law Reports" which shall inform all interested bodies—both governmental and non-governmental—of developments in population laws.

D. *Regional Organizations*

The Symposium on Law and Population,

Considering the desirability for close collaboration in the population field between countries in the same region;

Welcoming the increasing emphasis given to population questions by the regional economic commissions of the United Nations as well as by other regional organizations, both governmental and non-governmental;

Bearing in mind that substantial progress has been made in the field of law and population in selected countries of different regions and that other countries could benefit from the experience of these selected countries; and,

Noting in this context, the success of the Rio Seminar on Law and Population sponsored by the Inter-American Bar Association in August 1973;

Recommends that regional organizations intensify regional cooperation in the field of law and population, including in particular;

1. The sponsorship of regional meetings and seminars on law and population; and

2. The incorporation of a regular law component into the regional demographic and training centres.

1. *Study on the Interrelationship of the Status of Women and Family Planning*, U.N. Doc. No. E/CN.6/575, prepared by the Special Rapporteur, Commission on the Status of Women.
2. *The Effect of Family Law and Practice*, U.N. Doc. No. E/CN.6/575/Add. 1, pages 69-89.
3. *Status of Women, Family Planning and the Population Dynamics*, by Mrs. Vida Tomsic.
4. *Some Considerations of Incentives and Disincentives in the Promotion of Family Planning*, by V.I. Chacko.
5. *Legislation and Demographic Changes*, by Alexandre Paraiso.
6. *Family Relations Law*, by Mrs. Nani Soewondo.
7. *Laws Regulating the Manufacture and Distribution of Contraceptives*, by Dr. D. Malcolm Potts.
8. *Laws Relating to Paramedical Role in Contraception*, by Dr. Allan G. Rosenfield.
9. *Voluntary Sterilization: A Human Right*, by Harriet F. Pilpel.
10. *Legal Problems Related to Abortion and Menstrual Regulation*, by Anne Marie Dourlen-Rollier.
11. *The Law on Abortion (Tunisia)*, by Mohieddine Mabrouk.
12. *Laws Relating to the Role of Paramedicals in Voluntary Male Sterilization and Menstrual Regulation*, by Dr. F.M. Shattock.
13. *Coordination of Population Laws and Policies: National Governments*, by Elizabeth Odio.
14. *Local Government and Population Policy*, by Reuben R. Canoy.
15. *Population in the UN System: Developing the Legal Capacity and Programs of UN Agencies*, by Daniel G. Partan.
16. *Report of the Symposium on Population and Human Rights*, Amsterdam, 21 January 1974, U.N. Doc. E/CONF.60/CBP/4, prepared by Population Committee for World Population Conference, Bucharest, Romania, 19-30 August 1974.
17. *Report of UNESCO Workshop on the Teaching of Population Dynamics in Law Schools*, Paris, 18-22 February 1974.

LIST OF PARTICIPANTS, ORGANIZATIONS AND OBSERVERS

COUNTRY	NAME	TITLE	ADDRESS
BANGLADESH	K.A.A. Quamruddin	Director, Bangladesh Institute of Law and International Affairs	11/B Fuller Road Dacca
BELGIUM	Gerard Sledsens	Representative, Pathfinder Fund	11 rue Omed Roriche Tunis
BRAZIL	Carlos Dunshee de Abranches	Professor, InterAmerican Bar Association and University of Guanabara	Av. Roosevelt, 23 Rio de Janeiro
	Benjamin Moraes	Professor, Universidad Federale de Rio de Janeiro	Rua Bulhoes Carvalho 25, Apart. 401 20.000 Rio de Janeiro
	Walter Rodrigues	Executive Director, Sociedade Bem Estar Familiar Brasil	Rua Laranjeiras 308 Rio de Janeiro GB
CANADA	John Humphrey	Professor of Law, McGill University	1455 Sherbrooke St. W. Montreal, Quebec
CHILE	Francisco Cumplido	Professor, Latin American Faculty of Social Sciences	Jose Manuel Infante 51 Casilla 3213 Santiago
	Guillermo Espejo Adriasola	M.D., Representative Ministry of Public Health	Casilla 9926 Santiago
	Jose Sulbrandt	Sociologist, Latin American Faculty of Social Sciences	Jose M. Infante 51 Santiago
CHINA	Wang Ping-Yun	Conseiller commercial près l'Ambassade de la République populaire de Chine	41 Ave. Lesseps Tunis

COSTA RICA	Mario Blanco	Chief, International Organizations and Technical Assistance	Ministry of Foreign Affairs San Jose
	Elizabeth Odio	Professor, Law Faculty, Director Law and Population Project	University of Costa Rica Ciudad Universitaria "Rodrigo Facio" San Jose
	Eduardo Ortiz	Dean, Law Faculty University of Costa Rica	University of Costa Rica San Jose
DAHOMEY	Alexandre Paraiso	Judge, Supreme Court Dahomey	B.P. 867 Cotonou
DOMINICAN REPUBLIC	César Augusto García	Anthropologist, Consejo Nacional de Problacion y Familia	Ministry of Public Health, Santo Domingo
	Ramón Antonio García	Professor of Law Universidad Madre y Maestra	General Cabrera 27 Santiago de los Caballeros
EGYPT	Georges M. Abi-Saab	Professor of International Law and Organization, Graduate Institute of International Studies	57 rue de Moillebeau 1211 Geneva 28
	Adel Azer	Expert, Center for Social & Criminological Research	Gezira P.O. Cairo
	Leila I. Takla	Doctor, Member of Parliament	House of Parliament Cairo
ETHIOPIA	Worku Tafara	Dean, Faculty of Law	Haile Sellassie I University P.O. Box 1176 Addis Ababa

FRANCE	Anne Marie Dourlen-Rollier	Secretary-General, Association Nationale pour l'Etude de l'Avortement	47 Bd. Garibaldi 75015 Paris
GERMANY, FEDERAL REPUBLIC	Klaus Detering	M.D., Schering AG.	D-1 Berlin 65 Mullerstrasse 170-171
	Eva-Maria Wiese	Sociologist, Head, Foreign Section, PROFAMILIA	53 Bonn Bungartstrasse 14
GHANA	Michael Asamoa Akyeampong	Principal Secretary Ministry of France	P.O. Box M 40 Accra
	Emmanuel V.O. Dankwa	Lecturer in Law, University of Ghana	Law Faculty Legon
HUNGARY	Livia Lengyel	Interpreter, Hungarian Central Statistical Office	1525 Budapest Keleti Karoly ut 5-7
	Egon Szabady	Vice-President Office Central Hongrois de Statistique	1525 Budapest Keleti Karoly ut 5-7
INDIA	Valale I. Chacko	Chief Executive Advisor	United Planters Association of Southern India "Glenview" Post Box 11, Coonor 1 (Nilgiris)
INDONESIA	Saran Gurdev Singh	Reader in Law, Jammu University	703 Model Town Jullundur (Punjab)
	Oemar Seno Adji	Supreme Court Chief Justice	Jl. Gatot Subroto C5 Djakarta
	Sri Hanifa	Lecturer, Faculty of Law	University of Indonesia Jl. H.A. Salim 80 Djakarta
	Lillahi Grahana Sidharta	First Secretary, Indonesian Embassy	Hotel Amilcar Tunis
	Soerdjono Soekanto	Lecturer of Law	University of Indonesia Jl. Prapapan III/29 Djakarta

	Nani Soewondo	Chairman, IPPA Law and Population Committee	Jalan Saharjo 3g Djakarta Selatan
	Mely Tan	Head, Social Sciences Division, National Institute of Economic and Social Research	Jl. Gondangdia Lama 39 Djakarta
IRAN	Ahmad Ghoreishi	Dean, Law School	National University of Iran Tehran
	Jehan Shah Saleh	Senator and Professor	Tehran University House of Senate Niavaran, Tehran Ave. Kakh Ave. Shenshad 3 Tehran
	Parviz Saney	Professor of Law National University of Iran	
ITALY	Rev. Pedro C. Beltrao, S.J.	Professor, Universita Gregoriana	4 Pza. Pilotta 00137 Rome
JAPAN	Minoru Muramatsu	Chief, Section of Demography, Department of Public Health Demography	Institute of Public Health 4-6-1 Shirokanedai Minato-ku Tokyo
LAOS	Maniso Abhay	Executive Director Lao Family Welfare Association	Sakarine Road Vientiane
	Tougeu Lyfoung	Director General	Ministry of Justice Vientiane
LEBANON	Georges Dib	Professor of Law	Lebanese University Beirut
	Hassan Rifai	Minister of Planning	Ministère du Plan Beirut

MALAGASY REPUBLIC	Rachel Razafimandranto	Magistrat, Comité National Permanent de la Population	46 rue Georges V Tananarive
MAURITIUS	Jacques Vallet	President, Permanent Arbitration Tribunal	Government of Mauritius, Port Louis
MEXICO	Gerardo M. Cornejo	Executive Director, Fundacion para Estudios de la Poblacion, A.C.	Insurgentes Sur 1752 Mexico 20, D.F.
MOROCCO	Birgitta Danielson	Junior Professional Officer, United Nations Development Programme	Rabat-Chellah
NEPAL	Dhruba Bar Singh Thapa	Dean Institute of Law	Tribhuvan University Post Box No. 1247 Kathmandu
NETHERLANDS	M.M.J. Reyners	Chef d'Equipe Adjoint Equipe Medical Néerlandais	Le Kef Tunis
	Dr. Van der Straate	Chef d'Equipe Equipe Médicale Néerlandais	Le Kef Tunis
NIGERIA	A.A.O. Okunniga	Senior Lecturer, Faculty of Law	University of Ife Ile-Ife
PAKISTAN	Rahman Hussanally	Professor of Law	Law College 142A Allamo Iqbulk Karachi
	Khalid Mohammad Ishaq	Lawyer	126 Manecji Street Garden East Karachi
PHILIPPINES	Rudolph A. Bulatao	Assistant Professor of Sociology	University of the Philippines Diliman, Quezon City

	Irene Cortes	Dean, College of Law	University of the Philippines, Quezon City
	Carmelo V. Sison	Assistant Professor of Law, Project Coordinator	University of Philippines Law Center, Quezon City
ROMANIA	Ioan Copil	Counselor, National Commission of Demography	Consiliul de Staat, Comisia Nationala de Demografie, Bucharest I, Calea Victoriei 49-53
	Vladimir Trebici	Professor, Academy of Economic Studies	Bucharest
	Victor Zlatescu	Counselor, Legislative Council	Bucharest
EL SALVADOR	Jose Enrique Silva	Ministro de la Presidencia	Apartado postal 06-125), San Salvador
SENEGAL	Cheikh T. Sar	Magistrat, Cour d'Appel	Palace of Justice, Dakar
SINGAPORE	Riaz Hassan	Senior Lecturer, Department of Sociology	University of Singapore, Singapore 10
	Kenneth Kim Seng Wee	Faculty of Law, University of Singapore	Bukit Timah Road, Singapore 10
SRI LANKA	Wickrema Weerasooria	Co-Director, Law and Population Project, Sri Lanka	% Monash University, Faculty of Law, Clayton, Victoria, Australia
SWEDEN	Alvar F. Nelson	Professor of Law, University of Uppsala	Box 512, 75120 Uppsala

SWITZERLAND	Hans Hoffman-Nowotny	Professor of Sociology University of Zurich	Zeltweg 63 CH 8032 Zurich
SYRIA	Hajar Sadek	Deputy, Member of Executive Office of Women	Syrian Family Planning Association Ministry of Health Damascus
THAILAND	Damrong Dharmaraksa	Lecturer, Faculty of Law	Chulalongkorn University 138 Sorkumvit 4 Bangkok 5
	Phijaisaxdi Horayangkura	Lecturer, Faculty of Law	Chulalongkorn University 6/2 Pramuan Road Bangkok 5
TOGO	Anani Ahianyo-Akakpo	Director-General National Institute of Scientific Research	P.O. Box 1914 Lomé
	Messanvi Leon Foli	Professor, Faculty of Law	University of Benin Lomé
TRINIDAD & TOBAGO	Fenton Ramsahoye	Deputy Director Council of Legal Education	University of the West Indies St. Augustine Campus Trinidad
TUNISIA	Abdelwaheb Abdallah	Chercheur au CERES (Section juridique) Attaché de Cabinet Ministere de l'Education Nationale	
	Ridha Abdallah	Attaché de Cabinet Chercheur au CERES (Section juridique)	
	Mohamed Ayad	Démographe, Division de la Population, Office Nationale du Planning Familial et de la Population	Bab Saâdoun Tunis

Name	Title	Address
Naziha Lakhal Ayat		11 rue du Croquet El Amrane
Fatyhia Bahri		11 rue du Croquet El Amrane
Samia Ben Ammar	Résidente du Comité National pour l'UNICEF	Le Colisee 45 Ave. Habib Bourguiba Tunis
Ismail Ben Salah	Avocat Général à la Cour de Cassation Ministère de la Justice	
Bechir Ben Slama	Député à l'Assemblée Nationale, Rapporteur de la Commission Culturelle et Sociale	
Jalila Ben Mustapha	Député à l'Assemblée Nationale, Membre de la Commission Culturelle et Sociale	
Tahar Ben Youssef	Attaché de Cabinet Ministère de la Santé Publique	Bab Saâdoun
Mongi Bchir	Chef de la Division de la Population Office Nationale du Planning Familial et de la Population	
Boubaker Belaid	Association Tunisienne du Planning Familial	
Benzina Bencheikh	Association Tunisienne du Planning Familial	

Name	Title	Organization
Souad Beyrakdar	Sociologist, Chef de Service des Etudes, Office Nationale des Travailleurs Tunisiens à l'Etranger, de l'emploi et de la formation professionnelle	Ministère des Affaires Sociales
Mahmoud Bouali	Bibliotécaire	Ministère des Affaires Etrangères, Tunis, Tunis
Abdelwahab Bouhdiba	Directeur, Centre d'Etudes et de Recherches Economiques et Sociales	
Fredj Chaieb		Institut de Presse, Blvd. 9 Avril 1938, Tunis
Mezri Chekir	President, Director-General, National Office of Family Planning and Population	Ministry of Public Health, Tunis
Mounira Chelli	Psycho-sociologist	Division de la Population, Office Nationale du Planning Familial et de la Population
Hedi Djemai	Section de Demographie, Centre d'Etudes et de Recherches Economiques et Sociales	23 rue d'Espagne, Tunis
Ahmed Elloumi	Administrateur	Conseil Economique et Sociale

Habib Guerfal	Président de l'Organisation Tunisienne de l'Education et de la Famille	78 Ave. de la Liberte Tunis
Mohsen Harbi	Attaché de Cabinet	Ministère de la Justice Tunis
Monique Harcha	Adjoint à la Direction Service Oeucumenique a Tunis	
Yolande Jemiai	Demographer	Division de la Population Office Nationale du Planning Familial et de la Population Bab Saâdoun
Lotfi Labbane	Director	Association Tunisienne 80 Ave. Hedi Chake Tunis
Noe Ladhari	Director	Ministère des Affaires Sociales Tunis
Mohieddine Mabouk	Director, Law and Population Project Maître-Assistant	Faculty de Droit de Tunis 12 rue des Bougainvillees Le Bardo Tunis
Mohamed Mansour	Juge et Chercheur au CERES	
Fathia Mzali	Présidente, Union Nationale des Femmes Tunisiennes	Bd. Bab Benat Tunis

Sadok Sahli	Section de Démographie	Centre d'Etudes et de Recherches Economiques et Sociales 23 rue d'Espagne Tunis
Najet Sayah	Directrice	Institut de Protection de l'Enfance Tunis
O. Sfar	President	Association Tunisienne du Planning Familial 80 Ave. Hedi Chakar Tunis
TURKEY Bulent Nuri Esen	Professor	Faculty of Law University of Ankara Ankara
Sevinc Kavadarli	Research Associate	Institute of Population Studies Kibris Sok 20/2 Farabi, Ankara
UNITED KINGDOM John Cummins	Attaché commercial	Embassy of the United Kingdom Tunis
Richard G. Lawson	Faculty of Law	The University Southampton England SO9 5NH
Rev. Arthur McCormack, S.J.		St. Joseph's College Lawrence Street Mill Hill London NW 7
Dr. F. M. Shattock	Professor, Liverpool School of Tropical Medicine	Pembroke Place Liverpool L3QA England

	Name	Title	Address
UNITED STATES OF AMERICA	Leo Gross	Professor of International Law	Fletcher School of Law and Diplomacy Tufts University Medford, Mass. 02155
	Edmund H. Kellogg	Deputy Director	Law and Population Programme Tufts University Medford, Mass. 02155
	Wayles Kennedy	Senior Sector Advisor, Human Resources	AID Mission to Tunisia % American Embassy Tunis
	Daniel Partan	Professor of Law	Boston University School of Law 765 Commonwealth Ave. Boston, Mass. 02145
	Gerald Patrick	Policy Development Division	Office of Population Agency for International Development Washington, D.C. 20523
	John M. Paxman	Research Associate	Law and Population Programme Tufts University Medford, Mass. 02155
	Harriet F. Pilpel	Lawyer	Planned Parenthood-World Population 437 Madison Avenue New York, N.Y. 10020
	Granville Sawyer	President	Texas Southern University 3201 Wheeler Street Houston, Texas

	NAME	TITLE	ADDRESS
VIETNAM, REPUBLIC OF	Tôn-Thât-Niem	Senator	197 Hông-Thâp-Tú Saigon
	Khûu Thí Ngôc Sáng	First Secretary	Embassy of the Republic of Vietnam Tunis
YUGOSLAVIA	Vida Tomsic	President	Federal Council for Family Planning 61000 Ljubljana Valvazorjeva 7

ORGANIZATION	NAME	TITLE	ADDRESS
INTERNATIONAL PLANNED PARENTHOOD FEDERATION	Rebecca Cook	Assistant Executive Secretary	18-20 Lower Regent Street London SW1Y4 PW
	Julia Henderson	Secretary-General	18-20 Lower Regent Street London SW1Y4 PW
	Isam Rushdi Nazer	Regional Director	P.O. Box 1567 Beirut, Lebanon
	David Malcolm Potts	Consultant	8 Langbourne Ave. London N6 GAL
POPULATION COUNCIL	Alain Marcoux	Associate Director, Technical Assistance Division	% The Ford Foundation 60 Ave. Mohamed V. Tunis
	Alan Rosenfield		245 Park Avenue New York, N.Y. 10017
UNITED NATIONS	Helvi Sipila	Assistant Secretary-General for Social Development and Humanitarian Affairs	United Nations New York, N.Y. 10017

Organization	Name	Title	Address
	Riad Tabbarah	Acting Chief, Population Policy Section, Population Division	United Nations New York, N.Y. 10017
UNITED NATIONS DEVELOPMENT PROGRAMME	David Blickenstaff	Resident Representative	61 Blvd. Bab Benat Tunis
UNITED NATIONS ECONOMIC COMMISSION FOR AFRICA	A.M. Akiwumi	Regional Adviser on Legal Aspects of Economic Cooperation	Africa Hall Addis Ababa Ethiopia
UNITED NATIONS ECONOMIC COMMISSION FOR LATIN AMERICA	Raul Atria	Political Scientist	CELADE Santiago, Chile
UNITED NATIONS EDUCATIONAL, CULTURAL & SCIENTIFIC ORGANIZATION	Bertil Mathsson	Programme Specialist	Population Research & Coordination Unit Place de Fontenoy Paris 7, France
UNITED NATIONS FUND FOR POPULATION ACTIVITIES	Hasse Gaenger	UNFPA Coordinator	61 Blvd. Bab Benat Tunis
	Halvor Gille	Deputy Executive Director	485 Lexington Avenue New York, N.Y. 10017
	Majeed Khan	UNFPA Coordinator	UNDP, PO Box 1505 Colombo, Sri Lanka

Organization	Name	Title	Address
UNITED NATIONS	Luke T. Lee	Consultant on Law and Population	485 Lexington Avenue New York, N.Y. 10017
INTERNATIONAL LABOUR ORGANIZATION	Kailas C. Doctor	Head, Population Focal Point	1211 Geneva 22 Switzerland
UNITED NATIONS WORLD HEALTH ORGANIZATION	Jean de Moerloose	Chief, Health Legislation	1211 Geneva 27 Switzerland
ASSOCIATION FOR VOLUNTARY STERILIZATION	Ira Lubell	Director, International Project	708 Third Avenue New York, N.Y. 10017
FORD FOUNDATION	Michael Lemelle	Associate Representative	60 Ave. Mohammed V Tunis
FORD FOUNDATION	Michael S. Teitelbaum	Program Officer	320 East 43rd Street New York, N.Y.
INSTITUT NATIONAL D'ETUDES DEMOGRAPHIQUES	Paul Paillat	Chief, Department of Social Demography	27 rue du Commandeur Paris 16, France
INTERNATIONAL DEVELOPMENT RESEARCH CENTRE	Joseph Ingram	Executive Assistant	P.O. Box 8500 Ottawa, Ontario
INTERNATIONAL UNION FOR THE SCIENTIFIC STUDY OF POPULATION	Bruno Remiche	Executive Secretary	Rue Forgeur 5 4000 Liège, Belgium

SECTION 6

Closing Addresses

Statement

By
Julia Henderson
Secretary-General of International
Planned Parenthood Federation

I would like to start with a tribute to Professor Luke T. Lee and his colleagues in the Law and Population Project who have developed this programme and gained widespread support. I can remember the days when he was a "voice crying in the wilderness," trying to convince demographers, doctors, social scientists, development experts and family planning administrators of the importance of giving more attention to the legal aspects of the population question. This Symposium proves that this is an idea whose time has come. Most of you here at this Symposium have studied the laws of your own countries. You have formed some opinion about changes which are required. At this Symposium you have identified common problems and attempted to discover the areas in which you could agree on legal solutions. You have agreed as jurists on a remarkable number of recommendations on basic policy issues in the field of population, some of which are very controversial both in political and medical circles.

The International Planned Parenthood Federation, as the oldest international organisation in the field of planned parenthood, has had a long-standing concern for legal reform. Most of its programmes started in defiance of the law. Most of the pioneers of our organisation, Lady Rama Rau from India, Senator Kato from Japan, Margaret Sanger from the United States, and Mrs. Ottesen-Jensen from Sweden have faced court actions or even gone to jail in the conviction that every family had the right to determine the number and spacing of its children. We have recently published a history of these pioneers in an IPPF chronicle entitled "Be Brave and Angry"—a quotation from Mrs. Ottesen-Jensen. In every continent today, the IPPF has a Family Planning Association actively engaged in promoting legal reform on basic questions of fertility control law, status of women, age of marriage and the liberalization of abortion. I encourage those of you who are working on law and population studies in your countries to work with these Associations in promoting legal reform.

It seems clear that the World Plan of Action now in its final draft will be agreed upon—in fact, many of you here at this Symposium will be involved in the Government delegations at Bucharest. What happens after Bucharest will perhaps be the best monument to the efforts of all who have worked for this World Population Conference. Bucharest can only accomplish an increase in the political awareness of all countries on the population problem. However, the real job is to be done after Bucharest in the implementation of the World Population Plan of Action. Certainly the implementation of the objectives of the World Plan of Action will require many legal reforms in order to assure family planning as a basic human right and a reality for all people.

Address

By
Slaheddine Baly
Minister of Justice
Republic of Tunisia

I arrive after the battle, and all has been said.

However, even though I have not had the high honor of contributing to the Symposium's work, I have followed its debate with interest. Through the exchange of experiences and information, through the quality of research which you undertake, and by virtue of your devotion to reasoned enthusiasm and laudable scientific curiosity, this Symposium will have an impact beyond its objectives. As a result, we will witness a radiation which will have happy consequences for the international community.

The history of law is intimately linked to the history of civilization. When a law falls into disuse, when it no longer has application, it inevitably is altered to conform with established contemporary principles. Law is essentially revolutionary; it carries nations toward progress and contributes to the advancement of human societies. To illustrate the evolution of ideas through the ages, as well as the evolution of laws, Plato believed that slavery was a normal thing. Aristotle himself berated his fellow citizens for the liberal rights they had timidly granted women and, by this very fact, he felt that their grave transgression was responsible for the fall of Sparta. Man and law have advanced measurably since those ancient times. Nevertheless, we are still surrounded by the vestiges of early civilizations.

A few weeks ago, jurists from thirty-four different countries gathered in an IDEF Congress in Tunis to deal with the subject of the legal, political and social condition of women. I have the impression that the memories I hold of that meeting have been regenerated and enriched by the recommendations of this Symposium on Law and Population. Its work has ended today in Tunis but, I am sure, it will provide a documentary basis and tools for the upcoming World Population Conference.

Our concern for women in Tunisia is not just a philosophical attitude. It is a composite of a respect for human beings, of a breaking away from out-dated ideas, of a healthy interpretation of the idea of equality and of a pressing invitation to an awakening of consciousness with the goal of arriving at the advancement of our society. Since the dawn of our independence, it was established that the harmonious development of the new Tunisia implied an acceleration of economic growth, accompanied by a demographic policy which was integrated into our development plans. Legislation leaning towards the planning of births did not grow out of a pessimistic Malthusianism. The objective was to create a society which fit our aspirations, a balanced society where all enjoy the benefits of education, and all have the right to work, to health, to culture, in short, to a worthwhile life.

What was needed to accomplish this was President Bourguiba's prestige, his moral authority, his vision of things, his relentless action to promote a revolutionary and daring legislative reform in order to bring men back to a sane conception of their rights and duties, and to raise women to the level of their responsibilities. Thus, confirmed in their person, enjoying the fullness of their legal, political and social rights, aware both of their bodies and of the decisive role they play within the family, women now take part in the great options and, in a setting of mutual respect and understanding, they share with men the task of building a better world.

The theme which has dominated your deliberations is a problem which affects all of humanity. As I see it, the international statements on population made by the Heads of State in 1966 and in 1967, the Resolution adopted by the 1968 United Nations Conference on Human Rights held in Teheran, and the 1969 United Nations Declaration on Social Progress and Development are the fundamental principles of a positive international law. Through militant action, free from restrictions, free from a certain amount of self-denial and from an out-dated fatalism, it is possible to use law as a tool for creating a new and universal society.

The Symposium on Law and Population has allowed us to get to know one another better. Now we can appreciate each other more. It has also allowed us to realize that there is a universal awakening with regard to a problem which is vital to us and to future generations.

I pay tribute to the representatives from the United Nations Fund for Population Activities for their activities regarding population, as well as to the various specialized United Nations agencies, to the International Planned Parenthood Federation and the International Advisory Committee on Population and Law and to all those who assisted them in the preparation of this Symposium.

I declare that the work of the Symposium on Law and Population has come to an end.

APPENDIXES

Legal Restrictions on the Distribution of Contraceptives in the Developing Nations: Some Suggestions for Determining Priorities and Estimating Impact of Change*

By
John U. Farley** and Steven S. Tokarski***

ABSTRACT

In order for countries to succeed in reducing their population growth rates to levels desired under established policies a long term and concerted campaign must be waged by both the public and private sectors, and the skills of medical, legal, political and numerous other professions must be employed. Nevertheless, the continuing pressure of 3-4 percent population growth rates on the world's natural resources (particularly food and fuel) compels the consideration of simpler, less costly measures which hold the promise of some immediate relief.[1] A study of eight developing countries by the Westinghouse Population Center suggests that the relaxation of legal restrictions on the distribution and use of contraceptive products may present an opportunity for effecting a fairly immediate and significant reduction in population growth rates.

---

* The authors gratefully acknowledge the assistance of the Westinghouse Population Center, especially Gary L. Damkoehler and Robert H. Smith, in the preparation of materials for this article.
** Ph.D. Professor, Graduate School of Business, Columbia University. Professor Farley has been active in research in family planning for a decade.
*** M.B.A. Mr. Tokarski was formerly a research associate with the Westinghouse Population Center, is currently a student at the Columbia University School of Law and is a Staff Member, Columbia Human Rights Law Review.
1. If current fertility levels continue into the future, world population will be nearly 7 billion in the year 2000, over 21 billion in 2050, and about 34 billion in 2070—or nearly ten times today's size within a century. *See* WORLD POPULATION: STATUS REPORT 12 (Reports on Population/Family Planning No. 15, 1974). *See also*, F. Thomas, REFERENCE TABLES TO "THE FUTURE OF POPULATION GROWTH" (1973).

Introduction

Various aspects of law are recognized to have some impact on population development, particularly on the recent efforts in many countries to reduce population growth by the implementation of family planning programs. Official recognition of the importance of law in population planning is evidenced by the Declaration on Population by thirty heads of state in 1967[2] and by the unanimous adoption of the Teheran Proclamation by the United Nations Conference on Human Rights in 1968.[3,4] On a more pragmatic level, substan-

---

2. Conclusions of the Declaration were:
"As Heads of Governments actively concerned with the population problem, we share these convictions:
"*We believe* that the population problem must be recognized as a principal element in long range national planning if governments are to achieve their economic goals and fulfill the aspirations of their people.
"*We believe* that the great majority of parents desire to have the knowledge and the means to plan their families; that the opportunity to decide the number and spacing of children is a basic human right.
"*We believe* that lasting and meaningful peace will depend to a considerable measure upon how the challenge of population growth is met.
"*We believe* the objective of family planning is the enrichment of human life, not its restriction; that family planning, by assuring opportunity to each person, frees man to attain his individual dignity and reach his full potential.
"Recognizing that family planning is in the vital interest of both the nation and the family, we, the undersigned, earnestly hope that leaders around the world will share our views and join with us in this great challenge for the well-being and happiness of people everywhere." *See Declaration on Population: The World Leaders' Statement* 3 in 1 Studies in Family Planning 26 (1968).
3. U.N. Conference on Human Rights at Teheran, U.N. Doc. A/CONF. 32/41 (1968). Resolution XXIII, on "Human Rights Aspects of Family Planning," is reprinted with the text of the Proclamation of Teheran in 63 Am. J. of Int'l Law 674 (1969). It contains the following operative paragraphs:
1. *Observes* that the present rapid rate of population growth in some areas of the world hampers the struggle against hunger and poverty, and in particular reduces the possibilities of rapidly achieving adequate standards of living, including food, clothing, housing, medical care, social security, education and social services, thereby impairing the full realization of human rights.
2. *Recognizes* that moderation of the present rate of population growth in such areas would enhance the conditions for offering greater opportunities for the enjoyment of human rights and the improvement of living conditions for each person.
3. *Considers* that couples have a basic human right to decide freely and responsibly on the number and spacing of their children and a right to adequate education and information in this respect.
4. *Urges* Member States and United Nations bodies and specialized agencies concerned to give close attention to the implications for the exercise of human rights of the present rapid rate of increase in world population.
In 1974, the World Plan of Action, adopted by 135 participating nations at the Conference on Population in Bucharest, went even further by extending the right to education and information to individuals as well as couples. *See A Report on Bucharest* 371 in 5 Studies in Family Planning 12 (1974).
4. For other examples of international concern for population problems, *see* D. Partan, Population in the United Nations System (Law and Population Book Series No. 3, 1973).

tial legal research has been conducted in the effort to compile those elements of various legal systems thought to have an effect on population growth rates.[5]

While the connection between law and family planning is now widely accepted,[6] analysis in this field has rarely advanced beyond speculation that a particular statute or regulation has the effect of contributing to increasing or decreasing population growth rates.[7] It is acknowledged, for example, that some laws are likely to have a greater impact than others and that some changes can be achieved only at great political, economic or other social cost.[8] Yet in many countries, even those with national population policies, no attempt has been made to identify priorities from among the many changes suggested by legal studies. This is due in part to the difficulty of performing quantitative analysis in so complicated a subject area as family planning.[9] Projection of the impact of one law or even of a set of laws requires isolation of legal factors from religion, family economic status and culturally based beliefs and practices. Nevertheless, sufficient data are now available in some countries to allow rough calculations that identify changes in law that would have immediate and not insignificant impact at relatively low cost.

Information gathered in a study of eight developing nations[10] shows that

---

5. Most notable of these efforts is the Law and Population Programme of the Fletcher School of Law and Diplomacy, Tufts University. *See especially*, M. COHEN, LAW AND POPULATION CLASSIFICATION PLAN (1973).

6. The connection between law and population has been recognized at the policy level for many years:

> "The attitudes of a state always have a hold on the development of its population, whatever the end pursued by law, and that, even when the law pretends indifference.
>
> "In its turn, the population, by its very structure, exercises an influence on every sort of law: constitutional, organic and statutory."

J. Doublet, *Des Lois Dans Leurs Rapports Avec La Population* 39-56 in 4 POPULATION 1 (1949). *Cited in* L. Lee, *Law and Family Planning* 81 in 2 STUDIES IN FAMILY PLANNING 4 (1971).

7. D. Berman, *Working Paper for Proceedings of the Sixteenth Hammerskjold Forum* in ASSOCIATION OF THE BAR OF THE CITY OF N.Y., THE ROLE OF LAW IN POPULATION PLANNING (1972).

8. B. Berelson, *Beyond Family Planning* 163 SCIENCE 533 (1969). *See also* T. Lyons Jr., *The Political Process and Legal Change* in PROCEEDINGS OF THE AMERICAN SOCIETY OF INTERNATIONAL LAW REGIONAL MEETING AND THE JOHN BASSETT MOORE SOCIETY OF INTERNATIONAL LAW SYMPOSIUM, THE WORLD POPULATION CRISIS: POLICY IMPLICATIONS AND THE RULE OF LAW (1971).

9. "For example, in failing to forecast the continuing decline in fertility that began in the United States during the late 1950's the demographer in the mid-sixties had no basis for believing that the rash of teenage marriages would subside; women's liberation would become a major social force; the divorce rate could take another sharp swing upward; family planning services, including abortion, would become both acceptable and available to large segments of the population; or that both inflation and unemployment would soar during the last two years of the decade." Berman, supra note 7, at 5.

10. During 1971-2 the Westinghouse Population Center (Columbia, Md.) and research firms in eight countries (Turkey, Iran, Thailand, S. Korea, the Philippines, Venezuela, Panama and Jamaica) sponsored by the U.S. Agency for International Development, conducted a three part study of the current and potential role of the commercial sector in family planning: (1) a survey of importers and distributors of contraceptives in each country to examine sales levels of

substantial groups of persons in the developing nations have already decided
to limit their family size but cannot do so because contraceptive products are
either physically or economically unavailable to them. Analysis of the same
data shows also that elimination of legal restrictions directly affecting contraceptive product distribution is likely to result in a visible reduction of
population growth rates over a relatively short period of time. This analysis
proceeds in the following steps: (1) outline of the current laws affecting the
availability and use of contraceptive products; (2) identification of potential
users of contraceptives who are currently barred from access to contraceptive
products and information; (3) proposed changes and estimation of impact; (4)
obstacles to implementation; and (5) a look to the future.

I. Outline of Current Laws Affecting the Availability and Use of Contraceptive Products

The spectrum of laws affecting population growth rates is very broad,
touching both the public and private sectors[11] and both product and natural
methods[12] of contraception.[13] Analysis presented here, however, is primarily

---

commercially distributed contraceptives and to determine the factors impeding and/or facilitating
commercial distribution; (2) a survey of operators of retail outlets was undertaken with the
following objectives: to profile retail outlets which sell contraceptive products; to determine
customer profiles; to determine the degree of knowledge sellers have about family planning and
their attitude towards selling family planning products; to determine the role played by
contraceptive sellers in family planning; to determine the types of contraceptives sold in retail
outlets; and to determine the source of supply of retail outlets and degree of availability of
contraceptive products; (3) a stratified multi-stage random sample survey of the fertile population
of each country was conducted in order to evaluate the potential for increasing availability and
usage of contraceptive products. Data relevant to marketing decisions were sought as well as
information of a more traditional, demographic nature. In particular, data were collected in order
to distinguish groups that might differ in their receptiveness to family planning (i.e. to identify
market segments) and to target policies toward these groups. A structured questionnaire was used
to survey the fertile population and to obtain information relevant to the hypothesized factors
affecting the use of contraceptive products. To obtain a comprehensive picture of the target
population, both men and women were interviewed. A sample of 1,000 cases evenly divided
between males and females was selected for the survey. The questionnaire was prepared in
English, translated locally in each country and was then pre-tested for appropriateness, wording,
sequencing of questions and revised accordingly. All respondents were married (except where
cultural circumstances legitimized unmarried couples) and the female was fertile and between the
ages of 15 and 44 years. It should be noted that not all rural areas were sampled and that
data indicating usage of contraceptives is probably slightly overstated. *See* Westinghouse
Population Center, Distribution of Contraceptives in the Commercial Sector of
Selected Developing Countries: Summary Report (1974). (Hereinafter cited as Westinghouse, Summary Report).

11. In this article, the terms "private sector" and "commercial sector" are defined to
include profit making companies engaged in the manufacture, distribution and sale of contraceptive products. The "public sector" is defined as official family planning programs supported by the
national or local government and nongovernmental organizations engaged in family planning
activities supported by private or nonprofit institutional funds.

12. In this article, the term "product methods" includes only contraceptive products that
may be self-administered: oral contraceptives, condoms, spermicides, injectible contraceptives.
The term "natural methods" is used to mean rhythm and withdrawal.

13. L. Lee, *Law and Family Planning* 81 in 2 Studies in Family Planning 4 (1971).

concerned with laws regulating availability and use of contraceptive products which may be self-administered (oral contraceptives and condoms) and which are available through the private sector. Before considering the laws affecting contraceptive distribution, a brief description of family planning delivery systems is in order.

Traditionally, family planning program services and information have been provided through regular medical channels (operating hospitals, private physicians and the social security network are often used)[14] which are themselves subject to many of the barriers discussed above. Where national family planning policies and programs exist, implementation is often through clinics specially staffed for distributing information and contraceptives, and clinics operated by volunteer organizations are also important in many cases.[15] In general, though, family planning is a low priority activity of the conventional medical system.[16]

Because organized family planning services originated in the public sector or with volunteer organizations, private sector activity has been viewed as superfluous, frequently ignored and occasionally discouraged. As a result, until recently, little special attention was paid to the impact upon population policy of laws affecting commercial sales, distribution or promotion of contraceptive products. Contraceptives were often grouped with other products (oral contraceptives with ethical drugs[17] and condoms with miscellaneous rubber goods) and were subjected to the same rate of taxation and type of regulations and restrictions as these other products. Since direct consumer advertising of explicit information on ethical products is generally prohibited or controlled, couples who have decided to limit or space children may not know where to obtain or how to use oral contraceptives. Similar limitations often govern communication about other contraceptives.

Over the past few years, increased attention has been focused on the actual and potential role of the commercial sector in supplying contraceptive products in the developing nations. One reason for this interest is the surprising ability of this system (even when confronted by legal barriers) to move contraceptives at relatively high prices, often in competition with government programs which usually provide materials free or at nominal cost (Table 1). There are several reasons for this. First, in most developing nations medical resources and governmental spending power are simply not sufficient to provide services to the entire eligible population, particularly in rural areas

---

14. D. Seidman, *Alternative Modes of Delivering Family Planning Services* 6-12 in 1 STUDIES IN FAMILY PLANNING 52 (1970). *See also* B. Berelson, *Beyond Family Planning* 163 SCIENCE 533 (1969).
15. Id.
16. Id.
17. An ethical drug is one which may be legally obtained only by physician prescription in a registered pharmacy. Proprietary drugs are sold over-the-counter in both pharmacies and other retail stores.

TABLE 1

PERCENT OF TOTAL FERTILE COUPLES SURVEYED, IN EIGHT COUNTRIES,
CURRENTLY USING A CONTRACEPTIVE PRODUCT, BY SOURCE
OF SUPPLY, 1972[18]

Country	Private Sector	Public Programs	Total % Using Contraceptives
Turkey	27%	5%	32%
Iran	16%	17%	33%
Thailand	20%	20%	40%
S. Korea	10%	25%	35%
Philippines	3%	10%	13%
Venezuela	19%	18%	37%
Panama	27%	13%	40%
Jamaica	20%	17%	37%

where the majority of these populations live.[19] The private sector in these same countries, however, can reach almost all segments of the population and can in many cases deliver products more cheaply than clinic based government programs. For example, the large numbers of pharmaceutical and non-pharmaceutical outlets (which usually do not now sell contraceptives) to be found even in the most remote rural areas, are channels through which more products and even some information could be delivered. Moreover, pharmaceutical manufacturers and importers have the selling skills, and local advertising agencies have expertise in communications to help design and implement needed advertising or promotional campaigns.[20] Private sector potential, however, is particularly limited, in part because of legal regulations affecting availability of contraceptives as well as their price.

Laws affecting contraception can be broken down into two groups. First, there are laws which are primarily directed toward family planning and birth control practices. The "primary-effect" category includes laws regulating abortion and sterilization; laws establishing family planning programs and clinics; laws authorizing or prohibiting para-medical personnel from prescribing contraceptives; laws relating to public education about sex and birth control practices; and laws which regulate the use, sale, display, advertising, importation and manufacture of contraceptive products.

Relaxation of any of these legal constraints can be expected to increase the quantity and variety of contraceptives available through the commercial

18. Westinghouse, SUMMARY REPORT, *supra* note 10, at 25.
19. "The inequities of a physician-distributed method such as oral contraceptives are apparent in the following example. Over half of the 5,000 physicians in Thailand are practicing in Bangkok (population 3 million), and a majority of the rest are practicing in large capital cities and towns. There are less than 200 rural health centers with a physician for the 80% of the population living in rural areas, and very few doctors are in private practice in these areas." L. Atkinson, R. Castadot, A. Cuadros & A.G. Rosenfield, *Oral Contraceptives: Considerations of Safety in Non-Clinical Distribution* 246 in 5 STUDIES IN FAMILY PLANNING 8 (1974).
20. *See* Farley & Leavitt, *Private Sector Logistics in Population Control: A Case in Jamaica* 449-459 in 5 DEMOGRAPHY 1 (1968) and LEVIN & BELSKY, COMMERCIAL PRODUCTION AND DISTRIBUTION OF CONTRACEPTIVES 1 (Reports on Population/Family Planning No. 4, 1970).

sector. Any legal changes which would facilitate the freer flow of materials and information should be particularly effective in reaching those segments of the fertile population which are receptive to the notion of contraceptive usage, but are presently unable to gain access to contraceptive products. The impact of such changes on segments which display negative or indifferent attitudes toward the use of contraceptives would clearly be more limited.

There is also a large variety of laws (not included in this study) which though mainly designed to implement other social or administrative policies, incidentally affect population patterns. Laws which have a secondary effect on population include laws relating to family and personal status (minimum marriage age, divorce and remarriage, adoption and succession), social welfare measures (family and child allowances, maternity leave and benefits, child and female labor laws, old age security, housing policies), educational programs (compulsory education, education for women, medical education), public health and medical practices (regulation of medical practice, required health standards for public services), taxes (income tax exemptions related to family size) and controls on migration, internal movement and urbanization. More specifically, insofar as social security programs replace children as the guarantors of support during old age, the perceived importance of children for this role may decline. Families might be induced to plan to have fewer children or to increase the years separating each birth. It may be reasonable to anticipate that population growth rates will decline as a result of the institution of a social security program or of some of the other "secondary-effect" measures listed above. However, these broad social policies are rarely, if ever undertaken for the purpose of meeting population program goals. In many cases, they are adopted because of their primary effect and little or no thought is given to their secondary effect on population growth.[21] In addition, the timing and size of any decline in growth is not readily determinable without considerable expensive and time consuming research. Consequently, the "secondary-effect" measures are not likely to be effective in achieving any immediate change in population patterns.

In the eight countries surveyed the "primary" legal impediments to the more extensive use of birth control methods varied in type and number. These laws are derived from diverse sources and generally do not comprise a monolithic body of national law relating to the distribution and usage of contraceptives. Some of these laws originate from public health codes or from regulatory schemes covering commercial trade, both domestic and foreign, while others represent examples of governmental supervision over quality and safety in the medical and pharmaceutical spheres of activity.

---

21. R. Ravenholt, POLICY, TECHNOLOGY AND THE CONTROL OF FERTILITY, in PROCEEDINGS OF THE AMERICAN SOCIETY OF INTERNATIONAL LAW REGIONAL MEETING AND THE JOHN BASSETT MOORE SOCIETY OF INTERNATIONAL LAW SYMPOSIUM, THE WORLD POPULATION CRISIS: POLICY IMPLICATIONS AND THE RULE OF LAW (1971).

Legal restrictions affecting the availability of contraceptive products generally fell into the following categories:

(1) *Laws Related to Price*
   (a) High duties and taxes on raw materials needed for local production of contraceptive products and on imported finished contraceptive products;[22]
   (b) Government controls on price and fixed margin controls often encouraged resale through multiple levels of wholesalers with resultant higher prices to ultimate consumers.[23]
(2) *Laws Restricting Channels of Distribution and Sales Outlets*
   (a) Laws restricting distribution of oral contraceptives, vaginal tablets, and in some cases, condoms, to registered pharmacies;[24]
   (b) Requirements of physician's prescription and medical supervision for oral contraceptives and some vaginal products, and restriction of activity of para-medical personnel;[25]
(3) *Laws Contributing to Inadequate, Irregular Supply*
   (a) Complicated customs clearance procedures, time consuming import license requirements and restrictions on the availability of foreign exchange;[26]
   (b) Restrictive quotas or total exclusion of imported contraceptives;[27]
   (c) Limitations on local manufacturing; alternatively, a requirement of domestic production;[28]
   (d) Re-export requirements imposed on imported raw materials;[29]
   (e) Internal regulations relating to approval of drugs prior to sale on the market and trade agreements according preferential treatment to certain countries' products; (these restrictions limit not only the quantity of supply but limit the variety and range of products available on the market);[30]
   (f) Lack of legal incentives (tax credits, etc.) to encourage holding inventory at the retail level;[31]
(4) *Laws Barring Advertising and Dissemination of Information*
   (a) Prohibition or censorship of advertisement and/or store display of contraceptives, vaginal tablets and condoms;[32]

22. Westinghouse, SUMMARY REPORT, *supra* note 10, at 106-135.
23. Id.
24. Id.
25. Id.
26. Id.
27. Id.
28. Id.
29. Id.
30. Id.
31. Id.
32. Id.

(b) Restrictions on the role of para-medical and non-medical personnel as family planning consultants;[33]

(c) Laws restricting promotion of contraceptive products to conventional detailing to physicians, i.e. sampling and retail promotions;[34]

(The important identifiable barriers in each country appear in Table 2.)

II. IDENTIFICATION OF POTENTIAL USERS OF CONTRACEPTIVES WHO ARE CURRENTLY BARRED FROM ACCESS TO CONTRACEPTIVE PRODUCTS AND INFORMATION

Legal systems, particularly those components with the primary effect just discussed, do not deal with population dynamics in the aggregate, since population growth rates are the product of independent decisions made by large numbers of couples acting in private, outside the general control of law enforcement. Consequently, analysis must focus on the effect of law on the decision making process of individual couples. One major component of this process is the decision (implicit or explicit, conscious or by default) to practice some form of modern contraception. For the purpose of developing workable proposals to influence this decision it is necessary to focus on specific groups in the fertile population most likely to be affected by the lowering of legal barriers[36]—i.e. comprising the most promising segments for family planning:

---

33. Id.

34. Id.

35. Information summarized in Table 2 was gathered from the following sources: U.S. Dept. of Commerce Regional Desk Officers; Dept. of Health in each country; Customs Bureau in each country; Office of Price Control where present; and interviews with importers, manufacturers, distributors and retailers of contraceptive products. It appears in the Westinghouse, SUMMARY REPORT *supra* note 10, at 106-135.

36. From the marketer's point of view, there are three basic steps in developing a plan for increasing the use of contraceptives. The first step is to group the total fertile population according to those likely and unlikely to be receptive to the promotion of contraceptive products. Current contraceptive practice, the desire for more children (complete or incomplete ideal family size), and the intention to use a contraceptive product in the future are the factors which best indicate to which group a fertile couple should be assigned. While the value of these factors as absolute predictors is as yet undetermined, they do seem a fair indication of current receptiveness to promotion of contraceptive products. The second step is to analyze demographic and behavioral profiles in order to develop appropriate means of reaching each group (target audience) and introducing it to the use of contraceptive methods. The third step is to determine which activities will have the greatest impact toward reaching this objective, so that resources available to the private and public sectors can be allocated to them. Participants in random sample surveys conducted in eight countries were segregated into three groups (Level I): those using contraceptive products, those using natural methods and those not using any method. Each of these groups was then subdivided into groups of couples expressing the desire to have more children or to stop having children and into groups who believe that God rather than their own actions determined family size (Level II). In addition, non-users and those using natural methods were also subdivided according to whether or not they intend to use contraceptive products in the future (Level III). The figure below displays these market segments.

TABLE 2

ELEMENTS OF LAW IDENTIFIED AS IMPEDIMENTS TO INCREASED DISTRIBUTION OF CONTRACEPTIVES IN SELECTED DEVELOPING COUNTRIES, 1972[35]

Legal Restrictions*	Turkey	Iran	Thailand	S. Korea	Philippines	Jamaica	Panama	Venezuela
(1) Laws Related to Pricing								
(a) high duties and taxes	x	—	—	x	x	x	x	—
(b) government price controls	x	x	—	—	—	x	x	x
(2) Laws Restricting Channels of Distribution and Sales								
(a) distribution in pharmacies only 1. oral pills	x	x	x	x	x	x	x	x
2. condoms	—	—	—	—	—	—	—	x
(b) physician prescription required for oral contraceptives	x	x	x	x	x	x	x	x
(3) Laws Contributing to Inadequate and Irregular Supply								
(a) complicated customs procedure, import licence requirements and restrictions on foreign exchange	x	x	x	x	x	x	x	x
(b) quotas or total exclusion of imported contraceptives	—	x	—	x	x	—	—	—
(c) limitations on local manufacture or requirement of domestic production	—	—	x	x	—	—	—	—
(d) re-export requirement imposed on imported raw materials	—	—	—	x	—	—	—	—
(e) internal regulation of drug licencing	x	—	—	—	—	—	x	—
(f) preferential trade agreements	—	—	—	—	—	—	x	x
(g) lack of legal incentives to increase retail inventory	x	x	x	x	x	x	x	x

TABLE 2 (continued)

Legal Restrictions*	Turkey	Iran	Thailand	S. Korea	Philippines	Jamaica	Panama	Venezuela
(4) *Laws Barring Advertising and Dissemination of Information*								
(a) prohibition or censorship of advertising 1. oral pills	x	x	x	x	x	x	x	x
2. condoms	x	x	—	—	x	x	x	x
(b) restrictions on role of para-medical and non-medical personnel	x	x	—	—	x	x	x	x
(c) restrictions on promotion of contraceptives	x	x	—	—	x	x	x	x

* A description of the study which gathered this information is found in footnote 10.

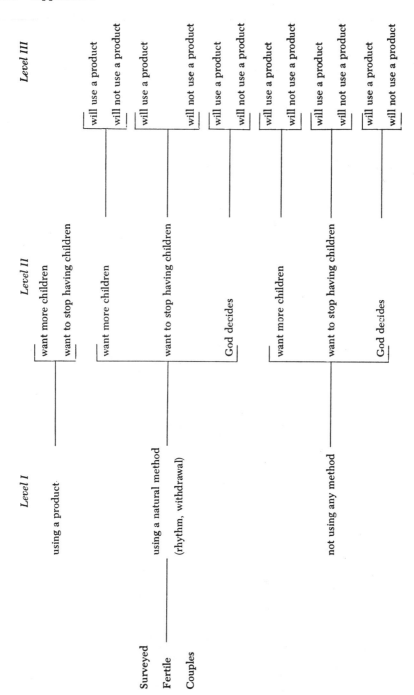

(1) Couples currently practicing some contraceptive method and not desiring to have more children in the future.
(2) Couples not practicing contraception who
      (a) do not desire to have more children, and
      (b) are willing to use a modern contraceptive method.

The percentage of the fertile population in each of these groups in eight developing nations appears in Table 3.

TABLE 3
PROPORTIONS OF SAMPLES,* IN EIGHT COUNTRIES, COMPRISING MOST
PROMISING SEGMENTS FOR FAMILY PLANNING, 1972[37]

Country	Current Product Users Wishing To Stop Having Children**	Non-Users, Who Do Not Want To Have More Children, and Are Willing To Use Some Form of Birth Control Device
Turkey	21%	23%
Iran	26%	16%
Thailand	26%	18%
S. Korea	30%	20%
Philippines	9%	17%
Venezuela	22%	11%
Panama	26%	11%
Jamaica	4%	13%

* Sampling frame leads to some overstatement of usage and perhaps intention as well.
** The remainder of product users are probably using contraceptives for child-spacing. However, there is not sufficient data to analyze this group carefully.

In practice, the law affects these and other segments of the population in different ways. For example, those not practicing contraception and wanting to stop having children will be more affected by various prohibitions on the flow of information than will those already practicing a modern family planning method. In addition, a given person may shift several times over a lifetime from one category to another (i.e., starting as a non-contraceptor wanting more children early in marriage, becoming a practicer wanting more children later in life as spacing of children becomes a concern, and finally, as the family approaches completion, perhaps shifting into the category of wanting to stop having children). The strategy of approach for each group might also be different:

(1) Those couples practicing contraception who want to have more children might be encouraged to continue practice for a longer than usual period between children.
(2) Those couples not practicing contraception who do not want more

children and who would consider using some form of contraception might respond to easier access to information and materials.

Of course, both strategies imply that removing legal restrictions is only a part of the solution because attitudinal and behavioral problems not amenable to legal solution also constitute major barriers to influencing these couples' decisions towards the practice of family planning. For example, nearly two-thirds of the couples surveyed were not using any effective contraceptive method (Table 4) and between one-quarter and one-half stated that they would *never* use any contraceptive product.[38] Probably more important, most couples expressed a desire for large families. Three or more children (Table 5)

TABLE 4

PERCENTAGE OF SURVEYED COUPLES IN EIGHT COUNTRIES USING
MODERN CONTRACEPTIVE METHODS,* 1972[39]

Country	Percent of Sample Using Modern Contraceptive Method	Percent of Sample Not Using Modern Contraceptive Method
Turkey	32%	68%
Iran	33%	67%
Thailand	40%	60%
S. Korea	35%	65%
Philippines	13%	87%
Venezuela	36%	64%
Panama	40%	60%
Jamaica	38%	62%

* Oral contraceptives, condoms, spermicides or injectibles. IUD excluded.

TABLE 5

EXPRESSED IDEAL FAMILY SIZE OF FERTILE COUPLES
IN EIGHT COUNTRIES, 1972[40]

Country	Number of Children Desired			
	1 to 3	More than 3	God Decides	Don't Know
Turkey	NA	NA	NA	NA
Iran	28%	48%	21%	3%
Thailand	43%	39%	3%	15%
S. Korea	56%	42%	2%	0%
Philippines	30%	55%	14%	1%
Venezuela	42%	57%	0%	1%
Panama*	27%	69%	1%	3%
Jamaica*	27%	55%	7%	11%

* First column designates 1 or 2 children, second designates more than 2.

38. Id.
39. Id. at 17-24.
40. WESTINGHOUSE POPULATION CENTER, DISTRIBUTION OF CONTRACEPTIVES IN THE COMMERCIAL SECTOR OF IRAN 76-132 (1974); WESTINGHOUSE POPULATION CENTER, DISTRIBUTION OF CONTRACEPTIVES IN THE COMMERCIAL SECTOR OF THAILAND 103-160 (1974); WEST-

was the expressed ideal family size of 40% of South Korean and Thai couples and as many as 70% of Philippine and Iranian couples (if "God decides" is included as meaning more than three children). As to reasons for non-practice of family planning (Table 6), non-users most often cited the "danger" or

TABLE 6
REASONS NON-USERS OF CONTRACEPTIVES CITE FOR NOT PRACTICING FAMILY PLANNING, EIGHT COUNTRIES, 1972[41]

Country	"Dangerous"	Prefer Natural Methods*	"Immoral"	Want More Children
Turkey	34%	11%	NA	4%
Iran	11%	15%	19%	1%
Thailand	36%	1%	5%	16%
S. Korea	7%	10%	—	41%
Philippines	39%	5%	7%	24%
Venezuela	38%	15%	9%	7%
Panama	11%	3%	—	19%
Jamaica	11%	10%	10%	9%

* Rhythm or withdrawal.

"immorality" associated with contraceptives or that they wanted more children.

Nevertheless, there is now a significant group of fertile couples who do not want to have more children (Table 7). Also, while most couples desire

TABLE 7
PERCENT OF FERTILE COUPLES IN EIGHT COUNTRIES, BY DESIRE FOR MORE CHILDREN, 1972[42]

Country	Want More Children	Want To Stop Having Children
Turkey	34%	61%
Iran	29%	55%
Thailand	39%	57%
S. Korea	32%	67%
Philippines	39%	50%
Venezuela	42%	46%
Panama	38%	58%
Jamaica	62%	38%

more than three children, many couples surveyed said that they already had more children than they considered desirable (Table 8). While some of these

INGHOUSE POPULATION CENTER, DISTRIBUTION OF CONTRACEPTIVES IN THE COMMERCIAL SECTOR OF SOUTH KOREA 82-136 (1974); WESTINGHOUSE POPULATION CENTER, DISTRIBUTION OF CONTRACEPTIVES IN THE COMMERCIAL SECTOR OF THE PHILIPPINES 70-132 (1974); WESTINGHOUSE POPULATION CENTER, DISTRIBUTION OF CONTRACEPTIVES IN THE COMMERCIAL SECTOR OF VENEZUELA 63-72 (1974); WESTINGHOUSE POPULATION CENTER, DISTRIBUTION OF CONTRACEPTIVES IN THE COMMERCIAL SECTOR OF PANAMA 71-156 (1974); WESTINGHOUSE POPULATION CENTER, DISTRIBUTION OF CONTRACEPTIVES IN THE COMMERCIAL SECTOR OF JAMAICA 61-168 (1974).
    41. Westinghouse, SUMMARY REPORT 92.
    42. Id. at 87.

TABLE 8
RELATIONSHIP OF ACTUAL AND EXPRESSED FAMILY SIZE OF FERTILE
COUPLES IN EIGHT COUNTRIES, 1972[43]

Country	Ideal Family Less than Current Actual Family Size[a]	Ideal Family and Current Actual Family Size Are Equal[b]	Ideal Family Greater than Actual Family Size[c]
Turkey	15%	34%	51%
Iran	24%	33%	43%
Thailand	11%	34%	55%
S. Korea	25%	38%	37%
Philippines	19%	34%	47%
Venezuela	35%	32%	33%
Panama	26%	41%	33%
Jamaica	20%	17%	63%

[a] Already have more children than they want.
[b] Have as many children as they want.
[c] Want more children.

couples will not use contraceptive methods for one reason or another, a not insignificant minority said they were willing to use a contraceptive product (Table 3, supra). Changes in regulations affecting contraceptives, particularly those affecting price and availability, could help these segments of the population implement their decision to limit family size.

III. SUGGESTIONS FOR CHANGE AND ESTIMATION OF IMPACT

Potential users are confronted by four types of barriers: (1) prohibitively high cost of products; (2) inadequate and irregular supply of products; (3) restricted access to sources of supply; and (4) lack of information concerning contraceptives. Some remedies for these problems are presented here and in the case of the problem of product cost, followed by an effort to calculate the impact of the remedy on population growth rates. Estimation of the impact of price reductions is possible because survey data are available regarding price sensitivity of consumers in seven of the eight developing nations surveyed. While lack of similar data concerning the other potential remedies precludes an attempt at making even rough estimates, the information that is available (see below) clearly implies that wider distribution of contraceptives is likely to achieve significant results at low cost to national governments. In addition, market experiments currently under way in at least three developing nations may soon generate data which will make these calculations possible.[44]

---

43. Id.
44. Market experiments are now in progress in Jamaica (supervised by the Westinghouse Population Center, Columbia, Md.), Kenya and Sri Lanka (supervised by Population Services International New York, New York).

A. *Prohibitively High Cost of Products*

The sheer cost of contraceptives relative to income prices them out of the range of a large part of the population in the developing nations.[45] The average cost of using an oral contraceptive or condoms effectively for one year ranged from 2% to 6% of per capita GNP (Table 9) in the eight countries surveyed as compared to a small fraction of one percent of income in the developed countries.

TABLE 9
MEDIAN COST OF CONTRACEPTIVE USE PER YEAR IN EIGHT
SELECTED COUNTRIES, 1971[46]

Country	GNP/ Capita	Oral Pill Price/ Year for Regular User	Oral Pill Price/Yr. as % of GNP/ Capita	Estimated Condom Price/ Yr. for a Regular Condom User	Condom Price/Yr. as % of GNP/ Capita
Turkey	$350	$9.10	2.6%	$7.20	2.1%
Iran	327	11.05	3.4%	6.00	1.8%
Thailand	400	7.80	2.0%	8.40	2.1%
S. Korea	200	7.00	3.5%	12.00	6.0%
Philippines	200	11.70	5.9%	10.80	5.4%
Venezuela	1,100	29.00	2.6%	27.60	2.5%
Panama	600	24.00	4.0%	19.20	3.2%
Jamaica	543	16.90	3.1%	18.00	3.3%

At the same time, duties and taxes on imported raw materials or finished contraceptive products contribute to these high prices (Table 10). The taxes are, of course, based on legislation enacted prior to the initiation of a population policy but in most cases left unchanged after an official policy is adopted or a program is started. Mexico, for example, recently reversed its pro-natalist policy but did not remove barriers to the import of contraceptives. Table 11 shows that retail price reductions resulting from abolition of taxes and duties may range as high as 30% on oral contraceptives and over 50% for condoms. In virtually all cases, there is potential for some substantial consumer price reduction, provided the benefits are passed on through the conventional mark-up structure usually used with these products.

Estimation of the impact of price reductions resulting from the elimination of taxes and duties may be done in the following way. First, taxes and duties are subtracted from the landed price of oral contraceptives and the prevailing market margins are added to calculate the decrease in retail price (see Table 11). Next, the price sensitivity of the most responsive market segment (non-users who want to stop having children and are willing to use a

---

45. Levin & Belsky *supra* note 20.
46. Westinghouse, SUMMARY REPORT 73.

TABLE 10

IMPORT TARIFFS AND OTHER CONTROLS FOR CONTRACEPTIVES IN EIGHT COUNTRIES, 1972[47]a,b

Country	Oral Pills		Condoms	
	Raw Materials	Finished Goods	Raw Materials	Finished Goods
Turkey	5% ad valorem[c] 10% cif[e] +35% fees[f]	5% ad valorem 10% cif +35% fees	NI[d]	22% cif +45% fees
Iran	5-20%[g] +15-20% fees	10% cif +15-20% fees	NI	30% cif
Thailand	30% cif +1.5% sales tax	10% cif +7.7% sales tax	3% on packaging materials	60% cif +7.7% sales tax
S. Korea	5% cif	Import Prohibited	30% cif (70% on latex)	Import Prohibited
Philippines	10% cif +30-40% packaging	30% cif	NI	20% cif +7% sales tax
Venezuela	1% cif	1% cif	1% cif	20% cif
Panama	NI	20% ad valorem +2.5% fees	NI	10% ad valorem +2.5% fees
Jamaica	NI	(US Prod.) 36.5% +5% fees (GB Prod.) 24.5% +5% fees	NI	22% +0.125/hundred wt.

a Source: U.S. Dept. of Commerce and Westinghouse Population Center.
b Duties and taxes have changed in many countries since these data were collected.
c ad valorem—appraised value.
d NI—no importation.
e cif—cost, insurance, freight.
f fees—licenses and consular fees.
g Depends on form.

47. Id. at 55.

TABLE 11
PROJECTED CHANGE IN RETAIL PRICE OF ORAL CONTRACEPTIVES AS A
RESULT OF ELIMINATION OF TARIFFS AND TAXES
IN EIGHT COUNTRIES, 1972[40]

Country	Current Median Price Per Cycle (US $)	Projected Percent Decrease in Price	Estimated Price Per Cycle After Removal of Tariffs and Taxes (US $)
Turkey	$0.70	NA	$NA
Iran	0.85	25.9%	0.63
Thailand	0.60	3.3%	0.58
S. Korea	0.54	11.1%	0.49
Philippines	0.90	13.3%	0.78
Venezuela	2.23	7.6%	2.06
Panama	1.85	13.5%	1.60
Jamaica	1.35	23.7%	1.03

contraceptive product; column 1 in Table 12) is examined. The response of couples in this segment to the question, "How much would you be willing to pay per month to stop having children?"[49] allows estimation of the percent of couples in the group that would be able to purchase contraceptives at the reduced price calculated above (Table 12, column 2). Third, the projected percentage increase of all couples able to purchase contraceptives is obtained by multiplying this figure by the total population percentage this segment represents (columns 1 and 2 in Table 12). In the countries surveyed, the projected increase ranges up to 12.6% of all fertile couples (Table 12, column 3).

Extrapolation of the next effect of this estimated increase in contraceptors on the population growth rate of each country is, of course, a complicated task even with the use of state-of-the-art demographic tools. Analysis here is limited to attempting only a rough calculation using the approach illustrated by the following model.

> In a country with a total population of ten million persons, the following factors influencing population growth might be expected:[51]
>
> (1) Fertile age, married females   2 million
> (2) Live births per year (at 45 per
>   1,000 persons in the population)   450,000

48. Id. at 55 & 71.

49. *See* WESTINGHOUSE POPULATION CENTER, DISTRIBUTION OF CONTRACEPTIVES IN THE COMMERCIAL SECTOR OF IRAN 160 (1974).

51. Forty-five percent of the population may be expected to be between the ages of 15 and 44; slightly less than half of these are female and (assuming an early age of marriage/consentual union) most are married. D. BOGUE, PRINCIPLES OF DEMOGRAPHY 147-366 (1969). Birth and death rates used to derive net increase in population here are similar to those common in many of the developing nations. D. NORTMAN, POPULATION AND FAMILY PLANNING PROGRAMS: A FACTBOOK 7 (Reports on Population/Family Planning No. 2, 1974).

TABLE 12

PROJECTED INCREASE IN PERCENTAGE OF FERTILE COUPLES ABLE TO PURCHASE ORAL CONTRACEPTIVES
AS A RESULT OF REMOVAL OF TARIFFS AND TAXES IN EIGHT COUNTRIES, 1972[50]

Country	Percent of Non-Users, Willing To Use a Contraceptive, Wanting To Stop Having Children	Percent of Non-Users, Willing To Use a Contraceptive, Wanting To Stop Having Children, Who Said They Would Pay as Much as the Reduced Price*	Projected Additional Percent of Fertile Couples Able To Purchase Oral Contraceptives as a Result of Decrease in Price
Turkey	NA	NA	NA
Iran	16%	79%	12.6%
Thailand	16%	0%	0%
S. Korea	20%	30%	6.0%
Philippines	17%	26%	4.4%
Venezuela	11%	17%	1.8%
Panama	11%	32%	3.5%
Jamaica	13%	25%	3.3%

* See Table 11.

50. See note 40 supra.

(3) Deaths per year (at 15 per 1,000
    persons in the population)   150,000
(4) Net increase in persons per year   300,000
(5) Percent net increase in population
    per year   3.0%

Perhaps 10%, or 200,000 couples might be practicing family planning, and these can be considered highly motivated contraceptors.[52] If reduction in price leads to doubling of this level of family planning practice, the net annual increase in population might be reduced as follows:

(6) Additional contracepting couples due
    to reduced price (10% of all couples)   200,000
(7) Estimated live births per year averted
    as a result of this increase (10%
    of live births)   45,000
(8) Live births per year after change   405,000
(9) Net increase in persons per year   255,000
(10) Percent net increase in population
    after change   2.55%

Table 13, based on the method of estimation explained above, shows that modest though not negligible reductions in population growth rates, ranging up to 0.56%, may be achieved in almost all cases. The size of this reduction becomes more important when it is remembered that it is likely to occur in a reasonably short period of time after it is perceived by consumers and that it may be achieved at very low and totally non-recurring cost.[53]

In addition to the high taxes and duties, there is another kind of legal barrier to reduction of retail cost of contraceptive products. Government controls on margins, ordinarily meant to hold down prices, may also contribute to the relatively high cost of contraceptives. Permissible margins may be unnecessarily high for a product purchased repeatedly, or so low that they may encourage re-sales through multiple levels of wholesaler/retailers before reaching the consumer level. The resultant middleman's margin adds substantially to the price to consumers. Fixed percentage margins also have the disadvantage of encouraging concentration of marketing efforts on the higher

52. A contracepting couple may be considered highly motivated if husband and wife are willing to consistently use an effective method, e.g. never miss taking oral pills, use condoms during every act of intercourse.

53. The cost of making price reductions known to the public and of wider distribution would be borne by the private sector and the loss of revenue to the government resulting from elimination of taxes and duties is not significant, see note 73 infra.

TABLE 13

PROJECTED IMPACT OF REDUCTION OF RETAIL CONTRACEPTIVE PRICE ON POPULATION GROWTH RATES OF SELECTED DEVELOPING COUNTRIES[54]

Country	Population (Millions)	Fertile Age Females (Millions)	Live Births Per Year (000s)	Deaths Per Year (000s)	Net Increase in Persons Per Year	Additional % Contracepting Due to Lower Price	Births Averted Per Year After Change (000s)	Live Births Per Year After Change (000s)	Net Increase in Persons Per Year	Current Growth Rate	Growth Rate After Change	Net Change in Growth Rate
Iran	31.1	6.2	1,400	528	872	12.6%	176.0	1,224	696	2.8%	2.24%	0.56%
Thailand	39.9	8.0	1,716	399	1,317	0.0%	None	1,716	1,317	2.3%	2.30%	0.00%
S. Korea	34.5	6.9	1,040	379	661	6.0%	62.4	977	598	2.0%	1.73%	0.27%
Philippines	42.2	8.4	1,900	506	1,394	4.4%	83.6	1,816	1,310	3.3%	3.10%	0.20%
Venezuela	11.9	2.4	488	95	393	3.3%	8.8	479	384	3.3%	3.22%	0.08%
Panama	1.6	0.3	59	14	45	3.5%	2.1	57	43	2.8%	2.68%	0.12%
Jamaica	2.1	0.4	73	14	59	1.8%	2.4	71	57	2.8%	2.66%	0.14%

54. Westinghouse, SUMMARY REPORT, *supra* note 10, and 1973 WORLD POPULATION DATA SHEET (Population Reference Bureau, 1973).

priced products.[55] Price controls should be instituted only after a realistic appraisal of their probable effects and should seek to link the prospects for a reasonable margin with the sale of contraceptives to more consumers more efficiently.

B. Restrictions on Distribution Channels and Sales Outlets

Because oral contraceptives are usually classified as ethical drugs, their sale is in many cases restricted to pharmacies and they can legally be obtained, in theory, only with a physician's prescription. The number of physicians and pharmacies in most developing nations is small relative to the population, and is usually concentrated in the larger cities and towns.[56] Often, half of the population is "medically indigent," i.e. individuals never see a physician for any reason during their lifetime; even those who do receive medical care have little access to preventive medical services such as family planning. People living in rural or semi-rural areas must either make special long trips to medical centers or else be in effect denied access to contraceptives because transportation to urban areas is irregular or too expensive for frequent trips required for resupply.

Though there is generally little opposition to increasing the available sales outlets for condoms (except in the case of Colombia where sellers want to maintain control of the market), proposals for liberalizing the manufacture, sale and distribution of oral contraceptives have usually met with strong opposition from the medical and pharmaceutical professions. Many physicians argue that most kinds of contraceptives, particularly oral pills, require regular medical supervision in order to monitor the possible serious medical complications. They further contend that no single oral pill formula is appropriate to the physiology of most women, so a physician's examination must precede initiation of use of oral contraceptives.[57] However, danger from the unsupervised use of oral contraceptives must be compared with the danger of recurrent pregnancy and childbirth.[58] Pregnancy related fatalities are of much greater magnitude than fatalities related to oral pill usage.[59] Furthermore, the

---

55. See P. KOTLER, MARKET MANAGEMENT: ANALYSIS, PLANNING AND CONTROL 362-385 (1967).

56. See note 19 supra.

57. For discussion of the relative safety and potential long term effects of oral contraceptive use, see Lehfeldt, Current Status of Oral Contraceptives in OBSTETRICS AND GYNECOLOGY ANNUAL 261 (1973); Bingel & Benoit, Oral Contraceptives' Therapeutics Versus Adverse Reactions With an Outlook to the Future in 62 JOURNAL OF PHARMACEUTICAL SCIENCES 179-200 (1973); Andrews, Oral Contraception, A Review of Reported Physiological and Pathological Effects in 26 OBSTETRICAL AND GYNECOLOGICAL SURVEY 477-499 (1971); WORLD HEALTH ORGANIZATION, METHODS OF FERTILITY REGULATION: ADVANCES IN RESEARCH AND CLINICAL EXPERIENCE (Technical Report Series No. 473, 1971).

58. Ravenholt, Piotrow & Speidel, Use of Oral Contraceptives: A Decade of Controversy in 8 INT'L. GYNECOLOGY AND OBSTETRICS 941-956 (1973).

59. The following passage, from Atkinson, Castadot, Cuadros & Rosenfield, Oral Contraceptives: Considerations of Safety in Nonclinical Distribution 244-245 in 5 STUDIES IN FAMILY PLANNING 8 (1974) makes this point very clearly. Citations are omitted.

"The risks associated with OCs (oral contraceptives) cannot be evaluated without taking into consideration the risks of not practicing contraception or of using other contraceptive methods (cite omitted). The nonpractice of contraception leads to pregnancy, which is a cause of mortality varying from around 25 maternal deaths per 100,000 live births (cite omitted) in those countries providing the best available medical care to most of their population, to 500 per 100,000 in many rural areas of Africa, Asia and Latin America. (cite omitted)

In Table (below), we have compared mortality due to pregnancy and due to method use, by specified method, for the two levels of medical care. The pregnancy rates among OC and IUD users are derived from Tietze (cite omitted) for the United States (2 and 3.5 per 100 woman-years, respectively) and from Sivin's Worldwide Survey of the Postpartum Program (cite omitted) for urban centers of the developing countries (2.6 and 2.2 per 100 woman-years, respectively), and, consequently, these urban use-effectiveness rates might not be representative of the rural areas considered here. The pregnancy rates for "no protection" are derived from Tietze (cite omitted) and take into account the effect of breast feeding on fertility. The rates for condom/diaphragm are from Potts (cite omitted).

The mortality levels associated with OCs and the IUD are based on rates from the United States and Great Britain (cite omitted) and might not be appropriate for other areas. One could assume that the death rates in the developing world are lower among OC users (probable lower incidence of thromboembolic disease) and higher among IUD users (infection less likely to be treated). Although the various rates used in the calculations for this table are approximations only, they seem to provide a reasonable indication of the comparative risks taken by users versus nonusers of contraceptives.

Although there is adequate evidence that oral contraceptives in the United States, Great Britain, and probably other industrialized countries cause a small excess mortality from thromboembolic disease (cite omitted), there is a remarkable scarcity of such evidence from less affluent regions (cite omitted). Part of this might be due to inadequate surveillance and reporting, but some of us who have practiced obstetrics in Africa, Asia and Latin America believe that thromboembolic complications are much less frequent in those areas than in the United States. Initial reports (cite omitted) tend to support these observations. Such a lower incidence rate might be related to different styles of life such as diet, level of activity, lack of smoking, and so on.

In conclusion, the mortality associated with oral contraception is lower than the mortality associated with pregnancy and the less effective methods for each level of health care. The differences are emphasized as the level of health care decreases. The mortality associated with the use of OCs does not seem very different from the mortality associated with the IUD, hence depriving us of clear-cut alternatives in this respect." (Emphasis added.)

CONTRACEPTIVE AND MATERNAL MORTALITY PER 1,000,000 WOMEN
AT RISK BY LEVEL OF HEALTH CARE

Item	No Contraception[a]	Condom/ Diaphragm	IUD	OC
A. Maternal mortality of 250 per 1,000,000				
Pregnancies in any year	600,000	150,000	35,000	20,000
Deaths				
Due to pregnancy	150	38	9	5
Due to method	0	0	10[c]	30[c]
Total deaths	150	38	19	35
	No Contraception[a]	Other Methods[b]	IUD	OC
B. Maternal Mortality of 500 per 1,000,000				
Pregnancies in any year	400,000	112,000	22,000	26,000
Deaths				
Due to pregnancy	2,000	560	110	130
Due to method	0	0	10[c]	30[c]
Total deaths	2,000	560	120	160

arguments made by medical groups ignore certain key market realities in many developing nations. For example, oral contraceptives, like many other ethical drugs, are generally available over-the-counter in pharmacies in many countries despite legal prohibition on sale without prescription.[60] Enforcement agencies and pharmacists apparently recognize that enforcing the prescription requirement would generally hurt those who do not have access to the medical system. Removal of these restrictions, which are nonetheless troublesome and partially effective, would only recognize *de jure* what has been widely accepted *de facto*. This could also provide the additional benefit of extending sales of pills to the much broader system of non-pharmaceutical sales outlets and allowing direct advertising aimed at consumers. Of course, each nation must determine on the basis of available data whether the risks and benefits associated with oral contraceptives warrant blanket prohibitions against their sale without prescription or whether some alternate measures may be formulated to insure the public health and safety. Nations have already weighed these factors and decided to eliminate prescription requirements for oral contraceptives (Antigua, Chile, Fiji, Jamaica, Pakistan, the Philippines and South Korea) or to allow para-medical personnel to insert IUDs (Mexico, the Philippines and South Korea).[61]

C. *Legal Barriers to Adequate and Regular Supply of Contraceptives*

Effective practice of family planning depends, of course, on the availability of a regular and continuous supply of oral contraceptives or condoms for couples choosing those particular methods, as well as on information for their proper use. In some countries legal regulations and procedures lead to an irregular flow of products, particularly at the import stage.[62] Customs procedures and foreign exchange regulations may result in port delays which leave retailers out of stock of particular brands or even of particular products for long periods of time.[63] Again, these regulations (and the resulting delays) are not specific to contraceptives, but to the customs categories into which contraceptives are classified. If, consistent with government policy, con-

---

[a] Rates for women of reproductive age in fertile unions, with consideration of extent and duration of breast feeding as estimated by Tietze (cite omitted).
    [b] Other methods include condom (70%), spermicides, diaphragm and a small number of Depo-Provera acceptors (cite omitted).
    [c] Those figures are approximations and the differences between IUDs and OCs are not of statistical significance.

    60. Black, *Oral Contraceptive Prescription Requirements and Commercial Availability in 45 Developing Countries* 250 in 5 STUDIES IN FAMILY PLANNING 8 (1974).
    61. C.E. DEAN & P. T. PIOTROW, EIGHTEEN MONTHS OF LEGAL CHANGE 4 (Law and Policy Series E No. 1, 1974).
    62. Westinghouse, SUMMARY REPORT 106-135.
    63. Id.

traceptives were dealt with as a special category for customs clearance and currency regulation, the import process would be streamlined and the flow of products expedited.

As with other slow-moving products, retailers hold small inventories of contraceptive products.[64] Stock-outs of such products are common and are in fact a normal part of day-to-day business operation of small retailers. As many as 20% of the rural couples questioned in five countries (Table 14) said that their source of supply had been out of stock on at least one occasion. This is an especially critical problem because many couples not currently using contraceptives expect to walk to their source of supply and many current users must travel relatively long distances to obtain their supply (Table 14). These stock-outs reflect both the current low sales volume per outlet and also the retailer's inability to obtain credit which would allow each outlet to carry more stock. Should exogenous events (such as reduction in price or a major promotion campaign, for example) lead to a significant increase in demand, some retailers will still be unable to increase their inventory because of lack of credit. Expansion of credit to retailers might be accomplished by such means as tax credits at the retail level (in return for cooperation with other aspects of the government program) as an incentive for stocking a larger than normal inventory of contraceptive products.

D. *Advertising and Information*

Classifying oral contraceptives as ethical drugs also results in prohibitions, either legal (as is the case in Panama)[66] or based on professional standards (as is the case in Jamaica),[67] on advertising to the public and restrictions on the role of pharmacists and other para-medical personnel in providing information and advice. Manufacturers cannot or do not post signs to indicate that oral contraceptives are available. The situation with condoms is rather similar, largely because of a tradition of secretiveness involved in their sale. Not surprisingly, improper and ineffective use of contraceptive products resulting from consumer misinformation was widespread in the eight countries surveyed (Table 15). Also, this is an especially appropriate area for change because potential users were favorably disposed toward both mass media advertising and point of purchase display of oral contraceptives and condoms (Table 16). Relaxation of these restrictions should increase the flow of information and availability of products to current consumers, and visibility of products might encourage potential consumers.[70] The enhanced visibility of

---

64. Id. at 56-65.
66. WESTINGHOUSE POPULATION CENTER, DISTRIBUTION OF CONTRACEPTIVES IN THE COMMERCIAL SECTOR OF PANAMA 23-24 (1974).
67. WESTINGHOUSE POPULATION CENTER, DISTRIBUTION OF CONTRACEPTIVES IN THE COMMERCIAL SECTOR OF JAMAICA 22-25 (1974).
70. Simon, *Some 'Marketing Correct' Recommendations for Family Planning Campaigns* 504-507 in 5 DEMOGRAPHY 1.

TABLE 14

PRODUCT "STOCK-OUTS" AND TRAVEL PATTERNS FOR ORAL CONTRACEPTIVES IN EIGHT COUNTRIES, 1972[65]

Country	Percent of Rural Users Ever Experiencing Stock-Out	Percent of Non-Users Who Would Expect To Walk To Source of Supply	Percent of All Oral Pill Users Traveling Less Than 1 Mile for Supply
Turkey	NA	76%	NA
Iran	12%	55%	62%
Thailand	19%	31%	37%
S. Korea	12%	69%	31%
Philippines	20%	34%	17%
Venezuela	NA	39%	NA
Panama	20%	53%	34%
Jamaica	NA	35%	NA

65. Id. at 75.

TABLE 15
MISUNDERSTANDING OF USE OF CONTRACEPTIVES AMONG CONTRACEPTIVE
USERS IN SELECTED DEVELOPING NATIONS, 1972[68]

Country	Oral Pill Users *Not* Understanding That One Pill is to be Used Each Day	Condom Users *Not* Understanding That a Condom Should be Used at Each Act of Intercourse
Turkey	31%	29%
Iran	11%	16%
Thailand	16%	51%
S. Korea	14%	40%
Philippines	8%	55%
Venezuela	21%	39%
Panama	18%	NA
Jamaica	15%	51%

products might also encourage those who are unaware of contraceptive methods generally to undertake conscious efforts to plan their families.

IV.   BARRIERS TO ACTION

The proposed changes in law discussed above are generally consonant with the expressed policies of many countries which have national family planning programs. In addition, they are justifiable on the ground that they provide individuals the opportunity to make voluntary, rational choices regarding family size and spacing, a human right recognized by many nations.[71] Nevertheless, some obstacles may arise if an attempt is made to implement the proposed changes.

Vested commercial interests may also resist changes in the legal system. However, manufacturer, importer and retailer interviews conducted in eight countries[72] indicated that this is not a critical problem at the moment. Most businessmen in the countries studied seemed more concerned with bringing the birth rate into some balance than with protecting the relatively modest revenue implications for the multiproduct firms now handling contraceptives.

Medical and pharmaceutical organizations concerned with health and safety and other professional organizations may resist measures to make oral contraceptives more readily available to consumers as may various religious and civic organizations.[73] The traditional medical aversion to advertising may

68. Westinghouse, SUMMARY REPORT 95-97.
71. *See* note 3 *supra.*
72. Westinghouse, SUMMARY REPORT 13-66.
73. Dr. Halfdan Mahler, Director General of the World Health Organization, commented on this issue in a 1971 interview. "For me there is only one fundamental issue. You have a certain technology, with certain resources, and certain political, social and cultural constraints. Within

TABLE 16

EXPRESSED ATTITUDE TOWARD USE OF ADVERTISING, OF NON-USERS OF CONTRACEPTIVES
NOT WANTING MORE CHILDREN AND WILLING TO USE A CONTRACEPTIVE, IN
SELECTED DEVELOPING NATIONS, 1972[69]

Country	Percent Thinking Use of In-Store Signs is a Good Idea	Percent Thinking Radio and Cinema Ads Are a Good Idea	Reasons Cited for Thinking Signs Are a Good Idea	
			Indicates Availability	Provides General Information
Turkey	NA	NA	NA	NA
Iran	19%	66%	3%	84%
Thailand	49%	57%	69%	—
S. Korea	66%	80%	32%	38%
Philippines	59%	69%	77%	—
Jamaica	84%	87%	73%	10%
Panama	54%	75%	34%	26%
Venezuela	43%	70%	52%	12%

69. *See* note 40 *supra.*

also retard the wide-scale dissemination of information which may be necessary to cultivate a general level of support for legal reform among both the indifferent and the skeptical. Legal changes must be presented not as a first wedge for an across-the-board incursion into the established medical preserve, but as a special phenomenon which requires unusual measures such as mass advertising and over-the-counter sales of certain ethical drugs.

The existence of price controls and other pricing regulations may complicate effecting changes in prices and margin structures. However, since these price control agencies are generally concerned with maximum prices,[74] any structural changes which promise generally lower prices should be acceptable. Similarly, reductions in governmental revenues implied by reductions in tariffs or duties on these specific products are generally small[75] and should not constitute a major barrier provided that the government is serious in implementing its population policies.

Finally, the level of political support of population policies (and specifically the support for measures aimed at encouraging family planning and lowering fertility rates) will be tested by the legislative action required to effect any of the changes suggested here. The time and effort required to secure real support for action (as opposed to basic agreement in principle) will also vary from setting to setting. Open market experiments now in progress should help clarify the scope and degree of the political, medical and commercial problems discussed here and facilitate development of measures to overcome these barriers.[76]

V. A Look to the Future

It should be apparent from this discussion that means for clear quantitative evaluation of the impact of "primary effect" changes in regulations such as those suggested here, as well as means for evaluation of secondary effects of more general programs are lacking. In fact, one problem faced by population programs is the lack of adequate methodologies to connect the effect of

---

this setting you have to do the maximum in order to benefit the health care consumer. Therefore I would consider it nonsensical to insist upon using only doctors or other categories of professionally qualified personnel, if you can standardize and simplify your technology to make it safe and applicable through either trained midwives or even people working part-time in health and part-time in other kinds of jobs. I don't think health care will ever be successful at the periphery in many of the developing countries unless other imaginative solutions for delivery are found. This I believe to be the fundamental issue. Our work should not be hampered by any vested interest of the medical profession which still hangs as a cloud over many of the things we do. *See Dr. Mahler: WHO Must Be the Family Planning Coordinator* 12 in 1 PEOPLE 1 (1973).

74. W.J. Keegan, MULTINATIONAL MARKETING MANAGEMENT 267 (1974).

75. Business Management Research Center of Korea University, Research on Prices of Contraceptives and Improvement of Related Tax Systems (1974).

76. *See* note 40 *supra*.

programs with changes in the birth rate. Absent more research on these issues, estimates of impact must be based on rough calculations like those presented earlier. The significance of any single change is likely to be so modest and the number of factors in the environment so large, that concrete assessment of the impact of a single policy change in terms of birth rate reduction is unlikely. However, it is easy to overlook relatively simple, practical and helpful steps like those suggested here that offer partial solutions in approaching the larger systems problem involved in achieving more ambitious demographic goals. Given the many difficulties that more comprehensive population programs face and will continue to face in terms of both available resources and basic levels of interest of target groups, active search for partial solutions should continue in any case. While the search for simpler and more effective methods of contraception should proceed, it is important to be sensitive to the fact that the relatively minor commitment of resources to activities like removal of legal constraints may be a very effective means of population policy in the short-run and will continue to have some impact over longer periods by assuring broader and more effective distribution of any new contraceptive technologies that might be developed.

A Selective Bibliography on Law and Population

By
Sanda M. Kayden* and Ilene P. Karpf*

OUTLINE

EXPLANATORY NOTE

The books and articles cited in this bibliography are not intended to be a complete review of the literature on law and population. The compilers have emphasized in their inquiry literature dealing with laws which have a "primary effect" on population, that is, laws which are primarily directed toward affecting population. Literature dealing with laws having a "secondary effect" on population is beyond the scope of this bibliography. Laws having a secondary effect on population may be briefly defined as laws "which though designed to implement other social or administrative policies, incidentally affect population patterns."

A fuller explanation of "primary" and "secondary effect" laws may be found in the Farley-Tokarski article in this volume.

* Staff Members, Columbia Human Rights Law Review.

I. Books and Articles

A. *Abortion*

1. *Abortion Decision: Right of Privacy Extended,* 27 U. Miami L. Rev. 481 (1973).
2. *Abortion: The Father's Rights,* 42 U. Cin. L. Rev. 441 (1973).
3. *Abortion: The Five-Year Resolution and Its Impact,* 3 Ecology L.Q. 311 (1973).
4. *Abortion: The Future Cases: Father's Rights,* 8 U. San Francisco L. Rev. 472 (1973).
5. *Abortion and the Husband's Consent,* 13 J. Family L. 311 (1973-74).
6. Abortion Reform Law Association, A Guide to the Abortion Act of 1967 (London: ALRA 1968).
7. *Abortion: Roe v. Wade and the Montana Dilemma,* 35 Montana L. Rev. 103 (1974).
8. Akingba, J., The Problem of Unwanted Pregnancies in Nigeria Today (Lagos: The University of Lagos Press 1971).
9. Alan & Susan, *Abortions for Poor and Nonwhite Women: A Denial of Equal Protection?* 23 Hastings L.J. 147 (1971).
10. *Analysis of the Constitutionality of the Nebraska Abortion Statute,* 7 Creighton L. Rev. 27 (1973).
11. Anderson et al., *Abortion after Roe and Doe: A Proposed Statute,* 26 Vand. L. Rev. 823 (1973).
12. Anderson, *Abortion and the Husband's Consent,* 13 J. Family L. 311 (1973-74).
13. Berkov & Sklar, The Impact of Legalized Abortion on Fertility in California, International Population and Urban Research (Berkeley: U. of Cal. Press 1972).
14. Bhashti, A., *Islamic Attitudes Towards Abortion and Sterilization,* 7 Birthright 49 (1972).
15. Brody, *Abortion and the Law,* 12 J. Philosophy 357 (1971).
16. Bryn, *Abortion Amendments: Policy in the Light of Precedent,* 18 St. Louis U.L.J. 380 (1974).
17. Bryn & Hellegers, *Wade and Bolton: Fundamental Legal Errors and Dangerous Implications,* 19 Catholic L.J. 243 (1973).
18. Burke, *Abortion: Law, Ethics, and the Value of Life,* 49 Manch. Med. Gaz. 4 (1970).
19. Butler, *Right to Abortion Under Medicaid,* 7 Clearinghouse Rev. 713 (1974).
20. Callahan, D., Abortion: Law, Choice and Morality (New York: MacMillan 1972).
21. Cane, *Whose Right to Life? Implications of Roe v. Wade,* 7 Family L.Q. 413 (1973).

22. Cheung, *Abortion Decision—A Qualified Constitutional Right in the United States: Whither Canada?* 51 CAN. B. REV. 643 (1973).

23. Conley & McKenna, *Supreme Court on Abortion—A Dissenting Opinion,* 19 CATHOLIC L.J. 19 (1973).

24. *Consent Provisions in Abortion Statutes,* 1 FLA. ST. U.L. REV. 645 (1973).

25. *Constitutional Law—A New Constitutional Right to an Abortion,* 51 N.C.L. REV. 1573 (1973).

26. *Constitutional Law—Minor's Right to Refuse Court-Ordered Abortion,* 7 SUFFOLK U.L. REV. 1157 (1973).

27. *Constitutional Validity of the Tennessee Abortion Statute,* 4 MEMPHIS ST. U.L. REV. 593 (1974).

28. Corriden, *Church Law and Abortion,* 33 THE JURIST 184 (1973).

29. Crawford, *Abortion Act,* 2 LANCET 1138 (1970).

30. *Culmination of the Abortion Reform Movement—Roe v. Wade and Doe v. Bolton,* 8 U. RICHMOND L. REV. 75 (1973).

31. Curren, *Abortion: Law and Morality in Contemporary Catholic Theology,* 33 THE JURIST 162 (1973).

32. DAVID, H., ABORTION RESEARCH: INTERNATIONAL EXPERIENCE (Lexington, Mass.: Lexington Books 1974).

33. DAVID, H., FAMILY PLANNING AND ABORTION IN THE SOCIALIST COUNTRIES OF CENTRAL AND EASTERN EUROPE (New York: Population Council 1970).

34. DAVID, H. & CAMBIASO, EDS., ABORTION AND FAMILY PLANNING PRACTICES IN LATIN AMERICA (Washington, D.C.: Pan American Health Organization 1974).

35. David & Wright, *Abortion Legislation: The Romanian Experience,* 2 STUDIES IN FAMILY PLANNING 205 (1971).

36. DAVID, H. ET AL., ABORTION LEGISLATION: A SUMMARY INTERNATIONAL CLASSIFICATION (Washington, D.C.: AIR/Trans-national Family Research Institute 1972) (updated to March 1974).

37. de Moerloose, *Abortion Throughout the World,* 2 NURSING TIMES 678 (1971).

38. Ely, *The Wages of Crying Wolf: A Comment on Roe and Doe,* 82 YALE L.J. 920 (1973).

39. Epstein, *Substantive Due Process By Any Other Name: The Abortion Cases,* 1973 SUP. CT. REV. 159 (1973).

40. *Euthanasia and Abortion,* 38 COLO. L. REV. 178 (1966).

41. Frederiksen & Brackett, *Demographic Effects of Abortion,* 83 PUB. HEALTH REP. 999 (1968).

42. Gaffney, *Law and Theology: A Dialogue on the Abortion Decisions,* 33 THE JURIST 134 (1973).

43. GARDNER, R., ABORTION: THE PERSONAL DILEMMA (Grand Rapids, Michigan: Eerdmans 1973).
44. George, *The Abortion—Law Mill*, 167 N.Y.L.J. 1 (1972).
45. GERMAN DEMOCRATIC REPUBLIC, LAW ON THE INTERRUPTION OF PREGNANCY, ABORTION RES. NOTES 1(2): Supp. 2 (1972).
46. Goldman, *Abortion: Jewish Law and the Law of the Land*, 135 ILL. MED. J. 93 (1969).
47. GRANFIELD, D., THE ABORTION DECISION (New York: Doubleday 1971).
48. GUTTMACHER, A., THE CASE FOR LEGALIZED ABORTION NOW (Berkeley, Calif.: Diablo Press 1967).
49. HALL, R., ED., ABORTION IN A CHANGING WORLD (New York: Colum. U. Press 1970).
50. Harrison, *Supreme Court and Abortion Reform: Means to an End*, 19 N.Y.L.F. 685 (1974).
51. Heyman & Barzelay, *Forest and the Trees: Roe v. Wade and its Critics*, 53 B.U.L. REV. 765 (1973).
52. HIGERS, T. & HORAN, D., EDS., ABORTION AND SOCIAL JUSTICE (New York: Sheed & Ward 1972).
53. *Hill-Burton Hospitals After Roe and Doe: Can Federally Funded Hospitals Refuse to Perform Abortions?*, 4 N.Y.U. REV. L. & SOC. CHANGE 83 (1974).
54. HORDEM, A., LEGAL ABORTION: THE ENGLISH EXPERIENCE (London: Pergamon 1972).
55. HUSER, R., THE CRIME OF ABORTION IN CANON LAW (Washington, D.C.: Catholic U. Press 1942).
56. *Implications of the Abortion Decisions: Post Roe and Doe Litigation and Legislation*, 74 COL. L. REV. 237 (1974).
57. *In Defense of Liberty: A Look at the Abortion Decisions*, 61 GEO. L.J. 1559 (1973).
58. JAIN, S. & SINDIG S., NORTH CAROLINA ABORTION LAW, 1967: A STUDY IN LEGISLATIVE PROCESS. Monograph #2, Carolina Population Center (Chapel Hill: U.N.C. Press 1968).
59. LADER, L., ABORTION II: MAKING THE REVOLUTION (Boston: Beacon 1973).
60. *Landmark Abortion Decisions: Justifiable Termination or Miscarriage of Justice?* 4 PACIFIC L.J. 821 (1973).
61. *The Law and the Unborn Child*, 46 NOTRE DAME LAW. 349 (1971).
62. LEE, L., BRIEF SURVEY OF THE ABORTION LAWS OF THE FIVE LARGEST COUNTRIES, Monograph #14, Law and Population Programme (Medford, Mass.: The Fletcher School of Law and Diplomacy 1973).
63. LEE, L., INTERNATIONAL STATUS OF ABORTION LEGISLATION, Mono-

graph #16, Law and Population Programme (Medford, Mass.: The Fletcher School of Law and Diplomacy 1973).

64. Levene & Rigney, *Law, Preventive Psychiatry, and Therapeutic Abortion,* 151 J. NERV. MENT. DIS. 51 (1970).

65. Loewy, *Abortive Reasons and Obscene Standards: A Comment on the Abortion and Obscenity Cases,* 52 N.C.L. REV. 223 (1973).

66. Lucas & Lamm, *Abortion: Litigative and Legislative Processes: A Symposium,* 1 HUMAN RIGHTS 23 (1973).

67. MARX, P., THE DEATH PEDDLERS: WAR ON THE UNBORN (Collegeville, Minn.: St. John's U. Press 1971).

68. Means, *The Phoenix of Abortional Freedom: Is a Penumbral or Ninth Amendment Right about to Arise from the Nineteenth Century Ashes of a Fourteenth Century Common-Law Liberty,* 2 N.Y.L.F. 335 (1971).

69. MEDICAL PROTECTION SOCIETY, THE ABORTION ACT OF 1967 (London: Pitman Publishing Co. 1969).

70. *Minor's Right to Abortion and the Requirement of Parental Consent,* 60 VA. L. REV. 305 (1974).

71. NAZER, I., ED., INDUCED ABORTION: A HAZARD TO PUBLIC HEALTH? Proceeding of the First Conference of the IPPF Middle East and North Africa Region, Beirut, Lebanon, Feb. 1971 (Beirut: IPPF Middle East and North Africa Region 1972).

72. NEWMAN, S., BECK & LEWIT, ABORTION, OBTAINED AND DENIED (Bridgeport, Conn.: Key Book Service, Inc. 1971) (Distrib. for Population Council).

73. Nielsen, *Toward a Socratic View of Abortion,* 18 AM. J. JURIS. 105 (1973).

74. NOONAN, J., ED., THE MORALITY OF ABORTION, LEGAL AND HISTORICAL PERSPECTIVES (Cambridge, Mass.: Harv. U. Press 1970).

75. OSOFSKY, H., AND OSOFSKY J. EDS., THE ABORTION EXPERIENCE (New York: Harper & Row 1973).

76. PERLINE, E., ABORTION IN CANADA (Toronto: New Press 1971).

77. Pilpel & Zuckerman, *Abortion and the Rights of Minors,* 23 CASE W. RES. L. REV. 779 (1972).

78. Polityka, *From Poe to Roe: A Bickelian View of the Abortion Decision: Its Timing and Principle,* 53 NEB. L. REV. 31 (1974).

79. Potts, *Legal Abortion in Eastern Europe,* 59 EUGENICS REV. 230 (1967).

80. REPORT OF THE COMMITTEE TO STUDY THE QUESTION OF LEGALIZATION OF ABORTION (New Delhi: Ministry of Health and Family Planning 1966).

81. Rice, *Dred Scott Case of the Twentieth Century,* 10 HOUSTON L. REV. 1059 (1973).

82. *Right of a Husband or a Minor's Parent to Participate in the Abortion Decision,* 28 U. MIAMI L. REV. 251 (1973).
83. *Right to Abortion: Expansion of the Right to Privacy Through the Fourteenth Amendment,* 19 CATHOLIC LAW 36 (1973).
84. Roberts & Skelton, *Abortion and the Courts,* 1 ENVIRON. L.J. 225 (1971).
85. *Roe v. Wade and Doe v. Bolton: Compelling State Interest in Substantive Due Process,* 30 WASH. & LEE L. REV. 628 (1973).
86. Roemer, *Abortion Law: The Approaches of Different Nations,* 57 AM. J. PUB. HEALTH 1910 (1967).
87. Rubin, *Abortion Cases: A Study in Law and Social Change,* 5 N.C. CENTRAL L.J. 215 (1974).
88. ST. JOHN-STEVAS, N., THE RIGHT TO LIFE (New York: Holt, Rinehart & Winston 1964).
89. SARVIS, B. & H. RODMAN, THE ABORTION CONTROVERSY (New York: Colum. U. Press 1973).
90. SCHULDER, D. & KENNEDY, F., ABORTION RAP (New York: McGraw Hill 1971).
91. Simon, *Abortion Decision and ⌐ ⌐to Rico,* 34 REV. C. ABO. P.R. 505 (1973).
92. SMITH, D., ED., ABORTION AND THE LAW (Cleveland: Western Reserve U. 1967).
93. THERAPEUTIC ABORTION AND THE LAW IN SWEDEN (Stockholm: The Swedish Institute 1971).
94. Tietze, *Abortion in Europe,* 57 AM. J. PUB. HEALTH 1923 (1967).
95. TIETZE, THE POTENTIAL IMPACT OF LEGAL ABORTION ON POPULATION GROWTH AND THE AMERICAN FUTURE (1972).
96. Tietze, *Two Years Experience with a Liberal Abortion Law: Its Impact on Fertility Trends in New York City,* 5 FAM. PLANN. PERSPECT. 36 (1973).
97. Tribe, *Forward: Toward a Model of Roles in the Due Process of Life and Law,* 87 HARV. L. REV. 1 (1973).
98. VAN DER TAK, J., ABORTION, FERTILITY AND CHANGING LEGISLATION: AN INTERNATIONAL REVIEW (Lexington, Mass.: Lexington Books 1974).
99. Veitch & Tracey, *Abortion in the Common Law World,* 4 AM. J. COMP. L. 652 (1974).
100. VIEDERMAN, S., ED., POPULATION EDUCATION IN SOCIAL EDUCATION, Vol. 36, No. 4 (April 1972).
101. Vieira, *Roe and Doe: Substantive Due Process and the Right of Abortion,* 25 HASTINGS L. REV. 867 (1974).
102. WEINBERG, R., LAWS GOVERNING FAMILY PLANNING (Dobbs Ferry, N.Y.: Oceana 1968).

103. Wheeler, *Roe v. Wade: The Right of Privacy Revisited,* 21 KANSAS L. REV. 527 (1973).
104. *Whose Right to Life? Implications of Roe v. Wade,* 7 FAMILY L.Q. 413 (1973).
105. WILLIAMS, G., THE SANCTITY OF LIFE AND THE CRIMINAL LAW (London: Faber & Faber 1958).
106. Williamson, *Abortion: A Legal View,* 72 N.Z. MED. J. 257 (1970).
107. WORLD HEALTH ORGANIZATION, ABORTION LAWS: A SURVEY OF CURRENT WORLD LEGISLATION (Geneva: World Health Organization 1971).

B. *Birth Control*

1. *Birth Control and the Liability of Physicians and Pharmacists,* 6 U.D.C.L. REV. 255 (1973).
2. CHASTEEN, E., THE CASE FOR COMPULSORY BIRTH CONTROL (Englewood Cliffs, N.J.: Prentice Hall 1971).
3. Cushner, *In Pregnancy Termination, the Impact of New Laws,* 6 J. REPROD. MED. 274 (1971).
4. Davis & Blake, *Birth Control and Public Policy,* 29 COMMENTARY 42 (1960).
5. DIENES, C., LAW, POLITICS AND BIRTH CONTROL (Urbana: U. Ill. Press 1972).
6. Dienes, *Moral Beliefs and Legal Norms: Perspectives on Birth Control,* 11 ST. LOUIS U.L.J. 536 (1967).
7. Dienes, *Progeny of Comstockery—Birth Control Laws Return to Court,* 21 AM. U.L. REV. 1 (1971).
8. Dixon, *The Griswold Penumbra: Constitutional Charter for an Expanded Law of Privacy?* 64 MICH. L. REV. 197 (1965).
9. Dowse & Peel, *The Politics of Birth Control,* 13 POLITICAL SCIENCE 179 (1965).
10. *Eisenstadt v. Baird: State Statute Prohibiting Distribution of Contraceptives to Single Persons Void on Equal Protection Grounds,* 3 N.Y.U. REV. L. & SOC. CHANGE 56 (1973).
11. Emerson, *Nine Justices in Search of a Doctrine (Griswold v. Conn.),* 64 MICH. L. REV. 219 (1965).
12. FERRARI, G., ED., LEGISLATION DIRECTLY OR INDIRECTLY AFFECTING FERTILITY IN ITALY (Florence: Dipartimento Statistico Matematico 1973).
13. FRYER, P., THE BIRTH CONTROLLERS (New York: Stein & Day 1966).
14. Gardner, *Towards an International Population Program,* INT'L ORG. 1 (1968).
15. Greenberg, *Birth Control in Jewish Law,* 50 COMMENTARY 64 (1970).

16. Hall, *Legal Initiatives in Fertility Control; The Singapore Experience*, 3 LAWASIA 339 (1972).
17. Hardin, *Parenthood: Right or Privilege?* 49 SCIENCE 42 (1970).
18. Hudson, *Birth Control Legislation*, 9 CLEV.-MAR. L. REV. 1 (1960).
19. IPPF, EUROPEAN REGION, A SURVEY OF THE LEGAL STATUS OF CON-TRACEPTION, STERILIZATION, AND ABORTION IN EUROPEAN COUNTRIES (London: IPPF 1973).
20. Johnson, *Control of Human Fertility in Australia: Law and Policy*, 1 MED. J. AUS. 73 (1965).
21. Katin, *Griswold v. Connecticut: The Justices and Connecticut's 'Uncommonly Silly Law'*, 42 NOTRE DAME LAW 680 (1967).
22. Kauper, *Penumbras, Peripheries, Emanations, Things Fundamental and Things Forgotten: The Griswold Case*, 64 MICH. L. REV. 235 (1965).
23. LEE & PAXMAN, LEGAL ASPECTS OF MENSTRUAL REGULATION, Monograph No. 19. Law and Polpulation Programme (Medford, Mass.: The Fletcher School of Law and Diplomacy 1974).
24. MEASURES, POLICIES AND PROGRAMMES AFFECTING FERTILITY, WITH PARTICULAR REFERENCE TO NATIONAL FAMILY PLANNING PROGRAMMES. St/SOA/Series A/51 (New York: United Nations 1972).
25. *Minors and Contraceptives: A Constitutional Issue*, 3 ECOLOGY L.Q. 843 (1973).
26. Mueller, *Oral Contraceptives—Government-Supported Programs Are Questioned*, 163 SCIENCE 553 (1969).
27. Muramatsu, *An Analysis of Factors in Fertility Control in Japan*, 19 BULL. INST. PUB. HEALTH 97 (1970).
28. PEEL & POTTS, TEXTBOOK OF CONTRACEPTIVE PRACTICE (Cambridge, England: Cambridge U. Press 1969).
29. *Pill—A Legal and Social Dilemma*, 45 TEMP. L.Q. 484 (1972).
30. Pilpel, *Birth Control and a New Birth of Freedom*, 28 OHIO ST. L.J. 679 (1966).
31. Pilpel & Wechsler, *Birth Control: Teenagers and the Law*, 1 FAM. PLANN. PERSPECT. 29 (1969).
32. Pilpel & Wechsler, *Birth Control, Teenagers and the Law: A New Look, 1971*, 3 FAM. PLANN. PERSPECT. (1971).
33. PLANNED PARENTHOOD FEDERATION OF AMERICA—WORLD POPULATION EMERGENCY CAMPAIGN, BIRTH CONTROL AND PUBLIC POLICY (New York: Planned Parenthood Federation of America 1962).
34. Ravenholt & Pietrow, *Use of Oral Contraceptives in Developing Countries*, 8 PAKISTAN J. MED. RESEARCH (1969).
35. Rowan, *Blacks Being Misled on Birth Control*, Kansas City Star, Feb. 2, 1970.
36. ST. JOHN-STEVAS, N., THE AGONIZING CHOICE: BIRTH CONTROL, RELIGION AND THE LAW (London: Eyre & Spottiswoode 1971).

37. SILVERMAN, M. & LEE, P., PILLS, PROFITS AND POLITICS (Berkeley: U. of Cal. Press 1974).
38. Smith, *The History and Future of the Legal Battle Over Birth Control*, 49 CORNELL L.Q. (1964).
39. Solloway, *The Legal and Political Aspects of Birth Control in the United States*, 15 LAW & CONTEMP. PROB. 600 (1960).
40. STEPAN, J. & KELLOGG, E., THE WORLD'S LAWS ON CONTRACEPTIVES, Monograph No. 17, Law and Population Programme (Medford, Mass.: The Fletcher School of Law and Diplomacy 1973).
41. Tunkel, *Modern Anti-Pregnancy Techniques and the Criminal Law*, 1974 CRIM. L. REV. 461 (1974).
42. WESTOFF, C. & WESTOFF, L., FROM NOW TO ZERO: FERTILITY, CONTRACEPTION AND ABORTION IN AMERICA (Boston: Little, Brown 1971).
43. Young et al., *Court-Ordered Contraception*, 55 A.B.A.J. 223 (1969).

C. *Population Planning*

1. Agarwala, *Population Control in India*, 71 LAW & CONTEMP. PROB. 577 (1960).
2. AGENCY FOR INTERNATIONAL DEVELOPMENT, ASSISTANCE FOR FAMILY PLANNING PROGRAMS IN DEVELOPING COUNTRIES (January 1967).
3. AGENCY FOR INTERNATIONAL DEVELOPMENT, POPULATION PROGRAM ASSISTANCE (1967 through 1970).
4. ALLISON, A., ED., POPULATION CONTROL (Middlesex, England: Penguin Books Ltd. 1970).
5. AMERICAN ASSEMBLY, THE POPULATION DILEMMA (Englewood Cliffs, N.J.: Prentice-Hall 1963).
6. ANDERSON, ED., CHANGING LAW IN DEVELOPING COUNTRIES (New York: Praeger 1963).
7. BACHRACH, P. & BERGMAN, E., POWER AND CHOICE: FORMULATION OF AMERICAN POPULATION POLICY (Lexington, Mass.: Lexington Books 1973).
8. Baker, *Population Control in the Year 2000—The Constitutionality of Placing Anti-Fertility Agents in the Water Supply*, 1 OHIO ST. L.J. 20 (1971).
9. BEHRMAN, S. ET AL., FERTILITY AND FAMILY PLANNING: A WORLD VIEW (Ann Arbor: U. Mich. Press 1969).
10. Berelson, *Beyond Family Planning*, 163 SCIENCE 533 (1969).
11. BERELSON, B., ED., FAMILY PLANNING PROGRAMS: AN INTERNATIONAL SURVEY (New York: Basic Books 1969).
12. BERELSON, B., ED., FAMILY PLANNING AND POPULATION PROGRAMS: A

REVIEW OF WORLD DEVELOPMENTS (Chicago: U. Chi. Press 1966).

13. BERELSON, B., ED., POPULATION POLICY IN DEVELOPED COUNTRIES (New York: McGraw Hill 1974).

14. BERGMAN, E. ET AL., EDS., POPULATION POLICY-MAKING IN THE UNITED STATES (Lexington, Mass.: Lexington Books 1974).

15. Berman & Dolan, *Oral Contraceptives: An Interests Analysis*, 21 KAN. L. REV. 493 (1973).

16. *Beyond the Eye of the Beholder: Aesthetics and Objectivity*, 71 MICH. L. REV. 1438 (1973).

17. Bitker, *Genocide Revisited*, 56 A.B.A.J. 71 (January 1970).

18. Blacker, *Stages in Population Growth*, 39 EUGENICS REV. 88 (1947).

19. Blaustein, *Arguendo: The Legal Challenge of Population Control*, 1 LAW & SOC'Y REV. 106 (1968).

20. BRAYER, F., ED., WORLD POPULATION AND U.S. GOVERNMENT POLICY AND PROGRESS (Wash., D.C.: Georgetown U. Press 1968).

21. Brodie, *Family Planning Service and Population Research Act of 1970*, 5 FAMILY L.Q. 424 (1971).

22. Bronfenbrenner & Buttrick, *Population Control in Japan: An Economic Theory and Its Application*, 3 LAW & CONTEMP. PROB. 553 (1960).

23. BROWN, H. & A. SWEEZY, EDS., POPULATION PERSPECTIVE, 1971 (S. Fr., Cal.: Freeman, Cooper & Co. 1972).

24. BROWN, H. & A. SWEEZY, EDS., POPULATION PERSPECTIVE, 1972 (S. Fr., Cal.: Freeman, Cooper & Co. 1973).

25. BROWN, H. ET AL., POPULATION PERSPECTIVE, 1973 (S. Fr., Cal.: Freeman, Cooper & Co. 1973).

26. BULATAO, B., ATTITUDES TOWARD LEGAL MEASURES FOR POPULA-TION CONTROL: SOCIAL-PSYCHOLOGICAL FACTORS AFFECTING ETHICAL-CULTURAL ACCEPTABILITY (Quezon City: U. Philippines 1974).

27. Bulatao & Lee, *The Impact of Law on Fertility Behavior: Perspectives of Philippine Influentials*, 3 PHILIPPINE L.J. 324 (1973).

28. Caldwell, *The Control of Family Size in Tropical Africa*, 2 DEMOG-RAPHY 598 (1968).

29. CALLAHAN, D., ED., THE AMERICAN POPULATION DEBATE (Garden City: Doubleday Anchor 1971).

30. CALLAHAN, D., ETHICS AND POPULATION LIMITATION (An Occasional Paper of the Population Council) (New York: The Population Council 1969-70).

31. CENTER FOR FAMILY PLANNING PROGRAM DEVELOPMENT, FAMILY PLANNING PROGRAMS IN THE UNITED STATES (New York: C.F.P.P.D. 1969).

32. Chamberlain, *Population Control—The Legal Approach to a Biological Imperative,* 1 ECOLOGY L.Q. 143 (Winter 1971).
33. CHAPLIN, D., ED., POPULATION POLICIES AND GROWTH IN LATIN AMERICA (Lexington, Mass.: Lexington Books 1971).
34. Chisholm, *Dangerous Complacency Towards Biological Warfare,* THE HUMANIST (Jan. Feb. 1960).
35. Clark , *Law as an Instrument of Population Control,* 40 U. COLO. L. REV. 179 (1968).
36. Clark, *Population Redistribution Proposal: Put Orwell at the Pump,* 51 J. URBAN LAW 1 (1973).
37. Claxton, *Population and Law,* 5 INT'L LAW 1 (1971).
38. CLINTON, R. AND GORDON K., EDS., RESEARCH IN THE POLITICS OF POPULATION (Lexington, Mass.: Heath 1972).
39. COHEN, M., LAW AND POPULATION CLASSIFICATION. Monograph #5, Law and Population Programme (Medford, Mass.: The Fletcher School of Law and Diplomacy 1972).
40. COMMISSION ON POPULATION GROWTH AND THE AMERICAN FUTURE, POPULATION AND THE AMERICAN FUTURE (Interim Report March 1971).
41. COMMISSION ON POPULATION GROWTH AND THE AMERICAN FUTURE, POPULATION AND THE AMERICAN FUTURE (Final Report 1972).
42. COMMITTEE ON LEGAL ASPECTS OF THE INDONESIAN PLANNED PARENTHOOD ASSOCIATION, LEGAL ASPECTS OF FAMILY PLANNING IN INDONESIA. Monograph #4, Law and Population Programme (Medford, Mass.: The Fletcher School of Law and Diplomacy 1972).
43. *Constitutional Problems of Population Control,* 4 J. LAW REFORM 63 (1970).
44. Cook, *Formulating Population Policy: A Case Study of the United States,* 3 ENVIR. AFFAIRS 47 (1974).
45. COOK, R., POPULATION AWAKENING (New York: Victor Fund for the Int'l Planned Parenthood Fund 1966).
46. COOK, R., POPULATION LAW: A SYSTEMS APPROACH TO SINGAPORE'S FAMILY PLANNING AND ABORTION ACTS OF 1969 (New York: The Population Council 1970).
47. Cortes, *Population and the Law: The Fundamental Rights Aspects in the Philippine Setting,* 3 PHILIPPINE L.J. 303 (1973).
48. Davis, *Population Policy: Will Current Programs Succeed?* 158 SCIENCE 732 (Nov. 10, 1967).
49. Davis, *Overpopulated America,* 162 THE NEW REPUBLIC, No. 2, Issue 2872 (Jan. 10, 1970).
50. Dembitz, *Law and Family Planning,* 1 FAMILY L.Q. 103 (1967).

51. DEPT. OF STATE, POLICY PLANNING COUNCIL, FOREIGN IMPLICATIONS OF THE WORLD POPULATION EXPLOSION (Publication No. PPC-61-3 —).

52. Dileo, *Directions and Dimensions of Population Policy in the United States: Alternatives for Legal Reform*, 46 TUL. L. REV. 184 (1971).

53. DOBERENZ & TAYLOR, EDS., PROCEEDINGS OF THE SECOND ANNUAL SYMPOSIUM ON POPULATION GROWTH AND FAMILY PLANNING PROGRAMS (Green Bay: U. Wisc., January 8 & 9 1971).

54. Dombroff & Lifhitz, *Overpopulation: No Strength in Numbers*, 6 FAMILY L.Q. 93 (1972).

55. Dornberg, *Eastern Europe: Programming the Population*, 5 Ms. 128 (1974).

56. DOUBLET, J. & DE VILLEDARY, H., LAW AND POPULATION GROWTH IN FRANCE. Monograph #12, Law and Population Programme (Medford, Mass.: The Fletcher School of Law and Diplomacy 1973).

57. Drinan, *The Loving Decision and the Freedom to Marry*, 29 OHIO ST. L.J. 358 (1968).

58. Driver, *Population Policies of State Governments in the United States: Some Preliminary Observations*, 15 VILL. L. REV. 743 (1970).

59. EDGAR, H. AND GREENAWALT K., THE LEGAL TRADITION AND SOME POPULATION CONTROL PROPOSALS (Hastings-on-Hudson, N.Y.: The Hastings Center, —).

60. The Effect of Family Law and Practice, U.N. Doc. No. E/CN.6/575/Add.1, 69-89 (19—).

61. ELDRIDGE, H., POPULATION POLICIES: A SURVEY OF RECENT DEVELOPMENTS (Wash., D.C.: Int'l Union for the Scientific Study of Population 1954).

62. Elkins, *Constitutional Problems of Population Control*, 4 U. MICH. J.L. REFORM. 120 (1970).

63. Erlich & Erlich, *Introduction to Symposium: Population and the Law*, 23 HASTINGS L.J. 1345 (1972).

64. EWALD, JR., ED., ENVIRONMENT AND POLICY (Bloomington: Ind. U. Press 1968).

65. Fagley, *A Protestant View of Population Control*, 25 LAW & CONTEMP. PROB. 470 (1960).

66. Falk, *World Population and International Law*, 63 AM. J. INT'L L. 514 (1969).

67. Faundes & Luukkainen, *Health and Family Planning Services in the Chinese People's Republic*, 3 STUDIES IN FAM. PLANN. 165 (1972). (1972).

68. FELDMAN, D., BIRTH CONTROL IN JEWISH LAW (New York: N.Y.U. Press 1968).

69. FINLAY, H. AND GLASBEEK, S., FAMILY PLANNING AND THE LAW IN AUSTRALIA (Sydney: Family Planning Assoc. of Australia 1973).

70. Fletcher, *Legal Aspects of the Decision Not to Prolong Life*, 65 J. AM. MED. ASSOC. 68 (1968).

71. FREEDMAN, R. ET AL., FAMILY PLANNING, STERILITY AND POPULATION GROWTH (New York: McGraw-Hill 1959).

72. Friedman, *Interference with Human Life: Some Jurisprudential Reflections*, 70 COLUM. L. REV. 1058 (1970).

73. GADALLA, POPULATION PROBLEMS AND FAMILY PLANNING PROGRAMS IN EGYPT (Reprint, Series No. 14) (Cairo: Am. U. in Cairo: Social Research Center 1968).

74. GARDNER, R., POPULATION GROWTH: A WORLD PROBLEM, STATEMENT OF U.S. POLICY (Dept. of State January 1963). Originally printed as U.N. Doc. X/C.2/L.657 (1963).

75. Goldenberg, *Crimes Against Humanity—1945-1970*, 10 W. ONT. L. REV. 1 (1971).

76. Golding & Golding, *Ethical and Value Issues in Population Limitation and Distribution in the United States*, 24 VAND. L. REV. 495 (1971).

77. Gray, *Does Population Control = Zero Black Children?* OB. GYN. NEWS (June 1, 1971).

78. GRAY, V., POLITICAL ISSUES IN U.S. POPULATION POLICY (Lexington, Mass.: Lexington Books 1974).

79. Greenawalt, *Criminal Law and Population Control*, 24 VAND. L. REV. 465 (1971).

80. Greene, *Federal Birth Control: Progress Without Policy*, REPORTER (Nov. 18, 1965).

81. GREEP, R., ED., HUMAN FERTILITY AND POPULATION PROBLEMS (Cambridge, Mass.: Schenkman 1968).

82. Gross, *Family Planning as a Human Right; Some Jurisprudential Reflections on Natural Rights and Positive Law*, 2 LAW Q.J. OF THE INDIAN LAW INST. 85 (1974).

83. HALL, P., LAW AND POPULATION GROWTH IN SINGAPORE. Monograph #9, Law and Population Programme (Medford, Mass.: The Fletcher School of Law and Diplomacy 1973).

84. HARDIN, G., ED., POPULATION, EVOLUTION AND BIRTH CONTROL (S. Fr.: W. H. Freeman 1964).

85. HARKAVY, O., F. JAFFE & S. WISHIK, IMPLEMENTING DHEW POLICY ON FAMILY PLANNING AND POPULATION (New York: Colum. U. Press 1967).

86. HART, H., LAW, LIBERTY AND MORALITY (New York: Vintage Books 1966).

87. HAUSER, ED., THE POPULATION DILEMMA (Englewood Cliffs, N.J.: Prentice-Hall, 1963).
88. HAUSER, WORLD POPULATION PROBLEMS (New York: Foreign Policy Assoc. 1965).
89. Hellegers, *Law and the Common Good*, COMMONWEAL (June 30, 1967).
90. Hill et al., *Population Control in Puerto Rico*, 15 LAW & CONTEMP. PROB. 3 (1960).
91. HILL, R. ET AL., THE FAMILY AND POPULATION CONTROL (Chapel Hill: U.N.C. Press 1959).
92. HSU, S., FROM TABOO TO NATIONAL POLICY: THE TAIWAN FAMILY PLANNING UP TO 1970 (Taiwan: Chinese Center for Int'l Training in Family Planning).
93. INDONESIA PLANNED PARENTHOOD ASSOCIATION, LEGAL ASPECTS OF FAMILY PLANNING (Djakarta, Indonesia: I.P.P.A. 1971).
94. INTERNATIONAL PLANNED PARENTHOOD FEDERATION, FAMILY PLANNING IN THE MIDDLE EAST AND NORTH AFRICA (Beirut, Lebanon: I.P.P.F. 1973).
95. INTERNATIONAL PLANNED PARENTHOOD FEDERATION, POPULATION (London, England: I.P.P.F. 1973).
96. INTERNATIONAL SOCIAL SECURITY ASSOCIATION, FAMILY ALLOWANCES, DEVELOPMENTS IN FAMILY ALLOWANCES LEGISLATION SINCE 1953 (Report 16, 17) (Geneva: I.S.S.A. 1965).
97. Jaffe, *Population Trends and Controls in Underdeveloped Countries*, 3 LAW & CONTEMP. PROB. 509 (1960).
98. JOHNSON, LIFE WITHOUT BIRTH (Boston: Little, Brown & Co. 1970).
99. Katz, *Legal Dimensions of Population Policy*, 69 SOC. SCI. Q. 731 (1969).
100. Kellogg, *Population Growth and Indonesian Law*, 3 CORNELL INT'L L.J. 93 (1970).
101. Kindregan, *States' Power Over Human Fertility and Individual Liberty*, 23 HASTINGS L.J. 1401 (1972).
102. KISER, C., ed., *Forty Years of Reseach in Human Fertility*, 49 MILBANK MEMORIAL FUND Q. No. 4, Part 2 (1971).
103. KISER, C., ED., RESEARCH IN FAMILY PLANNING (Princeton, N.J.: Princeton U. Press 1968).
104. KLOSS, D. & RAISBECK B., LAW AND POPULATION GROWTH IN THE UNITED KINGDOM. Monograph #11, Law and Population Programme (Medford, Mass.: The Fletcher School of Law and Diplomacy 1973).
105. KOYA, Y., PIONEERING IN FAMILY PLANNING (Tokyo: Med. Pub. 1967).
106. Lamm, *The Reproductive Revolution*, 56 A.B.A.J. 41 (1970).
107. Lanlan, *Birth-Rate Decline in Warsaw Pact Area Threatens Soviet Growth Plans*, 20 NATO REV. 15 (Jan./Feb. 1972).

108. Law and Population in the Philippines, Law and Population Programme (Medford, Mass.: The Fletcher School of Law and Diplomacy 1974).

109. Lee, *Human Rights and Population: A Strategy for Action,* 12 Va. J. Int'l L. 309 (1972).

110. Lee, L., Law, Human Rights and Population: A Strategy for Action. Monograph #6, Law and Population Programme (Medford, Mass.: The Fletcher School of Law and Diplomacy, 1972).

111. Lee, L., Law and Family Planning. Monograph #1, Law and Population Program (Medford, Mass.: The Fletcher School of Law and Diplomacy, 1971).

112. Lee, *Law and Family Planning,* 4 Studies in Fam. Plann. 1 (1971).

113. Lee, L., and Larson A., eds., Population and the Law (Durham, N.C.: Rule of Law Press; Leyden: A.W. Sijthoff, 1971).

114. *Legal Analysis and Population Control: The Problem of Coercion,* 84 Harv. L. Rev. 1856 (1971).

115. Linner, B., Sex and Society in Sweden (New York: Harper & Row 1971).

116. Longo, *Constitutional Problems of Population Control,* 4 J. Law Reform 63 (April, 1970).

117. McCormack, The Population Problem (New York: Thomas Y. Crowell Co. 1970).

118. McCracken, *The Population Controllers,* 5 Commentary 45 (1972).

119. Mackey, J., ed., Morals, Law and Authority (Dayton, Ohio: Pflaum 1969).

120. Maggs, P. Law and Population Growth in Eastern Europe. Monograph #3, Law and Population Programme (Medford, Mass.: The Fletcher School of Law and Diplomacy 1971).

121. Maggs, P., Legal Regulation of Population Movement To, From, and Within the United States—A Survey of Current Law and Constitutional Limitations. Paper #25 (Honolulu: East-West Center).

122. Maramatsu, M. & Harper, P., eds. Population Dynamics, Inter-National Action and Training Programs (Baltimore: The Johns Hopkins U. Press 1965).

123. Mayer, *Toward a Non-Malthusian Population Policy,* — Colum. Forum 5 (1969).

124. Measham, A., Family Planning in North Carolina: The Politics of a Lukewarm Issue (Chapel Hill: Carolina Population Center, 1972).

125. Measures, Policies and Programmes Affecting Fertility with Particular Reference to National Family Planning Pro-

GRAMMES (Provisional Report of the Secretary General) U.N. Doc. E/CN.9/232 (Sept. 17, 1969).

126. Montgomery, *Population Explosion and U.S. Law*, 22 HASTINGS L.J. 629 (1971).

127. Moore, *Legal Action to Stop Our Population Explosion*, 12 CLEV.-MAR. L. REV. 314 (1963).

128. Miller & Davidson, *Observations on Population Policy-Making and the Constitution*, 40 GEO. WASH. L. REV. 618 (1972).

129. MINISTRY OF HEALTH AND SOCIAL AFFAIRS, NATIONAL FAMILY PLANNING PROGRAM (Korea: Ministry of Health and Social Affairs 1972).

130. Muller & Jaffe, *Financing Fertility-Related Health Services in the United States, 1972-1978: A Preliminary Projection*, 4 FAM. PLANN. PERSP. 6 (1972).

131. MURAMATSU, JAPAN'S EXPERIENCE IN FAMILY PLANNING, PAST AND PRESENT (Tokyo: Family Planning Federation of Japan 1967).

132. Nanda, *The Need for a Global Population Policy—Now*, DENVER L.J. 17 (Special Issue 1971).

133. NATIONAL ACADEMY OF SCIENCES, ED., RAPID POPULATION GROWTH: CONSEQUENCES AND POLICY IMPLICATIONS (Baltimore: Johns Hopkins Press 1971).

134. *National Population Programs and Policy: Social and Legal Implications—A Symposium*, 15 VILL. L. REV. 785 (1970).

135. PAKISTAN—A PROFILE (Lahore, Pakistan: The Pakistan Population Planning Council and the Family Planning Association of Pakistan 1973).

136. PARKES, A., ED., TOWARDS A POPULATION POLICY FOR THE UNITED KINGDOM (London: The London School of Economics 1970).

137. PARSONS, J., POPULATION VERSUS LIBERTY (London: Pemberton 1971).

138. PARTAN, D., POPULATION IN THE UNITED NATIONS SYSTEM: DEVELOPING THE LEGAL CAPACITY AND PROGRAMS OF U. N. AGENCIES (Leyden: A.W. Sijthoff; Durham, N.C.: Rule of Law Press 1972).

139. PETERSON, W., POPULATION (New York: The Macmillan Co. 1961).

140. PHILIPPINE LAWS AFFECTING POPULATION (Manila: U. Philippines L. Center).

141. Phillips & Deutsch, *Pitfalls of the Genocide Convention*, 56 A.B.A.J. 641 (1970).

142. PHILLIPS & MORRIS, MARRIAGE LAWS IN AFRICA (New York: Oxford U. Press 1971).

143. PILPEL, H., BRIEF SURVEY ON U.S. POPULATION LAW. Monograph #2 Law and Population Programme (Medford, Mass.: The Fletcher School of Law and Diplomacy 1971).

144. Piotrow, P., World Population Crisis: The U.S. Response (New York: Praeger 1973).
145. Planned Parenthood Federation of America, Laws Relating to Birth Control and Family Planning in the United States (New York: P.P.F.A. 1968).
146. Pohlman, E., Incentives and Compensations in Population Programs (Chapel Hill: Carolina Population Center 1971).
147. Pohlman, E., ed., Population: A Clash of Prophets (New York: New American Library 1973).
148. *Population Control*, 25 Law & Contemp. Prob. 377 (1960).
149. *Population Control—The Legal Approach to a Biological Imperative*, 1 Ecology L.Q. 143 (1971).
150. The Population Crisis Committee, Population Problems and Policies in Economically Advanced Countries (New York: The Population Crisis Committee in association with the Ditchley Foundation 1972).
151. *Population Density Crisis*, 10 Calif. W. L. Rev. 147 (1973).
152. *Population and the Law: A Symposium*, 6 Trial 10 (1970).
152. Population Policy in Czechoslovakia (Prague: Orbis 1974).
153. *Population Policy-Making: Reproductive Freedom and the 'Compelling' State Interest*, 42 U.M.K.C.L. Rev. 201 (1973).
154. *Population: the Problem, the Constitution, and a Proposal*, 11 J. Fam. L. 319 (1971).
155. The Population Problems Research Council, ed., Family Planning in Japan—A Private Survey by the Mainichi Newspapers (Tokyo: P.P.R.C., The Mainichi Newspapers 1970).
156. Population Program of India (New Delhi: Ministry of Health, Family Planning and Urban Devel. 1967).
157. Population—Special Issue in Finance and Development (Vol. 10, No. 4) (Wash., D.C.: Intern'l Monetary Fund and the World Bank Group 1973).
158. President's Committee on Population and Family Planning, Population and Family Planning: The Transition from Concern to Action (1968).
159. Program on Population and Ethics, Ethics, Population and the American Tradition (Hastings-on-Hudson, N.Y.: Institute for Society, Ethics and the Life Sciences 1971).
160. Program Quarterly, No. 67 (S. Fr. Cal.: The Asia Foundation 1973).
161. *Progress and Problems of Fertility Control around the World*, 2 Demography 539 (Special Issue 1968).
162. Rauch, *Federal Family Planning Programs: Choice or Coercion?* 15 Social Work — (1970).

163. Ravenholt, *The A.I.D. Population and Family Planning Programs—Goals, Scope and Progress*, 5 DEMOGRAPHY 564 (1968).

164. Reiss, *Law and Sociology: Some Issues for the 70's*, 5 U. RICHMOND L. REV. 20 (1970).

165. REPORT ON POPULATION AND LAW CONFERENCE (Seoul: Population Research Council 1972).

166. REVELLE, R., ED., RAPID POPULATION GROWTH: CONSEQUENCES AND POLICY IMPLICATIONS (Baltimore: The Johns Hopkins Press 1971).

167. THE ROLE OF WOMEN IN THE FAMILY: STATUS OF WOMEN AND FAMILY PLANNING (Progress Report by the Special Rapporteur, Mrs. Helvi Sipilä) U.N. ECOSOC Doc. E/CN.6/564 (1971).

168. ROSEN, R., LAW AND POPULATION GROWTH IN JAMAICA. Monograph #10, Law and Population Programme (Medford, Mass.: The Fletcher School of Law and Diplomacy 1973).

169. St. John-Stevas, *A Roman Catholic View of Population Control*, 25 LAW & CONTEMP. PROB. 445 (1960).

170. Samuel, *Development of India's Policy of Population Control*, 44 MILBANK MEMORIAL FUND Q. 1 (19—).

171. SANEY, LAW AND POPULATION GROWTH IN IRAN. Monograph #21, Law and Population Programme (Medford, Mass.: The Fletcher School of Law and Diplomacy 1974).

172. SAYNEY, P., ED., IRANIAN LAWS AFFECTING POPULATION (Teheran: Law and Population Project 1974).

173. SENATE COMM. ON LABOR AND PUBLIC WELFARE, DECLARATION OF UNITED STATES POLICY OF POPULATION STABILIZATION BY VOLUNTARY MEANS, S. Doc. No. —, 92d Cong., 1st Sess. (1971).

174. SENATE COMM. ON LABOR AND PUBLIC WELFARE, FAMILY PLANNING PROGRAM, HEARINGS BEFORE THE COMMITTEE. 89th Cong., 2d Sess. (1966).

175. SENATE COMM. ON LABOR AND PUBLIC WELFARE, PROGRESS REPORT ON THE FIVE-YEAR PLAN FOR FAMILY PLANNING SERVICES AND POPULATION RESEARCH PROGRAMS SUBMITTED BY THE SECRETARY OF HEALTH, EDUCATION, AND WELFARE. 92d Cong., 2d Sess. (1972).

176. SENATE COMM. ON LABOR AND PUBLIC WELFARE, REPORT OF THE SECRETARY OF HEALTH, EDUCATION, AND WELFARE SUBMITTING A FIVE-YEAR PLAN FOR FAMILY PLANNING SERVICES AND POPULATION RESEARCH PROGRAMS, S. Doc. No. 92d Cong., 1st Sess. (1971).

177. SHEPS, M. & RIDLEY, J., PUBLIC HEALTH AND POPULATION CHANGE (Pitt., Pa.: U. of Pitt. Press 1965).

178. Sirilla, *Family Planning and the Rights of the Poor*, 13 CATHOLIC L.J. 42 (1967).

179. Sison, *Population Laws of the Philippines*, 3 PHILIPPINE L.J. 356 (1973).
180. SOCIETY OF FRIENDS: AMERICAN FRIENDS SERVICE COMMITTEE, WHO SHALL LIVE? MAN'S CONTROL OVER BIRTH AND DEATH: A REPORT (New York: Hill & Wang 1970).
181. Spengler, *Population Control: Multidimensional Task*, 24 VAND. L. REV. 525 (1971).
182. Spengler, *Population Pressure, Housing and Habitat*, 32 LAW & CONTEMP. PROB. 191 (1967).
183. Starkman, *Control of Life: Unexamined Law and the Life Worth Living*, 11 OSGOODE HALL L.J. (1973).
184. Steinberg, *Law, Development and Korean Society*, J. COMP. ADMIN. (1971).
185. STYCOS & BLACK, CONTROL OF HUMAN FERTILITY IN JAMAICA (Ithaca, N.Y.: Cornell U. Press 1964).
186. SWEE-HOCK, SINGAPORE: POPULATION IN TRANSITION (Phila.: U. of Pa. Press 1970).
187. SYMONDS, R. & CARDER, M. UNITED NATIONS AND THE POPULATION QUESTION 1945-1970 (Toronto: McGraw-Hill 1973).
188. Taylor, *Five Stages in a Practical Population Policy*, 10 INT'L DEVEL. REV. 14 (1968).
189. THOMLINSON, R., THAILAND'S POPULATION (Bangkok: The Population Council and Chulalongkorn U. 1971).
190. Tietze, *The Current Status of Fertility Control*, 3 LAW & CONTEMP. PROB. 441 (1960).
191. UCHE U. LAW AND POPULATION GROWTH IN KENYA. Monograph #22, Law and Population Programme (Medford, Mass.: The Fletcher School of Law and Diplomacy 1974).
192. UNITED NATIONS, HUMAN FERTILITY AND NATIONAL DEVELOPMENT (New York: United Nations 1971).
193. UNITED NATIONS, MEASURES, POLICIES AND PROGRAMMES AFFECTING FERTILITY, WITH PARTICULAR REFERENCE TO NATIONAL FAMILY PLANNING PROGRAMS (Department of Economic and Social Affairs, Population Studies No. 51 1972).
194. THE UNITED NATIONS AND POPULATION: MAJOR RESOLUTIONS AND INSTRUMENTS (New York: U.N. Fund for Population Activities 1973).
195. UNIV. OF PHILIPPINES POPULATION INSTITUTE, PHILIPPINE POPULATION: PROFILES, PROSPECTS, PROBLEMS (Philippines: U. of Philippines Population Institute 1970).
196. Weintraub, *Population and Law: Legal Control of the Demographic Process*, 5 EUROPEAN DEMOGRAPHIC INFORMATION BULL., No. 3 (1974).
197. WHELPTON, P., CAMPBELL A., & PATTERSON J., FERTILITY AND FAM-

ILY PLANNING IN THE UNITED STATES (Princeton, N.J.: Princeton U. Press 1961).

198. WOGAMAN, J., ED., THE POPULATION CRISIS AND MORAL RESPONSI- BILITY (Wash., D.C.: Public Affairs Press 1973).

199. WOLF, B., ANTI-CONTRACEPTION LAW IN SUB-SAHARAN FRAN- CAPHONE AFRICA: SOURCES AND RAMIFICATIONS. Monograph #15, Law and Population Programme (Medford, Mass.: The Fletcher School of Law and Diplomacy 1973).

200. WORLD POPULATION YEAR, THE UNESCO COURIER (Place de Fon- tenoy, Paris: UNESCO, Special Issue May 1974).

201. YETTE, S., THE CHOICE: THE ISSUE OF BLACK SURVIVAL IN AMERICA (New York: Putnam 1971).

202. YOUNG, L., ED., POPULATION IN PERSPECTIVE (New York: Oxford U. Press 1968).

D.   *Sterilization*

1. Addison, *Legal Aspects of Sterilization and Contraception*, 35 MEDICO L.J. VICTORIA 164 (—).

2. Bartholomew, *Legal Implications of Voluntary Sterilization Operations*, 2 MELBOURNE U.L. REV. 77 (1960).

3. Bligh, *Sterilization and Mental Retardation*, 51 A.B.A.J. 1059 (1965).

4. Bravenec, *Voluntary Sterilization as a Crime: Application of Assault and Battery and of Mayhem*, 6. J. FAM. L. 94 (1966).

5. Champlin and Winslow, *Elective Sterilization*, 113 U. PA. L. REV. 415 (1965).

6. *Compulsory Eugenic Sterilization: For Whom Does Bell Toll?* 6 DUQUESNE U.L. REV. 145 (1967-68).

7. *Compulsory Sterilization: Weeding Mendel's Garden*, 22 DRAKE L. REV. 355 (1973).

8. *Contraceptive Sterilization: the Doctor, the Patient and the U.S. Con- stitution*, 25 U. FLA. L. REV. 327 (1973).

9. Ferster, *Eliminating the Unfit—Is Sterilization the Answer?* 27 OHIO ST. L.J. 591 (1966).

10. GILLETTE, P., THE VASECTOMY INFORMATION MANUAL (New York: Outerbridge & Lazard 1972).

11. Gray, *Compulsory Sterilization in a Free Society: Choices and Dilemmas*, 41 U. CIN. L. REV. 529 (1972).

12. Green, *Sterilization and the Law*, 5 MALAYAN L. REV. 105 (—).

13. *Hathaway v. Worcester City Hospital—The Right To Be Sterilized*, 47 TEMP. L.Q. 403 (1974).

14. *Human Sterilization*, 35 IOWA L. REV. 251 (1950).

15. *Individual and the Involuntary Sterilization Laws, 1966*, 31 ALBANY L. REV. 97 (1967).

16. Kindregan, *Sixty Years of Compulsory Eugenic Sterilization: 'Three Generations of Imbeciles' and the Constitution of the United States*, 43 CHI.-KENT L. REV. 123 (1966).
17. KONOTEY-AHULU, F., MEDICAL CONSIDERATIONS FOR LEGALIZING VOLUNTARY STERILIZATION. Monograph #13, Law and Population Programme (Medford, Mass: The Fletcher School of Law and Diplomacy 1973).
18. McWhirtes and Weijer, *Alberta Sterilization Act: A Genetic Critique*, 19 U. TORONTO L.J. 424 (1969).
19. Miller and Dean, *Civil and Criminal Liability of Physicians for Sterilization Operations*, 16 A.B.A.J. 158 (1930).
20. Paul, *Return of Punitive Sterilization Proposals*, 3 LAW & SOC. REV. 77 (1968).
21. STEPAN, J. AND KELLOGG, E., THE WORLD'S LAWS ON VOLUNTARY STERILIZATION FOR FAMILY PLANNING PURPOSES. Monograph #8, Law and Population Programme (Medford, Mass.: The Fletcher School of Law and Diplomacy 1973).
22. *Sterilization: A Continuing Controversy*, 1 U. SAN FRAN. L. REV. 159 (1966).
23. *Sterilization and Family Planning: The Physician's Civil Liability*, 56 GEO. L.J. 976 (1968).
24. *Sterilization of Mental Defectives*, 3 CUMBER-SAM. L. REV. 458 (1972).
25. Watkins and Watkins, *Alabama's Sterilization Law*, 35 ALA. L. REV. 85 (1974).
26. *Woman's Right to Voluntary Sterilization*, 22 BUFFALO L. REV. 291 (1972).

E. *Migration*

1. AGARWALA, B., LAW RELATING TO ENTRY INTO AND EXIT FROM INDIA (Delhi: Metropolitan Book Co. 1970).
2. *Aliyah of Soviet Jews: Protection of the Right of Emigration Under International Law*, 14 HARV. INT'L L.J. 89 (1973).
3. BOUSCAREN, A., INTERNATIONAL MIGRATIONS SINCE 1945 (New York: Praeger 1963).
4. ESPINA, V., IMMIGRATION & ALIEN REGISTRATION LAWS OF THE PHILIPPINES (Manila: Educational Book Store 1965).
5. HOOD, D. AND BELL, B., IN-MIGRATION AS A COMPONENT OF HAWAII'S POPULATION GROWTH: ITS LEGAL IMPLICATIONS (Honolulu: Legislative Reference Bureau 1973).
6. KANSAS, S., UNITED STATES IMMIGRATION: EXCLUSION, DEPORTATION, AND CITIZENSHIP OF THE UNITED STATES OF AMERICA (New York: Matthew Bender 1940).

7. KLAASEN, L. AND DREWE, P., MIGRATION POLICY IN EUROPE: A COM-
   PARATIVE STUDY (Lexington, Mass: Lexington Books 1973).
8. McDONALD, I., RACE RELATIONS AND IMMIGRATION LAW (London:
   Butterworths 1969).
9. MORRISON, P., MIGRATION FROM DISTRESSED AREAS: ITS MEANING
   FOR REGIONAL POLICY (Santa Monica, Cal: Rand 1973).
10. MORRISON, P., POPULATION MOVEMENTS AND THE SHAPE OF URBAN
    GROWTH: IMPLICATIONS FOR PUBLIC POLICY (Santa Monica, Cal:
    Rand 1973).
11. PARRY, C., NATIONALITY AND CITIZENSHIP LAWS OF THE COMMON-
    WEALTH AND OF THE REPUBLIC OF IRELAND (London: Stevens
    1961).
12. Plender, *The Exodus of Asians from East and Central Africa: Some
    Comparative and International Law Aspects*, 19 AM. J.C.L. 287
    (1971).
13. PLENDER, R., INTERNATIONAL MIGRATION LAW (Leydon: A. W. Sijthoff
    1972).
14. Ryan, *Immigration, Aliens and Naturalization in Australian Law* in
    INTERNATIONAL LAW IN AUSTRALIA (O'Connell ed.) (Sydney: Law
    Book Co. 1965).
15. SADLER, B., LEGAL AND ETHICAL IMPLICATIONS OF REDUCING IMMI-
    GRATION AS PART OF A COMPREHENSIBLE POPULATION POL-
    ICY (Hastings-on-Hudson, N.Y.: Information Program, Hastings
    Center, n.d.).
16. SINHA, A., THE LAW OF CITIZENSHIP AND ALIENS IN INDIA (New York:
    Asia Publishing House 1962).

F. *Sex Education*

1. AMRITHMAHAL, G. R., TRAINING OF FAMILY PLANNING WORKERS.
   IPPF-SEAOR Monograph No. 1 (Malaysia: IPPF-SEAOR —).
2. HARTMAN, D., FUNCTIONAL EDUCATION FOR FAMILY LIFE PLANNING,
   II (Monograph) (New York: World Education 1973).
3. KLINE, D. AND HARMAN, D., EDS., ISSUES IN POPULATION EDUCATION
   (Lexington, Mass: Lexington Books 1974).

G. *Land Control*

1. Aloi, *Recent Developments in Exclusionary Zoning—The Second Generation Cases and the Environment*, 6 S.W.U.L. REV. 88 (1974).
2. Ausness, *Land Use Controls in Coastal Areas*, 9 CALIF. W. L. REV.
   391 (1973).
3. Babcock, *Sanbornton and Morales: The Two Faces of 'Environment,"* 2
   ENVIR. AFFAIRS 758 (1973).

4. Bittker, *The Case of the Checker-Board Ordinance: An Experiment in Race Relations*, 71 YALE L.J. 1387 (1962).
5. Bosselman, *Can the Town of Ramapo Pass a Law to Bind the Rights of the Whole World?* 1 FLA. ST. U.L. REV. 231 (1973).
6. CLARK, C., POPULATION, GROWTH AND LAND USE (London: Macmillan 1967).
7. Clark & Grable, *Growth Control in California: Prospects for Local Government Implementation of Timing and Sequential Control of Residential Development*, 5 PACIFIC L.J. 570 (1974).
8. *Constitutional Law—Equal Protection—One-Family Zoning Ordinances*, 19 N.Y.L.F. 351 (1973).
9. *Constitutional Law—Equal Protection—Zoning Ordinance Restricting Use of One-Family Dwellings to No More than Two Unrelated Persons Unconstitutional*, 51 J. URBAN L. 307 (1973).
10. Cope, *Zoning: The definition of 'Family'*, 62 ILL. BAR J. 30 (1973).
11. Costonis, *Development Rights Transfer: An Exploratory Essay*, 83 YALE L.J. 75 (1973).
12. Cunningham, *Land-Use Control—The State and Local Programs*, 50 IOWA L. REV. 367 (1965).
13. Cutler, *Legal and Illegal Methods for Controlling Community Growth on the Urban Fringe*, 1961 WIS. L. REV. 370 (1961).
14. Elliot & Marcus, *From Euclid to Ramapo: New Directions in Land Development Controls*, 1 HOFSTRA L. REV. 56 (1973).
15. *Exclusionary Zoning: A Question of Balancing Due Process, Equal Protection and Environmental Concerns*, 8 SUFFOLK U.L. REV. 1190 (1974).
16. *Exclusionary Zoning: An Overview*, 47 TULSA L.J. 1056 (1973).
17. Fagin, *Regulating the Timing of Urban Development*, 20 LAW & CONTEMP. PROB. 298 (1955).
18. Freilich, *Development Timing, Monitoring and Controlling Growth*, 1974 PLANNING, ZONING, & EMINENT DOMAIN INSTITUTE 147 (1974).
19. Freilich, *Missouri Law of Land Use Controls: With National Perspectives*, 42 U.M.K.C. L. REV. 1 (1973).
20. *Golden v. Planning Board: Time Phased Development Control Through Zoning Standards*, 38 ALBANY L. REV. 142 (1973).
21. HAAR, C., ED., LAW AND LAND: ANGLO-AMERICAN PLANNING PRACTICE (Cambridge, Mass.: Harv. U. Press and M.I.T. Press 1964).
22. Heyman, *Innovative Land Regulation and Comprehensive Planning*, 13 SANTA CLARA L. REV. 183 (1972).
23. *Judicial Review of Land Bank Dispositions*, 41 U. CHI. L. REV. 377 (1974).
24. Lamm, *Legal Control of Population Growth and Distribution of a Quality Environment: The Land Use Alternatives*, 49 DENVER L.J. 1 (1972).

25. *Land Planning in a Democracy: A Symposium*, 20 LAW & CONTEMP. PROB. 197 No. 2 (1955).

26. *Local Versus State and Regional Zoning: The Tragedy of the Commons Revisited*, 47 CONN. B.J. 249 (1973).

27. Lundberg, *Land Use Planning and the Montana Legislature: An Overview for 1973*, 35 MONT. L. REV. 38 (1974).

28. Makuch, *Zoning: Avenues of Reform*, 1 DALHOUSIE L.J. 294 (1973).

29. MISFUD, F., CUSTOMARY LAND LAW IN AFRICA (Rome: Food and Agriculture Organization of the United Nations 1967).

30. Miller, *Current Status of Conditional Zoning*, 1974 PLANNING, ZONING & EMINENT DOMAIN INSTITUTE 121 (1974).

31. Minetz, *Zoning Ordinances which Restrict the Definition of a Family and Constitutional Considerations*, 62 ILL. BAR J. 38 (1973).

32. Navasky, *The Benevolent Housing Quota*, 6 HOW. L.J. 30 (1960).

33. *Phased Zoning: Regulation of the Tempo and Sequence of Land Development*, 26 STAN. L. REV. 585 (1974).

34. *Planned Unit Development and North Carolina Enabling Legislation*, 51 N.C.L. REV. 1455 (1973).

35. Reuter, *Eternalities in Urban Markets: An Empirical Test of the Zoning Ordinance of Pittsburgh*, 16 J. LAW & ECON. 313 (1973).

36. Sager, *Tight Little Islands: Exclusionary Zoning, Equal Protection and the Indigent*, 21 STAN. L. REV. 767 (1969).

37. Schiller, *Population Resettlement Plans May Save Dying Towns*, 6 NAT'L CIVIC REV. 291 (1972).

38. *State Land Use Control: Why Pending Federal Legislation Will Help*, 25 HASTINGS L.J. 1165 (1974).

39. Stever, *Land Use Controls, Takings and the Police Power—A Discussion of the Myth*, 15 N.H. BAR J. 149 (1974).

40. Sussna, *Attempt at Realism—Or Another Look at Exclusionary Zoning*, 1974 PLANNING, ZONING, & EMINENT DOMAIN INSTITUTE 83 (1974).

41. *Time Control, Sequential Zoning: The Ramapo Case*, 25 BAYLOR L. REV. 318 (1973).

42. *Town Ordinance Conditioning Approval of Residential Subdivision Plan on the Availability of Necessary Municipal Services Held Valid*, 1 FORDHAM URBAN L.J. 516 (1973).

43. *Up the Down-Sliding Scale: Boraas v. Village of Belle Terre and the Equal Protection Assault on Restrictive Definitions of "Family" in Zoning Ordinances*, 49 NOTRE DAME LAW 428 (1973).

44. *Validity of Zoning an Entire Municipality Exclusively Residential*, 7 URBAN L. ANN. 304 (1974).

45. Vestarl & Reid, *Toward a Rational Land Use Planning: An Interdisciplinary Approach*, 1 FLA. ST U L. REV. 266 (1973).

46. Williams, *Planning Law and Democratic Living*, 20 LAW & CONTEMP. PROB. 317 (1955).

47. Woodroff, *Land Use Control Policies and Population Distribution in America*, 23 HASTINGS L.J. 1427 (1972).

H. *Bibliographies*

1. CARDER, M., ET AL., EMERGING POPULATION ALTERNATIVES: AN ANNOTATED BIBLIOGRAPHY (Washington, D.C. 1974) (EMPA c/o American Freedom From Hunger Foundation).
2. DRIVER, E., WORLD POPULATION POLICIES: AN ANNOTATED BIBLIOGRAPHY (Lexington, Mass: Lexington Books 1972).
3. FLOYD, M., ABORTION BIBLIOGRAPHY FOR 1970 (Troy, N.Y.: Whitston 1972).
4. GOODE, S., POPULATION AND THE POPULATION EXPLOSION: A BIBLIOGRAPHY FOR 1970 (Troy, N.Y.: Whitston 1973).
5. WOJCICHOWSKY, S., ETHICAL-SOCIAL-LEGAL ANNOTATED BIBLIOGRAPHY ON ENGLISH LANGUAGE STUDIES ON ABORTION 1967-1972 (Toronto: Toronto Institute of Public Communications 1973).

I. *Conferences and Reports*

1. BERMAN, D. AND FOX, D., THE ROLE OF LAW IN POPULATION PLANNING—WORKING PAPERS AND PROCEEDINGS IN THE 16TH HAMMERSKJOLD FORUM (Dobbs Ferry, N.Y.: Oceana 1972).
2. HUMAN RIGHTS AND POPULATION: FROM THE PERSPECTIVES OF LAW, POLICY AND ORGANIZATION, Proceedings of the 2nd Annual Meeting of the International Advisory Committee on Population and Law in Tokyo, October 30-31, 1972 (1973).
3. NATIONAL POLICY PANEL REPORTS, WORLD POPULATION: A CHALLENGE TO THE UN AND ITS SYSTEM OF AGENCIES (New York 1969).
4. PAXMAN, J., ED., THE WORLD POPULATION CRISIS: POLICY IMPLICATIONS AND THE ROLE OF LAW, Proceedings, Regional Meeting of the American Society of Int'l Law at the University of Virginia, March 12, 13, 1971 (Charlottesville, Va.: John Bassett Moore Society of Int'l Law 1971).
5. POPULATION GROWTH: FAMILY PLANNING PROGRAMS, Proceedings of Symposium (Green Bay: University of Wisconsin 1971).
6. PROCEEDINGS OF THE EIGHTH INTERNATIONAL CONFERENCE OF THE INTERNATIONAL PLANNED PARENTHOOD FEDERATION, Santiago, Chile, April, 1967 (London: Int'l Planned Parenthood Federation 1967).
7. REPORT OF THE SYMPOSIUM ON POPULATION AND HUMAN RIGHTS, Amsterdam, January 21, 1974, U.N. Doc. E/Conf. 60/CBP/4 (Bucharest, Romania: Population Committee for World Population Conference 1974).

8. REPORT OF UNESCO WORKSHOP ON THE TEACHING OF POPULATION DYNAMICS IN LAW SCHOOLS (Paris: February 18-22, 1974).

9. A REPORT ON THE NEW ENGLAND REGIONAL CONFERENCE ON POPULATION, November 29-December 1, 1972 (New York, N.Y.: The Population Council 1973).

10. RFSU INTERNATIONAL SYMPOSIUM ON SEXOLOGY—BACKGROUND AND DEVELOPMENT IN SWEDEN (Stockholm: Swedish Association for Sex Education, RFSU 1970).

11. SADIK, N. ET AL., EDS., POPULATION CONTROL, Proceedings of the Pakistan International Family Planning Conference at Dacca (Islamabad: Pakistan Family Planning Council 1964).

12. SCHIMA, ET AL., EDS., ADVANCES IN VOLUNTARY STERILIZATION: PROCEEDINGS OF THE SECOND INTERNATIONAL CONFERENCE, GENEVA, SWITZERLAND, February 25-March 1, 1973 (New Jersey: Excepta Medica 1974).

13. SEMINAR ON LAW AND POPULATION (Jakarta: National Training and Research Center, Indonesian Planned Parenthood Association 1974).

14. SEMINAR ON LAW AND POPULATION (Colombo, Sri Lanka: Law and Population Project 1974).

15. SIXTH GENERAL ASSEMBLY AND CONFERENCE ON THE ADMINISTRATIVE IMPLICATIONS OF RAPID POPULATION GROWTH IN ASIA, 3 vols. (Manila: Europa Secretariat General 1971).

16. STUDY ON THE APPLICATION OF INTERNATIONAL BILATERAL AND MULTILATERAL INSTRUMENTS RELATING TO LEGISLATION ON FAMILY BENEFITS. Report IV (Geneva: Int'l Social Security Association 1968).

17. SYMPOSIUM ON LAW AND POPULATION: TEXT OF RECOMMENDATIONS, Tunis, June 17-21, 1974. Monograph #20, Law and Population Programme (Medford, Mass: The Fletcher School of Law and Diplomacy 1974).

18. SZABADY, E., ED., REPORT ON LEGISLATION AFFECTING DIRECTLY OR INDIRECTLY FERTILITY IN HUNGARY (Budapest 1972).

J. *Human Experimentation*

1. Cook, *Eugenics of Euthenics*, 37 ILL. L. REV. 287 (1943).

2. *Fetal Experimentation: Moral, Legal and Medical Implications*, 26 STAN. L. REV. 1191 (1974).

3. *Governmental Control of Research in Positive Eugenics*, 7 U. MICH J.L REF. 615 (1974).

4. Grad, *Legislative Responses to the New Biology: Limits and Possibilities*, 15 U.C.L.A. L. REV. 480 (1968).

5. Hardin, *Population, Biology and the Law*, 48 J. URBAN LAW 563 (1971).
6. KATZ, J., EXPERIMENTATION WITH HUMAN BEINGS (New York: Russell Sage Foundation 1972).
7. LINDMAN AND MCINTYRE, EDS., THE MENTALLY DISABLED AND THE LAW (Chicago: American Bar Foundation 1961).
8. Peters, *The Brave New World: Can the Law Bring Order Within Traditional Concepts of Due Process?* 4 SUFFOLK U.L. REV. 894 (1970).
9. Vukowich, *Dawning of the Brave New World-Legal, Ethical and Social Issues of Eugenics*, 1971 U. ILL. L.F. 189 (1971).
10. Weigel, *Eugenics and Law's Obligation to Man*, 14 S.T.L.J. 361 (1973).

II. PERIODICAL SERIES

1. AGENCY FOR INTERNATIONAL DEVELOPMENT, POPULATION PROGRAM ASSISTANCE (Washington, D.C.).
2. AGENCY FOR INTERNATIONAL DEVELOPMENT, WAR ON HUNGER (Washington, D.C.).
3. AMERICAN UNIVERSITIES FIELDSTAFF, INC., FIELDSTAFF REPORTS (Hanover, N.H.)
4. ASSOCIATION FOR VOLUNTARY STERILIZATION, NEWS (New York, N.Y.).
5. CENTER FOR ECONOMIC & SOCIAL INFORMATION, DEVELOPMENT FORUM (Geneva).
6. THE CENTRE FOR ECONOMIC AND SOCIAL INFORMATION AT UNITED NATIONS EUROPEAN HEADQUARTERS, ENVIRONMENT (Geneva).
7. CENTER FOR FAMILY PLANNING PROGRAM DEVELOPMENT, FAMILY PLANNING DIGEST (New York, N.Y.).
8. CENTER FOR FAMILY PLANNING PROGRAM DEVELOPMENT, FAMILY PLANNING POPULATION REPORTER (Washington, D.C.).
9. COMMITTEE FOR INTERNATIONAL COORDINATION OF NATIONAL RESEARCH IN DEMOGRAPHY, CICRED (Paris).
10. DEPT. OF MEDICAL AND PUBLIC AFFAIRS, THE GEORGE WASHINGTON UNIVERSITY MEDICAL CENTER, POPULATION REPORT (Washington, D.C.).
11. EAST-WEST CENTER, WORKING PAPERS OF THE EAST-WEST POPULATION INSTITUTE (Honolulu, Hawaii).
12. THE FAMILY PLANNING ASSOCIATION OF PAKISTAN, 1972 ANNUAL REPORT (Lahore, Pakistan 1972).
13. THE FUND FOR THE REPUBLIC, INC., THE CENTER MAGAZINE AND CENTER REPORT: A PUBLICATION OF THE CENTER FOR THE STUDY OF DEMOCRATIC INSTITUTIONS (Santa Barbara, Cal.).
14. INSTITUTE OF SOCIETY, ETHICS AND THE LIFE SCIENCES, THE HASTINGS CENTER REPORT (Hastings-on-Hudson, N.Y.).

15. INTERGOVERNMENTAL COORDINATING COMMITTEE OF SOUTH-EAST ASIA, IGCC NEWS (Selanger, Malaysia).
16. INTERNATIONAL COUNCIL OF VOLUNTARY AGENCIES, ICVA NEWS (New York, N.Y.).
17. INTERNATIONAL DEVELOPMENT RESEARCH CENTRE, THE IRDC REPORTS (Ottawa, Canada).
18. INTERNATIONAL LEAGUE FOR THE RIGHTS OF MAN, ANNUAL REPORTS (New York, N.Y.).
19. INTERNATIONAL LEGAL CENTER, NEWSLETTER (New York, N.Y.).
20. INTERNATIONAL PERSPECTIVES ON POPULATION PROGRAMS & POLICIES, POPULATION DYNAMICS QUARTERLY (Washington, D.C.).
21. INTERNATIONAL PLANNED PARENTHOOD ASSOCIATION, FAMILY PLANNING IN FIVE CONTINENTS (Herfordshire, Great Britain).
22. INTERNATIONAL PLANNED PARENTHOOD FEDERATION, NEWS (New York, N.Y.) (supplements included).
23. INTERNATIONAL PLANNED PARENTHOOD FEDERATION, PEOPLE (London).
24. INTERNATIONAL PLANNED PARENTHOOD FEDERATION, SITUATION REPORT (London).
25. INTERNATIONAL PROJECT ASSOCIATION IN VOLUNTARY STERILIZATION, INC., IPAVA NEWSLETTER (New York, N.Y.).
26. INVENTORY ANALYSIS TASK GROUP, EAST-WEST COMMUNICATION, REPORTS ON COUNTRY PROGRAMS AND FUTURE NEEDS FOR INTERNATIONAL ASSISTANCE IN POPULATION/FAMILY PLANNING IEC (Honolulu).
27. LEGAL-MEDICAL STUDIES, INC., REPORTER ON HUMAN REPRODUCTION AND THE LAW (Boston).
28. THE PATHFINDER FUND, FAMILY PLANS (Chestnut Hill, Mass.).
29. PLANNED PARENTHOOD FEDERATION OF AMERICA, FAMILY PLANNING PERSPECTIVES (New York, N.Y.).
30. PLANNED PARENTHOOD FEDERATION OF KOREA, PPFK ACTIVITY REPORT (Seoul, Korea).
31. PLANNED PARENTHOOD-WORLD POPULATION, MEMORANDUM (Washington, D.C.).
32. POPULATION ASSOCIATION OF AMERICA, DEMOGRAPHY (Washington, D.C.).
33. POPULATION ASSOCIATION OF AMERICA, PAA AFFAIRS (Washington, D.C.).
34. THE POPULATION COUNCIL, ANNUAL REPORTS (New York, N.Y.).
35. THE POPULATION COUNCIL, COUNTRY PROFILES (New York, N.Y.).
36. THE POPULATION COUNCIL, CURRENT PUBLICATIONS IN POPULATION/FAMILY PLANNING (New York, N.Y.).
37. THE POPULATION COUNCIL, POPULATION COUNCIL PERIODICAL INDEX (New York, N.Y.).

38. THE POPULATION COUNCIL, REPORTS ON POPULATION/FAMILY PLANNING (New York, N.Y.).
39. THE POPULATION COUNCIL, STUDIES IN FAMILY PLANNING (New York, N.Y.).
40. THE POPULATION COUNCIL AND THE INTERNATIONAL INSTITUTE FOR THE STUDY OF HUMAN REPRODUCTION, POPULATION CHRONICLE (Columbia University, New York, N.Y.).
41. POPULATION CRISIS COMMITTEE, POPULATION CRISIS (Washington, D.C.).
42. POPULATION DIVISION, UNITED NATIONS ECONOMIC COMMISSION FOR ASIA AND THE FAR EAST, ASIAN POPULATION PROGRAMME NEWS.
43. POPULATION DIVISION OF ECONOMIC AND SOCIAL AFFAIRS, UNITED NATIONS, POPULATION NEWSLETTER (New York, N.Y.).
44. POPULATION PROGRAMME CENTRE, ECONOMIC COMMISSION FOR AFRICA, AFRICAN POPULATION NEWSLETTER (Addis Ababa).
45. POPULATION REFERENCE BUREAU, INC., INTERCHANGE (Washington, D.C.).
46. POPULATION REFERENCE BUREAU, INC., POPULATION BULLETIN (Washington, D.C.).
47. POPULATION REFERENCE BUREAU, INC., POPULATION PROFILE (Washington, D.C.).
48. POPULATION REFERENCE BUREAU, INC., PRB SELECTIONS (Washington, D.C.).
49. POPULATION SERVICES INTERNATIONAL, INTERCOM (Washington, D.C.).
50. THE SEX INFORMATION AND EDUCATION COUNCIL OF THE UNITED STATES, INC., SEICUS (New York, N.Y.).
51. TRANSNATIONAL FAMILY RESEARCH INSTITUTE, ABORTION RESEARCH NOTES (Washington, D.C.).
52. UNESCO, INTERNATIONAL CO-ORDINATING COUNCIL OF THE PROGRAMME ON MAN AND THE BIOSPHERE (MAB) (Geneva).
53. UNITED NATIONS FUND FOR POPULATION ACTIVITIES, POPULI (New York, N.Y.).
54. UNITED NATIONS FUND FOR POPULATION ACTIVITIES, WPY BULLETIN (New York, N.Y.).
55. UNITED NATIONS HIGH COMMISSION FOR REFUGEES, HCR BULLETIN (Geneva).
56. UNITED STATES ADVISORY COMMITTEE ON VOLUNTARY FOREIGN AID, WORLD EDUCATION REPORTS (New York, N.Y.).
57. UNITED STATES DEPT. OF HEALTH, EDUCATION, AND WELFARE, FAMILY PLANNING EVALUATION: ABORTION SURVEILLANCE REPORT—LEGAL ABORTIONS, UNITED STATES, ANNUAL SUMMARY, 1970 (1970).
58. THE VICTOR FUND AND THE VICTOR-BOSTROM FUNDS, THE VICTOR-BOSTRUM FUND FOR THE INTERNATIONAL PLANNED PARENTHOOD FEDERATION (Washington, D.C.).

59. WESTERN HEMISPHERE REGION, IPPF/WHR DOCUMENTATION AND PUBLICATION CENTER, NEWS SERVICE (New York, N.Y.).
60. WESTINGHOUSE POPULATION CENTER, SURVEYS OF CONTRACEPTIVE DISTRIBUTION (Columbia, Md.).
61. WORLD HEALTH ORGANIZATION, WHO CHRONICLE (Geneva).
62. ZERO POPULATION GROWTH, INC., EQUILIBRIUM (Palo Alto, Cal.).
63. ZERO POPULATION GROWTH, INC., NATIONAL REPORTER (Palo Alto, Cal.).